THE GOSPEL OF JOHN

Sacra Pagina Series

Volume 4

The Gospel
of
John

Francis J. Moloney, S.D.B.

Daniel J. Harrington, S. J.
Editor

A Michael Glazier Book
THE LITURGICAL PRESS
Collegeville, Minnesota

Cover design by Don Bruno.

A Michael Glazier Book published by The Liturgical Press.

1   2   3   4   5   6   7   8

Library of Congress Cataloging-in-Publication Data

Moloney, Francis J.
    The Gospel of John / Francis J. Moloney ; Daniel J. Harrington, editor.
        p.   cm. — (Sacra pagina series ; v. 4)
    "A Michael Glazier book."
    Includes bibliographical references and index.
    ISBN 0-8146-5806-7
    1. Bible. N.T. John—Commentaries.   I. Harrington, Daniel J.
II. Title.   III. Series: Sacra pagina series ; 4.
BS2615.3.M65   1998
226.5'077—dc21   97-49883
                                                                          CIP

CONTENTS

Editor's Preface   ix

Preface   xi

Note on References and the Translation   xv

Abbreviations   xvii

Introduction

A. The Johannine Literature   1

B. The Author   6

C. "The Jews" in the Fourth Gospel   9

D. Approaches to the Fourth Gospel   11

E. The Approach Adopted in this Commentary   13

F. The Theological Contribution and Contemporary Significance
   of the Fourth Gospel   20

G. The Structure of the Gospel   23

General Bibliography   25

Translation, Interpretation, Notes

I. THE PROLOGUE (1:1-18)   33

II. THE BOOK OF SIGNS (1:19–12:50)   48

   A. The First Days of Jesus (1:19-51)   48

   B. From Cana to Cana (2:1–4:54)   63

      Introduction   63

      The Response to Jesus Within Israel (2:1–3:36)   65

      i.   The First Miracle at Cana: Faith in the Word of Jesus (2:1-12)   65

ii.   Jesus and "the Jews" (2:13-22)   75

iii.   The Narrator's Comment (2:23-25)   84

iv.   Jesus and Nicodemus (3:1-21)   88

v.   Jesus and John the Baptist (3:22-36)   103

The Response to Jesus Outside Israel (4:1-54)   113

vi.   Jesus and the Samaritan Woman: I (4:1-15)   114

vii.   Jesus and the Samaritan Woman: II (4:16-30)   125

viii. Jesus' Comment (4:31-38)   136

ix.   Jesus and the Samaritan Villagers (4:39-42)   145

x.   The Second Miracle at Cana:
       Faith in the Word of Jesus (4:43-54)   150

C. The Feasts of "the Jews" (5:1–10:42)   164

Introduction   164

i.   Jesus and the Sabbath (5:1-47)   165
       a) Jesus' Healing Work on a Sabbath (5:1-18)   166
       b) Life and Judgment (5:19-30)   176
       c) Witness and Accusation (5:31-47)   185

ii.   Jesus and the Passover (6:1-71)   193
       Introduction   193
       a) An Introduction (6:1-4)   195
       b) The Miracle of the Loaves and Fishes (6:5-15)   196
       c) The Miracle on the Sea (6:16-21)   201
       d) A Second Introduction (6:22-24)   205
       e) The Discourse on the Bread From Heaven (6:25-59)   207
       f) The Crisis Created by the Word of Jesus (6:60-71)   226

iii.   Jesus and Tabernacles: I (7:1–8:59)   232
       The Feast of Tabernacles   232
       a) Before the Feast (7:1-9)   237
       b) At the Feast in Jerusalem (7:10-13)   239
       c) About the Middle of the Feast (7:14-36)   241
          1. Jesus, "the Jews," and "the People" (7:14-24)   242
          2. The Jerusalemites and "the People" (7:25-31)   246
          3. Jesus and "the Jews" (7:32-36)   248
       d) On the Last Day of the Feast (7:37–8:59)   251
          1. Jesus, "the People," and the Leaders (7:37-52)   251
          Excursus on John 7:53–8:11: The Woman Taken in Adultery   258
          2. Jesus Reveals Himself as the Light of the World (8:12-30) 265

      3. Jesus and "the Jews" in Conflict Over Their Respective
          Origins (8:31-59)   274

   iv. Jesus and Tabernacles: II (9:1–10:21)   289

   v.   Jesus and Dedication (10:22-42)   312

 D. Jesus Turns Toward "The Hour" (11:1–12:50)   322

   i.   A Resurrection That Will Lead to Death (11:1-54)   322

   ii.   The Hour Has Come (11:55–12:36)   346

   iii. Conclusion to the Ministry of Jesus (12:37-50)   362

III. THE BOOK OF GLORY (13:1–20:31)   370

 A. The Last Discourse (13:1–17:26)   370

   i.   Making God Known: The Footwashing and the Morsel (13:1-38)   370
       a) The Footwashing (13:1-17)   372
       b) To Make God Known (13:18-20)   379
       c) The Gift of the Morsel (13:21-38)   381

   ii.   Departure (14:1-31)   391

   iii. To Abide, to Love, and to Be Hated (15:1–16:3)   416
       a) To Abide (15:1-11)   418
       b) The Command to Love (15:12-17)   424
       c) To Be Hated by the World (15:18–16:3)   427

   iv.   Departure (16:4-33)   436

   v.   Making God Known: Jesus' Final Prayer (17:1-26)   458

 B. The Passion (18:1–19:42)   481

   i.   Jesus and His Enemies in a Garden (18:1-11)   482

   ii.   Jesus' Appearance Before "the Jews" (18:12-27)   486

   iii. Jesus Before Pilate (18:28–19:16a)   492

   iv.   The Crucifixion of Jesus (19:16b-37)   501

   v.   Jesus Is Buried in a Garden by His New-found Friends (19:38-42)   510

 C. The Resurrection (20:1-29)   515

   Introduction   515

   i.   Scenes at the Tomb (20:1-18)   518
       a) Visits to the Empty Tomb (20:1-10)   518
       b) Jesus Appears to Mary Magdalene (20:11-18)   524

   ii.   Scenes in the House (20:19-29)   529
       a) Jesus Appears to the Disciples but not Thomas (20:19-23)   529
       b) Jesus Appears to the Disciples and to Thomas (20:24-29)   536

IV. THE CONCLUSION TO THE GOSPEL (20:30-31)   542

V. EPILOGUE (21:1-25)   545

    Further Resurrection Appearances (21:1-25)   545

    Introduction   545

    i.   Jesus Appears to His Disciples at the Sea of Tiberias (21:1-14)   547

    ii. Jesus, Peter, and the Beloved Disciple (21:15–24)   554

    iii. A Second Conclusion to the Gospel (21:25)   562

    Conclusion: Does John 21 Belong to the Story?   562

Indexes

Scripture Index   569

Index of Ancient Writings   579

Index of Authors   586

EDITOR'S PREFACE

Sacra Pagina is a multi-volume commentary on the books of the New Testament. The expression *Sacra Pagina* ("Sacred Page") originally referred to the text of Scripture. In the Middle Ages it also described the study of Scripture to which the interpreter brought the tools of grammar, rhetoric, dialectic, and philosophy. Thus *Sacra Pagina* encompasses both the text to be studied and the activity of interpretation.

This series presents fresh translations and modern expositions of all the books of the New Testament. Written by an international team of Catholic biblical scholars, it is intended for biblical professionals, graduate students, theologians, clergy, and religious educators. The volumes present basic introductory information and close exposition. They self-consciously adopt specific methodological perspectives, but maintain a focus on the issues raised by the New Testament compositions themselves. The goal of *Sacra Pagina* is to provide sound critical analysis without any loss of sensitivity to religious meaning. This series is therefore catholic in two senses of the word: inclusive in its methods and perspectives, and shaped by the context of the Catholic tradition.

The Second Vatican Council described the study of the "sacred page" as the "very soul of sacred theology" (*Dei Verbum* 24). The volumes in this series illustrate how Catholic scholars contribute to the council's call to provide access to Sacred Scripture for all the Christian faithful. Rather than pretending to say the final word on any text, these volumes seek to open up the riches of the New Testament and to invite as many people as possible to study seriously the "sacred page."

DANIEL J. HARRINGTON, S.J.

PREFACE

The Fourth Gospel has stirred minds, hearts, and imaginations from Christianity's earliest days. The second-century Gnostics used it in the construction of their systems, and its significance for mainstream Christianity is obvious from the time of Irenaeus (c. 130–c. 200 C.E.). It was fundamental to the emergence of Christian theology, especially in the trinitarian and christological debates that produced the great ecumenical Councils, from Nicea (325) to Chalcedon (451). Any interpreter of the Fourth Gospel is the heir to rich and widely varied interpretative traditions. Indeed, it is my view that in 1, 2, and 3 John the Gospel received its first interpretation from within the communities for which it was produced. Such commentary has gone on unabated since then. Not even a scholar who devotes the major part of his or her academic activity to the Fourth Gospel can hope to keep up with the flow of monographs and journal articles dedicated to it. Fortunately, students of the Fourth Gospel have been blessed with some remarkable commentaries. Early in the century (1925), Marie-Joseph Lagrange produced a volume that is remarkable for its identification of exegetical difficulties, however much the contemporary scholar may agree or disagree with Lagrange's solutions to those problems. Originally published in 1941, Rudolf Bultmann's commentary remains a most stimulating and provocative reading of the Johannine text. German commentary on the Gospel, outstandingly represented by the two volumes of Jürgen Becker (1979–1981), continues the Bultmannian tradition. British scholars have long been fascinated by the Fourth Gospel. Sir Edwyn C. Hoskyns' moving study (1947) at times reads like the poetry of the Gospel itself, and C. H. Dodd's *Interpretation* (1953) provided an unparalleled study of its background and meaning. Since those days the multi-volume commentaries of Raymond E. Brown (1966–1970) and Rudolf Schnackenburg (1965–1975), and the precise but rich second edition of the work of C. K. Barrett (1978) have provided the reader with a wealth of background information and well-informed, judicious commentary. No other book of the New Testament has attracted so much attention from commentators.

Is there need for a further commentary on the Fourth Gospel? Within the overall purpose of the *Sacra Pagina* series of New Testament commentaries, I have attempted to introduce another form of commentary. Building upon my large-scale narrative-critical reading of the Fourth Gospel, published between 1993 and 1998 in three volumes, this contribution to the series devotes particular attention to the narrative design of the Gospel story. It attempts to trace the impact the Johannine form of the Jesus story makes on a reader. My aim has been to trace the way in which the author has told the story of Jesus to bring readers to a point of decision (cf. John 20:30-31). I will comment on the unfolding argument of an author who communicates with readers by means of a unique Gospel narrative. My presupposition is that—whatever the sources may have been—the present shape of the Gospel attempts to tell a story that articulates a coherent theology, christology, and ecclesiology. Whoever the historical author may have been, there is an identifiable "point of view" in the story that gives it a literary and theological unity.

The Johannine narrative falls into obvious blocks of material that, after the Prologue (1:1-18), deal with Jesus' public ministry (1:19–12:50), his final evening with the disciples (13:1–17:26), and the account of his death and resurrection (18:1–21:25). There are, however, more subtle turning points in the narrative (see, 2:1; 5:1; 11:1-4; 13:1; 18:1-3; 20:1; 21:1). At these moments in the narrative I will provide a general introduction to the section that follows. It is in these introductions that the distinctive vision of this commentary unfolds. The translation of the text of the Gospel and the more detailed Interpretation and Notes that follow will attempt to support the larger vision supplied by the general introductions. Following the lead of the commentary on Paul's letter to Rome in this series by my colleague, Brendan Byrne, s.j., I will keep the bulk of the commentary in the Interpretation. The Notes serve the purpose of justifying the particular positions adopted in the commentary, presenting and evaluating alternative points of view, and sharing those issues from the history of the Gospel's interpretation that shed light on the commentary. In line with this aim, the Interpretation precedes the Notes to each section. A number of critical issues in the history of Christian theology and in the history of contemporary biblical interpretation have arisen from the text of the Fourth Gospel. I cannot devote exhaustive and detailed attention to all these matters. Some will be mentioned in the Notes, but they are well covered by the classic commentaries on the Gospel. Other commentaries and major specialized studies will be listed in the general bibliography found at the end of the Introduction and in the briefer bibliographies under the heading "For Reference and Further Study" that conclude each section of my commentary.

There are many people who have made this study possible. I can only mention those whose immediate interest and support brought it to its conclusion. Marshall Johnson, then Director of Publishing at Fortress Press, graciously allowed me to write this commentary that is so dependent on the three volumes published by Fortress. Daniel Harrington has been an attentive, wise, and encouraging editor. I am particularly grateful to Linda Maloney, the Academic Editor of The Liturgical Press, for her patient, detailed, and respectfully critical preparation of my manuscript for publication. Brendan Byrne, already the author of an outstanding commentary in the series, encouraged me to take on this task, and read some early drafts of my work. I am most in debt to Nerina Zanardo, F.S.P., who has read the script several times, and to Rino Zanardo who graciously made "Xanadu" available for much of this work. I am responsible for all that appears in the pages that follow, but Nerina's careful reading of my work produces a better text than I could ever have done on my own.

Francis J. Moloney, S.D.B.
Australian Catholic University
Oakleigh, Victoria
Australia

NOTE ON REFERENCES
AND THE TRANSLATION

References to the Old Testament are from the Hebrew Bible, given according to the Revised Standard Version. Where a reference is directly to the LXX, this is indicated. References to Pseudepigrapha of the Old Testament are given according to the collection edited by J. H. Charlesworth (*The Old Testament Pseudepigrapha*. 2 vols. Garden City, N.Y.: Doubleday, 1983). References to Qumran material follow the edition of F. García Martínez (*The Dead Sea Scrolls Translated*. Leiden: E. J. Brill, 1994), except that in the case of the "Thanksgiving Psalms" (1QH) the more traditional column numbering has been retained.

The Greek of John's Gospel is reasonably simple and straightforward, and is admirably reflected in the Revised Standard Version. Rather than producing yet another translation, I will use it as the basis for my exposition. However, there are a number of places in the text, indicated in the Notes, where the interpretation of the Greek requires a different translation. At times there was also need to render the Revised Standard Version in more inclusive language. This has usually, but not always, been done with the aid of the New Revised Standard Version.

ABBREVIATIONS

Biblical Books and Apocrypha

Gen	Nah	1–2–3–4 Kgdms	John
Exod	Hab	Add Esth	Acts
Lev	Zeph	Bar	Rom
Num	Hag	Bel	1–2 Cor
Deut	Zech	1–2 Esdr	Gal
Josh	Mal	4 Ezra	Eph
Judg	Ps (*pl.:* Pss)	Jdt	Phil
1–2 Sam	Job	Ep Jer	Col
1–2 Kgs	Prov	1–2–3–4 Macc	1–2 Thess
Isa	Ruth	Pr Azar	1–2 Tim
Jer	Cant	Pr Man	Titus
Ezek	Eccl (*or* Qoh)	Sir	Phlm
Hos	Lam	Sus	Heb
Joel	Esth	Tob	Jas
Amos	Dan	Wis	1–2 Pet
Obad	Ezra	Matt	1–2–3 John
Jonah	Neh	Mark	Jude
Mic	1–2 Chr	Luke	Rev

Pseudepigrapha

Adam and Eve	Books of Adam and Eve
Apoc. Abr.	Apocalypse of Abraham
2 Bar.	Syriac Apocalypse of Baruch
3 Bar.	Greek Apocalypse of Baruch
As. Mos.	Assumption of Moses
Bib. Ant.	Pseudo-Philo, Biblical Antiquities
1–2–3 Enoch	Ethiopic, Slavonic, Hebrew Enoch
1 Esdr	1 Esdras (= 2 Esdras in Slavonic = 3 Esdras in Appendix to Vulgate)
4 Ezra	Apocalypse of Ezra (= 2 Esdras 3-14)
Jub.	Jubilees

Odes Sol.	Odes of Solomon
Ps. Sol.	Psalms of Solomon
T. Adam	Testament of Adam
T. Isaac	Testament of Isaac
T. Jacob	Testament of Jacob
T. Job	Testament of Job
T. Moses	Testament of Moses
T. Sol.	Testament of Solomon
T. 12 Patr.	Testaments of the Twelve Patriarchs
T. Benj.	Testament of Benjamin
T. Levi	Testament of Levi [etc.]

Other Jewish Literature

Josephus	*Ant.*	*Antiquities of the Jews*
	War	*Jewish War*
	Life	*Life*

Philo of Alexandria

References to the works of Philo are given according to the abbreviated Latin titles used in the Loeb edition (cf. vol. 1, pp. xxiii–xxiv).

Dead Sea Scrolls

CD	*Damascus Document* (from Cairo Genizah and Qumran)
1QH	*Thanksgiving Hymns*
1QS	Community Rule (Manual of Discipline)
3Q15	Copper Scroll
4QFlor	Florilegium

Rabbinic Literature

References to the Mishnah name the tractate with the prefix *m.*, while references to the Babylonian Talmud have the prefix *b.* before the tractate and references to the Jerusalem Talmud have the prefix *j.* before the tractate; the prefix *t.* indicates the Tosefta. The Midrashim Rabbah are indicated by the abbreviation of the biblical book, followed by *Rab.* (e.g., *Exod Rab.*). The Midrashim Tanhuma, Sifre, etc. are indicated by the prefix *Tanh.* etc. followed by the biblical book (e.g., *Tanh. Bereshit; Sifre Lev*). Other rabbinic documents are indicated in full.

Periodicals, Reference Works, and Serials

AB	Anchor Bible
ABD	*Anchor Bible Dictionary.* David N. Freedman, ed. 6 vols. New York: Doubleday, 1992

ABR	*Australian Biblical Review*
ABRL	Anchor Bible Reference Library
AGJU	Arbeiten zur Geschichte des antiken Judentums und des Urchristentums
AGSU	Arbeiten zur Geschichte des Spätjudentums und Urchristentums
AnBib	Analecta Biblica
ANRW	*Aufstieg und Niedergang der römischen Welt Teil II: Principat. Religion.* Wolfgang Haase and Hildegard Temporini, eds. Berlin: de Gruyter, 1979–
Anton.	*Antonianum*
AThANT	Abhandlungen zur Theologie des Alten und Neuen Testaments
Aug.	*Augustinianum*
BAGD	Walter Bauer, W. F. Arndt, and W. F. Gingrich, *A Greek-English Lexicon of the New Testament and Other Early Christian Literature.* 2nd ed. rev. and augmented by F. W. Gingrich and F. W. Danker. Chicago: University of Chicago Press, 1979
BBB	Bonner biblische Beiträge
BDF	F. Blass and A. Debrunner, *A Greek Grammar of the New Testament and Other Early Christian Literature.* Rev. and trans. by R. W. Funk. Chicago: University of Chicago Press, 1961
BeO	*Bibbia e Oriente*
BEsB	Biblioteca Escuela Bíblica
BET	Beiträge zur biblischen Exegese und Theologie
BEThL	Bibliotheca Ephemeridum theologicarum Lovaniensium
BEvTh	Beiträge zur evangelischen Theologie
BGBE	Beiträge zur Geschichte der biblischen Exegese
Bib.	*Biblica*
BibIntS	Biblical Interpretation Series
BiKi	*Bibel und Kirche*
BJ	Bible de Jérusalem
BJRL	*Bulletin of the John Rylands Library*
BLE	*Bulletin de littérature ecclésiastique*
BN	Biblische Notizen
BS	*Bibliotheca Sacra*
BSRel	Biblioteca di scienze religiose. Rome
BT	*The Bible Translator*
BTB	*Biblical Theology Bulletin*
BThSt	Biblisch-theologische Studien
BU	Biblische Untersuchungen
BWANT	Beiträge zur Wissenschaft vom Alten und Neuen Testament
BZ	*Biblische Zeitschrift*
BZNW	Beihefte zur Zeitschrift für die neutestamentliche Wissenschaft
CB	Coniectanea biblica
CBET	Contributions to Biblical Exegesis and Theology
CBQ	*Catholic Biblical Quarterly*
CBQ.MS	Catholic Biblical Quarterly Monograph Series

CCSL	Corpus Christianorum Series Latina. Turnhout: Brepols.
CJ	*Classical Journal*
CNT	Coniectanea neotestamentica
CRB	Cahiers de la Revue Biblique
DBS	*Dictionnaire de la Bible Supplement*. L. Pirot, A. Robert, H. Cazelles, and A. Feuillet, eds. Paris: Letouzey, 1928–
DR	*Downside Review*
ED	*Euntes Docete*
EDNT	*Exegetical Dictionary of the New Testament*
EeT	*Eglise et Théologie*
ET	*Expository Times*
EtB	Etudes Bibliques
EThL	*Ephemerides theologicae Lovanienses*
ETR	*Etudes théologiques et religieuses*
EvQ	*Evangelical Quarterly*
EvTh	*Evangelische Theologie*
FRLANT	Forschungen zur Religion und Literatur des Alten und Neuen Testaments
FTS	Frankfurter theologische Studien
FV	*Foi et Vie*
FzB	Forschung zur Bibel
GBSNT	Guides to Biblical Scholarship, New Testament Series
Gr.	*Gregorianum*
HeyJ	*Heythrop Journal*
HNT	Handbuch zum Neuen Testament
HThKNT	Herders theologischer Kommentar zum Neuen Testament
HThR	*Harvard Theological Review*
HUTh	Hermeneutische Untersuchungen zur Theologie
IBSt	*Irish Biblical Studies*
ICC	International Critical Commentary
IDB	The Interpreter's Dictionary of the Bible. 5 vols. New York and Nashville: Abingdon, 1962–1976
Interp.	*Interpretation*
IRM	*International Review of Missions*
IThQ	*Irish Theological Quarterly*
JB	The Jerusalem Bible
JBL	*Journal of Biblical Literature*
JNES	*Journal of Near Eastern Studies*
JSNT	*Journal for the Study of the New Testament*
JSNT.S	Journal for the Study of the New Testament Supplement Series
JSOT	*Journal for the Study of the Old Testament*
JSOT.S	Journal for the Study of the Old Testament Supplement Series
JThS	*Journal of Theological Studies*
Laur.	*Laurentianum*
LeDiv	Lectio Divina
LouvSt	*Louvain Studies*

LSJ	H. Liddell, R. Scott, and H. S. Jones, *A Greek-English Lexicon*. Oxford: Clarendon, 1968
LThPM	Louvain Theological and Pastoral Monographs
LTP	*Laval théologique et philosophique*
LV	*Lumière et Vie*
LXX	The Septuagint
Mar.	*Marianum*
MPG	J.-P. Migne, *Patrologia graeca*
MPL	J.-P. Migne, *Patrologia latina*
MSR	*Mélanges de science religieuse*
MSSNTS	Society for New Testament Studies Monograph Series
MT	The Masoretic Text
MThZ	*Münchener theologische Zeitschrift*
NAB	New American Bible
NCB	New Century Bible
NEB	New English Bible
Neotest.	*Neotestamentica*
NIC NT	New International Commentary on the New Testament
NIV	New International Version
NJB	New Jerusalem Bible
NJBC	*The New Jerome Biblical Commentary*. R. E. Brown, J. A. Fitzmyer, and R. E. Murphy, eds.. Englewood Cliffs: Prentice Hall, 1990
NRSV	New Revised Standard Version
NRTh	*Nouvelle Revue Théologique*
n. s.	new series
NT	New Testament
NT	*Novum Testamentum*
NT.S	Supplements to *Novum Testamentum*
NTA	Neutestamentliche Abhandlungen
NTD	Das Neue Testament Deutsch
NTG	*Novum Testamentum Graece* (Nestle-Aland. 27th Edition)
NTS	*New Testament Studies*
NVB	Nuovissima versione della bibbia dai testi originali
OBO	*Orbis biblicus et orientalis*
OBS	Oxford Biblical Series
ÖBS	Österreichische biblische studien
OT	Old Testament
ÖTBK	Ökumenischer Taschenbuchkommentar zum Neuen Testament
PNTC	Pelican New Testament Commentaries
QD	Quaestiones disputatae
RB	*Revue Biblique*
RevSR	*Revue des Sciences Religieuses*
RExp	*Review and Expositor*
RHPhR	*Revue d'histoire et de philosophie religieuses*
RivBib	*Rivista Biblica*
RSR	*Recherche de science religieuse*

RSV	The Revised Standard Version
RThom	*Revue Thomiste*
RTL	*Revue Théologique de Louvain*
Sal.	*Salesianum*
SBFA	Studii Biblici Franciscani analecta
SBL.DS	Society of Biblical Literature Dissertation Series
SBL.MS	Society of Biblical Literature Monograph Series
SBS	Stuttgarter Bibelstudien
SBT	Studies in Biblical Theology
ScEc	*Sciences ecclésiastiques*
Sem	*Semeia*
SJTh	Scottish Journal of Theology
SPFTM	Scripta Pontificiae Facultatis Theologicae 'Marianum'
SRivBib	Supplementi alla Rivista biblica
StANT	Studien zum Alten und Neuen Testament
StBi	Studi Biblici
StEv	*Studia Evangelica*
Str-B	H. Strack and P. Billerbeck, *Kommentar zum Neuen Testament aus Talmud und Midrasch*. 6 vols. Munich: C. H. Beck, 1922–1961
StTh	*Studia Theologica*
SVTQ	*St. Vladimir's Theological Quarterly*
TDNT	*Theological Dictionary of the New Testament*. G. Kittel and G. Friedrich, eds. 10 vols. Grand Rapids: Eerdmans, 1964–1976
ThDiss	Theologische Dissertationen
Theol.	*Theology*
ThLZ	*Theologische Literaturzeitung*
ThR	*Theologische Rundschau*
ThStKr	*Theologische Studien und Kritiken*
ThV	*Theologische Versuche*
ThZ	*Theologische Zeitschrift*
TOB	Traduction Oecuménique de la Bible
TS	*Theological Studies*
TThZ	*Trierer Theologische Zeitschrift*
TW	Theologie und Wirklichkeit
TynB	*Tyndale Bulletin*
UBSGNT	Greek New Testament. United Bible Society
VD	*Verbum Domini*
VigChr	*Vigiliae Christianae*
VT	*Vetus Testamentum*
WBC	Word Bible Commentary
WMANT	Wissenschaftliche Monographien zum Alten und Neuen Testament
WUNT	Wissenschaftliche Untersuchungen zum Neuen Testament
ZGB	Max Zerwick. *Biblical Greek Illustrated by Examples*. Rome: Biblical Institute Press, 1963
ZKTh	*Zeitschrift für katholische Theologie*
ZNW	*Zeitschrift für die Neutestamentliche Wissenschaft*
ZThK	*Zeitschrift für Theologie und Kirche*

INTRODUCTION

Introductions to commentaries on biblical books traditionally discuss the place, date, and origins of the particular book, the history of its composition, its language and style, and the Greek (or Hebrew) text of the book in question, and give an overview of the book's theology, the current state of scholarly reflection on it, and an initial introduction to the structure of the book as a whole. The Introduction that follows covers most of these issues, and they will appear in a more detailed fashion in the commentary. Readers wanting to find scholarly treatments of traditional introductory questions should consult the major commentaries (cf. Brown 1:xxi–cxlvi; Schnackenburg 1:11–217; Barrett 3–146; Lindars 24–73; Becker 1:15–61; Haenchen 1:1–97) and the excellent introduction to Johannine Christianity by John Painter (*Quest* 33–135). The pages that follow situate the present volume within the context of contemporary Johannine scholarship, but introductory matters must be dealt with as a part of that process: the place of the Fourth Gospel within the larger body of literature found within the New Testament, commonly called "the Johannine literature," the author, "the Jews" in the Fourth Gospel, and a survey of scholarly approaches to the Gospel. Against that background the approach adopted in this commentary will be introduced.

A. *The Johannine Literature*

Several documents in the New Testament have been regarded by Christian tradition as originating from a single person named "John." The Johannine literature comprises the Gospel of John, the three Letters of John, and the book of Revelation. Only Revelation refers to its author by the name "John" (cf. Rev 1:1, 4, 9; 22:8). Scholarly opinion would regard this John, an elder writing from the island of Patmos (Rev 1:9), as someone other than the author of the Gospel and the Letters, but tradition gradually associated all the so-called "Johannine" documents with the disciple of Jesus, John the son of Zebedee. In a chapter that should be read as an addendum to the original Gospel (ch. 21. See Interpretation and Notes to 21:1-25), the narrator of the story identifies the Beloved

Disciple found in the Gospel story as its author (see John 21:24: "This is the disciple . . . who has written these things"). As early as 180 C.E. Irenaeus made the link between John, the son of Zebedee, and the Beloved Disciple. From then on the apostle John was almost universally recognized as the author of the Fourth Gospel.

All the Johannine literature appears to have been written near the turn of the first century (ca. 100 C.E.). While Revelation is generally associated with the persecutions of the Roman emperor Domitian (81–96 C.E.), the Gospel and the Letters, although dated at about the same period, come from a different background. Debate over the place and time of the Gospel's appearance continues, but the following details indicate a date toward the end of the first century of the Christian era.

(1) The Gospel of John is marked by a conflict between Jesus and "the Jews" (cf., for example, 2:13-25; 5:10-18; 7:1-9, 14-31, 40-44; 8:12-20, 39-47, 48-59; 10:31-39; 11:45-52) that indicates the period when the hostility between the two emerging sects of Christianity and post-70 rabbinic Judaism was leading to a breakdown in relations. However widespread this breakdown might or might not have been toward the end of the first century, the Fourth Gospel reflects a situation in which people called "the Jews" (see below) are in relentless conflict with Jesus and his followers (cf. 9:22; 12:42; 16:2).

(2) On three occasions in the Gospel of John mention is made of the eviction from the synagogue of those who believe and confess that Jesus is the Christ. A technical word *(aposunagōgos)* is associated with this eviction (cf. 9:22; 12:42; 16:2). On two of those occasions the reason for exclusion from the synagogue is explicitly named as confession *(homologein)* that Jesus was the Christ (9:22; 12:42). The final breakdown between the Johannine community and the local synagogue seems to have been created by a public recognition of Jesus as the Christ. In the story of the man born blind (9:1-34) there is a gradual growth of faith in Jesus as the Christ that leads to the blind man's being cast out of the synagogue (see 9:34). The experience of the man born blind is widely regarded as a reflection of the experience of the Johannine Christians (cf. Martyn, *History and Theology* 24–62). The history of the process that led to the elimination of Christians from the synagogue worship is complex, but signs of a separation began to appear between 80 and 90 C.E. However local the experience of the Johannine Christians might have been, the Fourth Gospel reflects that process. The composition history of the Gospel may have been very complex, but the final Gospel, in its present shape, appeared late in the first century.

(3) Despite the efforts of several Belgian scholars under the leadership of Frans Neirynck (cf. *Jean et les Synoptiques: Examen critique de l'exégèse de M.-E. Boismard*, BEThL 49; Leuven: University Press, 1979), the painstaking work of M.-E. Boismard and Arnaud Lamouille *(Jean)*, and the

speculative connections made by Thomas L. Brodie (*The Quest for the Origin of John's Gospel. A Source-Oriented Approach*, New York: Oxford University Press, 1993), it is impossible to trace any direct literary relationship between John's gospel and the synoptic gospels. Behind this affirmation lies an answer to the question posed in 1938 by Percival Gardner-Smith (*St. John and the Synoptic Gospels*, Cambridge: Cambridge University Press, 1938): is it easier to explain the differences between the Fourth Gospel and the synoptic gospels with a theory of dependence, or the similarities between the Fourth Gospel and the synoptics without one? The complexity of the suggestions of Neirynck, Boismard-Lamouille, and Brodie points to the strength of the second possibility. Yet behind the Fourth Gospel one senses traditions from the story of Jesus that are also found in the synoptic gospels: the calling of disciples (1:35-51), the purification of the Temple (2:13-25), the curing of a paralytic (5:1-9), the multiplication of the loaves and fishes (6:1-15), walking on the water (6:16-21), Peter's confession (6:68-69), the curing of a blind man (9:1-7), the theme of Jesus as a shepherd (10:1-18), a woman washes Jesus' feet (12:1-8), the passion story (18:1–19:42), the resurrection story (20:1-29), the miraculous draught of fishes (21:1-14). While once it was taken for granted that John knew the synoptic gospels and was rewriting them, nowadays the position taken above is widely accepted. John's gospel comes later than the synoptics and does not depend directly upon them. Many of the stories are common, but they show that they have been developed over a longer period and reflect a slightly later stage in the history of the early Church (cf. Dodd, *Historical Tradition*). If, as is widely accepted, the gospels of Matthew and Luke appeared toward the middle of the eighties of the first century, the Fourth Gospel must have appeared after that date.

One can never be certain of the accuracy of the world an interpreter reconstructs from the evidence of an ancient text, but putting points (1), (2), and (3) together suggests that the Johannine community and its gospel had the following history. A group of like-minded Christians began within Judaism but was expelled from the synagogue and exposed to the wider world. Within that wider world the early Christians whose experiences produced this gospel had to come to a clear understanding of who Jesus Christ was, what he meant for them, and how they should live their Christian lives in response to the challenge of Jesus. Their story of Jesus no doubt had a long literary development, traces of which remain in the text. The Gospel of John in its final shape was written in a way that is rooted in the Jewish origins of the Christian Church yet open to the wider world, in a way that is somewhat foreign to the synoptic gospels. The use of the expression *logos* to refer to Jesus (cf. 1:1, 14), the importance of knowledge (cf., for example, 6:69; 17:3), a stress on a region "above" and another "below" between which both angels (cf. 1:51) and Jesus (cf. 3:13;

6:62) move, and a number of other words and ideas found only in this gospel (cf. Notes to the commentary for details) suggest that the world into which this gospel was written was markedly different from the one that received the earlier stories of Jesus. Although not all would agree (cf. Robinson, *Priority*), it is widely accepted that this particular story of Jesus, and the language used to tell it, belong to the end of the first century.

Whatever might be said of Revelation, the Johannine Gospel and the Letters belong together. They are written in much the same language and have many ideas that are parallel; yet there are differences. Most of all, one is a story of the life of Jesus (the Gospel) and the others are letters. The Letters do not tell the story of Jesus, but they presuppose it. Indeed, much that is in the Letters presupposes the Gospel of John. It is the stimulating, novel understanding of God, Jesus, the Spirit, and the Christian life found in the Gospel that has generated many of the difficulties the author of the Letters addresses (cf. the magisterial demonstration of this relationship in R. E. Brown, *The Epistles of John*. AB 30; Garden City, N.Y.: Doubleday, 1982, 47–115). The Letters were written later than the Gospel that, as was mentioned earlier, is marked by a strong conflict between Jesus and "the Jews." It appears that those who confessed that Jesus was the Christ had been thrown out of the synagogue (cf. John 9:22; 12:42; 16:2). There had been a painful breakdown between the Johannine community and the local synagogue. The Letters show no interest in this process that must have been long since past. The problem with people "outside" the Johannine communities had been resolved, for better or for worse. The Letters face an inevitable further stage in the story of the people for whom they were written: problems emerging "within" the communities. Indeed, it appears that the catalyst for the writing of the Letters is further breakdown. While the Gospel responds to a breakdown in the relationship between the Johannine Christians and the synagogue Jews, the Letters are occasioned by breakdowns among members of Johannine communities. Indeed, the Letters indicate that conflicting "Johannine" communities now exist: "They went out from us, but they were not of us; for if they had been of us, they would have continued with us; but they went out, that it might be plain that they all are not of us" (1 John 2:19. Cf. also 2 John 7).

While it is impossible to be certain of the identity of the author(s), the Gospel and the Letters come from the same background, even though the Letters reflect a situation of conflict quite different from the Gospel. The Letters also reflect a later situation where the original Johannine group is gradually spreading (and dividing) into a number of communities. This is evident in all the Letters, but especially in 3 John where the author of the Letter, an "elder," a senior figure in a Christian community, pleads with the leader of another community, Gaius, to disregard the thought and behavior of a third party, Diotrephes (3 John 9-10). Without the doctrines of the Gospel, however, there would be no letters written some time early in the second century of the Christian era. They attempt to resolve the theological and community problems generated by the highly original story of the life of Jesus found in the Gospel.

The Johannine churches were deeply divided. There are hints that the division led the parties in the argument into very different forms of Christianity during the second century. The author of the Letters and the Christians he represented may have become members of the larger established Church, while Diotrephes and his friends may have become Gnostics, but one cannot be sure of this. In the Johannine Letters we have only one side of the argument. No doubt Diotrephes and his community would have some hard things to say about the author of the Letters. The term "antichrist" (cf. 1 John 2:18, 22; 4:3; 2 John 7) may also have been used about him! We have only one end of a telephone conversation, and we must speculate about what was being said or not said at the other end. Nevertheless, the early Church found its faith reflected in these Letters, and thus they form a part of the New Testament, a Christian treasure house that continues to support and inspire believers through all ages.

The Fourth Gospel was probably written at the turn of the century, and the Letters shortly after that time. It was written in a place where Judaism, early Christianity, the complex religions of the Hellenistic and Greek world, and incipient Gnosticism rubbed shoulders—often painfully. Contemporary scholarship, reversing earlier suggestions that the Gospel was evidence for the hellenization of Christianity (e.g., C. H. Dodd), the christianization of gnosticism (e.g., Rudolf Bultmann) or the gnosticizing of Christianity (e.g., Ernst Käsemann), is looking more and more to the close links that exist between the Fourth Gospel and syncretistic and sectarian Judaism, especially evident in the Dead Sea Scrolls (cf. Painter, *Quest* 35–52). Some suggest that the author was an Essene, and that the Gospel is the product of this more "oriental" world (cf. Ashton, *Understanding the Fourth Gospel* 205–237). It is clear that the thought world of the type of syncretistic and sectarian Judaism evidenced by the Dead Sea Scrolls has influenced the traditions that produced the Gospel, but there are elements in the Gospel that cannot be satisfactorily explained by this background. The traditional site for the writing of the Gospel of John—Ephesus—remains one of the best locations for the blend of traditions that lies behind the Gospel. Arguments can be marshaled against this setting (cf. Smith, *Theology* 6), and if it were not for the tradition associating the Gospel with that city a more general statement about a place where an emerging Christian community dealt with its separation from Judaism and its insertion into the broader maelstom of religions and

religious practice in the late first century would suffice. Within such a setting a remarkable Gospel was forged. The result of decades of early
Christian experience, strongly influenced by the thought world of sectarian Judaism, of the telling and retelling of Christian stories over several
generations and into different situations, the Fourth Gospel cannot be
conveniently situated in any one cultural milieu (cf. Painter, *Quest*
119–131; Smith, *Theology* 10–20). It is Greek and Jewish, and its language,
background, and theological point of view would resonate within a number of worldviews. It looks back to the foundational story of Jesus of
Nazareth, but tells it in a way that addressed the religious and cultural
maelstrom of Asia Minor at the end of the first century. "An effort to
begin from a single presumed background in order to interpret the
Gospel against it will be too narrow, or ill focused, or both" (Smith, *Theology* 20). The Fourth Gospel tells an old story in a new way. It is more difficult to locate the Letters and the several "communities" behind them.
They are not, however, too far from one another geographically. There is
easy movement from one community to another (2 John 12; 3 John 3, 5-
6), but access to increasingly hostile communities made up of former
friends is clearly becoming a problem (2 John 10-11; 3 John 10). The
changed circumstances, however, do not detract from their "Johannine"
background. Indeed, the language, background, and theological point of
view of the Gospel lie behind the conflicts, especially in the areas of christology and Christian behavior, that are emerging among different Johannine communities. Both the letter writer and those he is accusing of
failure appear to be looking back to the Gospel for their christological and
Christian inspiration (cf. Brown, *Epistles* 73–86).

B. *The Author*

The Beloved Disciple who leaned on Jesus' breast at the Last Supper
(cf. 13:23) was present at the foot of the cross (cf. 19:25-27), and saw and
believed when he found the clothes of death empty and folded in the
tomb (cf. 20:3-10). John 21:24 claims that this character in the story is the
author of the Gospel: "This is the disciple who is bearing witness to these
things, and who has written these things; and we know that his testimony is true." The further identification of the Beloved Disciple with
John, the son of Zebedee, is well attested in Christian art and history. This
identification owes much to the work of Irenaeus (about 130–200 C.E.)
who is often credited with having rescued the Gospel of John from the
Gnostics of the second century, but Irenaeus may have been depending
on even earlier traditions (cf. Hengel, *Die Johanneische Frage* 9–95). The
Gnostics found the poetic, speculative nature of the Johannine story
suited their myth of a redeemer who descended to give knowledge

(Greek: *gnōsis*) to the unredeemed, wallowing in the darkness of ignorance. They found that the Johannine story of Jesus suited their schemes, and the earliest commentaries we have on the Fourth Gospel come from the Gnostic world (cf. Elaine H. Pagels, *The Johannine Gospel in Gnostic Exegesis: Heracleon's Commentary on John*. Nashville and New York: Abingdon, 1973). Part of Irenaeus's defense of the Gospel of John was to insist on the link between this story and an original disciple of Jesus. This authenticated the tradition: this story is not mere speculation; it goes back to the first-hand witness of John, the son of Zebedee.

Was Irenaeus right? It is impossible to give a certain answer one way or the other. The vast majority of contemporary scholars do not regard it as a significant question, claiming that there is insufficient evidence *within the Gospel* to substantiate such claims, and that Irenaeus might have been strongly influenced by the need to authenticate the Johannine tradition, to save it from the speculations of the Gnostic writings. Most who have pursued the matter in recent times conclude that the author was a founding figure in the community, possibly a disciple of Jesus, but not the son of Zebedee or one of the Twelve. From the story of the Gospel itself, however, an interesting figure emerges. As John the Baptist sends two of his disciples to follow Jesus (cf. 1:35-42), one of them is eventually named: Andrew (1:40). The other remains incognito. There is the repetition of this practice in the non-naming of a character in the story known as "the other disciple" (cf. 18:15, 16; 20:3, 4, 8). This enigmatic character eventually comes to be known as "the other disciple . . . whom Jesus loved" (cf. 20:2). In 20:2 it looks as if an early stage of the tradition simply had "the other disciple" (cf. 18:15, 16; 20:3, 4, 8), but that in a final edition (or at least a later stage in the writing of the Gospel) the words "whom Jesus loved" were added. This is "the Beloved Disciple" (cf. 13:23; 19:26), identified in the Epilogue to the Gospel (John 21) as the author of the Gospel (21:20, 23, 24). From such evidence it appears that the narrative of the Gospel has traces of its "author." He was an ex-disciple of the Baptist (although many scholars would discount the non-named character in 1:35-42. Cf. note to 1:40), with Jesus from the beginnings of his ministry, present at the climactic events of the first Easter, the founding father of a community whose Gospel we today call the Gospel of John. Precisely because of his centrality to the birth, development, and life of the community in which he was such an important figure, his desire to keep his name out of the account of the life of Jesus was respected even after he had died. However much they respected the desire to remain incognito, those responsible for the present shape of the Gospel could not resist inserting a description that expressed their memory and their admiration. They described "the other disciple" as "the disciple whom Jesus loved" (cf. 20:2).

It is presupposed by 21:20-23 that the disciple is dead when the Gospel reaches its final stages of writing. Chapter 21, the addendum to the Gospel, provides information about the slightly later situation of the Johannine community. As Peter "follows" Jesus (21:19), he looks back to the Beloved Disciple who is, in turn, following (v. 20). He inquires about the destiny of this other important figure (v. 21). Jesus tells Peter that he is not to concern himself about whether or not the Beloved Disciple will live on until Jesus returns (v. 22), but the narrator adds a further explanatory comment to the words of Jesus (v. 23). Jesus did not say that the Beloved Disciple would not die, but that whether or not he would die should not be Peter's concern. This comment is called for because "the rumor spread in the community that this disciple would not die" (v. 23). The author of John 21 is at pains to point out that this is not exactly what Jesus said. The community must be taught exactly what Jesus meant. What is the problem? The Beloved Disciple is no longer alive as this chapter is being written so that it might be added to the original Gospel. Part of the task of this additional chapter is to set right some of the misconceptions of the Johannine community. There were obviously some who expected the Beloved Disciple to be alive for the return of the Lord. However, he had died, and this had to be explained.

Was the anonymous, other, Beloved Disciple John the son of Zebedee? Irenaeus might have been correct in identifying the two figures, and the massive support that this identification has received across the centuries has given this identification a popularity lending the hypothesis a weight that the evidence cannot support. Whether or not the son of Zebedee was the author of the Fourth Gospel is the subject of never-ending debates. The weight of the evidence is against their being one and the same figure. Many confusing traditions surround the death of John, the son of Zebedee (cf. M.-É. Boismard, *Le Martyre de Jean l'Apôtre*. CRB 35; Paris: Gabalda, 1996), and the existence of several significant figures in the early Church called "John" may have led to this confusion. The fact that the author of Revelation is called "John" (cf. Rev 1:1, 4, 9; 22:8) has been a major element in the emergence of the traditional association with John the author and John, the son of Zebedee (for a comprehensive study of the traditions surrounding "John," see Culpepper, *John, The Son of Zebedee*). Yet there are still contemporary scholars who locate the apostle at the origins of the Fourth Gospel (cf. Morris 4–25; Carson 68–81; Robinson, *Priority* 92–122). However much the scholarly assessment of the internal and external evidence militates against the traditional identification of John the son of Zebedee with the Beloved Disciple, there is always the chance that the apostle John may have been in some way "author" of the Gospel we traditionally call "of John." It is arrogant to rule any possibility out of court. It should not worry us that we cannot be sure. The authority of this

Gospel flows from the way it tells the story of God and God's Son, Jesus Christ, and its challenge to all who would wish to be his followers. These issues do not depend upon the apostolicity of its author. Perhaps the most telling feature about the ancient text we call the Gospel of John is that it has stood the test of time. Today, after almost two thousand years of Christian history, we continue to read this life story of Jesus. It remains one of the most fascinating of all the Gospels, as the unflagging and voluminous commentary upon it indicates. Its perennial fascination is not determined by whether or not John the apostle was its author.

C. *"The Jews" in the Fourth Gospel*

Frequently during the Johannine story of Jesus the opponents of Jesus are bluntly called "the Jews." After initial hints that all is not well between Jesus and "the Jews" (cf. 1:19; 2:13-22) they gradually enter into public conflict (5:16-18), and a decision is made that Jesus must be slain (5:18). From that point on "the Jews" are presented as hostile to Jesus and to all who would confess that he is the Christ (cf. 9:22; 12:42; 16:2). They plot against him (cf. 11:45-53) and browbeat Pilate into handing him over to them for execution (18:28–19:16). Even after his death, when Pilate ironically places the title, "Jesus of Nazareth, the King of the Jews" on the cross, they reject this claim (19:17-22), and on the day of the resurrection the disciples are huddled behind closed doors "for fear of the Jews" (20:19). Uncritical reading has led to two dangerous consequences directly related to the misunderstanding of what is meant by "the Jews" in the Fourth Gospel.

(1) The Gospel of John has been accepted as the inspired and infallible Word of God that roundly condemns the Jewish people because of their rejection and eventual slaying of Jesus of Nazareth. For centuries this interpretation of the Fourth Gospel has legitimated some of the most outrageous behavior of European Christian people, including pogroms and the attempted genocide of the Holocaust.

(2) It is also possible to come to a different, but equally damaging conclusion. It could be claimed that the language used to speak of the Jews is so violently anti-Semitic that the Fourth Gospel should not be used in today's Christian churches, that it is time to lay the Gospel of John quietly to rest.

Inflammatory rejection of the Jewish people has marked much of the history of European Christianity and, because of this, of European culture as a whole. The Christian involvement in—or at best non-opposition to—the Holocaust, and a large part of European history and culture, including the European theological tradition, are but indications of the immeasurable damage that has resulted from the misreading of one of Christianity's foundational texts. However, there is a rich and significant presence of the Fourth Gospel in Christian life, spirituality, and both Western and Eastern liturgical traditions. It has inspired Christian iconography, being outstandingly present in the many paintings and statues of the crucified Jesus, his mother, and the Beloved Disciple (cf. 19:25-27), and has inspired music from J. S. Bach to Arvo Pärt, both of whom have written unforgettable renditions of the Johannine passion account. There can be no wholesale rejection of the Fourth Gospel, as neither the condemnation and persecution of "the Jews" nor the elimination of the Gospel of John from Christian literature can claim to be based upon a correct reading of the Fourth Gospel.

The expression "the Jews" in this gospel must always be placed within quotation marks because it does not represent the Jewish people. A critical reading of the Johannine Gospel makes it clear that "the Jews" are those characters in the story who have made up their minds about Jesus. They are one side of a christological debate, and this language was forged within the Johannine community, that formed the other side of the debate. The conflicts between Jesus and "the Jews" are more the reflection of a christological debate at the end of the first century than a record of encounters between Jesus and his fellow Israelites in the thirties of that century. *They do not accurately report the experience of the historical Jesus.* The Johannine community had come to believe that Jesus was the one sent by God, the Son of God, and as such the expected Messiah (cf. 20:31). This is the authorial point of view portrayed in Jesus' actions, words, death, and resurrection. The Gospel exists because an author wished to express this viewpoint by means of a gospel. However, while one group in the story is passionately committed to this viewpoint there is another group equally passionately committed to the belief that Jesus *is not the Messiah.* This group casts out the man born blind from the synagogue (9:22, 34); some of its members are afraid to confess that Jesus is the Christ lest they too be cast out of the synagogue (12:42); and Jesus warns his disciples that they will be thrown out of the synagogue and even slain by people who regard their actions as rendering praise to God (16:2). Because these people believe that Jesus' claims are false (7:10-13, 45-52) and that he is a blasphemer (5:16-18; 19:7) they are portrayed as systematically rejecting him and those who believe and follow him. This is the point of view represented by "the Jews."

Historically, these opponents of the Johannine point of view were doubtless ethnically Jewish people with a fierce commitment to the religion of Israel, especially as it was being established after the devastations of the Jewish War (66–73 C.E.). They were locked in bitter conflict with Johannine Christians. We cannot be sure how widespread this conflict was.

There is evidence, both in the New Testament and outside it, that Jews and Christians clashed. Some scholars have attempted to associate the experience of the Johannine Christians with Rabbi Gamaliel II and a formal separation between Jews and Christians in the eighties of the first century (Martyn, *History and Theology;* W. D. Davies, "Reflections on Aspects of the Jewish Background of the Gospel of John," *Exploring the Fourth Gospel* 43–64), but the evidence linking the decisions of Gamaliel II with the eventual breakdown of relationships between Jews and Christians is hard to evaluate with certainty (cf. P. W. van der Horst, "The Birkat ha-minim in Recent Research." *ET* 105 [1993–1994] 363–368). The situation behind the Fourth Gospel may have been a very local affair. Whatever may have been happening in the Mediterranean world at large, the Fourth Gospel comes from a situation where those who believed and confessed that Jesus was the Christ were forcibly excluded from the synagogue (9:22; 12:42). It is most likely that the separation from the synagogue was now behind the Christians, a thing of the past, but the memory of the pain and anger it generated is still very present. The fact that the Johannine Christians were being ejected from the synagogue indicates that *many members of the Johannine community were also ethnically Jewish,* and committed to the religion of Israel.

Jewish people as such are not represented by the term "the Jews," and the Fourth Gospel must not be read as if they were. Both "the Jews" and many members of the Johannine community were Jews, and the expression "the Jews" in the Gospel indicates those people who have taken up a theological and christological position that rejects Jesus and the claims made for him by his followers. Thus they also reject his followers. The expression "the Jews" does not represent a race. Indeed, the expression could be applied to anyone of any age and any nation who has decided, once and for all, that Jesus of Nazareth is not the Messiah, but a sinner whose origins are unknown (9:24-29). As a recent important study of the Fourth Gospel has said so well, one must "recognise in these hot-tempered exchanges the type of family row in which the participants face one another across the room of a house that all have shared and all call home" (J. Ashton, *Understanding the Fourth Gospel* 151). Over the centuries since the appearance of the Fourth Gospel this text has been used violently to demolish one of the families in that row. This has greatly impoverished those who claimed to have unique rights to the home.

D. *Approaches to the Fourth Gospel*

One of the features of the growth of historical criticism was the dethroning of the Gospel of John as a historical document. Once scholars began to see the importance of the Gospel of Mark and its use as a source for both Matthew and Luke, it became clear that there was very little of the Gospel of John that belonged to the life of Jesus. This led to its being read as a "spiritual gospel," as it had already been called by Clement of Alexandria in the Second Century (Eusebius, *Hist. Eccl.* 6.14.7). It was a deeply religious, semi-philosophical, Hellenistic, and perhaps Gnostic reflection on the significance of Jesus. It had little or no connection with the life story of the man known as Jesus of Nazareth. The major influences on the formation of the Gospel were Greek, Hermetic, or Gnostic traditions, and great scholarship was devoted to the recovery of the various religions reflected in the Gospel (cf. the commentaries of Bauer and Bultmann, and the critique of this position in Painter, *Quest* 52–61). Some important archaeological discoveries and a gradual recognition that even Mark, the earliest of the gospels, was a subtle and profound theological treatise led to a "new look" at the Fourth Gospel. It is not as if the Fourth Gospel is the only "theological" gospel, and it is not as if it alone used places, feasts, and characters in the story in a non-historical symbolic fashion. All the gospels are "theological" in their own way, and many of the Fourth Gospel's place names and descriptions of Jerusalem at the time of Jesus have proved to be accurate. From about 1959 onwards, beginning with a celebrated article by J. A. T. Robinson ("The New Look on the Fourth Gospel," *Twelve New Testament Studies.* SBT 34; London: SCM Press, 1962, 94–106), there has been a greater appreciation of the Gospel of John as a Christian document that reflected events from the life of Jesus, and the subsequent experience of a Christian community that derived its Christianity from a telling and retelling of that life.

This rebirth of interest in the Fourth Gospel as a historical document, however, has not led scholars back to the naïve use of the story as an accurate record of the life, teaching, death, and resurrection of Jesus. The story of Jesus recorded in this gospel, rather, reflects *the history of an early Christian community.* Over the past three decades the major studies of the Fourth Gospel have attempted to lay bare the stages of the faith growth of the Johannine community, peeling back the various literary strata found in the present form of the Gospel (cf. the commentaries of Schnackenburg, Brown, and Becker). In more recent times some of the most creative work has been done by scholars who have attempted to retrace the faith journey of the members of the Johannine community itself (cf. Martyn, *History and Theology;* Brown, *Community*). The community began as a small group of Jerusalem Christians and its members developed an increasingly unique understanding of Jesus as they responded to a variety of experiences, both religious and social. People foreign, and even hostile to the traditions of Israel were admitted to the community (cf. 4:1-42), and this led to a stage when the members of the Johannine Community could no longer be accepted by their fellow Jews. Thus they were expelled from the synagogue (cf. 9:22; 12:42; 16:2). Free from this controlling tradition, a further vigorous affirmation developed of a unified and potentially dangerous understanding of God, the Christ of God, and his Church. From this long journey of faith and experience the Gospel of John emerged, the end product of a long and complicated literary history. The squabbles reflected in the Letters of John show that the potential dangers behind the message of the Gospel were realized. There were now at least two types of Johannine Christians: those who held to the perspective of the Letter writer, and those against whom he was writing: "They went out from us, but they did not belong to us; for if they had belonged to us, they would have remained with us. But by going out they made it plain that none of them belongs to us" (1 John 2:19).

Much that is exciting, illuminating, and helpful has happened in Johannine studies. However, after the foundational work of R. A. Culpepper *(Anatomy)* contemporary scholarship is increasingly devoting its attention to the impact that the whole story of Jesus, as it is told in this particular gospel, makes upon a reader. For the greater part of the twentieth century massive erudition has been shown in the rediscovery of the Jewish, Greek, and Gnostic religions that influenced the writing of the Gospel, in the dissecting of the Gospel into a variety of literary strata, and in the tracing of the community's history. It is now time to focus on the power of the story as we have it in its final form. Although traditional historical criticism must go on (cf. Painter, *Quest;* Schnelle, *Antidocetic Christology*), the narrative of the Gospel of John must be appreciated as a whole, as a unified, coherent utterance, and not be dissected into its constituent parts to be left, in pieces, on the scholar's table.

E. *The Approach Adopted in this Commentary*

The following commentary works from the conviction that it is possible to identify a strong narrative unity across the Fourth Gospel. In assessing that narrative unity, however, we must never lose sight of the world behind the text. My observations on the use of the expression "the Jews" are but one, admittedly critical example of the importance of that "world." However, I will concentrate on the world in the text, attempting to show how the story has been designed and told in order to influence the world in front of the text. Biblical scholarship has gradually come to appreciate more fully that there are more than two "worlds" involved in the interpretation of an ancient text. Historical-critical scholarship has devoted almost two hundred years to the rediscovery of *the world behind the text,* so that there be no abuse of *the world in the text.* Contemporary critics are devoting more attention to *the world in front of the text* (cf. Sandra M. Schneiders, *The Revelatory Text. Interpreting the New Testament as Sacred*

Scripture. San Francisco: Harper, 1991), as there is now a greater interest in approaching each single document, however limited and flawed it might be, as a work of art. This commentary is a contribution to such an approach through its reading of the Fourth Gospel.

Contemporary gospel studies are showing an increasing interest in what has come to be known as narrative criticism. Adapting and applying theories of narrative developed by literary theorists, Old Testament scholars were the first to seize upon this possible approach, given the large amount of narrative text found within the pages of the Bible. New Testament critics have not been slow to follow (on the Fourth Gospel, see Culpepper, *Anatomy;* Moloney, *Belief in the Word* 1–22). Behind each "story" there is a *real author* who has a definite person or group of people in mind as he or she tells the story. Thus there is an intended *real reader.* Neither of these figures can be found *in* the story itself. One produces it and the other takes it in hand to read it, or listens to it. An author constructs a narrative as a means to communicate a message to an audience. The Fourth Gospel is one such writing, but it is something more. The real author, whoever he (or she) might have been, is long since dead, as are the original recipients of the book. However, the Gospel still has a widespread readership. There is something about this book that has generated interested readers for almost two thousand years.

Although the real author and the real reader(s) do not play an active role in the events of the narrative, they leave their traces. Narratives have deliberately contrived plots and characters who interact throughout the story along a certain time line through a sequence of events. An author devises certain rhetorical features to hold plot and character together so that the reader will not miss the author's point of view. These rhetorical features are *in* the narrative. Although narrative theoreticians dispute the exactness of the scheme one can broadly claim that the communication between a real author and a real reader who are *outside* the text takes place through an implied author, a narrator, a narratee, and an implied reader who are *inside* the text. However obscure the details of the concrete situations of the original real author and the original real reader(s) may be, we still have the text, and much can be gleaned from it. This language may sound overly complex but it reflects everyone's reading experience. Whether or not one knows who the historical author is or was, and whether or not a story was directed specifically to the reader who has it in hand, any reader senses the presence of a story-teller, called throughout this commentary "the narrator," and behind the narrator hides an author who is directing affairs. A lost letter picked up by a disinterested third party quickly tells the reader something of the person writing the letter. The rhetoric of the letter also reveals something of the author's understanding of and approach to the reader. The person who has found the letter knows neither the real author nor the original intended reader, but the real reader—the person who picked up the letter from the pavement—is able to identify the communication attempted by the letter. The person who found the letter traces an author "implied" and a reader "implied" by the letter. Indeed, a very beautiful letter may even move the "eavesdropper." When that happens a mutuality is established between the reader "implied" by the letter and the real reader of the letter. One does not have to be part of the original communication process between the original writer of the letter and its original reader to be moved and inspired by the power of the emotions expressed by the letter. The literary form of a letter is very different from the sometimes complex literary shape of a narrative, especially one that was written almost two thousand years ago. However, the process of communication between an author and a reader takes place in both. Contemporary narrative approaches to the gospels attempt to enter into the process of communication between an author and a reader whom we do not know, and who are long since dead, so that the contemporary reader might be moved and inspired by the passionate convictions of the author.

Although not ignoring historical questions that inevitably lie "behind" the text of the Gospel this commentary focuses on the literary features found in the narrative of the Fourth Gospel. Much attention will be given to the literary shape of each section of the story; the way each section follows logically from what went before and leads directly into what follows; the roles of the various characters in the story; the passing of time; unresolved puzzles that emerge, forcing the reader to look farther into the narrative to tie these puzzles together; the consistency of the underlying point of view of an author who has shaped and told a story of the life of Jesus in a way unparalleled by any other early Christian writing. Like the reader who "eavesdropped" on the letter found on the pavement and was moved by the sincerity and power of the emotions communicated by the letter, we are "eavesdropping" on an ancient story of Jesus. "Eavesdropping" on this particular story, however, has been going on for some time, and it has served as an inspiration for Christians from all walks of life for almost two thousand years. This commentary will trace, via the literary features of the story-telling, the communication that is taking place *in the narrative* between an author and a reader.

We must allow ourselves to be seduced by the perspective of the author—but which author? It is possible for an author to write a narrative that communicates a point of view not reflective of his or her own situation in life, humor, personality, or personal experience. As George Steiner has correctly remarked: "Aristophanes may, at heart, have been the saddest of men—the which proposal is itself a piece of romanticised inversion. Our persuasion that some deep turbulence of spirit and sexuality attended the composition of *King Lear* and *Timon of Athens* may be nothing but trivial rationalisation. We have no shred of evidence either way" (G. Steiner, *Real Presences. Is there anything in what we say?* London: Faber & Faber, 1989, 169). There is, therefore, an author *in the text* of the Fourth Gospel, just as there was an author *in the text* of the letter described above. Whatever the perspective of a historical flesh-and-blood author may have been, we can only claim to trace the theological point of view of an author in the text itself. Such an author is generally called the *implied author*. This feature of any narrative is not a historical person, however well the point of view may or may not reflect the choices of that figure from the past who should be called the *real author*. Differently from some contemporary narratives, it can generally be assumed (but never proved) that the real author *of* and the implied author *in* New Testament narratives speak with the same voice. It is difficult to imagine that such a passionate book as the Fourth Gospel is anything but the communication of a historical person's deeply held and passionate belief in what God has done in and through Jesus.

Like the historical author of the book, now long since dead and beyond our knowledge and scientific control, the flesh-and-blood historical first real readers are likewise outside our control. We cannot be sure of the reception this passionate story of Jesus received. The ongoing existence of the Gospel demonstrates that it was received, treasured, and passed on, but the evidence of the Johannine Letters indicates that the readers did not always agree on what the author wanted to communicate. Indeed, they quickly broke into argument, and even division, over the christological and Christian significance of the Gospel. This is understandable. How I might respond to a narrative in any of the gospels may vary from day to day, depending on any number of circumstances. We are well aware of the numerous circumstances that affect the reading process, for better or worse. Yet *within the narrative* there is a reader addressed by the implied author, as there was an identifiable reader implied by the letter described above. As the narrative unfolds the reader is gradually provided with information and experiences such a reader cannot avoid. This reader is shaped by the desires of the author and emerges as the text unfolds. This reader does not suffer from the vagaries that can impinge upon the reading process. Critics speak of a literary construct within the narrative itself, whose responses are totally controlled by the implied author. Such a "reader" is generally called the *implied reader*. The implied reader is not a historical person. Historically there are only real readers. The implied reader is produced by the unfolding narrative. By tracing the developing knowledge and experience of the implied reader as each page of the text is opened I am better able to appreciate the temporal flow of the narrative and grow in my appreciation of the unfolding narrative.

Stanley Fish has described the use of the implied reader by a narrative critic as follows:

> The basis of the method is a consideration of the *temporal* flow of the reading experience, and it is assumed that the reader responds in terms of that flow and not to the whole utterance. That is, in an utterance of any length, there is a point at which the reader has taken in only the first word, and then the second, and then the third, and so on, and the report of what happens to the reader is always a report of what happened *to that point.* (S. Fish, *Is There a Text in This Class? The Authority of Interpretative Communities.* Cambridge: Harvard University Press, 1988, 26–27).

At any given stage in the unfolding narrative the commentary will only refer back to that part of the story told so far. As each page is opened, much is learned about Jesus and the Father who sent him, but there is still more to learn from those parts of the story that lie ahead. Only when the author has obviously signed off from the telling of the story (cf. 20:30-31) does the reader come to rest. But the citation from Fish needs expansion, as it does not fully exhaust the experience of the readers of ancient, canonical texts like the Fourth Gospel. The reader gradually emerges from the unfolding narrative shaped by the author, knowing only what has been read so far, and the reader is able to move backward to recall events already narrated. But it is impossible that the reader in a Christian gospel has no knowledge or experience of the story of Jesus of Nazareth and Christian life and its practices. The direct importation of literary scholarship into New Testament studies has sometimes presupposed such a "virginal" reader, but this is unrealistic. The author of the Fourth Gospel takes it for granted that the reader knows many things already. The implied reader knows Greek! The reader in the Fourth Gospel is able to understand double meanings behind Greek words (e.g., 3:3-5, 14; 8:28; 12:32) and subtle ironies (e.g., 9:28-29; 19:14-15); language that was used in the sacramental life of the community (6:51-58; 19:35) and references to Jesus' resurrection are taken as understood from quite early in the story (cf. 2:22). Much more than a knowledge of the syntactically correct and simple Greek of the text of the Fourth Gospel (cf. Barrett 5–11) is presupposed of its reader. The unexplained use of certain Jewish messianic categories (e.g., in 1:19-51), religious customs (e.g., 2:6; 5:9; 6:4; 7:2; 10:22), and the geography of Palestine (e.g., 5:2; 18:1; 19:17) indicates that such things are taken as known. The reader knows everything that the author does not explain. The reader in the Fourth Gospel story may be credited with a knowledge of the Jesus story, but its Johannine form is being presented to bring the reader (or listener) to accept a particular point of view. The reader knows that Jesus died on a cross, but the author of this gospel insists that this death is both a "lifting up" (cf. 3:14; 8:28; 12:32) and a glorification (11:4; 12:23). Indeed, on two occasions the author of the Fourth

Gospel does not hesitate to tell the reader why the story is being written in this particular way (19:35; 20:30-31).

It would be dishonest not to recognize that every word of the Gospel is historically and culturally conditioned. The fact that it is written in *koiné* Greek is prima facie evidence of this truth. There is inevitably something "strange" and "foreign" about the biblical text that demands that we wrestle with it. First-century history and culture must play a part in interpretation. The Fourth Gospel, like all biblical texts handed down to us by Jewish and Christian tradition, is a difficult text, and a great deal of this difficulty comes from its strangeness when read in our present cultural context. The original readers of the Gospel are an important point of reference in following the interplay between author and reader in the text. Adela Yarbro Collins has rightly insisted that we should

> give more weight to the original historical context of the text. This context cannot and should not totally determine all subsequent meaning and use of the text. But if . . . all meaning is context bound, the original context and meaning have a certain normative character. I suggest that Biblical theologians are not only mediators between genres. They are also mediators between historical periods. . . . Whatever tension there may be between literary- and historical-critical methods, the two approaches are complementary (A. Yarbro Collins, "Narrative, History and Gospel," *Sem* 43 [1988] 150, 153).

Every narrative generates a reader as it unfolds, but it would be a mistake to think that one has performed one's task of interpretation once one has traced the temporal flow of a narrative through the experience of an emerging reader. Such a use of literary techniques will still only tell us how an author achieves an effect, but there are other elements that must be kept in mind for a sound, critical reading of an ancient, normative text. *The world behind the text* must be respected and studied in order to understand its strange distance from our world and our concerns. What must be asked is: how does the reader *in the text* who emerges as this ancient story of Jesus unfolds speak to the knowledge and experience of the twenty-first century Christian reader *of the text?* There is, of course, a context that unites the original and all subsequent readers of the Gospel of John: a context generated by Christian faith, a community of believing readers. The secret of the lasting value of a narrative lies in the mutuality that is created between the implied reader *in the text* and the real reader *of the text,* and the common context of Christian belief helps this mutuality. A story that tells of Jesus the Christ should appeal to Christians. Nevertheless, there are libraries of Christian books that have not! What is it in the Fourth Gospel that has generated its ongoing readership? There must be an understanding and respect for the world behind the text that shaped the reader *in the text,* but there is more. When I read a good novel for the first time I become the implied reader. I become part of the story, caught in its characters, events, time, and places as the pages turn. This is the case with any good book, but in a classic there is an even deeper relationship between the reader in the text and the reader of the text. It is the mutuality generated between the implied reader *in the text* and the real reader *of the text* that makes any given text a classic. As David Tracy has said: "The classic text's real disclosure is its claim to attention on the ground that an event of understanding proper to finite human beings has here found expression" (D. Tracy, *The Analogical Imagination: Christian Theology and the Culture of Pluralism* (New York: Crossroad, 1981, 102).

The practice of reading and the community of readers that has produced the Bible are an example of that truth. The Fourth Gospel can lay claim to being a Christian classic. As we continue to read the Fourth Gospel after nearly two thousand years of reading in a variety of contexts we can be sure that there has been a mutuality between its implied and real readers. The unfolding narrative of the Fourth Gospel raises problems that the reader will solve through the ongoing reading of the story of Jesus. Did these solutions speak to the members of the Johannine community, the original intended readers who were part of the world of the narrative of the gospels in a way that the contemporary real reader can never be? They read Greek, or at least understood it as it was read; they caught the subtleties of double-meaning words and ironies. None of this can to be taken for granted for most contemporary readers of the Fourth Gospel. Do the questions raised and the solutions offered by this story of Jesus still speak to real readers at the beginning of the third millennium? Is this text a classic? Does its ongoing claim to a readership rest on "the ground that an event of understanding proper to human beings has here found expression" (Tracy)? Narrative critical *theory* rightly distinguishes between an implied reader who emerges from the unfolding narration, the intended reader for whom the narrative was originally written (for whom it was originally "intended" by a real author), and the real reader, whoever, wherever, and whenever he or she may take the text in hand. Reading *practice* does not make such neat distinctions. Neither will the commentary that follows. Our experience of reading is that some stories speak to us while others do not.

The commentary, while based on an awareness of an emerging reader *in the text,* is only concerned with today's reader *of the text.* It attempts to show that readers at the turn of the second and third millennia still find that their response to this gospel, in dialogue with the experience of almost two thousand years of Christian life, resonates with the experience of the implied reader and the original readers in the Johannine community. We may find (and no doubt many do find) that such a response is fatuous in our mundane world. But that is not the only thing that might happen. Sometimes we may have a further response that is independent of the implied reader and thus outside the control of the author. It is unavoidable that our response, either of empathy or antipathy, will be the result of our privileged position as the recipients of almost two thousand years of the Christian practice of reading the gospels. As Honoré de Balzac's narrator informs his implied reader at the beginning of *Père Goriot:* "You may be certain that this drama is neither fiction nor romance. *All is true,* so true that everyone can recognise the elements of the tragedy in his own household, in his own heart perhaps" (H. de Balzac, *Old Goriot,* Penguin Classics; Harmondsworth: Penguin Books, 1951, 28).

In the reading of the Fourth Gospel that follows my aim is to trace the reader's emerging experience as this particular story of the life, teaching, death, and resurrection of Jesus is told. Two thousand years of Christian history are a fair indication that generation after generation of Christian readers have "entered the fictional contract" of the Fourth Gospel; they have become one with the implied reader (cf. Seymour Chatman, *Story and Discourse. Narrative Structure in Fiction and Film.* Ithaca, N.Y.: Cornell University Press, 1978, 150). I will deliberately avoid the jargon that has been developed within literary criticism and briefly outlined above. I will simply refer to "the author" and "the reader." There is a theoretical distinction among various elements that combine to form a satisfactory reading experience, but the commentary attempts to create a meeting of horizons among the worlds behind the text, in the text, and in front of the text. Traditional critical scholarship and a contemporary literary approach are combined to create a space where a satisfied Christian reader is born.

F. *The Theological Contribution and Contemporary Significance of the Fourth Gospel*

The christology and theology of this gospel provided the raw material out of which the great Christian doctrines were forged (cf. T. E. Pollard, *Johannine Christology and the Early Church.* MSSNTS 13; Cambridge: Cambridge University Press, 1970). Major questions about Jesus, God, and the Christian life were left unanswered by Jesus and the apostolic Church. As Christianity became part of the world and culture of the Mediterranean basin and beyond, these unresolved questions emerged with increasing urgency. Who was Jesus of Nazareth? How did he relate to God? If he was the Son of God, what was the nature of his relationship with God? Was he "of the same being" as the Father? If so, he was divine. But if he was divine, how was he human? These questions plagued the emerging Christian Church, and Christian society once the Empire embraced Christianity with the decision of Constantine to grant religious tolerance to all and to restore confiscated property to the Christians in 313 C.E.

It took almost four hundred years before the great ecumenical councils of Ephesus (431 C.E.) and Chalcedon (451 C.E.) formulated the Christian responses to these questions, and it was the Fourth Gospel that provided the language for its debates. Jesus was the Son of Man, the Son of God, and the Word of God; he and the Father were one, and he was in the Father and the Father in him. Indeed, the challenge to account for the human and the divine in Jesus lies at the heart of both the Fourth Gospel and all subsequent christological debate. Chalcedon may have formulated an accepted christological creed, but it did not bring christological debate to an end.

This commentary points out the way the Fourth Gospel presents the God of Israel as Father, and Jesus as Son, in an all-determining *relationship*. The later Church took a different direction and used the Johannine language in its debates about the *metaphysics* of the Son of God. This shift of focus asked the language of the Fourth Gospel to respond to questions the Johannine narrative did not pose. As the history of theology witnesses, this shift generated many problems then, and these problems remain. One of the important contributions that contemporary biblical scholarship has made to theology can be seen in the theological return to more reflection about Jesus Christ's relationship with God and creation.

The Fourth Gospel also generates questions about God that it does not resolve. The traditional God of Israel is firmly in place, but God is now the Father of Jesus and Jesus is a Son, united in a oneness of will and love with the Father. The Old Testament had already spoken of the spirit of God, and the New Testament, especially Paul and Luke, made regular reference to the Spirit (e.g., Romans 8; Luke 24:44-49; Acts 2:1-13). In the Fourth Gospel the Paraclete, the Holy Spirit, becomes a character whom the Father will send after the departure of Jesus. The Spirit Paraclete will be the presence of Jesus in his absence, leading, instructing, comforting Christians, and judging the world (cf. 14:15-17, 25-26; 15:26-27; 16:7-11, 12-15). There are several places in the Gospel where the interplay between Father, Son, and Holy Spirit is intense (e.g., 14:1-31). Once again these different "characters in the story" are clearly in relationship. God is the Father of the Son, Jesus Christ. The Father sends and loves the Son as the Son loves the Father. The gift of the Paraclete is intimately linked with continuation of the ministry of the absent Jesus, and the Paraclete is sent by both the Father and the departed Jesus.

However, the Fourth Gospel never attempts to resolve the nature of this relationship. Here we have the beginnings of the traditional Christian doctrine of the Trinity. The Christian doctrine of one God and three Persons is an attempt to explain in philosophical, often *metaphysical* terms what was described as a series of *relationships* in the Fourth Gospel. The early Church debated these questions with much passion, shifting the discussion from relationship to metaphysics until the first steps in the formulation of a traditional doctrine of the Trinity were taken at the Council of Nicea in 325 C.E. Nicea may have formulated a Trinitarian creed but it did not bring Trinitarian debate to an end. What was said above about contemporary christological thought could also be said about contemporary writing on the Trinity. Without abandoning its philosophical inquiry, much contemporary theology is enriched by a return to reflection on the relationships that exist within and beyond the Godhead.

More could be said about the theological contribution of this gospel, but it must be left for the commentary: the saving effect of the crucifixion of Jesus, the unique revelation of God that takes place in Jesus Christ, the Christian sacraments of Baptism and Eucharist, the communitarian nature of the Christian life, the tension between a realized and an end-time understanding of life, eternal life and judgment to mention the more important issues. Little wonder that the Fourth Gospel has been one of the most loved documents throughout the Christian centuries.

Nevertheless, there is more to its fascination than its contribution to Christian thinking and to the formulation of the great Christian doctrines. It has, above all, captured the minds and hearts of its readers. So central have some passages become for Christians that they have developed a life of their own (cf. 1:14; 3:16-17; 8:32; 10:30, 38; 11:26-27, etc.). As the commentary attempts to draw out the Gospel's impact upon a reader it will attempt to highlight the narrative power of the Johannine story. But there is something behind this story generating this narrative power that has never failed to capture willing readers of the story. The Fourth Gospel records the Jesus-story of a community in transition (see above, A. *The Johannine Literature*). No longer able to live their new faith in Jesus as the Christ, the Son of God within the world in which Christianity came to birth, the Johannine Christians took their story of Jesus into a new world (cf. 9:22; 12:42; 16:2). In crossing the bridge from one world into another they inevitably, and perhaps unconsciously, produced a story of the life, death, and resurrection of Jesus that has addressed the perennial situation of all Christians. The summons to believe that Jesus is the Christ, the Son of God, and that he has made God known so that all who believe might have life (cf. 20:31; 17:3), addresses a people in transition.

Christian belief unfailingly calls people of all generations into transition. A follower of Jesus cannot rest easily within a "closed system" of religious beliefs and commitments, however well-articulated and precious they may be. New worlds are forever challenging the believer to tell and live the old story in a new way, and the Fourth Gospel did this paradigmatically in the early Church. Much of the commentary that follows points out that the Johannine Jesus repeatedly demands "more" from those who claim to have come to believe and understand him and the God he makes known. It is this "more" that renders the heart of the Christian restless, and that gives this ancient text, for all its oddities, a power of its own.

G. *The Structure of the Gospel*

Although there are dissenting voices (cf. Brodie 21–45), the vast majority of interpreters accept that there are four major sections to the Fourth Gospel: the Prologue (1:1-18), the ministry of Jesus, often called the book of signs (1:19–12:50), the account of Jesus' final night with his disciples, the passion and the resurrection (13:1–20:29), and a solemn conclusion to the Gospel (20:30-31). Contemporary scholarship, with its interest in the literary unity of the narrative as it has come down to us, is questioning a long-held common opinion that John 21 was an addendum to the original Gospel. This commentary will argue that it is added. The detailed subdivision of the major sections is more difficult to determine. The structure proposed below presupposes the detailed argument of the commentary, especially in the general introductions found at the beginning of each major section. For reasons of clarity, however, I will not list the smaller blocks of material that form my subdivisions. It is sufficient for the reader to appreciate the outline of the Gospel's argument that will determine the structure of the commentary. The reasons behind the detailed articulation of each section of this overall structure will be provided during the course of the commentary.

OUTLINE OF THE STRUCTURE OF THE GOSPEL

I. THE PROLOGUE (1:1-18)
II. THE BOOK OF SIGNS (1:19–12:50)
    A. The First Days of Jesus (1:19-51)
    B. From Cana To Cana (2:1–4:54)
       i. The First Miracle at Cana (2:1-12)
          ii. Jesus and "the Jews" (2:12-22)
          iii. The narrator's comment (2:23-25)
          iv. Jesus and Nicodemus (3:1-21)
          v. Jesus and John the Baptist (3:22-26)
          vi. Jesus and the Samaritan woman (4:1-15)
          vii. Jesus and the Samaritan woman (4:16-30)
          viii. Jesus comments (4:31-38)
          ix. Jesus and the Samaritan villagers (4:39-42)
      x. The Second Miracle at Cana (4:43-54)

C. The Feasts of "the Jews" (5:1–10:42)
   i. Jesus and the Sabbath (5:1-47)
   ii. Jesus and the Passover (6:1-71)
   iii. Jesus and Tabernacles, I (7:1–8:59)
   iv. Jesus and Tabernacles, II (9:1–10:21)
   v. Jesus and Dedication (10:22-42)
D. Jesus turns toward "the hour" (11:1–12:50)
   i. A resurrection that will lead to death (11:1-54)
   ii. The hour has come (11:55–12:36)
   iii. Conclusion to the ministry of Jesus (12:37-50)
III. THE BOOK OF GLORY (13:1–20:31)
A. The Last Discourse (13:1–17:26)
   i. Making God known: the footwashing and the morsel (13:1-38)
      ii. Departure (14:1-31)
         iii. To abide, to love, and to be hated (15:1–16:3)
      iv. Departure (16:4-33)
   v. Making God known: Jesus' final prayer (17:1-26)
B. The Passion (18:1–19:42)
   i. Jesus and his enemies in a garden (18:1-11)
      ii. Jesus' appearance before "the Jews" (18:12-27)
         iii. Jesus before Pilate (18:28–19:16a)
      iv. The crucifixion of Jesus (19:16b-37)
   v. Jesus buried in a garden by his new-found friends (19:38-42)
C. The Resurrection (20:1-29)
   i. Scenes at the tomb (20:1-18)
      (a) Visits to the empty tomb (20:1–10)
      (b) Jesus appears to Mary Magdalene (20:11–18)
   ii. Scenes in the house (20:19-29)
      (a) Jesus appears to the disciples, but not Thomas (20:19–23)
      (b) Jesus appears to the disciples, and to Thomas (20:24–29)
IV. THE CONCLUSION TO THE GOSPEL (20:30-31)
V. EPILOGUE: Further Resurrection Appearances (21:1-25)
   i. Jesus appears to his disciples at the Sea of Tiberias (21:1-14)
   ii. Jesus, Peter, and the Beloved Disciple (21:15-24)
   iii. A second conclusion to the Gospel (21:25)

GENERAL BIBLIOGRAPHY

It is impossible to provide a complete bibliography. Interested readers should consult Gilbert van Belle, *Johannine Bibliography 1966-1985. A Cumulative Bibliography on the Fourth Gospel.* BETL 82; Leuven: University Press, 1988. This volume runs to 563 closely printed pages, and the flood of publications has not abated since 1985. I have largely limited the general bibliography that follows to English works. There are some major commentaries and studies in other languages, however, that are so important that they must be listed. In the bibliographies that follow the sections of the commentary I have given more specialized references, some of which are in other European languages. I have, however, concentrated on providing a majority of studies in English. Books listed here are referred to in an abbreviated form in the Introduction and throughout the commentary.

Commentaries

Barrett, C. K. *The Gospel according to St. John.* 2nd ed. London: S.P.C.K., 1978.

Bauer, Walter. *Das Johannesevangelium erklärt.* HNT 6. Tübingen: J. C. B. Mohr (Paul Siebeck), 1933.

Beasley-Murray, G. R. *John.* WBC 36. Waco: Word Books, 1987.

Becker, Jürgen. *Das Evangelium des Johannes.* 2 vols. ÖTBK 4/1–2. Gütersloh: Gerd Mohn, and Würzburg: Echter Verlag, 1979–1981.

Bernard, J. H. *A Critical and Exegetical Commentary on the Gospel according to St John.* 2 vols. ICC. Edinburgh: T&T Clark, 1928.

Boismard, M.-E., and Arnaud Lamouille. *L'Evangile de Jean.* Synopse des Quatre Evangiles en Français III. Paris: Cerf, 1977.

Brodie, Thomas L. *The Gospel According to John. A Literary and Theological Commentary.* New York: Oxford University Press, 1993.

Brown, Raymond E. *The Gospel According to John.* 2 vols. AB 29, 29a. Garden City, N.Y.: Doubleday, 1966–1970.

Bultmann, Rudolf. *The Gospel of John. A Commentary.* Oxford: Blackwell, 1971.

Bussche, Henri van den. *Jean. Commentaire de l'Évangile Spirituel.* Bruges: Desclée de Brouwer, 1976.

Carson, D. A. *The Gospel according to John.* Grand Rapids: Eerdmans, 1991.

Delebecque, Edouard. *Evangile de Jean. Texte Traduit et Annoté.* CRB 23. Paris: Gabalda, 1987.

Ellis, Peter F. *The Genius of John. A Compositional-Critical Commentary on the Fourth Gospel.* Collegeville: The Liturgical Press, 1984.

Gnilka, Joachim. *Das Johannesevangelium.* Die Neue Echter Bibel. 2nd ed. Würzburg: Echter Verlag, 1985.

Haenchen, Ernst. *John 1–2.* 2 vols. Hermeneia. Philadelphia: Fortress, 1984.

Hoskyns, Edwyn C. *The Fourth Gospel.* Edited by F. N. Davey. London: Faber & Faber, 1947.

Kysar, Robert. *John.* Augsburg Commentary on the New Testament. Minneapolis: Augsburg Publishing House, 1986.

Lagrange, M.-J. *Evangile selon saint Jean.* EtB. Paris: Gabalda, 1936.

Léon-Dufour, Xavier. *Lecture de l'évangile selon Jean.* 3 vols. Parole de Dieu. Paris: Editions du Seuil, 1988, 1990, 1993.

Lightfoot, R. H. *St. John's Gospel.* Edited by C. F. Evans. Oxford: Oxford University Press, 1956.

Lindars, Barnabas. *The Gospel of John.* NCB. London: Oliphants, 1972.

Loisy, Alfred. *Le quatrième évangile.* Paris: Emile Nourry, 1921.

Macgregor, G. H. C. *The Gospel of John.* Moffat Commentary. London: Hodder and Stoughton, 1928.

Marsh, John. *Saint John*. PNTC. Harmondsworth and Baltimore: Penguin Books, 1968.

Moloney, Francis J. *Belief in the Word. Reading John 1–4*. Minneapolis: Fortress, 1993.

_____. *Signs and Shadows. Reading John 5–12*. Minneapolis: Fortress, 1996.

_____. *Glory not Dishonor. Reading John 13–20 (21)*. Minneapolis: Fortress, 1998.

Morris, Leon. *The Gospel According to John*. NIC NT. Revised Edition. Grand Rapids: Eerdmans, 1995.

Schnackenburg, Rudolf. *The Gospel According to St John*. 3 vols. HThKNT IV/1–3. London: Burns & Oates; New York: Crossroad, 1968–1982.

Segalla, Giuseppe. *Giovanni*. NVB 36. Roma: Edizioni Paoline, 1976.

Stibbe, M. W. G. *John*. Readings: A New Biblical Commentary. Sheffield: JSOT Press, 1993.

Talbert, C. H. *Reading John. A Literary and Theological Commentary on the Fourth Gospel and the Johannine Epistles*. London: S.P.C.K., 1992.

Westcott, B. F. *The Gospel According to Saint John*. London: John Murray, 1908.

Witherington, Ben. *John's Wisdom. A Commentary on the Fourth Gospel*. Louisville: Westminster/John Knox, 1995.

General

Ashton, John. "The Identity and Function of the *Ioudaioi* in the Fourth Gospel," *NT* 27 (1985) 40–75.

_____. *Understanding the Fourth Gospel*. Oxford: Clarendon Press, 1991.

Ashton, John, ed. *The Interpretation of John*. Issues in Religion and Theology 9. London: S.P.C.K., 1986.

Ball, David M. *'I Am' in John's Gospel. Literary Function, Background and Theological Implications*. JSNT.S 124. Sheffield: Sheffield Academic Press, 1996.

Barrett, C. K. *Essays on John*. London: S.P.C.K., 1982.

_____. *The Gospel of John and Judaism*. London: S.P.C.K., 1975.

Beutler, Johannes. *Martyria: Traditionsgeschichtliche Untersuchungen zum Zeugnisthema bei Johannes*. FTS 10. Frankfurt: Josef Knecht, 1972.

Bittner, Wolfgang J. *Jesu Zeichen im Johannesevangelium: Die Messias-Erkenntnis im Johannesevangelium vor ihrem jüdischen Hintergrund*. WUNT 2nd ser. 26. Tübingen: J. C. B. Mohr (Paul Siebeck), 1987.

Blank, Josef. *Krisis: Untersuchungen zur johanneischen Christologie und Eschatologie*. Freiburg: Lambertus Verlag, 1964.

Boer, Martinus C. de. *Johannine Perspectives on the Death of Jesus*. CBET 17. Kampen: Kok Pharos, 1996.

Brown, Raymond E. *The Community of the Beloved Disciple*. New York: Paulist, 1979.

Bühner, Jan-Adolf. *Der Gesandte und sein Weg im 4. Evangelium: Die kultur- und religionsgeschichtlichen Grundlagen der johanneischen Sendungschristologie sowie ihre traditionsgeschichtliche Entwicklung*. WUNT 2nd ser. 2. Tübingen: J. C. B. Mohr (Paul Siebeck) 1977.

Bultmann, Rudolf. "Die Bedeutung der neuerschlossenen mandäischen und manichäischen Quellen für das Verständnis des Johannesevangeliums," *ZNW* 24 (1925) 100–146.

Burge, Gary M. *The Anointed Community. The Holy Spirit in the Johannine Community.* Grand Rapids: Eerdmans, 1987.

Cassidy, Richard J. *John's Gospel in New Perspective. Christology and the Realities of Roman Power.* Maryknoll: Orbis, 1992.

Charlesworth, James H. *The Beloved Disciple. Whose Witness Validates the Gospel of John?* Valley Forge, Pa.: Trinity Press International, 1995.

Collins, Raymond F. *These Things Have Been Written. Studies on the Fourth Gospel.* LThPM 2. Louvain: Peeters, 1990.

Cullmann, Oscar. *The Johannine Circle: Its place in Judaism, among the disciples of Jesus and in early Christianity: A study in the origin of the Gospel of John.* London: SCM Press, 1976.

Culpepper, R. Alan. *Anatomy of the Fourth Gospel.* New Testament Foundations and Facets. Philadelphia: Fortress, 1983.

_____. *John, The Son of Zebedee. The Life of a Legend.* Studies on Personalities of the New Testament. Columbia: University of South Carolina Press, 1994.

_____. "The Gospel of John and the Jews," RExp 84 (1987) 273–288.

_____. *The Johannine School: An Evaluation of the Johannine School Hypothesis Based on an Investigation of the Nature of Ancient Schools.* SBL.DS 26. Missoula, Mont.: Scholars, 1975.

Culpepper, R. Alan, and C. Clifton Black, eds. *Exploring the Fourth Gospel. In Honor of D. Moody Smith.* Louisville: Westminster/John Knox, 1996.

Dodd, C. H. *Historical Tradition in the Fourth Gospel.* Cambridge: Cambridge University Press, 1963.

_____. *The Interpretation of the Fourth Gospel.* Cambridge: Cambridge University Press, 1953.

Duke, Paul D. *Irony in the Fourth Gospel.* Atlanta: John Knox Press, 1985.

Forestell, J. Terence. *The Word of the Cross: Salvation as Revelation in the Fourth Gospel.* AnBib 57. Rome: Biblical Institute Press, 1974.

Fortna, Robert T. *The Fourth Gospel and its Predecessor: From Narrative Source to Present Gospel.* Studies in the New Testament and its World. Edinburgh: T&T Clark, 1989.

_____. *The Gospel of Signs: A Reconstruction of the Narrative Source Underlying the Fourth Gospel.* MSSNTS 11. Cambridge: Cambridge University Press, 1970.

Guilding, Aileen. *The Fourth Gospel and Jewish Worship. A Study of the Relation of St. John's Gospel to the Ancient Jewish Lectionary System.* Oxford: Oxford University Press, 1960.

Haenchen, Ernst. "Johanneische Probleme," ZThK 56 (1959) 19–54.

Hahn, Ferdinand. "'Die Juden' im Johannesevangelium," in Paul-Gerhard Müller and Werner Stenger, eds., *Kontinuität und Einheit: Für Franz Mussner.* Freiburg: Herder, 1981, 430–438.

Hare, Douglas R. A. *The Son of Man Tradition.* Minneapolis: Fortress, 1990.

Hengel, Martin. *Die johanneische Frage. Ein Lösungsversuch mit einem Beitrag zur Apokalypse von Jörg Frey.* WUNT 67. Tübingen: J. C. B. Mohr (Paul Siebeck), 1993.

_____. *The Johannine Question.* London: SCM Press, 1989. A collection of lectures on the Johannine question, expanded into the above scholarly volume in German.

Jonge, Marinus de. "Signs and Works in the Fourth Gospel," in Tjitze Baarda, A. F. J. Klijn, and W. C. van Unnik, eds., *Miscellanea Neotestamentica*. NT.S 48. Leiden: E. J. Brill, 1978, 107–125.

Käsemann, Ernst. *The Testament of Jesus according to John 17*. London: SCM Press, 1966.

Kieffer, René. *Le monde symbolique de saint Jean*. LeDiv 137. Paris: Cerf, 1989.

Knöppler, Thomas. *Die theologia crucis des Johannesevangeliums. Das Verständnis des Todes Jesu im Rahmen der johanneischen Inkarnations- und Erhöhungschristologie*. WMANT 69. Neukirchen-Vluyn: Neukirchener Verlag, 1994.

Koester, Craig. "Hearing, Seeing and Believing in the Gospel of John," *Bib*. 70 (1989) 327–348.

_____. *Symbolism in the Fourth Gospel. Meaning, Mystery, Community*. Minneapolis: Fortress, 1995.

Kysar, Robert. *The Fourth Evangelist and His Gospel. An examination of contemporary scholarship*. Minneapolis: Augsburg, 1975.

_____. "The Fourth Gospel: A Report on Recent Research." *ANRW* 2.25.3, 2389–2480.

_____. *John, the Maverick Gospel*. Atlanta: John Knox Press, 1976.

_____. *John's Story of Jesus*. Philadelphia: Fortress, 1984.

Lee, Dorothy A. *The Symbolic Narratives of the Fourth Gospel: The Interplay of Form and Meaning*. JSNT.S 95. Sheffield: JSOT Press, 1994.

Léon-Dufour, Xavier. "Towards a Symbolic Reading of the Fourth Gospel," *NTS* 27 (1980–1981) 439–456.

Leroy, Herbert. *Rätsel und Missverständnis: Ein Beitrag zur Formgeschichte des Johannesevangeliums*. BBB 30. Bonn: Peter Hanstein, 1968.

Lieu, Judith M. *Image and Reality. The Jews in the World of the Christians in the Second Century*. Edinburgh: T&T Clark, 1996.

Loader, William R. G. "The Central Structure of Johannine Theology." *NTS* 80 (1984) 188–216.

_____. *The Christology of the Fourth Gospel*. BET 23. Frankfurt: Peter Lang, 1989.

Maccini, Robert G. *Her Testimony is True. Women as Witnesses according to John*. JSNT.S 125. Sheffield: Sheffield Academic Press, 1996.

Manns, Frederic. *L'Evangile de Jean à la lumière du Judaïsme*. SBFA 33. Jerusalem: Franciscan Printing Press, 1991.

Martyn, J. Louis. *History and Theology in the Fourth Gospel*. 2nd ed. Nashville: Abingdon, 1979.

_____. *The Gospel of John in Christian History. Essays for Interpreters*. New York: Paulist, 1978.

Meeks, Wayne A. "The Man from Heaven in Johannine Sectarianism," *JBL* 91 (1972) 44–72.

_____. *The Prophet-King: Moses Traditions and the Johannine Christology*. NT.S 14. Leiden: E. J. Brill, 1967.

Menken, Maarten J. J. *Old Testament Quotations in the Fourth Gospel. Studies in Textual Form*. CBET 15. Kampen: Kok Pharos, 1996.

Mlakuzhyil, George. *The Christocentric Literary Structure of the Fourth Gospel*. AnBib 117. Rome: Biblical Institute Press, 1987.

Moloney, Francis J. "Johannine Theology," *NJBC* 1417–1426.

_____. *The Johannine Son of Man.* BSRel 14. 2nd ed. Rome: LAS, 1978.

Neyrey, Jerome H. *An Ideology of Revolt: John's Christology in Social-Science Perspective.* Philadelphia: Fortress, 1988.

Nicholson, Godfrey C. *Death as Departure: The Johannine Descent-Ascent Schema.* SBL.DS 63. Chico, Cal.: Scholars, 1983.

Obermann, Andreas. *Die christologische Erfüllung der Schrift im Johannesevangelium. Eine Untersuchung zur johanneischen Hermeneutik anhand der Schriftzitate.* WUNT 2nd ser. 83. Tübingen: J. C. B. Mohr (Paul Siebeck), 1996.

O'Day, Gail R. *Revelation in the Fourth Gospel. Narrative Mode and Theological Claim.* Philadelphia: Fortress, 1986.

Odeberg, Hugo. *The Fourth Gospel Interpreted in Its Relation to Contemporaneous Religious Currents in Palestine and the Hellenistic-Oriental World.* Uppsala: Almqvist, 1929; Chicago: Argonaut, 1968.

Onuki, Takashi. *Gemeinde und Welt im Johannesevangelium: Ein Beitrag zur Frage nach der theologischen und pragmatischen Funktion des johanneischen "Dualismus."* WMANT 56. Neukirchen-Vluyn: Neukirchener Verlag, 1984.

Painter, John. "Inclined to God: The Quest for Eternal Life—Bultmannian Hermeneutics and the Theology of the Fourth Gospel." In R. A. Culpepper and C. Clifton Black, eds., *Exploring the Gospel of John. In Honor of D. Moody Smith.* Louisville: Westminster/John Knox, 1996, 346–368.

_____. *John: Witness and Theologian.* London: S.P.C.K., 1975.

_____. *The Quest for the Messiah. The History, Literature and Theology of the Johannine Community.* 2nd Ed. Edinburgh: T&T Clark, 1993.

Pancaro, Severino. *The Law in the Fourth Gospel: The Torah and the Gospel, Moses and Jesus, Judaism and Christianity according to John.* NT.S 42. Leiden: E. J. Brill, 1975.

Petersen, Norman R. *Literary Criticism for New Testament Critics.* GBSNT. Philadelphia: Fortress, 1978.

_____. *The Gospel of John and the Sociology of Light. Language and Characterization in the Fourth Gospel.* Valley Forge: Trinity Press International, 1993.

Pollard, T. E. *Johannine Christology and the Early Church.* MSSNTS 13. Cambridge: Cambridge University Press, 1970.

Porsch, Felix. *Pneuma und Wort. Ein exegetischer Beitrag zur Pneumatologie des Johannesevangeliums.* FTS 16. Frankfurt: J. Knecht, 1974.

Potterie, Ignace de la. *La Vérité dans Saint Jean.* 2 vols. AnBib 73–74. Rome: Biblical Institute Press, 1977.

Quast, Kevin. *Peter and the Beloved Disciple: Figures for a Community in Crisis.* JSNT.S 32. Sheffield: JSOT Press, 1989.

Reim, Günter. *Studien zum alttestamentlichen Hintergrund des Johannesevangeliums.* MSSNTS 22. Cambridge: Cambridge University Press, 1974.

Reinhartz, Adele. *The Word in the World: The Cosmological Tale in the Fourth Gospel.* SBL.MS 45. Atlanta: Scholars, 1992.

Rensberger, David K. *Johannine Faith and Liberating Community.* Philadelphia: Westminster, 1988.

Robinson, John A. T. *The Priority of John.* London: SCM Press, 1985.

Rodriguez Ruiz, Miguel. *Der Missionsgedanke des Johannesevangeliums. Ein Beitrag zur johanneischen Soteriologie und Ekklesiologie.* FzB 55. Würzburg: Echter Verlag, 1987.

Sabugal, Santos. *Christos: Investigación exegética sobre la cristologia joannea.* Barcelona: Herder, 1972.

Schenke, Ludger. *Das Johannesevangelium: Einführung—Text—dramatische Gestalt.* Stuttgart: Kohlhammer, 1992.

Schnelle, Udo. *Antidocetic Christology in the Gospel of John: An Investigation of the Place of the Fourth Gospel in the Johannine School.* Minneapolis: Fortress, 1992.

Schuchard, B. G. *Scripture within Scripture: The Interrelationship of Form and Function in the Explicit Old Testament Citations in the Gospel of John.* SBL.DS 133. Atlanta: Scholars Press, 1992.

Schweizer, Eduard. *Ego Eimi . . . Die religionsgeschtliche Herkunft und theologische Bedeutung der johanneischen Bildreden, zugleich ein Beitrag zur Quellenfrage des vierten Evangeliums.* FRLANT 38. Göttingen: Vandenhoeck & Ruprecht, 1939.

Scott, Martin. *Sophia and the Johannine Jesus.* JSNT.S 7. Sheffield: JSOT Press, 1992.

Segovia, Fernando F. *The Farewell of the Word. The Johannine Call to Abide.* Minneapolis: Fortress, 1991.

Smalley, Stephen S. *John: Evangelist and Interpreter.* Exeter: Paternoster Press, 1978.

Smith, D. Moody. *John.* Proclamation Commentaries. Philadelphia: Fortress, 1976.

_____. "Judaism and the Gospel of John," in J. H. Charlesworth, ed., *Jews and Christians: Exploring the Past, Present, and Future.* Shared Ground among Jews and Christians 1. New York: Crossroad, 1990, 76–99.

_____. *The Composition and Order of the Fourth Gospel: Bultmann's Literary Theory.* New Haven: Yale University Press, 1965.

_____. *The Theology of the Gospel of John.* New Testament Theology. Cambridge: Cambridge University Press, 1995.

Staley, Jeffrey L. *Reading with a Passion. Rhetoric, Autobiography, and the American West in the Gospel of John.* New York: Continuum, 1995.

Stemberger, Günter. *La symbolique du bien et du mal selon saint Jean.* Paris: Editions du Seuil, 1970.

Stibbe, Mark W. G. *John as storyteller: narrative criticism and the Fourth Gospel.* MSSNTS 73. Cambridge: Cambridge University Press, 1992.

Stimpfle, Alois. *Blinde Sehen: Die Eschatologie im Traditionsgeschichtlichen Prozess des Johannesevangeliums.* BZNW 57. Berlin: de Gruyter, 1990.

Strachan, Robert H. *The Fourth Gospel: Its Significance and Environment.* 3rd ed. London: SCM Press, 1941.

Thomas, J. C. "The Fourth Gospel and Rabbinic Judaism," *ZNW* 82 (1991) 159–182.

Thompson, Marianne Meye. *The Humanity of Jesus in the Fourth Gospel.* Philadelphia: Fortress, 1988.

Thüsing, Wilhelm. *Die Erhöhung und Verherrlichung Jesu im Johannesevangelium.* NTA 21/1–2. 3rd ed. Münster: Aschendorff, 1979.

Tilborg, Sjef van. *Imaginative Love in John.* BibIntS 2. Leiden: E. J. Brill, 1993.

Tröger, Karl-Wolfgang. "Ja oder Nein zur Welt: War der Evangelist Johannes Christ oder Gnostiker?" *ThV* 7 (1976) 61–80.

Wahlde, Urban C. von. *The Earliest Version of John's Gospel: Recovering the Gospel of Signs.* Wilmington: Michael Glazier, 1989.

Wengst, Klaus. *Bedrängte Gemeinde und Verherrlichter Christus: Der historischer Ort des Johannesevangeliums als Schlüssel zu seiner Interpretation.* BThSt 5. 2nd ed. Neukirchen-Vluyn: Neukirchener Verlag, 1983.

Whitacre, Rodney A. *Johannine Polemic: The Role of Tradition and Theology.* SBL.DS 67. Chico, Cal.: Scholars, 1982.

Young, F. W. "A Study of the Relation of Isaiah to the Fourth Gospel," *ZNW* 46 (1955) 215–233.

Zumstein, Jean. "Der Prozess der Relecture in der johanneischen Literatur," *NTS* 42 (1996) 394–411.

_____. "L'évangile johannique, une stratégie du croire," *RSR* 77 (1989) 217–232.

TRANSLATION, INTERPRETATION, NOTES

I. THE PROLOGUE (1:1-18)

I

(a) 1. In the beginning was the Word, and the Word was turned toward God, and what God was the Word also was. 2. He was in the beginning with God.

(b) 3. All things were made through him, and without him nothing was made. What took place 4. in him was life, and the life was the light of humankind.

(c) 5. The light shines in the darkness, and the darkness has not overcome it.

II

(a) 6. There was a man sent from God, whose name was John. 7. He came for testimony, to bear witness to the light, that all might believe through him. 8. He was not the light, but came to bear witness to the light.

(b) 9. The true light that enlightens everyone was coming into the world.

(c) 10. He was in the world, and the world was made through him, yet the world knew him not. 11. He came to his own home, and his own people received him not. 12. But to those who received him, who believed in his name, he gave power to become children of God; 13. who were born, not of blood nor of the will of the flesh nor of the will of a man, but of God.

(d) 14. And the Word became flesh and dwelt among us, the fullness of a gift that is truth. We have gazed upon his glory, glory as of the only Son from the Father.

III

(a) 15. John bore witness to him, and cried, "This was he of whom I said, 'He who comes after me ranks before me, for he was before me.'"

(c) 16. And from his fullness have we all received, a gift in place of a gift.

(d) 17. For the law was given through Moses; the gift that is the truth came through Jesus Christ. 18. No one has ever seen God; the only Son, who is turned toward the Father, he has made him known.

INTERPRETATION

Introduction. The first page of the Fourth Gospel is one of the most dense passages in the New Testament, a synthesis of the author's christology and theology. There have been many attempts to discern the literary structure of this ancient Christian hymn. Most follow a movement in time, from preexistence (vv. 1-2) into creation (vv. 3-5), proceeding through the story of the human condition until the high point of the incarnation (vv. 6-14). The final part of the hymn deals with the subsequent reception of the incarnate *Logos* (vv. 15-18) (cf., for example, Lagrange 2–34). Others have traced a chiastic structure, which means that the same themes are repeated around a central statement: e.g., A–B–C–B´–A´ (cf. R. A. Culpepper, "The Pivot" 1–31). This Christian hymn, however, may follow some of the well-established patterns of biblical poetry, especially the use of parallelism. A hint that such may be the case is found in the twofold reference to John the Baptist (vv. 6-8, 15), which troubles most attempts to find a formal literary structure for John 1:1-18. These Baptist passages indicate that the hymn has three sections:

> I. The Word in God becomes the light of the world (vv. 1-5)
> II. The incarnation of the Word (vv. 6-14)
> III. The revealer: the only Son turned toward the Father (vv. 15-18).

Within these three sections there is a statement and restatement of the same message. Like the motion of a wave running up the seashore each section carries the same message farther. Not all four themes are dealt with in each section, but the hymn states and restates them in the following fashion:

> (a) The Word is announced or described (vv. 1-2 [I], 6-8 [II], 15 [III]),
> (b) The revelation brought by the Word is coming into the world (vv. 3-4 [I], 9 [II]).
> (c) Humankind responds (vv. 5 [I], 10-13 [II], 16 [III]),
> (d) and the object of belief is described: the only Son of the Father (vv. 14 [II], 17-18 [III]).

The Prologue plays an important role in the rhetoric of the Fourth Gospel. John 1:1-18 informs the reader that Jesus Christ is the incarnation of the preexistent Word and that life, light, and divine filiation flow from an acceptance of the story of the unseen God revealed by the incarnate Word. This story perfects the former gift of the Law given through Moses. However, this theology and christology have only been *affirmed.* The reader has been told *who* Jesus is and *what* he has done, but an important question remains unanswered: *how* did this action of God in the human story take place? Only a Johannine story of Jesus can answer that question.

The Word in God becomes the light of the world (vv. 1-5). The first words of the Prologue, "In the beginning *(en archē)* was the Word," establish a parallel between the opening of the Gospel and the biblical account of the beginnings of the human story in Gen 1:1. Before the *archē* of Gen 1:1 there were only God, the waters of chaos, and darkness, but the author of the Fourth Gospel announces that even then the Word "was" *(ēn).* The use of the imperfect tense of the verb "to be" places the Word outside the limits of time and place, neither of which existed *en archē* (Gen 1:1). The Word preexists the human story, and the Word does not preexist for its own sake but in a relationship with God *(pros ton theon).* The preposition *pros* means more than the static "with." It has a sense of motion toward the person or thing that follows. The translation therefore reads "The Word was *turned toward* God." There is a dynamism in the relationship that must somehow be conveyed. But there is more. The author has chosen the Greek expression *ho logos* to hint, from the start, that from the intimacy of God a word will be spoken. A word exists to say something, and thus revelation, one of the dominating themes of the Gospel, appears in the first verse.

This verse concludes with a description of the consequences of the intense intimacy between the Word and God. Although the traditional translation is "and the word was God," there is a danger that this might lead the contemporary reader of the English text to collapse the Word and God into one: they are both God. The author has gone to considerable trouble to indicate that an identification between the Word and God is to be avoided. The Greek sentence *(kai theos ēn ho logos)* places the complement *(theos:* God) before the verb "to be" and does not give it an article. It is extremely difficult to catch this nuance in English, but the author avoids saying that the Word and God were one and the same thing. The translation "what God was the Word also was" indicates that the Word and God retain their uniqueness, despite the oneness that flows from their intimacy.

Verse 2 repeats substantially what has already been said, but "the Word" (v. 1) is indicated by a personal pronoun, "this man" *(houtos).* The pronoun looks both backward to the masculine word *logos* and forward to a figure with a human story. Who might "this man" be? Much has been claimed in these first verses: the preexistence of the Word, its intimate relationship to God, and the first hints of an eventual revelation that will take place in the human story by means of the story told by the Word. *The Word has been described.* What Barrett said of v. 1 can be applied to vv. 1-2: "John intends that the whole of his gospel shall be read in the light of this verse. The deeds and words of Jesus are the deeds and words of God; if this be not true the book is blasphemous" (Barrett, *Gospel* 156).

Verses 3-4 have been the source of many scholarly problems, most of which are associated with the interpreter's theological understanding of this passage. The use of the aorist and the sudden shift from the regular use of the imperfect of the verb "to be" looks back to a point of time in the past when all things *(panta)* came into being *(egeneto)* through the Word, and nothing *(oude hen)* in creation took place without this mediating presence. There was a moment in the past when the revealing act of creation took place *(egeneto)* through the Word *(di 'autou)*. The tense of the verb changes again as a new sentence begins with *ho gegonen*. A shift from the aorist tense of v. 3ab to the perfect tense in v. 3c indicates that an event took place in the past, but the significance of that event continues into the present *(gegonen)*. In vv. 3c-4 one finds the Gospel's first reference to the incarnation. The Word broke into the human story (perfect tense) and made life an ongoing possibility. The appearance of the Word of life brought light. The life that is light broke into the human story in an event that happened in the past, the effects of which are still part of the present story. The Word speaks out of intimacy with God (vv. 1-2), and thus makes God known, both in creation (v. 3ab) and in the presence of the Word itself in the human story (vv. 3c-4). This knowledge provides the life for which humanity yearns, a life that gives sense and direction: light.

A history of salvation can be plotted from the preexistence of the Word to the life and light brought into the human story through the presence of an as yet unidentified human figure:

1. A preexistent Word with God *(pros ton theon)*.
2. God's manifestation in creation *(di 'autou)*, wherein the Word can already be experienced.
3. The Word in the human story as the life that is the light of humankind *(en autǭ)*.

However much still has to be told about *how* it happened, vv. 3-4 affirm that *the revelation brought by the Word is coming into the world.*

The final verse of this first section is marked by a further change in the tense of the verb: the light shines (present tense: *phainei*) in the darkness. There is a close link between v. 4 and v. 5, but while the former announces that the Word is light in the world the latter indicates that this light continues to be present despite the hostile reception given to it. Though it may appear to the contrary, both in terms of crucifixion as the end of Jesus' story and the ongoing experience of the presence of evil in the world, the light that is the Word shines on. The author introduces a form of the verb *lambanein*, "to receive," which will appear regularly across the Gospel to speak of how *humankind responds* to the revelation of God that takes place in Jesus. The darkness has not overcome the light *(ou katelaben)*. It may appear that *humankind responds* negatively to the presence of life and light, but such is not the case. The light continues to shine in the darkness. It is too early in the Prologue to do any more than announce a hostile human response. Further details on the one who is to be accepted in belief will be developed in the two following sections (see vv. 14, 17-18).

The incarnation of the Word (vv. 6-14). The elevated poetry of vv. 1-5 disappears momentarily as vv. 6-8 give a more narrative description of the figure and role of John the Baptist. Regarded by many as a secondary addition to the Prologue, these verses are essential to its present structure and message. The hints of the Word's involvement in the events of history found in vv. 3c-5 continue as a historical figure with the proper name "John" enters the story *(egeneto)*. John was not just any man, for he had been sent by God (v. 6). This is an important claim, as no one else in the Johannine story apart from Jesus is described as having been sent by God. John was part of a divine plan: he came to give witness to the light, so that others might come to believe by means of the life-giving presence of the light. The theme of the Word as the light continues from vv. 4b-5. John was not the light; his role was to give witness to the light. There must be no confusion. John the Baptist was a great figure but he was not the light. Nevertheless his appearance in vv. 6-8 opens the second section of the Prologue (vv. 6-14) with a description of the Word as the light, the one through whom people can come to life-giving belief. The Prologue is now firmly anchored in history and, like vv. 1-5, its second section (vv. 6-14) opens with a *description of the Word* and a careful separation of the role of the Baptist from the role of the Word.

The one and only authentic light *(to phōs to alēthinon)* who gives life-giving light to everyone *is coming into the world* (v. 9). The hints of incarnation already found in vv. 3c-4 are now bluntly stated. Reference to the coming of the Word into the world cannot be put off till v. 14. It has been part of the first section of the Prologue (vv. 1-5) and returns in v. 9. The Word was in the world that has its very existence through him (v. 10b; cf. v. 3ab) but the world has not known him. From this general statement the author moves to a more specific identification of the place and people who would not receive him: he came to his own place *(eis ta idia)* and his own people *(hoi idioi)*. Gnostic documents speak of the place for which the soul longs, its own true home, as *ta idia* (cf. *Odes Sol.* 7:12; 26:1; *Mandean Liturgy* 114:4-5). This language may have been familiar to many of the first readers of the Fourth Gospel, but its meaning has been radically transformed. For the Fourth Gospel *ta idia* is not some heavenly place of ideal existence as among the Gnostics. The Word came into the human story only to be rejected by his own people. Some in Israel did not receive *(ou parelabon)* the Word. A form of the verb *lambanein* again appears to describe the first moment in *humankind's response*. Unlike v. 5 where this message of a negative response was found for the first time, the negative response from those to whom the Word came (v. 11) is matched by the description of the positive response of others, and the results of such a response (vv. 12-13).

In v. 12 the verbs "to receive" *(lambanein)* and "to believe" *(pisteuein)* are placed in parallel: "To those who receive him" *(hosoi de elabon auton);* to those who believed in his name *(tois pisteusousin eis to onoma autou).* To receive the Word means to believe in his name. In v. 5 and v. 11 the rejection of the Word was described with the negative use of forms of the verb "to receive." There is a right and a wrong way "to receive" the Word. The right way "to receive" is "to believe" in his name. In terms of the Prologue itself the Word as yet has no name, no role in the human story. Nevertheless the results of belief in the name of the Word are described in the past tense: he gave them (aorist: *edōken autois*) power to become children of God. The power given is not a promise but an achieved fact for those who receive and believe. A Johannine understanding of life and eternal life has been broached for the first time. One does not have to wait for an end-time to become a child of God. The choice of the aorist infinitive "to become" *(genesthai)* indicates that Johannine faith and so-called "realized eschatology" demand continual commitment. In a traditional eschatology the believer waits for resurrection and the end of time for the final gifts of life and eternal life. In the Fourth Gospel these gifts are anticipated. They are available to the believer *now,* and are thus "realized."

One *becomes* a child of God through a process of growth, yet such a childhood cannot be explained by human experience or understanding because it is not the result of human initiative (v. 13). The ancients saw the generation of a child as the result of the mechanical coagulation of the woman's blood resulting from its mingling with the male seed. But children of God are not born "of blood." Children are also generated as a result of human concupiscence, but children of God are not born "of the flesh." There are times when parents decide that they wish to have a child, and act accordingly, but children of God are not born "of the will of a human being." Children of God are generated by God *(ek theou egennēthesan).*

Many regard v. 14 as the high point of the Prologue, the place where the incarnation of the Word is announced. But the indication that the Word was coming into the world has already been found in vv. 3c-4 and v. 9. The fact of the coming into the world has been established. This is now restated (v. 14a), but the bulk of v. 14 *describes him in whose name one must believe: the only Son of the Father* (v. 14bcd). As the Baptist came into the human story (cf. v. 6: *egeneto anthrōpos*) so also the Word enters the human story: the Word became flesh *(sarx egeneto).* The preexistent Word, so intimately associated with God (vv. 1-2), now enfleshed, can be the communication and revelation of God in the human situation, where he now dwells (v. 14b). This second affirmation, that the Word dwelt among us, draws the world of the reader into the hymn. The verb chosen to speak of the dwelling of the Word among us *(eskēnōsen)* may simply mean "to dwell" or "to live" and be linked with the dwelling of Wisdom in Israel reported in Sir 24:8: "my Creator chose the place for my tent. He said, 'Make your dwelling *(kataskēnōson)* in Jacob, and in Israel receive your inheritance'" (cf. also 24:10). The Greek verb *skēnein* may also be linked to the Hebrew verb *šākan,* used of the dwelling of YHWH in Israel (Exod 25:8; 29:46; Zech 2:14) and the root of an important word in Rabbinic Judaism to speak of the resting of the glory *(kābōd)* of YHWH over the tabernacle (cf. Exod 25:8; 40:35). His dwelling "among us" looks to the experience of a believing community that can further claim to have gazed upon his glory *(tēn doxan autou).* During the historical existence of the Word believers represented by the author of the Gospel saw the *doxa.* The Old Testament often spoke of the visible manifestation of YHWH to the people in terms of the Hebrew word *kabōd* that was (strangely) rendered in the LXX as *doxa* (cf., for example, Exod 33:22; Deut 5:21; 1 Kgs 8:11; Isa 10:1; Hab 2:14). Given the intimacy of the relationship existing between the Word and God from before all time (cf. vv. 1-2) the author can claim that to gaze on the incarnation of the Word was to see the revelation of the divine in the human story.

This affirmation is further substantiated in v. 14d. The glory seen was "glory as of the only Son from the Father." The relationship earlier described as between the Word and God is now articulated as between "Son" and "Father." A relationship fundamental for the story which is about to begin has been stated. As in vv. 1-2, however, the author carefully maintains the distinction between the Son and the Father. The believer does not see the glory of the Father in the Son, a glory "as of" *(hōs).* The glory that the Son had with the Father before all time (cf. 17:5) is unknown and unknowable to the human situation (cf. v. 18). The author states that what the human story can see of the divine has been seen in the incarnation of the Word, the only Son from the Father. A further description is added. Although the last phrase is traditionally translated "full of grace and truth," reflecting the Hebrew of Exod 34:6 *(ḥesed weʾemet),* it is also possible that the Greek word *charis* in the Johannine Prologue retains its original meaning: an unsolicited gift. The translation offered above takes this approach and then reads the noun that follows the connecting "and" (epexegetical *kai)* as a further explanation of the unsolicited gift. This produces the translation: "the fullness of a gift that is truth" (cf. Note). The community behind the story that begins with this Prologue has gazed upon the visible manifestation of God, in the enfleshed Word, the only Son from the Father, the fullness of a gift that is truth.

The revealer: the only Son turned toward the Father (vv. 15-18). History again enters the hymn as the Baptist cries out his first words of witness.

The first *description of the Word* (vv. 1-2) is recalled as the direct speech of the Baptist proclaims that one who is coming (*erchomenos*: present participle) follows John in terms of the temporal sequence of events. However, in terms of his place in God's design he existed (*gegonen*: perfect tense of *ginomai*) before him. In a return to the imperfect tense of the verb "to be" of v. 1, John explains how this is so: "because he *was* before me (*hoti prōtos mou ēn*)."

Enough has been said of *the coming of the Word into the world* (cf. vv. 3c-4, 9, 14). The author moves immediately to a final treatment of *humankind's reception and response to the gift of the Word*. Again using language that may have rung a bell for many of the Gospel's original readers and listeners, the author explains that from his fullness (*ek tou plērōmatos autou*) we have all received (v. 16). Again, however, this well-known language is being used in a startlingly new way. For the Gnostics the *plērōma* existed in the heavenly spheres; for the Fourth Gospel the believers receive from this fullness within their human existence. They receive a gift that perfects, and thus brings to an end, a former gift. Traditionally the Greek word *charis* has been read as "grace," and the critics have wondered about the meaning of the preposition that joins the two uses of the word in the expression *charin anti charitos*. It is difficult to understand, if one takes the expression in a Christian theological sense, how one "grace" can be set against another "grace," but there might be two "gifts" where one perfects another (cf. Note).

These two gifts, and their relationship, are immediately explained by v. 17. There have been two unique gifts of God to the human story. In the first place God gave the Law through Moses (*dia Mōüseōs edothē*). However, there is now another gift, already mentioned in v. 14 ("the fullness of a gift that is truth") and in v. 16 ("a gift in place of a gift"): the gift that is the truth (v. 17b: *hē charis kai hē alētheia*). The two nouns from v. 14 reappear, this time with a definite article, again joined by an epexegetical *kai*. The gift that is the truth surpasses and perfects the former gift given through Moses (cf. v. 17a), and it took place (*egeneto*) through Jesus Christ (*dia Iēsou Christou*). This is not a negative assessment of the former gift; it is a Christian perspective that respects the gift of God given through Moses but insists that the former gift is now perfected in the gift of the truth that took place in and through the event of Jesus Christ. At the end of the central section of the Prologue (vv. 6-14) *the object of Christian belief has been described as the only Son of the Father* (v. 14). This Son (v. 14), the incarnate Word (vv. 1-2, 14), *has now been further described:* he is the perfection of God's gifts, and he has a name: Jesus Christ (v. 17). There is one further point the author must make before he turns to the narrative. As the story is about to begin there must be a further description of what Jesus Christ has done. However much the Christian community may claim to have seen the revelation of the glory of God in the Son (v. 14), no one has ever seen God (v. 18a). There is only one historical figure who has told the story of God's way with the world (*exēgēsato:* see Note): the only begotten Son. Throughout the story that is about to be told the Son's attention will be unbrokenly focused on the Father. As in the preexistent relationship between the Word and God, so also the Son, Jesus Christ, is continually "turned toward the Father" (*ho ōn eis ton kolpon tou patros.* See Note). The reader next encounters the word *kai* (v. 19). The events that are about to be told are linked with the Prologue. Indeed, the narrative must make sense of the Prologue as the Prologue has been written to make sense of the narrative.

Conclusion to 1:1-18. The Prologue to the Fourth Gospel is one of the most celebrated passages in the New Testament. The Johannine symbol of the eagle depends upon it. More importantly, it expresses the major christological beliefs of Christianity: the Word preexisted creation with God; creation was through the Word; divine filiation is possible for believers; Jesus Christ is the incarnation of God, the Word become flesh; he shares in the divinity of God, yet he has taken on the human condition totally; Jesus is the unique, once-and-for-all revelation of God in the human story; the perfection of God's earlier gift of the Law to Moses takes place in and through Jesus Christ. Despite this intense focus on christology that has marked the use of the Prologue over the Christian centuries, at the heart of this passage lies a theology. What the Prologue says about Jesus depends entirely upon what the author wants to say about God's having been made known in and through Jesus Christ.

The product of a Christian experience that looks back with respect to its Jewish origins, the Prologue has to be understood in the light of the traditional understanding of the God of Genesis and the God of Sinai. The obvious link between Genesis 1 and the opening of the Prologue sets the stage. Before there was anything, there was God. John 1:1 affirms that there was also the Word. The role of the Word, as with any word, is to be uttered. The Word that was turned toward God makes God known, and this revelation has consequences for creation and the darkness of the human situation. It is now possible to become children of God. It is not as if God has never shown any concern for the ambiguity of the human situation. In former times he made himself known; he revealed his glory (Exod 19:16-25) through the gift of the Law on Sinai, through Moses (Exod 20:1-26). The Prologue affirms that Christians have access to the perfection of this former gift. They can see the revelation of the glory of God in his Son, Jesus Christ. God has gifted us twice. His former gift of the Law through Moses has been perfected in the fullness of his gifts in and through Jesus Christ. Only the Son has ever seen God, and the story of his life will tell the story of God's loving action within the human story.

NOTES

1. *The Word:* There has been much discussion of the background for the use of the phrase *ho logos* in the Prologue of the Fourth Gospel. The expression can be found throughout the religious literature of antiquity, from Herodotus to Philo in the Greek-Hellenistic world, and throughout the various Gnostic systems. It has many parallels with Hellenistic Judaism's *sophia* and throughout the Hebrew Bible, especially the prophets' speaking the word of YHWH. The rabbinic and targumic literature often avoided the use of the name and presence of God by replacing it with the Aramaic *memra:* "the word." Christian pre-Johannine uses of "the Word of God" speak of the Christian message of salvation (cf. Luke 8:11; Acts 13:5; 1 Thess 2:13; 2 Tim 2:9; Rev 1:9, etc.). It is hard to decide categorically whether any one of the influences determined the use of *ho logos,* but—as often with this Gospel—its use would have been familiar to a multiplicity of readers and listeners. In the end the Johannine use of *logos* is determined by the universal truth that a word is essentially about communication.

   toward God: It is often denied that in the *koiné* Greek of the New Testament the preposition *pros* followed by the accusative retained this idea of "motion toward." The intimacy of the overall context must determine what is possible, however much the Greek of the time may have lost some of these nuances; cf. E. Delebecque, *Saint Jean* 143.

   what God was the Word was: Syntactically *kai theos ēn ho logos,* placing the complement, *without* an article, before the verb "to be" and following it with the subject *with* an article maintains a distinction between *ho logos* and *ho theos* in v. 1b but indicates that their intimacy makes one what the other is. As God is divine so the Word is divine, but the Word is not equated with God.

3–4. *all things were made:* The Greek verb *ginomai* is versatile and thus has many possible meanings. My reading of v. 3ab interprets the *panta* as a reference to creation and the aorist tense of *ginomai (egeneto)* as the act of creation. This meaning applies to the use of *egeneto* in both v. 3a and 3b. In v. 3c the tense changes as the perfect tense of the verb appears, *gegonen.* Here the reference is no longer to the act of creation but to an act that "took place" or "happened" in the past and continues into the present: the presence of the life and light in the human story that "took place" or "happened" through the Word. Most scholars, who are loath to admit that the coming of the Word into the world could be present so early in the Prologue, interpret this presence of life and light in terms of the Wisdom traditions in the Jewish Scriptures, or speak more vaguely of the promise of what is yet to come.

   without him nothing was made. What took place in him: There is a notorious textual problem involved in vv. 3-4. As our oldest manuscript tradition was written in capital letters, without spaces between the words and without punctuation, it is difficult to be certain where the major break came. A number of possibilities have been suggested over the years and are still represented in modern translations. My translation places the break after "and without him nothing was made." The change of tense in the verb in the next words (cf. Note above) leads into the words of the present v. 4 without any break: "What took place in him was life." For a detailed discussion of the textual problem see E. L. Miller, *Salvation-History* 79–86.

the life was the light of humankind: Like the expression *ho logos,* the important Johannine symbols of "light" and "life" are well represented in pagan, Jewish, early Christian, and Gnostic literature. It is now widely held that the terminology came into the Johannine tradition from biblical and Jewish traditions (cf. H. Preisker, "Jüdische Apokalyptik" 673–678) but, like *ho logos,* the expressions would have been readily recognized by readers and listeners from a number of religious, national, and social backgrounds.

5. *the darkness has not overcome it:* The symbol of "the darkness" *(hē skotia),* the obvious counterpart to "the light," determines the meaning of the verb *katalambanein* in v. 5. The verb can have the meaning of "to grasp intellectually," and a number of interpreters have understood the passage to indicate that the darkness was not able to comprehend the light. But the darkness is not to be located in the minds and hearts of humanity, unable to accept the light and truth brought by the Word. This would be foreign to the Johannine theology of revelation and consequent judgment (cf. 3:11-21, 31-36; 12:44-50). The human being is free to accept or reject the light. The darkness, therefore, is a power for evil which militates against the light. Thus the verb must be given its other possible meaning "to overcome" (BAGD 412–413) The darkness has not overcome the light, which continues to shine in the midst of darkness.

6–8. *There was a man sent from God:* It has often been pointed out that the sections of the Prologue dedicated to the Baptist are clumsy. Despite widespread disagreement on other details, all scholars who attempt to reconstruct a pre-Johannine hymn omit vv. 6-8 and v. 15 as clumsy Johannine additions. Many believe that these additions were an attempt on the part of the Johannine author to assert the superiority of Jesus over the Baptist in a Christian community that may have had a strong Baptist cult (cf. v. 8). For a survey of this discussion see M. Theobald, *Die Fleischwerdung des Logos* 67–119.

there was a man: John the Baptist is introduced with the aorist tense of the verb *ginomai.* The sentence abruptly introduces the events of a given time and place: *egeneto anthrōpos:* "a man appeared." Apart from the indication here that the Baptist is "from God" the only other character in the story to be so described is Jesus (cf. 1:14; 6:46; 7:29; 9:16, 33; 16:27; 17:8). Whatever one might make of the negative statements of v. 8, the Johannine Gospel cannot be regarded as an anti-Baptist document.

to bear witness to the light: The association of the Baptist with witnessing *(eis martyrian, hina martyrēsē)* sets the stage for the role of the Baptist in the Gospel story. He is never presented as a messianic forerunner. His only function is to witness to Jesus.

9. *the true light . . . was coming into the world:* This sentence is open to at least two translations. As well as the one given above, it could refer back to the Baptist: "He was the true light that enlightens every person coming into the world." On the translation adopted here see P. Borgen, "Logos was the True Light"

95–110. The use of the adjective *true (alēthinon)* is found in the Fourth Gospel to point to that which is authentic and genuine, over against all false claimants. In this case, among many possible "lights" there was only one "true light."

10. *he was in the world:* The Johannine use of "the world" *(ho kosmos)* is open to at least three interpretations, all present in this sentence: v. 10a: created reality (cf. 11:9; 17:5, 24; 21:25); v. 10b: the arena where the saving revelation of God in and through Jesus Christ takes place (cf. 1:29; 3:16; 4:42; 6:51; 8:12; 9:5); v. 10c: a place where the power of darkness reigns as the prince of this world (cf. 7:7; 12:31; 14:17, 22, 27, 30; 15:18-19; 16:8, 11, 20, 33; 17:6, 9, 14-16). Cf. N. H. Cassem, "A Grammatical and Contextual Inventory" 81–91.

    the world knew him not: The negative form of the verb *ginōskein,* found here for the first time *(ouk egnō),* is used throughout the Gospel to indicate a willful refusal on the part of the hostile world to accept the revelation brought by the Word (cf. 3:10; 8:27, 43, 55; 10:6, 38; 16:3; 17:23, 25a).

11. *he came to his own home:* The aorist *ēlthen* looks back to the moment in the past when the Word came into the world. As throughout the Prologue and the Gospel, the negative use of a form of the basic verb *lambanein* is used to speak of the rejection of the Word who came to his own *(ou parelabon).* For fuller discussion and documentation on the use of *ta idia* and *hoi idioi* in Hellenistic mysticism and Gnosticism, see Schnackenburg, *Gospel* 1:259–260.

12. *to those who received him . . . who believed in his name:* A positive use of the verb *lambanein (elabon)* speaks of the reception of the Word, set in parallel with the verb *pisteuein (tois pisteusousin).* There is a close relationship between "receiving" the Word and "believing" in the Johannine understanding of the Christian response. What this means will be further developed in the Gospel story (cf. especially 2:1–4:52).

    children of God: Never in the Johannine Gospel are the believers called sons of God *(huioi tou theou).* Only Jesus is "the Son of God." The theological notion of filiation is rendered by the expression "children of God" *(tekna tou theou).*

    he gave power to become: The use of the aorist *edōken* indicates that the power to become children of God is already given and not a mere possibility, even though the aorist infinitive *genesthai* shows that continual commitment is required.

13. *who were not born:* There is some textual support in early Patristic traditions and in the Greek miniscules for the single reading "he who was not born" *(ho ouk . . . egennēthē).* This is read by some important scholars as a reference to the tradition of the virginal conception. Cf. I. de la Potterie, "Il parto verginale del Verbo incarnato" 127–174. The translation follows the major Greek uncial tradition and the majority of scholars in reading the plural *(hoi ouk . . . enennēthēsan)* as a reference to "children of God" being the result of divine initiative. Cf. J. W. Pryor, "Of the Virgin Birth" 296–318; Theobald, *Die Fleischwerdung des Logos* 238–247.

not of blood: The unusual plural "from bloods" *(ex haimatōn)* is probably to be understood as the mixing of the female and the male "bloods". Cf. Bernard, *Commentary* 1:18.

of the will of a man: This seemingly exclusive translation renders the Greek *ek thelematos andros,* which reflects the patriarchal world of the first century where the male partner was regarded as determining initiator of a process that led to the birth of a child.

14. *the word became flesh:* There is a close parallel between the proclamation of the coming of the Baptist in v. 6: *egeneto anthrōpos,* and the coming of the Word in v. 14: *ho logos sarx egeneto.*

    the fullness of a gift that is truth: The Greek adjective *plērēs* is indeclinable when followed by a genitive (cf. BAGD 669–670), and the translation reads it as a noun (cf. BDF § 263): "the fullness." This "fullness" is further described by the two genitives that follow: *charitos kai alētheias.* The translation gives *charis* its normal meaning of a kindness, a manifestation of good will, a gift, an unexpected favor (cf. LSJ 1978–1979). The expression appears only in the Johannine Prologue and nowhere else in the Gospel. Much interpretation and translation has been unduly influenced by the important theological use Paul made of the word to speak of God's unsolicited love for an undeserving, sinful humanity. The Fourth Gospel must be allowed to have its own use of this word, whatever it may mean in the Pauline literature. The second noun *(alētheias)* joined to the *charitos* by means of *kai* and in the same case (genitive) is an example of an epexegetical *kai* or a so-called *hendiadys,* where the second noun is not something added to the former, but explains it: a gift that is truth (BDF § 442.9, 16). This produces the translation given above: "the fullness of a gift that is truth." Cf. de la Potterie, "*Charis* paulinienne et *charis* johannique" 265–282; Edwards, "*Charin anti charitos* (John 1.16)" 3–15.

15. *he who comes:* The expression "the coming one" *(ho erchomenos)* can have messianic overtones in other places in the New Testament. This possibility does not seem to apply here. Cf. E. Arens, *The* ELTHON *Sayings in the Synoptic Tradition: A Historico-Critical Investigation.* OBO 10. Göttingen: Vandenhoeck & Ruprecht, 1976, 288–300.

16. *and from his fullness we have all received:* The Greek word *hoti* that begins this clause is taken by many Church Fathers and some modern scholars as an indication that the Baptist is still talking. Some scribes sensed the difficulty and replaced *hoti* with *kai.* Although clumsy, *hoti* can be read as "and." It is best taken in this way. See Schnackenburg, *Gospel* 1:275–276. The expression translated "fullness" *(plerōma)* looks back to the word *plērēs* in v. 14. However, this is a noun widely used in the Gnostic systems, especially in Valentinian Gnosticism, to speak of the heavenly "fullness" of the initiate's desires. Cf. Gerhard Delling, "*plērēs*" *ktl,* TDNT 6:300–301; Kurt Rudolph, *Gnosis: The Nature and History of an Ancient Religion* (Edinburgh: T&T Clark, 1983) 320–322. As with the use of *ta idia* (cf. v. 11) the word would be familiar to a wide readership but its sense is radically altered. Here the believing community "receives" from the fullness of something given within the context of human events.

Again the word *lambanein* appears to describe the way the revelation of the Word is encountered by the believers (cf. also vv. 5, 11, 12).

a gift in place of a gift: The puzzle of two different "graces" being opposed *(kai charin anti charitos)* has generally been eased by translating the proposition *anti* as "upon," rendering the sense as "grace upon grace," generating the meaning of a superabundance of grace. The evidence for this meaning of *anti* has been questioned (see Edwards, *"Charin anti charitos"* 5-6), and my earlier rendering of *charis* as "a gift" enables a different translation that allows *anti* to retain its accepted meaning: "a gift *in place of* a gift" (cf. BAGD 73).

17. *the law:* In the description of two different "gifts" the first verb is the aorist passive of the verb *didōmi* indicating that the Law given through Moses *(dia Mōüseōs)* is a gift of God. The second verb, *egeneto,* looks back to the use of the same verb in v. 14 *(kai ho logos sarx egeneto)* and indicates that it comes through the incarnation of the Word, given a recognizable, historically identifiable name for the first time in the Prologue *(dia Iēsou Christou).* Both are gifts of God. One cannot "replace" the other. One prolongs and perfects the never-ending graciousness of God. The gift of the Law is perfected in the gift of the incarnation.

The gift that is the truth: To describe what took place in Jesus Christ, the latter gift, the author again uses an epexegetical *kai,* or *hendiadys.* The two nouns in the same case, joined by *kai,* repeat v. 14e, but this time the nouns have the definite article: *hē charis kai hē alētheia:* "the gift that is the truth." The term *alētheia* is widely used in Greek and Gnostic religions. However, the Johannine use of *alētheia* is closely linked with the idea of the authentic revelation of God. Cf. de la Potterie, *La Vérité* 1:23–36. A paraphrase that catches the full meaning of v. 17b is: the fullness of a gift that is the definitive revelation of God in the human story that took place in Jesus Christ.

18. *no one has ever seen God:* The strong affirmation that no one has ever seen God *(theon oudeis hōraken pōpote)* is a polemical rejection of all claims, perhaps both Jewish and Gnostic, that the great saints of Israel or the Gnostic savior-messenger could have ever seen God. Cf. W. Carter, "The Prologue and John's Gospel" 43–48; C. H. Talbert, "The Myth of a Descending-Ascending Redeemer in Mediterranean Antiquity." *NTS* 22 (1975–1976) 418–443.

the only Son: There are very good witnesses that read "the only God" *(monogenēs theos)* rather than "the only Son" *(monogenēs huios),* including $\mathfrak{P}^{66}$, $\mathfrak{P}^{75}$, the first hand of Sinaiticus, Vaticanus, and the Ephraim Rescript. Against this, despite its somewhat weaker textual support, it appears that a reference to Jesus Christ as "the only God" would be somewhat clumsy in this context and within the overall christology and theology of the Fourth Gospel (cf. 3:16, 18; 1 John 4:9). The confusion may have come from an error of transcription in the abbreviated forms of *theos* and *huios.* See Brown, *Gospel* 1:17.

who is turned toward the Father: A parallel is often rightly drawn between v. 1: *ho logos ēn pros ton theon* and v. 18: *ho ōn eis ton kolpon tou patros.* However, there is an important distinction between the two affirmations concerning the intimate relationship between the Word and God (v. 1) and Jesus Christ and the Father (v. 18). The author has caught this by means of the expression *eis ton kolpon*. The expression does not indicate an indwelling, or a return to the preexistent status of the Word, as many would claim. The Greek word *kolpon* indicates the bosom, breast, or chest, an external part of the body (cf. 13:23). Jesus Christ is turned toward the Father at all times during the story that is about to be told. The present participle *ho ōn* makes the durative aspect of this oneness clear. The Prologue does not close with words on the life of the Son *in* the Father outside time. Jesus Christ, the only begotten Son, during the whole of his historical existence, was turned toward the bosom of the Father.

he has made him known: The primary meaning of the final word of the Prologue *(exēgēsato)* comes from a verb widely represented in the literature of the Hellenistic religions that has the basic meaning "to tell at length," "to relate in full," "to recount a narrative" (cf. Barrett, *Gospel* 170; LSJ 593). In John 1:18 the use of this verb produces syntactic difficulties, as it has no object. However difficult, it closes the introductory hymn and leads into the prose narrative of the life of Jesus, which tells of God's way with the world through the gift of Jesus Christ (cf. vv. 14-17). The object of the verb (God) must be supplied by the reader: "He has told God's story." The *kai* that follows immediately leads the reader into that story. Cf. Delebecque, *Saint Jean* 63; Robert, "Le mot finale du prologue johannique" 279–288.

FOR REFERENCE AND FURTHER STUDY

Ashton, John. "The Transformation of Wisdom: A Study of the Prologue of John's Gospel," *NTS* 32 (1986) 161–186.

Barrett, C. K. "The Prologue of St John's Gospel," *New Testament Essays*. London: S.P.C.K., 1972, 27–48.

Borgen, Peder. "Logos was the True Light: Contributions to the Interpretation of the Prologue of John." In idem, *Logos was the True Light and Other Essays on the Gospel of John*. Relieff 9. Trondheim: Tapir, 1983, 95–110.

Carter, Warren. "The Prologue and John's Gospel: Function, Symbol and Definitive Word," *JSNT* 39 (1990) 35–58.

Cassem, N. H. "A Grammatical and Contextual Inventory of the use of *kosmos* in the Johannine Corpus with some Implications for a Johannine Cosmic Theology," *NTS* 19 (1972–1973) 81–91.

Culpepper, R. A. "The Pivot of John's Prologue," *NTS* 27 (1981) 1–31.

Edwards, R. B. "*Charin anti charitos* (John 1.16): Grace and Law in the Johannine Prologue," *JSNT* 32 (1988) 3–15.

Fennema, D. A. "John 1.18: God the only Son," *NTS* 31 (1985) 124–135.

Hayward, C. T. R. "The Holy Name of the God of Moses and the Prologue of St John's Gospel," *NTS* 25 (1978–1979) 16–32.

Hofius, Otfried. "'Der in des Vaters Schoss ist' Joh 1,18," *ZNW* 80 (1990) 163–171.

Hooker, Morna D. "The Johannine Prologue and the Messianic Secret," *NTS* 21 (1974–1975) 40–58.

Käsemann, Ernst. "Structure and Purpose of the Prologue to John's Gospel." In idem, *New Testament Questions of Today*. London: SCM Press, 1969, 138–167.

La Potterie, Ignace de. "'C'est lui qui a ouvert la voie'. La finale du prologue johannique," *Bib* 69 (1988) 340–370.

_____. "*Charis* paulinienne et *charis* johannique." In E. Earle Ellis and Erich Grässer, eds., *Jesus und Paulus: Festschrift für Werner Georg Kümmel zum 70. Geburtstag.* Göttingen: Vandenhoeck & Ruprecht, 1975, 252–282.

_____. "Il parto verginale del Verbo incarnato: 'Non ex sanguinibus . . . sed ex Deo natus est' (Gv 1,13)," *Marianum* 45 (1983) 127–174.

_____. "Structure du Prologue du Saint Jean," *NTS* 30 (1984) 354–381.

Lacan, M.-F. "Le Prologue de saint Jean: Ses thèmes, sa structure, son mouvement," *LumVie* 33 (1957) 91–110.

Miller, E. L. *Salvation-History in the Prologue of John: The Significance of John 1:3-4.* NT.S 60. Leiden: E. J. Brill, 1989.

Moloney, Francis J. *Belief in the Word* 23–52.

Panimolle, Salvatore. *Il dono della Legge e la grazia della verità (Gv 1:17).* Teologia Oggi 21. Rome: Editrice A.V.E., 1973.

Preisker, Herbert. "Jüdische Apokalyptik und hellenistischer Synkretismus im Johannes-Evangelium, dargelegt an dem Begriff 'Licht'," *ThLZ* 77 (1952) 673–678.

Pryor, J. W. "Of the Virgin Birth or the Birth of Christians?" *NT* 28 (1985) 296–318.

Robert, René. "Le mot final du prologue johannique: A propos d'un article récent," *RevThom* 89 (1989) 279–288.

Theobald, Michael. *Die Fleischwerdung des Logos: Studien zum Verhältnis des Johannesprologs zum Corpus des Evangeliums und zu 1 Joh.* NTA n.s. 20. Münster: Aschendorff, 1988.

Tobin, T. H. "The Prologue of John and Hellenistic Jewish Speculation," *CBQ* 52 (1990) 252–269.

II. THE BOOK OF SIGNS (1:19–12:50)

A. THE FIRST DAYS OF JESUS (1:19-51)

(a) *The first day:* 19. And this is the testimony given by John when the Jews sent priests and Levites from Jerusalem to ask him, "Who are you?" 20. He confessed and did not deny, but confessed, "I am not the Messiah." 21. And they asked him, "What then? Are you Elijah?" He said, "I am not." "Are you the prophet?" He answered, "No." 22. Then they said to him, "Who are you? Let us have an answer for those who sent us. What do you say about yourself?" 23. He said,

"I am the voice of one crying out in the wilderness,

'Make straight the way of the Lord,'"

as the prophet Isaiah said.

24. Now they had been sent from the Pharisees. 25. They asked him, "Why then are you baptizing if you are neither the Messiah, nor Elijah, nor the prophet?" 26. John answered them, "I baptize with water. Among you stands one whom you do not know, 27. the one who is coming after me; I am not worthy to untie the thong of his sandal." 28. This took place in Bethany across the Jordan where John was baptizing.

(b) The second day: 29. The next day he saw Jesus coming toward him and declared, "Here is the Lamb of God who takes away the sin of the world! 30. This is he of whom I said, 'After me comes a man who ranks ahead of me because he was before me.' 31. I myself did not know him; but I came baptizing with water for this reason, that he might be revealed to Israel." 32. And John testified, "I saw the Spirit descending from heaven like a dove, and it remained on him. 33. I myself did not know him, but the one who sent me to baptize with water said to me, 'He on whom you see the Spirit descend and remain is the one who baptizes with the Holy Spirit.' 34. And I myself have seen and have testified that this is the Son of God."

(c) The third day: 35. The next day John again was standing with two of his disciples, 36. and as he watched Jesus walk by he exclaimed, "Look, here is the Lamb of God!" 37. The two disciples heard him say this, and they followed Jesus. 38. When Jesus turned and saw them following he said to them, "What are you looking for?" They said to him, "Rabbi" (which translated means Teacher), "where are you staying?" 39. He said to them, "Come and see." They came and saw where he was staying, and they remained with him that day. It was about four o'clock in the afternoon. 40. One of the two who heard John speak and followed him was Andrew, Simon Peter's brother. 41. He first found his brother Simon and said to him, "We have found the Messiah" (which is translated Anointed). 42. He brought Simon to Jesus, who looked at him and said, "You are Simon son of John. You are to be called Cephas" (which is translated Peter).

(d) The fourth day: 43. The next day Jesus decided to go to Galilee. He found Philip and said to him, "Follow me." 44. Now Philip was from Bethsaida, the city of Andrew and Peter. 45. Philip found Nathanael and said to him, "We have found him about whom Moses in the law and also the prophets wrote, Jesus son of Joseph from Nazareth." 46. Nathanael said to him, "Can anything good come out of Nazareth?" Philip said to him, "Come and see." 47. When Jesus saw Nathanael coming toward him he said of him, "Here is truly an Israelite in whom there is no deceit!" 48. Nathanael asked him, "Where did you get to know me?" Jesus answered, "I saw you under the fig tree before Philip called you." 49. Nathanael replied, "Rabbi, you are the Son of God! You are the King of Israel!" 50. Jesus answered, "Do you believe because I told you that I saw you under the fig tree? You will see greater things than these." 51. And he said to him, "Amen, amen, I say to you, you will see heaven opened and the angels of God ascending and descending upon the Son of Man."

Introduction. As the presentation of the overall literary structure of the Gospel has shown, this story may provide an elusive reading experience but the author's rhetorical strategies are generally clearly marked. The repetition of material on John the Baptist in 1:1-18 (cf. vv. 6-8 and 15) was a good example of this technique. The beginning of the narrative proper has the same feature. The description of events surrounding a Jerusalem delegation to the Baptist occupies the first day of the story (vv. 19-28). Three further days are subsequently highlighted: "the next day" (v. 29: *tę epaurion*); "the next day again" (v. 35: *tę epaurion palin*); "the next day" (v. 43: *tę epaurion*). The fourth day concludes with the first major self-revelation of Jesus in v. 51, and 2:1 returns to the theme of "days": "On the third day *(tę hēmerą tę tritę)* there was a marriage at Cana in Galilee." These "days" have often been noticed by scholars. Many have linked them with the seven days of creation (cf., for example, Boismard, *Du Baptême à Cana* 14–15; Saxby, "The Time-Scheme" 9–13), while others see little significance in the use of "days" (cf. Schnackenburg, *Gospel* 1:297, 308, 313; Léon-Dufour, *Lecture* 1:150–151 n. 1).

Fundamental background to these days, which close in 2:11 with the revelation of the *doxa* of Jesus to the disciples, is the description of the gift of the Law in Exodus 19. After the people's confession of their preparedness to do all that YHWH commanded (cf. Exod 19:7-9), YHWH tells Moses, "Go to the people and consecrate them today and tomorrow . . . and prepare for the third day, because on the third day (LXX: *tę tritę hēmerą*) YHWH will come down upon Mount Sinai in the sight of all the people" (19:10-11). Moses obediently tells the people, "Prepare for the third day" (v. 15). The description of the gift of the Law then begins: "On the morning of the third day (LXX: *tę tritę hēmerą*) there was thunder and lightning, as well as a thick cloud (MT: *kābēd*) on the mountain." The glory of God is revealed "on the third day." This biblical account was the basis for the Jewish liturgical celebration of Pentecost, described in the targums, rabbinic literature, and especially in the *Mekilta on Exodus* (see Note). In the ancient celebration of Pentecost, commemorating the gift of the Law on Sinai, the three days of Exodus 19 remain but they are prefaced by four days of more remote preparation. These four extra days of preparation for the revelation of God and the gift of the Law culminate in the fourth day, which is both the final day of remote preparation and the first of the three days that come to the celebration from the biblical account of Exodus 19. On the third day the *doxa* of God is revealed. (On the link between Sinai, the Hebrew *kābōd*, and the Johannine use of *doxa*, see Moloney, *Belief in the Word* 57–59). This time-scheme shapes the order of the events reported in John 1:19–2:12. There are four days of preparation:

Day One (Vv. 19-28): The Baptist points away from himself to another whom those who have been sent from Jerusalem do not know.

Day Two (Vv. 29-34): The Baptist witnesses to Jesus as the Lamb of God and Son of God.

Day Three (Vv. 35-42): Some disciples of the Baptist "follow" Jesus, and Simon is told that he will become Cephas.

Day Four (Vv. 43-51): This final day of general preparation, which is simultaneously the first of the three days from Exodus 19, has a different character. Jesus takes the initiative in calling a disciple and revealing himself. He calls Philip and reveals himself to Nathanael and the other disciples.

These days come to their climax in 2:1-12, which opens with the exact words of LXX Exod 19:16: "on the third day," and closes with an indication that as the *doxa* of God was revealed at Sinai (cf. LXX Exod 19:16) the *doxa* of Jesus is seen by the disciples (John 2:11). As the *Mekilta* (19:10) comments: "That was the sixth day of the week on which the Torah was given."

This background indicates that 1:19–2:12 should be read as a unit, but there are indications in the text that 2:1-12 has close links with 4:46-54. Both passages describe a miracle that took place at Cana in Galilee, and in telling the second of the Cana stories the author goes to some trouble to recall 2:1-12 (cf. 4:46, 54). More detailed links across the two miracle stories indicate that 2:1–4:54 is a literary unit that can be entitled "from Cana to Cana." Still, there is an important link between 1:19-51 and 2:1-12. Read against the background of the Jewish celebration of Pentecost, the first days of Jesus (1:19-51) cannot be fully understood without the revelation of the *doxa* (2:1-12). The Prologue states that "The Law was given through Moses; the gift that is the truth came through Jesus Christ" (1:17). This statement is now being acted out in the story, as the celebration of the gift of the Law at Pentecost is perfected in the revelation of Jesus' *doxa* and the incipient belief of the first disciples. But the obvious links with 4:46-54 must not be ignored. The first Cana miracle acts as a bridge. It prepares the way for a later account of a miracle at Cana and serves as an introduction to the narrative that runs from 2:1–4:54; it also concludes 1:19–2:12. The first attempts to articulate an understanding of Jesus in 1:19-51 will lead to a puzzling promise to stumbling disciples (cf. 1:50-51). Questions will be raised by the narrative of 1:19-51 that demand an answer, and a major part of the answer to some of those questions will be provided by 2:1–4:54.

Day One: 1:19-28. Major themes from the Prologue, the witness of the Baptist (cf. vv. 6-8, 15) and the question of Jesus' identity *(passim)*, continue in the first days of Jesus. The link between the Prologue and the narrative is indicated by the first word in the narrative: "and." Important characters from the story of Jesus are also introduced, although only by means of their representatives. "The Jews" in Jerusalem send priests and Levites to determine the identity of the Baptist. The Prologue indicates the God-designed role of the Baptist and of Jesus, but this is unknown to "the Jews." The question they raise will hang over the rest of the story: "Who are you?" From the first line of the narrative proper tension exists between "the Jews" and God's agents in the human story, Jesus Christ his Son, the incarnate Word (cf. vv. 14-18), and the witness, John the Baptist (cf. vv. 6-8; 15).

The Baptist introduces the messianic theme into the interrogation by denying that he is the Messiah (v. 20). The pleonastic introduction to these first words of the Baptist, "He confessed and did not deny but confessed," is an indication that the right confession of messiahship will be important to the right understanding of the identity of both the Baptist and Jesus. His interlocutors suggest that if he is not the Messiah he might be one of the expected precursor figures, Elijah (cf. Mal 4:5; Sir 48:10-11) or the prophet who would usher in the messianic era (cf. Deut 18:15, 18; 1QS 9:11; 4QFlor). The Baptist's vigorous denial of this (v. 21: *ouk eimi*) is remote preparation for Jesus, who alone can claim "I am he" (*egō eimi*) (Cf. E. D. Freed, "*Ego eimi* in John 1:20 and 4:25" 288–289). But an answer must be had for "the Jews" in Jerusalem (v. 22), and the Baptist explains his mission in terms of Isa 40:3. The exclusive use of this passage, selected from a larger collection of OT texts used in the tradition to explain the Baptist's role (cf. Mark 1:2-3; Matt 3:2-3; Luke 3:4-5), maintains this author's concentration on the Baptist as a witness. He bears witness to a future moment: the coming of "the Lord" (v. 23). The *expected* messianic criteria are being eclipsed as the Baptist points forward to "the Lord."

There is little indication of messianic baptism in first-century Judaism but the envoys from Jerusalem, further identified as having been sent by the Pharisees, ask why John is baptizing. This may have connections with the baptismal practices of the Qumran sectarians (cf. 1QS 4:20-22) and the association of his activity with the Messiah, Elijah, and the prophet (vv. 24-25; cf. v. 21) indicates that the discussion is still being determined by the overall context of Jewish messianic expectation. The representatives of the Jewish world are determined not to move from *their* criteria, but the Baptist merely baptizes with water; there is one among them whom they do not know, whose sandal the Baptist is not worthy to untie (vv. 26-27). The coming of this figure (v. 23; cf. 1:6-8, 15), whom the world of Judaism (priests, Levites, "the Jews," Pharisees, those "from Jerusalem") does not know (cf. v. 26), lies in the future beyond the criteria of Jewish messianic expectation.

The first day of the story of Jesus has passed without mention of his presence. It closes formally in v. 28 with an indication of the place where

John was baptizing: Bethany across the Jordan. The characters who played such an active role in this first day, representatives of the world of Judaism, are dismissed. Nowhere else in 1:19-51 is a day brought to such a formal close as this first day. The preparation has begun for the future coming of the Lord, the one whose sandal a figure as great as John the Baptist was not worthy to untie.

Day Two: 1:29-34. This day is dominated by John the Baptist, who continues to give witness to Jesus, fulfilling the promise of the Prologue (vv. 29, 30, 32, 34. Cf. Morna D. Hooker, "John the Baptist" 354–358). The only other character vaguely present to the narrative is Jesus who is "coming toward" the Baptist *(erchomenon pros auton).* Jesus plays no active role, but acts as the catalyst that triggers the witness of vv. 29-34. The Baptist bears witness, but no surrounding listeners are described or identified. The information provided by the Prologue is further developed as the Baptist identifies Jesus as the preexistent one (v. 30; cf. vv. 1, 15), the Lamb of God who takes away the sin of the world (v. 29), the one upon whom the Spirit descended (v. 32) in fulfillment of a divine promise (v. 33a), the one who baptizes with the Holy Spirit (v. 33a): the Son of God (v. 34). The unreported baptism of Jesus by John, motivated by the Baptist's mission to enable the revelation of Jesus to Israel (v. 31), gives substance to the Baptist's witness. He did not know Jesus (vv. 31a, 33a), but God, who sent John (cf. v. 6), had revealed truths about Jesus to his missionary (v. 33). This revelation has taken place in the unreported event of the baptism of Jesus. The Spirit has descended as a dove from heaven and remained upon Jesus (v. 32; cf. Isa 11:2; Mark 1:10; Matt 3:16; Luke 3:22). The Johannine presentation of the Spirit will develop as the Gospel unfolds. The Spirit of God has entered the human story by descending and remaining upon Jesus, just as the Baptist had been told. On the basis of what he has seen the Baptist bears witness (v. 34).

Jesus appears in the story already an adult, baptized by John, witnessed to by a God-sent witness. Jesus is the Lamb *of God* and the Son *of God,* the one upon whom the Spirit remains and who baptizes with the Holy Spirit. The response of the Baptist to his interrogators on the first day (vv. 19-28) is further clarified. Jesus is "the Lord" (v. 23), the one who is to come, whom Israel does not know (v. 26). No messianic expectation contains what God is doing in and through Jesus Christ, the incarnate Son of the Father (vv. 14-18). He has his origins in God and brings the Holy Spirit into the human story. Such affirmations cannot be *proved.* The witness of the Baptist must be accepted, but questions remain. It is not enough to claim *that* Jesus is the Lamb of God who takes away the sin of the world, the one who brings the Holy Spirit, the Son of God. This second day of preparation for the gift of the *doxa* further informs the reader of the story, but not the other characters *in the story,* of *who* Jesus is and *what* he does. The question of *how* all this takes place becomes more urgent.

Day Three: 1:35-42. Another set of characters is introduced as the next day opens: two disciples of the Baptist. John is "standing" *(heistēkei)* with them (v. 35). Jesus remains in the distance, but in motion, walking by *(peripatounti).* The Baptist points toward Jesus and repeats to his disciples the witness of his words in vv. 29-34: "Behold the Lamb of God" (v. 36). The initial response of the disciples is encouraging. They respond to the witness of the Baptist by moving from their static position (cf. v. 35: *heistēkei*) to become "followers" of Jesus (v. 37: *ēkolouthēsan tǭ Iēsou*). There is a movement *away* from the Baptist *toward* Jesus. Motion continues as Jesus breaks his movement to "turn" and "see" the followers. He asks a question that hints at an answer to the issues raised by the Prologue and the story thus far: "What are you looking for?" (v. 38a). The response of the first followers is disappointing. They use a term of respect, "Rabbi," further clarified by the narrator, reinforcing the fact that the followers have not understood John's revelation of Jesus as the Lamb of God (cf. v. 36). Rabbi means "teacher." On the basis of this understanding of Jesus they ask a legitimate question. Like all Jewish Rabbis, Jesus must have a place where he gathers his disciples for instruction. It is this understanding of Jesus that motivates their question, "Where are you staying?" (v. 38b). Their response is limited, so soon after vv. 29-34 and the Baptist's words to his disciples in v. 36.

The disciples further respond to Jesus' invitation to "come and see." They accompany him, they see where he is staying and remain with him from about four o'clock in the afternoon till the end of the day (v. 39). These details should be taken at their face value. Nothing is reported of what was shared, and there is no evidence for a symbolic reading of Jesus' invitation and the time they spend with him. However, the scene has been set for the response of these first disciples, one of whom is explicitly named as Andrew, Simon Peter's brother. The second disciple remains unidentified. Andrew informs his brother Simon: "We have found the Messiah," and—as with the earlier recognition of Jesus as "Rabbi"— the narrator adds a note to indicate that the expression means "the anointed." However wonderful the claim to have found the Messiah might appear to be, it falls short of a correct recognition of Jesus as he has been described in the Prologue (vv. 1-18) and in the witness of the Baptist during the second day of preparation for the gift of the *doxa* (vv. 29-34). Such a claim has its own truth, but does Andrew understand Jesus' messianic status in a satisfactory fashion? There are hints that all is not well. Andrew has told Simon, "We have found" *(heurēkamen),* and this is not true (v. 41). The Baptist pointed his disciples toward Jesus, and they followed (vv. 36-37). They were invited by Jesus to come and see, and they did what they were told (v. 39). The initiative for their presence with Jesus and their understanding of him does not belong to them. A lie has been told, and this is further reinforced by Jesus' words to Simon. Once Andrew led Simon to Jesus he looked at him and spoke to him (*emblepsas autǭ ho Iēsous eipen*). The initiative is entirely with Jesus. He tells Simon who he is, where he comes from (son of John) and who he will be in the future (Cephas). Again the narrator adds a note, indicating a future that the reader of the Gospel may know came true: the man once called Simon son of John will become Cephas, Peter. The words to Simon are an indication to the disciples that there is more to a proper understanding of Jesus than finding in this rabbi the fulfillment of *their* messianic expectations.

Day Four: 1:43-51. The first of the three days dedicated to intensive preparation for the gift of the *doxa* (cf. Exod 19:10-15) has a character of its own. As the first words indicate, Jesus will be at the center of the action. He decided (*ēthelēsen*) to go to Galilee, he found (*heuriskei*) Philip, and he said (*legei*) to him: "Follow me" (*a kolouthei moi*). This disciple follows Jesus because he is called by Jesus. Philip, like Andrew and Peter (cf. Mark 1:16-20; Luke 5:1-11), is from Bethsaida in Galilee, and this gathering of disciples journeys to Galilee. Philip professes his understanding of Jesus to another potential disciple, Nathanael, but he repeats the lie of Andrew: "We have found. . . ." The only person Philip found is Nathanael (v. 45a), but he *was found* and called by Jesus. Traditional hopes are again expressed by Philip's description of Jesus as "him about whom Moses in the law and also the prophets wrote" (v. 45b). As with Andrew's confession (cf. v. 41) there is a sense in which these words are true, but Philip, like Andrew, does not fully understand their Johannine meaning. He describes Jesus as "Jesus *of Nazareth,* the son *of Joseph*" (v. 45c), but a proper understanding of Jesus as the fulfillment of OT expectation would eclipse the promises of the OT; Jesus is the Son *of God,* the Lamb *of God.* He cannot be understood as "of Nazareth," or "of Joseph." Indeed, perhaps citing from a proverbial statement of the time (cf. K. Dewey, "*Paroimiai* in the Gospel of John," *Sem* 17 [1980] 90–91), Nathanael's question points to exactly that weakness in Philip's understanding of Jesus: "Can anything good come *out of Nazareth?*" (v. 46a). There is profound irony here. The earliest Church recognized Jesus as being "of Nazareth," but the Johannine story insists that the believer look beyond his historical origins. In this Nathanael poses a good question. However, the supreme good is the one known to the Christian tradition as "Jesus of Nazareth" (see Duke, *Irony* 24–25). Yet Philip's mistake, which attempts to understand Jesus in terms of his physical and geographical origins (cf. v. 45: "of Joseph," "from Nazareth"), persists. Philip repeats Jesus' earlier invitation to the first disciples as he asks Nathanael to come and see (v. 46b; cf. v. 39).

Nathanael does not come to faith by seeing Jesus; Jesus has seen him first. He is greeted as an Israelite without guile (cf. Ps 32:2; Isa 53:9), unlike the wily Jacob (cf. Gen 27:35-36) (v. 47). Nathanael, omitting any salutation of honor or respect, asks Jesus directly where he got to know him *(pothen me ginōskeis)*. The question of origins is still present: what are the origins of Jesus' knowledge? Jesus tells him that he had seen him under the fig tree before Philip called him (v. 48). There has been much speculation about the image of the fig tree: the comfort of the home (cf. 1 Kgs 4:25; Mic 4:4; Zech 3:10), Nathanael's dedication to the study of the Law, and the fig tree as a symbol of good and evil (cf. Hahn, "Die Jüngerberufung" 187–188; Koester, "Messianic Exegesis" 23–24). Some or all of this may be involved in the use of the image, but it must not distract from the major thrust of the passage: Jesus has shown a knowledge of things that marks him out as a wonder-worker. This moves Nathanael to salute Jesus: "Rabbi, you are the son of God! You are the King of Israel!" (v. 49). These words climax a series of confessions of Jesus from the first disciples (cf. vv. 41, 45) but, like the earlier confessions, it falls short of the mark. The terms Nathanael uses to address Jesus can be understood as the expressions of first-century messianic hope. He joins the earlier disciples in addressing Jesus as "Rabbi" (cf. v. 38). "King of Israel" is associated with Davidic messianic traditions, and the expression "son of God," on the basis of 2 Sam 7:14 and Ps 2:7, was part of widespread Jewish royal messianic expectation. (Cf. B. J. Byrne, *'Sons of God—Seed of Abraham': A Study of the Idea of the Sonship of God of All Christians in Paul against the Jewish Background.* AnBib 83. Rome: Biblical Institute Press, 1979, 9–78, especially 16–18 and 59–62). Exalted as these confessions may be they are bound by Nathanael's own culture, religion, and history.

A number of scholars, assessing Nathanael's confession as an expression of full Johannine faith, regard vv. 50-51 as an addition to this fourth day. Jesus' words initially address only Nathanael: "Do you believe because I told you *(soi)* that I saw you *(se)* under the fig tree? You will see *(opsē)* greater things than these" (v. 50). This is the first time the verb *pisteuein* has appeared since the Prologue. Jesus questions the basis of Nathanael's belief in him and points out that the sight of greater things will follow a different form of faith. Nathanael has believed on the basis of the wonder of Jesus' having seen him under the fig tree, but more is required for the sight of greater things. What might these greater things be? What more is required from the believer to have sight of them? The answer to the first of these questions is provided in v. 51, and the answer to the second is at the heart of the Cana to Cana section of the Gospel (2:1–4:54). Jesus rebuked only Nathanael (v. 50), but his further words to him (v. 51a) promise the sight of greater things for all the disciples: "Amen, amen I say to you *(humin)*, you will see *(opsesthe)* heaven opened

and the angels of God ascending and descending upon the Son of Man"
(v. 51bc).

The expectations of "the Jews" (vv. 19-28) and the disciples (vv. 35-50)
must be surpassed. There is need for greater faith so that the greater
things might be seen. In a cosmology where God was "above" and the
earth "below," the tearing open of the heavens, especially when the passive verb *(aneōgota)* is used to describe the tearing open, promises a communication between God and the human story (see Gen 7:11; Isa 64:1;
24:18; Ezek 1:1; Mark 1:10; Matt 3:16; Luke 3:21; Rev 4:1). The scene is set
for a "sight" that looks back to the story of Jacob's dream:

> And he dreamed that there was a ladder set up on the earth, the top of
> it reaching to heaven; and the angels of God were ascending and de-
> scending on it. . . . Then Jacob woke from his sleep and said, "Surely
> the LORD is in this place—and I did not know it!" And he was afraid, and
> said, "How awesome is this place! This is none other than the house of
> God, and this is the gate of heaven" (Gen 28:12, 16-17).

Following a Jewish interpretation (cf. Moloney, *Son of Man* 26–30), Jesus
shifts the movement away from the ladder. The angels ascend and descend upon the Son of Man. The Son of Man becomes "this place," "the
gate of heaven," where the revelation of God can surely be found. The
"greater things" that will result from greater faith are associated with the
sight of the heavenly in the Son of Man.

Throughout the first three days of remote preparation for the gift of
the *doxa* various characters, ignorant of the Prologue (vv. 1-18) and the
witness of John the Baptist (vv. 29-34), raise the question of the expected
Messiah. The Baptist will not allow them to fit him into those categories
(vv. 19-28). After hearing that Jesus is the Lamb of God disciples of the
Baptist move away from their former master toward Jesus. However
much they move geographically, these initial disciples cannot move beyond their own messianic expectations (vv. 35-42). On the final day, the
first of the three days of immediate preparation for the gift of the *doxa*, a
disciple called by Jesus makes the same mistake (vv. 43-45), as does one
singled out by Jesus for his lack of guile (vv. 46-49). The special feature of
Jesus' final words on this fourth day (vv. 50-51) is their vigor, stressing the
need to transcend contemporary messianic expectations. Faith based on
miracles will not suffice; something more is needed. This greater faith
will enable all disciples to see the revelation of the heavenly in Jesus, the
Son of Man. The setting of these "days" against the background of the
celebration of Pentecost and the commemoration of the gift of the *doxa* on
"the third day" creates an expectation that sight of the "greater things"
may not be too far away. Such expectation is nourished by words that follow 1:19-51: "And on the third day . . . *(kai tē hēmera̧ tȩ̄ tritȩ̄)*" (2:1).

NOTES

19. *And this is the testimony given by John:* The consistent use of *martyria* to speak of the Baptist's role points to this author's departure from the synoptic tradition. The Baptist is not a "precursor" but a "witness." This is developed in v. 21.

    "The Jews" sent priests and Levites from Jerusalem: On "the Jews" see the remarks in the Introduction.

    Who are you?: Although asked of John the Baptist, the question *su tis ei?:* "who are you?" could be taken as the *leitmotif* of the Fourth Gospel. Response to that question will determine the success or failure of all who encounter the Johannine Jesus.

20. *He confessed and did not deny, but confessed:* The pleonastic introduction to Jesus' rejection of any messianic role, *hōmologēsen kai ouk ērnēsato kai hōmologēsen,* recalls the situation of the Johannine community whose uncompromising confession of Jesus as the Messiah was leading to exclusion from the synagogue (see Introduction). The only other places in the Fourth Gospel where the verb *hōmologein* appears are 9:22 and 12:42, in which some form of exclusion from the synagogue is at stake.

24. *Now they had been sent from the Pharisees:* There are several places in the Gospel where the expressions "the Jews" and "the Pharisees" are used without distinction, as here (see v. 19; cf., for example, 9:13, 18, 40). For some this has been an indication of different sources behind the Fourth Gospel (cf. Urban C. von Wahlde, "The Terms for Religious Authorities in the Fourth Gospel: A Key to Literary Strata?" *JBL* 98 [1979] 251–253). Whatever the prehistory of the text, it can be read in its present shape by regarding "the Pharisees" as a further specification of "the Jews." The problem of the rejection of Jesus' claims is common to both groups.

27. *I am unworthy to untie the thong of his sandal:* The task of untying the thong of the sandal was given to the least and lowest of all in the hierarchy of servants and slaves.

28. *This took place in Bethany:* Several names are given for this location in the ancient manuscripts. The confusion has been created by an attempt to distinguish this place from the more famous "Bethany" just outside Jerusalem. Cf. Barrett, *Gospel* 175.

29. *The next day:* For the texts and discussion of the "days" that prepared for the celebration of Pentecost, see Jean Potin, *La fête juive de la Pentecôte.* LeDiv 65. Paris: Cerf, 1971, 146–170 (for the targums); Serra, *Contributi* 75–86 (for the rabbinic literature), and Potin, *La fête juive* 314–317; Serra, *Contributi* 91–110 (for the *Mekilta*). For the text (Hebrew and English) of the *Mekilta* see J. Lauterbach, ed., *Mekilta de Rabbi Ishmael.* 3 vols. Philadelphia: Jewish Publication Society of America, 1961.

    The Lamb of God who takes away the sin of the world: Generations of scholars have grappled with the background and meaning of this expression. Several issues need to be faced. Most importantly, the crucial element is "of God." In accordance with biblical thought only God takes away or forgives sin. The use of the verb *airein,* "to take away," has both meanings here. Jesus' role as Lamb of God flows from his having come from God. He is the one through whom God will take away the sin of the world. But why use "the Lamb"? Some associate it with the Suffering Servant of Isaiah 53, others with the triumphant lamb of Revelation (cf. Rev 7:17; 17:14), still others with a Jewish tradition of a lamb who would lead the flock of God's people or, most commonly, with the Passover lamb. (For a survey, see Brown, *Gospel* 1:58–63.) While the Passover link is undeniable (cf. 19:14), it is probably best explained with reference to the broader ritual practice of Israel. Through the use of the lamb for the sacrificial rites of communion and for reconciliation after sin the people of Israel established and renewed their union with God and among themselves. Jesus is the lamb, but he is not a cultic offering. He is "of God." The traditional way of gaining pardon and communion has been transcended through the Lamb of God. Jesus is not a cultic victim but the one through whom God enters the human story, offering it reconciliation with him. As so often in the Fourth Gospel, an old symbol is being used in a new way. Cf. Forestell, *The Word of the Cross* 157–166.

32. *I saw the Spirit descending from heaven like a dove:* On the use of the dove in both the synoptic and Johannine traditions surrounding the baptism of Jesus see F.-L. Lentzen-Deis, *Die Taufe Jesu nach den Synoptikern: Literarkritische und gattungsgeschtliche Untersuchungen.* FTS 4. Frankfurt: Joseph Knecht, 1970. On the possibility that the messianic prophecy of Isa 11:2 has been fulfilled with the descent of the Spirit see W. J. Bittner, *Jesu Zeichen im Johannesevangelium: Die Messias-Erkenntnis im Johannesevangelium vor ihrem jüdischen Hintergrund.* WUNT ser. 2, 26. Tübingen: J. C. B. Mohr (Paul Siebeck), 1987, 245–246.

34. *The Son of God:* Part of the manuscript tradition ($\mathfrak{P}^5$, first hand of Sinaiticus, Old Latin, some Syriac translations) has "the chosen one of God." The textual tradition for "Son of God" is stronger and the reading "the Son" rather than "the Chosen" is more in harmony with Johannine language and theology. Some, however, have argued for "the Chosen" for precisely these reasons, regarding it as the *lectio difficilior.* See the discussion supporting the reading "the Son of God" in F.-M. Braun, *Jean le Théologien II: Les grandes traditions d'Israel, L'accord des Ecritures d'après le Quatrième Evangile.* EtB. Paris: Gabalda, 1964, 71–73.

35. *Standing with two of his disciples:* This is the first time that disciples of the Baptist have been mentioned. They are not to be supposed as hearers of the Baptist's words in vv. 29-34. They hear that Jesus is the Lamb of God from the lips of the Baptist in v. 35 and move toward Jesus on the basis of that witness.

37. *They followed Jesus:* The language of "following" *(akolouthein)* is associated with discipleship across all canonical gospels. The word has at least two possible meanings: a spiritual "following" in which the disciples learn from and model themselves on the one followed, and a physical "following" in which the disciple treads the same path as the master. In the gospel traditions both meanings are involved. See G. Schneider, *EDNT* 1:49–54.

38. *Rabbi (which translated means Teacher):* It is often claimed that the parenthetic interpretations the author adds to explain Hebrew or Aramaic terms in the Fourth Gospel are an indication that the original listeners and readers knew no Hebrew or Aramaic (cf. Lindars, *Gospel* 113). While this may be partly true it is also a technique used by the author to strengthen the theological and christological point of view of the Gospel. Here the disciples call Jesus "Rabbi." This title falls well short of the author of the Fourth Gospel's understanding of Jesus. The addition of the Greek explanation of Rabbi, "which means teacher," is not only a translation but also a comment on the poor quality of the first disciples' initial understanding of Jesus.

39. *It was about four o'clock in the afternoon:* The translation renders the Greek "it was about the tenth hour," giving the expression no symbolic value. Cf. Schnackenburg, *Gospel* 1:309.

40. *One of the two who heard John speak and followed him was Andrew:* Although Andrew is identified, no information is provided on who the other ex-disciple of the Baptist might have been. Many scholars see this silence as a hint of an ex-disciple of the Baptist wishing to remain silent, thus initiating the presence of an anonymous figure in the story who eventually becomes known as the Beloved Disciple. Most recently see Charlesworth, *The Beloved Disciple* 326–336. Many disagree and see the issue as irrelevant. For the discussion see Frans Neirynck, "The Anonymous Disciple in John 1," *EThL* 66 (1990) 5–37.

41. *He first found:* Responding to criticism of the lack of seven days for the week of creation, Boismard (*Moïse ou Jésus: Essai de Christologie Johannique*. BEThL 84. Leuven: University Press, 1988, 79–81) reads *proi* rather than *protos* and thus generates an extra "day" at this point. The text would then read, "the next day he found his brother," rather than "he first found his brother." There is sparse textual support for this reading, which is little more than speculation.

    We have found: The claim on the part of the first disciples to have found Jesus and to have come to a decision about his person and role is a blatant untruth. This is seldom noticed by commentators. The theological point that is made by this untruth is that true discipleship flows from the initiative of Jesus. This is the case across both the synoptic and Johannine traditions. For the Johannine Gospel true discipleship involves a correct understanding of who Jesus is. The first disciples fail on both counts.

    The Messiah (which is translated Anointed): On the explanation of "the Messiah" as "the anointed one," see the note to v. 38.

42. *You are to be called Cephas (which is translated Peter):* Given the widespread presence of Simon Peter in the gospel traditions and his indisputable role as the appointed leader of the Twelve and other disciples it is most likely that the author of the Fourth Gospel plays on the readers' awareness of the Cephas/Peter figure in this promise. Jesus promises something to Simon that the readers know came true. Simon did become Cephas/Peter. As in vv. 38 and 41, the addition of the Greek explanation of the Aramaic name Cephas not only responds to the needs of non-Jewish readers but also strengthens the narrative

agenda of the author. The readers know that what Jesus said would happen has happened.

43. *Jesus decided . . . He found . . . :* The fourth day is different from the three preceding days, strongly marked as it is by the initiative of Jesus. This interpretation supplies "Jesus" as the subject of the verb *ēthelēsen.* This verb has no subject, but "said" has Jesus as its subject. I am supposing that Jesus is the subject throughout. Some scholars would claim that Philip decided to go to Galilee. My reading indicates that the first of the three days, leading into the celebration of the gift of the *doxa,* is under way.

44. *Now Philip was from Bethsaida, the city of Andrew and Peter:* The city of Bethsaida lies northeast of the Lake of Galilee and close to the border with the Decapolis. The names of these first disciples are Greek (cf. Mark 1:16-20; Luke 5:1-11), and it is to these disciples that the Greeks will come later in the Gospel (cf. 12:20-22).

45. *Philip found Nathanael and said to him, "We have found . . .":* See the note on v. 41. Here the lie is particularly obvious because of the play on the verb "to find": He *found* Philip . . . Philip *found* Nathanael . . . "We have *found.*"

46. *Can anything good come out of Nazareth?* The proverbial nature of this question suggests that it may have been a common enough saying. However, there is no evidence for such a proverb outside John 1:46.

47. *An Israelite in whom there is no deceit:* Nathanael is described as a person who is honest in his frankness (unlike Jacob in Gen 27:35-36), without lies (cf. Ps 32:2; Isa 53:9), who does not prostitute himself to false gods (Rev 14:5). He is worthy to recognize all that has been promised in the Scriptures (cf. v. 45).

48. *I saw you under the fig tree before Philip called you:* This earlier sight of Nathanael cannot be called a miracle in the Johannine sense of miracles being "signs," but it generates a response in Nathanael that recognizes that something miraculous is happening. Hahn, "Die Jüngerberufung" 187, sensitive to the technical question of miracles in John, rightly comments on "das wunderbare Wissen Jesu." It is this context of "wonder" that generates Nathanael's response in v. 49.

49. *Rabbi, you are the Son of God! You are the King of Israel!:* Many commentators regard Nathanael's confession as the final and correct confession of faith from the first disciples. Cf., for example, Hahn, "Die Jüngerberufung" 189; Barrett, *Gospel* 185–186; Schnackenburg, *Gospel* 1:317–319; Pancaro, *The Law in the Fourth Gospel* 288–304. This interpretation reads "Son of God" as a correct christological confession of the Johannine Jesus. The Interpretation argues that it is an expression of Jewish messianic hopes and thus falls short of the Johannine view, which transcends those hopes. This interpretation takes into account the wider context of responses from the disciples that fall short of true Johannine christological confessions and the immediate context of the surrounding titles "Rabbi" and "King of Israel." It leads into the words of Jesus in v. 50, which do not approve of what has been said in v. 49. This problem is often resolved by claiming that vv. 50-51 have been added to a passage

that originally concluded with the confession of v. 49. Cf., for example, Boismard, *Du Baptême à Cana* 105; Brown, *Gospel* 1:88; Fortna, *Gospel of Signs* 179–189; Kuhn, *Christologie und Wunder* 153–159. See the survey of the discussion in Neyrey, "The Jacob Allusions" 586–589.

50. *Do you believe because I told you that I saw you under the fig tree?:* This is the first indication in the Gospel of Jesus' difficulty in accepting belief generated by his miracles. This complicated question is largely conditioned by the contemporary debate about the existence of a Signs Source, that is, a body of synoptic-like miracle stories that has been used for the construction of the Fourth Gospel. It will be discussed in more detail in the Notes on 2:23-25. Miracles are never ends in themselves, as the believer must look beyond the fact of the miracle to a deeper understanding of what God is doing in and through the miracle worker. However, as 20:30-31 indicates, the author has chosen to tell miracle stories ("signs") so that the readers might come to believe that Jesus is the Christ, the Son of God, and that they might have life in his name.

You will see greater things than these: There is a hint that what will be seen will result from something that transcends what the disciples can see from their own initiative.

51. *Amen, amen I say to you:* The double introductory "amen" is found only in the Fourth Gospel. A single "amen" is found regularly in the synoptic gospels, especially in Matthew (thirty-one times). The double "amen" appears in the Fourth Gospel twenty-six times. It generally leads into a significant statement that is intimately connected with what went before. Cf. de la Potterie, *La Vérité* 1:57–58.

The angels of God ascending and descending upon the Son of Man: For a full discussion of the scholarship surrounding this first Son of Man passage in the Fourth Gospel see Moloney, *Son of Man* 23–41, especially the conclusions on pp. 33–41.

For Reference and Further Study

Barrosse, Thomas. "The Seven Days of the New Creation in St. John's Gospel," *CBQ* 23 (1959) 507–516.

Boismard, M.-É. *Du Baptême à Cana (Jean 1,19–2,11).* LeDiv 18. Paris: Cerf, 1956.

Burge, G. M. *The Anointed Community* 50–62.

Freed, E. D. "*Ego eimi* in John 1:20 and 4:25," *CBQ* 41 (1979) 288–291.

Hahn, Ferdinand. "Die Jüngerberufung Joh 1,35-51." In Joachim Gnilka, ed., *Neues Testament und Kirche: Für Rudolf Schnackenburg.* Freiburg: Herder, 1974, 172–190.

Hooker, Morna D. "John the Baptist and the Johannine Prologue," *NTS* 16 (1970) 354–358.

Koester, Craig. "Messianic Exegesis and the Call of Nathanael (John 1:45-51)," *JSNT* 39 (1990) 23–34.

Kuhn, H.-J. *Christologie und Wunder: Untersuchungen zu Joh 1,35-51.* BU 18. Regensburg: Pustet, 1988.

Moloney, Francis J. *Belief in the Word* 53–76.

_____. *Son of Man* 23–41.

Neyrey, Jerome H. "The Jacob Allusions in John 1:51," *CBQ* 44 (1982) 586–605.

Olsson, Birger. *Structure and Meaning in the Fourth Gospel: A Text Linguistic Analysis of John 2:1-11 and 4:1-42.* CB, NT ser. 6. Lund: Gleerup, 1974, 70–73, 102–104, 276.

Rad, Gerhard von, and Gerhard Kittel. *"dokeō" ktl. TDNT* 2:232–235.

Rowland, C. C. "John 1.51, Jewish Apocalyptic and Targumic Tradition," *NTS* 30 (1984) 498–507.

Saxby, Harold. "The Time-Scheme in the Gospel of John," *ET* 104 (1992) 9–13.

Schenke, Ludger. "Die literarische Entstehungsgeschichte von Joh 1,19-51," BN 46 (1989) 24–57.

Serra, A. M. *Contributi dell'antica letteratura giudaica per l'esegesi di Gv. 2:1-12 e 19:25-27.* SPFTM 31. Rome: Herder, 1977, 45–89, 259–301.

_____. "Le tradizioni della teofania sinaitica nel Targum dello Pseudo Jonathan Es. 19.24 e Giov. 1:19-2:12," *Mar.* 33 (1971) 1–39.

Trudinger, L. P. "The Seven Days of the New Creation in St John's Gospel: Some Further Reflections," *EvQ* 44 (1972) 154–158.

B. FROM CANA TO CANA (2:1–4:54)

Introduction to 2:1–4:54. The words that open the account of the first Cana miracle, "And on the third day" (2:1), indicate that the theme of "days" that marked 1:19-51 is coming to its conclusion. In the Jewish celebration of Pentecost, following the account of Exod 19:16, on the third day the glory of God is revealed in the gift of the Law (cf. 2:11) after four days of preparation (cf. 1:19, 29, 35, 43). However, several features of 2:1-12 separate this miracle story from 1:19-51. There is a change of place. In 1:43 Jesus decided to go to Galilee, and in 2:1 he is there. Along with the disciples of Jesus (v. 2) new characters enter the story, the mother of Jesus (v. 1) and several participants at the wedding feast: servants (v. 5), the steward (v. 8), the bridegroom (v. 9), Jesus' brethren (v. 12). There is a change in literary form as the account moves from the initial response of "the Jews" and the first disciples to the Baptist and Jesus (1:19-51) to a miracle story (2:1-12). The most significant feature that points to 2:1-12 as both the close of the "days" and the beginning of a further stage is Jesus' return to Cana in Galilee in 4:43-54. The narrator goes to considerable pains to link the second Cana miracle (4:43-54) with the story of Jesus' first visit to Cana. The account of the second Cana miracle begins "Then he came again to Cana in Galilee where he had changed the water into wine" (4:46). A number of structural elements in 4:43-54 are matched in

2:1-12. As the second miracle story closes the narrator comments, "Now this was the second sign that Jesus did after coming from Judea to Galilee" (v. 54). These comments single out a new stage in the unfolding structure of the Gospel as a whole. It reports a journey from Cana to Cana.

Once this literary frame between the two Cana stories is recognized (2:1-12 and 4:43-54) the reported encounters that fill 2:13–4:42 take on an identifiable role within the author's point of view. One moves systematically through episodes that report meetings between Jesus and others: Jesus and "the Jews" meet in the purification of the Temple (2:13-22). After a *comment* from the narrator (2:23-25) Jesus meets two other figures from the world of Israel: Nicodemus (3:1-21) and John the Baptist (3:22-36). Jesus next moves to the world that is both geographically and spiritually beyond the boundaries of Israel. In the absence of the disciples (cf. 4:8) he has two moments of encounter with the Samaritan woman (4:1-15 and 4:16-30). The disciples' return (cf. 4:27) allows Jesus to *comment* on the events that are going on around the unwitting disciples (4:31-38) and these episodes conclude with Jesus' reception by the Samaritan villagers (4:39-42). Each of these encounters between Jesus and others, Jews and non-Jews, tells of Jesus' self-revelation and the response of others to that revelation. On two occasions the narrative slows down and the narrator (2:23-25) and Jesus (4:31-38) comment on the surrounding events.

This overview of 2:1–4:54 suggests that the section, entitled Cana to Cana, may be structured in the following fashion:

  i. The first miracle at Cana (2:1-12)
     ii. Jesus and "the Jews" (2:13-22)
    iii. *Comment* (2:23-25)
    iv. Jesus and Nicodemus (3:1-21)
     v. Jesus and John the Baptist (3:22-36)
    vi. Jesus and the Samaritan woman (4:1-15)
   vii. Jesus and the Samaritan woman (4:16-30)
  viii. *Comment* (4:31-38)
    ix. Jesus and the Samaritan villagers (4:39-42)
  x. The second miracle at Cana (4:43-54).

This scheme shows the literary frame created by the use of the two Cana stories and the careful assembly of the intervening material. Encounters between Jesus and characters from Israel follow the first Cana miracle, and parallel encounters between Jesus and characters from Samaria lead into the second Cana miracle. The two comments, one from the narrator following the encounter between Jesus and "the Jews" and the other before the encounter between Jesus and the Samaritan villagers, are also symmetrically placed in the narrative.

The first days of Jesus closed with a promise that the disciples would see greater things, but this promise was tied to his demand that their faith exceed the belief demonstrated across those days. It was not enough to believe that Jesus was the fulfillment of their messianic hopes, nor was it enough to be moved to faith in Jesus by his wonderful knowledge of things that should have been hidden from him. Greater faith will lead them to see the revelation of the heavenly in Jesus, the Son of Man. This promises that the story that lies ahead will tell of how God is made known in and through Jesus. However, it must also involve the response to such revelation. Both issues will be dealt with in the Cana to Cana section but with a stronger focus on how different people from both inside and outside Israel respond to the person and word of Jesus.

The Response to Jesus Within Israel (2:1–3:36)

i. The First Miracle at Cana:
Faith in the Word of Jesus (2:1-12)

1. And on the third day there was a marriage at Cana in Galilee, and the mother of Jesus was there. 2. Jesus also was invited to the marriage, with his disciples.
3. When the wine failed, the mother of Jesus said to him, "They have no wine." 4. And Jesus said to her, "O woman, what have you to do with me? My hour has not yet come." 5. His mother said to the servants, "Do whatever he tells you."
6. Now six stone jars were standing there, for the Jewish rites of purification, each holding twenty or thirty gallons. 7. Jesus said to them, "Fill the jars with water." And they filled them up to the brim. 8. He said to them, "Now draw some out, and take it to the steward of the feast." So they took it. 9. When the steward of the feast tasted the water now become wine and did not know where it came from (though the servants who had drawn the water knew), the steward of the feast called the bridegroom 10. and said to him, "Every man serves the good wine first; and when all have drunk freely, then the poor wine; but you have kept the good wine until now."
11. This, the first of his signs, Jesus did at Cana in Galilee, and manifested his glory; and his disciples believed in him.
12. After this he went down to Capernaum, with his mother and his brothers and his disciples; and there they stayed for a few days.

INTERPRETATION

Introduction to 2:1-12. The action of the narrative is framed by the movement of characters in the story, Jesus, his mother, and the disciples (vv. 1-2, v. 12). In v. 12 Jesus' brothers, who will reappear later (cf. 7:1-10) join the movement. Within this literary frame where people move from one place to another two exchanges lead to action, one initiated by the mother of Jesus (vv. 3-5) and the other by Jesus (vv. 7-10). Finally, the narrator comments on the significance of the event (v. 11). The story has the following shape:

(a) *Vv. 1-2:* The time, place, and reason for the gathering *(eklēthē)* of named characters (the mother of Jesus, Jesus, the disciples) are established. They are "there" (v. 1: *ekei*).

(b) *Vv. 3-5:* The mother of Jesus speaks to Jesus and responds to his rebuke by telling the attendants to do whatever he tells them.

(c) *Vv. 6-10:* The main action of the story—filling of the jars, the steward's recognition of good wine, his reaction and words to the bridegroom—is triggered by Jesus' speaking to the servants, who do what he tells them.

(d) *V. 11:* The narrator comments on the manifestation of the glory of Jesus and the faith of the disciples.

(e) *V. 12:* The account closes as the characters from vv. 1-2, who have made a journey (cf. 2: *eklēthē*) to be "there" (cf. v. 1: *ekei*) at Cana, move away (v. 12: *katebē*) to be in another place (v. 12: *ekei*) at Capernaum.

The narrative is rich in Johannine symbolism and anticipates many of the themes that will develop through the story. The miracle and its consequences take place after a discussion over "the hour" (2:4; cf. 4:21, 23; 5:25, 28; 7:30; 8:20; 12:23, 27; 13:1; 17:1; 19:27). This is the first of a number of events each described as a "sign" *(sēmeion:* cf. 2:23; 3:2; 6:2, 14, 26, 30; 7:31; 9:16; 10:41; 11:47; 12:18, 37. Cf. 20:30-31). The theme of water will return in chs. 2, 4, 5, 7, 9, and 19, and the revelation of the *doxa* is an important theme throughout the Gospel (see *doxa* in 1:14; 5:41-44; 7:18; 11:4, 40; 12:43; 17:5, 22-24, and *doxazein* in 8:54; 11:4; 12:23, 28; 13:31-32; 17:1-5). "Everywhere in the Fourth Gospel we are further confronted by this self-contained allusiveness" (Hoskyns, *Fourth Gospel* 67).

Introduction (vv. 1-2). The words "on the third day" recall the moment of God's revelation at Sinai (v. 1a). The four days of 1:19-51 look forward to "the third day" (see Exod 19:16). The setting of a marriage feast also summons up biblical images of the messianic era and the messianic fullness, marked by wine and abundance of fine foods (cf. Hos 2:19-20; Isa 25:6-8; Jer 2:2; Song of Songs). The first character introduced is the mother of Jesus (v. 1b). The singling out of this character hints that she may have an important role to play in the narrative that follows. She is accompanied at the celebration by her son and his disciples (v. 2). The scene has been set as a group of people headed by the mother of Jesus has gathered (*eklēthē*) for the celebration of a wedding "on the third day."

Action initiated by the mother of Jesus (vv. 3-5). The mother draws Jesus' attention to a fact that the narrator has already commented on: there was no wine (v. 3). She was the first character introduced and she initiates action with her statement. She is met by a sharp, twofold response from Jesus. Jesus asks, "O woman, what have you to do with me?" (v. 4b: *ti emoi kai soi?*). There have been many attempts to soften this retort, but whatever one makes of it, it is not the type of response one would expect from a son to a mother. The expression "is abrupt and draws a sharp line between Jesus and his mother" (Barrett, *Gospel* 191). The narrator did not announce her name but introduced her as "mother" (v. 1). Jesus calls her "woman," and his question puts a distance between his mother and himself. He then makes a statement that indicates that Jesus' life is marked by a sequence of events leading to an "hour": "My hour has not yet come" (v. 4c). This is the first reference to a theme that will develop as the narrative unfolds. The Prologue concludes with an insistence that the Word become flesh is the Son (1:14-18), and the witness of the Baptist repeats it (1:29-34). Jesus is the Son of God, and the life story of the Son will be determined by his relationship with the Father. However, the hour of Jesus is an event that will take place in the human sphere, a part of the story of Jesus of Nazareth that is "not yet." This introduces tension. The story that is only now beginning looks forward to the completion of "the hour" of Jesus. Jesus' initial question and his words concerning "the hour" indicate that there is a distance between himself and his mother and that "the law according to which he works is imposed on him by another" (Schnackenburg, *Gospel* 1:329). A world exists between Jesus and God, and the mother of Jesus is outside that world. The words of Jesus in v. 4 firmly inform his mother that such is the case. It is a gentle rebuke that keeps her in her place.

If the reply of Jesus to his mother is surprising, equally surprising is her reaction to it. In the face of a rebuke, and from her position outside the inner world of the relationship between Jesus and the Father, she tells the servants to do *whatever he tells them* (v. 5: *ho ti an legē humin poiēsate*). However much the interpretation of this scene has been influenced by the Marian traditions of the Christian Churches, nothing in the narrative explains how she can turn away from the rebuke of her son, correctly indicating that she has no knowledge or understanding of God's designs for his Son. Yet she tells the servants, in a carefully worded command, that they should put into action *anything* that he tells them to do. The Prologue announces Jesus as the *logos* of God but this new character, the mother of Jesus, does not know this. Yet with unconditional trust in the efficacy of his word *(ho ti an legē)* she issues instructions to the servants. She is the first person in the narrative to show, at the level of the action of the story, that the correct response to the presence of Jesus is trust in his word. Her brief appearance at the beginning of this miracle story acts as the trigger initiating a series of events that leads to the miracle (vv. 8-10), the manifestation of the *doxa* of Jesus and the faith of the disciples (v. 11). Following hard upon the response of the emissaries of "the Jews" (vv. 19-28), the initial confessions of faith of the first disciples (vv. 35-49), and the promise of Jesus that greater faith would lead to the sight of greater things, the mother of Jesus is the first to show the quality of true belief. She trusts unconditionally, indeed even in the face of apparent rejection and rebuke, in the efficacy of the word of Jesus.

Action initiated by Jesus (vv. 6-10). The narrator sets the scene for the following section with an important description of stone jars (v. 6). There are six of them, one short of the perfection of the number "seven." This is probably a hint that a former gift is to be perfected (cf. 1:16-17). Later Jewish texts indicate that stone was useful for purificatory purposes because it did not contract uncleanness. They are very large jars, each one containing some twenty-four gallons. There will be a superabundance of wine produced from this water, and the problem raised by the mother is about to be resolved. The water in the jars, used for Jewish purification rituals, will be transformed into a "sign" (v. 11: *sēmeiōn*) in and through which the *doxa* will be revealed.

As the mother of Jesus told the servants to do whatever he told *(legē)* them, Jesus tells *(legei)* them what they are to do (v. 7a), and they respond with wordless obedience. The mother's command is perfectly executed: Jesus tells them to fill the jars with water, and the servants fill them up to the brim. The transformation of the water into wine is not reported. Jesus issues a second set of instructions, again in direct speech (v. 8: *legei*), that they draw from the jars and take what they draw forth to the steward of the feast. They again do exactly as they are told. The mother's command, that they do *whatever* Jesus tells them, is being followed to perfection. The steward tastes the water that is now wine. He does not know the origin of the wine *(pothen estin)*, while the servants do. They had drawn the water, and they are aware that the wine is the result of a chain of responses to a series of "words": the word of the mother concerning the word of her son (v. 5), and two words from Jesus (vv. 7-8). The importance of acceptance of the "word" of Jesus is a crucial theme.

The bridegroom is summoned and asked to explain the strange appearance of the good wine as the celebration draws to a close (vv. 9c-10). The bridegroom is only spoken to; he never plays an active role in the story. The words of the steward imply that the bridegroom is responsible for this remarkable fullness of good wine. The next time a bridegroom appears in the story (cf. 3:29) it will be in the words of John the Baptist, who speaks of Jesus as the bridegroom, and himself as the friend of the bridegroom. At one level of the narrative the steward instructs the bridegroom on common sense, but on another level the encounter raises a question about the source of the fullness provided by the bridegroom. "The steward here seems to be wholly unaware of the supply of wine, of the shortage or of the drawing of water. He merely states that the wine is excellent *(kalos)* and that the bridegroom's actions are not those of ordinary men" (B. Olsson, *Structure and Meaning* 62). In v. 4 the mother of Jesus was told that the hour had not yet come. The steward seems to think that it has, as he tells the bridegroom, who has provided the wine, that he has kept the good wine *until now (heōs arti).* But Jesus announced at the beginning of the account that the hour has not yet come (v. 4: *oupō hēkei).* However rich the gift of the wine may have been, the larger story of Jesus points beyond this particular story. This is an important moment, but not the final moment, in the revelation of Jesus.

The narrator's comment (v. 11). The tension between the "not yet" of the hour of Jesus (cf. v. 4) and the "now" of the miracle story (cf. v. 10) is present in the narrator's comment that in this, the beginning of his signs (v. 11: *archēn tōn sēmeiōn),* the *doxa* of Jesus was manifested, and the disciples believed in him. This is a "beginning." The Prologue announced that the *doxa* was seen in the incarnation of the *logos* in the person of Jesus Christ, and that this was the fullness of the gift of God, perfecting the former gift of the Law. This is now happening in the story. "The transformation of water into wine . . . is the first act of the Word in the world, and a type of the transformation to come. Perhaps it is the grace beyond grace, the messianic wine of being that replaces the inferior wine of the Torah, which is appropriate only to becoming" (Alter, "John" 449). The disciples, who attempted to contain Jesus within the limitations of their own messianic hopes in 1:35-51, come to belief when Jesus manifests his *doxa.* The promise implied by the days of preparation for the Jewish celebration of the gift of the Law at the feast of Pentecost is realized in the revelation of the *doxa* of Jesus "on the third day" (v. 11. Cf. v. 1). However, as Israel faced a long history of loyalty, mediocrity, and failure *after* the gift of the Law, so also the disciples are only on the threshold of their experience of the revelation of God in and through Jesus. The unconditional faith of the mother of Jesus in the word of her son initiated a series of events that led to the revelation of the glory of God. What Jesus *said* was done, and his glory was manifested as a consequence of an unconditioned acceptance of his word. But there will be an "hour" in the future when this revelation will come to a final consummation. The mother of Jesus, the woman, will return at that "hour" (cf. 19:25-27).

Conclusion (v. 12). The major players, Jesus, his mother, and his disciples are reassembled, and Jesus' brothers are added to the group. When the brothers return in 7:1-10 the reader will recall that they have been with Jesus from his first days, and from the first manifestation of his glory. The group journeys away from Cana to stay at Capernaum "for a few days" (v. 12). This closing comment keeps the narrative moving. A group that gathered at Cana in v. 1 *(ekei)* sets out from Cana in v. 12 to stay in another place *(ekei)* for a brief time. The narrator's remarks on characters, space, and time lead away from Cana, further into the narrative.

NOTES

1–12. *The literary form of a miracle story.* Bultmann has described this passage as a typical miracle story (Bultmann, *Gospel* 115). In his *History of the Synoptic Tradition* (Oxford: Blackwell, 1963, 318–331) he argues that miracle stories have the following form:

  (a) A problem is described in some detail to indicate the gravity of the situation.
  (b) A request is made.
  (c) The miracle is performed, accompanied by a description of how it is done.
  (d) The successful outcome of the miracle is described.
  (e) The wonder of all who saw it or heard of it is described.

The Cana miracle has contacts with this tradition, but cannot be described as a "typical miracle story." It unfolds in the following fashion:

  1. *Problem:* "The wine failed" (v. 3a).
  2. *Request:* "The mother of Jesus said to him, 'They have no wine'" (v. 3b).
  3. *Rebuke:* "O woman, what have you to do with me? My hour has not yet come" (v. 4).
  4. *Reaction:* "His mother said to the servants, 'Do whatever he tells you' *(ho ti an legē humin poiēsate)*" (v. 5).
  5. *Consequence:* A miracle that leads to the faith of others (the disciples) (vv. 6-11).

Those parts of the story where the mother of Jesus plays an important role disturb the traditional form of a miracle story. She points out that there is a problem (v. 3a), but her words generate a rebuke that in turn leads to the mother of Jesus' words to the servants: "Do whatever he tells you" (v. 5). The final element in the story is also somewhat foreign. There is no report of wonder or of the effect the miracle had on the guests. The result of the miracle is the manifestation of the glory of Jesus and the faith of the disciples (v. 11). The author has composed this miracle story, no doubt using sources from the Johannine tradition. At 1:51 the question of the appropriate response to Jesus was raised. By the time the narrative reaches 2:12 an initial answer to that question has been provided.

1. *there was a marriage:* Many attempts have been made to discover a pre-Johannine miracle story (cf. Fortna, *Signs* 29–38; idem, *Predecessor* 48–58), perhaps with its origins in a Dionysiac celebration (cf. Bauer, *Johannesevangelium* 47; Bultmann, *Gospel* 118–119). Whatever its origins, the present shape of 2:1-12 reveals a careful ordering of the material from both a literary and theological perspective.

   the mother of Jesus was there: Exaggerated Marian reflections, especially from the Catholic tradition, have led to an exegesis of this passage that paradoxically minimalizes the role played by the mother of Jesus (cf. Zappella, "Gv 2:1-12" 59–78). A balance must be found, as the text indicates that her role is crucial to the correct reading of the passage. The fact that she is the first person introduced to the account, even preceding Jesus, is a sign that what she says and does is crucial to the story (cf. Smitmans, *Das Weinwunder* 54–63).

2. *with his disciples:* It is sometimes suggested that Jesus and his disciples may have been uninvited, and thus were the cause of the shortage of wine (Derrett, "Water into Wine" 80–97). There is no hint of this in the text.

3. *When the wine failed:* Some early manuscripts, including the first hand of Sinaiticus and the Old Latin, have a longer reading at v. 3a: "Now they had no wine, for the wine provided for the feast had been used up." The shorter reading, "when the wine gave out," is attested in both the Bodmer papyri, and must be accepted as the original (cf. Olsson, *Structure and Meaning* 33–34).

4. *what have you to do with me?:* The interpretation of *ti emoi kai soi* is notoriously difficult. Is it a statement or a question? Once that has been decided, what does it mean in this context? For a survey of scholarly discussion see Michaud, "Le signe de Cana" 247–253. It is widely used in the OT (cf. Lagrange, *Evangile* 56) and appears in the synoptic tradition (cf. Maynard, "TI EMOI KAI SOI" 583–584). As C. H. Giblin has shown ("Suggestion, Negative Response" 197–211), it is part of a Johannine narrative technique, following a Semitic practice, that is "an agreement to disagree, so that the party voicing disagreement expresses a concern . . . not to become 'involved' with the specific concerns of the party addressed" (p. 203). Some element of harshness cannot be eliminated from these words (cf. Maynard, "TI EMOI KAI SOI" 584–585).

   My hour has not yet come: The "hour" of Jesus unfolds gradually across the Gospel. For the major part of Jesus' ministry it is "not yet" (cf. 2:4; 7:4, 30; 8:20). However, though its first association is with a marriage feast it is eventually associated with violence (cf. 7:30; 8:20). Toward the close of the public ministry, as the threat of Jesus' violent end approaches through a "lifting up" on a cross, the "hour" of violence "has come," and is associated with Jesus' glorification (cf. 12:23, 27). This theme continues into the final section of the Gospel (cf. 13:31) and is further explained as the hour through which Jesus must pass in order to return to the Father (cf. 13:1, 32; 17:5) and the hour that creates a new family of Jesus (19:27).

5. *Do whatever he tells you:* Despite many reflections on this passage claiming that Jesus responds to his mother's request (cf. Lagrange, *Evangile* 57; Schnackenburg, *Gospel* 1:331), this is not said in the text. From a position "outside" the oneness that exists between the Father and the Son, which determines "the hour" of Jesus, she shows her openness to trust in "whatever" the word of Jesus might bring. The narrative has not provided the mother of Jesus with a shred of information that might allow her to give such commands to the servants. Her confident command depends entirely upon a yet-to-be-verified belief. "Nowhere is perhaps such trust shewn" (Westcott, *Gospel* 37).

   It is possible that the account of the gift of the Law at Sinai (Exodus 19; 24) and subsequent Jewish reflection on that foundational account may still be present to the narrative. On three occasions as the people of Israel receive the Law from the hands of Moses they commit themselves as a people of God by crying out: "All that the Lord has spoken we will do" (Exod 19:8. See also Exod 24:3, 7). As once the *debarīm* (words) of the Law offered life to a people, here the mother of Jesus trusts that the *dabar* (word) of her son will do likewise. (Cf. Serra, *Contributi* 139–181.)

6. *six stone jars:* For a collection of later rabbinic documents that indicate the usefulness of stone for purificatory purposes see Str-B 2:406. For the calculation of *metrētas duo ē treis* as eighteen to twenty-four gallons see Barrett, *Gospel* 192. There is no need to link the purification mentioned here with any particular feast, or with rites before or after a meal. The issues that determine the significance of the description of the jars are their association with rites "of the Jews" and the number "six." These details give a Jewish setting to the wedding feast at Cana.

7. *Jesus said to them:* The importance of the "word" of Jesus emerges as Jesus speaks. The narrative depends on a series of encounters where there are never more than two active characters on stage at any one time (cf. Martyn, *History and Theology* 3–16, 49–57), and where all that happens is the result of a "word" (cf. vv. 3, 4, 5, 7-8, 10). Cf. Olsson, *Structure and Meaning* 86–88.

9. *where it came from:* The Prologue has already indicated the importance of the question of the origins of Jesus. Throughout the first days of Jesus the representatives of "the Jews" and the first disciples fall short in their attempts to understand the Baptist and Jesus because they do not understand the importance of Jesus' origins. This theme returns in the steward's not knowing where the wine came from. "The origins of the gift, like the origins of the giver, are hidden from him" (Gnilka, *Johannesevangelium* 23 [author's translation]). There is little to support the suggestion that the wine has links with the early Church's eucharistic celebrations (cf. Cullmann, *The Early Church* 66–71; Suggit, "John 2:1-11" 141–158).

   the steward of the feast called the bridegroom: There are at least two levels of reading operating in the identification of *ho nymphios* ("the bridegroom") as Jesus. A surface reading reports what any steward may have done on finding that excellent wine had been kept till late in the proceedings. The fact that the bridegroom never speaks, but simply hears the blustering of the steward introduces irony (cf. Duke, *Irony,* 83–84). The provider of the wine, whose origins are unknown to the steward (cf. v. 9), is instructed by a character who responds to the events in a totally "earthly" fashion. As the following comment from the narrator indicates, much more than good wine is provided by the "sign." For the patristic interpretation of the bridegroom as Jesus see Smitmans, *Das Weinwunder* 207–217.

11. *the first of his signs:* The indication that this is the *archē tōn sēmeiōn* has led many to see the miracle at Cana as the first miracle in the Signs Source (cf. Bultmann, *Gospel* 118; Gnilka, *Johannesevangelium* 22). Whatever its background, it will be argued that this numbering is more an indication of the passage's relationship to 4:46-54 than the clumsy remnant of an earlier source.

 [he] manifested his glory: The verb *phaneroun* is widely used in the Fourth Gospel (cf. 1:31; 3:21; 7:4; 9:3; 17:6; 21:1 [twice], 14). It is closely associated with the Johannine idea of Jesus' revelation of God (cf. Schnackenburg, *Gospel* 1:335–337; Bittner, *Jesu Zeichen* 97–98). This is the only place where it is used with *doxa (ephanerōsen tēn doxan autou).* The solemnity of the language recalls the revelation of the glory of Yhwh manifested "on the third day" at Sinai (Exod 19:16), surpassed in the manifestation of the *doxa* of Jesus "on the third day" at Cana (John 2:1). For a full discussion of the Sinai connection see Olsson, *Structure and Meaning* 69–73; Theobald, *Die Fleischwerdung* 290–292. Biblical scholars who seek to apply anthropological concepts to the Johannine text play down the links with the Sinai tradition, giving *doxa* its social meaning of "honor" in a society shaped by an honor-shame anthropology. For an application of this paradigm to John 2:1-11 see Collins, "The Question of *Doxa*" 100–109. This commentary will regularly associate the noun *doxa* and the verb *doxazein* with the Sinai tradition, so closely linked with the central Johannine notion that what God gave Israel at Sinai was a first gift and that this gift has been perfected in the gift that takes place through Jesus Christ (cf. 1:17; 1:19–2:12; 2:11). See the remarks of the professional anthropologist J. K. Chance, "The Anthropology of Honor and Shame: Culture, Values, and Practice." *Sem* 68 (1994) 139–149. Chance is critical of the lack of sophistication in biblical scholars' application of these categories, concluding that "there is more to Mediterranean culture than honor and shame," and asking that biblical scholars "recognize the possibilities for heterogeneity in the societies they study" (148). A crucial element in the NT traditions is the link with the OT. In the Fourth Gospel, Torah and Jesus Christ are profoundly related. See Pancaro, *The Law in the Fourth Gospel.*

12. *After this he went down to Capernaum:* This verse has been the subject of much controversy as "it is difficult to treat this verse as a real connective between Cana and the next scene at Jerusalem, for a journey to Capernaum is a long detour from the road to Jerusalem" (Brown, *Gospel* 1:113. Cf. Dodd, *Tradition* 235). Supporters of the Signs Source theory claim that in the source the verse led immediately into the second miracle story in 4:46-54 (cf. Bultmann, *Gospel* 114 n. 4; Fortna, *Signs* 102–103; Boismard, *Moïse ou Jésus* 44–46). However

inappropriate the geographical movement might be, in literary terms the narrative axes of character, space, and time are gathered in this way to lead into the next event in the life of Jesus (cf. Schnackenburg, *Gospel* 1:342–343).

FOR REFERENCE AND FURTHER STUDY

Boismard, M.-E. *Du Baptême à Cana.*

Brown, Raymond E. "The 'Mother of Jesus' in the Fourth Gospel," in Marinus de Jonge, ed., *L'Evangile de Jean: Sources, rédaction, théologie.* BEThL 44. Leuven: University Press, 1977, 307–310.

Collins, M. S. "The Question of *Doxa:* A Socioliterary Reading of the Wedding at Cana," *BTB* 25 (1995) 100–109.

Collins, R. F. "Cana (Jn. 2:1-12)–The first of his signs or the key to his signs?" *IThQ* 47 (1980) 79–95.

_____. "Mary in the Fourth Gospel–a decade of Johannine Studies." *LouvSt* 3 (1970) 99–142.

Cullmann, Oscar. *Early Christian Worship.* SBT 10. London: SCM Press, 1953.

Derrett, J. D. M. "Water into Wine," *BZ* 7 (1963) 80–97.

Geoltrain, Pierre. "Les noces à Cana: Jean 2,1-12: Analyse des structures narratives," *FV* 73 (1974) 83–90.

Giblin, C. H. "Suggestion, Negative Response, and Positive Action in St. John's Gospel (John 2.1-11; 4.46-54; 7.2-14; 11.1-44)," *NTS* 26 (1979–1980) 197–211.

Grassi, Joseph A. "The Wedding at Cana (John II 1-11): A Pentecostal Meditation?" *NT* (1972) 131–136.

Maynard, A. H. "TI EMOI KAI SOI," *NTS* 31 (1985) 582–586.

Michaud, J.-P. "Le signe de Cana dans son contexte johannique," *LTP* 18 (1962) 239–285; 19 (1963) 257–283.

Moloney, Francis J. *Belief in the Word* 77–92.

_____. "From Cana to Cana (Jn 2:1–4:54) and the Fourth Evangelist's Concept of Correct (and Incorrect) Faith," in E. A. Livingstone, ed., *Studia Biblica 1978. II. Papers in The Gospels. Sixth International Congress on Biblical Studies. Oxford 3–7 April 1978.* JSNT.S 2. Sheffield: JSOT Press, 1980, 185–213.

_____. *Mary: Woman and Mother.* Collegeville: The Liturgical Press, 1989, 31–50.

Olsson, Birger. *Structure and Meaning* 18–114.

Serra, A. M. *Contributi* 29–257.

Smitmans, Adolf. *Das Weinwunder von Kana: Die Auslegung von Jo 2,1-11 bei den Vätern und heute.* BGBE 6. Tübingen: J. C. B. Mohr (Paul Siebeck), 1966.

Suggit, J. N. "John 2:1-11: The sign of greater things to come," *Neotest.* 21 (1987) 141–158.

Vanhoye, Albert. "Interrogation johannique et l'exégèse de Cana." *Bib.* 55 (1974) 157–177.

Zappella, M. "Gv 2,1-12: La figura della madre di Gesù nel conflitto delle interpretazioni. Rassegna bibliografica (1970–1988)," *Quaderni Monfortani* 5 (1987) 59–78.

ii. Jesus and "the Jews" (2:13-22)

13. The Passover of the Jews was at hand, and Jesus went up to Jerusalem.
14. In the Temple he found those who were selling oxen and sheep and pigeons, and the money changers at their business. 15. And making a whip of cords, he drove them all, with the sheep and oxen, out of the Temple; and he poured out the coins of the money changers and overturned their tables. 16. And he told those who sold the pigeons, "Take these things away; you shall not make my Father's house a house of trade." 17. His disciples remembered that it was written, "Zeal for your house will consume me."
18. The Jews then said to him, "What sign have you to show us for doing this?" 19. Jesus answered them, "Destroy this Temple, and in three days I will raise it up." 20. The Jews then said, "It has taken forty-six years to build this Temple, and will you raise it up in three days?"
21. But he spoke of the Temple of his body. 22. When therefore he was raised from the dead, his disciples remembered that he had said this; and they believed the Scripture and the word that Jesus had spoken.
[23. When he was in Jerusalem during the Passover festival in the festival crowd many believed in his name because they saw the signs that he was doing. 24. But Jesus on his part would not entrust himself to them, because he knew all people 25. and needed no one to bear witness of them; for he himself knew what was in each person.]

INTERPRETATION

Introduction to 2:13-22. The account of the purification of the Temple is well represented in the synoptic tradition (cf. Mark 11:15-17; Matt 21:12-13; Luke 19:45-46). The author of the Fourth Gospel has used a unique version of the tradition at the beginning, rather than at the end of the story of Jesus. Whatever the prehistory of the Johannine use of the story, it has been carefully shaped. The narrator provides an obvious introduction (v. 13) and a conclusion that serves to close this episode and to lead into the story of Nicodemus (vv. 23-25). Verses 23-25 are included within this structure. These verses conclude the episode of the purification of the Temple but they also look forward to the story of Nicodemus's visit to Jesus (3:1-21). They deserve separate treatment because of their role as commentary upon the unfolding story of responses to Jesus (cf. Topel, "A Note" 216–217). The account itself opens with the description of Jesus' actions (vv. 14-17), highlighted by his words (cf. v. 16), followed by the reaction of "the Jews," also marked by direct speech (cf. vv. 18-20) and a closing comment on the action from the narrator (vv. 21-22). Taking these elements into account, the narrative has the following shape:

(a) *V. 13:* The scene is set. Time, place, and the reason for Jesus' movement from Galilee to Jerusalem are established.

(b) *Vv. 14-17:* Jesus' action, its motivation, and the response of the disciples are described.

(c) *Vv. 18-20:* A verbal exchange follows the action. This section is dominated by direct speech: "'The Jews' said" (v. 18); "Jesus answered" (v. 19); "'The Jews' said" (v. 20).

(d) *Vv. 21-22:* The narrator comments to inform the reader of the true meaning of Jesus' words and the limited nature of the disciples' faith.

[(e) *Vv. 23-25:* A concluding passage both closes the account of Jesus' stay in Jerusalem and opens the following episode by commenting on the limits of a faith based on signs.]

There is a strong concentration on the Jewish context of all that happens in this scene. The Jewish feast of Passover is the motivation for Jesus' going to Jerusalem and his presence in the Temple. For the first time in the narrative "the Jews" become active protagonists. Following the model of unquestioning trust in the word of Jesus provided by the mother of Jesus, a Jewish woman at a Jewish celebration in a Jewish town, the response of "the Jews" to Jesus takes place in the city of Jerusalem, at a Jewish feast. The literary shape of this passage has close links with 2:1-12. Both have an introduction (vv. 1-2, 13), a combination of dialogue and action (vv. 3-10 [dialogue–action–dialogue], 14-20 [action–dialogue]) and concluding comments from the narrator (vv. 11-12, 21-25). While 2:1-12 is described as a "sign" by the narrator (v. 11), 2:13-25 is highlighted by a request for a "sign" (v. 18) and concludes with many in Jerusalem going to Jesus because of "the signs" that he did (v. 23).

Introduction (v. 13). After the pause at Capernaum (cf. 2:12) Jesus "went up" *(anebē)* to Jerusalem. The motivation for this journey is the Jewish feast of Passover, celebrated on the 14 and 15 Nisan (March-April). Before the destruction of the Temple (70 C.E.) the annual visit to Jerusalem for the celebration of Passover was a major event for the city of Jerusalem. The feast was a combination of earlier feasts linked with the Exodus that "became not only powerful symbols of hope and redemption but also central religious experiences in the life of Israel and of people who identified with biblical Israel" (Bokser, "Unleavened Bread" 755–756).

Jesus' action in the Temple (vv. 14-17). Jesus discovers merchants in the Temple area (v. 14: *kai heuren en tǭ hierǭ*) who were selling the oxen, sheep, and pigeons necessary for the Temple cult. They were also changing Roman money into Tyrian money so that people might pay the Temple tax with coins not bearing effigies (cf. Beasley-Murray, *John* 38). These activities, which while not praiseworthy were not intrinsically wrong (cf. Israel Abrahams, *Studies in Pharisaism and the Gospels.* Cambridge: Cambridge University Press, 1917, 1st ser., 82–89), are set in disarray as Jesus drives out with a whip of cords those selling animals, scatters the coins, and overturns the tables of the money changers. Jesus does not speak, but every verb in vv. 14-15 has Jesus as its subject, and the actions described take place in rapid succession. The action provides the opportunity for the words of Jesus (cf. v. 16). The word for "Temple," *hieron* (vv. 14, 15), is used in this description of Jesus' aggressive action to speak of the Temple as a whole.

Cages, unlike oxen and sheep, cannot be sent scurrying away. Jesus tells the pigeon sellers, "Take these things away" and continues to address his Jewish listeners, telling them what motivates his action. The words of Jesus attack the abuse of the *hieron*. The Temple should never be an *oikos emporiou*. For Jesus it is not merely a building where people gather *(to hieron)*, degenerated into a marketplace *(oikos emporiou)*; it is "the house of my Father" *(ton oikon tou patros mou)*. The contrast between the two uses of the word "house" *(oikos)* recalls Zech 14:21b: "And there shall no longer be traders in the house of the LORD of hosts on that day" (cf. Dodd, *Interpretation* 300). The *hieron* is now called an *oikos*. It is not only an area where people gather to worship God *(hieron)*, but a place among men and women where the God of Israel, whom Jesus calls "my Father," has his dwelling *(oikos)*. The synoptic gospels have Jesus cite Isa 56:7, claiming that the Temple is "*my* house" (cf. Mark 11:17; Matt 21:13; Luke 19:46). The Johannine christology does not adopt this Jesus-centered focus. While Jesus challenges Israel's abuse of the Temple, he looks beyond himself for the motivation of such a challenge. Israel relates to God through its Temple but Jesus tells his listeners that their Temple belongs to him in a special way; it is the house of his Father. The *hieron* has degenerated into an *oikos emporiou*, but the sent one of the Father has reclaimed it as *ton oikon tou patros mou*.

The first reaction to Jesus' claim comes from the disciples (v. 17). They accept what he said, interpreting it by recalling *(emnēsthēsan hoi mathētai)* LXX Ps 68 [69]:10. However, there is an important alteration in the tense of the verb in the psalm. The LXX Greek text of Psalm 68 explains the sufferings and abuse of the person dedicated to Temple prayer in the aorist tense: "Zeal for your house *has consumed (katephagen)* me." The recollection of the disciples cites the psalm with the verb in the future tense: "Zeal for your house *will consume (kataphagetai)* me." At this stage of the story they can only guess that the actions performed by Jesus will eventually lead to a life and death struggle. In this they are correct, but they align Jesus with figures from the past whose commitment to the honor of God cost them their lives: Phineas, Elijah, or Mattathias (cf. Num 25:11; 1 Kgs 19:10, 14; Sir 48:1; 1 Macc 2:24-26). Jesus' *present* action *will lead* to a similar fate (cf. Hoskyns, *Fourth Gospel* 194). An important element of truth is present in the disciples' recognition of Jesus' future, and an echo of the Passion is heard. However, the disciples make no commitment to Jesus' major claim, that the *hieron* of "the Jews" is in fact the *oikos* of the Father of Jesus.

Jesus and "the Jews" (vv. 18-20): If the disciples take the actions of Jesus at their face value and (via LXX Ps 68:10) show their admiration and concern over the future of a person who behaves like this, it is "the Jews" who seek further evidence for Jesus' actions (v. 18). The author introduces them into this narrative, for the first time, with a solemn pleonastic construction, literally translated: "Therefore 'the Jews' answered and said" (v. 18a: *apekrithēsan oun hoi Ioudaioi kai eipan autǭ*). They demand that Jesus give them a "sign" (*sēmeion*), a miraculous proof to guarantee belief. The introduction to Jesus' response repeats the solemn pleonastic construction that introduced the direct speech of "the Jews," literally translated: "Jesus replied and said to them" (v. 19a: *apekrithē Iēsous kai eipen autois*). The author uses these solemn introductions to draw the reader's attention to the importance of the *words* that are spoken. Jesus' response is highlighted by the use of a third word to describe the Temple: "Destroy this Temple *(ton naon)* and in three days I will raise it up" (v. 19b). More than a building is in question, as Jesus speaks of a *naos* that will be destroyed and raised up in three days. Such words must baffle "the Jews," but the light will shine in the darkness (cf. 1:5) and although his own would not accept him, to those who did receive him and believe in his name he would give authority to become children of God (cf. 1:11-13). In the immediate past episode (2:1-12) the mother of Jesus believed in the word of Jesus. How will "the Jews" respond to this baffling word of his? Jesus is not speaking about the destruction of the Jerusalem Temple or of his raising up a Temple of stone *(to hieron)*, but of a future event when, in a very brief time after its destruction, he will raise up the Temple *(ho naos)*.

This is the "word of Jesus" that demands assent, but "the Jews'" reply shows their inability to make the distinction between a *naos* that Jesus will raise after three days and a *hieron* made of stone. Both words can refer to the building of the Temple, but Jesus has distinguished between them. "The Jews" see the words as identical; giving Jesus' words their surface meaning, they *misunderstand* them. Instead of seeing Jesus as the *naos* they "apply them [Jesus' words] literally to the visible temple of stone which rises before their eyes" (Schnackenburg, *Gospel* 1:350). "The Jews," unlike the mother of Jesus, are unable and unwilling to accept the word of Jesus. Using Jesus' word *(ho naos)* they speak of the forty-six years that elapsed during its building. They identify the *hieron* with the *naos*. Jesus has replied in direct speech (in v. 19) and "the Jews" take the words of Jesus, throwing them back at him in their rejection of the *sēmeion* he offers as a guarantee for belief in the authority of his actions and his words (cf. v. 18). Insolently adding the word "you" (*su*) to the words of Jesus, they use those words to formulate a mocking question:

Jesus	"The Jews"
And in three days	And *you* in three days
I will raise it up	will you raise it up?
(kai en trisin hēmerais	*(kai* **su** *en trisin hēmerais*
egerō auton)	*egereis auton?)*

The mother of Jesus accepted the word of Jesus telling the servants to do whatever he told them (2:5), but "the Jews" formally refuse to accept his word. The first appearance of "the Jews" in the Fourth Gospel portrays them in a situation of unbelief, rejecting the word of Jesus.

The narrator's comment (vv. 21-22): The narrator, as in 2:11, draws back from the narrative to offer a correct understanding of Jesus' words (v. 21; cf. v. 19) and to comment on the initial response of the disciples (v. 22; cf. v. 17). The disciples have unwittingly seen Jesus' actions as paving the way for conflict and death (v. 17), but the words of Jesus to "the Jews" have indicated that he has authority to raise up "the Temple" after three days (v. 19). The narrator explains that the Temple that will be destroyed and raised up after three days is not the *hieron* of stone, but the *naos* of his body (v. 21). Jesus Christ is the gift that replaces a former gift (cf. 1:17). The transformation of water from six jars used for the Jewish rites of purification into a good wine was a first "sign" (cf. 2:11) of the fullness of the gifts of God that perfects the former gift of God to Israel. The narrator now informs the reader that more astonishing transformations are still to be seen. The steady use of the future tense in the verbs of vv. 17, 19-20 promises that Jesus' passion for the ways of his Father will lead to his being consumed, and that after a very short time he will raise up the Temple of his body (v. 21). The presence of God in the Temple will be perfected by the revelation of God that will take place in the destruction and the resurrection of the Temple of the body of Jesus. At a time when there is no longer a Temple in Jerusalem, believing readers of the Fourth Gospel will experience the presence of the crucified yet risen Jesus as their "Temple."

The narrator closes his reflections on this event by looking beyond the time of the story into a future experience of the disciples. In v. 17 the disciples "remembered" the word of Scripture that spoke of a holy person's passion for the house of God, but in v. 22 it becomes evident that such a "remembering" is insufficient. It falls short of a correct understanding of Jesus' passion for the ways of his Father. The narrator points out that there will be a time, "when therefore he was raised from the dead," that they will have a deeper "remembering" (*emnēsthēsan*), and they will come to believe and rightly understand the word of Scripture and the word of Jesus. The story points forward to the resurrection of Jesus for the resolution

of the limited belief of the disciples. Something will happen at the death
and resurrection of Jesus that will transform the disciples. They will believe the Scripture and the word that Jesus has spoken *(episteusan tȩ
graphȩ kai tǭ logǭ hon eipen ho Iēsous).* This final comment from the narrator is a further indication of the nature of true Johannine belief: one must
believe in the word of Jesus.

The mother of Jesus has led the way in this (cf. 2:5), but "the Jews"
have rejected the word of Jesus (cf. vv. 19-20). If the traditional christological confessions used over the first days of Jesus (vv. 35-51) did not
reflect authentic belief (cf. vv. 38, 41, 45, 49), what more is required? An
answer is emerging from the response of the mother of Jesus and "the
Jews" to the word of Jesus (2:1-5, 19-20).

NOTES

13. *The Passover of the Jews:* The Passover "of the Jews" is mentioned in passages
that frame the action (2:13, 23). Feasts are often referred to throughout this
Gospel, and there has been considerable discussion over their significance for
both the theology and the structure of the Fourth Gospel as a whole. The feast
of the Passover associated with the event of the purification of the Temple has
no immediate literary or theological connection with the systematic use of the
feasts "of the Jews" in chs. 5–10 or the final Passover that serves as the time
frame for chs. 11–20. It serves here to maintain the focus on the traditional
practices of Israel and "the Jews," who play a central role in 2:13-25. Brown
rightly sees the three Passovers in the Fourth Gospel as "setting for a particular narrative" and not "signposts for a division of the Gospel" (*Gospel*
1:cxxxix).

The close literary relationship between the narratives in 2:1-12 and 2:13-25
has often been noticed. See, for example, Koester, "Hearing, Seeing and Believing" 327–348.

Jesus went up to Jerusalem: It is difficult to be certain of the time or the precise
details of this event in the life of the historical Jesus. More likely it took place
toward the end of his career and was one of the reasons for the decision that
he should be eliminated (cf. Brown, *Gospel* 1:116-120). For the Fourth Gospel
it is placed at the beginning of the story as an excellent literary introduction
to the theme of conflict between Jesus and "the Jews," and it forms part of a
series of responses from within the world of Israel.

The use of the verb *anabainein,* "go up" (to Jerusalem) reflects the city's location in the Judean hill country. However, the verb came to be used (as here)
as a technical term for a pilgrimage to the capital and its Temple (cf. Barrett,
Gospel 197).

14. *In the Temple:* The Temple-centered celebration of Passover is taken for
granted. With many others, Brown, *Gospel* 1:115 affirms that *hieron* means the
outer court of the Temple while *naos* refers to the sanctuary. In fact *hieron*

refers to the Temple as a whole (cf. BAGD 372). This is the meaning intended by the author in vv. 14-15. It enables the misunderstanding that will occur in vv. 19-21.

15. *he drove them all:* As the majority of commentators affirm, *pantas* in v. 15 includes all the human beings associated with the selling and money changing, rather than just the animals (cf. H. K. Moulton, *"pantas* in John 2.15." BT 18 [1967] 126–127).

    out of the Temple: Derrett ("The Zeal of the House" 79–94) suggests that Jesus is acting out the promise of the Servant in Isa 59:14-20. The Messiah comes to check that the Temple is a fit place to which the nations may resort. But there are few literary contacts, and the Servant-Messiah christology is somewhat foreign to Johannine theology.

16. *my Father's house:* Essential to the above interpretation is the Jewish belief that the God of Israel dwelt in the Temple (cf. Roland de Vaux, *Ancient Israel: Its Life and Institutions.* London: Darton, Longman & Todd, 1961, 325–330), on the Temple mountain.

    he told those who sold the pigeons: It appears that Jesus' words are directed only to the pigeon sellers. However, there are almost certainly two parts to Jesus' words. He addresses the pigeon sellers, telling them to take their cages away, because one cannot drive out birds. He then addresses a larger group of unidentified listeners with his words about the Temple. This is demanded by the entrance of "the Jews" in v. 18, asking for a sign to substantiate his authority for such behavior. They have been present throughout, even though they were not mentioned in vv. 14-16.

17. *His disciples remembered:* The disciples appear in the narrative unexpectedly, as it was not said that they traveled from Capernaum (v. 12) to Jerusalem (v. 13).

    "Zeal for your house": Psalm 68 is used elsewhere in the NT in Passion apologetic (cf. Rom 11:9; 15:13; Matt 27:48; John 15:25; 19:28-29; Acts 1:20). For an assessment of the Johannine use of the psalm see Barnabas Lindars, *New Testament Apologetic: The Doctrinal Significance of Old Testament Quotations.* London: SCM Press, 1961, 104–108.

    will consume me: There are variants in the textual traditions. The tense of the verb in the LXX is sometimes changed to the future to accommodate the Johannine use of the psalm, and the tense in John 2:17 is sometimes aorist to accommodate the LXX text (cf. Bernard, *Commentary* 192).

18. *What sign?:* The use of the word *sēmeion* by "the Jews" so soon after the narrator's use of the same word to speak of the miracle at Cana (cf. 2:11) warns against a blanket understanding of the word in the Fourth Gospel. Unlike the narrator who uses "sign" to speak of the visible revelation of the *doxa* (2:11), here "the Jews" are asking that a prophetic act of zeal be authenticated (cf. Lagrange, *Evangile* 67–68). In the Fourth Gospel Jesus never works "signs" as miraculous proofs to guarantee belief (cf. Brown, *Gospel* 1:115).

19. *Jesus answered them:* Despite the refusal to provide a "sign" to guarantee his prophetic authority, Jesus' response to "the Jews" must be understood as the

promise of a "sign." However, he transforms their expectation both in post-poning the time when the sign will be given and in the nature of the sign.

Destroy this Temple: As with *hieron,* used in vv. 14-16 to indicate the whole Temple area, so also the word *naos,* used here, can mean the whole Temple area (cf. BAGD 533–534). The subsequent misunderstanding of the Jews (cf. v. 20) depends on the fact that both words *can* mean the same thing. They take it for granted that such is the case. However, for Jesus there is a distinction between the *hieron* of the Temple building and the *naos* of his body.

Destroy this Temple . . . I will raise it up: The verbs for "destroy" *(luein)* and "raise up" *(egeirein)* can be applied equally well to the tearing down and re-construction of a building or the destruction and resurrection of the body of Jesus (cf. Schnackenburg, *Gospel* 1:349).

in three days: The use of the expression "on the third day" in 2:1 is linked to Exod 19:16 and is not *primarily* a reference to the Christian tradition of resur-rection "on the third day" (cf. 1 Cor 15:4; Matt 16:21; 17:23; 20:19; Luke 9:22; 18:33; 24:7, 46). It is a conventional expression for a short period of time. As Lindars elegantly expresses it, "Even if the temple be destroyed, I will build it up in a trice" (Lindars, *Gospel* 143). The Johannine community may not have been familiar with "third day" resurrection language. It never appears in John 20–21. However, readers rightly see the connection with the resurrection tradition, as is almost unanimously claimed by the commentators. Whether or not traditional resurrection language is involved, clearly the promise of resurrection is the "sign" that will authenticate Jesus' claim that the Temple is the house of his Father. Dodd, *Interpretation* 209, with reference to 6:30 argues that the "sign" of a destroyed and restored Temple has already taken place in the expulsion of the sacrificial animals. Such an interpretation eliminates the narrative tension created by the close relationship found in Jesus' words in v. 19 and the explicit reference to the resurrection in v. 22.

20. *forty-six years:* As the period of forty-six years does not fit the facts (cf. Barrett, *Gospel* 200), the figure has been given various symbolic interpretations: Jesus' age, the numerical value of the name "Adam," Gnostic numeric speculations, etc. The exact number of years need not trouble the reader. The issue is that "the Jews'" focus is limited to the construction of a building and they miss the point of Jesus' reference to himself. See Brown, *Gospel* 1:115–116; Barrett, *Gospel* 200–201.

21. *But he spoke:* The narrator's emphatic use of *ekeinos,* "this man," to open his remark separates Jesus' promise of the destruction and resurrection of the Temple, which the narrator shares, from the misunderstanding of "the Jews" in v. 20. There is, therefore, a sharp contrast between the "common sense" re-sponse of "the Jews" (v. 20) and the point of view of the narrator expressed in v. 21.

the Temple of his body: The genitive "of his body" in the expression "the Temple of his body" *(peri tou naou tou sōmatos autou)* must be understood as either ap-positional (the Temple, that is, his body) or explicative (the Temple that is his body). See Bultmann, *Gospel* 127 n. 5. It has been argued that the expression "the Temple of his body" *(tou sōmatos autou)* refers to the eucharistic experience of the community (cf. Cullmann, *Early Christian Worship* 71–74; Derrett, "Fresh Light" 52–58). The most explicit eucharistic passage in the Gospel (6:51-58) uses the word *sarx* (recalling 1:14), rather than *sōma*.

22. *his disciples remembered:* The further mention of the disciples, their "remembering," the stress upon what Jesus had said, and the *tę graphę* link this verse closely with v. 17. However positive the disciples' understanding of Jesus' actions in their remembering LXX Ps 68:10 [MT 69:9] might appear to be, v. 22 indicates that they have not fully understood his passion for God. They did not understand the Scripture on the occasion of the purification of the Temple, but later, at a time that lies ahead of the reader of this unfolding story, they will come to believe in the Scripture and the word of Jesus about the raising up of a destroyed body.

they believed the Scripture and the word: The interpretation offered here sees the risen and departed Jesus as the perfection of the former promise, and the presence of the "Temple," even though the Temple of stone in Jerusalem no longer stands (cf. Schnackenburg, *Gospel* 1:356–357). This christological interpretation is often exaggeratedly taken further, via the Pauline notion of the body of Christ, into an ecclesiological interpretation: the rebuilt Temple is the Christian Church (cf. Westcott, *Gospel* 42; Dodd, *Interpretation* 302–303; van den Bussche, *Jean* 156–159). There is insufficient evidence of this notion in the Johannine theology as a whole.

FOR REFERENCE AND FURTHER STUDY

Barrett, C. K. "The House of Prayer and the Den of Thieves." In E. Earl Ellis and Erich Grässer, eds., *Jesus und Paulus. Festschrift für Werner Georg Kümmel zum 70. Geburtstag.* Göttingen: Vandenhoeck & Ruprecht, 1975, 13–20.

Bokser, B. M. "Unleavened Bread and Passover, Feasts of," *ABD* 6:755–765.

Campbell, R. J. "Evidence for the Historicity of the Fourth Gospel in John 2:13-22," *StEv* 7 (1982) 101–120.

Derrett, J. D. M. "Fresh Light on the Lost Sheep and the Lost Coin," *NTS* 26 (1979–1980) 36–60.

_____. "The Zeal of the House and the Cleansing of the Temple," *DR* 95 (1977) 79–94.

Hiers, R. H. "Purification of the Temple: Preparation for the Kingdom of God," *JBL* 90 (1971) 82–90.

Koester, Craig. "Hearing, Seeing and Believing in the Gospel of John," *Bib.* 70 (1989) 327–348.

Moloney, Francis J. *Belief in the Word* 93–104.

_____. "Reading John 2:13-22: The Purification of the Temple," *RB* 97 (1990) 432–452.

Neirynck, Frans. "L'expulsion des vendeurs du Temple (2,13-22)," *EThL* 53 (1977) 446–449.

Topel, L. J. "A Note on the Methodology of Structural Analysis in Jn 2:23-3:21," *CBQ* 33 (1971) 211–220.
Trocmé, Etienne. "L'expulsion des marchands du Temple," *NTS* 15 (1968–1969) 1–22.

iii. The Narrator's Comment (2:23-25)

23. When he was in Jerusalem during the Passover festival in the festival crowd many believed in his name because they saw the signs that he was doing. 24. But Jesus on his part would not entrust himself to them, because he knew all people 25. and needed no one to bear witness of them; for he himself knew what was in each person.

INTERPRETATION

Introduction. As the first days of Jesus drew to a close Jesus promised a greater sight, but indicated that this sight would be possible only for those whose faith exceeded that of the first disciples (1:49-51). In 2:23-25 the narrator returns to this theme. The reader is addressed directly in a commentary on the quality of faith generated by beholding the signs that Jesus did in Jerusalem. This passage serves as a conclusion to the events and verbal encounters that took place in the Temple (vv. 13-22) and also leads into the next example of faith in Israel: Nicodemus (3:1-21).

Many believe and Jesus does not respond (vv. 23-24): There is a return to v. 13 in v. 23: Jesus is in Jerusalem for the celebration of Passover. The account of events begun in v. 13 is drawing to a close. Although no miraculous activity has been reported many people move toward Jesus in belief *(polloi episteusan eis to onoma autou)* because they saw the signs *(ta sēmeia).* There are hints of a mass movement toward Jesus, but little grounds for any such movement. The very strangeness of this description indicates that the narrator is making a significant point. Nathanael's initial response to Jesus (1:49-51) proved that signs were not enough. The sign at Cana did produce faith (2:11), but this sign was not sought; it was given as the result of unconditional faith in the efficacy of Jesus' word (2:5). "The Jews" requested a sign and they were given one (cf. 2:18-20), but this did not bring them to faith because it was not what they were expecting.

The narrator uses the verb *pisteuein* twice. Its first use describes the faulty belief in Jesus based on the signs he has done in Jerusalem (v. 23). The same verb is then used, in the negative, to describe Jesus' response to such belief *(ouk episteuen auton autois).* The Prologue has announced a reciprocity between Jesus and the believer (cf. 1:12-13), but this studied repetition of the same verb, first in the positive and then in the negative, shows that such reciprocity is absent here. Those who move toward Jesus as a result of miracles do not experience the same trusting commitment of Jesus toward them. The promised reciprocity of 1:12-13 is absent. Nowhere is the dynamic nature of the Johannine notion of belief so clearly presented.

The reason for Jesus' response (v. 25): Jesus' unwillingness to trust himself to those who believe because of signs arises from his knowledge of all people *(dia to auton ginōskein pantas).* In this confidential aside from the narrator such a remark is acceptable. The Prologue (cf. especially 1:3-4, 10) teaches that the Word who became flesh in Jesus Christ stands behind the creation of all things. Jesus thus knows that signs-faith is not a sufficient response to the fullness of the gift of God that he brings into the human story. However much there was need for a witness to Jesus (cf. 1:6-8, 15, 29-34), Jesus needs no witness concerning the human situation. He knew what was in humankind.

NOTES

23. *during the Passover festival in the festival crowd:* The simple translation of *en tǭ pascha en tę heortę* as "during the Passover festival" (NRSV), should be fully rendered: "at the Passover feast in the festival crowd" (Joachim Jeremias, *The Eucharistic Words of Jesus.* London: SCM Press, 1971, 71–73. Cf. also Barrett, *Gospel* 202). This suggestion accentuates the presence of a Jewish crowd celebrating a Jewish feast, continuing the concentration on the geographical and religious setting of the episodes that run from 2:1–4:54.

the signs that he was doing: The reference to "signs" done in Jerusalem creates difficulties for the smooth running of the narrative. The story has not reported any "signs" in Jerusalem, and these "signs" upset the numbering of a first and second miracle at Cana (cf. 2:11; 4:54). It may be a trace of an early stage in the Gospel's history, and some would see it as an important early reaction from the Evangelist against the theological perspective of the Signs Source (see below). Some narrative critics call it "anachrony" (cf. Gerard Genette, *Narrative Discourse: An Essay in Method,* Ithaca: Cornell University Press, 1980, 35–47). The ongoing narrative takes it for granted that they happened, but the signs are not the major focus of this reflection. They serve the purpose of the author by providing the occasion for a well-timed reflection on Jesus' response to those who come to him on the basis of his signs. See the apt remarks of Schnackenburg, *Gospel* 1:342.

the signs: In the wake of the History of Religions movement in Germany, under the influence of the earlier commentaries of Julius Wellhausen (1908) and Walter Bauer (1933), and in the light of new discoveries of Gnostic material, Rudolf Bultmann (1941) argued that the Fourth Gospel is the product of at least four major elements. The evangelist used a synoptic-like collection of miracles. This is called the "Signs Source." It reflects an earlier positive christological understanding of Jesus as a wonder-worker. A further source comes from a collection of proto-Gnostic revelatory discourses that were christianized to present Jesus as the unique Revealer. The major work of the evangelist, which can be regarded as the third element in the development of the Gospel, was the marriage of these two basic sources with their conflicting christologies. The evangelist produced a gospel that portrayed Jesus as the revelation of God, summoning readers to acceptance of the Revealer (*that* he is the Revealer more than *what* he had to reveal), and thus to authentic life. In order to achieve this the evangelist insinuated a critical view of the theology and christology of the Signs Source. John 2:23-25 is regarded as evidence of the hand of the evangelist, correcting the theological tendency of the Signs Source. This radical gospel was edited by a so-called Ecclesiastical Redactor. The final stage of the gospel introduced more conservative elements, such as an end-time eschatology and explicit references to the sacraments in the early Church. Bultmann's theory is further complicated by his suggestion (not followed by most who broadly accept his source theory) that the present canonical text does not reflect the *original order* of the Gospel. Continuing and further developing a proposal of Bernard (*Commentary,* 1928), his commentary follows a proposed original order, a rearrangement of the canonical Gospel. Although this source theory may sound somewhat fantastic to the uninitiated it has strongly influenced a number of scholars (including H. Becker, S. Schulz, H. Strathmann, W. Wilkens, G. Richter, J. Becker, J. Gnilka, and E. Haenchen), and M.-E. Boismard has developed an even more complex theory of the development of the Fourth Gospel. The presence of a Signs Source, although not always called by that name, is widely accepted by a large number of more mainstream commentators (including Raymond E. Brown, Rudolf Schnackenburg, and Barnabas Lindars) and has been the subject of some influential monographs (e.g., W. Nicol, *The Sēmeia in the Fourth Gospel*; R. T. Fortna, *The Gospel of Signs*; idem, *The Fourth Gospel and Its Predecessor*; S. Temple, *The Core of the Fourth Gospel*; H. M. Teeple, *The Literary Origin*; G. Reim, *Alttestamentlichen Hintergrund* 206–246, 269–282; U. C. von Wahlde, *The Earliest Version*). For a thorough presentation and critique of Bultmann's theory see D. M. Smith, *Composition and Order,* and for a convincing recent critique of the Signs Source theory see Udo Schnelle, *Antidocetic Christology* 150–164. A survey of this quest to discover the sources of the Gospel can be found in Robert Kysar, "The Fourth Gospel: A Report on Recent Research" 2389–2480.

24. *he did not entrust himself to them:* The expression *pisteuein auton autois* is a reflexive use of the verb *pisteuein* found nowhere else in the NT. It is, however, found outside the NT (cf. Barrett, *Gospel* 202). The twofold use of the verb *pisteuein* creates the desired impact on the reader and makes the author's point clear, but it is difficult to speak of Jesus' "faith" in others. Thus the author resorts to the reflexive, which is satisfactorily rendered "trust himself to them." However, the translation loses the subtlety of the play on words (*episteusan*

. . . ouk episteuen). The change of tenses from aorist to imperfect is also significant. "There is . . . a contrast of tenses." The first verb marks a definite, completed act, "the second a habitual course of action" (Westcott, *Gospel* 45).

believed in his name . . . he would not entrust himself to them: The Fourth Gospel never uses the noun *pistis,* but has ninety-eight uses of the verb *pisteuein.* This fact alone indicates the dynamic, active nature of the Johannine understanding of belief in Jesus. When this is coupled with the author's frequent use of the preposition *eis* after the verb *pisteuein* this dynamism is further enhanced. However, as 2:23 already shows, one must be careful not to read *every* use of *pisteuein eis* as an indication of correct Johannine belief.

he knew all people: The criticism aimed at the many in Jerusalem who come to Jesus because of the signs is not a condemnation. It does not mean that they can go no further in their journey of faith. See Hodges, "Problem Passages" 139–152; Hahn, "'Die Juden' im Johannesevangelium" 432–434.

25. *he himself knew what was in each person . . . there was a person:* This awkward translation attempts to show the link, made in the original Greek, between the introduction (2:23-25) and the Nicodemus episode (3:1-21): "bear witness of them *(peri tou anthrōpou)* . . . he knew what was in each person *(en tō anthrōpō)* . . . There was a person *(ēn de anthrōpos)."* See Moloney, *Son of Man* 46–47. The awkwardness is caused by the fact that the Greek word *anthrōpos* means "human being" (as in 2:25) but is sometimes used to mean "male human being" (as in 3:1). The ambiguity is similar to that produced in English by using "man" to refer to humanity in general and "a man" to refer to a male individual. Greek does have a specific word to refer to a male human being, *anēr,* but the NT writers use *anēr* and *anthrōpos* interchangeably. In the present instance the shift from the generic to the specific does not detract from the link between 2:23-25 and 3:1-21.

For Reference and Further Study

John 2:23-25:

Hodges, Z. C. "Problem Passages in the Gospel of John. Part 2: Untrustworthy Believers – John 2:23-25," *BiblSac* 135 (1978) 139–152.

La Potterie, Ignace de. *"Ad dialogum Jesu cum Nicodemo (2:23–3:21). Analysis litteraria,"* VD 47 (1969) 141–150.

Moloney, Francis J. *Belief in the Word* 104–106.

Topel, L. J. "A Note," 211–220.

Sources in the Fourth Gospel:

Bauer, Walter. *Johannesevangelium.*

Becker, Heinz. *Die Reden des Johannesevangeliums und der Stil der gnostischen Offenbarungsrede.* Göttingen: Vandenhoeck & Ruprecht, 1956.

Becker, Jürgen. *Johannes.*

Bernard, J. H. *St John.*

Boismard, M..-E., and Arnaud Lamouille. *L'Evangile de Jean.*

Bultmann, Rudolf. "Die Bedeutung," 100–146.

_____. *John.*

Fortna, Robert T. *The Fourth Gospel and Its Predecessor.*

_____. *The Gospel of Signs.*

Gnilka, Joachim. *Johannesevangelium.*

Haenchen, Ernst. *John 1–2.*

Nicol, W. *The Sēmeia in the Fourth Gospel. Tradition and Redaction.* NT.S 23. Leiden: E. J. Brill, 1972.

Reim, Günter. *Studien zum Alttestamentlichen Hintergrund* 206–246, 269–282.

Richter, Georg. *Studien zum Johannesevangelium.* Ed. J. Hainz. BU 13. Regensburg: Pustet, 1977.

Schnelle, Udo. *Antidocetic Christology* 150–164.

Schulz, Siegfried. *Das Evangelium nach Johannes.* NTD 4. Göttingen: Vandenhoeck & Ruprecht, 1972.

Smith, D. Moody. *The Composition and Order of the Fourth Gospel.*

Strathmann, Hermann. *Das Evangelium des Johannes.* 10th ed. NTD 4. Göttingen: Vandenhoeck & Ruprecht, 1963.

Teeple, Howard M. *The Literary Origin of the Gospel of John.* Evanston: Religion and Ethics Institute, 1974.

Temple, Sydney. *The Core of the Fourth Gospel.* London: Mowbrays, 1975.

Wahlde, Urban C. von *The Earliest Version of John's Gospel.*

Wellhausen, Julius. *Das Evangelium Johannis.* Berlin: Georg Reimer, 1908.

Wilkens, Wilhelm. *Zeichen und Werke: ein Beitrag zur Theologie des 4. Evangeliums in Erzählungs und Redestoff.* AThANT 55. Zürich: Zwingli Verlag, 1969.

iv. Jesus and Nicodemus (3:1-21)

1. Now there was a person, one of the Pharisees, named Nicodemus, a ruler of the Jews. 2a. This man came to Jesus by night and said to him, 2b. "Rabbi, we know that you are a teacher come from God; for no one can do these signs that you do, unless God is with him."
3. Jesus answered him, "Amen, amen, I say to you, no one can see the kingdom of God without being born again, from above." 4. Nicodemus said to him, "How can a person be born after having grown old? Can one enter a second time into the mother's womb and be born?" 5. Jesus answered, "Amen, amen, I say to you, no one can enter the kingdom of God without being born of water and the Spirit. 6. That which is born of the flesh is flesh, and that which is born of the Spirit is spirit. 7. Do not marvel that I said to you, 'You must be born anew.' 8. The wind blows where it wills, and you hear the sound of it, but you do not know whence it comes or whither it goes; so it is with every one who is born of the Spirit."
9. Nicodemus said to him, "How can this be?" 10. Jesus answered him, "Are you a teacher of Israel, and yet you do not understand this?

11. Amen, amen, I say to you, we speak of what we know, and bear witness to what we have seen; but you do not receive our testimony. 12. If I have told you earthly things and you do not believe, how can you believe if I tell you heavenly things?

13. No one has ascended into heaven, but one has descended from heaven, the Son of Man. 14. And as Moses lifted up the serpent in the wilderness, so must the Son of Man be lifted up, 15. that whoever believes in him may have eternal life."

16. For God so loved the world that he gave his only Son, that whoever believes in him should not perish but have eternal life. 17. For God sent the Son into the world, not to condemn the world, but that the world might be saved through him. 18. Those who believe in him are not condemned; those who do not believe are condemned already, because they have not believed in the name of the only Son of God. 19. And this is the judgment, that the light has come into the world, and people loved darkness rather than light, because their deeds were evil. 20. For all who do evil hate the light, and do not come to the light, so that their deeds may not be exposed. 21. But those who do what is true come to the light, that it may be clearly seen that their deeds have been done in God.

INTERPRETATION

The Place of 3:1-21 within 3:1-36. The narrative dedicated to Nicodemus and to the final appearance of John the Baptist follows the reflection on the faith of many who came to believe in Jesus because of the signs he did (2:23-25). The final remark of the narrator (2:25: "for he himself knew what was in each person") and the introduction of Nicodemus to the story (3:1: "Now there was a person, one of the Pharisees") are closely linked. Elements in the literary structure of 3:1-36 also indicate that the presentations of Nicodemus and John the Baptist are closely related (cf. Rensberger, *Johannine Faith* 58–61). The two reports form a diptych, as both contain a narrative in which first Nicodemus (vv. 1-10) and then the Baptist (vv. 22-30) play central roles. Both characters are firmly situated within the world of Judaism. Nicodemus is described as "one of the Pharisees . . . a ruler of the Jews" (v. 1) and "a teacher of Israel" (v. 10). He meets Jesus in the city of Jerusalem as there has been no change of place since Jesus' arrival in the city (cf. 2:13). Although the Baptist is probably active at a Samaritan site (cf. Boismard, "Aenon" 218–229) his association with Israel is traditional, and the discussion that leads to his words on his relationship to Jesus is "between John's disciples and a Jew over purifying" (v. 25). The narrative sections are followed by discourse-type material (vv. 12-21, 31-36), each developing the two-stage argument. Both open with the claim that Jesus is the unique revealer of the heavenly (vv. 12-15, 31-35), and then move to the logical consequence of such a claim: salvation or condemnation flows from the acceptance or refusal of this revelation (vv. 16-21, 35). Whatever traditions might lie behind 3:1-36 its close association with 2:23-25 and its internal unity show that it continues a series of encounters between Jesus and characters from the world of Israel.

Introduction to 3:1-21. As with 2:1-12 and 13-22, words of Jesus and Nicodemus' responses to those words determine the account in 3:1-10. In vv. 11-12 further words of Jesus open with the double use of "amen" (see 1:51). These words have been interpreted as a conclusion to the discussion with Nicodemus, as Jesus introduces them by speaking directly to Nicodemus (v. 11a: "I say to you [singular]: *legō soi*"), but in the same sentence he addresses a plural audience (v. 11b: "you [plural] do not receive: *ou lambanete*"). The use of the plural flows into v. 12, and the direct address to Nicodemus disappears. Verses 11-12 form a "bridge passage" that both concludes vv. 1-12 and opens vv. 11-21. At best Nicodemus remains in the background, listening to Jesus' brief discourse (vv. 11-21). The discourse addresses the reader, and comments authoritatively upon the encounter between Jesus and Nicodemus. The passage unfolds as follows:

(a) *Vv. 1-2a:* The scene is set at night, and two characters are introduced: Jesus and Nicodemus.
(b) *Vv. 2b-11/12:* The dialogue between Jesus and Nicodemus:
    i. *V. 2b:* Nicodemus addresses Jesus, reflecting his understanding of Jesus.
    ii. *Vv. 3-8:* Jesus' teaching on rebirth in the Spirit, during which Nicodemus' misunderstanding (v. 4) enables further development in Jesus' teaching.
    iii. *Vv. 9-10:* Nicodemus' closing words show his inability to understand Jesus' teaching. Jesus responds directly to Nicodemus.
    iv. *Vv. 11-12:* Bridge passage: Jesus initially addresses Nicodemus and thus brings the encounter with Nicodemus to a close, but then addresses a larger audience and thus opens the discourse of vv. 11-21.
(c) *Vv. 11/12-21:* The discourse of Jesus
    i. *Vv. 11-12:* Bridge passage: Jesus words, closing vv. 1-12 and opening vv. 11-21.
    ii. *Vv. 13-15:* The revelation of the heavenly in the Son of Man, who comes from heaven.
    iii. *Vv. 16-21:* The salvation or condemnation that flows from the acceptance or refusal of this revelation.

Introduction (vv. 1-2a). The Jewish setting for the meeting between Jesus and Nicodemus is guaranteed by the ongoing presence of Jesus in Jerusalem (cf. 2:13), and the description of the man called Nicodemus as "a

Pharisee . . . a ruler of the Jews." He is a new character in the narrative and comes to Jesus "by night." The Word is "life and light" (1:4), and the light was coming into the world (1:9). The light shines in the darkness and the darkness does not overcome it (1:5). The movement of Nicodemus, a leader of "the Jews," toward Jesus, coming from the darkness of the night into the light, is a significant movement toward believing, receiving the one sent to make God known (cf. 1:11-14).

The dialogue between Jesus and Nicodemus (vv. 2b-12). Nicodemus' words to Jesus, however, indicate that his movement toward Jesus parallels that of the many in Jerusalem who came to him and believed in his name because of the signs he did (2:23-25): "Rabbi, we know that you are a teacher come from God; for no one can do these signs that you do, unless God is with him" (3:2b). Almost every element of Nicodemus' address is found in an earlier, partial, confession of faith in Jesus. The first disciples called Jesus "Rabbi" (1:38), and after some time with him they confidently asserted "we have found" (1:41, 45). Nathanael believed that Jesus was Rabbi, son of God and King of Israel on the basis of Jesus' miraculous knowledge (1:49) and many in Jerusalem came to him because of the signs he did (2:23). Nicodemus joins these first, fragile believers in Jesus, and goes further in accepting that Jesus is a teacher from God and that the signs he does are an indication that God is with him, a dignity reserved for the great figures of Israel (cf. LXX Exod 3:12 [Moses]; Jer 1:8 [Jeremiah]).

> Men like Nicodemus have identified themselves with definitions they know too exactly. They want someone new to confirm a notion already fixed inside the heads of those who know best. For them revelation has become, quite unconsciously, a kind of technology (Bishop, "Encounters" 2:292).

But however partial Nicodemus' first response to Jesus has been there is a progression from the open hostility shown toward Jesus by "the Jews" who rejected his word (2:18-20). There is no conflict or rejection from this leader of "the Jews," only an approach to Jesus that cannot reach beyond the limitations of the "definitions" he "knows too exactly." The exchange that follows develops from Nicodemus' limited—but positive—understanding of Jesus.

Jesus' response attempts to build on this limited understanding. Without any clarification he states: "No one can see the kingdom of God without being born *anōthen* (again/from above)" (v. 3). Jesus plays on the double meaning of *anōthen* in his demand for a rebirth that a person might "see" *(idein)* the kingdom of God. Israel was familiar with the notion of God as king, but Jesus' demand that one be born again/from above to *see* the kingdom of God challenges Nicodemus to expand his notion of what that kingdom might be. He approached Jesus as a rabbi, a miracle worker, and a teacher (v. 2), but finds himself confronted with an affirmation beyond his comprehension. He thus falls back upon the tried and true, asking a question that shows he has neither grasped the full significance of the two possible meanings of *anōthen* nor is able to move outside the world he controls and understands: "How can a person be born again after having grown old? Can one enter *deuteron* (a second time) into the mother's womb and be born?" (v. 4). Jesus has used a word *(anōthen)* that has two meanings. One lies on a temporal-horizontal axis ("again") and the other on a spatial-vertical axis ("from above"). Jesus' first words to Nicodemus on his initial approach (v. 3) can only be understood if the word *anōthen* be given *both meanings*. One can only *see* the kingdom of God as a consequence of an experience that combines both the horizontal and the vertical, but Nicodemus eliminates the meaning "from above" by using a word *(deuteron)* that only has a temporal meaning: "a second time" (v. 4). Jesus' words to Nicodemus ask for a birth that combines both the horizontal experience of time and the vertical experience of the in-breaking of God "from above." Nicodemus' response is limited to the horizontal, the experience of a "second time" physical birth of a child from a mother, which is impossible.

Nicodemus' "misunderstanding" allows Jesus to explain further (v. 5). He repeats v. 3, replacing *anōthen* with expressions that spell out what is meant by "anew" (of water) and "from above" (and the Spirit). He also develops his word on the "sight" of the kingdom of God by speaking of "entering" the kingdom: "Amen, amen, I say to you, no one can enter *(eiselthein)* the kingdom of God without being born *of water and the Spirit*" (v. 5). A human experience "of water" and a spiritual experience "of the Spirit" are required for entrance into the kingdom of God. A gift "from above" is essential for the sight of and entry into the kingdom. This tallies with all that has been told so far; belief in Jesus is not the result of human response. Birth into a new situation, where believers become the children of God as a result of the initiative of God, has already been announced in the Prologue as the result of believing in and receiving Jesus (1:12-13). But there is also a historical experience, a rebirth "of water" associated with the gift of the Spirit. In 1:29-34 the Baptist told the reader that his baptism was "with water" (1:31). The Baptist witnessed to one among them, but unknown, who would baptize "with the Holy Spirit" (1:33). Rebirth from above is thus marked by the continuation of the ritual of a baptism "of water," now perfected with the baptism of the Spirit brought by Jesus. Nicodemus, who has not read the Prologue or heard the Baptist's witness to Jesus, for the moment must struggle with the words of Jesus. He is baffled, but the promises of the Prologue and the prophecies of John the Baptist are being realized in these words.

Seeing and entering the kingdom of God are consequences of a ritual of water that accompanies the gift of the Spirit. Commentators rightly remark that the expression "the kingdom of God" comes to this gospel from earlier Christian tradition. In that tradition Jesus often speaks of the kingdom as a present reality (cf., for example, Mark 1:15; 9:1; Matt 5:10; 6:10, 33; Luke 9:2, 11; 17:21; Rom 14:17), but the image of "the kingdom of God" is basically eschatological. This eschatological language has been adapted to correspond to the more realized Johannine understanding of the Christian experience. The kingdom of God refers to a community of believers, a group of Christians who profess and attempt to live the Johannine understanding of Jesus. The original readers of this gospel were aware of a passage away from a former situation of life style and belief, be it Temple or synagogue, into a community bound by Christian belief and practice. The result of a gift *from above* "of the Spirit," being born *again* "of water" enabled people to see and *enter* into the kingdom of God. From its beginnings the gift of the Spirit "from above," which enabled this passage, was accompanied by a ritual of rebirth solemnized by water baptism (vv. 3, 5).

Jesus comments on Nicodemus' failure to grasp his teaching: "That which is born of the flesh is flesh, and that which is born of the Spirit is spirit" (v. 6). To be born of the flesh means to be content with what one can observe and control. Living in the "flesh" means making judgments on the basis of what one senses (cf. 7:24; 8:15). Birth in the Spirit leads into a different way of seeing and understanding but Jesus turns directly to Nicodemus, urging him not to marvel at his word (v. 7: *mē thaumasēs hoti eipon soi*) that rebirth must take place through a gift "from above" *(anōthen)*. Misunderstanding should cease, and to guide Nicodemus Jesus resorts to a brief parable on "the wind/the Spirit" (v. 8). The same Greek word *(to pneuma)* can be used for "the wind" and "the Spirit." Making a play on this word, Jesus starts with a reflection on the everyday experience of "the wind." The wind *(to pneuma)* is a mystery; one can experience it; it is a part of life. But one can never claim to have discovered and explained where it comes from or where it is going (cf. Qoh 11:5; Sir 16:21, where this same point is made). On the basis of this observable truth about the wind *(to pneuma)*, Jesus affirms that it is also thus with those born of the Spirit *(to pneuma)*. "The Spirit, like the wind, is entirely beyond both the control and the comprehension of man: it breathes into this world from another" (Barrett, *Gospel* 211). One can never determine its origin and destiny. Nicodemus' limited response would be overcome if he could recognize that he is summoned into the realm of God, where those born of the Spirit have their origin and destiny in the mystery of God.

Nicodemus remains nonplused. His response to Jesus' teaching is not one of refusal or rejection. However, it is a stunned confession, reflecting his inability to move away from his own categories into the mysterious life in the Spirit that Jesus is offering: "How can this be?" (v. 9). There is weakness in this response, and Jesus chides as he reminds him that he is "a teacher of Israel" (v. 10a). He should have been able to grasp some of the meaning of Jesus' teaching. The idea of a life "in the Spirit" that transcends the human spirit and understanding was not new in Israel. It was part of its religious tradition (cf. Exod 15:8; Isa 40:7; 44:3; 59:21; Ezek 11:19-20; 36:26-27; Joel 28:29; Job 34:14; Pss 18:15; 51:10; Wis 9:16-18; 1QS 3:13–4:26), and Jesus will shortly refer to such teaching as "earthly things" (v. 12: *ta epigeia*).

The bridge passage (vv. 11-12). Jesus responds to Nicodemus (v. 11a: *amēn, amēn legō soi*) with an address from a singular person *(legō)* to a singular listener *(soi),* but immediately multiplying both the speakers and the audience: "We speak of what we know *(hoti ho oidamen laloumen)* and bear witness to what we have seen *(kai ho heōrakamen martyroumen)*; but you do not receive our testimony *(tēn martyrian hēmōn ou lambanete)*." This shift from the one-to-one discussion between Jesus and Nicodemus begins the bridge passage from the narrative of vv. 1-10 to the discourse in vv. 13-21. Jesus and a representative of Judaism have shared a discussion but now one senses the presence of two larger groups: the community of Jesus speaks to Israel. Jesus comments upon what has happened thus far (v. 11). Nicodemus' responses within the discussion have shown he is unable to accept Jesus' authoritative voice (cf. vv. 2, 4, 9), announcing unquestionable truths that he did not receive from hearsay (cf. vv. 3, 5, 6, 8). Jesus speaks what he knows and Nicodemus is unable to receive such truths. However, although initially addressed to Nicodemus *(legō soi)* these words now come from a Jesus-community *(laloumen, martyroumen)* proclaiming the words of Jesus into the world of "the Jews" who will not receive them *(ou lambanete)*. What has been said so far comes from the best of Israel's tradition, but these truths are described as "earthly things" (v. 12a: *ta epigeia*). If Nicodemus, a ruler of "the Jews" and a teacher of Israel, is unable to believe these things, how much more difficulty will "the Jews" have in believing Jesus' further revelation of "the heavenly things" (v. 12b: *ta epourania*). Jesus, however, will not be deterred. He has shared the richness of *ta epigeia* with Nicodemus in vv. 1-10; he will now proceed to tell of *ta epourania* in vv. 13-21. The point of vv. 11-12 is not so much to show that Judaism is wrong, but to tell those who might be happy to settle for Israel's religious traditions (earthly things) that more is necessary (heavenly things) for salvation. A newness is made possible because of the revelation that comes from above. What follows is a synthesis of the Gospel message on Jesus as the "heavenly revealer" (vv. 13-15) and the subsequent salvation or condemnation that flows from an acceptance or refusal of this revelation (vv. 16-21).

The revelation of the heavenly (vv. 13-15). Jesus affirms the uniqueness of the revelation of the Son of Man by means of a strong contradiction (*oudeis*) of any suggestion that the great revealers of Israel had been to heaven, seen the heavenly secrets, and returned to reveal them. No one has ever ascended into heaven (v. 13a). There is only one who can authoritatively reveal the heavenly things: the Son of Man who has come down from heaven (v. 13b). This is the basis for his earlier words to Nicodemus. He knows what he is saying and he has seen that to which he bears witness (v. 11). Jesus proclaims what has already been said in the Prologue: "No one has ever seen God; the only Son, who is turned toward the Father, he has made him known" (1:18). This second reference to the Son of Man also catches up the earlier promise made to the first disciples: greater faith will produce greater sight. They will see the revelation of the heavenly in the Son of Man (1:51). Only Jesus, the word become flesh (1:14), the Son of God (1:18), the Son of Man (1:51; 3:13) reveals the heavenly things.

But how will this revelation take place? Joined by the use of the expression "the Son of Man," vv. 13-14 are intimately linked. While v. 13 affirms *that* Jesus is the unique revealer of God, v. 14 tells *how* this revelation will take place. As Moses raised up (*hypsōsen*) the serpent on a stake, so must the Son of Man be lifted up (*hypsōthēnai dei*). As an Exodus people, suffering in their sinfulness, gazed upon the raised serpent to be restored to health (cf. Num 21:8-9), so eternal life will come to the one who, gazing upon the elevated Son of Man, believes (v. 15). One of the central themes of the Gospel again receives expression: the wonderful gifts of God to the chosen people, Israel, are now brought to perfection in the gift of the Son (cf. 1:17). Very soon after the use of the double-meaning words *anōthen* and *to pneuma* the double-meaning verb *hypsōthēnai* appears for the first time (cf. 8:28; 12:32). It means both a physical lifting up, as Moses did with the serpent upon the spear, and an exaltation. The death of Jesus has provided essential background knowledge for the understanding of the clash between light and darkness (1:5), the rejection of the Word by "his own people" (1:11), the hour of Jesus that was "not yet" (2:4), and the first rumblings of an eventual conflict as Jesus and "the Jews" met for the first time (2:13-22). How Jesus is to die (cf. 12:33; 18:32) is now indicated: he will be "lifted up." The first use of this double-meaning verb indicates that Jesus' crucifixion will also be his exaltation. For the moment this is simply affirmed, but another central message of the Fourth Gospel has been broached: Jesus is the revelation of God (v. 13) and this revelation will reach its high point in the "lifting up/exaltation" of Jesus on a cross (v. 14). Belief in this revelation brings eternal life (v. 15). The introduction of the promise of eternal life (v. 15) leads to a development of the theme of salvation throughout vv. 16-21.

Salvation and condemnation (vv. 16-21). Another major theme of this gospel emerges for the first time in vv. 16-17. The saving love of God stands behind the mystery of the "lifting up" of the Son, "sent" to bring the possibility of eternal life and the salvation of the world. The message of vv. 13-15 lingers as Jesus indicates the immensity of God's loving gift of the Son for the life of the world. The Son was sent that the world might be saved, not judged. A universal element enters Jesus' words despite the strongly Jewish context of the encounter with Nicodemus that prefaced this brief discourse. "God so loved the world" (v. 16); "God sent the Son into the world" (v. 17). This recalls the promise of the Prologue (cf. 1:12-13) and prepares for the shortly-to-be-introduced narrative dedicated to Jesus' encounters with Samaritans and a Gentile (4:1-54). But the loving gift of the Son for the salvation of the world raises the issue of judgment. Despite God's gift of the Son for the salvation—and not the judgment—of the world (vv. 16-17), a judgment takes place. It flows from the acceptance or refusal of the unique revelation of God that takes place in the Son. The language of the Prologue returns as Jesus speaks of "life," "light," and "darkness" (vv. 18-21; cf. 1:4-8). Belief leads to freedom from condemnation and to life, but unbelief produces condemnation and death (v. 18). Neither the Son nor the Father acts as judge. To refuse belief brings self-condemnation, shown in evil deeds and the presence of darkness (vv. 18-19). The time of judgment is *now* as the believer is faced with the revelation of the Father in the Son. Johannine realized eschatology stresses the importance of the response of the believer, not the sovereign action of God.

Yet the believer's decision for or against God's revelation in the Son cannot be limited to some all-determining moment of truth and light when faced with a once-and-for-all inbreaking of the Word of God. Jesus' discourse concludes with words on the situations of the believer and the unbeliever that flow from a longstanding preparedness to accept or refuse the revelation of God (vv. 20-21). The doing of evil results from loving the darkness and choosing it, hiding one's ambiguity in the darkness (v. 20), just as a life of good deeds leads to one's coming into the light. It is not as if one lives in the light, basking in the blessedness of such a situation. Ongoing commitment to good deeds is required to become more deeply involved in the light and to be part of the ongoing revelation of that light: "that it may be clearly seen that their deeds have been done in God" (v. 21b).

Conclusion to 3:1-21. Jesus alone makes God known (vv. 13-15) and judgment flows from the acceptance or refusal of that revelation (vv. 16-21). In the light of this discourse of Jesus, Nicodemus' hesitations, and especially his desire to keep his acceptance of Jesus within the limitations of his own understanding and experience (cf. vv. 2, 4, 9), must be understood as not responding to Jesus' requirement of the greater faith that produces greater sight (cf. 1:50-51). Nicodemus' faith does not match the criteria mapped out in vv. 11-21, but all is not lost. This "ruler of the Jews" (v. 1) and "teacher of Israel" (v. 10) demonstrates an initial openness to Jesus. Unlike "the Jews" in vv. 13-22, never does Nicodemus take the word of Jesus and reject it (cf. vv. 18-20). His difficulties come from his inability to reach beyond what he can measure, control, and understand. He could not grasp that the only way to full acceptance of Jesus was to recognize that he offered a gift "from above" (v. 3). Nicodemus will return on two further occasions in later episodes and make a journey of faith within the unfolding narrative (cf. 7:50-52; 19:38-42). However, at this stage of his story, following the absence of faith among "the Jews" who rejected the word of Jesus (2:13-22), Nicodemus is an example of a character who demonstrates a *partial faith*. Nicodemus' understanding of Jesus is not wrong, but he does not allow himself to be led by the gift of the Spirit "from above" (v. 3: *anōthen*) into an acceptance of the "heavenly things" (v. 12: *ta epourania*).

NOTES

1. *Now there was a person, one of the Pharisees, named Nicodemus:* Doubtless the end result of a long pre-Gospel storytelling tradition (cf. Boismard and Lamouille, *Jean* 112–117), 3:1-36 is increasingly understood as a carefully articulated literary unit. For a survey of attempts to trace that unity see H. Thyen, "Aus der Literatur zum Johannesevangelium," *ThR* 44 (1979) 110–118.

   Throughout the Fourth Gospel the terms "the Pharisees" and "the Jews" are often interchanged (see already 1:19, 24). The Greek word *archōn* ("leader," "prince") is applied in this gospel only to the leaders of "the Jews" (cf. 3:1; 7:26, 48; 12:42) and "the prince of this world" (cf. 12:31; 14:30; 16:11). As the story unfolds, the leaders of "the Jews" are increasingly shown to be the historical representatives of the prince of this world.

2. *Rabbi, we know that you are a teacher come from God:* The plural is used to indicate Nicodemus' representative status. Jesus is not only speaking with Nicodemus, but also with Israel. The confident "we know" is not only a personal opinion but a doctrinal declaration (cf. Gaeta, *Il dialogo* 45). This statement from Nicodemus determines the dialogue form of the narrative (cf. Dodd, "Dialogue Form" 60–67) and sets the agenda of correct and incorrect understanding of Jesus (cf. Neyrey, "John III" 118–119). While most of Nicodemus' confession is readily recognized as the expression of first-century Jewish categories, some have seen his description of Jesus as a teacher *from God* as expressing a Johannine perspective. This need not be the case, as the phrase "expressed the general belief of Judaism" about great Israelites (Bernard, *Commentary* 1:101; Barrett, *Gospel* 205).

3. *Amen, amen, I say to you:* The Johannine double "amen" plays an important role in 3:1-21. As always it carries the discussion further by introducing a new idea, closely related to what has gone before. It appears in v. 3 to open Jesus' response to Nicodemus' confession. In v. 5 it introduces Jesus' expansion on what was said in v. 3. In v. 11 it opens Jesus' words that both close vv. 1-10 and open vv. 13-21. This threefold use of the expression, therefore, is an important literary indication of the unity of 3:1-21.

no one can see: Jesus' words *(ou dynatai)* pick up and repeat Nicodemus' "no one can do these signs" *(oudeis dynatai)* from v. 2. Jesus repeats, but develops and deepens the superficial statement from Nicodemus.

without being born again, from above: A number of commentators argue that the best translation for *gennēthę* is "be begotten" (e.g., Brown, *Gospel* 1:130; Beasley-Murray, *John* 45). It is better to translate "born" to maintain the spatial and temporal possibilities of *gennēthę anōthen:* rebirth *from above.* "Re-begotten" hardly suits. Many commentators claim that Jesus' use of *anōthen* only means "from above" and that Nicodemus totally misunderstands this in his use of *deuteron* (v. 4). Both the temporal and the spatial dimensions of the word are called for by its expansion into "of water (again) and the Spirit (from above)" in v. 5. "*Anōthen* is capable of two meanings and here it probably has both" (Barrett, *Gospel* 205).

4. *How can a person:* Greek *anthrōpos,* meaning "human being," appears again. It is possible that the author means "a man," since Nicodemus is male and asks the question of himself, now adult and being instructed on the need to be born again.

enter a second time: Nicodemus' use of *deuteron* indicates that he chooses only the temporal meaning of *anōthen.* The Johannine misunderstanding technique demands that—on this occasion—*both* the temporal and the spiritual be involved. It is here that Bultmann's widely accepted explanation of the Johannine misunderstanding technique is imprecise (Bultmann, *Gospel* 135 n. 1). He claims that it is a question of seeing the right meaning of the word but thinking "that its meaning is exhausted by the reference to earthly matters." As can be seen in this case, the earthly matters still have a role to play in the correct understanding of *anōthen,* but they do not exhaust the significance of the word. Both the earthly and the spiritual must be maintained.

5. *enter the kingdom of God:* On the Johannine contact with earlier tradition in the use of "kingdom of God" see Lindars, "John and the Synoptic Gospels" 287–294. The verbs *idein* (v. 3) and *eiselthein* (v. 5) in association with "the kingdom of God" are often described as identical in significance, as "seeing" means to experience (e.g., Strachan, *Fourth Gospel* 130; Barrett, *Gospel* 207). The verbs must be given the full weight of a physical, historical experience: rebirth in water and the Spirit enables *the sight of* and *entrance into* the Christian community. A ritual experience marking the entrance into a community is involved. Most commentators affirm that for this gospel the traditional term "the kingdom of God" is to be identified with "eternal life" (cf. Lagrange, *Evangile* 74; Bernard, *Commentary* 1:101–102; Bultmann, *Gospel* 152 n.

2; Lightfoot, *St. John's Gospel* 130–131; Vellanickal, *Divine Sonship* 208–213) or "the heavenly realm on high to which the divine envoy leads" (Schnackenburg, *Gospel* 1:366–367). Westcott (*Gospel* 48–50) argued that it meant the community of believers. The suggestion returns in various ways but has not gained much support. See the suggestions of Leroy, *Rätsel und Mißverständnis* 129–136; Rossetto, "Nascere dell'acqua" 56–58; Rensberger, *Johannine Faith* 55–56, 58, 66–70; Onuki, *Gemeinde und Welt* 63–64. Some recent structuralist approaches have stressed that "the realm of the kingdom is nothing else than the Johannine community of faith" (Patte, "Jesus' Pronouncement" 41). See also Michel, "Nicodème" 231–236; Gaeta, *Il dialogo* 49.

born of water and the Spirit: The remaining dialogue (vv. 5-8) concentrates upon "spirit"; "water" is never again mentioned. Was the reference to "water" added by later scribes to render a "spiritual" text more ecclesial (Bultmann, *Gospel* 138 n. 3)? It is likely that it was added to the text at some stage of the history of the Johannine community. The earliest form of this text would have spoken of the need for rebirth in the Spirit for entry into the community. However, the community's break with the synagogue and a growing awareness of its uniqueness led to the introduction of the reference to water, to make an explicit reference to the ritual of water baptism, a public sign that *externally* marked the *internal* experience and commitment to the beliefs of the Johannine community. See I. de la Potterie, "Naître de l'eau" 351–374.

6. *That which is born of the flesh:* The interpretation of the use of *sarx* in the Fourth Gospel must be determined by its Johannine context and not by other uses of the word in the NT. The majority of uses refers to the flesh of Jesus (1:14; 6:51, 52, 53, 54, 55, 56), where it must be given a positive meaning. God is revealed in the physical manifestation of Jesus. On other occasions it refers to the flesh of human beings (1:13; 3:6; 8:15; 17:2). Each of these usages must be interpreted in its context. They generally refer to the human being (1:13; 3:6; 17:2). There is a close link between 1:13 and 3:6. In both passages no judgment is made upon what is born of the flesh except to say that it is physical flesh. The most pejorative use of *sarx* in the Fourth Gospel is condemnation of a judgment that comes from a human, superficial assessment of things seen, heard, and experienced (8:15; cf. 7:24).

7. *Do not marvel:* There is a slight irregularity in the Greek syntax of this command. After *mē* one would expect the present imperative form of the verb, forbidding the continuation of the attitude of marveling. Instead the aorist subjunctive appears. This makes the imperative more vivid and absolute (cf. Bauer, *Johannesevangelium* 55; ZGB 80.

8. *The wind blows where it wills:* The interpretation offered above reads v. 8abc as referring to the natural wind and only v. 8d as an application of phenomena associated with the wind to the Spirit. Some commentators claim that v. 8abc has a double meaning, wind and Spirit, particularly on the basis of the use of the word *phonē.* The "sound" of the wind may also refer to the "voice" of the Spirit. The chosen interpretation insists on the parabolic nature of the saying,

with the application coming only at the close of an example drawn from nature.

9. *How can this be?:* There is a consistency in Nicodemus' inability to grasp Jesus' word and person. He expresses a limited understanding of Jesus (v. 2); he misunderstands Jesus' words (v. 4); he comes to a stunned puzzlement (v. 9). No malice or overt rejection is involved. "The *pōs* of this question is typical of the 'common sense' point of view" (Bultmann, *Gospel* 143 n. 2).

10. *Are you a teacher of Israel?:* The use of the definite article *(ho didaskalos)* is not intended to single out Nicodemus as the *only* teacher in Israel. It is rhetorical and indicates an important teacher, but not the only one (cf. Bultmann, *Gospel* 144 n. 2). On the irony involved in Jesus' question see Duke, *Irony* 45–46.

11. *Amen, amen I say to you:* The Johannine use of the double "amen" again appears, marking an important new moment in the narrative, but closely related to all that has gone before. See the note to v. 3.

    There is uncertainty among scholars over the speaker of this discourse. The interpretation takes it to be Jesus. For a summary of the discussion, also concluding that Jesus is the speaker, see Brown, *Gospel* 1:149.

12. *earthly things . . . heavenly things:* The logic of the narrative demands that the "earthly things" *(ta epigeia)* that Jesus has told look back to vv. 1-10. Given the significance of Jesus' words concerning rebirth in the Spirit it can be asked how such issues are regarded as "earthly things." The position taken above, that however exalted they might be within the Johannine context they are but the christianization of a rich vein in Israel's thought, has the support of major commentators (cf. Barrett, *Gospel* 202–203; Blank, *Krisis* 62–63). The discussion between Jesus and Nicodemus (vv. 1-10) reflects debates that went on between the Johannine community and the members of the synagogue.

    If I have told you: Jesus has spoken in the plural in v. 11 ("we speak of what we know . . ."), but returns to the singular in v. 12. This change may reflect different sources but it is possible that while a debate over the meaning of *ta epigeia* has been part of the conflict between community and synagogue (v. 11) the revelation of *ta epourania* comes only from Jesus, and thus the singular "I" returns. See previous note.

13. *No one has ascended into heaven:* Many take the link between the ascent motif (v. 13a) and the Son of Man (v. 13b) as associated with either the Gnostic idea of the ascension of the Primal Man or the Lukan idea of Jesus' ascension. Some see it as both. Against this is the use of the parallel between Moses' action with the serpent in v. 14. There is no hint in the OT that the serpent ascended. It remains fixed so that it can be seen. The background to v. 13 is contemporary Jewish speculation concerning the ascent of Israel's revealer-figures, Moses, Abraham, Isaiah, Enoch, and other great saints (cf. *Tg. Onq., Tg. Ps.-J.,* and *Frg. Tgs.* on Deut 30:11-14; *Tg. Ps.* 68:19; *Mart. Isa.* 2:9; 3:7-10; *1 Enoch* 71; *2 Bar.* 2:1-8; *3 Bar.; Adam and Eve* 25–28; *2 Enoch* 1; *T. Abr.,* Rec. A: 10-15; Rec. B: 8-12). All such revelatory ascensions into heaven so that the transported visionary might return to make God known are categorically denied by means of *oudeis* (cf. 1:18). For a discussion of these ascending figures see

Talbert, "The Myth of a Descending-Ascending Redeemer" 418–443; Moloney, *Son of Man* 53–55.

but one has descended from heaven: Over against the negation of any figure who has been proposed as having *ascended to heaven* to become a revealer figure there is the positive affirmation of the unique revealer, the Son of Man who *has come down from heaven. Anabēbeken* in v. 13a and the *katabas* of v. 13b are deliberately opposed. The revealer is not one who went up, but the only one who came down. Jesus is "from heaven," the sent one of the Father. For a full discussion of these issues, see Moloney, *Son of Man* 51–60.

(who is in heaven): Early scribes, attracted by the reference to ascension, added "who is in heaven" to the present v. 13 (cf., for example, the first hand of Alexandrinus, Koridethi, some Latin and Syriac versions). Although largely Egyptian ($\mathfrak{P}^{66.75}$, Sinaiticus, Vaticanus, Regius, Freer Gospels, the Coptic and Ethiopic versions), the best witnesses exclude it. It should be excluded as a very early scribal addition.

14. *as Moses lifted up the serpent:* The background to the parallel (Num 21:8-9) between Moses in the desert and the Son of Man must be kept firmly in place. There is a close relationship between what Moses did with the serpent and what *must* happen to the Son of Man *(kathōs Mōüsēs hypsōsen ton opsin . . . houtōs hypsōthēnai dei ton huion tou anthrōpou).* The parallel runs into v. 15. As the Israelites gazed upon the elevated serpent to be returned to health, so also the one who believes in the revelation of God (v. 13) that takes place on a cross (v. 14) will have eternal life (v. 15).

    so must the Son of Man be lifted up: As with the use of *anōthen,* where both the physical meaning of "again" and the more spiritual meaning of "from above" are needed for a correct understanding of the passage, so also with the use of *hypsōthēnai.* Both the physical lifting up of Jesus on a stake as Moses lifted up the serpent and the theological meaning of "exaltation" must be involved in the interpretation of v. 14. What this association of "lifting up" and "exaltation" might mean is yet to be determined. After 1:5; 2:4, 18-22, and the Christian awareness that Jesus died on a cross the "lifting up" is associated with the death of Jesus, but the link between death and glory will develop. As the narrative unfolds it will become the *leitmotif* of the passion narrative.

16. *he gave his only Son:* A link between the cross and the "gift" of the Son is sometimes seen in the use of the verb *didōmi* (e.g., Brown, *Gospel* 1:134). But the gospels use the technical term *paradidōmi* for the cross (cf. Mark 9:31; 10:33; 14:21, 41; Matt 17:22; 20:18; 26:2, 24, 25; Luke 18:32; 22:22; 24:7). It does appear, however, in Gal 1:4. The broader context of vv. 13-15, leading into v. 16, certainly provides a message of God's love and the cross as the gift of the Son (cf. Brown, *Gospel* 1:147).

17. *that the world might be saved:* The language of vv. 11-17 is typical of later Gnostic literature. The Son speaks of what he has seen (v. 11); the revelation of earthly and heavenly things (v. 12); the descent of the Son of Man (v. 13); the "lifting up" of the Son of Man (v. 14); the Father sends the Son to save the world (v. 16), not to judge the world (v. 17). "It is this passage more than any

other which supports Bultmann's theory of adaptation from a pre-Gnostic source. . . . It is more reasonable to suppose that John presents what is basically Jewish and Christian teaching, in words that may be expected to be meaningful to a Gentile audience familiar with the ideas of Hellenistic religious aspirations" (Lindars, *Gospel* 147–148). This passage is another fine example of the author's use of language and ideas that tell the traditional story in a new way.

18. *are not condemned . . . are condemned already:* The Johannine expressions *krinein* and *krisis* appear here (vv. 18-19) for the first time in the narrative. The association of a realized eschatology with a theology of self-judgment is one of the Fourth Gospel's contributions to Christian thought. One does not wait till the end of time (traditional eschatology) for the return of the Son of Man who will exercise a final judgment (cf. Matt 25:31-46). One judges oneself by the acceptance or refusal of the revelation of God in and through Jesus Christ and by the good and bad deeds that flow from this decision. See Blank, *Krisis* 41–52, 75–108; Dodd, *Interpretation* 208–212.

19–21. *And this is the judgment, that the light has come into the world:* These verses contain a suggestion of predestination. The light comes into the world of certain people and not into others (v. 19). Consequently some do evil and remain in the darkness (v. 20) and some do good, live in the light, and their good deeds are seen (v. 21). As the above interpretation attempts to show, this is not the only way the passage can be read. See further Blank, *Krisis* 75–108; Stemberger, *La symbolique du bien et du mal* 26–33.

For Reference and Further Study

Bassler, Jouette M. "Mixed Signals: Nicodemus in the Fourth Gospel," *JBL* 108 (1989) 635–646.

Bishop, J. "Encounters in the New Testament." In Kenneth R. R. Gros Louis, ed., *Literary Interpretations of Biblical Narratives.* 2 vols. Nashville: Abingdon, 1982, 2:285–294.

Cosgrove, C. H. "The Place where Jesus is: Allusions to Baptism and Eucharist in the Fourth Gospel," *NTS* 35 (1989) 522–539.

Dodd, C. H. "Dialogue Form in the Gospels," *BJRL* 37 (1954–1955) 54–67.

Gaeta, Giancarlo. *Il dialogo con Nicodemo.* Brescia: Paideia, 1974.

Jonge, Marinus de. "Nicodemus and Jesus: Some Observations on Misunderstanding and Understanding in the Fourth Gospel," *BJRL* 53 (1970–1971) 337–359.

Kysar, Robert. "The Making of Metaphor: Another Reading of John 3:1-15." In Fernando F. Segovia, ed., *"What is John?" Readers and Readings of the Fourth Gospel.* Atlanta: Scholars, 1996, 21–41.

La Potterie, Ignace de. "Naître de l'eau et naître de l'Esprit," *ScEc* 14 (1962) 351–374.

Lindars, Barnabas. "John and the Synoptic Gospels: A Test Case," *NTS* 27 (1980–1981) 287–294.

Michel, Marc. "Nicodème et le non-lieu de vérité," *RevSR* 55 (1981) 227–236.

Moloney, Francis J. *Belief in the Word* 106–121.

_____. *Son of Man* 42–67.

_____. "When is John Talking about Sacraments?" *ABR* 30 (1982) 10–33.

Neyrey, Jerome H. "John III – A Debate over Johannine Epistemology and Christology," *NT* 22 (1981) 115–127.

Patte, Daniel. "Jesus' Pronouncement about Entering the Kingdom like a Child: A Structural Exegesis," *Sem* 29 (1983) 3–42.

Rossetto, Giovanni. "Nascere dall'alto: Gv 3:3-8," in Pius-Ramon Tragan, ed., *Segni e Sacramenti nel Vangelo di Giovanni.* Studia Anselmiana 66. Rome: Editrice Anselmiana, 1977, 45–71.

Suggit, J. N. "Nicodemus – the True Jew," *Neotest.* 14 (1981) 90–110.

Talbert, C. H. "The Myth of a Descending-Ascending Redeemer in Mediterranean Antiquity," *NTS* 22 (1975) 418–443.

v. Jesus and John the Baptist (3:22-36)

22. After this Jesus and his disciples went into the Judean countryside, and he spent some time there with them and baptized. 23. John also was baptizing at Aenon near Salim because water was abundant there; and people kept coming and were being baptized 24. For John had not yet been put in prison.

25. Now a discussion about purification arose between John's disciples and a Jew. 26. They came to John and said to him, "Rabbi, the one who was with you across the Jordan, to whom you testified, here he is, baptizing, and all are going to him."

27. John answered, "No one can receive anything except what has been given from heaven. 28. You yourselves are my witnesses that I said, 'I am not the Christ, but I have been sent ahead of him.' 29. He who has the bride is the bridegroom. The friend of the bridegroom, who stands and hears him, rejoices greatly at the bridegroom's voice. For this reason my joy has been fulfilled. 30. He must increase, but I must decrease."

31. The one who comes from above is above all; the one who is of the earth belongs to the earth and speaks about earthly things. The one who comes from heaven is above all. 32. He bears witness to what he has seen and heard, yet no one receives his testimony. 33. Whoever has received his testimony sets seal to this, that God is true. 34. He whom God has sent speaks the words of God, for it is not by measure that he gives the Spirit. 35. The Father loves the Son and has given all things into his hand.

36. The one who believes in the Son has eternal life; the one who does not obey the Son shall not see life, but the wrath of God rests upon such a one.

INTERPRETATION

Introduction to 3:22-36. There are indications that this passage has been composed from several preexisting traditions. The opening (vv. 22-24) and closing (vv. 31-36) have a certain clumsiness. However, whatever its origins the passage serves well to focus on the author's major concern: a narrative presentation of the right relationship that must exist between Jesus and John the Baptist. Jesus and John both baptize, but in different locations. The time of this activity is before the imprisonment of John. However awkward, the time, the two places, the characters in question and their baptismal activity have been established in vv. 22-24. Within this setting a discussion over "purification" between the disciples of the Baptist and "a Jew" leads the disciples to tell their master about Jesus' baptizing activities. This enables the Baptist to give his final witness to Jesus (vv. 25-30). As with Jesus' encounters with "the Jews" (cf. 2:23-25) and Nicodemus (cf. 3:11-21), the Baptist's witness to Jesus closes with a reflection on the events narrated (cf. vv. 31-36). Who is speaking in vv. 31-36: John the Baptist, Jesus, or the narrator? The question is still debated. Taken as a final reflection from the narrator, 3:22-36 unfolds in the following fashion:

> (a) *Vv. 22-24:* Introduction. The time, the two places, and the baptizing activity of the major characters of the narrative (Jesus and John the Baptist) are introduced.
> (b) *Vv. 25-30:* John the Baptist bears witness
> > i. *Vv. 25-26:* A statement from the disciples of the Baptist raises the question of the nature of the relationship between Jesus and the Baptist.
> > ii. *Vv. 27-30:* The response of the Baptist, his final witness to Jesus.
> (c) *Vv. 31-36:* The discourse-commentary of the narrator
> > i. *Vv. 31-35:* The revelation of the heavenly in the Son, who comes from heaven.
> > ii. *V. 36:* The salvation or condemnation that flows from the acceptance or refusal of this revelation.

The narrative repeats the shape of 3:1-21. Both have an introduction (vv. 1-2a, 22-24) to a discussion (vv. 2b-12, 25-30) that leads into a discourse (vv. 11-21, 31-36). An interesting feature of 2:1–3:36 emerges. Both 2:1-12 and 2:13-25 were structurally similar, as are 3:1-21 and 3:22-36. These passages are further united by the fact that they deal with the response of Jews to Jesus: the mother of Jesus (2:1-12), "the Jews" (2:13-25), Nicodemus (3:1-21), and John the Baptist (3:22-36). Whatever the prehistory of the narrative and discourse material used to create 2:1–3:36, this part of the story has its own thematic and literary unity.

Introduction (vv. 22-24). There is a break from the preceding scene, marked by an expression often used in the Fourth Gospel to indicate a new stage in the narrative: "after this" *(meta tauta)*. Jesus and his disciples move away from the city of Jerusalem into the broader geographical context of "the land of Judea." In this new place Jesus and his disciples remained together, and Jesus baptized. The imperfect tense of the verb "to baptize" *(ebaptizen)* indicates that he resumed a habitual practice (v. 22). In a different place, Aenon near Salim, John is also practicing baptism. The location of Aenon is not known for certain, but its description as a place where there was much water has led many to suggest a location in Samaria (cf. Boismard, "Aenon près de Salem" 218–229). The imperfect passive form of the verb "to baptize" reappears to describe the fact that people came to John and were baptized *(ebaptizonto)* (v. 23). Two characters have been located in different places and both have been described as practicing baptism. There is no hint in these introductory remarks that there was any qualitative difference between the two baptisms. The focus is on the baptizers, not the respective merits of their baptismal rites. In a final introductory note the reader is informed that all this took place before John had been put in prison (v. 24). The description of the characters, the time, the place, and their parallel activities sets the scene for the brief narrative that follows (vv. 25-30).

The two baptizers (vv. 25-26). Two significant characters are practicing baptism (vv. 22-24), and a discussion arises between the disciples of the Baptist and "a Jew." The debate "over purifying" *(peri katharismou)* is stated in the most general terms (cf. 2:6), but in this context it must be related to vv. 22-24. There is an unresolved problem between the disciples of the Baptist and "a Jew" concerning the baptisms administered by Jesus and by John (v. 25). Only this interpretation of the discussion concerning "purification" makes sense of the question the disciples pose to their master: "Rabbi, he who was with you beyond the Jordan, to whom you bore witness, here he is, baptizing, and all are going to him" (v. 26). The rhetoric involved is subtle. In a debate over the respective merits of two baptizers one of them is asked to offer his opinion. The disciples recall John's role in the story so far as having witnessed to Jesus (cf. 1:6-8, 15, 19-34). In what may be a tiny piece of historical evidence they recall a time when Jesus was beyond the Jordan with John (cf. Murphy-O'Connor, "John the Baptist and Jesus" 367–376). Now the two have separated (vv. 22-23), and the disciples are concerned because Jesus has not only taken over a baptizing ministry that parallels the ministry of John, but "all are going to him."

The Baptist's final witness to Jesus (vv. 27-30). One might expect the Baptist to defend his role, but after 1:6-8, 15, 19-34 this will not happen, as John's only function is to bear witness to Jesus. John does not respond to his disciples' question concerning baptism; he shifts the discussion into the realm of revelation. Both John the Baptist and Jesus Christ receive their authority from God (cf. 1:1-2; 3:13-14, 16-17 [Jesus]; 1:6, 33 [the Baptist]). The issue that determines the respective roles of Jesus and John the Baptist is not the rite of baptism but "what is given to him from heaven" (v. 27). In the immediately previous encounter between Jesus and Nicodemus, Jesus instructed Nicodemus on the heavenly origin of what he had to offer and of what he had seen and heard (cf. vv. 3, 5, 7-8, 11-12). The Baptist accepts this point of view and is thus able to return to his earlier witness to Jesus (cf. 1:19-28): he is not the Christ, but the one sent before him (v. 28). Although he is not the anointed one of God the Baptist has been "sent by God" (1:6) and his witness to Jesus corresponds with God's design. There is an unquestionable authority to John's witness, but he is not the Christ.

Having established his role as sent by God but not the Christ, the Baptist describes his relationship with the Christ. The Baptist's use of marriage imagery has two sources. The Scriptures often speak of Israel as the bride of God (cf. Isa 62:4-5; Jer 2:2; Ezek 16:8; 23:4; Hos 2:21) and the Christian Church continued this imagery to speak of itself as the bride of Christ (cf. 2 Cor 11:2; Eph 5:25-27, 31-32; Rev 21:2; 22:17). This is sufficient background for the Baptist to affirm that "not he but Christ is the head of the New Israel" (Barrett, *Gospel* 222–223), but the image of the friend of the bridegroom who stands and hears him *(akouōn autou)* and rejoices greatly in his voice *(tēn phonēn)* (v. 29), draws from marriage practice of the time. Paralleling himself with the friend of the bridegroom who accompanies him until such time as he takes possession of his bride, he places himself in a subordinate position, "hearing" the bridegroom's "voice." This hearing has taken place and thus the Baptist can announce, in the present tense, that his joy is now full *(peplērotai)*. Full of joy, he is prepared to decrease as Jesus comes upon the scene (vv. 29-30). This description of the decreasing importance of the Baptist and the centrality of Jesus reflects what happens from this point on in the story, but there is more to these words of the Baptist than a description of what will happen from now on. In 2:5 the mother of Jesus became the first person in the story to place unconditional belief and trust in the word of Jesus. Although there is no use of the expression *logos* or related words they are paralleled by the word *phōnē* in v. 29. John the Baptist demonstrates openness to the word of Jesus even though it means he must disappear from the scene. This leads to a comment from the narrator (vv. 31-36) that has parallels with vv. 11-21.

The narrator's comment: the revelation of the heavenly (vv. 31-35). Jesus is the authoritative revealer whose revelation is not accepted (vv. 31-32; cf. vv. 11-12). Because he is revealer his uniqueness and authenticity come "from above" (v. 31; cf. v. 13). The life that comes from the revelation brought by the Son cannot be provided by any person or institution belonging to "the earth." Hence the question of origins emerges as the one "from above" brings a revelation of the truth that exceeds the limited truths the world and its knowledge can offer. God makes "the word" known through the spoken word of the sent one, pouring out the Spirit without reserve (vv. 33-34; cf. v. 17). Behind this authoritative revelation of the Son is the love that unites the Father and the Son, leading the Father to give the Son the task of making God known (v. 35; cf. v. 16).

The narrator's comment: salvation and condemnation (v. 36). In vv. 11-21 equal space was given to the theme of the revelation brought by the Son of Man (vv. 11-15) and the salvation or condemnation that flows from the acceptance or refusal of that revelation (vv. 16-21). In vv. 31-36 the narrator concentrates on the theme of revelation (vv. 31-35), but concludes with the themes of death and judgment in v. 36. Belief produces eternal life, while the wrath of God is the fruit of a refusal to accept this revelation (v. 36; cf. vv. 20-21).

Conclusion to 3:22-36. This episode comes at the end of a triptych of encounters between Jesus and characters from the world of Judaism: "the Jews," Nicodemus, and John the Baptist. The theme of "the word" has been central. According to the Prologue (1:1-18) the saving revelation of God takes place in the incarnation of "the Word," Jesus Christ (1:14-18). Within the narrative, therefore, the "word of Jesus" has been the place where the characters in the story encounter what God is doing in and through Jesus. By this criterion "the Jews" demonstrate a total lack of faith while the faith of Nicodemus is limited by his determination to understand Jesus according to his own categories. Finally, John the Baptist sees himself as the friend of the bridegroom, rejoicing to hear his voice. He shows an openness to the word of Jesus, cost what it may: "He must increase but I must decrease" (v. 30). The earlier experience of the mother of Jesus comes to mind. She told the servants to do whatever Jesus told them despite the fact that she had been sharply rebuked by her son (2:4-5). John the Baptist, like the mother of Jesus, has been presented as an example of *authentic belief*, laying himself open to the word of Jesus (3:29).

Conclusion to 2:13–3:36: The narrative of 2:13–3:36 articulates a point of view about how one should respond to Jesus and the fruits of such a response. Using "the word" of Jesus as the criterion, the story points to the possibility of no faith (2:13-22: "the Jews"), partial faith (3:1-21: Nicodemus), and authentic Johannine belief (3:22-36: John the Baptist) *within the world of Judaism.* The narrator comments on the limitations of a faith generated by Jesus' miraculous signs (2:23-25). Closely associated with these models of belief is the Johannine message on the importance of belief in the revelation of God in and through the word of Jesus for life and salvation (cf. especially 3:11-21, 31-36). The concentration on characters *within the world of Judaism* indicates that Israel has not been excluded from the Johannine theology of revelation and salvation. However much the bitter encounters between Jesus and "the Jews" may intensify as the story unfolds, these encounters that open Jesus' public ministry have *shown* (2:13–3:36) what was *told* in the Prologue (1:16-18). God's former gift of the Law has been perfected in the gift of the revelation of God in the word of Jesus Christ. As the Johannine community had its roots in Judaism, Johannine Christianity was the fruit of authentic belief among Jews (Martyn, *History and Theology*; Brown, *Community*). John 2:13–3:36 indicates that such belief is always possible in Israel. The narrative now turns "to the world on and beyond the borders of Judaism" (Barrett, *Gospel* 220).

NOTES

22. *into the Judean countryside:* Critics point to the seeming contradiction between 3:1-21, where Jesus is in Jerusalem, and his journey *eis tēn Ioudaian gēn*. It is often read as a clumsy remnant of a source. However, the reading of the Greek adopted in the interpretation indicates that Jesus moved from the Judean city of Jerusalem into the surrounding Judean countryside. For further discussion of the difficulty, and support for the position adopted here, see Westcott, *Gospel* 57; Bultmann, *Gospel* 170 n. 3.

23. *Aenon near Salim:* For a survey of possible sites see Brown, *Gospel* 1:151. On its Samaritan location, as well as Boismard (see above) see Murphy-O'Connor, "John the Baptist and Jesus" 363–366. For a symbolic interpretation of the place name and the scene as a whole see Krieger, "Fiktive Orte" 121–123. This is not called for. As well as the recent case made for a Samaritan site for Aenon, such a geographical location also serves the narrative well. The mention of a Samaritan location is a hint that the focus on Jewish people in Jewish places is coming to an end and opens the way for Jesus' proximate presence in Samaria (cf. 4:4)

24. *For John had not yet been put in prison:* For reconstructions of the possible background to this relationship between Jesus and John the Baptist see Murphy-O'Connor, "John the Baptist and Jesus" 359–374; Légasse, "Le Baptême administré par Jésus" 17–25; Witherington, "Jesus and the Baptist" 225–244. By piecing together various elements from the gospels, including the Fourth Gospel, we may list the bare bones of events as follows: an initial association between the two men (related by blood?) on the other side of the Jordan (John 3:26); a separation possibly caused by the increasing hostility developing between the Baptist and both political and religious leaders; the Baptist continues his ministry in Samaria (politically distant from his opponents) while Jesus baptizes in Judea (3:22-23); the imprisonment of the Baptist (3:24); the ministry of Jesus begins; the execution of the Baptist; Jesus emerges as a fig-

ure with close links to the now executed Baptist but exceeding him in his claims concerning the kingdom of God, which raise further questions concerning his identity.

25. *A discussion arose between John's disciples and a Jew:* There is some textual confusion over *meta Ioudaiou*. Some manuscripts have *meta tōn Ioudaiōn* which would make excellent sense and should be rejected precisely because it is the *lectio facilior.* There is also a popular (but unattested) reading of *meta Iēsou,* which would also make good sense. Schnackenburg (*Gospel* 1:413–414) makes the good suggestion that "the Jew" may have come from Judea, where Jesus was baptizing. This would lead logically into the question of v. 26. The presence of "the Jew" also retains the narrative focus on the world of Judaism.

    about purification: There is no reason, beyond the context, to link "purification" with baptism. The discussion between the disciples of the Baptist and "a Jew" could have been about any number of the complex issues that surround ritual purity. The focus on baptism in vv. 22-23 and the question posed to John by his disciples (v. 26) point to baptism. The water practices of the Qumran sectarians were associated with purification (cf. 1QS 3:1-9; 5:13-14; CD 10:10-13. On the complex question of purity at Qumran see García Martínez and Barrera, *The People* 139–157).

26. *here he is, baptizing:* There is no interest in the relative merits of the two baptisms. The focus is entirely upon the two baptizers. Historically the baptism administered by Jesus would have been parallel to that of the Baptist. See Légasse, "Le Baptême administré par Jésus" 25–29; Murphy-O'Connor, "John the Baptist and Jesus" 367–374. Barrett suggests (*Gospel* 221) that the discussion probably arose from the Baptist's lack of concern in his baptismal ministry to observe the details of Jewish ablutions.

    all are going to him: It is often pointed out that the *pantes* is an exaggeration, possibly produced by anger. In literary terms, however, v. 26, "and all are going to him" counters the indications of the Baptist's successful ministry in v. 23: "the people came and were baptized." The *pantes* creates the impression that John's once-successful mission is falling away dramatically.

27. *John answered:* The solemn nature of the Baptist's response is marked by the use of the pleonastic *apekrithē kai eipen* to introduce his words.

    No one: The affirmation in v. 27 is general. It is a statement about the source of ultimate truth for anyone (*ou dynatai anthrōpos lambanein*) and does not apply, as some would maintain (e.g., Becker, *Evangelium* 1:154), only to the Baptist. On the basis of this general statement the Baptist will develop his assessment of the relationship between himself and Jesus.

28. *I am not the Christ:* As throughout the Fourth Gospel, the Baptist acts as the unique witness to Jesus (cf. 1:6-8, 15; 19-34). Many have claimed that part of the Fourth Gospel's agenda is to subordinate John the Baptist to Jesus. Originally the suggestion of Baldensperger, this position has been further developed and argued strongly by Bultmann (*Gospel* 167–172) and others, who see the insertions on the Baptist in the Prologue (1:6-8, 15) as anti-Baptist material added to an original pro-Baptist hymn. For Bultmann the original hymn

was from Mandean circles and was in praise of the Baptist. In Johannine circles it has been christianized and used as a hymn to honor Jesus Christ, the incarnate Logos. But one does not receive the impression that the present Gospel is in any way anti-Baptist. The Baptist plays a positive role whenever he actively appears in the story (1:6-8, 15, 19-34; 3:22-29), and he is positively assessed by Jesus later in the narrative (5:33-36). Whatever the nature of the Baptist material in its pre-Gospel form and context it has been skillfully inserted into the present Gospel. See Hooker, "John the Baptist" 354–358; Stowasser, *Johannes der Täufer.*

29. *the friend of the bridegroom:* For a collection of later Jewish material on marriage practices and the friend of the bridegroom see Str-B 1:45–46, 500–504. See especially *Tosefta Ketuboth* 1:4 (Jacob Neusner, *The Tosefta Translated from the Hebrew: Third Division Nashim [The Order of Women]*. New York: Ktav, 1979, 61). See also van Selms, "The Best Man and the Bride" 65–75; Boismard, "L'ami de l'epoux" 289–295.

the bridegroom's voice: Given the importance of the expression *logos,* the verb *legein,* and associated words, it is strange that the author uses *phonē* in the Baptist's description of his role as standing and hearing, rejoicing at the bridegroom's voice. One can never be sure why an author chooses certain words but "it is highly probable that we are here in touch with pre-canonical tradition" (Dodd, *Tradition* 287). The tradition already said what the real author wished to communicate and thus he left these words of the Baptist in the form in which they came to him. See the note on v. 36.

Commentators pay little attention to the culminating statement of vv. 29-30. Infante, "L'amico dello sposo" 12–14, sees it as crucial but focuses on the Baptist's joy. In the light of the attention given to this question across 2:1–3:36 the interpretation suggests that the crucial element in the Baptist's response is his openness to the voice (the word) of Jesus, cost what it may. His response matches that of the mother of Jesus (2:1-12).

30. *He must increase but I must decrease:* The Baptist's use of the words "increase" *(auxanein)* and "decrease" *(elattousthai)* became important in the Patristic interpretation of the passage as a whole. The verbs were applied to an image of the waxing and waning of the sun. On the basis of this image the Fathers claimed that John pointed to a turning point where the old gives way to the new. For a survey see Schnackenburg, *Gospel* 1:417–418.

Augustine offers a splendid interpretation of this passage: *Ego sum in audiendo, ille in dicendo; ego sum illuminandus, ille lumen; ego sum in aure, ille Verbum* ("I am in the place of hearer; he, of speaker; I am as the one that must be enlightened, he is the light; I am as the ear, he is the word." *In Iohannis Evangelium* 13.12: CCSL 36:137).

Many commentators see the early sections of the Fourth Gospel as the transcending of Israel. This is true only insofar as "transcending" does not mean "replacing" Israel. It must be observed that two Jews, the mother of Jesus and John the Baptist, are presented as models of faith. Neither of them becomes a model of authentic Johannine belief by rejecting his or her Jewishness. They both unconditionally accept the word of Jesus (cf. 2:5; 3:29-30).

31. *The one who comes from above:* The numerous parallels between 3:11-21 and 31-36 have often been noticed. See Brown, *Gospel* 159–160; Segalla, *Giovanni* 185–187; Moloney, *Son of Man* 44–45. Despite the parallels there are also some important differences. In vv. 13-15 the christological title "the Son of Man" is used: this is the unique revealer who must be lifted up on a cross. In vv. 31-34 Jesus is presented as the one sent from above who "speaks" (v. 31), who "bears witness" (v. 32), who gives authentic testimony (v. 33), who "utters the words of God" (v. 34). It is likely that vv. 31-36 formed an earlier focus on Jesus as the sent one of God (vv. 31-35) and on judgment as "eternal life" or "the wrath of God" (v. 36). Verses 11-21 are the product of further Johannine reflection on the basic themes of revelation and consequent judgment, but developed in terms of the lifting up of the Son of Man on the cross as the revelation of God's love (vv. 11-16) and on judgment as loving darkness rather than light, hating the light and coming into the light (vv. 17-21). See Moloney, *Son of Man* 50–51, and especially Boismard and Lamouille, *Jean* 113–117. On the significance of the retention of this older form of a reflection upon the themes of revelation and judgment see the note to v. 36.

    A number of scholars have noticed the symmetrical literary structure of 3:1-36 although they do not follow the details of the position adopted in this commentary. See Ibuki, *"kai tēn phonēn autou akoueis"* 9–33; Thyen, "Aus der Literatur" 112; Klaiber, "Der irdische" 211–213, 232–233; Wilson, "Integrity" 38–40.

    The one who comes from above . . . the one who is of the earth: Some scholars regard "from above" as a reference to Jesus and "the one who is of the earth" as a reference to the Baptist (cf. Barrett, *Gospel* 224–225; Klaiber, "Der irdische" 205–233). This suggestion generally regards vv. 31-36 as a continuation of the words of the Baptist (e.g., Bauer, *Johannesevangelium* 63–65; Barrett, *Gospel* 224; Wilson, "The Integrity" 36–38). Some regard the speaker as Jesus (e.g., Schnackenburg, *Gospel* 1:380–381). This suggestion, however, is made possible by transposing vv. 31-36 to follow v. 12, producing the sequence v. 12; vv. 31-36; vv. 13-21 (Schnackenburg, "Die situationsgelösten Redestücke" 88–99). The interpretation regards it as a final reflection from the narrator, and while "the one who comes from above" clearly refers to Jesus "the one who is of the earth" has a more general application. It describes all those who (like "the Jews" and Nicodemus) are unable to transcend the things of this world *(epigeia)* and thus cannot accept the revelation of the heavenly *(epourania)* that takes place in Jesus.

32. *He bears witness . . . yet no one receives:* The translation "yet" renders an adversative *kai* (cf. Schnackenburg, *Gospel* 1:384). Jesus reveals on the basis of direct access to God, *but* this is refused (cf. vv. 11-12).

33. *whoever has received his testimony:* The verb *lambanein* is again used to indicate acceptance in faith.

34. *it is not by measure that he gives the Spirit:* There is a longstanding discussion over who gives the Spirit, the Father of Jesus or Jesus. See the survey in Brown, *Gospel* 1:161–162. Both are possible. Because the Fourth Gospel is primarily

theological rather than christological (see *NJBC* 1420–1421) the interpretation opts for God, but the difference is not great. See also Loader, *Christology* 25–26.

35. *the Father loves the Son:* This is the first mention of the relationship of love that exists between the Father and the Son. The affirmation of this relationship, and its consequence, that the Father has given all things *(panta)* into his hand, states the basis of the authority of Jesus' words and actions. In the Fourth Gospel the words and actions of Jesus flow from this relationship.

36. *the wrath of God:* The use of "wrath of God" *(hē orgē tou theou)* indicates that these words on judgment come from older tradition. The OT provides the language of wrath, and it appears in the preaching of John the Baptist to speak of the oncoming judgment (cf. Matt 3:7; Luke 3:7). The earlier passage (vv. 18-21) reflects a later development of the theme of judgment, using Johannine expressions: judgment and judging *(krisis* and *krinein)*, light *(phōs)* and darkness *(skotia)*, belief in the name *(eis to onoma)* of the only Son of God *(monogenous huiou tou theou)*, and good deeds being clearly seen *(hina phanerōthē)*. The use of the more traditional expression of the themes of revelation and judgment in vv. 31-36 focuses strongly upon Jesus as *the one who speaks the word of the Father* (vv. 32-34). The author thus pointedly closes 2:1–3:36, describing responses to Jesus within Judaism. The focus throughout these episodes has been on various protagonists' responses to *the word of Jesus*.

FOR REFERENCE AND FURTHER STUDY

Baldensperger, Wilhelm. *Der Prolog des vierten Evangeliums. Sein polemisch-apologetischer Zweck.* Freiburg: J. C. B. Mohr (Paul Siebeck), 1898.

Boismard, M.-E. "L'ami de l'epoux (Jo III,29)." In André Barucq, Jean Duplacy, Augustin George, and Henri de Lubac, eds., *A la Rencontre de Dieu: Mémorial Albert Gelin.* Le Puy: Xavier Mappus, 1961, 289–295.

García Martínez, Florentino, and J. T. Barrera. *The People of the Dead Sea Scrolls. Their Writings, Beliefs and Practices.* Leiden: E. J. Brill, 1993.

Ibuki, Yu. *"kai tēn phonēn autou akoueis:* Gedankenaufbau und Hintergrund des 3. Kapitels des Johannesevangeliums," *Bulletin of Seikei University* 14 (1978) 9–33.

Infante, Renzo. "L'amico dello sposo, figura del ministero di Giovanni Battista nel Quarto Vangelo," *RivBib* 31 (1983) 3–19.

Klaiber, Walter. "Der irdische und der himmlische Zeuge: eine Auslegung von Joh 3.22-36," *NTS* 36 (1990) 205–233.

Krieger, N. "Fiktive Orte der Johannes-Taufe," *ZNW* 45 (1953–1954) 121–123.

Légasse, Simon. "Le Baptême administré par Jésus (Jn 2,22-26; 4,1-3) et l'origine du baptême chrétien," *BLE* 78 (1977) 3–30.

Loader, William R. G. "The Central Structure of Johannine Theology," *NTS* 30 (1984) 188–216.

Moloney, Francis J. *Belief in the Word* 121–131.

Murphy-O'Connor, Jerome. "John the Baptist and Jesus: History and Hypotheses," *NTS* 36 (1990) 359–374.

Schnackenburg, Rudolf. "Die situationsgelösten Redestücke in John 3," *ZNW* 49 (1958) 88–99.

Selms, Adrianus van. "The Best Man and the Bride – from Sumer to St. John," *JNES* 9 (1950) 65–75.

Stowasser, Martin. *Johannes der Täufer im Vierten Evangelium.* ÖBS 12. Klosterneuberg: Österreichisches Katholisches Bibelwerk, 1992.

Thyen, Hartwig. "Aus der Literatur zum Johannesevangelium," *ThR* 44 (1979) 97–134.

Wilson, J. "The Integrity of John 3:22-26," *JSNT* 10 (1981) 34–41.

Witherington, Ben. "Jesus and the Baptist – Two of a Kind?" In David Lull, ed., *SBL 1988 Seminar Papers.* Atlanta: Scholars Press, 1988, 225–244.

The Response to Jesus Outside Israel (4:1-54)

The place of 4:1-54 within 2:1–4:54. After the first Cana miracle (2:1-12) there was a strong concentration on the response of Jewish people to the word of Jesus (2:13–3:36). The mother of Jesus displayed an unquestioning acceptance of the word of Jesus, and this act of faith led to the first of Jesus' signs, the manifestation of his glory, the perfection of the former gift of the glory at Sinai (2:1-12). The criterion of acceptance of the word of Jesus was established, after Jesus' criticism of the limited faith of the first disciples (1:35-51). On the basis of this criterion Jewish characters manifested no faith ("the Jews"), limited faith (Nicodemus), and authentic Johannine belief in the word of Jesus (John the Baptist). The episodes that follow (4:1-42) take place in Samaria.

The focus on Samaria is highlighted by the fact that the encounters between Jesus and the Samaritans happen *in one place*, with only a slight displacement at the end of the passage (v. 40). Even Jesus' words to the disciples happen in the same place. The *time sequence* of the narrative is linear. As the disciples go to buy food (v. 8), Jesus talks with a Samaritan woman. As the disciples come back she returns to the village (v. 28), and her fellow villagers begin to come toward Jesus (v. 30). While they are on their way Jesus speaks to the disciples (vv. 31-38). The Samaritans arrive, invite him to stay with them (v. 40), and eventually come to faith in him. After his two days with them he departs to Galilee (v. 43). With the exception of a brief discourse that Jesus delivers to his disciples (vv. 31-38), *all the characters* who encounter Jesus are Samaritans: the Samaritan woman (4:1-15, 16-30) and Samaritan villagers (vv. 39-42). In v. 42 Jesus departs to Galilee, and there encounters a *basilikos*, a royal official (vv. 43-54). He is not a Samaritan, but may be a Gentile. It can be established that there are two moments in the Samaritan woman's encounter with Jesus (vv. 1-15 and 16-30). Thus 4:1-54 is made up of four episodes. Three of them report responses of people from the world outside Israel to the word of Jesus (vv. 1-15, 16-30, 39-42), and they close with the story of the second Cana miracle (vv. 43-54). The brief discourse Jesus delivers to his shocked disciples (vv. 31-38) comments on his activity among the Samaritans and points to their future missionary involvement in a non-Jewish world (vv. 39-42).

The repetition of the succession of events in 2:1–3:36 is striking. The Jewish world witnesses a Cana miracle, no faith ("the Jews"), a comment from the narrator, limited faith (Nicodemus), and authentic belief in the word of Jesus (John the Baptist) (2:1–3:36). We have yet to consider the nature of the responses of the representatives of the world outside Israel (the Samaritan woman and the Samaritan villagers), but there are three responses to Jesus, with a comment from Jesus preceding his final encounter with the Samaritan villagers. As the Jewish responses to Jesus *began* with the first Cana miracle (2:1-12), the Samaritan responses *close* with the second Cana miracle (4:43-54). As these episodes come to an end the reader is reminded that "this was now the second sign that Jesus did when he had come from Judea to Galilee" (v. 54). This section of the story has come full cycle.

vi. Jesus and the Samaritan Woman: I (4:1-15)

1. Now when Jesus knew that the Pharisees had heard that Jesus was making and baptizing more disciples than John 2.—although Jesus himself did not baptize, but only his disciples—3. he left Judea and started back to Galilee. 4. But he had to pass through Samaria. 5. So he came to a Samaritan city called Sychar, near the field that Jacob had given to his son Joseph. 6. Jacob's well was there, and Jesus, tired out by his journey, sat down beside the well. It was about midday.
7. A woman of Samaria came to draw water, and Jesus said to her, "Give me a drink." 8. His disciples had gone away into the city to buy food. 9. The Samaritan woman said to him, "How is it that you, a Jew, ask a drink of me, a woman of Samaria?" For Jews use nothing in common with Samaritans.
10. Jesus answered her, "If you knew the gift of God, and who it is that is saying to you, 'Give me a drink,' you would have asked him, and he would have given you living water." 11. The woman said to him, "Sir, you have no bucket, and the well is deep. Where do you get that living water? 12. Are you greater than our father Jacob, who gave us the well, and with his children and his flocks drank from it?" 13. Jesus said to her, "Everyone who drinks from this water will be thirsty again, 14. but whoever drinks of the water that I will give them will never be thirsty. The

water that I will give will become in them a spring of water welling up to eternal life."
15. The woman said to him, "Sir, give me this water, so that I may never be thirsty or have to keep coming here to draw water."

INTERPRETATION

Introduction to 4:1-15. In 4:1-6 Jesus moves away from Judea on a journey to Galilee via Samaria. The motivations are given for Jesus' departure from Judea (v. 1) and for his presence in Samaria (v. 4). The time and place of the encounters that will fill vv. 7-42 are provided (vv. 5-6). This detailed introduction sets the scene for all the Samaritan episodes that follow. Once this is established, the first of two moments of encounter occurs between Jesus and a Samaritan. Jesus initiates a dialogue with the woman through the use of an imperative (v. 7: *dos moi*). He will not address her in this way again until the dialogue changes direction in v. 16 where a triple imperative appears *(hypage phōnēson . . . elthe enthade)*. In vv. 7-15 Jesus and the Samaritan woman are at cross purposes over thirst, wells, the gift of water, and life. These themes disappear in vv. 16-30, where the question of the person of Jesus and the place and nature of true worship are discussed. The first moment of Jesus' encounter with the Samaritan woman (vv. 1-15) is shaped in the following fashion:

(a) *Vv. 1-6:* General introduction and setting for 4:1-42.
(b) *Vv. 7-15:* A discussion between Jesus and a Samaritan woman.
  i. *Vv. 7-9:* An initial encounter that prepares the ground for the first discussion. Jesus asks for water. The woman responds with mocking surprise.
  ii. *Vv. 10-14:* Jesus dominates the discussion and shifts it from ordinary water to the gift from God that he can give. The woman is perplexed.
  iii. *V. 15:* The woman rejects Jesus' words, unable to discuss anything more than everyday water and journeys to the well.

There is a battle of wills in this first part of the discussion. Jesus' command arouses an arrogant response from the woman (vv. 7-9) but he wrests back the authority, speaking of a gift (cf. vv. 10-14) that the woman completely misunderstands (v. 15).

Introduction (vv. 1-6). The motivation for Jesus' departure from Judea into Galilee is the Pharisees' having heard that Jesus was making and baptizing more disciples than John (vv. 1, 3), but there is no reason why such knowledge should lead to flight from Judea. As yet there is no reason for Jesus to fear the Pharisees simply because of a successful baptismal ministry. The real problem is found in the troublesome v. 2. It is often regarded as an addition to the original Gospel, given its apparent denial of 3:22 and 4:1, but what is at stake is a proliferation of baptizers! Both historically and for the Fourth Gospel the significance of Jesus did not arise from his baptismal ministry. He is the one who makes God known (cf. 1:14, 18; 3:11-21, 31-36). He baptized (3:22; 4:1), but this ministry is carried on by the disciples, not by Jesus (v. 2). Jesus must not be known and remembered as a baptizer, however important the rite might be in the community of his followers. The narrator, who told of Jesus' baptizing ministry in 3:22, now adds a comment withdrawing Jesus from such a ministry. It is not Jesus who baptizes, but his disciples. The Pharisees have good reason to move against the religious threat of a spreading Jesus-movement. Once there was one baptizer, John (1:28); then there were two, John and Jesus (3:22-23); now there are many baptizers, all the disciples of Jesus (4:2). There is a proliferation of baptizers, and the purpose of the baptismal activity of the disciples of Jesus is to draw more people to their master. When Jesus comes to know that the Pharisees are aware of this he withdraws from Judea and heads toward Galilee.

There were two ways to make the south-north journey from Judea to Galilee: via Samaria or via the other side of the Jordan. The former was the shorter route and it was safer under the unified administration of the Romans than it had been in former times. However, it was still fraught with danger (cf. Josephus, *Ant.* 20.118; *War* 2.232). The narrator reports that Jesus was under constraint: he *had to* pass through Samaria (v. 4: *edei de auton dierchesthai dia tēs Samareias*). Geographically this is not true and it may not even have been wise. The motivation for Jesus' journey through Samaria is some constraint under which Jesus acts out his story. Although it is not clear, at this stage, why this should be the case, Jesus' presence in Samaria is the result of divine necessity. He *must* move into the world beyond Israel.

Although there is some debate over the exact location of Sychar, the narrator's description of the city, "near the field that Jacob gave to his son Joseph" (v. 5) introduces biblical and Jewish themes of the gift of water that Jacob gave (cf. Gen 48:22; cf. also Gen 33:19; Josh 24:32). This will provide important background to Jesus' discussion with the woman over wells and the gift of water (vv. 7-15). It is precisely at Jacob's well that Jesus sits, weary from the journey, at the sixth hour, the middle of the day (v. 6). Much good sense lies behind vv. 4-6. Jesus rests at a well during his long journey, at the middle of the day. However, the Samaritan location and the fact that this is Jacob's well introduce the themes of a gift and the refreshment offered by a well that transcend the simple logic of a midday stop at a well during a long journey.

Jesus asks the woman for water (vv. 7-9). A Samaritan woman appears on the scene. On two accounts Jesus should not speak to her: she is a woman and she is a Samaritan (v. 7a: *gynē ex tēs Samareias*). Yet Jesus opens the discussion with an imperative: "Give me a drink" (v. 7b). The disciples have already left the scene, gone away into the village to buy food (v. 8), and thus do not witness the scandalous encounter. This is a timely exit, and on their return the woman will flee (cf. v. 28). The woman's response highlights the irregularity of the encounter. It also has a nuance of mockery (v. 9a). Only here in the Fourth Gospel is Jesus called a *Ioudaios*. From a Samaritan point of view the woman opens her words insultingly *(pōs su Ioudaios)*. She asks how a Jew could ask for a drink from a Samaritan, and the narrator adds a point of clarification: "for Jews use nothing in common with Samaritans" (v. 9b). In this brief first moment of encounter three elements emerge. Jesus is prepared to share with the Samaritan woman (v. 7), and the theme of water is introduced (vv. 7, 9). Third, the fourfold insistence on the Samaritan side of the encounter (vv. 7, 9 [three times]) stresses that the world of the Samaritans is not the world of Judaism (cf. Sir 50:25-26; Josephus, *Ant.* 9.288–290; 10.184).

Jesus promises living water, the gift of God (vv. 10-14). Jesus does not answer the woman's question. He announces that if she knew two truths, the gift of God *(tēn dōrean theou)* and "who is speaking to you" *(tis estin ho legōn soi)*, she would need only to ask the one speaking, and "living water" would be given to her (v. 10). The two elements that form v. 10a serve as the basis for the entire discussion between Jesus and the woman. The first part of the discussion will concentrate on the living water, the gift of God (vv. 10-15: *tēn dōrean theou;* cf. v. 14), and the second will be concerned with who it is who is speaking (vv. 16-30: *tis estin ho legōn soi;* cf. v. 26).

The genitive in *tēn dorean theou* is objective, indicating that Jesus promises a gift that has its origins in God. But "living water" *(hydōr zōn)* is open to two meanings. On the one hand it can mean flowing water from a stream or spring, as opposed to the still water of a cistern or a pond. But the expression also has a long history in biblical and other religious traditions from antiquity that point beyond the physical reality of water (cf. Barrett, *Gospel* 233–234 for Jewish, Christian, and Hellenistic examples). The gift of God that the one speaking to her would give is the lifegiving revelation of the heavenly, which only Jesus makes known. He alone makes God known (1:18; 3:13) and thus offers the possibility of eternal life to those who are born again of water and the Spirit (3:5). Fruit of the saving love of God, the gift of Jesus offers the possibility of eternal life to humankind (3:16). But the woman chooses the physical meaning of "living water." Given the depth of the well and the fact that Jesus possesses no bucket she asks, more respectfully, *"kyrie . . . pothen oun echeis to hydōr to zōn"* (v. 11). The mocking title "a Jew" (v. 9) is replaced by "Sir" *(kyrie)* and the question "where from" *(pothen)* is legitimate as long as one is thinking of ordinary wells and water. But, ironically, she is asking more than she realizes. She is only able to explain the origins of the water in terms of the Jacob tradition she knows: the water in the well has its origins in the gift of the patriarch Jacob. He, his family, and his entourage drank from it and they were all satisfied with water from this well. The woman takes it for granted that the giver of the gift was Jacob, and that he cannot be surpassed.

Surely the origins of the well given by Jacob cannot be matched by this Jew: "Are you greater than our father Jacob?" (v. 12). Not only is she unable to reach beyond the physical understanding of "living water" but she is locked within her own traditions. "Her reply in vv. 11-12 is, in effect, a defence of the ancestral water" (Okure, *Johannine Approach* 99). She cannot imagine that Jesus might be greater than Jacob. Although it will receive more detailed treatment in vv. 16-30, the question of *tis estin* is already present in the woman's inability to accept that Jesus might be greater than the patriarch Jacob. She shows no openness or acceptance of Jesus' promise of the gift of God. Her inability to accept the word of Jesus becomes more evident in his further promise of vv. 13-14, and her reply in v. 15. In v. 10 Jesus spoke to the woman ("if you [singular] knew") of a gift of God. Jesus' development of this promise in vv. 13-14 addresses a universal audience, and he identifies himself as the one who gives the gift. Beginning his words with reference to everyday water, Jesus points out that everyone *(pas ho)* who drinks of the water from that well will eventually be thirsty again (v. 13). He then promises that whoever *(hos d'an)* drinks of the water that he will give will never thirst, because the gift that Jesus gives will be a spring of water welling up to eternal life (v. 14). Not only is *this water* from *this well* surpassed by the gift of Jesus, but this gift will be for all who would choose to take from it. It is associated with some future moment in the Jesus story. He "will give" *(dōsō)* it and it "will become in them *(genēsetai)* a spring of water welling up to eternal life" (v. 14). It is not *this time* that determines the gift Jesus has to give, but some time in the future when he will give a gift of water welling up to eternal life. The promise of Jesus transcends this person, this place, this water, this well, and this time.

The Woman's Response (v. 15). The response of the woman parallels that of the Jews in 2:20. She takes Jesus' words on the gift of water and the spring in v. 14 and makes them her own (cf. O'Day, *Revelation* 64–66). However, in doing so she transforms the word of Jesus from the promise of a future gift of water welling up to eternal life into her own agenda of this well, this place, and this water, satisfying her thirst: "Sir, give me this water *(touto to hydōr),* so that I may never be thirsty or have to keep coming here *(mēde dierchōmai enthade)* to draw water" (v. 15). All reference to the future gift of water that will produce eternal life disappears. The contrast between the words of Jesus and the response of the woman is obvious:

Words of Jesus	Words of the Woman
(Whoever drinks) of the water that	Give me this water,
I will give them will never be thirsty	so that I may never be thirsty
ek tou hydatos hou egō dōsō	*dos moi touto to hydōr*
autǭ ou mē dipsesę̄	*hina mē dipsō*
(The water . . .) will become in them	or have to keep coming here to
a spring of water welling up	draw water.
to eternal life.	
genēsetai en autǭ	*mēde dierchōmai*
pegē hydatos hallomenou	*enthade antlein.*
eis zōēn aiōnion.	

The words of Jesus have been misunderstood in a physical and selfish sense. As "the Jews" rejected the words of Jesus in 2:20, so does the Samaritan woman in 4:15. She too is presented, at the conclusion of this first moment of her encounter with Jesus, as having no faith. However, there is a contrast between "the Jews" and the Samaritan woman. The end response of the two characters ("the Jews" and the Samaritan woman) might be the same, as Jesus' words are rejected, but the hostility of "the Jews" is not found in the woman. Indeed, there are signs of a growing respect, as she initially addresses Jesus as "a Jew" (v. 9), but later as "Sir" (vv. 11, 15). "The Jews" disappeared from the narrative after 2:13-22, but they will return, publicly hostile, in 5:16-18. The Samaritan woman remains in the narrative. Her rejection of the word of Jesus in vv. 7-15 does not bring her role to a conclusion. She will eventually wonder whether Jesus is the Christ (cf. vv. 25, 29b) and will point other Samaritans toward Jesus (v. 29a).

NOTES

1. *Now when Jesus knew:* Equally ancient witnesses give either *ho kyrios* ("the Lord": Bodmer papyrus, Alexandrinus, and others) or *ho Iēsous* ("Jesus": Sinaiticus, Bezae, Koridethi, and others) for the first appearance of Jesus in v. 1. It is difficult to decide on the original text. It is possible that originally there was no noun, and thus both "Jesus" and "the Lord" would be secondary (cf. Brown, *Gospel* 1:164). The interpretation hesitantly chooses *ho Iēsous*, supposing that *ho kyrios* was supplied to avoid the clumsy twofold use of *Iēsous* in the one sentence (cf. Boismard and Lamouille, *Jean* 128).

2. *although Jesus himself did not baptize:* No doubt the present 4:1-6 had a long history, and v. 2 is a late part of that story. There are many indications of the secondary nature of vv. 1-3 in its present form. It is a long and unwieldy sentence, made so by the introduction of v. 2 which opens with *kaitoige* (although), a *hapax legomenon* in the NT, and uses the name "Jesus" without an article. So careful a scholar as Dodd (*Tradition* 237, 285–286) has rightly

argued that the same person cannot have written 3:22 and 4:2. Yet someone is responsible for the text as we now have it. Every effort should be made to catch the intention of the text as it comes to us before we abandon this quest and admit that the author has lost control of the sources, to conclude the passage is an incomprehensible pastiche. For a complete and critical survey of source and redactional theories, defending the unity of the text as it stands, see Leidig, *Jesu Gespräch* 1–77.

Along the lines suggested in the interpretation Loisy, *Evangile* 177, claims that vv. 1-3 have been arranged in their present form to throw the dignity of Jesus into greater light.

3. *He left Judea:* It is often objected that flight from Judea to Galilee to escape the attention of the Pharisees is pointless, as there would be Pharisees in Galilee. But the Fourth Gospel has a unique presentation of the Pharisees, closely related to the presentation of "the Jews," which may not exactly reflect the widespread presence of the Pharisees in the first century. They are seen as Jewish officials residing in Jerusalem (cf. 1:24; 7:32 [twice], 45-48; 8:13; 9:13, 15; 11:46-47, 57; 12:19, 42). See Haenchen, *John* 1:218.

4. *He had to pass through Samaria:* Not all scholars would accept the interpretation of *edei* as an indication of Jesus' response to divine constraint. Often Josephus, *Life* 269 is cited against this position. However, the passage from Josephus simply states that "for rapid travel it was essential *(edei)* to take that route." *Antiquities* 20.118 associates the shorter journey toward Jerusalem with the celebration of festivals in the city. Neither applies to John 4:4 as there is no indication of the need for a rapid journey, and Jesus' journey is away from Jerusalem. For a summary of the history of the interpretation of *edei* and a conclusion that supports the above position see Okure, *Johannine Approach* 83–86.

The interpretation regards the Samaritan encounters as representative of Jesus' presence to a non-Jewish world as the Samaritans were a people of mixed blood (cf. 2 Kgs 17:24-42). They no longer accepted a cult centered on Jerusalem and broke with the Jews who returned from Babylon (cf. the different but equally hostile reports of Nehemiah 13 and Josephus, *Ant.* 11.297–347). This situation had worsened by the time of Jesus. For a survey of the evidence see Jeremias, *Jerusalem* 352–358; Cross, "Aspects of Samaritan and Jewish History" 201–211.

5. *called Sychar:* For a survey of the various sites suggested for Sychar see Briend, "Puits" 386–398.

the field that Jacob gave to his son Joseph: The text of Gen 48:22 reads: "I now give to you one portion more than your brothers," but the word for "portion" is *shekem,* and the author reads this as the city of Shechem, as did the LXX (cf. Barrett, *Gospel* 231).

Jacob: The background of the Jacob traditions is largely ignored by the commentators. As is clear from the above interpretation, Jacob traditions are important to my reading of the text. The most important links with the Johannine tradition are found in the targums on Genesis 28–29 and Num 21:16-

18, and in *Pirqe de-Rabbi Eliezer* 35–36. See Jaubert, "La Symbolique" 1:63–73; Diaz, "Palestinian Targum" 76–77; Olsson, *Structure and Meaning* 168–173; Neyrey, "Jacob Traditions" 421–425; Léon-Dufour, *Lecture* 347–349; Perkins, *NJBC* 956–957.

6. *sat down beside the well:* The elaborate "sat down beside the well" *(ekathezeto houtōs epi tę̄ pēgę̄)* expresses a genuine settling down for a rest. The use of the verb *kathezomai* in the NT has a durative sense (Bernard, *Commentary* 1:135).

   It was about midday (the sixth hour): One cannot be sure about the enumeration of the hours in the Fourth Gospel, but there is widespread agreement among scholars that midday is meant by *hōra ēn hōs hektē*. Culpepper (*Anatomy* 219) argues that the hours of the day in the Fourth Gospel (cf. 1:39; 4:52; 19:14) are best calculated by the Roman system, starting from noon. If this is the case then 4:6 indicates 6.00 P.M.

7. *a woman of Samaria:* The description of the woman as *gynē ek tēs Samareias* is often read as an indication that the woman represents all Samaritans. The thrust of 4:7-30 is to show the response of *this* woman to the word of Jesus (cf. Okure, *Johannine Approach* 111 n. 63, 129–131). The passage as a whole (i.e., vv. 1-42) is directed to the response of Samaritans, representatives of the world beyond the borders of Israel, but this becomes clear only at the end of the passage when Samaritans make a confession of faith in Jesus (cf. v. 42).

   Give me a drink: Many critics see an evocation of OT well-scenes here (cf. Gen 24:10-19 [Isaac's servant and Rebekah]; Gen 29:1-14 [Jacob and Rachel]; Exod 2:15b-21 [Moses and Zipporah]). See, for example, Dagonet, *Selon Saint Jean* 47–53; Duke, *Irony* 101–103; Carmichael, "Marriage" 332–346; Eslinger, "The Wooing" 167–183. For the interpretation, especially in the light of the influence of Jacob traditions, there is insufficient evidence for this link. For a summary of this discussion and support for the position taken here see Okure, *Johannine Approach* 87–88.

8. *his disciples had gone away:* Critical questions can be raised. Why do all the disciples need to go to the village to purchase food, leaving Jesus alone? Why does the woman come to the well at the hottest time of the day? Such questions do not allow the author sufficient license in the construction of the drama. They become irrelevant, or at best quaint, when the literary and theological agenda of the author is fully appreciated. See O'Day, *Revelation* 50–53.

9. *For Jews use nothing in common with Samaritans:* The verb *synkraomai* is generally translated as "to have dealings with." Daube, *The New Testament* 373–382, has made a good case for the translation adopted here. See also Barrett, *Gospel* 332–333. Not all would agree (cf. Haenchen, *John* 1:219–220, and the compromise suggested by Lindars, *Gospel* 181). On the hostility between Jews and Samaritans see Str-B 2:438.

10. *If you knew the gift of God . . . who it is that is saying to you:* For a full development of the argument that the encounter between Jesus and the woman progresses along the axes of vv. 7-15 ("the gift of God") and vv. 16-26 ("who it is that is saying to you") see Okure, *Johannine Approach* 92. It had been earlier

suggested by Schmidt, "Die Komposition" 150, in 1929. For reasons that will be developed below, the second part of the encounter between Jesus and the woman is to be extended to v. 30.

The discussion of the meaning of "the gift of God" and its relationship with the "living water" is neverending. The main question is: does it refer to the gift of Jesus or to the gift of the Spirit? For the case in defense of the Spirit see Braun, "Avoir soif et boire" 249–251. More recent scholarship has tended to adopt a middle position. For example, Beasley-Murray (*John* 60) looks to 6:35, 51 and 7:37-39 to claim that it is "life mediated by the Spirit," while Olsson (*Structure and Meaning* 212–218) concludes that it is the revelation of Jesus, giving life through the action of the Spirit. Much of this depends on later teaching on the Paraclete, and the interpretation is more closely linked to the immediate context of the passage. For a survey of the discussion and support for the christological position adopted here see Okure, *Johannine Approach* 96–97.

the gift of God: A sacramental interpretation of the passage is excluded. For this see Cullmann, *Early Christian Worship* 80–84.

11. *Sir:* The use of the expression *kyrie* is an indication that she is growing in respect for Jesus. It is a first step (cf. v. 15) toward her eventual suspicion that Jesus might be the Messiah (vv. 25, 29) (cf. Friedrich, *Chi è Gesù* 35).

    the well is deep: In v. 10 Jesus spoke of "who it is that is saying to you," and then "he would have given you living water." The woman reverses the order in vv. 11-12, speaking first of the water and then asking Jesus how it relates to Jacob (cf. Léon-Dufour, *Lecture* 355).

12. *Are you greater than our father Jacob?:* The woman's question, which begins with *mē,* expects a negative answer. It is unthinkable that anyone could be greater than Jacob. The issue is that the gift of Jesus surpasses the gift of Jacob. This is important in deciding what is meant by "the gift of God" (v. 10). The focus is entirely on Jesus; there is no question of the Spirit in this comparison of the gifts of Jacob and Jesus. On Jacob as "father" of the Samaritans see Olsson, *Structure and Meaning* 139–141. The woman remains "outside" the world of Jesus and is unable to understand or accept what he is saying (cf. O'Day, *Revelation* 61–62).

    and with his children and his flocks: It is often claimed that there is no known tradition about Jacob and his children and his flocks or entourage (*thremmata* is a *hapax legomenon* and may also mean his slaves) at the well. The Jewish traditions, especially as they are reflected in the targums on Genesis 28–29, go part of the way in providing such background.

13. *Everyone who drinks from this water:* The shift from the "gift of God" and the "living water" the Samaritan woman could receive in v. 10 to the universal possibility of the gift of "eternal life" in v. 14 is made possible by means of Jesus' statement of a universal truth concerning drinking water from this well. Everyone drinking *(pas ho pinōn)* ordinary water will eventually become thirsty again. This is a universal truth that cannot be disputed.

14. *but whoever drinks:* On the basis of what has been said concerning all who drink ordinary water Jesus makes a further universal statement, but a subtle change in the form of the verb adds to the impact of his words. The change from the participle of v. 13 *(pas ho pinōn)* to the aorist subjunctive of v. 14 *(hos d'an piē)* points to a universal, once-and-for-all drinking, eliminating a continual need to return to the source of the water (cf. Barrett, *Gospel* 234). The water Jesus will give will touch the depths of the human spirit, resolving its desires and questions once and for all (cf. Lenglet, "Jésus de passage" 497–498).

of the water: The image of "water" as a spiritual gift is widespread in ancient religions (cf. Bauer, *Johannesevangelium* 68–69). It has strong links, although in a somewhat contrasting fashion, with the Wisdom traditions (cf. Bernard, *Commentary* 1:140–142).

a spring of water: Two words have been used for "well" and "spring": *phrear* (vv. 11, 12) and *pēgē* (vv. 6, 14). It is possible that Jesus may be using the correct word for the life-giving water that comes from a *pēgē* (vv. 6, 11) while the woman refers to the dead water of a *phrear* (vv. 11, 12). However, the change of expression may only be stylistic.

welling up: More than "welling up" is implied by the use of the verb *hallesthai* which generally refers to quick, leaping movements of human beings. Only here is it known to be used to describe the movement of water. This verb is probably a further link with Jewish tradition of Jacob's gift of an overflowing well. The targums use the Aramaic word *sālaq,* which means "to go up," "to pile up" (cf. Olsson, *Structure and Meaning* 182).

to eternal life: The Johannine expression *eis ton aiōna* (cf. 6:51, 58; 8:35, 51-52; 10:28; 11:26; 12:34; 13:8; 14:16) is not a promise of eternal bliss after death. It promises a fullness of life, beginning now (cf. Schnackenburg, *Gospel* 1:430–431).

15. Some critics read the woman's response as positive, as a preparedness on her part to abandon Jacob's well and accept water provided by Jesus. See, for example, Olsson, *Structure and Meaning* 182–183; Carmichael, "Marriage" 337–343; Léon-Dufour, *Lecture* 1:419. The context demands, however, that the woman be judged in terms of her acceptance or refusal of the word of Jesus. On this criterion "the first round in the conversation ends in complete failure. The woman remains level-headed, incredulous" (Boers, *Neither on this Mountain* 169).

The parallel, yet not identical rejection of the word of Jesus by "the Jews" (2:20) and the Samaritan woman (4:15) reflects the experience of the Johannine community. Cast out of the synagogue (cf. 9:22; 12:42; 16:2), the members of the Johannine community have experienced a postwar Judaism that is struggling to affirm its own identity. Part of this struggle is the rejection of the community's claim that Jesus has made God known. This ongoing hostility is reflected in John 2:13-20. The Samaritan woman, however, reflects the community's missionary experience. An initial communication of the word of Jesus might often meet puzzlement, ignorance, and rejection, but not hostility and a final exclusion of the Johannine missionary. In the (Samaritan?) mission the task goes on. This is reflected in John 4:7-15, and the continuation of Jesus' dialogue with the woman in vv. 16-30 (cf. Schnackenburg, *Gospel* 1:419; Leroy, *Rätsel und Mißverständnis* 97–99).

Lightfoot (*Gospel* 121–122) highlights a number of hints across vv. 1-15 that look forward to the passion of Jesus: weariness (cf. 19:1-2), his desire for water (19:28), and "the sixth hour" (19:14). See also Hudry-Clergeon, "De Judée en Galilée" 821–823.

Attempts to structure John 4 chiastically (cf. Roustang, "Les moments" 352; Hudry-Clergeon, "De Judée en Galilée" 830; Cahill, "Narrative Art" 42) focus too closely on John 4 as a literary unit and thus miss the important narrative and theological relationship this chapter has with John 2–3.

For Reference and Further Study

Studies of John 4:1-42 are given here.

Bligh, John. "Jesus in Samaria," *HeyJ* 3 (1962) 329–346.

Boers, Hendrikus. "Discourse Structure and Macro-Structure in the Interpretation of Texts: John 4:1-42 as an Example." In Paul Achtemeier, ed., *Society of Biblical Literature 1980 Seminar Papers*. Chico, Cal.: Scholars, 1980, 159–182.

_____. *Neither on This Mountain Nor in Jerusalem*. SBL.MS 35; Atlanta: Scholars, 1988.

Braun, François-Marie. "Avoir soif et boire (Jn 4,10-14; 7,37-39)." In Albert Descamps and André de Halleux, eds., *Mélanges Bibliques en hommage au R. P. Béda Rigaux*. Gembloux: Duculot, 1970, 247–258.

Briend, Jacques. "Puits de Jacob," *SDB* 9, cols. 386–398.

Cahill, P. Joseph. "Narrative Art in John IV," *Religious Studies Bulletin* 2 (1982) 41–48.

Carmichael, Calum M. "Marriage and the Samaritan Woman," *NTS* 26 (1979–1980) 332–346.

Cross, Frank M. "Aspects of Samaritan and Jewish History in Late Persian and Hellenistic Times," *HThR* 59 (1966) 201–211.

Dagonet, Philippe. *Selon Saint Jean: Une Femme de Samarie*. Paris: Cerf, 1979.

Daube, David. *The New Testament and Rabbinic Judaism*. London: Athlone, 1956.

Diaz, J. R. "Palestinian Targum and New Testament," *NT* 6 (1963) 75–80.

Eslinger, Lyle M. "The Wooing of the Woman at the Well: Jesus, the Reader and Reader-Response Criticism," *Literature and Theology* 1 (1987) 167–183.

Friedrich, G. *Chi è Gesù? Il messagio del quarto evangelista nella pericopa della samaritana*. Biblioteca Minima di Cultura Religiosa. Brescia: Paideia, 1975.

Hudry-Clergeon, Charles. "De Judée en Galilée: Etude de Jean 4:1-45," *NRTh* 103 (1981) 818–830.

Jaubert, Annie. "La Symbolique des Puits de Jacob. Jean 4,12." In *L'Homme devant Dieu: Mélanges offerts au Père Henri de Lubac*. 3 vols. Théologie 56. Lyon: Aubier, 1963–1964.

Jeremias, Joachim. *Jerusalem in the Time of Jesus*. London: SCM Press, 1969.

Leidig, Edeltraud. *Jesu Gespräch mit der Samaritanerin und weitere Gespräche im Johannesevangelium*. ThDiss 15. Basel: Friedrich Reinhardt, 1981.

Lenglet, Adrien. "Jésus de passage parmi les Samaritains," *Bib.* 66 (1985) 493–503.

Moloney, Francis J. *Belief in the Word* 132–145.

Neyrey, Jerome H. "Jacob Traditions and the Interpretation of John 4:10-26," *CBQ* 41 (1979) 419–437.

O'Day, Gail R. "Narrative Mode and Theological Claim: A Study in the Fourth Gospel," *JBL* 105 (1986) 657–668.

_____. *Revelation in the Fourth Gospel: Narrative Mode and Theological Claim.* Philadelphia: Fortress, 1986, 49–66.

Okure, Teresa. *The Johannine Approach to Mission: A Contextual Study of John 4:1-42.* WUNT 2nd ser. 32. Tübingen: J. C. B. Mohr (Paul Siebeck), 1988, 79–131.

Olsson, Birger. *Structure and Meaning* 115–217.

Painter, John. "Inclined to God," 346–368.

Pazdan, Mary Margaret. "Nicodemus and the Samaritan Woman: Contrasting Models of Discipleship," *BTB* 17 (1987) 145–148.

Roustang, François. "Les moments de l'acte de foi et ses conditions de possibilité. Essai d'interpretation du dialogue avec la Samaritaine," *RSR* 46 (1958) 344–378.

Schneiders, Sandra M. *The Revelatory Text.* San Francisco: Harper, 1994, 180–199.

vii. Jesus and the Samaritan Woman: II (4:16-30)

16. Jesus said to her, "Go, call your husband, and come back." 17. The woman answered him, "I have no husband." Jesus said to her, "You are right in saying, 'I have no husband'; 18. for you have had five husbands, and the one you have now is not your husband. What you have said is true!" 19. The woman said to him, "Sir, I perceive that you are a prophet.

20. Our ancestors worshiped on this mountain, but you say that the place where people must worship is in Jerusalem." 21. Jesus said to her, "Woman, believe me, the hour is coming when you will worship the Father neither on this mountain nor in Jerusalem. 22. You worship what you do not know; we worship what we know, for salvation is from the Jews. 23. But the hour is coming, and now is, when the true worshipers will worship the Father in spirit and in truth, for such the Father seeks to worship him. 24. God is spirit, and those who worship him must worship in spirit and in truth." 25. The woman said to him, "I know that Messiah is coming, he who is called Christ. When he comes, he will show us all things." 26. Jesus said to her, "'I am' is the one speaking to you."

27. Just then his disciples returned. They were dumbfounded that he was speaking with a woman, but no one said, "What do you want?" or, "Why are you speaking with her?" 28. So the woman left her water jar and went back to the city. She said to the people, 29. "Come and see a man who told me everything I have ever done. Can this be the Christ?" 30. They went out of the village and were coming to him.

INTERPRETATION

Introduction to 4:16-30. The first part of the encounter between Jesus and the Samaritan woman (vv. 7-15) developed the theme stated in v. 10a: "the gift of God" *(tēn dōrean tou theou)*. The second moment unfolds the theme of 10b: "Who it is that is saying to you" *(tis estin ho legōn soi)*. There is a smooth passage from v. 15, with the woman's asking that she no longer "come here" *(dierchōmai enthade)* and Jesus' command, in v. 16, that she call her husband and "come here" *(elthe enthade)*. The imperatives in v. 16 mark the beginning of the section, and most critics see v. 26 as its closure. There, catching up the words of v. 10b, Jesus tells the woman, "'I am' is the one speaking to you" *(egō eimi ho lalōn soi)*. But this leaves vv. 27-30 linked neither with the encounter between Jesus and the woman (vv. 16-26) nor with what follows (vv. 31-38). The disciples' silent puzzlement (v. 27) and the woman's continued wondering in her return to the village (vv. 28-29) are better seen as the continuation of the issue of Jesus' identity (cf. v. 10b). The section closes as the Samaritan villagers set out to the place where Jesus is to be found (v. 30). They will be approaching Jesus as he speaks to his disciples in vv. 31-38.

There are indications that the literary structure of vv. 16-30, Jesus' second encounter with the Samaritan woman, parallels the first (vv. 7-15), although the theme shifts from the gift of living water (cf. v. 10a) to the identity of the person of Jesus (cf. v. 10b). It unfolds in the following fashion:

(a) *Vv. 16-19:* Jesus' initiative reopens a faltering discussion. The woman's response raises the issue of the identity of Jesus.

(b) *Vv. 20-26:* Jesus takes the initiative and shifts the discussion away from prophecy to true worship. This leads to a progression in the woman's understanding of Jesus. She suspects that Jesus might be the long-awaited Messiah. In response to this confession Jesus reveals himself as *egō eimi* ("I am").

(c) *Vv. 27-30:* The disciples' return leads to the woman's departure. But her words to the Samaritan villagers show that she has not been able to grasp the full significance of Jesus' self-revelation. The Samaritans set out to make their own discovery.

The two moments in Jesus' encounter with the Samaritan woman (vv. 7-15 and 16-30) are marked by the following parallels:

1. A relationship is established, initiated by a command from Jesus (vv. 7-9 // vv. 16-20).
2. Jesus' words transcend the apparent basis of the relationship (v. 10 // vv. 21-24).
3. The woman makes an intermediate response to Jesus' words (vv. 11-12 // v. 25).

4. A final intervention from Jesus (vv. 13-14 // v. 26).
5. The woman's concluding response (v. 15 // vv. 28-29).

Despite the literary links there is an important difference between vv. 7-15 and vv. 16-30. In v. 15 the Samaritan woman rejects the word of Jesus, while in v. 25 and v. 29 she suggests that Jesus might fit her categories of Messiah-Christ. Only the final remark from the narrator, telling of the movement of the Samaritans toward Jesus does not have a parallel in vv. 7-15. It will serve as important background for Jesus' words to the disciples in vv. 31-38, and opens the way for their response to Jesus, reported in vv. 39-42.

Jesus the prophet (vv. 16-19). Jesus' threefold command, "go . . . call . . . come" (v. 16) changes the direction of a faltering discussion. The woman's marital situation becomes the immediate focus of concern, and the question of the gift of water disappears. The woman's reply, that she has no husband (v. 17a), is to be regarded as an accurate reflection of her situation. She regards herself as not married to the man with whom she is currently living. Jesus compliments her for telling the truth: "You say well *(kalōs eipas)* 'I have no husband'" (v. 17b). He then proceeds to tell her of the details of her marital history in a way that parallels his earlier revelation of Nathanael's private life (1:48; cf. Okure, *Johannine Approach* 110–113). She has lived an irregular married life and is currently in a sinful situation, but the point of v. 18 is not to lay bare her sinfulness. There is no need to read the five husbands symbolically. The focus is on Jesus' power to know the secrets of her intimate life. Jesus' further compliment, telling her that what she has said has been said truly (v. 18c: *touto alēthes eirēkas*), demands that the story of the woman's inner life be read as a statement of fact. Jesus' knowledge of these "facts" is the turning point of the narrative. His claim to give living water was beyond her grasp, but a person who tells her about the secrets of her life commands her attention. She shows the first signs of openness to Jesus as she confesses: "Sir, I perceive that you are a prophet" (v. 19). There is no definite article before "prophet" and the woman's use of the verb "to perceive" *(theōreō)* makes this a limited confession. No deep spiritual insight is present in her coming to the conviction that this man must have prophetic qualities. However, there is a marked progression from her addressing him as "a Jew" (v. 9) and "sir" (vv. 11, 15, 19a). Her suggestion that Jesus might be a Jewish prophet raises a further issue, which she broaches, but that Jesus transcends (vv. 20-26).

Jesus transcends the woman's beliefs (vv. 20-26). A Jewish prophet, belonging to a tradition famous for its defense of the cult of YHWH in Jerusalem, must be challenged in the unlikely event of a dialogue with a Samaritan. The woman raises the question of Gerizim and Jerusalem (v.

20) not to steer Jesus away from her personal secrets but, on the basis of her perception that Jesus is a prophet, to delve into "an age-old problem debated between Samaritans and Jews" (Schnackenburg, *Gospel* 1:434; cf. *Gen. Rab.* 32.10; 81.9). All interest in the woman's marital situation disappears from the narrative as the person and role of Jesus as "prophet" are at stake. "As a prophet, He should know" (Lightfoot, *Gospel* 123).

Jesus' response to this comment from the woman transcends her limited notion of his being a Jewish prophet and her commitment to local traditions attached to Mount Gerizim, in whose shadow the dialogue is taking place. He attempts to draw the woman into a deeper understanding of his person and role, introducing his response with the words, "Woman, believe me" (v. 21a: *pisteue moi, gynē*). This appeal is followed by a promise of a future time when the debate between the Jews and the Samaritans will become irrelevant. The woman might be waiting for the revelation of a new "place," but Jesus has spoken of the worship of God as the worship of "the Father" (v. 21c). In v. 12 the woman spoke of Jacob's gift to his sons and asked if Jesus was greater than this "father"; in v. 20 she challenges Jesus to better "the ancestors [fathers]" who worshiped on Gerizim. Such notions are eclipsed by Jesus' words on the worship of God as worship of "the Father." The questions of the "place" that transcends Gerizim and Jerusalem, and "when" this might happen, remain.

Before resolving those questions, however, Jesus speaks to the immediate situation of the Samaritan woman and "the Jew" (v. 22). Jesus is a Jew, and he speaks strongly of the superiority of the Jewish traditions. They bear within them the authentic revelation of God, while the vague Samaritan traditions have no such authority. Jesus owns his origins among the Jewish people by using the plural "we," as he criticizes the Samaritan people and their traditions with the use of the plural "you." Jesus is part of a long tradition in which God has made himself known. Not only is he part of that story, but the man whom the woman had earlier called "a Jew" (v. 9) is the one who brings salvation. In the Jew, Jesus, salvation has come: salvation is from the Jews (v. 22b). This is an encounter between Jesus and the non-Jewish world (cf. vv. 4, 7, 9), and thus the traditions of Judaism, culminating in the salvation that Jesus brings, and the traditions of Samaritanism are contrasted. Jesus is revealing himself and the way to the Father to a non-Jewish world.

The theme first broached in v. 21 returns. There Jesus spoke of a new time and place for the worship of the Father. Johannine realized eschatology appears as Jesus first informs the woman of the new time: "The hour is coming *and now is*" (v. 23a). What Jesus is about to announce as the new "place" for true worship is already present because Jesus is present. In this present time, when both Gerizim and Jerusalem are transcended, the true worshiper worships the Father in spirit and in truth, but it is the Father who seeks out such worshipers. The act of worshiping is described by the use of the verb *proskynein*. It implies the act of bending or prostrating oneself in the direction of the one worshiped. In this context, where holy mountains and their sanctuaries are being excluded, true worship is the orientation of oneself toward the Father in such a way that God becomes the imperative of one's life. The expression "in spirit and in truth" combines important Johannine terms (cf. already in the narrative, 1:9, 14, 17; 3:3-5, 21) to insist that Jesus reveals a God and Father who is to be worshiped with one's life. The Father seeks out *(zētei)* true worshipers (v. 23c). "The 'seeking' by the Father signifies, not a passive desire on his part, but his causative action in the individual without which a genuine human response is impossible" (Okure, *Johannine Approach* 116). The basis for all that Jesus has taught the Samaritan woman is the way God acts. God is not a mountain, a place, or a sanctuary. God is spirit (v. 24a), an all-pervading personal presence to the believer. This may be remarkable language for the Samaritan woman but it has appeared in earlier treatments of Jesus' creative life-giving presence (cf. 1:12-13; 3:3-8). The hour has now come when the only acceptable act of worship *(dei proskynein)* is the total orientation of one's life and action toward the Father, sharing already in the gift of the Father *(en pneumati)*, a gift that is all that it claims to be *(kai alētheia)*.

Jesus' response to the traditional question of the right place of worship, Gerizim or Jerusalem, transcends what the woman might expect from "a prophet" (cf. v. 19). Jesus' identity (cf. v. 10b) is still to be discovered, so she hesitatingly falls back on another of her traditions. In an exact parallel with Nicodemus (cf. 3:2: *oidamen hoti*), she says "I know that *(oida hoti)* Messiah is coming, he who is called Christ; when he comes he will show us all things" (v. 25). It is often asserted that the Samaritan figure of the *Ta[?]eb* stands behind the woman's use of the terms "Messiah" and "Christ," as it can be claimed that the *Ta[?]eb* was a figure who would show all things. One cannot discount that this Samaritan background may be present, but it is fraught with difficulties (cf. note on v. 25). The woman raises the question of a Messiah and Christ without using the definite article, as she did when she accepted that Jesus was a prophet (cf. v. 19). Both the Semitic and the Greek words for an anointed figure, on the lips of the woman, take her growth in the understanding of Jesus a step further. She has addressed Jesus as "a Jew" (v. 9), "Sir" (vv. 11, 15, 19a), "a prophet" (v. 19b), and now she suggests that he might be "a Messiah-Christ" (v. 25). The criterion the woman offers for her burgeoning messianic confession is "he will show us all things." Jesus' knowledge of her private life (cf. vv. 16-18) still dazzles her. She makes no reference to the more recent part of her discussion with Jesus, true worship and the proclamation that salvation comes from the Jews (vv. 21-24). Jesus has told her that the possibility of true worship "now is" (v. 23), but the woman ignores this possibility, suggesting that Jesus might be the Messiah-Christ who is to come: "when he comes, he will show us all things" (v. 25b).

Most critics (and English translations) see Jesus' response in v. 26 as an acceptance of the woman's suggestion that he might be the Christ: "I who speak to you am he" (RSV). This does not appear to be the case. In v. 10b the agenda for vv. 16-30 was set: *tis estin ho legōn soi* ("who it is who is saying to you"). Jesus' response to the woman's suggestion answers the question of the *tis estin*, "who is it?" Repeating the words of v. 10b, the query of the first two words is replaced with the formula of revelation *egō eimi ho legōn soi* ("'I AM' [is] the one speaking to you." Cf. NRSV: "I am he, the one who is speaking to you."). Who is the person speaking to the woman? Jesus' answer is: *egō eimi*. One of the author's major claims for Jesus (cf. 8:24, 28, 58; 13:19; 18:5) appears for the first time (cf. note on v. 26). The expression has a long history in the literature of Israel. Its distant roots lie in the revelation of God's name to Moses in Exod 3:14, but the expression became particularly important to the prophets (cf. especially Isa 43:10; 45:18). It has always been used to refer to the living presence of God who makes himself known among his people. In a way that parallels Jesus' attempts to lead Nicodemus beyond the limitations of his understanding of Jesus (cf. 3:1-10), he challenges her to transcend the conclusion she has reached because he told her the secrets of her intimate life. The identity of Jesus (v. 10b: *tis estin*) reaches beyond a Messiah-Christ. He is the one who makes known the living God (v. 26). Because this is true Jesus has been able to tell the woman "The hour is coming, and now is, when true worshipers will worship the Father in spirit and in truth" (v. 23a). Jesus' words on true worship and his self-revelation as I AM have not been understood by the Samaritan woman (cf. v. 29).

The Disciples Return (vv. 27-30). The unresolved christological confession of the woman is part of the disciples' experience as they return to the scene and marvel that Jesus is talking with a woman (v. 27a). The disciples join a scene already almost at its conclusion. The imperfect use of the verb "to speak" *(elalei)* shows that the disciples are aware that Jesus has been speaking to this woman for some time. Their wonder is expressed through the emotion-laden verb *thaumazein*. They are shocked. Despite their amazement and shock they say nothing, and the narrator has to state their unspoken questions for them: "What do you want? . . . Why are you speaking with her?" (v. 27b). Behind these unspoken questions lurks the disciples' puzzlement: who is this man Jesus? "The awe of his friends makes the mystery of the revealer stand out more strongly" (Schnackenburg, *Gospel* 1:443; cf. O'Day, *Revelation* 74–75).

The woman flees, leaving her water jar behind. This detail has been the subject of considerable speculation. It is simply a sign that although she may have departed from the scene the Samaritan story has not yet come to an end. The woman's jar is still with Jesus as she returns to the village and repeats to her fellow-villagers what she said to Jesus: "Come, see a man who told me all that I ever did. Can this be the Christ?" (v. 29). She invites them to see "a man," and repeats the grounds for her suspicion that he might be the Christ: Jesus' knowledge of her marital situation and his telling her all that she ever did. The question she poses to her fellow-villagers expresses her ongoing uncertainty about the identity of Jesus: *mēti houtos estin ho christos* (cf. note on v. 29). It is on the basis of the words of the woman (v. 29), which repeat what she had said earlier to Jesus (cf. v. 25), that the Samaritans left the village (aorist tense) and set out toward Jesus (imperfect tense). But they will have their own response to the word of Jesus, which will transcend the words of the woman (vv. 39-42). As they move toward Jesus, he addresses his shocked disciples.

The Samaritan woman's response to Jesus in vv. 7-15 was to reject the word of Jesus. Although lacking the hostility of the rejection Jesus met from "the Jews" (cf. 2:13-22), her first moment of encounter with Jesus repeats the unbelieving response of "the Jews." Her further discussion with Jesus parallels Nicodemus' struggle to reach beyond the limitations of his own history, religion, and culture (3:1-10). She is prepared to accept that he might be "a prophet" (v. 19) and even "a Messiah-Christ" (v. 25), but she can go no further even though Jesus makes himself known to her as I AM (v. 26). She is still asking, as the episode closes, "Can this be the Christ?" (v. 29). Like Nicodemus she has arrived at a partial, conditioned belief in Jesus.

NOTES

16. *go . . . call . . . come:* The imperatives on the lips of Jesus, repeating his original initiative in v. 7, are an obvious marker of a new section. The radical change of direction in the conversation as Jesus asks her to bring her husband to him is a further sign that the encounter has entered another phase.

17. *I have no husband:* John Bligh ("Jesus in Samaria" 335–336) suggests that these words indicate she has marital designs on Jesus. There is insufficient evidence in the text for this claim, especially in the light of the interpretation's rejection of links between this encounter and the tradition of OT well-scenes. See note to v. 7. Okure (*Johannine Approach* 108–110) argues that it is the woman's way of trying to bring the discussion to a close.

18. *you have had five husbands:* Much is made of the five husbands, a number beyond the possibilities allowed by Jewish practice (cf. Str-B 2:437), as a possible symbolic use of the number five to refer to the five gods of Samaria (cf. Josephus, *Ant.* 9.288), or the five books of the Samaritan Pentateuch (Origen, *In Johannem* 13.8 [MPG 14:410–411]), or the five foreign cities that brought their

gods (there were in fact seven, but recourse is had to Josephus for the number five) with them (cf. 2 Kgs 17:27-31). The man with whom she is presently living, who is not her husband, has been identified with Simon Magus (cf. Purvis, "The Fourth Gospel" 193–195). These symbolic readings are widespread among those who see the Samaritan woman as a representative figure for all Samaritans (cf. Loisy, *Evangile* 182; Cullmann, "Samaria" 187–188). In the light of Jesus' comments in v. 17 ("you are right in saying") and v. 18 ("this you said truly"), Barrett (*Gospel* 235) is correct when he comments: "It is quite possible, and may well be right, to take these words as a simple statement of fact, and an instance of the supernatural knowledge of Jesus."

19. *Sir, I perceive:* For *theōreō* as a verb that indicates arrival at intellectual perception from growing experience see BAGD 360, s.v. *theōreō*, par. 1.

    that you are a prophet: Some see her acceptance of Jesus as "a prophet" as a reference to the Samaritans' messianic expectation on the basis of their interpretation of Deut 18:15-19 (cf. Boismard, *Moïse ou Jésus* 29–30, 67–68).

20. *Our ancestors worshiped on this mountain:* Samaritan tradition locates Abraham's sacrifice of Isaac, and Jacob's vision, on Mount Gerizim. The *shekinā* associated with the Mosaic revelation also dwells there, even though by the time of Jesus the temple on the mountain had long since been destroyed (by John Hyrcanus in 128 B.C.E.). On these and other claims for Mount Gerizim see Montgomery, *The Samaritans* 236–239; Hall, *Samaritan Religion* 229–232.

21. *Woman, believe me:* Not all would accept that this is a genuine request from Jesus that the woman be open to a deeper understanding of his person and role. For some (e.g., Bernard, *Commentary* 1:146) it is equivalent to the use of the double "amen." For the position adopted see, for example, Schnackenburg, *Gospel* 1:435; Dagonet, *Selon Saint Jean* 98–99.

22. *You worship what you do not know; we worship what we know:* Some have claimed that the "you" and "we" reflect Jews and Samaritans ("you") over against Jesus and his followers ("we"). For a history of this discussion see de la Potterie, "Nous adorons" 78–85. In defense of the interpretation given above, that the words of Jesus reflect his support of Jewish traditions over against Samaritan traditions, see Leidig, *Jesu Gespräch* 103–133.

    for salvation is from the Jews: The Johannine Jesus speaks in coherence with the rest of the early Church, which was never ashamed of the fact that its origins lay within the story of the Jewish people (cf. Brown, *Gospel* 1:172). Many critics disagree, and regard v. 22 as a gloss, as it is not consistent with what is said about "the Jews" throughout the Gospel (e.g. Bauer, *Johannesevangelium* 70; Bultmann, *Gospel* 189–190 n. 6). For detailed criticism of this position see Leidig, *Jesu Gespräch* 49–70. Much attention has been given to this verse in recent time. See, for example, Thyen, "Das Heil" 163–184; Hahn, "Das Heil" 67–84; Haacker, "Gottesdienst ohne Gotteserkenntnis" 110–126; Betz, "To Worship God" 53–72. For a detailed summary and a comprehensive presentation of the history of salvation and christological perspectives that lie behind the interpretation offered above see de la Potterie, "Interprétation de Jn 4,22" 85–115.

23. *the hour is coming and now is:* This is the first use of an expression that accurately describes the balance between traditional end-time eschatology and the more Johannine realized eschatology. The expression "brackets future and present without eliminating either" (Beasley-Murray, *John* 62).

true worshipers will worship: The verb "to worship" *(proskynein)* is closely related to the Hebrew verb *hishtahawā*, used to speak of a cultic inclining of oneself or a physical bending down. See Greeven, *"proskynein"* 6:760–761; Okure, *Johannine Approach* 116.

in spirit and in truth: The narrative has already told of the revelation of the true word (1:9) become flesh as the fullness of a gift that is truth (1:14, 17). In his encounter with Nicodemus, which has parallels with 4:16-30, Jesus promised that those who are born again of water and the Spirit (3:3-5) are caught up into the mystery of God that has no determined beginning or end (3:9-10), and they live in the light and do the truth (3:21). This background determines the meaning of worshiping "in spirit and in truth" as unconditional worship of God with one's life. See Otto Betz, "To Worship God" 53–72; Schnackenburg, "Die 'Anbetung in Geist und Wahrheit'" 88–94; Freed, "The Manner of Worship" 33–48.

for such the Father seeks to worship him: The initiative of the Father, acting in the believer to generate an unconditional openness to God, has been described by Barrett (*Gospel* 238): "This clause has as much claim as 20:30f. to be regarded as expressing the purpose of the Gospel."

24. *must worship:* The use of *dei proskynein* indicates that this is the only possible way to worship God properly. The unconditional and total directing of one's life toward God is the only acceptable act of worship.

25. *I know:* Some ancient witnesses read "we know" *(oidamen)*, reflecting the early interpretation that the woman's words reflect Samaritan belief in general. These witnesses have probably been influenced by the *oidamen* of v. 22 and/or the "will tell us *(hēmin)* all things" at the end of the sentence. The singular must be retained (cf. Haenchen, *John* 223–224).

I know that Messiah is coming, he who is called Christ: Some critics read "who is called the Christ" as a translation of the Hebrew/Aramaic expression "Messiah," added parenthetically to the words of the woman (e.g., Barrett, *Gospel* 239). The interpretation reads the whole sentence as coming from the woman (cf. Bultmann, *Gospel* 192 n. 2).

When he comes, he will show us all things: The Samaritan *Taʾeb* would tell of secrets hitherto unknown, and many have seen a close link between the woman's words and Samaritan messianic expectation (cf. Lagrange, *Evangile* 115; Schnackenburg, *Gospel* 1:441; Bowman, "Samaritan Studies I" 299; Sabugal, *Christos* 226–232). But the earliest known written source that mentions the *Taʾeb* is the *Memar Markah*, which dates from the fourth century C.E. The earliest manuscript we have of this document dates from the fourteenth century. See McDonald, *The Theology* 42–43; Purvis, "The Fourth Gospel" 162–168. For a recent survey of the possible evidence for the figure in John 4, Josephus, and the Samaritans see Hall, *Samaritan Religion* 226–327. Hall concludes: "The evidence fails to establish even the probability—although it does not preclude the possibility—that some form of messianic belief existed among the Samaritans at that time" (pp. 298–299). See also the full-scale study of Dexinger, *Der Taheb*. He also concludes that more evidence is needed to link the Samaritan Pentateuch's use of the prophet like Moses in Deut 18:18 and the fourth-century *Taʾeb*.

all things: Critics discuss whether "all things" *(hapanta)* refers to Jesus' earlier knowledge of her marital situation (cf. v. 18), his discussion of true worship (vv. 21-24), or both. The narrative, especially vv. 27-30, 39-42, demands that "all things" refers only to v. 18, as it is associated with things that she has done (cf. v. 29).

26. *"I am" is the one speaking to you:* Most critics and translations interpret Jesus' response as an acceptance of the woman's suggestion that he might be the Messiah (cf. Westcott, *Gospel* 73–74; Lagrange, *Evangile* 115; Barrett, *Gospel* 239; Segalla, *Giovanni* 196–197; Leidig, *Jesu Gespräch* 154–155; Haenchen, *John* 1:224). Some suggest that it is both an acceptance of the woman's suggestions and the use of a term "in which Jesus reveals his divine being" (Schnackenburg, *Gospel* 1:442. Cf. also Brown, *Gospel* 172–173, 177; Freed, "*Egō eimi* in John 1:20" 289–290). Boers, *Neither on This Mountain* 178–179, offers a further alternative. The woman's statement (v. 25) is a "negative sanction" showing her conviction that Jesus is not the expected Messiah. Jesus' reply (v. 26) affirms that he is. The interpretation above is based on the conviction that Jesus either accepts or transcends the woman's suggestion. The narrative as a whole, especially when this section is read through to v. 30, demands that Jesus transcends the woman's confession in a way she does not understand. Only Bultmann (*Gospel* 192) sees v. 26 as a use of *egō eimi* as a revelatory formula. He also follows the narrative down to v. 30.

    The absolute use of *egō eimi* is hardly an expression of divinity or a revelation "of his divine being" (Schnackenburg, *Gospel* 1:442). See also Neyrey, *An Ideology of Revolt* 213–220. As with its use against idols of foreign gods in Second Isaiah (e.g., Isa 43:10; 45:18), it announces that in Jesus the revelation of the divinity takes place. The difference is slight but important, as in the former Jesus is metaphysically associated with the divinity, while in the latter it is his oneness with God that makes him the consummate revelation of God. This interpretation accords with the earlier reading of the Prologue, especially 1:1-2 (cf. Moloney, *NJBC* 1423–1424).

27. *they were dumbfounded:* For the use of the verb *thaumazein* to express amazement see BAGD 352. The translation "dumbfounded" is taken from Okure, *Johannine Approach* 133. For a summary of the Jewish evidence that would make Jesus' discussion so shocking see Barrett, *Gospel* 240. Sexual innuendo is not far from the surface in the disciples' unspoken questions: "What do you want? . . . Why are you speaking with her?" This is the last thing they would expect from the Jesus with whom they had been associated in 1:35-51; 2:1-12, 13-25.

28. *So the woman left her water jar:* The water jar has exercised the imaginations of centuries of commentators. Suggestions vary from a sign of her ongoing

sexual interest in Jesus to a symbol of her preparedness to be filled by the revelation Jesus will give. Her ongoing presence in the narrative is assured by
the words of the Samaritans to her in vv. 39-42. Thus the jar is a sign that she
will return to the story. See also Westcott, *Gospel* 74; Lindars, *Gospel* 193;
Becker, *Evangelium* 1:179; O'Day, *Revelation* 75.

29. *Can this be the Christ?:* The question opens with the expression *mēti* which
"introduces a hesitant question" (Barrett, *Gospel* 240). BDF 221 §427.2 suggests that the question hints at unlikelihood. The use of this expression tells
against those who claim, despite the grammatical difficulties, that v. 29 reflects "complete belief in Jesus" (Okure, *Johannine Approach* 169). "The Samaritan woman in the text is neither a missionary nor a true believer" (van den
Bussche, *Jean* 195).

The difficulties created by vv. 28-30, when v. 26 is read as Jesus' climactic
acceptance of the woman's messianic confession, are sometimes resolved by
rearrangement, or source theories. For example Haenchen (*John* 1:224) claims
that vv. 28-30 followed v. 18 in the evangelist's source. Thus the woman
makes no reference to the discussion of true worship, which was added by
the evangelist (along with the rest of vv. 19-27) to the source. Such suggestions impoverish the narrative, which must be read very closely *in its present
shape* to discover what its author is trying to say to the reader.

30. *They went out of the village and were coming to him:* The use of the aorist tense
(*exēlthon*) indicates a decisive departure from their place of origin. There is a
certain alacrity in the response of the Samaritans to the words of the woman.
The imperfect tense (*ērchonto*) indicates that they were in a protracted journey
toward Jesus. As the passage ends the movement toward Jesus is unfinished.
This is relevant background for Jesus' words to his disciples in vv. 31-38, and
especially for v. 35: "Lift up your eyes, and see how the fields are already
white for harvest."

FOR REFERENCE AND FURTHER STUDY

See also studies of 4:1-42 in the bibliography following the commentary on 4:1-15
Betz, Otto. "'To Worship in Spirit and in Truth': Reflections on John 4:20-26." In
 Asher Finkel and Lawrence Frizzel, eds., *Standing Before God: Studies on
 Prayer in Scriptures and in Tradition with Essays in Honor of John M. Oester-
 reicher.* New York: Ktav, 1981, 53–72.
Bowman, John. "Samaritan Studies I: The Fourth Gospel and the Samaritans,"
 BJRL 40 (1958) 298–327.
Cullmann, Oscar. "Samaria and the Origins of the Christian Mission." In A.J.B.
 Higgins, ed., *The Early Church.* London: SCM Press, 1956, 185–192.
Dexinger, Ferdinand. *Der Taheb. Ein "messianischer" Heilsbringer der Samaritaner.*
 Kairos, Religionswissenschaftliche Studien 3. Salzburg: Otto Müller, 1986.
Freed, Edwin D. "*Egō eimi* in John 1:20 and 4:25," *CBQ* 41 (1979) 288–291.

_____. "The Manner of Worship in John 4:23f." In *Search the Scriptures: New Testament Studies in Honor of Raymond T. Stamm.* Gettysburg Theological Studies 3. Leiden: E. J. Brill, 1969, 33–48.

Greeven, Heinrich. *"proskyneō," TDNT* 6:658–666.

Haacker, Klaus. "Gottesdienst ohne Gotteserkenntnis: Joh 4:22 vor dem Hintergrund des jüdisch-samaritanischen Auseinandersetzung." In Brigitta Benzing, Otto Böcher, and Gunter Mayer, eds., *Wort und Wirklichkeit: Studien zur Afrikanistik und Orientalistik Eugen Ludwig Rapp zum 70. Geburtstag Herausgegeben.* Meisenheim: Hain, 1976, 110–126.

Hahn, Ferdinand. "Das Heil kommt von den Juden: Erwägungen zu Joh 4,22b." In Brigitta Benzing, Otto Böcher, and Gunter Mayer, eds., *Wort und Wirklichkeit: Studien zur Afrikanistik und Orientalistik Eugen Ludwig Rapp zum 70. Geburtstag Herausgegeben.* Meisenheim: Hain, 1976, 67–84.

Hall, B. W. *Samaritan Religion from John Hyrcanus to Baba Rabba: A critical examination of the relevant material in contemporary Christian literature, the writings of Josephus, and the Mishnah.* Studies in Judaica 3. Sydney: Sydney University Press, 1987.

La Potterie, Ignace de. "'Nous adorons, nous, ce que nous connaissons, car le salut vient des Juifs': Histoire de l'exégèse et interpretation de Jn 4,22," *Bib.* 64 (1983) 74–115.

McDonald, John. *The Theology of the Samaritans.* London: SCM Press, 1964.

Moloney, Francis J. *Belief in the Word* 145–158.

Montgomery, J. A. *The Samaritans: The Earliest Jewish Sect: Their History, Theology and Literature.* Philadelphia: John C. Winston, 1907.

O'Day, Gail R. *Revelation in the Fourth Gospel* 66–77.

Okure, Teresa. *The Johannine Approach to Mission: A Contextual Study of John 4:1-42.* WUNT 2nd ser. 32. Tübingen: J. C. B. Mohr (Paul Siebeck), 1988, 79–131.

Olsson, Birger. *Structure and Meaning* 115–217.

Purvis, J. D. "The Fourth Gospel and the Samaritans," *NT* 17 (1975) 161–198.

Schnackenburg, Rudolf. "Die 'Anbetung in Geist und Wahrheit' (Joh 4:23) im Lichte vom Qumran-Texten," *BZ* 3 (1959) 88–94.

Thyen, Hartwig. "Das Heil kommt von den Juden." In Dieter Lührmann and Georg Strecker, eds., *Kirche: Festschrift für Günther Bornkamm zum 75. Geburtstag.* Tübingen: J. C. B. Mohr (Paul Siebeck), 1980, 163–184.

viii. Jesus' Comment (4:31-38)

31. Meanwhile the disciples besought him, saying, "Rabbi, eat." 32. But he said to them, "I have food to eat of which you do not know." 33. So the disciples said to one another, "Has anyone brought him food?" 34. Jesus said to them, "My food is to do the will of him who sent me, and to complete his work."

35. "Do you not say, 'Four months more, then comes the harvest'? I tell you, lift up your eyes, and see how the fields are already white for har-

vest. 36. The one who reaps receives wages, and gathers fruit for eternal life, so that sower and reaper may rejoice together. 37. For here the saying holds true, 'One sows and another reaps.' 38. I sent you to reap that for which you did not labor. Others have labored, and you have entered into their labor."

INTERPRETATION

Introduction to 4:31-38. The disciples' request that Jesus eat something and their wondering about the source of his nourishment leads into his comment that initially explains why he makes God known outside Israel and then tells the disciples that they must also be part of this mission. While this brief discourse is taking place the Samaritans are on their way toward the group (cf. v. 30). Jesus draws the disciples' attention to them (v. 35), and their arrival brings the discourse to a close (vv. 39-40). The discourse responds to wondering disciples and unfolds in the following fashion:

(a) *Vv. 31-33:* The disciples' command that Jesus eat some of their food leads to puzzlement concerning the source for Jesus' unique nourishment.

(b) *V. 34:* Jesus' answer to their wondering is the basis of his mission and serves as a starting point for the mission of the disciples.

(c) *Vv. 35-38:* A proverb on harvesting and a conclusion instruct the disciples on their future missionary activity.

The response Jesus gives to the disciples reaches beyond the characters in the story. In vv. 35-38 Jesus addresses his audience as "you" (*hymeis:* plural). Along with the disciples *in the story,* the readers *of the story* are addressed as Jesus provides the theological underpinning for his life and ministry (v. 34) and invites them to accept the challenge of mission (vv. 35-38). Although vv. 31-38 are occasioned by the disciples in vv. 31-33, Jesus' response in vv. 34-38 does not address the questions raised by the immediate situation of his presence at the well without any observable nourishment. It serves as commentary from Jesus on all that has happened thus far in the Samaritan section of the journey from Cana to Cana (2:1–4:54), just as 2:23-25 served as commentary from the narrator on all that had happened in the Jewish section of that journey.

The disciples' puzzlement (vv. 31-33). The very first phrase "meanwhile" (*en tō metaxu*) indicates that the encounter that follows is an "intermezzo." The adverbial use of the expression *metaxu* ("between, in the middle, what lies between") is rare in the NT (cf. Acts 13:42), but it catches exactly the role of the events and words that take place "in between" the departure of the woman (vv. 27-30) and the advent of the Samaritans (vv. 39-40).

Paralleling the first moment of the two encounters between Jesus and the Samaritan woman, this episode begins with an imperative form of the verb. The disciples beseechingly insist (*ērōtōn . . . legontes*) with Jesus, whom they continue to call "Rabbi" (cf. 1:38, 49; 3:2): "eat!" (*phage:* imperative mood). The disciples left Jesus at the well to buy food (v. 8), but on their return they find that he will not respond to their command (v. 31). Jesus' response leads them beyond the categories of ordinary food. He speaks of a food (*brōsin*) that he always has (*echō:* present tense) to eat (*phagein*), but of which they do not know (v. 32). They remain in that situation of unknowing because they refuse to be led beyond the notion of the physical food they are asking Jesus to eat. Their only explanation for Jesus' refusal to eat is that he must have had a source of food of which they were ignorant (v. 33). Unthinkable as it might be, there is a hint that he has accepted and shared food with the Samaritan woman (cf. v. 27b)! But they have joined the Samaritan woman, who was unable to accept Jesus' words on another water, a living water, because she was unable to transcend "this well" and "this water" (vv. 14-15). Jesus speaks of another food; the disciples can only think of "this food" (vv. 32-33). For all their cultural and religious sentiments of superiority (cf. vv. 8, 9, 27), the disciples are no better situated in their relationship with Jesus than was the woman after her first discussion with him (cf. vv. 7-15). Indeed, she has progressed further than they in the development of her understanding of Jesus (cf. vv. 16-30).

To do the will and complete the work of the Father (v. 34). The discourse of Jesus begins by returning to the word he used for "food" (v. 32: *brōma*), not understood by the disciples (v. 33): "my food is" (v. 34: *emon brōma estin*). The clarification of that which nourishes Jesus, which the disciples cannot understand, is fundamental to this gospel's presentation of Jesus' relationship with the Father, and the consequence of that relationship. Jesus explains: "My food is

so that	*hina*
(a) I might do the will	(a) *poiō to thelêma*
of the one who sent me	*tou pempsantos me*
and	*kai*
(b) complete his work."	(b) *teleiōsō autou to ergon.*

If we read the *kai* as epexegetical, (b) explains (a). The nourishment of Jesus is found in his doing the will of the one who sent him, which means he will bring to perfection the work of that figure. Jesus is the "sent one" of the Father (cf. 1:14, 18, 34; 2:16; 3:16-17, 35-36), and the driving force of his presence is to do the will of the one who sends him.

It is now clear why Jesus *had to (edei)* pass through Samaria (v. 4). Behind the events that have taken place in Samaria, regarded by the disciples as strange (and perhaps improper, cf. vv. 27, 33), stands the will of the one who sent Jesus (cf. Boers, *Neither on This Mountain* 191–192). His "food" is to be present in this non-Jewish land, dealing with non-Jewish people. Jesus' unconditional acceptance of the will of the Father also explains—in his own person—what he means when he speaks of true worship being the worship of the Father in spirit and truth (cf. vv. 21-24). But the doing of the will of the one who sent him means that he will bring to perfection *(teleiōsō)* the work *(to ergon)* of the Father. The future tense of the verb *complete/bring to perfection (teleiōsō)* points the reader toward some future moment when Jesus' unconditional response to the Father will lead to the perfection of the task set for him by the Father.

There will be a moment in the story, yet to be told, when *autou to ergon*, the overall scheme or plan of the task given to Jesus by the one who sent him, will be completed. Therein will Jesus find his nourishment, that is, this is the goal toward which his life is oriented. The Christian reader is aware that Jesus will come to the end of his life through death on a cross. This final event has already been alluded to in earlier parts of the narrative (cf. 1:5, 10-11, 51; 3:13-14), and perhaps linked to an hour that has not yet come (cf. 2:4). The narrator has also spoken of a time in the future "when therefore he was raised from the dead" (2:22). Jesus has now announced that the events that will mark the end of his life will also be the *teleiōsis tou ergou*, the perfection of the task given to him by the Father.

The mission of the disciples (vv. 35-38). The final words of the discourse shift from Jesus' description of his "food," that which drives and nourishes him in his mission to bring to completion the task entrusted to him by the one who sent him. His focus is now on the mission of the disciples. He instructs them that, although they may be following him into this mission, the harvest is there to reap. Jesus' opening words on the mission of the disciples remind them, in a proverb-like statement, of something they would commonly say: "Four months more, then comes the harvest" (v. 35a). They are reminded of common opinion, based on the physical reality of the fields around them, that the harvest is still some time away. Jesus contradicts this, telling them to lift up their eyes that they might see the advent of the Samaritans (cf. v. 30). Jesus stretches language. A harvest "already white" can only refer to sown fields ready for harvesting, but the coming Samaritans, responding to the initial and partial belief of the Samaritan woman, are "already white for harvest" (v. 35b). The crop in the fields around Jesus, the disciples, and the approaching Samaritans may still be some time away from harvesting, but the advent of the Samaritans is a sign to the disciples that Jesus' presence brings life to all who would "come toward him" (cf. v. 30). Johannine realized eschatology contradicts the expectations of the disciples. The "not yet" is here already, and the advent of the Samaritans is proof of it.

The life setting for this discourse is the (Samaritan?) mission of the Johannine community. Its members are told that the reception of non-Jews into the community is the result of the initiative of Jesus. He draws a distinction between the sower and the reaper in v. 36. The disciples are to work as reapers in a harvest that has been sown by Jesus through his encounter with the Samaritan woman. Nevertheless, the disciples are part of the harvesting process; they will reap the harvest symbolized by the Samaritans advancing toward them. They are paid, and gather fruit for eternal life, in their involvement in the mission. Because of this mutual involvement in mission, Jesus as the sower who initiates the movement toward true belief and the disciples who reap the harvest, sower and harvester rejoice together. All the verbs are in the present tense. The "not yet" is here already. There is no need, in the Johannine view of things, to do good deeds now in the hope that this will bring its reward of eternal life. The disciples already reap the fruits of a mission initiated by Jesus. This interpretation is reinforced by v. 37 which restates by means of a short proverb *(ho logos)* what has just been said and prepares the way for Jesus' final statement in v. 38. Against a background of prejudice (vv. 8, 9, 27), Jesus has drawn the Samaritans toward himself (vv. 7-30). The disciples are now associated with the divine urgency that brought Jesus into Samaria (cf. v. 4: *edei*). Jesus has told them to raise their eyes and gaze upon the advancing Samaritans (v. 35) that they may become reapers of a harvest they did not sow and thus enter the joy of Jesus' union with the Father (v. 36). This story shows that the proverb is true *(estin alēthinos):* one sows (Jesus) and another reaps (the disciples) (v. 37).

The above reading of vv. 35-37 clears the way for an interpretation of the much-debated v. 38: "I sent you to reap that for which you did not labor. Others have labored, and you have entered into their labor." The opening words of the statement repeat what has been said in vv. 35-36 but add a further qualification. As Jesus explained his "food" to the disciples he told them of his need to respond to the one who sent him (v. 34). He has now associated them with this mission: Jesus has sent the disciples *(egō apesteila hymas therizein).* In v. 2 the narrator announced that Jesus no longer baptized, as his many disciples were performing that ministry. They are already "sent ones of the sent one," and their commission to "lift up their eyes" and reap a harvest they did not sow (vv. 35-37) is part of their having been sent. The one who labored in the harvest is Jesus, and a deeper significance for the adjective *kekopiakas,* used to speak of Jesus' weariness in v. 6, emerges. His presence in Samaria, the result of the Father's will (vv. 4, 34), is for laboring. But Jesus now adds others to those whose labor has anticipated the missionary activities of the disciples: "others have labored" *(alloi kekopiakasin).* Who might they be?

The Johannine story provides the answer to this much-debated question. Two figures were sent by God: John the Baptist (cf. 1:6) and Jesus (3:17; 4:34). From the beginnings of his ministry the Baptist pointed beyond himself to a figure who might follow him within the limited measure of chronology, but who existed before time (cf. v. 15). He was coming to baptize with water and the Holy Spirit (1:33). Jesus taught Nicodemus that rebirth through water and the Spirit was the crucial rite through which one must pass to enter the life promised by Jesus (3:3-5). A discussion concerning the relative merits of the baptisms of Jesus and John remained unresolved (3:22-26), but in 4:1-2 the narrator announced that the baptism of Jesus was no longer administered by Jesus, but by his disciples. The baptisms of Jesus and John the Baptist have come to an end (cf. 3:24; 4:2). The disciples have emerged, sent ones of Jesus (4:38a), as the only baptizers. They come at the end of a long process that has its origins in God. They follow, chronologically, a missionary activity that started in the witness of the Baptist and led to the person of Jesus who has now associated them with himself so that they might reap a harvest they did not sow. The "others" who have labored, into whose labor the disciples now enter, are John the Baptist and Jesus.

Conclusion to vv. 31-38. After Jesus' first encounter with "the Jews" (2:13-22), the narrator drew back from the story and commented on the limitations of a faith based on the signs that Jesus did (2:23-25). Does this mean that the *events* of Jesus' life do not tell the story of God? Does Jesus only look to what is in the human heart (cf. v. 25)? If such is the case, then only "the spiritual" matters, and the oft-leveled charge that early Gnosticism inspired the Fourth Gospel may be well-founded. In 4:31-38 the reader finds a brief "intermezzo" (cf. v. 31: *en tǭ metaxu*) that interrupts Jesus' encounters with Samaritans. Structurally this interruption comes immediately *before* Jesus' short stay in the Samaritan village (vv. 39-42), his *final* Samaritan encounter. The earlier words from the narrator (2:23-25) came immediately *after* Jesus' first encounter with "the Jews."

The words from the narrator, insisting on the limited nature of belief arising from the signs Jesus did (2:23-25), need to be balanced by the firm belief of Christian tradition that the *events* of the life, death, and resurrection of Jesus are at the origins of Christian belief, life, and practice. Jesus' unconditional acceptance of the will of the one who sent him will lead to *events* that complete the task given to him: death and resurrection (v. 34). The association of the disciples in the missionary activity of Jesus (vv. 35-38) continues the revealing presence of Jesus in the world of events. However important it is to see through the signs of Jesus to come to authentic belief in the God who sends him (2:23-25), there are events in the human story, the death and resurrection of Jesus (4:34), that are the origin, model, and inspiration for a long history of disciples entering into the labor of others (v. 38), reaping where they did not sow (v. 37), rejoicing with the sower as they gather fruit for eternal life (v. 36). The interruptions to Jesus' encounters with Jews (2:23-25) and Samaritans (4:31-38) balance one another. True belief looks beyond the signs that Jesus did (2:23-25), but there are "signs," events in the lives of Jesus and his followers, that lead people to believe that Jesus is the Christ, the Son of God, and thus come to eternal life (4:31-38; cf. 20:30-31).

NOTES

31. *Meanwhile:* On the use of *metaxu* as an indication of an "intermezzo" see BAGD 513; Bauer, *Johannesevangelium* 72; Lagrange, *Evangile* 116.

    besought him, saying: The use of the imperfect *erōtōn* and the participle *legontes* conveys the idea of a continual insistence.

    Rabbi, eat: This verse contains the only words the disciples say to Jesus. They will wonder among themselves in v. 33. The notion of "eating" provides Jesus with the language he will use to develop the central statement of v. 34. It is thus widely accepted that in vv. 31-38 the disciples are not participating in a dialogue; they are listening to a discourse. See Bernard, *Commentary* 1:153; Lenglet, "Jésus de passage" 499; Olsson, *Structure and Meaning* 219–220.

32. *I have food to eat:* Grammatically it is possible that the verb *phagein* is used epexegetically after the noun *brōsin*. This means Jesus does not have the food for the purpose of eating, but the very nature of the food is that it be eaten by Jesus. It is this way of reading that enables the interpretation of the food as the nourishment that orients Jesus' life and death. See Barrett, *Gospel* 240; Bauer, *Johannesevangelium* 72.

    of which you do not know: An interesting literary feature is at play in the telling of Jesus' response to the disciples. The story thus far, especially the Prologue and the description of the encounters with the Samaritan woman, provides a point of view that, as yet, the disciples do not share. They remain perplexed. The reader does not have all the answers to the mystery of Jesus' words, but is much more "inside" Jesus' program than the disciples in the story (cf. O'Day, *Revelation* 77–79).

33. *Has anyone brought him food?:* The disciples' wondering among themselves about the possibility of anyone else having brought Jesus physical food implicitly suggests that he may have taken food from the Samaritan woman. Their problem with Jesus' encounter with the Samaritan woman (cf. v. 27) continues, even though she has left the scene (v. 28), and thus the issue of Jesus' presence among Samaritans, and even the possibility of scandalous interaction with one of their women, remains.

34. *My food is to do the will:* Contrary to N-A[27], the present tense *poiō* is to be read rather than the future *poiēsō*. Good witnesses read the present tense (among

them Sinaiticus, Alexandrinus, f^{13}, and Nestle-Aland's *Mehrheitstext*). The present tense links v. 34 with its immediate narrative context, pointing to the present nature of Jesus' acceptance of the Father's will. For its acceptance as the *lectio difficilior* see Schnackenburg, *Gospel* 1:447 n. 81; Olsson, *Structure and Meaning* 224.

of him who sent me: The notion of Jesus' being "sent" is already well established by this stage in the narrative (cf. 1:14, 18, 34; 2:16; 3:16-17, 35-36), but his doing the sender's will is a notion that appears here for the first time. It will return regularly in explanation of both who Jesus is and what he does (cf. 5:23-24, 30, 37; 6:38-39, 44; 7:16, 18, 28, 33; 9:4; 12:44-45, 49; 13:20; 14:24; 15:21; 16:5). See Segalla, *Volontà* 166–169. Leroy, *Rätsel und Mißverständnis* 149–155, sees Johannine descent christology behind "the one who sent me." He rightly argues that the *Sitz im Leben* of 4:34 was the need for the Johannine community to develop an authoritative catechesis, based on the obedience of the one sent from above, to counter early Gnostic tendencies. This is particularly helpful in assessing the relationship between 2:23-25 and 4:31-38.

to complete his work: The terms "to complete" (*teleioō* and the related *teleō;* cf. 5:36; 17:4, 23; 19:28, 30) and "the work" (*to ergon;* cf. 4:24; 17:4) play an important role in the Fourth Gospel's description of Jesus' life and death. Against Bultmann (*Gospel* 265) and Becker (*Evangelium* 1:179), a distinction between *ta erga,* "the works" of Jesus and *ton ergon,* "the work," should be maintained. The former, although related to the latter, refers to the deeds of Jesus that make God known. The latter is an expression that refers to the whole mission of Jesus, understood as responding exactly to the will of the Father. It could be said that "the works" belong to Jesus while "the work" is something the Father asks Jesus to bring to perfection. See Segalla, *Volontà* 169–173; Okure, *Johannine Approach* 141–142.

to complete: For the reading of *teleiōsō* as a future rather than an aorist subjunctive see Schnackenburg, *Gospel* 1:447 n. 81; Olsson, *Structure and Meaning* 225 n. 34. See also BDF 186, §369.3: "A special case is that in which a future connected by *kai* follows upon *hina* or *mē* with the subjunctive to designate some further consequence." See also 15:8, where the same construction, clearly pointing to the future, is found. Even without the future, the use of the aorist subjunctive after *hina* would indicate a prolepsis.

Jesus' words in v. 34 provide the swivel around which vv. 31-38 swing. The wondering disciples have provided Jesus with the language of food (vv. 31-33), and his words to them (vv. 35-38) associate the disciples with his doing the will of the one who sent him. They become the sent ones of the sent one (cf. v. 38a). For a study of 4:34 see Segalla, *Volontà* 149–177. On *brōsis* and *brōma* see ibid. 162–166.

35. *Do you not say?:* It is sometimes suggested that "Four months more . . ." may reflect a parable with a universal application, but there is no evidence for any such parabolic saying (cf. Okure, *Johannine Approach* 147–149). It may simply mean that these are the expressions the disciples would use when they looked upon fields still some months away from harvest time.

lift up your eyes: There is widespread scholarly support for the suggestion that this command from Jesus urges the disciples to see the oncoming Samaritans and not just the surrounding fields. Isaiah 49:18 very possibly lies behind this command.

the fields are already white: The Greek word for "already" (*ēdē*) can be read as either the last word of v. 35 or the first word of v. 36. The interpretation above, following the indications of 𝔓⁶⁵, reads "already" as the last word in v. 35. For this choice see Okure, *Johannine Approach* 150–151; Bauer, *Johannesevangelium* 73; Bernard, *Commentary* 1:157; Lagrange, *Evangile* 120. The majority of critics place it at the beginning of v. 36. They rightly point out that it is better Johannine style to place *ēdē* at the beginning of a sentence, immediately before the pronominal participle. See, for example, Westcott, *Gospel* 76; Schnackenburg, *Gospel* 1:449 n. 92; Lindars, *Gospel* 196. Despite the better style in locating the adverb at the beginning of v. 36, the Johannine theme of realized eschatology is better caught by placing it at the end of v. 35.

white for harvest: On the harvest as an eschatological symbol see Isa 27:12; Joel 4:13; Mark 4:1-9, 26-29; Matt 13:24-30; Rev 14:14-16. On the Johannine realization of this eschatological symbol see Léon-Dufour, *Lecture* 1:386–387.

36. *gathers fruit for eternal life:* For a discussion of the Samaritan mission as the possible *Sitz im Leben* of this promise see Brown, *Gospel* 1:175–176; Cullmann, *The Johannine Circle* 39–56; Olsson, *Structure and Meaning* 233–241; Okure, *Johannine Approach* 188–191. The fact that the disciples are commissioned to continue the missionary activity initiated by Jesus may indicate that Samaritans already form part of the Johannine community. This situation may need the support of an account of Jesus' initial presence among Samaritans, and his mandate to the disciples to continue—not initiate—such a mission. The members of the Johannine community are told that they are but reapers of a harvest sown by Jesus and that this activity forms part of the will of God. This is one of the main conclusions of Okure, *Johannine Approach* 185–188.

sower and reaper: The position taken in the interpretation, that Jesus is the sower and the disciples are the reapers, is not universally accepted. Some suggest that Jesus is the reaper and the Father is the sower (cf. Schnackenburg, *Gospel* 1:451). Others claim that Jesus is lord of the harvest, and therefore the lawgiver, priest, and prophet who went before him were the sowers (cf. Westcott, *Gospel* 76). These solutions are often arrived at with an eye to the identification of the "others" of v. 38.

37. *One sows and another reaps:* On the possible background to this proverb (*ho logos*), see Bauer, *Johannesevangelium* 75; Watson, "Antecedents" 368–370; Niccaci, "Siracide 6,19" 149–153.

38. *I sent you to reap:* It is sometimes claimed that the aorist *apesteila* ("I sent") creates an unresolvable temporal sequence, as the disciples have not yet been sent. This is generally resolved by theories of v. 38a being originally a post-resurrection mandate that has been drawn back, clumsily, into the Johannine pre-resurrection narrative (cf. Schnackenburg, *Gospel* 1:452–453). The dis-

ciples have already been initiated into the ministry of Jesus and John the Baptist in v. 2. The temporal axis of the narrative explains the aorist.

others have labored: For surveys of the scholarly discussion, and the many suggested explanations of the "others" who have labored before the disciples, see Okure, *Johannine Approach* 159–160; Olsson, *Structure and Meaning* 229–233. The attempt (cf. the interpretation above) to locate the "others" by tracing, within the temporal axis of the narrative, the activities of John the Baptist, Jesus, and then the disciples, may also reflect what happened historically (cf. Robinson, "The 'Others'" 510–515; Murphy-O'Connor, "John the Baptist and Jesus" 359–374).

FOR REFERENCE AND FURTHER STUDY

See also studies of 4:1-42 in the bibliography following the commentary on 4:1-15
Moloney, Francis J. *Belief in the Word* 158–168.
Niccaci, A. "Siracide 6,19 e Giovanni 4,36-38." *BeO* 23 (1981) 149–153.
O'Day, Gail R. *Revelation in the Fourth Gospel* 77–86.
Okure, Teresa. *The Johannine Approach to Mission* 133–168.
Olsson, Birger. *Structure and Meaning* 218–257.
Robinson, J. A. T. "The 'Others' of John 4,38." *StEv* 1 (1958) 510–515.
Segalla, Giuseppe. *Volontà di Dio e dell'Uomo in Giovanni (Vangelo e Lettere).* SRivBib 6. Brescia: Paideia, 1974.
Watson, Wilfred G. E. "Antecedents of a New Testament Proverb." *VT* 20 (1970) 368–370.

ix. Jesus and the Samaritan Villagers (4:39-42)

39. Many Samaritans from that city believed in him because of the word of the woman's testimony, "He told me everything I have ever done."
40a. So when the Samaritans came to him, they asked him to stay with them;
40b. and he stayed there for two days.
41. And many more believed because of his word.
42. They said to the woman, "It is no longer because of your words that we believe, for we have heard for ourselves, and we know that this is indeed the Savior of the world."

INTERPRETATION

Introduction to 4:39-42. Jesus remains at the well, but the disciples disappear into the background as Samaritans and the Samaritan woman come to Jesus. This brief passage is composed of four affirmations, three of them from the narrator and a final one from the Samaritans who address the woman, upon whose word they have come to Jesus (cf. vv. 29-30). It unfolds in the following five stages:

(a) *V. 39:* The narrator reports the initial belief of "many" Samaritans, based on the word of the woman.
(b) *V. 40a:* The narrator reports the Samaritans' request that Jesus stay with them.
(c) *V. 40b:* The narrator reports Jesus' positive response to their request.
(d) *V. 41:* The narrator reports that "many more" believe because of the word of Jesus.
(e) *V. 42:* In the only words from characters in the story, the Samaritans tell the woman that they no longer believe because of what she said. They know that Jesus is the savior of the world.

This brief but elegant episode serves as a climax to Jesus' presence in Samaria with non-Jews proclaiming him as a universal savior.

The initial belief of "many" Samaritans (v. 39). Many of the Samaritans from the village believed in Jesus on the basis of the words of the woman: "He told me everything I have ever done" (v. 39). The words of v. 29 are cited, but no reference is made to the discussion between the woman and Jesus dealing with the possibility of universal worship of God, "neither on this mountain nor in Jerusalem" (cf. vv. 21-24). At this stage the Samaritans are asking the question put to them by the woman in v. 29: "Can this be the Messiah" (v. 29; cf. v. 25). They join the woman in a partial faith, as they "believed in him because of the word of the woman's testimony" *(episteusan eis auton dia ton logon tēs gynaikos martyrousēs).*

The Samaritans request that Jesus stay with them (v. 40a). The Samaritans ask that Jesus remain with them *(menei par'autois).* The Samaritan woman attempted to break contact with Jesus in v. 9, but Jesus persevered with her. The issue of the conflict between Samaritan and Jew (cf. v. 9) appears to have been forgotten.

Jesus' response (v. 40b): Jesus is reported as staying with them "two days." At this stage the brief duration of time is simply stated. It will assume a great importance later in the narrative (cf. vv. 43, 46).

Many more believed (v. 41): Many *(polloi)* believed in Jesus because of the word of the woman (v. 39: *dia ton logon tēs gynaikos*) but the narrator announces that "many more" (v. 41: *pollǭ pleious*) believed in him "because of his word" (v. 41: *dia ton logon autou*). The contrast between the two motivations for belief could not be stated more clearly, even though *episteusan eis auton* is used in both v. 39 and v. 41. Before the Samaritans utter their confession of faith they have made a major step toward true faith: they have believed because of the word of Jesus (cf. 2:5; 3:29).

The faith of the Samaritans (v. 42). The woman who had left her jar at the well (cf. v. 28) has returned, and the Samaritans speak to her. They are aware of the qualitative difference between the "words" of the woman and the "word" of Jesus. A distinction, already made clear by the narrator in vv. 39 and 41, is articulated by the Samaritans in the only direct speech found in the narrative. They disassociate themselves with their initial belief (v. 39). They tell the woman that they "no longer" *(ouketi)* believe "because of your words" (v. 42a: *dia tēn sēn lalian*). Classical literature uses the word *lalia* to speak of "gossip, common talk" (BAGD 464), but it can hardly have that negative meaning here. Nevertheless, the use of the expression *logos* to speak of the witness of the woman in v. 39 has been changed to *lalia* now that the Samaritans have come to belief in Jesus because of his *logos*. There is only one revealing *logos,* and it comes from Jesus. They believe because they themselves *(autoi)* have had the experience of hearing (v. 42b: *akēkoamen*). John the Baptist's final appearance in the Gospel was marked by the use of the same verb. He described himself as the friend of the bridegroom who "stands and hears *(akouōn)* him" (3:29). On the basis of this hearing they claim to "know" *(oidamen)* that Jesus is the savior of the world (v. 42c). The first disciples claimed to have found the Messiah (1:41, 45), and Nathanael claimed to "know" that Jesus was a teacher come from God (cf. 3:2), but their finding and knowledge were based on their own religious and cultural traditions. The knowledge of the Samaritans is based entirely on the *logos* of Jesus.

The expression used by the Samaritans in their confession, "the Savior of the world," is found in only one other place in the NT (1 John 4:14), and the Hellenistic title "savior" *(sōtēr)* is not widespread (cf. Luke 1:47; Acts 5:31; 13:23; Phil 3:20; and the Pastorals). Both Jew and Greek hoped for a "savior" although they thought, spoke, and wrote about such a figure in very different ways. Jesus has already announced his role: "God sent the Son into the world not to condemn the world, but that the world might be saved through him" *(hina sōthȩ ho kosmos di'autou)"* (3:17). However much the author might be using an expression well known and widely used in a number of societies and cultures at the end of the first century, its Johannine meaning is determined by this Johannine context. The major thrust of the confession is the affirmation of Jesus' universal saving role. In his discussion with the woman he spoke of the universal possibility of right worship of the true God. Such a possibility "is coming and now is" (v. 23; cf. vv. 21-24). All subsequent discussion between Jesus and the woman (vv. 25-26), and her report to the Samaritan villagers (v. 29) failed to face this question. It appears to have been forgotten. The confession of the Samaritans brings it back to center stage.

> Jesus, the messiah, is neither the savior of the Samaritans nor of the Jews—"an hour comes when neither on this mountain nor in Jerusalem will you worship the Father" (v 21)—but the savior of the world—"the

true worshippers will worship the Father in spirit and truth" (v 23). True worship, worship in the spirit, constitutes a community beyond all earthly religious communities, a community of worship in which all of humanity is united. That is what the villagers recognise; it is the point of the story (Boers, *Neither on This Mountain* 199–200).

As John the Baptist heard the voice of the bridegroom and rejoiced to hear that voice, the Samaritans hear the word of Jesus and confess that this is indeed the savior of the world. As John the Baptist was prepared to decrease that Jesus might increase, so are the Samaritans prepared to abandon all debates of Gerizim or Jerusalem, and place their trust in Jesus as the savior of the world. The Samaritans' openness to the word of Jesus transforms them; they become examples of authentic Johannine belief.

Conclusion to 4:1-42: As with 2:13–3:36, the narrative of 4:1-42 articulates a point of view about how one should respond to Jesus, and the fruits of such a response. With "the word" of Jesus as the criterion, the story of Jesus' presence among the Samaritans points to the possibility of no faith (vv. 1-15: the Samaritan woman), partial faith (vv. 16-30: the Samaritan woman), and authentic Johannine belief (vv. 39-42: the Samaritan villagers) *in the world beyond the boundaries of Judaism.* These models of belief are closely associated with the Johannine message on the importance of belief in the revelation of God in and through the word of Jesus for life and salvation (cf. especially 4:13-14, 21-24, 34-38). Jesus has come to bring to perfection the work given to him by the Father, and he associates disciples with himself, as the fields are ripe for the harvest (vv. 31-38). The concentration upon characters *beyond the world of Judaism* indicates that no one, of whatever race, culture, or religion is to be excluded in the Johannine theology of revelation and salvation. Jesus' promise of 3:17, "For God sent the Son into the world, not to condemn the world, but that the world might be saved through him," is being acted out in the narrative.

NOTES

39. *because of the word of the woman's testimony:* Augustine has aptly commented upon this episode: *"Primo per famam, postea per presentiam"* ("First by reputation, then by his presence") (*In Iohannis Evangelium* 15:33; CCSL 36:164). However, too much modern philosophical thought has been introduced into the discussion, via Kirkegaard, by Bultmann (*Gospel* 200) of first hand and second hand hearers of the word. The presence of the word of the Gospel renders all "second hand" experiences "first hand." See, for example, Walker, "Jüngerwort und Herrenwort" 49–54. Okure, *Johannine Approach* 172–173 is rightly critical of this approach.

40. *for two days:* The reference to the time spent with the Samaritans may simply be a discrete amount of time, long enough for them to have exposure to Jesus. However, the precise reference to "two days," the repetition of the "two days" in v. 43, and the indication "he came again to Galilee" (v. 46) may point to a more precise identification of the time of Jesus' arrival in Cana (v. 46).

There may be missionary instruction in the description of Jesus' staying with the Samaritans for two days (cf. Schnackenburg, *Gospel* 1:455–456). Okure, *Johannine Approach* 179, links the two days with the stay of the genuine missionary in *Didache* 11.5.

41. *many more:* It is not said that the whole village believed. "Many" (v. 39) and "many more" (v. 41) indicate an increasing number, but not the totality. As always in the Fourth Gospel a choice is made (cf. Hudry-Clergeon, "De Judée en Galilée" 828–829).

because of his word: Most commentators see two stages of faith reflected in the Samaritans' response first to the word of the woman and then to the word of Jesus. The former is based on signs (Jesus' telling the woman her secrets) and the latter is a faith based on the word. Okure, *Johannine Approach* 170–181, argues the contrary in the light of her attempt to see the Samaritan woman in vv. 16-26 as having already arrived at authentic belief, and thus becoming a true missionary in vv. 28-30.

42. *because of your words:* Some scholars see no difference between the *lalia* of the woman and the *logos* of Jesus. Okure, *Johannine Approach* 171, argues strongly for an identical meaning for the two words (cf. also Barrett, *Gospel* 243; Walker, "Jüngerwort und Herrenwort" 52–53; Léon-Dufour, *Lecture* 1:392). The context, both remote and immediate, demands that some distinction is being made between the use of *logos* for the witness of the woman in v. 39 and her *lalia* in v. 42. The uniqueness of the *logos* of Jesus emerges very strongly (cf. Lagrange, *Evangile* 122; Brown, *Gospel* 1:174–175; Segalla, *Giovanni* 200–201).

no longer: The temporal dimension of *ouketi* indicates that the belief of the Samaritan villagers admits to two stages of faith. Earlier they believed on the basis of the woman's words (v. 39), but this is no longer the case (v. 42). This element in the narrative (not discussed by Okure, *Johannine Approach* 172) adds weight to the position adopted in the interpretation and in the previous note.

we have heard for ourselves: The focus given in the interpretation on "hearing" is demanded by the strong insistence in the original *autoi gar akēkoamen*. The use of *autoi* for "ourselves" stresses their experience, highlighting an important distinction between the reported words of the woman and the heard word of Jesus. Okure, *Johannine Approach* 173–174, attempts to lessen this by resorting to a poorly attested *autou* rather than *autoi*.

the Savior of the world: "The Samaritans speak the language of Johannine Christology" (Barrett, *Gospel* 243). For comprehensive surveys of the use of *sōtēr* in the ancient world see Bernard, *Commentary* 1:161–163; Schnackenburg, *Gospel* 1:457–458.

FOR REFERENCE AND FURTHER STUDY

See also studies of 4:1-42 in the bibliography following the commentary on 4:1-15
Moloney, Francis J. *Belief in the Word* 168–175.
O'Day, Gail R. *Revelation in the Fourth Gospel* 86–92.
Okure, Teresa. *The Johannine Approach to Mission* 168–191.
Olsson, Birger. *Structure and Meaning*.
Walker, Rolf. "Jüngerwort und Herrenwort: Zur Auslegung von Joh 4:39-42."
    ZNW 57 (1966) 49–54.

x. The Second Miracle at Cana: Faith in the Word of Jesus (4:43-54)

43. After the two days he went from that place to Galilee. 44. For Jesus himself testified that a prophet has no honor in his own country. 45. So when he came to Galilee, the Galileans welcomed him, having seen all that he had done in Jerusalem at the feast; for they too had gone to the feast. 46. So he came again to Cana in Galilee where he had made the water wine. And at Capernaum there was a royal official whose son was ill.
47a. When he heard that Jesus had come from Judea to Galilee,
47b. he went and begged him to come down and heal his son, for he was at the point of death. 48. Therefore Jesus said to him, "Unless you see signs and wonders you will not believe." 49. The official said to him, "Sir, come down before my little boy dies."
50a. Jesus said to him, "Go; your son is living."
50b. The man believed the word that Jesus spoke to him and went his way.
51. As he was going down, his slaves met him and told him that his child was living. 52. So he asked them the hour when he began to recover, and they said to him, "Yesterday at the seventh hour the fever left him." 53. The father knew that was the hour when Jesus had said to him, "Your son is living"; and he himself believed, along with his whole household. 54. This was now the second sign that Jesus did after coming from Judea to Galilee.

INTERPRETATION

Introduction to 4:43-54. The narrator's indications in vv. 43-45 both shift Jesus from Samaria to Galilee and comment on the nature of the reception Jesus receives from the Galileans. Although v. 46 probably introduced an originally independent story, now reported in vv. 46-54, vv. 43-46 serve the present shape of the narrative as an introduction to vv. 47-

54. On arrival at v. 47 the major characters, the place, the time, and the reason for Jesus' return to Galilee have been introduced. The story as a whole unfolds in the following way:

> (a) *Vv. 43-46:* Introduction of characters (Jesus [v. 43], the Galileans [v. 45], and the royal official [v. 46]), motivation (v. 44), place (vv. 45-46), and time (vv. 43, 46).
> (b) *Vv. 47-53:* Jesus and the royal official at Cana in Galilee.
>> i. *V. 47a:* The official approaches Jesus because of what he has heard from the Galileans.
>> ii. *Vv. 47b-49:* The perseverance of the official, requesting help for his dying son, despite Jesus' initial refusal.
>> iii. *V. 50a:* Jesus' word of positive response.
>> iv. *V. 50b:* The official believes in the word of Jesus.
>> v. *Vv. 51-53:* The result of the official's belief: his son lives, he "knows," and his household comes to belief.
> (c) *V. 54:* Conclusion to 4:46-54 and to 2:1–4:54.

There is a strong resemblance between the literary shape of vv. 47-54 and vv. 39-42: the official comes to Jesus on the word of someone else (v. 47a; cf. v. 39) and he makes a request of Jesus to which he eventually responds positively (vv. 47b-50a; cf. v. 40). Jesus' presence leads to belief in the word (v. 50; cf. v. 41), and the official "knows" the authority of Jesus (v. 53; cf. v. 42). Thus this final episode in the journey from Cana to Cana (2:1–4:54) completes a literary pattern common throughout this section of the Gospel where the literary shapes of successive narratives are very similar. The first Cana story (2:1-12) is matched by the purification of the Temple (2:13-25), and the encounter with Nicodemus (3:1-21) is structurally parallel with the Baptist's final witness (3:22-36). The two moments of Jesus' encounter with the Samaritan woman are shaped in the same way (4:1-15 and 4:16-30). The literary shape of the account of Jesus' stay with the Samaritan villagers (4:39-42) returns as Jesus comes back to Cana in Galilee (4:43-54). This literary pattern is important in a narrative that could tempt the reader to notice the Cana stories at the beginning and end, and then the parallel accounts of different faith responses told between them. The links existing between the stories that follow one another point to the fundamental importance of a sequential reading of the narrative. A reader does not read in chiasms, but moves from episode to episode, and only at the end recognizes an author's use of the technique of repetition.

Introduction (vv. 43-46). Jesus' departure to Galilee (v. 43) forms an excellent transition (cf. v. 40), but in v. 44 a notorious problem emerges. The narrator recalls a word of Jesus found in the tradition (cf. Mark 6:4; Matt 13:57; Luke 4:24; 13:33-34) to claim that the motive for Jesus' journey from Judea to Galilee was because a prophet has no honor in his own country.

Jesus is traditionally known as "of Nazareth" (cf. Matt 2:23) and as a Galilean (cf. Mark 14:70). There is no immediate background for such a negative statement, so how can this journey into Galilee, which is traditionally regarded as his own country, be motivated by the narrator's remark in v. 44? The Matthean and Lukan infancy narratives at least situate his birth in Judea, but "this Gospel does not even tell us that Jesus was born in Judea" (Brown, *Gospel* 1:187) because it has a singular belief concerning his origins. On only one occasion has anyone in the story suggested that Jesus was from Galilee. Philip told Nathanael that they had found the fulfillment of Israel's hopes, "Jesus of Nazareth, the son of Joseph" (1:45). But, as the interpretation of that passage has sought to show, this statement misunderstands Jesus. Again, the presence of the mother of Jesus at Cana (2:1) may be taken to indicate Galilean origins, but this alone need not necessarily indicate that Jesus was a Galilean.

For the Fourth Gospel the origins of Jesus are beyond human control, as "in the beginning was the Word and the Word was turned toward God" (1:1). However, in the light of 1:43 the first three days of Jesus' ministry take place in Judea (cf. 1:19-42). The fourth day (1:43-51) and the following revelation of the *doxa* (2:1-12) take place in Galilee. Jesus returned immediately to Jerusalem (2:13) and remained in Judea until he began his journey to Galilee via Samaria (cf. 4:3-4). As he departs from Samaria the narrator again mentions that he is heading for Galilee (4:43). Whatever the synoptic tradition might say, an impression of Jesus' regular presence in Judea is created. A journey into Galilee deserves special mention (cf. 1:43; 4:3-4, 43) as Jesus sets out on a journey from his normal place of residence and activity. Once this is accepted, v. 44 makes good sense. In Judea Jesus has met rejection from "the Jews" (2:13-22); many have come to him looking for miracles but Jesus has not trusted himself to them (2:23-25); a Jewish leader, Nicodemus, has been unable to accept Jesus' teaching (3:1-12). Jesus has moved away from Judea because of the danger of hostility from the Pharisees (4:1). As far as the Johannine story is concerned, the events narrated so far indicate that Jesus' words hold true: "a prophet has no honor in his own country" (v. 44).

The welcome afforded Jesus on arrival in Galilee looks enthusiastic, but there are reasons for concern. Looking back to the feast of the Passover that has just been celebrated in Jerusalem (cf. 2:13, 23-25), the narrator reports that the Galileans had been in Jerusalem and had seen the signs Jesus had done. Their enthusiastic reception of Jesus matches the response of those in Jerusalem who "believed in his name when they saw the signs that he did" (2:23). The Galileans were at the same feast and responded in the same fashion. Jesus did not trust himself to such enthusiastic believers (cf. 2:24-25). It is from this background that Jesus comes again *(palin)* to Cana in Galilee, and the narrator reminds the reader of the miracle Jesus had performed the last time he was there (v. 46a; cf. 2:1-12). As the introduction to the action closes, a major player appears. The narrator reports: "At Capernaum there was a royal official *(basilikos)* whose son was ill" (v. 46b). Recent research has shown that a figure described as a *basilikos* might be either Jewish or Gentile (cf. Wegner, *Der Hauptmann* 57–72. See note on v. 46). The use of the word in the present Johannine context leads to the suggestion that this man is a Gentile. He is the last in a series of characters who appear across 4:1-54. He is not from Cana, but from the border town of Capernaum, well known for the presence of Gentile soldiers. All the others characters in 4:1-54 are Samaritans, people from the world outside Judaism. It is most likely that this particular *basilikos* is understood and presented to the reader by the author as a final example of the reception of the word of Jesus from the non-Jewish world.

Jesus and the royal official in Cana (vv. 47-54). As the Samaritans had heard from the woman (v. 39), so also the official has "heard that Jesus had come from Judea to Galilee" (v. 47a). Verse 45 and this "hearing" of the official are closely linked. The basis of the official's movement toward Jesus (v. 47a) is his hearing from the Galileans of the wonders that Jesus did in Jerusalem (v. 45).

He begs Jesus to come to Capernaum to heal his son (v. 47b). In a way typical of miracle stories the gravity of his son's situation is described: "for he was at the point of death" (v. 47b). What follows is surprising, and quite untypical of miracle stories. Jesus responded without hesitation to the Samaritans who asked him to stay with them on the basis of what they had heard from the woman (cf. v. 40). In this more urgent situation of life and death Jesus rebukes the official (v. 48). No doubt the man approaches Jesus because he has heard from the Galileans that he is a wonderworker (vv. 45, 47a), and Jesus' rebuke warns against "signs and wonders." However, he does not address his words only to the official; he has a plural audience: "Unless you (plural) see signs and wonders you will not believe" *(ean mē sēmeia kai terata idēte, ou mē pisteusēte* [v. 48b]). The wider group, including the Galileans who had told the official of Jesus' wonders, are warned that true faith cannot be based on signs alone. This rebuke enables the author to state clearly the major theme of the passage: authentic belief. Two issues emerge from the official's insistence, despite Jesus' rebuke, that Jesus come down to Capernaum before his son dies (v. 49). Primarily there is a restatement of the urgency of the situation, introducing the expression *paidion* ("child," "little boy" in this case), to indicate the affectionate intimacy that exists between this concerned father and his child. But this is not the first time that a character has persevered in the face of a rebuke. Exactly the same process took place in the first Cana miracle, where the mother of Jesus trusted in the word of Jesus despite his rebuke (2:4-5; cf. Giblin, "Suggestion, Negative Response" 205).

As in the first Cana miracle, Jesus accedes to the man's persevering request. With increasing insistence Jesus has been asked to "come down" *(katabainein)* to heal the child (vv. 47, 49). Jesus does not accede to the request that he physically "come down" to Capernaum, but he heals the child by the authority of his word. The official is told to return home because his son is living. It is not the presence of Jesus that effects the healing, but his word: "Go; your son is living" (v. 50a). The response of the official, coming after a number of episodes where various responses to the word of Jesus have been highlighted, is impressive: "The man believed the word that Jesus spoke to him and went his way" *(episteusen ho anthrōpos tǭ logǭ hon eipen autǭ ho Iēsous kai eporeueto)* (v. 50). The verb *pisteuein* opens the sentence. The man believed, and the object of his belief is the word that Jesus had spoken to him *(tǭ logǭ hon eipen autǭ ho Iēsous)*. There are no "signs and wonders" supporting this belief. The official does not fall under the judgment of v. 48. Jesus had commanded him, "Go *(poreuou)*, your son is living" (v. 50a). The response of the man closes with a wordless acceptance of the command of Jesus: "and he went *(eporeueto)*" (v. 50b).

The words of Jesus, "Go, your son is living" (v. 50a), form the background for vv. 51-53. In v. 51a the man is "going down," continuing the obedient response to the command of Jesus initiated in v. 50a. The official's servants meet him, announcing, "Your son lives" (v. 51b). There is a slight but important difference between the words of Jesus and the words of the servants. Jesus speaks of the man's "son" (v. 50a: *ho huios sou*), but the servants tell him that his child *(ho pais autou)* lives. The story could have concluded very effectively here, but a number of literary and theological connections remain open. In the immediately previous encounter between Jesus and the Samaritans (vv. 39-42) the villagers' belief in the word of Jesus led them to knowledge (vv. 41-42). The same thing happens with the official. Requesting detail concerning the time of the recovery of his child, he is told that it was at the seventh hour of the previous day (v. 52). The words of Jesus then return for the third time: "The father knew *(egnō oun ho patēr)* that was the hour when Jesus said to him *ho huios sou zę̄*" (v. 53ab). He had believed in the word of Jesus (v. 50b), and now he "knows" the saving authority of that word. Like that of the Samaritans (cf. vv. 41-42), his faith in the word of Jesus produces not only a miracle, but knowledge (v. 53ab).

The final comment from the narrator creates difficulty: "and he himself believed *(kai episteusen autos)* along with his whole household" (v. 53c). Does the man only come to believe after he has heard the message of his son's recovery? It is not possible that the solemnity of v. 50b can be watered down to anything less than authentic Johannine belief in the word. The function of v. 53cd is to close the narrative in a way that parallels 2:11. In the first Cana story others came to belief as a result of the miracle (cf. 2:11). The narrator has reminded the reader of the first Cana story in v. 46. In 2:1-12 not only does the mother of Jesus place all her trust in the word of Jesus and thus act as the catalyst that produces the miracle. Her initial act of faith (2:5) leads to the faith of others, the disciples (2:11). In the second Cana story an initial act of faith (4:50b) has enabled a miracle that leads to the faith of others, the official's household (v. 53d). The use of the same verb *episteusan* for both the official and his household is difficult, as it suggests that they all came to belief at the same time. Given the parallel with 2:1-12, the verb must be read as a complexive rather than an ingressive aorist (cf. note). The whole experience of the official is a reflection of his belief, and through it his household believed. "The servants have confirmed the official's faith, but in doing so have themselves discovered faith" (Lindars, *Gospel* 205). One might paraphrase v. 53cd: "Not only did he believe, but also his whole household believed" (cf. Schnackenburg, *Gospel* 1:461).

Confirmation for this interpretation comes from further close reading of the text (cf. Lightfoot, *Gospel* 129). The main character in the story begins as a *basilikos*, a person with a political and social function (vv. 46, 49). But there is more to this person, as his use of the affectionate expression *paidion* hints (v. 49b). He is a human being with significant personal relationships. In reporting the official's act of faith the narrator calls him *ho anthrōpos* (v. 50b). At the end of the story, as the household tells him that his *pais* lives, and joins him in faith, he is called *ho patēr* (v. 53). "A certain official" (v. 46) who trusted unconditionally in the word of Jesus became "the man" (v. 50) and is finally described as "the father" (v. 53). His faith (v. 50b) and knowledge (v. 53ab) generate faith in others (v. 53cd). Both Cana miracle stories show that Johannine faith is not only a personal commitment to the word of Jesus; it leads others to faith (2:11; 4:53). The final Samaritan episode (vv. 39-42) makes a similar point. Faith in the word of the woman (v. 39) has been transcended by faith in the word of Jesus (v. 41) to produce knowledge and a confession of faith (v. 42). In a parallel fashion the official has an initial faith as a result of the report of the Galileans (vv. 45-47). This movement toward Jesus (v. 47) has been transcended by faith in the word of Jesus (v. 50) to produce knowledge and belief among others (v. 53). Augustine's comment on 4:39-42 applies equally well to vv. 43-54: *Primo per famam, postea per presentiam* (cf. note to v. 39).

The episode closes with a summarizing statement from the narrator, drawing attention to the fact that this is the second sign that Jesus did in Galilee. The use of "the second sign" (4:54: *palin deuteron sēmeion*) recalls "the first of his signs" (2:11: *archēn tōn sēmeiōn*), but the two Cana miracles conclude differently. In 2:12 the narrator gathered all the actors from the

miracle story and sent them on their way. This conclusion lead further
into the story. In 4:54 the narrator looks back to 2:1-12, thus closing the
episodes that run from Cana to Cana. The two Cana stories form an obvious frame around the narrative that extends from 2:1–4:54. The Jewish
mother's unconditional belief in the word of her son Jesus triggers a miracle that reveals the *doxa* and leads to the faith of others (2:1-12). A series
of encounters has followed this first miracle where characters from the
world of Judaism respond in various ways to the word of Jesus (2:13–
3:36). Further encounters between Samaritans, characters outside the
world of Judaism, repeat the responses of Jews to Jesus (4:1-42). A Gentile
official's unconditional belief in the word of Jesus triggers a miracle that
leads to the faith of others (4:43-54).

Conclusion to 2:1–4:54: The first Cana story (2:1-12), following the account of the limited belief of the first disciples and Jesus' promise of
greater sight (cf. 1:35-51), provides the criterion for the belief that will
allow access to such sight. The mother of Jesus believes in the word of her
son (2:5), the *doxa* of Jesus is manifested, and the disciples believe. On the
basis of this criterion the responses of a series of characters from Judaism
can be assessed: "the Jews" (2:13-22), Nicodemus (3:1-21), and John the
Baptist (3:22-36). As Jesus journeys into Samaria the responses of people
outside the world of Judaism can also be judged: the Samaritan woman
(4:1-15), the Samaritan woman (4:16-30), and the Samaritan villagers
(4:39-42). Jesus returns to Cana in Galilee where a Gentile official believes
in the word of Jesus, his son is restored to health, and his household believes (4:43-54). This carefully structured narrative and its central concern
with the question of authentic Johannine belief can be summarized as
follows:

2:1-12: *At Cana the mother of Jesus, a Jewish woman, demonstrates faith in the
word of Jesus and initiates a process which leads to a miracle, the revelation of the* **doxa** *and the belief of the disciples.*

> **2:13-22:** After the purification of the Temple "the Jews" reject the word of
> Jesus. They demonstrate the absence of authentic belief.

> **2:23-25:** *The narrator tells of Jesus' non-accepting* (ouk episteuen) *the many in
> Jerusalem who came to him and believed* (episteusan) *in him because of the
> signs that he did. Faith aroused by signs is insufficient.*

> **3:1-21:** The encounter with Nicodemus shows the good will of "a leader of
> the Jews" who comes by night to Jesus, and the good will of Jesus
> who tries to lead Nicodemus out of the world he knows and in
> which he is comfortable. Nicodemus is left speechless by Jesus'
> teaching, and is thus a model of imperfect or partial belief in Jesus.

> **3:22-36:** John the Baptist's final witness to Jesus describes his relationship
> as one of listening to the voice of the bridegroom, rejoicing in the

sound of his voice even though he himself must now decrease. His unconditional acceptance of the word of Jesus marks him out as a model of authentic belief.

4:1-15: After a long introduction to Jesus' presence in Samaria (vv. 1-6), the first moment in Jesus' encounter with the Samaritan woman results in her inability to understand and accept the "gift of God" offered by the word of Jesus. She demonstrates the absence of authentic belief (vv. 7-15).

4:16-30: Jesus perseveres with the woman, resurrecting the faltering encounter with a series of imperatives that draw her back into conversation. Although she remains silent about the time and place of true worship she suspects that Jesus might be the Messiah. Jesus attempts to transcend her messianic belief by telling her that I AM is speaking to her, but she fails to respond to this revelation. She returns to the villagers still wondering whether or not Jesus is the Messiah. Despite the progress she makes in her approach and understanding of Jesus, she remains a model of imperfect or partial belief in Jesus.

4:31-38: The Samaritan episodes are briefly interrupted by an "intermezzo," a reflection from Jesus on his doing the will of the one who sent him and bringing to completion the work that has been given to him as that which drives and nourishes him. The life, death, and resurrection of Jesus Christ are the source and inspiration for all that Jesus does, and for all those who are sent by him to continue a mission they did not initiate.

4:39-42: The Samaritan villagers transcend an initial belief in the word of the woman to believe in the word of Jesus. As a result of their hearing Jesus' word they transcend all differences between Jew and Samaritan to confess that Jesus is the savior of the world. Their unconditional acceptance of the word of Jesus marks them out as models of authentic belief.

4:43-54: At Cana a Gentile official demonstrates faith in the word of Jesus and initiates a process that leads to a miracle, his recognition of the authority of the word of Jesus and the belief of his household.

However central the theme of authentic Johannine belief is to 2:1–4:54, there is more to the shape and message of the passage than the statement and restatement of faith responses. An important linear development of the story takes place, controlled by Jesus' movements. He moves from Galilee to Jerusalem, into the Judean countryside, and back to Galilee via Samaria. The reader follows this journey, reported in a series of episodes that are linked by closely matched literary shapes. The shape of 2:1-12 is repeated in 2:13-25, and that of 3:1-21 is repeated in 3:22-36. The shape of 4:7-15 is repeated in 4:16-30, and that of 4:39-42 returns in 4:43-54. This technique insures the ongoing reading process that introduces the reader to fundamental Johannine questions emerging across these stories: Jesus is the unique revelation of God (cf. 3:13-14, 31-35), the unique Son of the Father (2:16; 4:34), the perfection of the former gift of the Law (cf. 2:6-7, 11; 4:10-14), the revelation of the *doxa* (2:11), the one who creates a new situation of freedom where people judge themselves by accepting or refusing what Jesus reveals (3:18-21, 36). The time has come for God to make known that salvation is available for all people, in all places (4:20-24, 42). Jesus initiates a mission in response to the will of the Father, and he draws his disciples into it (4:31-38). God is Spirit, and true life is lived in the Spirit (4:24; 3:6-8) after a ritual entry into a new community, a place where God reigns (3:3-5). The death of Jesus will not be the ignominious slaying of a failed Messiah but the "lifting up" of the Son of Man (3:14). Much of this is beyond the understanding of the disciples, but the time will come, after the death and resurrection of Jesus, when they will understand the word of Jesus and believe (2:19-22).

The reader is now instructed in some of the most important Johannine beliefs. What has been said in the Prologue (1:1-18) is being proclaimed and acted out in the story of Jesus (1:19–4:54). Above all, the reader now knows the nature of a right relationship with Jesus. The Prologue's teaching on the lifegiving power that comes from "believing" and "receiving" the incarnate word (1:12-13) happens in the story of Jesus as people accept or reject his word. However, much still remains to be revealed before the disciples will remember everything that Jesus has said and done, and believe in his word and in the Scriptures (cf. 2:22).

Notes

43-54. *The literary form of a miracle story.* The first Cana story (2:1-12) proved to be untypical of miracle stories. See note to 2:1-12. The second Cana miracle story is untypical in exactly the same way. It unfolds in the following fashion:

1. *Problem:* "There was a royal official whose son was ill" (v. 46).
2. *Request:* "He went and begged him to come down and heal his son" (v. 47).
3. *Rebuke:* "Unless you see signs and wonders you will not believe" (v. 48).
4. *Reaction:* "The man believed the word that Jesus spoke and went his way" (*episteusen ho anthrōpos tǭ logǭ hon eipen autǭ ho Iēsous kai eporeueto*) (v. 50).
5. *Consequence:* A miracle that leads to the faith of others (the official's household) (vv. 51-53).

As with 2:1-12, where the mother's encounter with her son disturbed the traditional form of a miracle story, so here the interaction between Jesus and the official disturbs the form (cf. Bauer, *Johannesevangelium* 78). He asks that his son be healed (v. 47), but his request generates a rebuke that leads to a further request, this time in direct speech (v. 49). Jesus responds with his word of healing (v. 50a) and the man believes the word of Jesus (v. 50b). The final element in the story is also somewhat foreign with no report of wonder or of the effect the miracle had on the official, his entourage, or the surrounding Galileans. The result of the miracle is the faith of the official's household (v. 53). The author has composed this miracle story, no doubt using sources from the Johannine tradition, so that the reader who arrives at 4:54 looks back to 2:1-12 and recognizes that a significant part of the Gospel story has been told by means of a journey that runs from Cana to Cana (2:1-4:54).

Some commentators suggest that 4:46-54 serves as an introduction to 5:1-47. Rather than closing a series of events that began in the first Cana story, they argue, 4:46-54 is a parabolic action about Jesus' gift of life and the power of the word, which transcend the witness of the old dispensation. In the discourse of 5:19-47 the themes of Jesus as the giver of life and the authority of his word, acted out in 4:46-54, are developed (cf. Dodd, *Interpretation* 318–319; Feuillet, "La signification théologique" 34–46). The passage may well prepare for 5:1-47 and thus serve as a bridge passage (cf. Brown, *Gospel* 1:cxli; 194–195), but its major focus is not the story about the restoration of life, but belief in the word of Jesus (cf. vv. 43-45, 48, 50, 53). The narrator's overt references to 2:1-12 (cf. vv. 43, 46, 54; cf. the following notes) cannot be ignored.

43. *After the two days:* When this indication of time is linked with v. 46: "So he came again to Cana in Galilee," it appears that Jesus arrived at Cana in Galilee "on the third day." This would be a further link with 2:1-12 (cf. 2:1), although the expression *tẹ̄ hēmerą tẹ̄ tritẹ̄* does not appear. The technical expression "on the third day" was called for in 2:1 because of its association with Exod 19:16, the celebration of Pentecost and the gift of the Law. It would be inappropriate in 4:43, 46, but the arrival of Jesus "on the third day" is still maintained (cf. Boismard and Lamouille, *Jean* 144–145, 151–152).

he went from that place to Galilee: Most critics rightly point out that v. 43 picks up v. 3, and that this marks the end of Jesus' Samaritan interlude. He resumes his interrupted journey.

44. *a prophet has no honor in his own country:* This is a widely attested proverb, found in profane literature as well as in the gospel tradition. See BAGD 637; Bauer, *Johannesevangelium* 77. Of the several scholarly positions concerning Jesus' *patris,* some regard the passage as impossible to explain and thus resort to a redactional theory. See, for example, Lagrange, *Evangile* 124; Schnackenburg, *Gospel* 1:463; Bernard, *Commentary* 1:163–165; Brown, *Gospel* 1:187; Becker, *Evangelium* 1:185; Beasley-Murray, *John* 73. A number of scholars claim that Nazareth and Galilee are regarded as Jesus' home and attempt to explain v. 44 in that light (cf. Pryor, "John 4:44" 254–258). For a survey see Willemse, "La patrie de Jésus" 350–353. Although on different grounds from those presented in the interpretation, the following argue that Jesus' *patris* is understood as Judea: Westcott, *Gospel* 77–78; Hoskyns, *Gospel* 260–261; Barrett, *Gospel* 246; Dodd, *Interpretation* 352; Feuillet "La signification théologique" 67–68; Lindars, *Gospel* 200–201; Willemse, "La patrie de Jésus"

354–364. Finally, there are several scholars who argue that the passage must be understood in the light of the Prologue. Jesus' true home points beyond all earthly places. See, for example, Loisy, *Evangile* 192–193; Reim, "John IV.44" 476–480; Lightfoot, *Gospel* 34–36; Marsh, *Saint John* 231–232.

45. *having seen all that he had done in Jerusalem at the feast:* A link with 2:23-25, where the last reference to a feast is found, is clearly intended (2:23: "He was in Jerusalem at the Passover feast"). There an unspecified "many" believe in the name of Jesus "when they saw the signs that he did" (v. 23). Jesus' response to this signs-faith is not recorded in 4:45, but it is implicit. The enthusiasm of the Galileans in v. 45 is based on a limited understanding of Jesus. This is what the official "heard" (v. 47), and more will be asked of the man.

46. *So he came again to Cana in Galilee:* This recalling of the first Cana miracle begins the narrative proper, after the lengthy (and somewhat clumsy) introduction of vv. 43-45. The transitional vv. 43-45 come from the narrator as commentary on the story thus far (cf. Dodd, *Tradition* 238–241). Verse 46 in some form (perhaps without the explicit reference to Cana and the miracle associated with that place) would have opened the pre-Johannine miracle story. See Schnackenburg, "Zur Traditionsgeschichte von Joh 4,46-54" 70–76. In its present form it should be associated with vv. 43-45 as it continues the introduction of the people, place, and time of the events that follow.

    And at Capernaum there was a royal official whose son was ill: The many similarities between John 4:46-54 and the Q account of the centurion of Capernaum (cf. Matt 8:5-13; Luke 7:1-10) indicate contact between the Q-tradition (which has its own difficulties) and the Johannine tradition at a pre-literary stage. However, there is too little contact to be able to construct a theory of dependence. Not all would agree. For a survey of the discussion down to 1984 see Neirynck "John 4,46-54" 367–375. Since then see Wegner, *Der Hauptmann* 18–74.

    a royal official: It is impossible to determine the ethnic origins of the *basilikos*. Recent research (cf. Wegner, *Der Hauptmann* 57–72) shows that there are four possible meanings for the word: from royal blood, servants to a royal household, soldiers of either the Herodian kings or of the emperor, or a royal scribe. The context, and the widespread use of the term in Josephus (for references see Wegner, *Der Hauptmann* 59 n. 8; Bauer, *Johannesevangelium* 77), suggest that the character in the Johannine story is a soldier of either the Herodian kings or of the emperor. This does not determine whether such a soldier would be Jew or Gentile. He could be either (cf. Schalit, *König Herodes* 167–183). It is tempting to resolve the problem by looking to the Q material, where he is a *hekatontarchēs*. That centurion is certainly Gentile, and probably Roman (cf. Wegner, *Der Hauptmann* 60–69). There is no conclusive proof for the link between a *basilikos* and a *hekatontarchēs* (cf. Mead, "The *basilikos*" 69–72, who claims that there is evidence for his being a Gentile, and Schwarz, "'kai ēn tis basilikos'" 138, who suggests an Aramaic *Vorlage* meaning advisor to the king). What can be asserted is that the figure could be *either* a Jew *or* a Gentile. As this passage is the concluding section of the Gospel dedicated entirely to Jesus' presence to non-Jews (4:1-54), this Johannine literary context has determined the decision taken in the interpretation, that he is a Gentile. Some witnesses have eased the situation by calling the man a *basiliskos* ("a chieftain"), which corresponds to the Latin *regulus*. It is certainly not original (cf. Lagrange, *Evangile* 125).

47. *When he heard:* The hearing of Jesus' arrival in Galilee from Judea depends upon v. 45. The Galileans, who belong to the "many" of 2:23-25, communicate their enthusiasm for Jesus based upon their having "seen all that he had done in Jerusalem at the feast" (v. 45; cf. 2:23). The official's initial movement toward Jesus reflects the belief of the "many" in 2:23-25. His request of Jesus is reported in indirect speech.

48. *Unless you see signs and wonders you will not believe:* A number of scholars attempt to eliminate the rebuke. Some resort to a redactional theory and suggest that vv. 48-49 were added to an original miracle story, as they contradict vv. 51-53 (cf. Schweizer, "Die Heiligung" 64–71; Haenchen, "Johanneische Probleme" 23–31). Others claim that vv. 50b-53 were added to the story to reinforce v. 48! (cf. Boismard and Lamouille, *Jean* 148; Lindars, *Gospel* 204–205). For surveys see Schnackenburg, "Zur Traditionsgeschichte" 62–63; van Belle, "Jn 4,48" 167–169. Bittner, *Jesu Zeichen* 128–134, eliminates the rebuke. He regards it as a proverb stating a broad truth about seeing signs and believing. This strains the grammar and misses the parallel with 2:4.

49. *Come down before my little boy dies:* The second request of the official is in direct speech. The actual "words" of the man are reported, in response to the "words" of Jesus in v. 48. The use of the diminutive *paidion* has been read by Westcott (*Gospel* 79) as indicating "a faith, however imperfect, which springs out of a father's love." This is an interesting remark, particularly in the light of the shift from *basilikos* (vv. 46, 49) to *ho anthrōpos* (v. 50) to *ho patēr* (v. 53).

50. *Your son is living:* Jesus' response to the direct speech of the official's second request (v. 49) is also in direct speech (v. 50a). The man will respond to the "word" of Jesus. Most English translations (e.g. RSV, NRSV, NEB, NAB, NJB) accommodate the translation of the verb *zē* to a future tense: "your son will live." It is best read as a genuine present tense, a declaration of what is happening because of the authority of Jesus' word (cf. v. 53) rather than the promise of something that will happen in the future (cf. BJ; TOB, Lagrange, *Evangile* 126).

The man believed the word: Some scholars attempt to resolve the tension created by the man's two moments of belief (vv. 50 and 53) by claiming that *pisteuein* followed by the dative (as in v. 50b) does not reflect true faith. For example, "The man is not yet a Christian believer; contrast v. 53. He believes that what Jesus has said is true" (Barrett, *Gospel* 248). Although it may be generally the case, one cannot claim that *pisteuein eis* with the accusative always indicates true faith, while *pisteuein* with the dative never does. Thus far, for example, *pisteuein eis* in 2:23 indicates imperfect faith, but *pisteuein* with the dative indicates correct faith in 2:22. *Pisteuein en* in 3:15 indicates correct faith, while *pisteuein dia* in 4:39 indicates incorrect faith and the same expression in 4:41 indicates correct faith.

51. *As he was going down:* Most commentators point to vv. 51-53 as creating a problem in the narrative. The "word faith" of v. 50b seems to be compromised by the faith produced by the verified miracle in vv. 51-53. Does this not prove that Jesus' accusation in v. 48 is correct (so Schnackenburg, *Gospel* 1:467-468)? This problem is eased in v. 50b if not regarded as an act of faith. See the note on v. 50. Thompson, *The Humanity of Jesus* 72–75, and Haenchen, *John* 1:235, claim that in v. 50 the man believes that his son will live, and in v. 53 he believes in Jesus. In the light of the parallel experience of the Samaritans in vv. 41-42, vv. 51-53 can be read as a movement from faith to knowledge (cf. Bittner, *Jesu Zeichen* 259–282).

    that his child was living: The translation reads *pais,* along with the best manuscripts. Origen and some Western texts read *huios.* The latter reading has been accepted by Kilpatrick, "John IV.51" 393, but rightly rejected by Freed, "John IV.51" 448–449. As well as the external textual support, the reading *pais* develops the internal theme of the status of the official emerging since his use of *paidion* in v. 49, and the narrator's description of him as "the man" (v. 50b) and "the father" (v. 53).

52. *"Yesterday at the seventh hour":* The "seventh hour" most probably indicates one o'clock in the afternoon, but there have been various symbolic readings of the number (cf. Robinson, "The Meaning and Significance" 255–262). Given the difficulty in locating a town called Cana, speculation and symbolic readings on the basis of the improbable excessive length of the journey (e.g., Loisy, *Evangile* 196–197; Robinson, "The Meaning and Significance" 259–261) are not helpful.

53. *and he himself believed:* The clumsiness of this second moment of belief has led most scholars to suggest that in the pre-Johannine version of the miracle story the man came to faith because of the miracle. Thus vv. 50-53 are original, and the earlier uncompromising acceptance of the word of Jesus is a Johannine addition to the earlier account. See Schnackenburg, "Zur Traditionsgeschichte" 67–70. The two aorists (v. 50 and v. 53) are to be distinguished. In v. 50 the aorist is ingressive: the man believed and departed. In v. 53 it is complexive, and thus covers the entire belief-experience of the official, the man and the father.

    along with his whole household: The way in which belief gathers others throughout John 4 is widely recognized by scholars as the result of the missionary *Sitz im Leben* of this material. The household's coming to faith as a result of the man's belief is a final example of the missionary function of authentic belief (cf. Boismard and Lamouille, *Jean* 150–151; Gnilka, *Johannesevangelium* 38).

54. *This was now the second sign:* Most scholars who attempt to reconstruct an original signs source (see note to 2:23-25) link 2:12 with 4:46-54. See, for example, Bultmann, *Gospel* 205–206; Fortna, *The Fourth Gospel* 58–65; Boismard and Lamouille, *Jean* 146, 149–150. These scholars regard the numbering of the signs (2:11: "the first of the signs" and 4:54: "the second sign") as traces in the present narrative of a source that originally numbered the miracles. The other

major trace of the source is in 20:30-31: "Now Jesus did many other signs in the presence of the disciples, which are not written in this book; but these are written than you may believe. . . ." Whatever the prehistory of the miracle stories in the Fourth Gospel, these suggestions miss the literary function of 2:1-12 and 4:43-54 in the present Gospel. The two Cana episodes point forward (2:1-12) and backward (4:43-54) as a frame around episodes that, among other things, deal with responses to the word of Jesus. "The curious word order *palin deuteron* implies that this second sign is a reiteration of the first sign or forms its logical complement" (Hanhart, "The Structure" 29).

FOR REFERENCE AND FURTHER STUDY

Belle, Gilbert van. "Jn 4,48 et la foi du centurion," *EThL* 61 (1985) 167–169.

Feuillet, André. "La signification théologique du second miracle de Cana (Jn IV,46-54)," *Études Johanniques*. Bruges: Desclée, 1962, 34–46.

Freed, Edwin D. "John IV:51, PAIS or HUIOS?" *JThS* 16 (1965) 448–449.

Giblin, C. H. "Suggestion, Negative Response and Positive Action in St John's Portrayal of Jesus (John 2.1-11; 4.46-54; 7.2-14; 11.1-44)," *NTS* 26 (1979–1980) 197–211.

Hanhart, Karel. "The Structure of John I 35-IV 54." In *Studies in John: Presented to Professor J. N. Sevenster on the Occasion of His Seventieth Birthday*. NT.S 24. Leiden: E. J. Brill, 1970, 21–46.

Kilpatrick, G. D. "John IV:51, ΠΑΙΣ or ΗΥΙΟΣ?" *JThS* 14 (1963) 393.

Matsunaga, K. "The Galileans in the Fourth Gospel," *Annual of the Japanese Biblical Institute* 2 (1976) 139–158.

Mead, A. H. "The basilikos in John 4.46-53," *JSNT* 23 (1985) 69–72.

Moloney, Francis J. *Belief in the Word* 176–191.

Neirynck, Frans. "John 4,46-54: Signs Source and/or Synoptic Gospels," *EThL* 60 (1984) 367–375.

_____. *Jean et les Synoptiques: Examen critique de l'exégèse de M.-É. Boismard*. BEThL 49. Leuven: University Press, 1979, 166–174.

Pryor, J. W. "John 4:44 and the *Patris* of Jesus," *CBQ* 49 (1987) 254–263.

Reim, Günter. "John IV.44—Crux or Clue?" *NTS* 22 (1975–1976) 476–480.

Robinson, B. P. "The Meaning and Significance of 'The Seventh Hour' in John 4:52." In E. A. Livingstone, ed., *Studia Biblica 1978: II, Papers in The Gospels: Sixth International Congress on Biblical Studies, Oxford 3-7 April 1978*. JSNT.S 2. Sheffield: JSOT Press, 1980, 255–262.

Schalit, Abraham. *König Herodes: Der Mann und sein Werk*. Berlin: Walter de Gruyter, 1969.

Schnackenburg, Rudolf. "Zur Traditionsgeschichte von Joh 4,46-54," *BZ* 8 (1964) 58–88.

Schwarz, Günther. "'*kai ēn tis basilikos*' . . . (Joh 4,46)," *ZNW* 75 (1984) 138.

Schweizer, Eduard. "Die Heiligung des Königlichen, Joh 4,46-54," *EvTh* 11 (1951–1952) 64–71.

Sturch, R. L. "The 'PATRIS' of Jesus," *JThS* 28 (1977) 94–96.

Wegner, Uwe. *Der Hauptmann von Kafarnaum (Mt 7,28a; 8,5-10.13 par Lk 7,1-10): Ein Beitrag zur Q-Forschung.* WUNT 2nd ser. 14. Tübingen: J. C. B. Mohr (Paul Siebeck), 1985.

Willemse, J. "La patrie de Jésus selon saint Jean IV.44," *NTS* 11 (1964–1965) 349–364.

C. THE FEASTS OF "THE JEWS" (5:1–10:42)

Introduction to 5:1–10:42. The Prologue affirms that God's former gift through the Law of Moses is perfected by the fullness of the gift of the truth in Jesus Christ (1:16-17). There is no conflict between the two gifts; one leads to the other, but the latter gift of the truth through Jesus Christ surpasses the gift of the Law through Moses. It is the fullness of God's gracious gifts. The first days of Jesus (1:19-51) indicated that access to this gift was through a faith that transcended traditional signs and expectations. The journey from Cana to Cana (2:1–4:54) told of the universal possibility of belief in the revelation of God in and through the word of Jesus. If access to the gift of God is to be had through belief in the word of Jesus, how do Johannine believers relate to the feasts of "the Jews," the way they had formerly celebrated and approached YHWH?

The celebration of a Jewish feast is called a *zikkārōn* (a noun derived from the Hebrew verb *zākar:* "to remember"), a memory that recalls God's active presence to the Jewish people in the past, *rendered present* in the liturgical celebration of the feast (cf. Chenderlin, *"Do this as my Memorial"* 88–167). Johannine Christians, now separated from their former friends and their former way of life in the synagogue (cf. 9:22; 12:42; 16:2), were also separated from these traditional celebrations. But they were not the only ones who needed to rethink their celebrations of God's presence. After the loss of the Temple in the post-70s of the first century the survival of the Pharisees led to a shift from Temple to synagogue-centered worship. Postwar Judaism was also rethinking its celebrations. "The liturgical feasts of the temple and the piety of the people were in a state of transition and adaptation. The old order and way of life having gone for the most part, the new order under the Pharisees labored and strained to find authority and acceptance in the wider Jewish community" (Yee, *Jewish Feasts* 21). Hence both Johannine Christians and their former Jewish friends who had expelled them from the synagogue were grappling with the way they might gain access to the saving presence of YHWH, traditionally celebrated at the feasts of Israel.

This is the background to the situation addressed by the words of 5:1: "After this there was a feast of the Jews." The celebration of the feast of

Passover motivates Jesus' presence in Jerusalem in 2:13-25, and the same feast provides chronological and theological background for 11:1–20:29. The days of preparation and the celebration of Pentecost led to the revelation of the *doxa* in 1:19–2:12. Some scholars have attempted to interpret the Fourth Gospel on the basis of the feasts (cf. Guilding, *The Fourth Gospel and Jewish Worship*), but it is better to allow the context to determine the use of the feasts rather than vice-versa. On the basis of this principle John 5–10 is dominated by Jewish feasts. After the introduction to the theme in 5:1, the following feasts serve as the chronological setting for the pages that follow: Sabbath (5:1-47; cf. 5:9b), Passover (6:1-72; cf. 6:4), Tabernacles (7:1–10:21; cf. 7:2), Dedication (10:22-42; cf. 10:22). As both "the Jews" and the Johannine Christians grappled with the loss of the Temple and the celebrations of the presence of God centered upon that sacred place, the author tells the story of Jesus' presence at feasts of "the Jews" to articulate the Johannine understanding of how God is present to God's people.

The chronology, the symbolism, and the theology of the Jewish tradition are not abandoned. They provide essential background for the Johannine understanding of the perfection of the former gift of the Law in and through the gift of Jesus Christ (cf. 1:16-17). Leo the Great (d. 461 C.E.) provides a perceptive Christian theological interpretation of the relationship between the Johannine and the Jewish understanding of the feasts of "the Jews": "Lord, you drew all things to yourself so that all nations everywhere in their dedication to you might celebrate . . . what was done only in the Jewish Temple and in signs and shadows" (*Sermon 8 on the Passion of the Lord.* MPL 54:341B).

i. Jesus and the Sabbath (5:1-47)

Introduction to 5:1-47. Jesus' presence in Jerusalem on a Sabbath day begins in 5:1 with an expression *(meta tauta)* used regularly in the Fourth Gospel to mark a new section. It translates literally "after these things." A new episode begins in 6:1, where the same expression appears: "After this *(meta tauta)* Jesus went to the other side of the Sea of Galilee" (6:1). The oneness of time, place, characters, and theme guarantees the unity of 5:1-47. Although there are debates about the internal articulation of each section, it is widely accepted that vv. 1-47 has three parts. In vv. 1-18 Jesus works a miracle, and this leads to his being challenged by "the Jews." He responds to them in two ways. In the first place, between the literary frame of v. 19 and v. 30 he defends his authority to work on a Sabbath (vv. 19-30). The final section of the chapter then continues the forensic nature of the debate between Jesus and "the Jews" as he introduces his witnesses (vv. 31-47).

a) *Jesus' Healing Work on a Sabbath* (5:1-18)

1. After this there was a feast of the Jews, and Jesus went up to Jerusalem.
2. Now at the Sheep-Pool in Jerusalem there is a place with five colonnades. Its name in the language of the Jews is Bethesda. 3a. In the colonnades lay many invalids, blind, lame, and paralyzed.
5. One man was there who had been ill for thirty-eight years. 6. When Jesus saw him lying there and knew that he had been there a long time he said to him, "Do you want to be healed?" 7. The sick man answered him, "Sir, I have no one to put me into the pool when the water is troubled, and while I am making my way someone else steps down ahead of me." 8. Jesus said to him, "Rise, take your mat and walk." 9. At once the man was healed, and he took up his mat and walked. Now that day was a sabbath.
10. So the Jews said to the man who had been cured, "It is the sabbath; it is not lawful for you to carry your mat." 11. But he answered them, "The one who healed me said to me, 'Take your mat and walk.'" 12. They asked him, "Who is the one who said to you, 'Take it and walk'?" 13. Now the one who had been healed did not know who it was, for Jesus had withdrawn, as there was a crowd in the place.
14. After this Jesus found him in the Temple and said to him, "See, you have been healed! Do not sin any more, so that nothing worse happens to you."
15. The man went away and told the Jews that it was Jesus who had healed him.
16. And this is why the Jews persecuted and prosecuted Jesus, because he did this on the sabbath. 17. But Jesus answered them, "My Father is still working, and I also am working." 18. This is why the Jews sought all the more to kill him, because he was not only breaking the sabbath but was also calling God his own Father, thereby making himself equal to God.

INTERPRETATION

Introduction to 5:1-18. The section opens with an introductory statement on Jesus' going to Jerusalem for a feast of the Jews (v. 1). This is followed by a more focused introduction (vv. 2-4) to the events and the discourse of vv. 5-47. The description of the dialogue and the events that constitute the miracle (vv. 5-9) concludes with a statement from the narrator: "Now that day was a sabbath" (v. 9b). Once this theme has been announced it dominates the account of the miracle (vv. 10-13) and its aftermath (vv. 15-18). Only one brief episode does not return to the fact that these things took place on the Sabbath: Jesus' meeting with the cured man in the Temple (v. 14). Attention to these details leads to the identification of the following narrative shape:

(a) *Vv. 1-3a:* Introduction
 i. *V. 1:* Thematic introduction to 5:1-47 and 5:1–10:42.
 ii. *Vv. 2-3a:* The setting for 5:5-47.
(b) *Vv. 5-18:* The Sabbath events
 i. *Vv. 5-9:* Jesus and the man. The miracle, concluding: "now that day was *a Sabbath.*"
 ii. *Vv. 10-13:* "The Jews" and the man. The interrogation of a man who carried his mat on *a Sabbath.*
 iii. *V. 14:* Jesus and the man. Separated from the rest of the action by the expression *meta tauta,* this encounter makes *no mention of the Sabbath.*
 iv. *V. 15:* "The Jews" and the man: The man informs "the Jews" that Jesus did the miracle on *the Sabbath.*
 v. *Vv. 16-18:* Jesus and "the Jews." Jesus is put on trial. "The Jews" seek to kill him for *a Sabbath offense.*

Sabbath is crucial to the story. "The Jews" have one understanding of the right way to worship God on the Sabbath, but Jesus has another.

Introduction (v. 1). The story takes a new direction as the narrator announces that after the events in Cana in Galilee *(meta tauta)* Jesus went up to Jerusalem. The motivation for this journey was "a feast of the Jews." No precise feast is mentioned or intended. The statement in v. 1 introduces the *theme* of a feast of "the Jews" that will be present in the narrative till 10:42. If a feast must be attached to v. 1, it is Sabbath (cf. v. 9b), but rather than introducing the particular feast of vv. 1-47 it indicates that a change of direction occurs in the narrative. The theme stated in 5:1 unfolds across the four feasts that set the chronological and theological agenda for 5:1–10:42 (cf. 5:9; 6:4; 7:2; 10:22). The issue of belief has been the *leitmotif* of 2:1–4:54; now, as Jesus goes up to Jerusalem, the story turns to the feasts of "the Jews." There has been growing hostility between Jesus and "the Jews" (cf. 1:19; 2:13-22). In 5:1 a negative tone is already struck as the narrator mentions a feast celebrated by "the Jews." The association of the feasts with "the Jews" reflects the *Sitz im Leben* of the Johannine community, celebrating the saving presence of God in a way that differed from that of "the Jews." Hostility, however local, was generated by the gradual separation of two Jewish communities. Already present in

1:19 and 2:13-22, it will intensify in the conflicts between Jesus and "the Jews" in John 5–10. The debates between Jesus and "the Jews" in these chapters reflect the pain of the Johannine and the synagogue communities toward the end of the first century, "the type of family row in which the participants face one another across the room of a house which all have shared and all call home" (Ashton, *Understanding the Fourth Gospel* 151).

The setting for 5:5-47 (vv. 2-3a). Jesus has been described as going up to Jerusalem, but the action is suspended in vv. 2-3. Details of a precise location for the following miracle are provided: the Sheep-Pool in Jerusalem, the place with five colonnades, called Bethesda in the language of the Jews (v. 2). The existence of a pool long associated with healing, including pagan healing, at the northern corner of Jerusalem, opposite the Antonia Fortress, is well established. The further description of the people gathered in the colonnades as invalids (v. 3a) "clearly suggests its continuity as a place of healing (going perhaps right back to Canaanite times)" (Robinson, *Priority* 57).

Jesus and the man (vv. 5-9). Within the context of a Jewish feast and a traditional healing site Jesus sees a man who has been ill for thirty-eight years (vv. 5-6). The narrator's comment, that "Jesus . . . knew that he had been there a long time" (v. 6b) recalls the encounters with Nathanael (1:47-48) and the Samaritan woman (4:18). Despite his knowledge of the man's circumstances Jesus asks him, "Do you want to be healed *(theleis hygiēs genesthai)*?" (v. 6c), and this question enables a dialogue. The man's response, "Sir, I have no one *(kyrie, anthrōpon ouk echō)* to put me into the pool" (v. 7) shows that he is unaware of who Jesus is. He is seeking another human being *(anthrōpon)* to perform a certain physical task so that he might be made well. Jesus commands the man, "Rise, take your mat and walk" (v. 8). The response of the man is an unquestioning obedience to the word of Jesus, but this is only possible because between the command and the response the narrator indicates that "the man was healed" (v. 9: *egeneto hygiēs*). It appears that the man is progressing from his initial response to Jesus in v. 7 to his obedience to the word of Jesus in v. 9a, but a warning tolls across the narrative in v. 9b: "Now that day was a sabbath." Jesus has approached the man, offered him healing (v. 6), and commanded him to perform certain actions (v. 8). The man is able to act because Jesus has effected a miracle (v. 9a). What has happened to the man, and his subsequent activity, come from the initiative of Jesus. But that day was a Sabbath (v. 9b)!

"The Jews" and the man (vv. 10-13). "The Jews" enter the story, accusing the man of the unlawful Sabbath work of carrying his mat (cf. *m. Šabb.* 7:2; cf. also 10:5; Exod 20:8-11; Jer 17:19-27). The man does not accept responsibility for this infringement of Sabbath practice; he only did what the

stranger asked him to do (v. 11; cf. vv. 8-9). The cured man has not moved beyond his initial understanding of Jesus (cf. v. 7: *anthrōpon ouk echō*). "The Jews" want to know "Who is the one? *(tis estin ho anthrōpos?)*" (v. 12), but the narrator comments that "the one who had been healed did not know who it was *(ouk ędei tis estin)*" (v. 13a). The two issues crucial to the story are the correct celebration of the Sabbath and the person of Jesus.

Jesus and the man (v. 14). The expression that opens v. 14 (*meta tauta*; cf. 2:12; 3:22; 4:43; 5:1) separates this encounter between Jesus and the man from what happens in the surrounding narrative. It is also the only scene that does not mention the Sabbath. Jesus takes the initiative and finds the man in the Temple (v. 14a). The Jewish institution of the Sabbath is briefly set aside, to be replaced by the institution of the Temple. Jesus recalls the miracle (v. 14b), but transcends the physical event and the issues it raises concerning the Sabbath. He commands the man: "Sin no more." Sin will lead to the man's being worse off than he was in his earlier long-suffering physical condition (v. 14; cf. v. 5). Someone more than "a human being" (cf. vv. 7, 12, 13), more than a miracle worker speaks in the Temple with an authority that transcends human authority. He transcends the theological and legal (v. 10) demands of the Sabbath. The rabbis associated sin with God's punishment through suffering and death (cf. Schnackenburg, *Gospel* 2:461 n. 20), but in the house of God (cf. 2:16) Jesus speaks in the name of God, breaking this traditional link between the physical and God's punishment. The man's physical problems have been overcome, but Jesus' warning hints that more is at stake. Sin will lead to a situation that is more damaging than physical illness. The characters in the story will continue to debate questions that surround the proper celebration of the Sabbath, but such issues are transcended by Jesus' words to the man in the Temple.

"The Jews" and the man (v. 15). There is separation between Jesus and the man, as the latter "went away" (v. 15a: *apēlthen ho anthrōpos*) to answer the question asked by "the Jews" in v. 12. There are no signs of "following" or faith in this "going away" to report the name of a human being, "Jesus," to "the Jews" (v. 15b). His most recent encounter in the Temple, where Jesus revealed himself as someone who transcends the Sabbath (v. 14), has made no lasting impact on the cured man. He has not moved since his original assessment of Jesus in v. 7: "Sir, I have no one *(kyrie, anthrōpon ouk echō).*" The man Jesus made him well.

Jesus and "the Jews" (vv. 16-18). The narrator states that the man's evidence against Jesus' being the one who broke Sabbath legislation is the reason for "the Jews'" instituting a legal process and persecuting him (v. 16). The verb *diōkein* means both "to persecute" and "to bring a charge against, to prosecute" (LSJ 440, s.v., § IV). The imperfect form of the verb *(ediōkon)* indicates that Jesus' actions on the Sabbath led to a constant persecution/prosecution of Jesus. From this point on there is a trial in process, and the protagonists are "the Jews" who act as accusers and Jesus who defends himself by revealing the truth. Jewish Sabbath theology lies behind the process. Jesus' words to "the Jews" are: "My Father is still working, and I also am working" (v. 17). It was clear to Jewish thinkers that God could not rest on the Sabbath. Creation continued, people died and were thus judged; children were born, and thus life was given. Despite Gen 2:2-3 God could not cease to be active, even on the Sabbath, or else history would come to an end (see especially *b. Taʿanit* 2a). But this prerogative of God could not be usurped by any creature. Sabbath was a "memory" (*zakōr*; cf. Exod 20:8) of a creating (cf. Gen 2:2-3; Exod 20:8-11) and redeeming (cf. Deut 5:15) God rendered present to a people. It celebrated God's sovereignty as creator and redeemer and called on the people to recognize this sovereignty publicly. Sabbath existed for the celebration of the unique sovereignty of Israel's Deity. Jesus' claim to be "also working" on the Sabbath is blasphemy to "the Jews" (cf. Gen 3:5; Isa 14:14; Ezekiel 28; Dan 11:31-36; 2 Macc 9:12), but for the one who believes that Jesus is the Word made flesh (1:14) it is but the logical consequence and perfection of God's former gift through Moses (cf. 1:16-17). Jesus claims that *his Father* works on the Sabbath and that he goes on working "still," up to and including the present time *(heōs arti)*. God has not stopped working. YHWH remains God of the Sabbath, but the issue is one of relationship. Jesus' claim to work on the Sabbath depends upon his relationship with the God of Israel, whom he continues to call "my Father" (v. 17; cf. 1:14, 18; 2:16; 3:35; 4:21-24). It is as the incarnate Son of the Father that Jesus is also working.

"The Jews" interpret Jesus' words accurately. According to their judgment he offends on three scores:

1. He has broken the Sabbath by telling the man to carry his mat and by healing (v. 18b).
2. He has called God his Father by claiming that the one who works on the Sabbath is his Father (v. 18c).
3. He has made himself equal to God by claiming that as God works on the Sabbath, so does he (v. 18d).

There are two different ways of interpreting Jesus' relationship to the Sabbath, and they both depend on an understanding of relationship with God. Ironically, "the Jews" have expressed a true understanding of Jesus. He cannot be controlled by traditional Sabbath laws (v. 18b). God is his Father (v. 18c), and he can thus lay claim to equality with God (v. 18d). But, unable to see beyond the limitations of their Sabbath traditions, they "sought all the more to kill him" (v. 18a; cf. Lev 24:10-16; Num 15:30-31).

A trial has been set in motion in which the accusers and the defendant have different answers to the same question. Jesus reinterprets the Sabbath traditions on the basis of his relationship with the God of Israel, his Father, while "the Jews" judge that he has broken the Sabbath legislation and thus deserves to die. "The one acting with the authority of God comes into conflict with the human custodians and exponents of God's law" (Schnackenburg, *Gospel* 2:97). A court scene follows, as Jesus presents his case (vv. 19-30) and calls witnesses (vv. 31-47). During this court scene Jesus may be the only one who speaks, but "the Jews" are always present.

NOTES

1. *After this there was a feast of the Jews:* The translation reads the text without a definite article before "feast" (*ēn heortē*), along with the majority of commentators (cf. Bauer, *Johannesevangelium* 79–81). The narrator speaks generally of "a feast" and many have attempted to resolve which particular feast is in question. Suggestions are Tabernacles, Passover, Pentecost, Purim, and Rosh Hashanah. For a survey, see Moloney, *Son of Man* 68 n. 3. Some (e.g., Becker, *Evangelium* 1:230) regard the feast as without meaning.

2. *Now at the Sheep-Pool in Jerusalem there is a place with five colonnades. Its name in the language of the Jews is Bethesda:* This translation is based on the text as it is found in 𝔓⁶⁶, 𝔓⁷⁵, and Vaticanus. The text has considerable disturbance due to the scribal insertion of vv. 3b-4 (cf. Barrett, *Gospel* 251; Brown, *Gospel* 1:206). Archaeological activity and the copper scroll from Qumran (3Q15 11.12) incline a number of recent scholars to the choice of "Bethesda" for the name of the place. There is a confused textual tradition, with other important witnesses reading Bethzatha and Bethsaida. See Jeremias, *Die Wiederentdeckung;* Weiand, "John V.2" 393–404; Duprez, *Jésus et les dieux guérisseurs* 57–127. For a summary see Davies, *The Gospel* 302–313. It is generally agreed that vv. 3b-4 ("for an angel of the Lord went down at certain seasons into the pool, and troubled the water; whoever stepped in first after the troubling of the water was healed of whatever disease he had") should be omitted. See Fee, "On the Inauthenticity" 207–218; Bruce M. Metzger, *A Textual Commentary on the Greek New Testament* (Stuttgart: German Bible Society, 1994), 179. Some (e.g., Duprez, *Jésus et les dieux guérisseurs* 128–130; Boismard and Lamouille, *Jean* 152–153) argue for their authenticity. It should be omitted because it is absent from the best and earliest manuscripts (e.g., 𝔓⁶⁶.⁷⁵, Sinaiticus, Vaticanus, Ephraemi Rescriptus, Claromontanus, etc.), it is marked by a number of words or expressions that appear only here, and it appears in various forms in different witnesses. It is a gloss, added to explain the miraculous power of the moving water.

In the colonnades lay many invalids, blind, lame, and paralyzed: The five colonnades have often been interpreted symbolically, especially in terms of the five books of the Law (cf. Marsh, *Saint John* 245–246). Archaeological work suggests that a symbolic interpretation (while not to be regarded as impossible) is not necessary. Jeremias's reconstruction has met with widespread acceptance (e.g., Schnackenburg, *Gospel* 2:94) but is regarded by Robinson, *Priority* 54, as "a construct of the imagination." Most (even Robinson, *Priority* 57) make a close link between the archaeological discoveries and an ancient healing site (cf. especially Duprez, *Jésus et les dieux guérisseurs*).

6. *Do you want to be healed?:* The Greek word *hygiēs* is used in the Fourth Gospel only in 5:6, 9, 11, 14, 15, and 7:23. Its use serves as a continual reminder of the physical event of this particular miracle, both throughout ch. 5 and in 7:14-24. See Pancaro, *The Law in the Fourth Gospel* 169–174.

7. *Sir, I have no one (no "man") to put me into the pool:* The term used in vv. 7, 11, 12, and 13 is *anthrōpos*, "human being," although the specific reference in vv. 11, 12, and 13 is to an individual male human being, either Jesus or the healed man. Jesus is regarded as a human being throughout, and it is this understanding of Jesus that limits "the Jews" (and the cured man) from accepting and rightly interpreting his Sabbath actions. The expression *anthrōpos* in the context of v. 7 may mean "slave" (Bauer, *Johannesevangelium* 51), but the links with vv. 11, 12, and 13 must be maintained. For some suggestions about the movement of the water and the practice of placing the sick in the troubled water see Robinson, *Priority* 57–59.

8. *Rise, take your mat and walk:* Jesus' command *(egeire aron ton krabatton sou kai peripatei)* is taken up in the response of the cured man in v. 9a: "he took up his mat and walked" *(ēren ton krabatton autou kai periepatei)*. This obedience to the word of Jesus, in a passage that immediately follows 2:1–4:54, suggests that the man achieves a faith response corresponding to that of the mother of Jesus (cf. 2:5), John the Baptist (3:29-30), the Samaritans (4:42), and the royal official (4:50). This initial impression leads nowhere.

9. *At once the man was healed:* The use of "was healed" *(egeneto hygiēs)* both looks back to Jesus' request in v. 5 and insists upon the initiative of Jesus in working the miracle. What happens to the man (healing) and what he does (carrying the mat) are the result of the initiative of Jesus, a fact that the man correctly points out to "the Jews" in v. 11.

   Now that day was a sabbath: It has often been suggested that this reference to the Sabbath may have been added to an original miracle story and then attached to the debate over Jesus' relationship with the Father (vv. 19-47: cf. Pancaro, *The Law in the Fourth Gospel* 9–16; Witkamp, "The Use of Traditions" 19–31). If this is so, it adds further strength to the case that the whole of 5:1-47 has been designed by the author of the Fourth Gospel to address the question of Jesus and the Sabbath.

10. *It is not lawful:* As well as the commentators, who single out the ways in which both the carrying of the mat and the working of a miracle breach Sabbath laws, see Thomas, "Fourth Gospel" 169–172.

11-12. *the one [the man] who healed me . . . who is the one [the man] . . .?:* Although the English "the one" or "the man" must be supplied as the subject of the verbal form in the Greek of v. 11, the word *anthrōpos* appears in v. 12. These two verses, which express wonder about the identity and authority of Jesus, look back to the cured man's original words to Jesus: "I have no one" (v. 7), and to Jesus' action in healing him (vv. 8-9). The focus of the narrative shifts away from the miracle to Jesus, even though—at this stage—he is absent (cf. Staley, "Stumbling" 60–61). The focus on Jesus will remain throughout the rest of the chapter.

Take your mat and walk: The rhythmic repetition of the same words in vv. 8, 9, 11, 12 locks the narrative together. At this stage, however, "the Jews" are not interested in the miracle but in the fact that "a man" commanded someone to do something that was against Sabbath law.

13. *the one who had been healed did not know who it was . . . as there was a crowd in the place:* In this remark from the narrator there may be a hint of the man's ongoing failure to separate Jesus from the rest of humankind. The man's ignorance of Jesus, despite the fact that he has been cured (another Greek word, *ho iatheis,* is used to describe the man here), arises from the fact that there are many people in the place. Jesus is just "one of the crowd."

14. *After this:* As throughout the Gospel this expression *(meta tauta)* is used to indicate a break in the story it is odd that it appears here, in the middle of the miracle and its aftermath. The interpretation given above singles out v. 14 as both structurally and theologically important.

See, you have been healed! Do not sin any more, so that nothing worse happens to you: Jesus' words initially look back to the earlier encounter between himself and the man. The word *hygiēs* returns, indicating a link between the interrogation of the man by "the Jews," where the same word appears (v. 11). The words on not sinning and the threat of something worse happening transcend both the surrounding discussion of Sabbath laws and the traditional link between sin and sickness. The man's physical sickness is over, and the "something worse" must be of a different order (cf. Lindars, *Gospel* 217; Lightfoot, *Gospel* 141). This encounter is an initial hint of the far-reaching claims Jesus will make for himself as lifegiver and judge in vv. 19-30.

15. *told the Jews that it was Jesus:* The narrative of a cure and its aftermath—interrupted by the expression *meta tauta* and the change of place in v. 14—is resumed. In the light of the interpretation suggested for v. 14 the cured man's inability to transcend the fact that "Jesus" had healed him is remarkable. He is going nowhere in faith, and has merely enabled the discussion between Jesus and "the Jews" to take place (cf. Culpepper, "John 5.1-18" 204–205; Staley, "Stumbling in the Dark" 58–64). He disappears from the narrative. Beck, "The Narrative Function" 143–158, argues that anonymous characters in the Fourth Gospel draw the reader into the narrative and into an identification with the character, culminating with an identification with the Beloved Disciple from ch. 13 onward (on ch. 5, cf. p. 151). The reader of the Fourth Gospel, however, hardly identifies with a man who is in league with "the Jews" (v. 15).

16. *And this is why the Jews persecuted and prosecuted Jesus:* I have translated the one Greek verb *(ediōkon)* with two English verbs. This is clumsy, but it is the only way to communicate the point made by the original Greek that introduces both the notion of an ongoing conflict between Jesus and "the Jews" and the forensic nature of the conflict. It is universally translated as "to persecute" (e.g., RSV, NRSV, JB, NJB, BJ, TOB). For the forensic meaning of *diōkein* in v. 16 see Harvey, *Jesus on Trial* 50–51. It is tempting—within the context of John 5—to limit the verb to its forensic meaning, but this would be to ignore the widespread use of the verb to mean "persecute" in the NT (cf. BAGD, 201, s.v., 2). Both are required. The imperfect tense of the verb indicates an action that was ongoing and repeated.

17. *My Father is still working, and I also am working:* For Jewish background to the idea that God must give life and judge on a Sabbath see *Mekilta Shabbata* 2:25; *Gen. Rab.* 11:5, 10, 12; *Exod. Rab.* 30:6, 9. See also Philo, *Cher.* 86–90; *Leg. all.* 1.5-6; *Letter of Aristeas* 210. On this see Dodd, *Interpretation* 320–323, and especially Bernard, "La guérison de Bethesda" 13–34. For surveys of the biblical and rabbinic understanding of Sabbath see Morgenstern, "Sabbath" 135–141; Hasel, "Sabbath" 5:849–856.

18. *the Jews sought all the more to kill him:* The earlier appearances of "the Jews" in the narrative have been increasingly hostile (1:19; 2:13-22). Here the hostility goes through a rapid escalation from v. 16, where the narrator announced that "the Jews" persecuted Jesus and put him on trial, to v. 18 where they are described as seeking to kill him *(ezētoun auton hoi Ioudaioi apokteinai).* A conflict unto death is now in motion.

    because he was not only breaking the sabbath: The Greek verb translated by "was breaking" *(elyen)* has a primary meaning of "loosened" or "broke." However, it could also mean "did away with" (BAGD, 483, s.v., 4). If this were the meaning, "the Jews" would be wrong. They are correct in suggesting that he broke their understanding of the Law. Jesus is not abolishing the Sabbath; he is reinterpreting it in terms of his relationship to the Father.

    but was also calling God his own Father: There is irony in this substantial complaint of "the Jews" against Jesus. In the Fourth Gospel the key to a proper understanding of Jesus lies in the relationship with the Father that they deny. The Word who existed before all time, turned toward God (1:1), has become flesh and dwells among us as the unique Son of the Father (1:14). No one has ever seen God, but the only Son is telling his story (cf. 1:18). "The Jews'" rejection of Jesus' words in v. 17 is a rejection of the Gospel's fundamental christological claim.

    thereby making himself equal to God: Only "the Jews" say that Jesus makes himself "equal to God" *(isos tō theō).* Jesus does not claim an equality that makes of him "another God," but a oneness that flows from his relationship with God. "They ('the Jews') can only understand equality with God as independence from God, whereas for Jesus it means the very opposite, as is brought out immediately in v. 19" (Bultmann, *Gospel* 245. Author's parenthesis). On the development and significance of this accusation in the Johannine community see Meeks, "Equal to God" 309–321. On Sabbath and blasphemy legislation, and the Johannine tendency to have Jesus breach it see Harvey, *Jesus on Trial* 67–81.

FOR REFERENCE AND FURTHER STUDY

Beck, D. R. "The Narrative Function of Anonymity in Fourth Gospel Characterization," *Sem* 63 (1993) 143–158.

Bernard, Jacques. "La guérison de Bethesda: Harmoniques judéo-hellénistiques d'un récit de miracle un jour de sabbat," *MSR* 33 (1976) 3–34; 34 (1977) 13–44.

Chenderlin, Fritz. *"Do This as My Memorial": The Semantic and Conceptual Background and Value of Anamnēsis in 1 Corinthians 11:24-25.* AnBib 99. Rome: Biblical Institute Press, 1982, 88–167.

Culpepper, R. A. "John 5.1-18: A Sample of a Narrative Critical Commentary." In M. W. G. Stibbe, ed., *The Gospel of John as Literature: An Anthology of Twentieth Century Perspectives.* NT Tools and Studies 17. Leiden: E. J. Brill, 1993, 193–207.

Davies, W. D. "Reflections on Aspects of the Jewish Background of the Gospel of John," *Exploring the Gospel of John* 43–54.

_____. *The Gospel and the Land: Early Christianity and Jewish Territorial Doctrine.* Berkeley: University of California Press, 1974, 302–313.

_____. *The Setting of the Sermon on the Mount.* Cambridge: Cambridge University Press, 1966, 256–312.

Duprez, Antoine. *Jésus et les dieux guérisseurs: A Propos de Jean V.* CRB 12. Paris: Gabalda, 1970.

Fee, G. D. "On the Inauthenticity of John 5:3b-4," *EvQ* 54 (1982) 207–218.

Ferraro, Giuseppe. "Il senso di *heōs arti* in Giov. 5,17," *RivBib* 20 (1972) 529–545.

Harvey, A. E. *Jesus on Trial: A Study in the Fourth Gospel.* London: SPCK, 1976.

Hasel, G. F. "Sabbath," *ABD* 5:849–856.

Jeremias, Joachim. *Die Wiederentdeckung von Bethesda.* Göttingen: Vandenhoeck & Ruprecht, 1966.

Meeks, Wayne A. "Equal to God." In Robert T. Fortna and Beverly Roberts Gaventa, eds., *The Conversation Continues: Studies in Paul and John: In Honor of J. Louis Martyn.* Nashville: Abingdon, 1990, 309–321.

Menken, M. J. J. *Numerical Literary Techniques in John: The Fourth Evangelist's Use of Numbers of Words and Syllables.* NT.S 55. Leiden: E. J. Brill, 1985, 97–137.

Moloney, Francis J. *Signs and Shadows* 1–10.

Morgenstern, Julian. "Sabbath," *IDB* 4 (1962) 135–141.

Painter, John. *Quest* 213–236.

Pancaro, Severino. *Law in the Fourth Gospel* 9–22.

Robinson, J. A. T. *The Priority of John.* London: SCM Press, 1985, 54–60.

Staley, J. L. "Stumbling in the Dark, Reaching for the Light: Reading Characters in John 5 and 9," *Sem* 53 (1991) 55–80.

Weiand, D. J. "John V.2 and the Pool of Bethesda," *NTS* 12 (1965–1966) 392–404.

Witkamp, L. T. "The Use of Traditions in John 5.1-18," *JSNT* 25 (1985) 19–31.
Yee, Gale A. *Jewish Feasts and the Gospel of John.* Zacchaeus Studies: NT. Wilming-
    ton, Del.: Michael Glazier, 1989.

b) *Life and Judgment* (5:19-30)

19. Jesus said to them, "Amen, amen, I say to you, the Son can do nothing on his own authority, but only what he sees the Father doing; for
whatever he does, that the Son does likewise. 20. For the Father loves the
Son, and shows him all that he himself is doing; and greater works than
these will he show him, that you may marvel.
21. For as the Father raises the dead and gives them life, so also the Son
gives life to whom he will.
22. The Father judges no one, but has given all judgment to the Son,
23. that all may honor the Son, even as they honor the Father. Anyone
who does not honor the Son does not honor the Father who sent him.
24. Amen, amen, I say to you, anyone who hears my word and believes
him who sent me has eternal life and does not come into judgment, but
has passed from death to life. 25. Amen, amen, I say to you, the hour is
coming, and now is, when the dead will hear the voice of the Son of God,
and those who hear will live.
26. For as the Father has life in himself, so he has granted the Son also to
have life in himself,
27. and has given him authority to execute judgment, because he is the
Son of Man. 28. Do not marvel at this; for the hour is coming when all
who are in the tombs will hear his voice 29. and come forth, those who
have done good to the resurrection of life, and those who have done evil
to the resurrection of judgment.
30. I can do nothing on my own authority; as I hear, I judge; and my
judgment is just, because I seek not my own will but the will of him who
sent me."

INTERPRETATION

Introduction to 5:19-30. Throughout vv. 19-47 only the voice of Jesus is
heard. He speaks in his own defense, in a discourse made up of two parts.
It opens with a concentration on the themes of life and judgment (cf. v. 21:
life; v. 22: judgment; v. 24: life and judgment; v. 25: life; v. 26: life; v. 27:
judgment; vv. 28-29: life and judgment). Those activities that rabbinic
thought allowed to God on a Sabbath form the backbone of a discourse

during which Jesus claims to work as the Father is working because of his relationship with the Father (cf. v. 17). The statement and restatement of the theme of Jesus' total dependence on the Father further indicates the unity of vv. 19-30:

> v. 19: The Son can do nothing on his own authority.
> *ou dynatai ho huios poiein aph' heautou ouden.*
> v. 30: I can do nothing on my own authority.
> *ou dynamai egō poiein ap' emautou ouden.*

What is said in the third person in v. 19 is restated in the first person in v. 30. The introduction, in v. 31, of the theme of witness ("If I bear witness to myself") introduces a further forensic question that will be pursued till v. 47.

Jesus' explanation of his relationship with the Father in vv. 19-30 is a continuous interplay between the themes of life and judgment, now and hereafter. This interplay produces a discourse shaped as follows:

(a) *Vv. 19-20:* A theological introduction deals with the relationship of love and dependence that exists between Father and Son, and the fruits this relationship could bear for those listening to the discourse.

(b) *V. 21:* As the Father gives life, the Son exercises an authority to give life (the expression *zōiopoiein* is used).

(c) *V. 22:* The basis of the Son's authority to judge: it is given to him by the Father *(ho patēr . . . dedōken).*

(d) *V. 23:* Jesus addresses the audience, insisting on the need to honor both the Father and the Son.

(e) *Vv. 24-25:* The hour is coming . . . when (they) will hear the voice *(erchetai hōra . . . akousousin tēs phonēs).* Jesus is the lifegiver, but judgment is closely associated.

(f) *V. 26:* The basis of the Son's authority to give life: it is given to him by the Father *(ho patēr . . . dedōken).*

(g) *V. 27:* The Son exercises his authority to judge as the Son of Man (the expression *krisin poiein* is used).

(h) *Vv. 28-29:* The hour is coming when (they) will hear the voice *(erchetai hōra . . . akousousin tēs phonēs).* Jesus is the judge, but life-giving is closely associated.

(i) *V. 30:* A theological conclusion deals with the dependence between the one who sends and the one sent, and the fruits this relationship could bear for those listening to the discourse.

This discourse develops Jesus' claim to work also on the Sabbath, as his Father is working still (v. 17). The Sabbath question continues to be central, even though the literary form shifts from a narrative built on action and dialogue (vv. 5-18) to a monologue (vv. 19-30). The same two players are present: as Jesus speaks, "the Jews" are addressed.

The Son and the Father (vv. 19-20). Jesus' words in vv. 19-20, which open with the solemn double "amen," respond directly to the problem created for "the Jews" by Jesus' Sabbath activity (v. 18). The Prologue and earlier words from Jesus have stressed the relationship between Jesus and the Father (cf. 1:1-5, 14, 17-18; 3:16-18, 35-36). Taking this relationship for granted, Jesus explains how it functions in the life of the Son (vv. 19-20a) and for the benefit of others (v. 20b). Jesus' defense of his claims does not eliminate the need to honor and praise the Sabbath God. The term used by "the Jews," who claim that Jesus makes himself equal to God (v. 18: *isos tō theō*) is never used by Jesus. It would be inappropriate. For "the Jews" Jesus' claim to equality was a claim to independence from the Father's authority to equality of status, "as if Jesus were setting himself up as a rival to God" (Pancaro, *The Law in the Fourth Gospel* 55), but all that the Son is and does flows from the Father. The negative structure of the sentence, "The Son can do nothing on his own authority *(ou dynatai ho huios poiein aph' heautou ouden)*" (v. 19a), stresses the "nothing" *(ou . . . ouden)*. The Son is not another Sabbath God, but in a totally dependent relationship where the Son has the privilege of intimacy. The Son sees all that the Father does, and is thus able to do exactly what the Father has done. This is the basis of Jesus' claim in v. 17: "I also am working." The Father goes on working (cf. v. 17: *heōs arti*), but the Son of the Father has entered the human story (cf. 1:14; 3:16) and Jesus points out that something new is happening: as the Father does, so also does the Son (v. 19b).

Not all parents show their children all their secrets, but in a relationship of love there are no secrets. The Father "shows him all *(panta deiknysin)* that he is doing." Affirmation turns to promise as Jesus tells "the Jews" that greater works will be shown to the Son "that you may marvel *(hina hymeis thaumazēte)*" (v. 20b). The relationship between the Father and the Son is not a closed circle. There is more to be seen and more to be marveled at, and Jesus' listeners can be drawn into the circle. "The Jews" have been shocked at Jesus' Sabbath activity (v. 18), but he promises them that greater works will be shown to the Son that they might be part of a revelation of God that reaches beyond their Sabbath expectations. The rest of Jesus' words in vv. 19-30 tell "the Jews" what these "greater works" are.

The Son gives life and all judging authority is granted to him (vv. 21-22). Formerly only the God of Israel was understood as raising the dead and giving life (cf. 1 Sam 2:6; Deut 32:39; Isa 25:8; Wis 16:13; 2 Kgs 5:7). This tradition lies behind Jesus' statement that the Father raises the dead and gives them life (v. 21a), but "just as" *(hōsper)* the Father gives life, "so also" *(houtōs)* the Son gives life. Jesus' discourse remains linked to the miracle, as he commanded the sick man, "Rise" (v. 8: *egeire*). Only the Lord of the Sabbath is the master of life and death, but because of the relationship that exists between the Father and the Son this activity has been passed on to the Son. The Son exercises a sovereign authority ("to whom he will") in giving life *(zōiopoiein)*. Another Sabbath activity reserved to God was judging (cf. Pss 67:5; 94:2; 105:7; Isa 2:4; 26:9; 33:2; Mic 4:3; Ezek 30:3). In the new situation heralded by Jesus' words in v. 17 the Father has ceased from all judging activity (v. 22a). At this stage of the discourse the Son's judging activity is not described, but the basis for any such activity is indicated: the Father gave all judgment to him (v. 22a: *ho patēr . . . tēn krisin pasan dēdōken tǭ huiǭ*). Because of the relationship between the Father and the Son, the Son gives life and all authority to judge has been given to him. Two major Sabbath activities traditionally credited to YHWH have now been associated with Jesus, the Son of the Father.

Honor the Father and the Son (v. 23). The detailed unraveling of what it means for the Son to do everything the Father does (cf. vv. 19, 21-22) pauses, as Jesus directly addresses his listeners accusingly (v. 23). The trial, the persecution, and the plot to kill Jesus (cf. vv. 16-18) lie behind Jesus' threat. Israel claims to honor God, lifegiver and judge, on the Sabbath, but "the Jews" are plotting to kill Jesus, the Son. This is an impossible contradiction and it is challenged by Jesus' insistence that his listeners must honor the Son if they wish to honor the Father. Again there is an interplay between the story of the miracle and its aftermath (vv. 5-18) and the discourse of vv. 19-30. Jesus' opponents' claims to the proper observance of the Sabbath are empty.

The hour is coming and now is (vv. 24-25). The discourse resumes the themes of lifegiver and judgment, marking the resumption with two further uses of the double "amen" (vv. 24, 25). Jesus continues to speak to "the Jews" *(legō hymin)*. Whereas previously Jesus spoke of the Son's lifegiving and judging presence (vv. 21-22) and the need to honor both Father and Son, what the reader has known now becomes explicit. Jesus replaces "the Son" with the first person singular. Jesus is the Son, lifegiver, and judge. Another feature of vv. 24-25 is their focus on the believer. The rest of the discourse spells out the way Jesus assumes the Sabbath roles of the Father. In these two verses, both beginning with "amen, amen, I say to you," the fruits of Jesus' lifegiving and judging presence are indicated. In v. 24 entrance into life and the avoidance of a negative judgment are explained in terms that come from the stories that filled the journey from Cana to Cana (2:1-4:54). The one who hears *(akouōn)* the word of Jesus and believes *(pisteuōn)* the Father who sent Jesus, the Son, *has already* passed (perfect tense: *metabēbeken*) from death to life *(eis tēn zōēn)*. Life can be achieved now through belief in the revelation of God in and through the Son of God (v. 25b). The passage from death to life is not a future promise; it happens now: *the hour is coming, and now is* (v. 25a). The event of Jesus Christ does not remove the celebration of the

Sabbath, but on a Sabbath festival (cf. vv. 1, 9) Jesus points to himself as the source of life and judgment, doing within the human story what the God of Israel has done from all time. The ongoing work of the Sabbath God has been "handed over" to the Son, Jesus. He is also working—*now* (cf. v. 17).

Jesus judges and all lifegiving authority is granted to him (vv. 26-27). As in v. 21 Jesus first states a principle central to Israel's theological tradition: the Father has life in himself. But he claims that "as" (*hōsper gar*) this is true of God, "so also" (*houtōs kai*) it is true of Jesus because the Father has granted it to the Son (*ho patēr . . . tō huiō edōken zōēn echein en heautō*. Cf. v. 22). He has earlier claimed that he gives life (v. 21) and now he explains how this is possible: the Father has granted the Son to have life in himself (v. 26). From this affirmation on the basis for his lifegiving authority Jesus goes on to state that the Son judges everyone because he is the Son of Man (v. 27: *krisin poiein;* cf. v. 21). He has earlier explained that the Father judges no one, but grants such authority to the Son (v. 22), and now he claims that he exercises judgment. The addition of the words "because he is the Son of Man" recall earlier references to this expression. As the first days of Jesus came to an end he promised those who believed the sight of greater things, the revelation of the heavenly in the Son of Man (1:50-51). Shortly after, in his dialogue with Nicodemus, he has carried that promise a few steps further, affirming that there was only one revealer of the secrets "from above," the Son of Man (3:13), and that this Son of Man must be lifted up on a stake so that all who believe in him might be saved (3:14-15). Some time in the future the Son of Man will be "lifted up." That event will also be a moment of revelation. It will make God known, and judgment will take place as people either believe or disbelieve that this Son of Man is the revelation of God (cf. 3:16-21, 31-36). God no longer actively judges (v. 22) but is made known in and through Jesus, the Son of Man. The Son exercises judgment as people accept or refuse the revelation of God in the figure of Jesus, the Son of Man (v. 27).

The hour is coming (vv. 28-29). In v. 25 Jesus announced "The hour is coming *and now is.*" These words proclaimed that the presence of Jesus already gave life and brought judgment (vv. 24-27). "The Jews" are now told not to marvel at this (v. 28a) because the handing over of Sabbath authority to Jesus does not remove the traditional understanding of the end time with its associated judgment unto life or death. In v. 28b the expression of v. 25 returns, focused entirely on the future: "the hour is coming." The words "and now is" have been omitted. Jesus' teaching in vv. 28b-29 matches traditional Jewish and early Christian eschatological expectations. Sometime in the future there will be an hour when the physically dead will hear the voice of the Son and come forth from their tombs into either the resurrection of life or the resurrection of judgment. The criterion for their post-tomb experience of resurrection will be their pre-tomb lives. "The Jews" are not to marvel at this marriage of the lifegiving and judging presence of Jesus and the traditional promise of resurrection and judgment after death. However stimulating the challenging realized eschatology of v. 24 might be, one must come to terms with the fact that the everyday experience of human life and death continues, despite the "eternal life" believers claim to possess *now*. There must also be a word addressing the other side of death, as those who hear the word of Jesus and believe in the one who sent him may have "eternal life" (cf. v. 24), yet they still die. The sovereignty of God honored by the celebration of Sabbath reaches beyond the limitations of time, as God is the Lord of all creation both here and hereafter. The physical reality of life and death is as much the domain of a Sabbath God as is the present role of lifegiver and judge. Acceptance and refusal of the Son *now* (vv. 24-27) must be related to life on the other side of the tomb (vv. 28-29). Those who hear the voice of the Son and have life *now* are spared neither the need to endure the vicissitudes of life nor the reality of physical death, but they will be summoned from their graves.

Conclusion (v. 30). In v. 30 much of v. 19 returns. As the discourse opened Jesus spoke of the dependence of the Son on the Father. Here the third person becomes the first person. Jesus is totally dependent, hearing and judging according to the will of the one who sent him (cf. 3:17, 34; 4:34; 5:23, 24). As God is the lifegiver and judge, so also is Jesus the lifegiver and judge (cf. v. 17). The setting of a Sabbath (v. 9b; cf. vv. 10, 16, 18) allows Jesus to reread traditional Sabbath theology and practice. A trial is in progress in which "the Jews" are the accusers (cf. v. 18) and Jesus is the defendant (vv. 19-30). At stake is Jesus' claim to work on a Sabbath, as the Father works (vv. 17-18). By v. 30 "the Jews" are being accused of not understanding the revelation of the Sabbath activity of God in Jesus. He has neither replaced God nor done away with the Sabbath celebration (vv. 19, 30). But they do not understand that the Son is lifegiver and judge, just as the Father is lifegiver and judge (cf. vv. 21, 26). The accusers are becoming the accused, guilty of not honoring the Father in not honoring the Son (v. 23).

NOTES

19. *Jesus said to them:* The discourse opens with a solemn introduction, literally "Jesus therefore answered and said to them" (*apekrinato oun ho Iēsous kai elegen autois*). A close link with vv. 1-18 is maintained by the connecting particle *oun* ("therefore"), and the indication that Jesus answers "the Jews."

    Amen, amen I say to you: As throughout the Fourth Gospel, this expression introduces a significant statement that is linked to what has gone before. See

Bernard, *Commentary* 1:67. It appears on two further occasions in vv. 19-30 (vv. 24, 25).

only what he sees the Father doing: Many scholars (e.g., Dodd, Gächter, Brown, Lindars, Talbert) have seen a traditional parable on a son's relationship to his father behind this passage. See Moloney, *Son of Man* 72–75. Whatever the tradition behind the passage, the absolute use of *ho huios* points to one of the author's fundamental christological claims for Jesus. See Ashton, *Understanding the Fourth Gospel* 292–329.

whatever he (the Father) does: The personal pronoun used for "he" in reference to the Father is the strong *ekeinos.* This "lays stress upon the separate divine Person" (Barrett, *Gospel* 259).

20. *the Father loves the Son:* This is the second time this has been affirmed (cf. 3:35). God's love for the world is also the motive for the sending of the Son (cf. 3:16). This theme will gather momentum, but in this context it is the reason for the Father's showing "all *(panta)* that he himself is doing." See Hoskyns, *Gospel* 267–268.

   greater works than these: Some interpreters claim that the "greater works" *(meizona)* look forward to Jesus' more spectacular works, the healing of the man blind from birth (ch. 9) and the raising of Lazarus (ch. 11). The interpretation offered above regards the greater works as the life and judgment that Jesus brings, not further miracles. It is the handing over of Sabbath privileges from the Father and the Son that could lead "the Jews" to marvel, not spectacular signs. See Schnackenburg, *Gospel* 2:104–105.

21. *As the Father . . . so also the Son:* The close association of the Father and the Son in giving life is made clear by "As . . . so also" *(hōsper . . . houtōs).* Jesus first affirms that the Son gives life, and later explains that this authority is given to him by the Father (v. 26).

   to whom he will: The sovereign freedom of Jesus in exercising his Sabbath privileges matches the traditional understanding of the sovereignty of YHWH over creation and the Sabbath.

22. *The Father judges no one:* The Johannine understanding of judgment is closely linked to the Gospel's realized eschatological perspective. There is no place for a final judgment from God. Human beings judge themselves as they accept or refuse the revelation of God in and through Jesus, and walk in the darkness of their evil deeds or the light of their good deeds as a result of their decision (cf. 3:17-21, 36). See Blank, *Krisis* 158–164.

   but has given all judgment to the Son: Unlike the development of the theme of the Son as lifegiver, which began by affirming his lifegiving activity (v. 21), the Son's judging activity is first shown to be authoritative because the Father grants it to him. At a later stage the Son will be described as judging (v. 27).

23. *Anyone who does not honor the Son does not honor the Father who sent him:* This statement from Jesus, which approaches an accusation, ties the discourse with the response of "the Jews" to Jesus' Sabbath activity in vv. 5-18. It continues the Sabbath theme, associating the Son with the honor due to the

Father, and shows that "the Jews" are doing neither. A number of attempts have been made to structure the discourse of vv. 19-30 around a chiasm, with the same themes being stated and restated around a central theme (cf. Vanhoye, "La composition" 270–274; Bernard, "La guérison" 17–20; Ellis, *Genius* 90–93; Mlakuzhil, *Christocentric* 126–128. See the critical survey in Moloney, *Son of Man* 74–76). This comment from Jesus has no parallel in the latter part of the discourse, and makes chiastic structures unwieldy.

24. *Amen, amen, I say to you:* This Johannine expression appears twice in two verses (vv. 24-25). Thus far Jesus has spoken of the lifegiving and judging role of the Son. Here he speaks of the fruits of the presence of his word for those who believe in him.

    has passed from death to life: The use of the perfect tense *(metabebēken)* of the verb ties the passage from a situation of sin ("death") to "life," to the acceptance of the word of Jesus within the present situation of the believer. This has been long regarded as "the strongest affirmation of realized eschatology . . . in the NT" (Beasley-Murray, *John* 76).

25. *The hour is coming and now is:* The association of the expression "and now is" *(kai nun estin)* with "the hour is coming" collapses traditional end-time eschatology into the present, yet the verbs of affirmation in the rest of v. 25 are in the future: "the dead will hear *(akousousin)* . . . those who hear will live *(zēsousin)*." While these futures are still to be read as belonging to the more realized view of "eternal life," they look forward to the introduction of the traditional end-time eschatology in vv. 28-29 (Cf. Stimpfle, *Blinde Sehen* 84). On "life" and "eternal life" in the Fourth Gospel see J. G. van der Watt, "The Use of *aiōnios* in the Concept *zōē aiōnios* in John's Gospel," *NT* 31 (1989) 217–228.

26. *as the Father has life . . . so he has granted the Son also to have life:* The Son's lifegiving activity was linked with the activity of the Father by means of "as . . . so also" *(hōsper . . . houtōs)* in v. 21. In v. 26 the basis of the Son's lifegiving authority is provided. It is granted him by the Father. Again the parallel between the Father and the Son is created by "as . . . so" *(hōsper . . . houtōs)*. God's Sabbath activity does not cease; it is granted to the Son (cf. v. 17).

27. *and has given him authority to execute judgment:* The handing over of all judgment to the Son was indicated in v. 22, and the judging activity of the Son is found in v. 27. There is an interesting interplay between the giving of life, which is exercised (v. 21) and given (v. 26), and judgment, which is given (v. 22) and exercised (v. 27).

    because he is the Son of Man: Although an article has been provided ("the Son of Man"), the Greek does not have one: *hoti huios anthrōpou estin* ("because he is son of man"). This is the only place in the NT where the term is found without an article, and it reproduces exactly what was found in the probable source for the expression, Dan 7:13, which also does not have an article: "You will see one like a son of man." As indicated in the interpretation, the earlier uses of this description of Jesus in the Fourth Gospel are crucial for a correct understanding of its meaning here. Jesus is the revelation of God in the human story, and judgment flows from acceptance or refusal of the revelation. Thus Jesus can say that the Son executes judgment *because he is the Son of Man* (see Moloney, *Son of Man* 68–86; Hare, *Son of Man* 90–96). However, due to the use of Dan 7:13 in both Jewish and Christian exegesis, "the Son of Man" was also strongly linked with an end-time eschatology in the tradition (cf. Mark 8:38; 13:26; 14:62; Matt 13:41; 16:28; 19:28; 24:29-30, 39; 25:31; Luke 11:30; 12:8; 12:40; 17:22, 24, 26, 30; 18:8; 21:36). Thus while the Johannine understanding of "the Son of Man" explains the realized way in which the Son executes judgment, the traditional end-time use of the term forms a bridge that leads into vv. 28-29 (cf. Moloney, *Son of Man* 80–82).

28. *the hour is coming:* The omission of "and now is" (cf. v. 25) introduces an end-time eschatological perspective. A number of scholars regard vv. 28-29 as coming from the hand of a later redactor who betrayed the original realized intention of the evangelist (e.g., Loisy, *Evangile* 213–214; Bultmann, *Gospel* 237–239, 261; Haenchen, *John* 1:253–254). Others (e.g., Schnackenburg, *Gospel* 2:145–150) see the apocalyptic elements as foreign to the Fourth Gospel but accept that the eschatological thought of the evangelist has not been betrayed. The majority of contemporary scholars accept both the authenticity of vv. 19-30 as a whole (cf. Vanhoye, "La composition" 262–268) and that an end-time eschatology is part of Johannine thought. See N. A. Dahl, "'Do Not Wonder!' John 5:28-29 and Johannine Eschatology Once More," *The Conversation Continues* 322–336; Carroll, "Present and Future," 63–69.

all who are in the tombs: Some scholars see those in the tombs as all those who came before Jesus and those who will come after him but never heard of him. They too would have their moment of judgment (e.g., Léon-Dufour, *Lecture* 2:61–62; van der Watt, "New Look," 76–85). This appears to read too much into the passage. It is not called for by the context, however true it might be when applied to later Christian concerns.

30. *the will of him who sent me:* In the Semitic world the one sent becomes the presence of the one who sends. Jesus' claim to be the Sent One of the Father fits into this scheme (cf. 4:34). See Bühner, *Der Gesandte* 181–267; Ashton, *Understanding the Fourth Gospel* 308–317.

FOR REFERENCE AND FURTHER STUDY

Carroll, J. T. "Present and Future in Fourth Gospel 'Eschatology,'" *BTB* 19 (1989) 63–69.

Dahl, N. A. "'Do Not Wonder!' John 5:28-29 and Johannine Eschatology Once More." In Robert T. Fortna and Beverly Roberts Gaventa, eds., *The Conversation Continues: Studies in Paul and John. In Honor of J. Louis Martyn.* Nashville: Abingdon, 1990, 322–336.

Moloney, Francis J. *Signs and Shadows* 10–19.

_____. *Son of Man* 68–86.

Painter, John. *Quest* 226–235.

Vanhoye, Albert. "La composition de Jean 5,19-30." In Albert Descamps and André de Halleux, eds., *Mélanges Bibliques en hommage au R. P. Béda Rigaux.* Gembloux: Duculot, 1970, 259–274.

Watt, J. G. van der "A New Look at John 5:25-29 in the Light of the Term 'eternal life' in the Gospel According to John," *Neotest.* 19 (1985) 71–86.

_____. "The Use of *aiōnios* in the Concept *zōē aiōnios* in John's Gospel," *NT* 31 (1989) 217–228.

c) *Witness and Accusation* (5:31-47)

31. "If I bear witness to myself, my testimony cannot be verified; 32. there is another who bears witness to me, and I know that the testimony that he bears to me is true.

33. You sent to John, and he has borne witness to the truth. 34. Not that I accept such human testimony, but I say this that you may be saved. 35. He was a lamp that was kindled and shining, and you were willing to rejoice for a while in his light.

36. But the testimony that I have is greater than that of John; for the works that the Father has granted me to accomplish, these very works that I am doing, bear me witness that the Father has sent me.

37. And the Father who sent me has himself borne witness to me. His voice you have never heard, his form you have never seen; 38. and you do not have his word abiding in you, for you do not believe him whom he has sent. 39. You search the scriptures, because you think that in them you have eternal life; and it is they that bear witness to me; 40. yet you refuse to come to me that you may have life.

41. I do not accept glory from human beings. 42. But I know that you have not the love of God within you. 43. I have come in my Father's name, and you do not receive me; if another comes in his own name, him you will receive. 44. How can you believe, who receive glory from one another and do not seek the glory that comes from the one who alone is God?

45. Do not think that I shall accuse you to the Father; it is Moses who accuses you, on whom you set your hope. 46. If you believed Moses, you would believe me, for he wrote of me. 47. But if you do not believe his writings, how will you believe my words?"

INTERPRETATION

Introduction to 5:31-47. The trial continues in vv. 31-47, but Jesus' defense of his own Sabbath activity (vv. 19-30) needs witnesses. As in vv.

19-30 only the voice of Jesus is heard, but "the Jews" of vv. 5-18 are addressed throughout (*hymeis:* vv. 33, 34, 35, 38, 39, 42, 44, 45. Second person plural verbs are used in vv. 37, 40, 43, 46, 47). Jesus accepts the need for witnesses (vv. 31-32) and supplies them (vv. 33-40), but as the discourse closes he points to the inability of "the Jews" to recognize the revelation of God (vv. 41-44), and threateningly tells them that their own writings accuse them (vv. 45-47). The discourse unfolds in the following fashion:

> (a) *Vv. 31-32:* Jesus raises the problem of an acceptable witness.
> (b) *Vv. 33-40:* Witnesses are presented to "the Jews."
>   i.   *Vv. 33-35:* John the Baptist
>   ii. *V. 36:* The works of Jesus
>   iii. *Vv. 37-40:* The word of the unseen Father.
> (c) *Vv. 41-44:* Jesus presents contrasting understandings of *doxa.*
> (d) *Vv. 45-47:* "The Jews" are accused by the writings of Moses.

A trial that began as Jesus' defense of his Sabbath actions (vv. 19-30; cf. vv. 16-18) closes with an accusation that "the Jews" are accused by their own Scriptures. The accusers have become the accused.

An acceptable witness (vv. 31-32). Jesus points out that the witness he has borne to himself cannot be verified (v. 31: *ouk estin alēthēs*). In Jewish practice it was not enough for the accused to prove the *truth* of certain facts; witnesses whose word could be trusted had to be brought forward (cf. Deut 19:15; *m. Roš Haš.* 3:1; *m. Ketub.* 2:9; Josephus, *Ant.* 4:219). Jesus accepts this situation, and points enigmatically toward "another" *(allos)* whom he knows bears a continuous witness (present tense: *martyrei*) of lasting value to him (v. 32). Jesus rests in the confidence of his knowledge, but more is needed for "the Jews." Although the reader might understand that the "other" is the Father of Jesus, this is not the case for "the Jews." Jesus thus turns to witnesses they have seen and heard: John the Baptist (vv. 33-35) and the works of Jesus (v. 36).

The witness of John the Baptist (vv. 33-35). Jesus reminds "the Jews" that they sent messengers to John the Baptist (cf. 1:19). That moment of witness is in the past (v. 33: *memartyrēken:* perfect tense). John witnessed to Jesus as the Lamb *of God* (1:19, 35) and the Son *of God* (1:34). Because of the never-failing witness of the "other" (cf. 5:32) Jesus needs no human witness, but "the Jews" do (v. 34a). Jesus is prepared to submit himself to the messiness of the human situation, including the trial now in process, so that his interrogators might be saved (v. 34b; cf. 1:14; 3:16-17). There may be conflict, and even a trial that seeks the death of Jesus (vv. 16-18), but Jesus does not exclude "the Jews" from his saving mission *(hina hymeis sōthēte).* Jesus' description of the Baptist as "a lamp that is kindled and shining" summons up primitive ideas of a lamp that becomes a witness to the Messiah (LXX Ps 131:16b-17; cf. Sir 48:1). This shining *(phainōn)* lamp brought joy. "The Jews" were prepared *(ēthelēsate)* to be joyful *(agalliathēnai)* but, as the present trial against Jesus shows, their joy stopped there (v. 35). "The Jews" joyfully accepted that the light of the Baptist gave witness to the coming Messiah, but they are now unable to accept the one to whom he gave witness (cf. 1:11). They were unable to look beyond the reflected light of the Baptist, to see him to whom he bore witness.

The witness of the works of Jesus (v. 36). Jesus has an even greater witness (v. 36a). He has a task *(to ergon)* to do that has its origins in God (cf. 4:34), and that task is performed through his continual response to the one who sent him. This response is seen in the many works *(ta erga)* that Jesus accomplishes (v. 36b; cf. v. 20). Jesus does not simply perform these works; he does them perfectly *(teleioun).* This is not to be regarded as self-witness (cf. v. 31). Jesus' perfect accomplishment of his tasks witnesses to the truth that he is the Sent One of the Father (v. 36c).

The witness of the word of the unseen Father (vv. 37-40). After the enigmatic summoning of the witness of the *allos* in v. 32 Jesus has called upon the Baptist (vv. 33-35) and his own works (v. 36). In the turn to the witness of the Father (vv. 37-40), the "other" of v. 32 is clarified. A marked difference is evident between the witnesses summoned in vv. 33-36 and that of the Father. The Baptist and the works of Jesus could be seen and heard, but this is not the case with the *martyria* of the Father who sent Jesus (v. 37a). "The Jews" have never heard his voice *(phōnēn autou)* and they have never seen his form *(eidos autou).* There is accusation, as Jesus spells out what is meant by "voice" and "form" in v. 38b: "for you do not believe him whom he has sent." "The Jews" take it for granted that they have the word of God abiding in them (v. 38a), but their rejection of the one whom God has sent makes such a belief presumptuous. Jesus is the *phōnē* and the *eidos* of God, but they do not hear or see him as such. Jesus is not the Father, but he is the one sent by the Father, and he tells the story of God in and through his story (cf. 1:18). The *phōnē* of God is the *logos* of Jesus.

Jesus continues to point to the failures of his accusers in vv. 39-40. The Jewish practice of study and reflection on the Scriptures is regarded as lifegiving (v. 39), but "the Jews" miss the lifegiving power that comes from a recognition that the biblical word bears witness to Jesus. Their decision to put Jesus on trial in an attempt to kill him is based on their scrutiny of the Scriptures and their interpretation of the Sabbath laws (cf. v. 18). But the Scriptures, where one finds the witness that the Father gives to Jesus (v. 37; cf. v. 31), and that are the witness of the unseen God to Jesus (cf. v. 37), are being abused by those who seek to kill him. They point to Jesus as the voice and form of God, and belief in him leads to the presence of the word of God dwelling in the believers, but their lack of belief disqualifies them from this presence (v. 38). "The Jews" mistakenly believe that they have life from their tradition and their reflection on Scripture (v. 39). They refuse to come to Jesus (v. 40a). Indeed, their decision to put Jesus on trial and attempt to kill him on the grounds of his blasphemous behavior on a Sabbath (vv. 16-18) excludes them from his lifegiving presence (v. 40b). The tables are being turned as the one on trial begins his accusation of the accusers.

Two different understandings of doxa (vv. 41-44). The trial scene is coming to an end, and Jesus now presents the two cases. The Greek word *doxa* has a secular and a biblical meaning. In common usage it refers to the esteem, praise, and glory that come from human achievement. Jesus indicates that he has no interest in "glory from human beings" (v. 41: *doxa tōn anthrōpōn*), but he is certain that "the Jews" do not have the love of God in them. From his intimate knowledge of God *(egnōka)* Jesus reproaches "the Jews" because, whatever their claims to life from the Scriptures, they show no sign of loving God (v. 42). Jesus, the accused, does not seek human recognition (v. 41) while "the Jews," the accusers, do not love God (v. 42). This leads them to the rejection of the one sent in the Father's name (v. 43a) and the easy acceptance of those who come in their own name (v. 43b). Jesus' authority comes from the Father as the one who sent him, but this is rejected as "the Jews" accept all those who might come with nothing more than the authority of their own name (v. 43a: *en tǭ onomati tou patros mou . . .*; v. 43b: *en tǭ onomati tǭ idiǭ*).

Two radically different perspectives emerge: Jesus looks to God while "the Jews" judge by external appearances. Jesus has rejected the *doxa* of human beings, but the opposite is the case with "the Jews." In the end, their inability to believe comes from settling for the esteem and honor they receive from one another, the *doxa* of human beings (v. 44a: *doxan para allēlōn*). Locked in the world they can understand and control, they are unable to seek and find the *doxa* that comes from God (v. 44b: *tēn doxan tēn para tou monou theou*). Jesus, Lord of the Sabbath, makes known the *doxa* of the only true God who has shown the Son all that he does so that the Son might show these, and even greater works (v. 20). In rejecting the revelation of the one and only God in the Son, "the Jews" have rejected the Sabbath God they claim to be defending (cf. vv. 16-18). "The failure to accept Jesus is really a preference of self" (Brown, *Gospel* 1:228).

Moses accuses "the Jews" (vv. 45-47). According to Jewish thought Moses was regarded as the mediator between God and Israel, the one who intercedes before God for Jews (cf. Exod 32:11-14, 30-33; Deut 9:18-29; *Exod. Rab.* 18:3; *T. Mos.* 11:17; *Jub.* 1:19-21; Josephus, *Ant.* 4:194–195). The Law, God's first great gift, had come to Israel through Moses (cf. 1:17a), but God's gifts have continued and been perfected in and through

Jesus Christ (1:17b). There is no conflict between the two gifts, as one takes the place of the other in God's design. But "the Jews" are rejecting Jesus Christ, and therefore Moses accuses them (v. 45). Jesus has earlier claimed that the Scriptures bear witness to him (v. 39b). This affirmation returns as an accusation in vv. 46-47. If they believed in Moses, they would believe Jesus, as the writings of Moses were about him (v. 46). But they have not believed in Moses. On the basis of their interpretation of the Mosaic Torah "the Jews" condemn Jesus (v. 18), but they are wrong. This is a misinterpretation of the Mosaic tradition. Thus Israel's great intercessor must turn against "the Jews" and condemn them. There is continuity between the writings of Moses (v. 47a: *ekeinou grammasin*) and the words of Jesus (v. 47b: *emois rhēmasin*) which perfect all that Moses said (cf. 1:16-17). But if "the Jews" are unable to believe the writings of Moses they cannot believe the words of Jesus, the revelation of God (v. 47).

Conclusion to 5:1-47. The celebration of the Sabbath is essential literary and theological background for John 5. A miracle worked on a Sabbath creates difficulties (vv. 1-13). After an encounter between Jesus and the cured man that suggests that Jesus cannot be limited to expected Sabbath behavior (v. 14) a trial opens (vv. 15-16) and a verdict is taken, that Jesus must die (vv. 17-18). Jesus defends himself by claiming that his lifegiving and judging activity on the Sabbath flows from his dependence upon his Father, who is still working (vv. 19-30). He next introduces his witnesses (vv. 31-32): John the Baptist (vv. 33-35), the works of Jesus (v. 36), and the Father (vv. 37-40). The inability of "the Jews" to accept these witnesses leads to an ironic change in the direction of the trial: the accusers become the accused (vv. 41-44). Their search for human praise and esteem cannot match Jesus' authority as the revelation of the one and only Sabbath God (v. 44: *ho monos theos;* cf. 2 Kgs 19:15, 19; Ps 85:10; Isa 37:20; Dan 3:25). They stand condemned, unable to read and understand rightly the writings of their great intercessor, Moses (vv. 45-47).

The Johannine community had been cast out of the synagogue (cf. 9:22; 12:42; 16:2), and its members struggled to understand how they were to relate to the God of Israel, the Father of Jesus, worshiped as the one and only creator God through the Jewish celebration of the Sabbath. Their ex-friends and fellow Jews were also coming to grips with a changed situation, without a priesthood, a holy city, or a Temple. The Johannine community was asked to believe that Jesus was the Son of God (vv. 19, 30), the perfection of the Mosaic tradition (1:16-17) who made God known (1:18). What had once been done in the Jewish Temple on the Sabbath was but a sign and a shadow of the perfection of the gift of God in the person of Jesus Christ (1:16-17), lifegiver and judge (5:19-30), the bringer of eternal life to all who would believe in his name (5:24). It was impossible to honor the traditional Sabbath God without honoring his Son (5:23).

Those who would use the Mosaic tradition to exact a judgment that could lead to the death of Jesus (vv. 16-18) are found wanting. Indeed, Moses accuses "the Jews" (v. 47). Like Jesus, the Johannine Christians have been condemned and expelled from the place where the traditions of Moses were celebrated on the Sabbath (cf. 9:22; 12:42; 16:2), but the author of the Fourth Gospel tells them that it is "the Jews" who have lost their way and are judged. "The Jews" who do not honor the Son do not honor the Father (v. 23). They do not accept Jesus' offer: to pass from death to life (v. 24). But as Jesus perfects the signs and shadows of the Jewish celebration of the Sabbath he enters into a conflict with "the Jews" that will prove to be fatal. Already there is an indication that the conflict between the Johannine Christians and "the Jews" will also lead to the death of Christians (cf. 16:2).

Notes

31. *I bear witness to myself:* The legal nature of the ongoing discourse is widely recognized. On the literary form see Becker, *Evangelium* 1:249–251, and on its possible rabbinic background see Thomas, "Fourth Gospel" 174–177. It is often pointed out that there is a contradiction between 5:31 and 8:14, where Jesus speaks of the truthfulness of the witness that he bears himself (e.g., Barrett, *Gospel* 264). The interpretation of each of these passages is strongly determined by their contexts, and they are not as contradictory as might at first appear.

    cannot be verified. A number of translations are possible for *ouk estin alēthēs*. The forensic nature of the discourse leads to the translation given. See Brown, *Gospel* 1:222. On the Jewish legal process that called upon witnesses who could be trusted see Harvey, *Trial* 19–20.

32. *there is another:* It is generally agreed that this "another" *(allos)* is the Father of Jesus, although this will not become clear until v. 37a. John Chrysostom interpreted the *allos* as John the Baptist, but this "makes havoc of the argument that follows" (Bernard, *Commentary* 1:248).

    I know: Jesus' use of the verb *egnōka* claims certain knowledge that the witness of the *allos* is true (Beutler, *Martyria* 256–257). Some textual evidence (Western readings of Original Sinaiticus, Bezae, Old Latin, Curetonian Syriac, Armenian, and Georgian) reads "you know" rather then "I know." This tradition reflects a scribal tendency to heighten the conflict between Jesus and "the Jews" and should be rejected.

33. *he has borne witness:* The perfect tense of the verb *(memartyrēken)* indicates that the witnessing took place in the past, but its significance endures.

35. *a lamp that was kindled and shining:* The passive participle, "kindled" *(ho kaiomenos)* indicates that the light the Baptist bears is the result of the initia-

tive of God, who sent him into the world to bear witness (cf. 1:6). The messianic ideas behind a lamp that would usher in the time of the Messiah come from Jewish interpretation of LXX Ps 131:16b-17: "Her faithful will shout for joy *(agalliasei agalliasontai)*. For I will cause a horn to sprout up for David; I have prepared a lamp for my anointed one *(lychnon tǭ christǭ mou)*." On this, see Neugebauer, "Miszelle" 130; Beutler, *Martyria* 258. It is rejected by some (e.g., Becker, *Evangelium* 1:253).

you were willing to rejoice: In the Fourth Gospel there is no rejection of the Baptist, no account of his death at the hands of Herod Antipas, and no report of his arrest. He fades from the scene because he regards it as necessary for Jesus to increase and for himself to decrease (3:30). On John the Baptist in 5:33-36 see Stowasser, *Johannes der Täufer* 221–231.

36. *the works that the Father has granted me to accomplish:* A distinction must be maintained between the singular "work" *(to ergon)* and the plural "works" *(ta erga)*, although some commentators collapse them into one (e.g., Bultmann, *Gospel* 265; Becker, *Evangelium* 1:253–254). The singular is a more theological concept that refers to the whole of Jesus' mission, consummated on the cross (cf. 4:34; 17:4; 19:30). The plural refers to the many deeds of Jesus that lead to Jesus' consummation of the *ergon*. They do show forth the *doxa* (cf. 2:11; 11:4, 40) and reflect Jesus' being the sent one of the Father. See Beutler, *Martyria* 259–260, and especially Vanhoye, "L'oeuvre du Christ" 415–419.

these very works . . . witness that the Father has sent me: Jesus does not witness to himself, but his perfect accomplishment of *ta erga* witnesses to the truth that he is the sent one of the Father. This point is made strongly in the Greek syntax, where the subject is repeated after a relative: *ta gar erga . . . auta ta erga ha poiō*. Never in the Fourth Gospel does Jesus speak of "*my* works." See Vanhoye, "Oeuvre du Christ" 394–408; Bernard, "Témoignage" 21–26.

37. *And the Father . . . has himself borne witness to me:* The progression from the Baptist (vv. 33-35) to the works of Jesus (v. 36) and the witness of the Father adopted in the interpretation is not accepted by all. In light of the discussion of the Scriptures in vv. 46-47 some would claim that vv. 37-40 refer to the OT with special reference to Sinai. See especially Pancaro, *The Law in the Fourth Gospel* 216–231.

his voice you have never heard, his form you have never seen: The interpretation sees the use of *phōnē* ("voice") and *eidos* ("form") as referring to "the Jews'" inability to recognize the revelation of God in Jesus (cf. Stimpfle, *Blinde Sehen* 102–103). Pancaro (*The Law in the Fourth Gospel* 216–226) argues that the two expressions refer to Sinai, and thus in vv. 37-38 Jesus presents the testimony given by the Father to Moses and Israel at Sinai, that is, the OT revelation. There is indeed a hint of the OT tradition of the inaccessibility of God (see Deut 4:12, 15), which is only overcome by the Son (cf. Segalla, *Giovanni* 219). For the christological interpretation adopted in the interpretation see von Wahlde, "The Witnesses to Jesus" 385–395; Painter, *Quest* 240–241; Thompson, "God's Voice" 177–204.

39. *you search the Scriptures:* The lifegiving Jewish practice of study and reflection on the Scriptures (cf. Psalm 119; Deut 8:3; Sir 17:11; 45:5; *Pirqe ʾAbot* 2:8; 6:7 and further rabbinic material in Str-B 2:467) is behind the use of the Greek verb *eraunate* ("you search"). See Bernard, "Témoignage" 35–42. The verb corresponds to the Hebrew *dāraš*, the technical term for biblical study and exposition. Dodd, *Interpretation* 329–330 n. 1 shows that the verb is indicative, not imperative. Jesus is not telling "the Jews" to do something; he is chastising them for their incorrect use of the Scriptures.

40. *yet you refuse to come to me that you may have life:* The author of the Fourth Gospel is not denying the importance of the Scriptures but taking the early Christian position that they point to Jesus. "Being the witness of God to his Son, the Scriptures are prophetic, not life-giving" (Hoskyns, *Gospel* 273).

42. *you have not the love of God:* Scholars discuss whether the expression "the love of God" *(tēn agapēn tou theou)* means "you do not love God" (objective genitive) or "you are not people whom God loves" (subjective genitive). For a summary of the discussion see Lindars, *Gospel* 213. As "the Jews'" active reading of the Scriptures and their rejection of Jesus on the basis of that reading is at the center of the argument, it is being read as an objective genitive. Jesus reproaches "the Jews" because, whatever their claims to life from the Scriptures, their rejection of the Son shows that they do not love God (cf. v. 23). The Fourth Gospel argues that God so loved the world that he gave his only Son (3:16). This love also includes "the Jews." See Pancaro, *The Law in the Fourth Gospel* 239–240. Schnackenburg, *Gospel* 2:127 and Brodie, *Gospel* 254 attempt to marry both the subjective and objective meanings.

44. *the one who alone is God:* The strong insistence on the uniqueness of God *(tou monou theou)* maintains the focus on the Sabbath Lordship of Israel's one and only God. Some very good witnesses ($\mathfrak{P}^{66}$, $\mathfrak{P}^{75}$, Vaticanus, Freer Gospels, Origen, Eusebius) omit *theou*. It should be retained (cf. Barrett, *Gospel* 269).

45. *Moses . . . on whom you set your hope:* For rabbinic material on Moses as Israel's intercessor before God see Str-B 2:562. See also Jeremias, *"Mōysēs"* 848–873; Meeks, *The Prophet-King* 159–161.
    it is Moses who accuses you: The use of the Greek verb *kategoreō* ("to accuse") in this context keeps the discussion within the framework of a legal process. For the forensic background to this word see BAGD 422, s.v.; LSJ 926–927. On the rabbinic and legal use of the expression, and the derived words *katēgoros* and *katēgōr* see Barrett, *Gospel* 270.

46. *If you believed Moses, you would believe me:* The interpretation insists that there is no conflict between the former gift of God through Moses and the perfection of the gift of God in and through Jesus. See the interpretation of 1:16-17. The preposition *anti* in 1:16b should not be read as a rejection of the Law. It is not correct to argue that Jesus Christ replaces "that which Judaism meant to offer, but failed to provide" (Dodd, *Interpretation* 86).

47. *if you do not believe his writings:* The final accusation of "the Jews" in v. 47 presupposes the argument of 5:1-47. They are accused by Moses, whose tradi-

tions they claim to be using in their accusation of Jesus (v. 18). But they were warned earlier in the trial that anyone who wishes to honor God must honor the Son (v. 23), and that only those who hear the word of Jesus and believe in the one who sent him can come to eternal life (v. 24). In defense of his Sabbath activity (vv. 1-18) Jesus' words on life and judgment (vv. 19-30) guide the understanding of his further words on witness and accusation (vv. 31-47). See Lee, *Symbolic Narratives* 108–125.

FOR REFERENCE AND FURTHER STUDY

Bernard, J. "Témoignage pour Jésus Christ: Jean 5:31-47," *MSR* 36 (1979) 3–55.
Beutler, Johannes. *Martyria* 254–265.
Jeremias, Joachim. "*Mōysēs*," *TDNT* 4 (1967) 848–873.
Moloney, Francis J. *Signs and Shadows* 19–29.
Neugebauer, Fritz. "Miszelle zu Joh 5,35," *ZNW* 52 (1961) 130.
Painter, John. *Quest* 235–252.
Pancaro, Severino. *The Law in the Fourth Gospel* 193–263.
Thompson, Marianne M. "'God's Voice You Have Never Heard, God's Form You Have Never Seen': The Characterization of God in the Gospel of John," *Sem* 63 (1993) 177–204.
Vanhoye, Albert. "L'oeuvre du Christ, don du Père (Jn 5,36 et 17,4)," *RSR* 48 (1960) 377–419.
Wahlde, Urban C. von. "The Witnesses to Jesus in 5:31-40 and Belief in the Fourth Gospel," *CBQ* 43 (1981) 385–408.

ii. Jesus and the Passover (6:1-71)

Introduction to 6:1-71. Matching 5:1, the expression *meta tauta* (6:1) introduces a new place (v. 1: the Sea of Galilee, which is the Sea of Tiberias), a new set of characters (v. 2: a multitude; v. 3: the disciples), and a change of time (v. 4: the Passover). The reason for this gathering is also given: "because they saw the signs he did on those who were diseased" (v. 2). Many modern and contemporary scholars have suggested that the present location of chapter 6 creates geographical difficulties that can only be resolved by rearranging chapters 4–7. If 6:1-71 is placed immediately after 4:43-54 Jesus' presence in Galilee is explained. The following events of chapters 5, 7, 9, and 10 all take place in Jerusalem. This suggestion, which has no support from textual traditions, focuses too strongly on geography. The issue that determines the order of events in John 5–10 is the celebration of the feasts of "the Jews" (cf. 5:1). After the general indication of the theme of feasts in 5:1, the fundamental observance of the Sabbath follows logically (cf. 5:9b). Other Jewish feasts then follow in the correct sequence of the Jewish year: 6:1-71: Passover (celebrated for seven days in the first month of the year), 7:1–10:21: Tabernacles (celebrated for seven days in the seventh month of the year), and 10:22-42: Dedication (celebrated for eight days in the ninth month of the year). The Johannine story of Jesus' presence at the feasts of "the Jews" captures the spirit of Jewish writing that preserves traditions that may be roughly contemporary with the writing of the Fourth Gospel: "If you will succeed in keeping the Sabbath, the Holy One, blessed be He, will give you three festivals: Passover, Pentecost, and Tabernacles" (*Mekilta* on Exodus 16:25. On the scholarly discussion of the order of John 4–7 see Moloney, *Son of Man* 87–89).

The celebration of Passover contains elements commemorating the passage from winter to spring and the liberation of the Jewish people from Egypt. It affirms liberation from every form of enslavement. Two independent feasts, Passover (originally associated with the slaying of a sheep or goat in a pastoral community) and Unleavened Bread (originally associated with eating unleavened bread in a community producing a barley harvest) were joined soon after Israel's settlement of Canaan. These feasts were then historicized and associated with God's deliverance of Israel from Egypt, and elements of the celebration recalled the biblical record of that event. The slaying of the Passover lamb recalled God's action in protecting the firstborn of the Israelites in Egypt (cf. Exod 11:1-10; 12:29-51), and the eating of unleavened bread recalled God's nourishing of Israel in the wilderness in the desert with manna (cf. Exod 16:1-36), regarded as "bread from heaven" (cf. Exod 16:4; Neh 9:15). After the loss of the Temple and its associated ritual sacrifices, postwar Judaism was gradually adapting and domesticating these rituals.

The Johannine community, now excluded from the Jewish ritual celebrations yet equally the product of a postwar Jewish world, developed a story that told of Jesus' presence at the Sea of Galilee at Passover time in the following fashion:

(a) *Vv. 1-4:* An introduction: where? when? who? why?
(b) *Vv. 5-15:* The miracle of the loaves and fishes.
(c) *Vv. 16-21:* Jesus comes to the disciples across the stormy sea.
(d) *Vv. 22-24:* A second introduction: where? when? who? why?
(e) *Vv. 25-59:* The discourse on the bread from heaven.
(f) *Vv. 60-71:* The crisis created by the word of Jesus:
    i. *Vv. 60-66:* Many disciples leave Jesus.
    ii. *Vv. 67-71:* Peter's confession leads Jesus to warn of Judas' betrayal.

The commentary will examine each of these sections separately. The discourse on the bread from heaven (vv. 25-59) will call for some further introductory remarks. This stage-by-stage reading of John 6 must not create the impression that it is a collection of independent items. The chapter is a coherent piece of carefully articulated Christian reflection on Jesus and the Jewish Passover.

a) *An Introduction* (6:1-4)

1. After this Jesus went to the other side of the Sea of Galilee, which is the Sea of Tiberias. 2. And a multitude followed him, because they saw the signs he did on those who were diseased. 3. Jesus went up on the mountain, and there sat down with his disciples. 4. Now the Passover, the feast of the Jews, was at hand.

INTERPRETATION

Who? Where? When? and Why? (vv. 1-4). The first introductory section describes the presence of Jesus (v. 1), the disciples (v. 3), and a multitude (v. 2) on the mountain (v. 3) on the other side of the Sea of Galilee (v. 1) as the feast of "the Jews," the Passover, approaches. The multitude follows Jesus because the people have seen the signs he did on the sick (v. 2). Jesus ascends an unnamed mountain and seats himself there with his disciples. The use of the definite article "the mountain" *(eis to oros)* may be a first hint that Jesus is adopting a position parallel to Moses who received the Law on a mountain (cf. Exod 19:20; 14:1-2; Isa 34:2-4). The critical stance Jesus has taken with other characters in the story who came to him because of the signs he did (cf. 1:49-51: Nathanael; 3:1-11: Nicodemus; 4:16-26: the Samaritan woman) and the narrator's comment in 2:23-25 indicate that the multitude still has much to learn.

NOTES

1. *to the other side:* The expression "to the other side" *(peran)* creates problems: the other side from where? "To the other side" may simply indicate a given place at the north end of the lake, close to Tiberias. See Delebecque, *Jean* 157–158.

2. *they saw the signs he did:* There are close verbal parallels between 2:23, 3:2, and 6:2. All three passages judge the response of people to "the signs he did" as insufficient. It is not as if signs are of no value for the Johannine understanding of Jesus (see 20:30-31), but they must lead the interested party or parties further.

3. *the mountain:* Scholars differ in their interpretation of the use of the definite article. An increasing number, however, make the link with the gift of the Law

at Sinai (e.g., Schnackenburg, *Gospel* 2:18; Brown, *Gospel* 1:232; Segalla, *Giovanni* 224; Perry, "The Evolution" 23–25). Some reject the connection (e.g., Becker, *Evangelium* 1:191). It should be read as a first hint that the gift made to the people in the Law through Moses is about to be perfected in and through the gift of Jesus Christ (cf. 1:16-17).

4. *the Passover, the feast of the Jews, was at hand:* Coming immediately after the account of Jesus' rereading of Sabbath theology and practice, this mention of the Passover in the introduction to 6:1-71 sets the theological agenda for the passage that follows. See Crossan, "It is Written" 5.

FOR REFERENCE AND FURTHER STUDY

Crossan, J. D. "It is Written: A Structuralist Analysis of John 6," *Sem* 26 (1983) 3–21.
Moloney, Francis J. *Signs and Shadows* 30–33.
_____. *Son of Man* 87–107.
Perry, J. M. "The Evolution of the Johannine Eucharist," *NTS* 39 (1993) 22–35.
Witkamp, L. T. "Some Specific Johannine Features in John 6.1-21," *JSNT* 40 (1990) 43–60.

b) *The Miracle of the Loaves and Fishes* (6:5-15)

5. Lifting up his eyes, then, and seeing that a multitude was coming to him, Jesus said to Philip, "How are we to buy bread, so that these people may eat?" 6. This he said to test him, for he himself knew what he would do. 7. Philip answered him, "Two hundred denarii would not buy enough bread for each of them to get a little." 8. One of his disciples, Andrew, Simon Peter's brother, said to him, 9. "There is a lad here who has five barley loaves and two fish; but what are they among so many?"

10. Jesus said, "Make the people sit down." Now there was much grass in the place; so the men sat down, in number about five thousand. 11. Jesus then took the loaves, and when he had given thanks he distributed them to those who were seated; so also the fish, as much as they wanted.

12. And when they had eaten their fill, he told his disciples, "Gather up the fragments left over, that nothing may be lost." 13. So they gathered them up and filled twelve baskets with fragments from the five barley loaves, left by those who had eaten. 14. When the people saw the sign he had done, they said, "This is indeed the prophet who is to come into the world!" 15. Perceiving then that they were about to come and take him by force to make him king, Jesus withdrew again to the mountain by himself.

INTERPRETATION

Introduction to 6:1-15. If one incorporates the introduction (vv. 1-4) into this section of the narrative the following shape emerges:

(a) *Vv. 1-4:* Setting the scene and the characters.
(b) *Vv. 5-9:* A problem posed by Jesus cannot be solved by the disciples.
(c) *Vv. 10-13:* A miracle takes place through the words and actions of Jesus.
(d) *Vv. 14-15:* The aftermath of the miracle.

Differently from the two Cana miracles (2:1-12; 4:43-54), the traditional form of a miracle story is found here. Nevertheless, a unique Johannine point of view has been insinuated into the telling of the traditional story (cf. Witkamp, "Some Specific Johannine Features" 46–51).

The problem (vv. 5-9). The distinction between the participants in the scene (vv. 1-4) is carefully maintained. Lifting up his eyes, Jesus sees the multitude coming to him, and he speaks to one of the disciples, Philip (cf. 1:43). In contrast to the synoptic accounts of this miracle (cf. Mark 6:37; 8:4; Matt 15:33), Jesus takes the initiative, indicating his concern that the people be fed (v. 5). A question that Moses asked of YHWH in the desert returns: "Where am I to get the meat to give all these people?" (Num 11:13), but Jesus' concern is rhetorical. In a crucial aside the narrator informs the reader that Jesus knew what he would do (v. 6b). The question tests the faith of the disciples (v. 6a). Moses, bread, and a moment of "testing" form the background for a story that takes place as "the Passover, the feast of the Jews, was at hand" (v. 4). Philip's response is limited to the material bread one would need to feed such a multitude (v. 7). As the disciples were present when Jesus spoke of the nourishment he had from his unconditional acceptance of the will of the one who sent him (4:32-34), Philip does not seem to have learned from that encounter. Andrew joins Philip in pointing to the paucity of their supplies: a lad is at hand with five barley loaves and two fish (vv. 8-9). Andrew and Philip have been with Jesus from the first days of the Gospel (cf. 1:43), but they have not learned from their master's attempt to draw them beyond the limitations of their expectations (cf. 1:35-51), in this case the need for a large sum of money to buy quantities of bread. Nevertheless the raw material for the events that follow has been provided: the loaves and the fish. The reader waits for Jesus' action, as "he himself knew what he would do" (v. 6b).

The miracle (vv. 10-13). Jesus commands the disciples to have the people recline, as if for a meal. In v. 3 Jesus "sat down" (*ekathēto*), but he asks that the people take up a position that prepares for a meal (v. 10: *anapesein*). The narrator adds two details: there was much grass in the place, and the men who arranged themselves for the meal were about five thousand in number. The latter detail indicates the immensity of the crowd and heightens the impact of the feeding. The green grass, however, recalls Ps 23:2: "He makes me lie down in green pastures." Jesus takes *(elaben)* the loaves, gives thanks *(eucharistēsas)*, and distributes *(diedōken)* them to the people stretched out for the meal *(tois anakeimenois)* (v. 11a). The distribution of the loaves recalls the formal setting of a eucharistic celebration. He also distributes the fish (v. 11b) and all are satisfied (v. 11c). The promise of Ps 23:1 is fulfilled: "The LORD is my shepherd, I shall not want."

Jesus commands the disciples again: "Gather up *(synēgagon)* the fragments *(ta klasmata)* left over, that nothing be lost *(hina mē ti apolētai)*" (v. 12). Eucharistic language colors this command. The *Didache* (9:4), *1 Clement* (34:7), and Ignatius (*Letter to Polycarp* 4:2) use the verb *synagein* to speak of the gathering of the faithful for Eucharist, and *ta klasmata* is the term used for the eucharistic fragments (*Didache* 9:3, 4). Jesus has fed a vast multitude in a way that recalls a Christian celebration of Eucharist, and this feeding takes place at Passover time, which celebrates the gift of the manna. The disciples are commanded to gather the fragments from this original meal *hina mē ti apolētai*. The Passover and Eucharist blend as the practice of the Exodus people is recalled. They gathered the manna each day, eating till they had their fill (cf. Exod 16:8, 12, 16, 18, 21). However, Moses commanded that the manna was *not to be stored,* and any manna that was hidden away perished (Exod 16:19-20). Jesus' gift to people who come to him in search of bread (cf. v. 5) must not be lost, and the disciples are to see to its preservation. An abundance of *klasmata* is still available. Unlike the manna given by God in the desert to the ancestors of Israel (Exodus 16), the *klasmata* given by Jesus on the occasion of the Passover feast have not perished; they are still available. Much that happened in the desert (Exodus 16) is repeated beside the lake (John 6:1-13), but there are some important Christian developments of that tradition. The traditional number twelve indicates a collection complete in itself (cf. Mark 6:43; Matt 14:20; Luke 9:17), and this collection of *klasmata* is gathered by the disciples, obedient to the word of Jesus (v. 13). They are commissioned to care for the *klasmata* that they may be available for future believers wishing to share from the bread that Jesus distributed on the occasion of the feast of the Passover. As throughout the miracle, there is a blending of Passover traditions and the Christian traditions that surround the ongoing celebration of Eucharist.

The aftermath (vv. 14-15). The sight of the miracle leads the people to a profession of faith: "This is indeed the prophet who is to come into the world" (v. 14). As with the disciples (1:35-49), Nicodemus (3:2), and the Samaritan woman (4:19, 25, 30), a sign has led to a limited faith. They have not progressed from v. 2: "A multitude followed him, because they saw the signs he did." They are looking for a figure who will satisfy their expectations and see Jesus as a Moses-like prophet, based on the word of YHWH to Moses in Deut 18:15-18: "The LORD your God will raise up for you a prophet like me from among your own people; you shall heed such a prophet. . . . I will raise up for them a prophet like you from among their own people; I will put my words in the mouth of the prophet, who shall speak to them everything that I command." They associate themselves with another Jewish hope, which awaited a second gift of the manna to mark the opening of the messianic era: "And it shall come to pass at that selfsame time that the treasury of manna shall again descend from on high, and they will eat of it in those years, because these are they who have come to the consummation of time" (*2 Bar* 29:8). Jesus is not prepared to accept their acclamation or their desire to impose their messianic criteria on him. He sees that they wish to force him into a royal role (*harpazein auton hina poiēsōsin basileia*) (v. 15a). He leaves them, retiring to the mountain from which he had descended to feed the multitude (v. 15b). His departure marks the end of the episode.

NOTES

5. *seeing that a multitude was coming to him:* From the start of the action the major groups involved in the narrative are kept separate. Earlier the narrator commented that the multitude "followed [Jesus]" (v. 2) but that he was "with his disciples" on the mountain (v. 3). From that position he lifts up his eyes to see the multitude approaching him. The disciples will largely disappear from the narrative, but on their return in v. 60 it is presupposed that they have been present throughout.

6. *for he himself knew what he would do:* This aside is a key to the interpretation of the miracle story and the subsequent discourse. In typically Johannine fashion Jesus "knew" (*ēdei*), and is thus in control of everything that is happening. The verb is the pluperfect form of *oida* ("to know"), and has an imperfect meaning: Jesus' knowing is ongoing. From this dominant position he attempts to lead the various characters in the narrative to a fuller understanding of the events reported and thus to a deeper level of belief.

7. *Two hundred denarii would not buy enough bread:* There are parallels between the disciples' response to Jesus and the subsequent miracle and the story of Elisha's feeding of one hundred men in 2 Kgs 4:42-44. For some (e.g., Bauer, *Johannesevangelium* 92) the Johannine text is constructed on the Elisha passage. See also Léonard, "Multiplication des pains" 265–270. On the disciples' failure see Lee, *Symbolic Narratives* 138–139.

8. *Andrew, Simon Peter's brother:* The deliberate reference to the relationship between Andrew and Simon Peter, immediately after Philip's response to Jesus

in v. 7, recalls the presence of these two disciples in the section entitled "The first days of Jesus" (1:40-43). They are shown not to have made any progress in their understanding of Jesus since that time (cf. the interpretation of 1:19-51).

10. *there was much grass in the place:* Many commentators have linked the grass with the Passover, held in spring (e.g., Westcott, *Gospel* 97). Although there are no explicit verbal links between the LXX Ps 22 [MT 23] and the Johannine passage, the context suggests that the psalm forms its background. See Schnackenburg, *Gospel* 2:16.

   so the men sat down, in number about five thousand: In singling out "men" (*andres*), for the very large number of five thousand, in contrast to "people" (*anthrōpous*) who are to sit down for the meal ("Make the people sit down"), the passage shows the patriarchy of the times.

11. *when he had given thanks he distributed them:* Some manuscripts (Sinaiticus, Bezae, and Old Latin) have "he rendered thanks and gave" (*eucharistēsen kai edōken*). This expression is very close to known early liturgical formulae and must be rejected as an attempt to have a text that is overtly eucharistic.

   "that nothing may be lost": As well as the contact with Exodus 16 and the command against preserving the manna developed in the interpretation there is a widely recognized Jewish tradition against waste. See especially *b. Ḥul.* 105b; *b. Ber.* 50b; *b. Šabb.* 147b. On this see Johnston, "The Johannine Version" 153–154. Second Kings 4:42-44 may have also been part of the background. After one hundred men ate from the barley loaves they "had some left" (v. 44). Some scholars make much of the Jewish notion of God's blessing in the gift of the surplus. See Daube, *The New Testament* 36–51; Dodd, *Tradition* 424 n. 4. This does not seem to be called for by the Johannine context. On the close links between the Johannine details and the eucharistic prayer in the *Didache* see Moule, "A Note" 240–243.

12. *that nothing may be lost:* Few commentators see the command as pointing to the *future responsibility* of the disciples, but see Crossan, "It is Written" 20; Witkamp, "Some Specific Johannine Features" 49. Witkamp, however, understands the *klasmata* as the future members of the gathered community who must not be lost. The verb *synagein* is used by Moses as he directs the Israelites to collect the manna (cf. Exod 16:16; cf. also 16:5, 21). There is no verbal contact between Jesus' command to gather the fragments that nothing may be lost and the description of the decaying manna in Exod 16:21, but the contrast between the results of the two gatherings is striking. The Exodus gathering leads to the corruption of the manna, while the gathering ordered by Jesus keeps the *klasmata* available for later use.

14. *When the people saw the sign:* The link made between the gift of the manna and the messianic era in *2 Baruch* is roughly contemporaneous with the Fourth Gospel. For later evidence, see *Mekilta on Exodus* 16:25; *Eccl. Rab.* 1:9; *Tanh. Shemot* 4:24.

the prophet who is to come into the world: For a discussion of the evidence for a first-century messianic interpretation of Deut 18:15-18 see Bittner, *Jesu Zeichen* 155–158. For the case against such an identification see Schnelle, *Antidocetic Christology* 103–104. Recent scholarship, following Horsley, "Popular Messianic Movements" 471–495, looks to a more general notion of a prophet-like Messiah. See, for example, Painter, *Quest* 260–264; Beasley-Murray, *John* 88–89.

15. *that they were about to come and take him by force to make him king:* The Greek uses an almost violent word *(harpazein)* to indicate that the people were about to force their will on him. See Brown, *Gospel* 1:235.

withdrew again to the mountain: There has been no mention of Jesus and the disciples ever coming down from the mountain (cf. v. 3). It must be presupposed that the miracle took place beside the lake, as the narrator indicates that he returns to the same mountain, but this time by himself *(eis to oros autos monos)*. The next sections (vv. 16-21; vv. 22-24) situate the disciples and the crowd beside the lake. Both groups embark on separate journeys across the lake (vv. 16-17; vv. 23-24). Only Jesus is separated from the lake, on the mountain. See Bauer, *Johannesevangelium* 93.

For Reference and Further Study

Crossan, J. D. "It is Written" 3–21.

Daube, David. *The New Testament and Rabbinic Judaism.* London: Athlone, 1956, 36–51.

Horsley, Richard A. "Popular Messianic Movements around the Time of Jesus," *CBQ* 46 (1984) 471–495.

Johnston, E. D. "The Johannine Version of the Feeding of the Five Thousand—an Independent Tradition?" *NTS* 8 (1962) 151–154.

Léonard, J. M. "Multiplication des pains: 2 Rois 4/42-44 et Jean 6/1-13," *ETR* 55 (1980) 265–270.

Moloney, Francis J. *Signs and Shadows* 33–39.

_____. "When Is John Talking About Sacraments?" *ABR* 30 (1982) 10–33.

Moule, C. F. D. "A Note on Didache IX 4," *JThS* 6 (1955) 240–243.

Perry, J. M. "The Evolution" 22–35.

Witkamp, L. T. "Some Specific Johannine Features" 46–51.

c) *The Miracle on the Sea* (6:16-21)

16. When evening came his disciples went down to the sea, 17. got into a boat, and were trying to go across the sea to Capernaum. It was now

dark, and Jesus had not yet come to them. 18. The sea rose because a strong wind was blowing. 19. When they had rowed about three or four miles they saw Jesus walking on the sea and drawing near to the boat. They were frightened, 20. but he said to them, "It is I; do not be afraid." 21. Then they were glad to take him into the boat, and immediately the boat was at the land to which they were going.

INTERPRETATION

Introduction to 6:16-21. A second miracle story now follows (vv. 16-21), matching the shape of the account of the multiplication of the loaves and fishes (vv. 5-15). Although this account is briefer, the same elements, common to most miracle stories, return.

(a) *Vv. 16-17:* Setting the scene and the characters.
(b) *V. 18:* The problem of the storm is reported.
(c) *Vv. 19-20:* Jesus comes to the disciples across the stormy waters.
(d) *V. 21:* The aftermath of the miracle.

This miracle story focuses on Jesus' coming to the disciples in a miraculous fashion, his making himself known to them (vv. 19-20), and their receiving him (v. 21). Thus although the shape of the story matches the account of the miracle of the loaves and fish, the action and the aftermath are not marked by the obtuseness of the disciples (vv. 5-9) and the ambiguity of the crowd (vv. 14-15).

The setting of the scene (vv. 16-17). As evening comes, the disciples go down to the sea (v. 16). The characters of vv. 1-4, who had been together in vv. 5-15, have been separated. Jesus has returned to the mountain (v. 15), the disciples are at the seashore (v. 16), and the multitude has not moved. The disciples struggle across the lake (see note on v. 17). The narrator specifies that the night had fallen and then comments that "Jesus had not yet *(oupō)* come to them" (v. 17b). The introduction to the episode indicates that Jesus will come to the disciples.

The storm (v. 18). The narrator briefly states that a storm arose: turbulent wind and rising seas. The eastern coast of the normally placid Sea of Galilee is formed by high country split by deep gorges. Sudden changes of weather can tunnel strong winds through the gorges and create difficult conditions on the lake.

Jesus comes on the waters (vv. 19-20). About halfway across the lake the disciples see Jesus walking on the surface of the water *(epi tēs thalassēs)*, drawing close to their boat. They are struck with fear. The drama of a difficult sea journey in the night (vv. 16-17), the storm (v. 18), and the fear of the disciples (v. 19) prepare for Jesus' words to them that provide the setting for an OT literary form for a theophany (e.g., Gen 15:1; 26:24; 46:3; Isa

41:13-14; 43:1, 3) and the OT theme of YHWH's unique authority over the terror of the sea (e.g., Exodus 14–15; Deut 7:2-7; Job 9:8; 38:16; Pss 29:3; 65:8; 77:20; 89:10; 93:3-4; Isa 43:1-5; 51:9-10). It is as Lord that Jesus comes across the waters, reveals himself to the disciples with the formula I AM *(egō eimi)*, and tells them not to fear (v. 20).

The aftermath (v. 21). The multiplication of the loaves and fish did not advance the crowds' understanding of Jesus (cf. vv. 2, 14-15). Jesus' self-revelation to the disciples leads them to receive him gladly *(ēthelon oun labein auton)*, and they find themselves "at the land to which they were going" (v. 21). As earlier in the story the acceptance of the word of Jesus led to a miracle (cf. 2:1-12; 4:46-54; 5:2-9a), the seemingly insurmountable problem of the journey to Capernaum on a stormy sea (cf. vv. 17-19a) is solved as the disciples "receive" Jesus. Where they will go from here, however, remains an open question (cf. Giblin, "The Miraculous Crossing" 98–101).

The narrative had reached a point at which the characters in the story were separated (vv. 15-16). Jesus and the disciples are then reunited (v. 20). The reunion is marked by Jesus' coming to the disciples as Lord, revealing himself as I AM, and being received by them (v. 21). None of this has happened to the crowds, who remain at the place of the miracle of the loaves and fish. The false messianic hopes of the crowds (vv. 14-15) have been corrected by Jesus' self-revelation (v. 20), and the disciples are willing recipients of that revelation (v. 21). The crowd, the disciples, and Jesus will shortly gather once more (vv. 22-24), and Jesus will deliver his discourse on the bread from heaven (vv. 25-59). The disciples, who have accepted the truth about Jesus, will strangely disappear from the action as Jesus speaks to the multitude and "the Jews" (vv. 25-29), but they will return to the action in vv. 60-71, and the quality of their faith will be tested.

NOTES

16. *his disciples went down to the sea:* At this point it is not explicitly stated that the crowd remained at the site of the miracle, but it must be presupposed. It will be confirmed in v. 23. On the importance of this separation of the characters see Witkamp, "Some Specific Johannine Features" 51–52; Borgen, "John 6" 269–271.

17. *they were trying to go across the sea:* The durative and conative force of the imperfect *ērchonto* ("they were going") must be given weight: "they were trying to go." See Barrett, *Gospel* 280.

    it was now dark: The use of "darkness" *(skotia)* is dramatic, but too much should not be read into it, nor is it symbolic of unfaith or the power of evil as some (e.g. Léon-Dufour, *Lecture* 2:120) would claim.

18. *the sea rose:* Sudden changes of weather are common on the Sea of Galilee.

19. *they saw Jesus walking on the sea:* There have been attempts to read *epi tēs thalassēs* as "beside the sea" (cf. Bernard, *Commentary* 1:185–186; Talbert, *Reading John* 133; Nisin, *Histoire* 275–276). This interpretation regards the journey of the disciples as along the coast of the lake, and the disciples see Jesus walking "beside the sea." There is no miracle involved. Grammatically this is a possible translation (cf. BAGD 286, s.v.), but the context demands the above interpretation.

20. *It is I; do not be afraid:* For the position adopted in the interpretation see Feuillet, "Les *Ego eimi* christologiques" 19–21; Schnackenburg, *Gospel* 2:27; Becker, *Evangelium* 1:194. There may also be a recalling of the Exodus tradition concerning the crossing of the Reed Sea found in Ps 77:18-19 (cf. Brown, *Gospel* 1:255–256; Kysar, *John's Story* 40–41; but see the reservations of Schnackenburg, *Gospel* 2:29–30). For a strong Mosaic reading of 6:1-21 see Perry, "Evolution" 22–26. Not all would accept that *egō eimi* is used as a revelatory formula here. Some see it simply as self-identification: "It's I, don't worry" (e.g., Bernard, *Commentary* 1:187; Barrett, *Gospel* 281). Heil, *Jesus Walking* 79–80, goes half way: "Jesus is the one acting on behalf of Yahweh" (p. 79), but "not to reveal" (p. 80).

21. *they were glad to take him into the boat:* The translation shows both their willingness *(ēthelon)* and their reception *(lambanein)* of Jesus. The verb *lambanein* has been used earlier in the Gospel (e.g., 1:12-13) to indicate the authentic reception of Jesus.

    but the boat was at the land to which they were going: There may be a hint of the fulfillment of Ps 107:23-32, especially v. 30: "And he brought them to their desired haven."

FOR REFERENCE AND FURTHER STUDY

Borgen, Peder. "John 6: Tradition, Interpretation and Composition." In Martinus C. de Boer, ed., *From Jesus to John: Essays on Jesus and New Testament Christology in Honour of Marinus de Jonge.* JSNT.S 84. Sheffield: JSOT Press, 1993, 268–291.

Feuillet, André. "Les *Ego eimi* christologiques du quatrième évangile," *RSR* 54 (1966) 5–22.

Giblin, C. H. "The Miraculous Crossing of the Sea (John 6.16-21)," *NTS* 29 (1983) 96–103.

Heil, John Paul. *Jesus Walking on the Sea: Meaning and Gospel Functions of Matt 14:22-33, Mark 6:45-52 and John 6:15b-21.* AnBib 87. Rome: Biblical Institute Press, 1981.

Moloney, Francis J. *Signs and Shadows* 38–40.

Nisin, Arthur. *Histoire de Jésus.* Paris: Seuil, 1961.

d) *A Second Introduction* (6:22-24)

22. On the next day the people who remained on the other side of the sea saw that there had been only one boat there, and that Jesus had not entered the boat with his disciples, but that his disciples had gone away alone. 23. However, boats from Tiberias came near the place where they ate the bread after the Lord had given thanks. 24. So when the people saw that Jesus was not there, nor his disciples, they themselves got into the boats and went to Capernaum, seeking Jesus.

INTERPRETATION

Introduction to 6:22-24. In a passage that matches vv. 1-4 the narrator establishes who is present, and where, when, and why a further gathering takes place.

> (a) Jesus (vv. 22, 24), the disciples (vv. 22, 24), and "the people who remained on the other side," who had eaten the bread (vv. 22, 23) are being brought together again.
> (b) They gather at Capernaum (v. 24).
> (c) It is "the next day" (v. 22).
> (d) The multitude was "seeking Jesus" (v. 24).

In a changed situation the questions of who, where, when, and why have been resumed from vv. 1-4, and given answers that fit the changed circumstances.

Who? where? when? and why? (vv. 22-24). "The people who remained on the other side" (v. 22), those who "ate the bread after the Lord had given thanks" (v. 23), are aware that Jesus and the disciples have been separated. They had observed on the day before that there was only one boat, but that Jesus had not departed with his disciples (v. 22). Yet neither Jesus nor his disciples are "there" (*ouk estin ekei*). They are left wondering and confused. Has another miracle happened? Anxious to find their miracle-working provider of the messianic manna (cf. vv. 14-15), they hail boats passing by from Tiberias and set off for Capernaum "seeking Jesus" (*zētountes tēn Iēsoun*).

An atmosphere of hustle and bustle is created as people crowd into boats to find their miracle-man (vv. 14-15). The eucharistic hints of the bread miracle (cf. esp. v. 11) have reappeared in v. 23: "where they ate the bread after the Lord had given thanks." The issue of the preserved *klasmata* (v. 13) remains open. The place for the assembly is Capernaum (v. 24; cf. vv. 16, 21), and it is "the next day," after the disciples' night encounter with Jesus (vv. 16-17). The "next day" brings the discourse and the events that are about to be reported closer to the celebration of the Passover feast (cf. v. 4).

NOTES

22. *On the next day:* This brief passage has a very confused textual tradition. For surveys see Roberge, "Jean VI, 22-24: Un problème de critique textuelle?" 275–289; idem, "Jean VI, 22-24: Un problème de critique littéraire" 139–151; Schenke, "Das Szenarium von Joh 6,1-15" 191–203; Neirynck, "L'*epanalepsis* et la critique littéraire" 325–332. On the often-questioned originality of vv. 22-24 see Schnelle, *Antidocetic Christology* 110–111.

    the people saw . . . that there had been: The interpretation requires that the verbs "saw" *(eidon)* and "had been" *(ēn)* are pluperfects. On this possibility see Lagrange, *Evangile* 170; Barrett, Gospel 285.

23. *boats from Tiberias:* The boats must be understood as passing by and not there by accident, "blown out of the harbor" (Westcott, *Gospel* 99) by the overnight storm. Several commentators (e.g., Bauer, *Johannesevangelium* 94) point out that this is a *deus ex machina* solution to resolve the problem of the separation of the characters. Such solutions are not foreign to the Fourth Gospel (cf. 2:6, 15; 3:25; 4:6-7, 45).

    the place where they ate the bread after the Lord had given thanks: These words not only recall the events of the day before, but also their significance. Eucharistic hints appear in the use of the singular noun "the bread" *(ton arton),* and the title of "Lord" for Jesus. See Léon-Dufour, *Lecture* 2:125–126. The Western textual tradition (Bezae, Old Latin, Sinaitic Syriac, Curetonian Syriac) omits "after the Lord had given thanks" *(eucharistēsontos tou kyriou),* but it should be retained (cf. Schnelle, *Antidocetic Christology* 110–111).

24. *they themselves got into the boats:* It is often pointed out that the whole crowd could not be intended. It would take a flotilla of boats from Tiberias to carry the "five thousand men" (see v. 10). The point at stake is that people who had witnessed the miracle and arrived at partial faith (cf. vv. 14-15) are still seeking Jesus. This is against those (e.g., Schnackenburg, *Gospel* 2:18) who claim that the enthusiasm reflected in the acclamations of vv. 14-15 has disappeared from the narrative.

FOR REFERENCE AND FURTHER STUDY

Moloney, Francis J. *Signs and Shadows* 41–42.
Neirynck, Frans. "L'*epanalepsis* et la critique littéraire. A propos de l'évangile de Jean," *EThL* 56 (1980) 303–338.
Roberge, Michel. "Jean VI, 22-24: Un problème de critique textuelle?" *LTP* 34 (1978) 275–289.
_____. "Jean VI, 22-24: Un problème de critique littéraire," *LTP* 35 (1979) 139–151.
Schenke, Ludger. "Das Szenarium von Joh 6,1-25," *TThZ* 92 (1983) 191–203.

e) *The Discourse on the Bread from Heaven* (6:25-59)

Introduction to 6:25-59. The rich interplay of theological themes and the complexity of the ongoing discussion with Jewish Passover traditions have made this section of the Fourth Gospel one of the most discussed texts in the New Testament. The interpreter faces a number of critical problems. Closely related questions concern the literary unity of the passage as we now have it and the possibility that at least part of the discourse reflects the Johannine celebration of the Eucharist. The relationship between these two questions arises from the fact that vv. 51-58 are widely accepted as overtly eucharistic, and some suggest that v. 51c may even reflect the eucharistic formula used in the Johannine community. However, many scholars regard precisely this section of the Gospel, for seemingly sound reasons (see notes), as a later eucharistic addition to a discourse that originally had no trace of such themes.

The interpretation that follows regards the discourse as a homiletic midrash on a text provided to Jesus by his interlocutors in v. 31: "He gave them bread from heaven to eat." The discourse is formed by a repeated play on words that come from this text. The first part of the discourse (vv. 32-48) is a midrashic paraphrase on the words of Scripture: "He gave them bread from heaven." The latter part (vv. 49-58) continues to use expressions plundered from "He gave them bread from heaven," but devotes particular attention to a midrashic commentary on the words "to eat" (Borgen, *Bread from Heaven* 28–57). Whatever its prehistory, once in existence the discourse has its own life. It does not start in v. 31, nor is there a new beginning in v. 49. The rhythm of question and answer determines its shape.

Five interventions from the crowd or "the Jews" give vv. 25-59 their shape.

> (a) *Vv. 25-29:* "Rabbi, when did you come here?" (v. 25). This trivial question leads Jesus to instruct the crowd on the need to search for the food that endures to eternal life: belief in the one whom God has sent.
>
> (b) *Vv. 30-33:* "Then what signs do you do?" (v. 30). Jesus is asked for miracle-working credentials that surpass Moses' gift of the manna (vv. 30-31). He points to another bread from heaven, *the true bread from heaven.*
>
> (c) *Vv. 34-40:* "Lord, give us this bread always" (v. 34). Jesus presents himself as the *true bread from heaven,* the only one able to make God known and give eternal life.
>
> (d) *Vv. 41-51:* "Is not this Jesus, the son of Joseph, whose father and mother we know? How does he say, 'I have come down from heaven'?" (v. 42). Jesus discusses the question of origins.

(e) *Vv. 52-59:* "How can this man give us his flesh to eat?" (v. 52). A final
question leads Jesus to instruct "the Jews" on the need to eat the flesh
and drink the blood of the Son of Man.

The discourse unfolds around these questions and answers, each section
developing a new thought around the single theme of the bread from
heaven. The interpretation will comment on each section in turn. The
section For Reference and Further Study follows the interpretation of vv.
51-59.

Verses 25-29

25. When they found him on the other side of the sea they said to him,
"Rabbi, when did you get here?" 26. Jesus answered them, "Amen,
amen, I say to you, you seek me, not because you saw signs, but because
you ate your fill of the loaves. 27. Do not labor for the food that perishes,
but for the food that endures to eternal life, that the Son of Man will give
to you; for on him God the Father has set his seal." 28. Then they said to
him, "What must we do to be devoting ourselves to the works of God?"
29. Jesus answered them, "This is the work of God, that you believe in
him whom he has sent."

INTERPRETATION

Introduction to the discourse (vv. 25-29). The people's question, "Rabbi,
when did you get here?" (v. 25), shows that they understand Jesus in their
terms ("Rabbi," cf. 1:28, 49; 3:2), and that they have trivialized his presence by asking the time of his arrival. The question is logical after the
puzzlement of v. 22, but when last with Jesus they wished to make him
king (cf. v. 15). They seem to have gone backwards in their understanding of Jesus, and his response to their question accuses them of seeking
him for baser reasons. The double "amen" introduces vv. 26-27. Jesus interprets their search for him (cf. v. 24) as no longer even motivated by the
sign of the miracle but because they enjoyed the bread he provided. He
instructs them that they are to work *(ergazesthe)* not for the bread (cf. v. 26:
artos) that fills their bellies, not for the food that perishes *(tēn brōsin tēn
apollumenēn),* but for the food that endures (v. 27: *tēn brōsin tēn menousan).*
Expressions from 4:32-34 return: "I have food *(brōsin)* to eat of which you
do not know. . . . My food *(emon brōma)* is to do the will of him who sent
me and to accomplish his work." There is a form of nourishment that
transcends earthly bread, and this must be the goal of the people's searching; it is for this that they must work (v. 27a). The final event in the miracle of the loaves and fish also returns. The disciples have gathered the

fragments *hina mē ti apolētai* ("that nothing may be lost"). There is a link between the need to abandon the search for the food that perishes (v. 27: *tēn brōsin tēn apollumenēn*) and the disciples' gathering of the *klasmata* so that they would not perish. Although it is by no means the main focus of the discourse at this stage, a subtle hint of the gift of the Eucharist is present.

The food that endures to eternal life will be given to them by the Son of Man (v. 27b). Jesus, the Son of Man, is the only revealer from God (3:13) to make God known (1:51) by means of a "lifting up" (3:14). The acceptance or refusal of the revelation brings about judgment (5:27). Questions multiply: what is this food and where can it be found? A further important question arises from the future tense of the verb: "that the Son of Man *will give* to you." When might this be? There will be a moment further on in the story when the revelation of God in the lifting up of the Son of Man will provide a food that will endure for eternal life. The promise of a nourishment that provided life matched Israel's belief that the Law provided life for those who lived by it (cf. Sir 17:11; 45:5; *Mekilta* on Exodus 15:26; *Exod. Rab.* 29:9; *Deut. Rab.* 8:3; *Tanh. Shemot* 4:19), and they "labored" *(ergazesthai)* on the Law so that they might have this life. Jesus points to an alternative nourishment as the source of eternal life: the future gift of the Son of Man. There can be no questioning this promise, however veiled its final significance might be at this stage of the story, for God the Father has set his seal upon the Son of Man (v. 27c). There is a uniqueness about the nourishment that the Son of Man will give because it is "God the Father who attests the authority and the truth of Jesus" (Barrett, *Gospel* 287). As an author puts his or her seal on a missive to show its authenticity and to give it authority, so has God the Father done with the Son of Man, his unique mediator between heaven and earth. He is the one who has come down from heaven (cf. 1:51; 3:13), bearing the credentials of God the Father (6:27c).

The crowd attempts to bypass the promise of the Son of Man, asking: "What must we do to be devoting ourselves to the works of God *(hina ergazōmetha ta erga theou)*" (v. 28). The question depends on the Jewish belief that the Law, given through Moses, allows direct access to God. Doing the works of the Law means doing things that please God (cf. CD 2:14-15). Jesus' response indicates that the way to God by means of the works of the Law is but a shadow of the possibility he offers them. Access to God is only through the Son who makes God known (cf. 1:18). The only way to do the work of God *(ton ergon tou theou)* is to believe in the one whom God has sent (v. 29).

As the Passover approaches (cf. vv. 4, 22) Jesus teaches that there will be a gift of God, made available through the Son of Man (v. 27), the one sent by God (v. 29), that surpasses all human nourishment (v. 26). Laboring for the possession of this nourishment (vv. 28-29), believing in the one whom God has sent (v. 29), will produce eternal life (v. 27). The program for the rest of the discourse has been established. "The whole discourse is summarized here" (Barrett, *Gospel* 282), and it is closely linked to themes that are important at the celebration of the Passover: nourishment, bread from heaven, and the revelation of God in the Law.

NOTES

25. *Rabbi, when did you get here?:* Not all would accept that the interruptions of the crowd (vv. 24, 30-31, 34) and "the Jews" (vv. 41, 52) play any part in the development of the argument across vv. 25-59. See, for example, Menken, *Numerical* 159–160. The question-and-answer form of the discourse does not reflect the structure of the Jewish Passover Haggadah as Gärtner, *John 6,* Kilmartin, "Liturgical Influence" 183–191, and Daube, *New Testament* 36–51, 158–169 suggest. The interpretation of the discourse offered here argues that these interruptions act as moments of ignorance or misunderstanding that set the agenda for the words of Jesus that follow (cf. Brown, *Gospel* 1:266–267). A similar function for the interruptions is suggested by Schenke, "Die formale" 21–41, and Phillips, "This is a Hard Saying" 38–43, 49–54. Phillips shows that the interruptions form different "enunciative posts."

26. *you seek me:* For Grob, "Vous me cherchez" 429–439, Jesus is not critical, but explains that the crowd does not hunger because it is "satiated" by the eschatological bread of the miracle. Roberge, "Jean 6,26" 339–349, accepts Grob's explanation of v. 26b, but reads the *zēteite* of v. 26a as an imperative. The crowd is commanded not to seek Jesus on the basis of signs but because of the promise of eschatological satisfaction, of which the miracle was a symbol.

27. *the Son of Man:* The threefold appearance of the title "the Son of Man" in John 6 (cf. vv. 27, 53, 62) is sometimes regarded as out of tune with the other Son of Man sayings in the Fourth Gospel. This is particularly true of scholars who link the Son of Man with a descending and ascending heavenly figure (e.g., Ashton, *Understanding the Fourth Gospel* 337–373). Most resort to a theory of a second edition of the Gospel in which these additional sayings were added (e.g., Ashton, *Understanding the Fourth Gospel* 356). If the fundamental function of the Son of Man in the Fourth Gospel is to make God known within the human experience of Jesus' life and death (cf. Moloney, *Son of Man* 208–220; Hare, *Son of Man* 79–111; Lindars, *Son of Man* 145–157) there is a unity across all the sayings, even though different aspects of Jesus' revealing role may be involved in each saying.

    will give: Many witnesses (Sinaiticus, Bezae, Old Latin, Curetonian Syriac) have the present tense "is giving." The evidence for the future tense provided by $\mathfrak{P}^{75}$ tips the scale. See Manns, *L'Evangile* 143. The future reading is important for the above interpretation that looks beyond the immediate context of the discourse for an explanation of what this gift might be and when it might be given.

for on him God the Father has set his seal: The unique nature of the one on whom God has set his seal is communicated by the use of the emphatic *houtos* ("this man") at the beginning of the affirmation *touton gar ho patēr esphragizen ho theos.* On the authoritative nature of "setting a seal" see Barrett, *Gospel* 287; Borgen, "John 6" 272–274. The aorist tense of "he has set his seal" looks back to the *egeneto* of 1:14, the moment in history when the Word turned toward God (1:1) became flesh. See Moloney, *Son of Man* 114–115.

28. *What must we do?:* This is the only interrupting question that does not begin a new section within the discourse. There are too many thematic and verbal links across vv. 25-29, highlighted by the movement from *ergazesthe* in v. 27, to *hina ergazōmetha* in v. 28, to Jesus' final words that equate *to ergon tou theou* with *pisteuēte eis hon apesteilen ekeinos* in v. 29.

    to be devoting ourselves to the works of God: There is a subtle shift in the use of *ergazesthai* in v. 27 and v. 28. The meaning of "work for" is used for a food produced by human hands (v. 27), but attention to the works of God requires the meaning of "work upon" See BAGD 307, s.v., 2e. The translation renders the notion as "to devote oneself to" (v. 28) which provides a good parallel with the rabbinic tradition of "working on" or "devoting oneself to" Torah. On devotion to the Law as pleasing to God see Schnackenburg, *Gospel* 2:39.

29. *that you believe in him:* The present subjunctive *pisteuēte* ("believe") has a durative meaning. The believing must go on. Among many, see Brown, *Gospel* 1:262.

Verses 30-33

30. So they asked him, "What sign do you do that we may see it and believe you? What will you do? 31. Our ancestors ate the manna in the desert; as it is written: 'He gave them bread from heaven to eat.'"
32. Jesus said to them, "Amen, amen, I say to you, it is not Moses who gave you the bread from heaven, but it is my Father who gives you the true bread from heaven. 33. For the bread of God is he who comes down from heaven and gives life to the world."

INTERPRETATION

The true bread of God from heaven (vv. 30-33). Two questions open the next stage in the discourse: "What sign *(sēmeion)* do you do that we may see it and believe you? What will you do?" (v. 30). They show that the crowd recognizes that Jesus' words on belief in the Sent One of the Father (v. 29) mean belief in him. The people tell Jesus why they trust in the

Mosaic tradition: "Our ancestors ate the manna in the desert; as it is written: 'He gave them bread from heaven to eat'" (v. 31). Judaism was familiar with the tradition of confirmatory miracles (cf. Schnackenburg, *Gospel* 2:39–40), and the crowd asks that Jesus conform to that tradition. Indeed, he must do more: "He who makes greater claims than Moses must provide a more striking attestation of his right" (Barrett, *Gospel* 288). Ironically, Jesus' interlocutors provide him with the text (v. 31b) that he will use for the backbone of his response. They also maintain the focus on the Passover background central to John 6.

When Israel looked back to the foundational experience of the Exodus a link was made between Moses and the gift of the manna, understood as bread from heaven (cf. Exod 16:4; Pss 78:24; 105:40; Neh 9:15; Wis 16:20). This never-failing nourishment from God was identified, in both the wisdom and Jewish midrashic traditions, with the gift of the Law (for texts see Borgen, *Bread from Heaven* 148–164; Manns, *L'Evangile* 154–158). Despite Jesus' warnings and promise (vv. 25-29), the people attempt to force Jesus into their Mosaic model: Moses, the manna, and Torah give life to Israel. What sign can Jesus do to surpass the sign of the gift of bread from heaven in the desert, and all that this has come to mean: the life-giving presence of the Torah to God's people? Within the context of the Jewish celebration of Passover, when the gift of the manna was recalled and celebrated, Jesus has summoned the crowd to labor for the bread that does not perish (v. 27; cf. vv. 12-13). Aroused by these words, the people demand that he offer them a sign that authorizes him to challenge the unique authority of Moses and the Torah, the ongoing presence of the manna, God's nourishment for the Jewish people.

A double "amen" (v. 32) opens Jesus' words that warn the people against setting too much store by Moses. Moses did not give the bread from heaven; God did. But that gift *once given (dedōken)*, is surpassed by a bread that God *now gives (didōsin):* the true bread from heaven *(ton arton ek tou ouranou ton alēthinon).* However wonderful the former gift of God once given, the true bread from heaven is the gift that the Father of Jesus (cf. 5:17) is now giving (v. 32). It comes down from heaven and gives life to the world (v. 33). The use of "true" *(alēthinos)* sets this bread over against all other breads, even the bread given to the ancestors of Israel through Moses. This is the authentic bread that is and does all that it claims to be and do. The present gift of God comes down from above and, unlike the Torah that gave life to Israel, gives life to the whole world. Both contrast and continuation are found here. In the past it was God who gave the bread, not Moses (cf. v. 32). Now this same God, the Father of Jesus, gives the true bread from heaven. The Mosaic manna provided nourishment for Israel; the true bread from heaven gives life to the whole world.

NOTES

30. *What sign do you do?:* At best one can conclude that the first part of Jesus' discourse (vv. 25-29) has led the audience back from their desire to fill their bellies (cf. v. 26) to the search for "signs" that marked their original appearance at the side of the lake (cf. v. 2).

31. *He gave them bread from heaven to eat:* No OT passage has these exact words. Borgen, *Bread from Heaven* 40–42 (and others) claim that Exod 16:4, 15 are combined to form the text. Many disagree. For example, Barrett, "The Flesh" 39–40; Geiger, "Aufruf an Rückkehre" 449–464; Menken, *Old Testament* 47–65; Painter, *Quest* 271–272; Schnelle, *Antidocetic Christology* 196 n. 129; Schuchard, *Scripture within Scripture* 33–46; and Obermann, *Die christologische Erfüllung,* 132–150, have argued for Ps 78:24. Rightly Manns, *L'Evangile* 153, comments: "It is most likely the text of Exod 16:4 and 16:15, a passage which is reflected in Ps 78:24 and Neh 9:15."

32. *Amen, amen, I say to you:* The use of the double "amen" in v. 29 and v. 32 is an indication that the first two sections of the discourse are vv. 25-29 (a question answered with a double "amen") and vv. 30-33 (a question answered with a double "amen"). For the rabbinic nature of this response of Jesus to the question raised in vv. 30-31 see Borgen, *Bread from Heaven* 61–69.

    who gave you the bread from heaven: The perfect tense of the verb *(dedōken)* must be maintained, even though Vaticanus, Bezae, and Clement of Alexandria have *edōken.* See Barrett, *Gospel* 289.

    the true bread from heaven: The placement of the adjective *(ton alēthinon)* after the noun, with its own article, is an emphatic use. On the importance of *both* gifts, but the superiority of the latter, see Barrett, *Gospel* 290. On the use of *alēthinos* as "genuine, being and doing what it claims to be and do," see Moloney, *Belief* 36, and the references mentioned there. For its use with this sense here see Leroy, *Rätsel und Mißverständnis* 103–107.

33. *he who comes down from heaven:* The Greek *ho katabainōn ek tou ouranou* could mean "that which comes down," and refer to Torah, or "he who comes down," and refer to Jesus (cf. Brown, *Gospel* 1:262–263). The ambiguity may be intended, as Jesus' next words will indicate that Jesus is the one who comes down (cf. v. 35).

Verses 34-40

34. They said to him, "Sir, give us this bread always." 35. Jesus said to them, "I am the bread of life; anyone who comes to me shall not hunger, and anyone who believes in me shall never thirst. 36. But I said to you that you have seen and yet do not believe. 37. Everyone the Father gives me will come to me; and anyone who comes to me I will not cast out. 38. For I have come down from heaven, not to do my own will, but the will of him who sent me; 39. and this is the will of him who sent me, that I should lose nothing of all that he has given me, but raise it up at the last

day. 40. For this is the will of my Father, that all who see the Son and believe in him may have eternal life; and I will raise them up on the last
day."

INTERPRETATION

Jesus is the bread of life (vv. 34-40). The response of the crowd to Jesus'
words on the true bread from heaven opens the next section. The people
ask, "Sir, give us this bread always *(pantote)*" (v. 34). They misunderstand
the nature of the bread and ask Jesus to give the bread from heaven again
and again *(pantote)*. Jesus responds by identifying himself with the once-
and-for-all gift of the bread: "I am the bread of life" (v. 35a). As with all
the "I am" sayings with a predicate, Jesus is not describing who he is but
what he does: he nourishes with a bread that produces life. Jesus claims
that he is perfecting the former gift, the lifegiving nourishment provided
by Torah. Gone are the limitations of chosen people, as Jesus promises
that anyone who would come to him *(ho erchomenos pros eme)* will not
hunger and that anyone who believes in him *(ho pisteuōn eis eme)* will not
thirst. Set in close parallel, to come to Jesus and to believe in Jesus mean
the same thing. Those who come to Jesus and believe in him will find rest
from the never-ending search for Wisdom: "Those who eat of me [Wis-
dom] will hunger for more, and those who drink of me will thirst for
more" (Sir 24:21; cf. also Isa 49:10). No longer will Moses, the manna,
Wisdom, or Torah provide sufficient nourishment. Jesus, the bread of life
(v. 35a), will satisfy the deepest needs of humankind, all hunger and all
thirst (v. 35b).

But the words of Jesus are *in the future tense.* Those who come and
believe shall not hunger *(ou mē peinasē)* and they shall not thirst *(ou mē
dipsēsei pōpote)*. Some time in the future Jesus will provide never-failing
food and drink. The links with Jewish tradition indicate that the revelation of God in and through Jesus will surpass the revelation of God in and
through the Law, but when might this happen? This promise of some future moment in which God will be made known recalls other unresolved
promises. When will the *klasmata,* gathered by the disciples so that they
might not perish (v. 13), be consumed? When will the never-perishing
food provided by the Son of Man (v. 27) be given? There will be some moment in the future when a food will be provided by the Son of Man that
will explain the *klasmata* and provide never-failing food and drink to
those who believe (vv. 13, 27, 35).

Jesus claims he has told them of their lack of belief, even though they
have seen (v. 36). These words are not found earlier in the Gospel, but
they refer back to Jesus' revelation through the miraculous gift of the

bread that the crowd has interpreted in terms of their Mosaic traditions. The key to a correct reading of v. 36 is v. 26. They have seen (vv. 5-15), but they have not believed (v. 26). Jesus is the nourishment of Israel and of the whole world (v. 35). He replaces the manna and Torah, but the people have not believed in this revelation even though they have seen it. The Father sends those who come to Jesus in faith, and Jesus willingly accepts "everyone" *(pan ho didōsin me ho patēr)*. He will not "cast out" *(ekballō)* anyone or anything given to him by the Father. As well as continuing the theme of universality broached in v. 35, the text addresses the Johannine community. Its members have been "cast out" (cf. 9:34) because of their faith in Jesus as the Christ. Their "coming to" and "belief in" Jesus place them in a new situation where such violence will never again be done to them.

As the word of God (cf. Isa 55:10-11) and the Law of God were understood as a gift of God come down from heaven (cf. Exod 19:11, 20; *m. Sanh.* 10:1; *b. Šabb.* 89b; *Pesiqta Rabbati* 53:2; *Exod. Rab.* 28:1-3), Jesus presents himself as the perfection of the former gift of the Law. Like the Law, his presence is a reflection of the will of the Father (cf. 4:34; 5:36). The Father gives (v. 37), the Father sends (v. 38a), and the one who is sent responds unconditionally to the will of the one who sent him (v. 38b). How this relates to and perfects the former understanding of the gift of the Law needs some further explanation. As the Law was to lead a chosen people to belong forever to YHWH, so it is with Jesus. In the new situation, where the Law has been replaced by Jesus and the new people of God includes whomsoever the Father gives him, the will of the Father is that not one of these be lost, either now or hereafter (v. 39). These words on life both here and hereafter are essential for a third-generation Christian Church facing the mystery of the death of its members (v. 39b; 16:2; 21:23).

In light of what he has claimed concerning his being the true bread, the gift of God from heaven that brings nourishment and life to those who come to him and believe in him, Jesus promises eternal life to those who would perfect their adherence to the Law by believing in the Son sent by the Father (v. 40a). It was through the concrete reality of the Law, words of God that spoke to the lived situation of a chosen people, that Israel would find the will of God. This "living presence," the visible assurance that God cares for and guides God's people, has been perfected. It is to be seen and believed in the presence of the Son: "*All* who see *(pas ho theorōn)* the Son and believe *(pisteuōn)* in him may have eternal life" (v. 40b). The *universal* and *never-ending* promise of life is made to *all* as Jesus will "raise them up at the last day" (v. 40c). Both the temporal dimensions of the Law, guarding and directing a people during its earthly pilgrimage, and the ethnic limitations of the Law, an exclusive covenant between

God and the people of Israel, have been perfected in Jesus. He promises life to *all*, both *now* and *forever*. The former gift of the bread from heaven has been perfected in Jesus, the true bread from heaven.

NOTES

34. *Sir, give us this bread always:* Most English translations of v. 34 have "Lord" for *kyrie*. The use of this passage out of context colors this translation, but an exalted title is uncalled for in the Johannine context. The normal term of respect, "Sir," is to be preferred.

    always: The Greek word *pantote* carries the idea of an ongoing giving, the continual repetition of the act of giving.

35. *I am the bread of life:* On the christological use of *egō eimi* with a predicate see, among many, the surveys of Bultmann, *Gospel* 225–226 n. 3; Barrett, *Gospel* 291–293; Schnackenburg, *Gospel* 2:79–89. On the rabbinic nature of vv. 34-40 and the parallels between Jesus' claims and claims made for Torah see Borgen, *Bread from Heaven* 69–80.

    shall not hunger . . . shall never thirst: For the wisdom background to v. 35 see Scott, *Sophia* 116–119. The use of the expression "never" (*pōpote*) in Jesus' response is a subtle correction of the crowd's mistaken request to have the bread from heaven "always" (v. 34: *pantote*). There is a strong emphasis on the never-failing gift of Jesus, the bread from heaven, expressed in the double negative *ou mē . . . pōpote*.

36. *you have seen:* There is good textual evidence for the presence of "me" ("you have seen me"). I am reading the more general affirmation, "you have seen." For a discussion of the evidence, and this conclusion, see Barrett, *Gospel* 293. It does have slightly better textual support (Sinaiticus, Old Latin, Sinaitic Syriac, Curetonian Syriac), and better suits the argument. However, for the inclusion of "me" see Brown, *Gospel* 1:270.

37. *Everyone the Father gives me:* The neuter singular *pan* is used for "everyone." This could indicate all creation, that is, "everything." A reference to "everyone" would call for the masculine plural *pantes*. The rest of v. 37 demands that human beings at least be a part of the meaning of *pan*, as Jesus does not reject anyone who comes to him. Optimistically, this may be one of the few places in the Fourth Gospel where an enthusiastic understanding of Jesus is the goal of all creation parallel to Colossians and Ephesians, a development of John 1:10. It would seriously disturb the logic of the argument at this stage of the discourse, and does not appear to be necessary. The neuter singular is found elsewhere in the Johannine writings with this more personal meaning (cf. 17:2; 1 John 4:2, 3; 5:4). See Bernard, *Commentary* 1:199.

38. *come down from heaven . . . to do . . . the will of the one who sent me:* The Sent One as the presence of the one who sent is widely accepted as reflecting Jewish thought. See Bühner, *Der Gesandte und Sein Weg* 118–267. In addition to this Borgen, *Bread from Heaven* 122–146, had earlier gathered an impressive

array of material from Philo on "a heavenly order reaching down to check the disorderly tendencies of the earth."

40. *all who see the Son and believe in him:* Brown, *Gospel* 1:270 correctly points out that a deeper sense in the "seeing" is involved here: *"theorein . . .* not only physically, but with spiritual insight." This understanding of "seeing" *(theōrōn)* makes it parallel with the use of "believing" *(pisteuōn).*

Verses 41-51

41. The Jews then murmured at him because he said, "I am the bread that came down from heaven." 42. They said, "Is not this Jesus, the son of Joseph, whose father and mother we know? How does he now say, 'I have come down from heaven'?" 43. Jesus answered them, "Do not murmur among yourselves. 44. No one can come to me unless drawn by the Father who sent me; and I will raise that person up at the last day. 45. It is written in the prophets, 'And they shall all be taught by God.' Every one who has heard and learned from the Father comes to me. 46. Not that anyone has seen the Father except the one who is from God; he has seen the Father. 47. Amen, amen, I say to you, whoever believes has eternal life. 48. I am the bread of life. 49. Your ancestors ate the manna in the wilderness, and they died. 50. This is the bread that comes down from heaven, so that one may eat of it and not die. 51. I am the living bread that came down from heaven; whoever eats of this bread will live for ever; and the bread that I shall give for the life of the world is my flesh."

INTERPRETATION

The question of origins (vv. 41-51): The unspecified crowd *(ho ochlos),* Jesus' interlocutor thus far, suddenly becomes "the Jews." Once this group emerges from the crowd hostility increases. Their "murmuring," recalling the behavior of the Israelites in the wilderness (cf. Exod 15:24; 16:2, 7; 17:3), indicates rebellion. Jesus' claim to be the bread from heaven in vv. 35-40 is challenged. How can he make that claim (vv. 41, 42b) when his human father and mother are known (v. 42a)? The theme of this section of the discourse has been struck: Jesus has made claims that can be understood only in terms of his origins: a descent *from his Father above.* His opponents will not consider such a possibility; they know *his father Joseph.* Moses had warned the murmuring people of Israel, "Your complaints are not against us, but against the Lord" (Exod 16:8). Jesus repeats this process as he reproaches the murmuring of "the Jews" (v. 43) by pointing to the Father, and explaining his role in terms of his origins with the Father. The Father sends Jesus, the Father draws believers to him, and the response of those drawn to the revelation of the Father in the Sent

One will be the measure of their everlasting life. It is Jesus who will raise up the believer on the last day (v. 44). While God determines the process, the encounter between the human being and the revelation of God in Jesus determines life, death, and everlasting life. This is only possible because Jesus is not the son of Joseph (vv. 41-42) but the Son of the Father.

The prophets had foretold that "they shall all be taught by God" (v. 45a, freely citing Isa 54:13). Thus Jesus asks that "the Jews" listen to God that they might be instructed. God taught Israel through the gift of the Law, but Jesus claims that all who have truly learned from God will come to him (v. 45). The instruction God gives to *all peoples* (v. 45a: *pantes*) draws them to Jesus (v. 45b: *pas . . . erchetai pros eme*). Continuing the theme of universality of vv. 35-40, Jesus now claims that in fulfillment of the prophetic promise (v. 45a) a process is in motion that leads to the true believer's coming to Jesus. No longer is Israel the object and the Law the source of God's instruction. It is aimed at all believers without limitation of race or nation, and it comes through Jesus.

Jesus is the one who makes the Father known. No one has ever seen the Father (cf. 1:18), but the one who has come from the Father makes him known (v. 46). As in 1:16-18, the relationship between Jesus and Moses is in question. However exalted were the claims of Moses, the Son who throughout his human story gazes toward the Father is the only one who has ever seen God (cf. interpretation of 1:18). The difference between Moses and Jesus is their respective origins. Jesus' origins *pros ton theon* (1:1) gave him a unique authority to make God known (1:18). Because this is the case the one who believes in the revelation of Jesus, the true bread who has come down from heaven, has eternal life. The comparison continues between the manna of the Law and Jesus, the true bread from heaven. It is no longer the Law that produces life. Jesus, the true bread from heaven, came to make the Father known and, in doing so, surpasses the former gift of a bread from heaven (cf. vv. 32-33). He is the bread of life (v. 48).

As the comparison of two "breads" draws to a conclusion Jesus recalls the experience of Israel's ancestors who ate the bread that came down from heaven in the form of manna: they all died (v. 49). The bread that comes down from heaven in the person of Jesus promises a life that is eternal: there will be no death for those who consume that bread (v. 50). There is a close parallel between the words of Jesus in v. 50: "This is the bread that comes down from heaven," and in v. 51: "I am the living bread that came down from heaven." As once Moses pointed to the manna and said, "This is the bread that the Lord has given you for food" (Exod 16:15), Jesus points to himself and says, "This is the bread" (v. 50). The Mosaic bread did not produce life (cf. v. 49), and even Moses is dead (cf. Deut 34:5-8). Now there is a bread that surpasses the bread given by

Moses: *houtos estin ho artos ho ek tou ouranou katabainōn* (v. 50) . . . *egō eimi ho artos ho zōn ho ek tou ouranou katabas* (v. 51). Jesus' identification of himself with the bread of life that came down from heaven is marked by an inceptive aorist: "he came." It looks back to the basis for Jesus' claims: the moment when the Word became flesh (1:14: *ho logos sarx egeneto*).

There has been an intensifying concentration on the person of Jesus: "This is the bread . . . I am the bread" (vv. 50, 51). The one who is the bread now makes a further surprising promise: "The bread that I shall give for the life of the world is my flesh" (v. 51c). The true bread that has come down from heaven *will* make God known in an unconditional gift of himself for the life of the world. When will this be? How will it happen? As in earlier statements that point to a future encounter between the darkness and the light (1:5), the hour of Jesus (2:5) and his being "lifted up" (3:14), much is still shrouded in mystery. But there are already clear hints that Jesus will be slain by "the Jews" in their rejection of him at the Temple in 2:13-23 and their plot to kill him in 5:18. The mystery does not lie in the *fact* that Jesus will die at the hands of "the Jews." The Johannine community and all subsequent believers have known that before reading the Gospel. But *how* does Jesus' experience of death provide nourishment for the life of the world?

This is not the first time Jesus has promised a future gift. In vv. 12-13 the disciples were commanded to gather the *klasmata* so that they might not be lost (*hina mē ti apolētai*). In v. 27 Jesus urged the crowds not to labor for a food that perishes (*tēn brosin tēn apollumenēn*), but for a food that endures, that would be provided by the Son of Man. In v. 35 Jesus' claim to be the bread of life leads to a further promise: all who come to him *will not* hunger, and all who believe in him *will not* thirst. The mounting impression is that there will be a definitive nourishment that will forever satisfy the needs of all who believe in Jesus. Jesus has outraged "the Jews" by telling them that he *will give* his flesh for the life of the world (v. 51). Their horrified question, asking *how* this is possible (v. 52), sheds light upon when and how Jesus' promise of the bread that surpasses all that the Passover celebrated will be given.

NOTES

41. *"the Jews"*: The sudden appearance of "the Jews" has led to suggestions concerning the history of the discourse. Painter (*Quest* 275–278) argues that the nature of the discourse changes here. He suggests that vv. 25-35 represent a "quest story" with its own history in the tradition, while vv. 36-71 represent "rejection stories" that come from a different background. He suggests that vv. 36-40 are a "transitional addition." See, however, the response to Painter in Borgen, "John 6" 283–285.

44. *unless drawn by the Father who sent me:* In the rabbinic sources the expression "to draw" is used to describe a bringing close to the Torah, and thus to conversion. See *Pirke Abot* 1:12.

45. *It is written in the prophets:* This vague reference to "the prophets" is made only here in the Fourth Gospel. On the text from Isaiah see Menken, *Old Testament Quotations* 67–77; Schuchard, *Scripture Within Scripture* 47–57; Obermann, *Die christologische Erfüllung* 151–167.

47. *Amen, amen, I say to you:* On the basis of the systematic use of the double "amen" to link what went before with what follows I have interpreted its use on this occasion as "because this is the case."

49. *Your ancestors ate the manna in the wilderness:* The verb "to eat" appears for the first time since v. 31. It marks the beginning of the midrashic treatment of the verb provided in v. 31: "He gave them bread from heaven *to eat.*" However, this does not mark the beginning of a new section of the discourse. The interventions of the crowd and "the Jews" open each section. Thus there is no break at v. 48, nor does v. 51c mark a new section as many commentators would insist. See the remarks of Barrett, *Gospel* 296.

51. *the bread that I shall give:* The future tense is not unanimous in the textual tradition. However, it must be retained on the basis of $\mathfrak{P}^{66}$, $\mathfrak{P}^{75}$, Vaticanus, Bezae, Old Latin, Vulgate, Sinaitic Syriac, Curetonian Syriac, and Sahidic.

the bread that I shall give for the life of the world is my flesh: Many elements in v. 51c reflect eucharistic traditions found elsewhere in the NT and in the early Church. The Johannine celebration of the Eucharist lies behind the use of key expressions: *ho artos* (bread), *sarx* (flesh), *egō dōsō* (I will give), *hyper* (for the sake of). See, for example, Jeremias, *Eucharistic Words* 106–108. These explicit eucharistic links are seen by most commentators as the introduction to vv. 51c-58, a discrete section within John 6 that deals with the Eucharist. It may be true that the "backbone of vss. 51-58 is made up of material from the Johannine narrative of the institution of the Eucharist" (Brown, *Gospel* 1:287), but behind the eucharistic language the interpretation given here insists that the fundamental issue is Jesus' self-gift for the life of the world. His body ("flesh") will be given over in crucifixion for the life of the world. For studies that support this conclusion see Schürmann, "Joh 6,51c—ein Schlüssel" 244–262; Menken, "John 6:51c-58" 9–13; Moloney, *Son of Man* 115; idem, "John 6" 243–251; Léon-Dufour, *Lecture* 2:159–162. Verse 51c does not introduce a eucharistic section (vv. 51c-58), but closes vv. 40-51 in a way that generates a horrified dispute among "the Jews." In v. 52 they ask *how* Jesus can make his flesh available to eat. Jesus responds to their question in vv. 53-58.

Verses 52-59

52. The Jews then disputed among themselves, saying, "How can this man give us his flesh to eat?" 53. So Jesus said to them, "Amen, amen, I say to you, unless you eat the flesh of the Son of Man and drink his blood you have no life in you; 54. those who eat my flesh and drink my

blood have eternal life, and I will raise them up at the last day. 55. For my flesh is food indeed, and my blood is drink indeed. 56. Those who eat my flesh and drink my blood abide in me, and I in them. 57. As the living Father sent me, and I live because of the Father, so the one who eats me will live because of me. 58. This is the bread that came down from heaven, not such as the ancestors ate and died; the one who eats this bread will live for ever." 59. This he said in the synagogue, as he taught at Capernaum.

INTERPRETATION

Jesus gives his flesh to eat (vv. 52-59). The question that emerges from the dispute among "the Jews" is a rejection of Jesus' outrageous suggestion: "How *(pōs)* can this man give us his flesh to eat?" (v. 52). But it allows Jesus to conclude his discourse on his perfection of the Mosaic gift of bread from heaven through his gift of himself as the true bread from heaven. Unable to go beyond the physical, "the Jews" by their question misunderstand Jesus' promise. Jesus insists on a gift of flesh and blood for life by stating negatively (v. 53) and positively (v. 54) that whoever eats the flesh and drinks the blood of Jesus, the Son of Man, has eternal life now and will be raised up on the last day. The midrashic play on the verb "to eat" provided by the Exodus passage in v. 31 has reached its high point. "Flesh" and "blood" emphasize that it is the incarnate life and very real death of the Son that are lifegiving food. Only the physical body of a human being produces flesh and blood. The argument of vv. 25-51 continues into vv. 52-59, especially in Jesus' words that point to the resolution of a series of promises (cf. vv. 12-13, 27, 35, 51c). Jesus will provide a food for the life of the world, and that food is his flesh and blood. As the ancestors of Israel were nourished by the gift of the Torah, Jesus will nourish the whole world with the gift of himself. The people of Israel were nourished by eating the manna, perennially recalled in the nourishment provided for them by their total receptivity to and absorption of the Law. Now "the Jews" are told of the absolute need to eat the flesh and drink the blood of the Son of Man. Unless they eat the flesh and drink the blood *(ean mē phagēte . . . kai piēte)* of the Son of Man they have no life (v. 53); whoever eats the flesh and drinks the blood *(ho trōgōn . . . kai pinōn)* of Jesus has eternal life (v. 54). The shift from the more respectable verb "to eat" *(phagein)* to another verb that indicates the physical crunching with the teeth *(trōgein)* accentuates that Jesus refers to a real experience of eating. Hints of the Eucharist continue to insinuate themselves into the words of Jesus (see below). Flesh is to be broken and blood is to be spilled. Violence has been in the air since Jesus' behavior on the Sabbath led "the Jews" to initiate a process that would lead to his death (5:16-18).

Jesus now associates the separation of flesh and blood in a violent death as the moment of total giving of himself. Jesus, the Son of Man, will give of his whole self for the life of the world (6:51c) by means of a violent encounter between himself and his enemies (1:5, 11; 2:18-20; 3:14; 5:16-18) in which his body will be broken and his blood will be poured out (6:53-54). This is the ongoing presence of Jesus in the gathered *klasmata* (vv. 12-13), the enduring gift that the Son of Man will give, the food that will not perish (v. 27) but will forever satisfy all hunger and thirst (v. 35).

The Passover context must not be forgotten. As once Israel ate of the manna in the desert and was nourished by adhesion to the Law given at Sinai, so now the world is summoned to accept the further revelation of God in the broken body and spilled blood of the Son of Man. In this way all will have life, now and hereafter (vv. 53-54). These claims are further developed through vv. 55-57. Earlier parts of the discourse are recalled as Jesus insists that his flesh really is food *(alēthēs estin brōsis)* and his blood really is drink *(alēthēs estin posis)*. This play on words recalls Jesus' promise of the *brōsis* (food) that the Son of Man would give (v. 27), and his claim that over against all other bread from heaven, and especially the gift of the Law from heaven, the Father gives "the true bread from heaven" (v. 32: *ton arton ek tou ouranou alēthinon*). Jesus is the true bread from heaven (v. 35). On the basis of the entire discourse Jesus lays claim to his flesh and blood as authentically *(alēthōs)* food and drink. The midrashic explanation of v. 31 continues: through a total absorption *(trōgein* is again used) of the revelation of God made available through the bloody death of Jesus, believers will come to a mutuality in which they live in Jesus and Jesus lives in them (v. 56). This mutual indwelling *(menein* is used; cf. 15:4-7) flows from the union that exists between the Father and the Son (v. 57). Jesus' words play on the verb "to live" *(zōein)*. He refers to the Father as "the *living* Father" *(ho zōn patēr)* who has sent his Son who has life in him because of the intimacy between the Father and the Son. If the one who sends is "living," then the one who is sent *lives* because of the one who sent him *(kagō zō dia ton patera)*. He thus has authority to pass on life to those who accept the revelation of the Father in the Son (v. 57). The idea of the reception of the revelation of God in and through the Son is not new (cf., for example, 3:11-21, 31-36), but the imagery has been changed by the Passover context. No longer does Jesus speak of "belief in" (cf. 3:12, 15, 18, 36), but of "the one who eats me" (v. 57b: *ho trōgōn me*). The expressions are parallel. As throughout the Gospel, unconditional commitment to the revelation of God in and through Jesus leads to life here and hereafter: the one who eats the flesh of Jesus *will live* because of him (v. 57b: *kakeinos zēsei di'eme*). As Jesus lives because of the Father (v. 57a), the believer lives and will live because of Jesus (v. 57b).

The discourse closes as it opened, comparing the bread that Israel's ancestors ate in the desert and the bread that comes down from heaven (v. 58; cf. vv. 30-33). All former gifts from heaven have been surpassed. Playing upon the two possibilities of life—physical life that the manna could not provide, and eternal life that the true bread of life does give (cf. vv. 49-50)—Jesus points to the death of Israel's ancestors and promises everlasting life to those who eat of the true bread from heaven. A new possibility has entered the human story. The Law was a gift of God (cf. 1:17), but it has been surpassed by Jesus, the bread from heaven (v. 35), promising his abiding presence (v. 56), communicating the life of the Father to all who consume this true bread (v. 57). On the occasion of the celebration of Passover Jesus announces that there is another bread from heaven that eclipses all the original bread offered to the ancestors of Israel (v. 58). "This he said in the synagogue, as he taught at Capernaum" (v. 59). Jesus has not moved. The discourse ends where it began: at Capernaum (vv. 24, 59). The narrator closes the discourse with a comment that reminds the reader that Jesus is in a Jewish center of worship during Passover time, uttering a message that presupposes, fulfills, and transcends a Jewish Passover tradition.

The Eucharist in John 6:51c-58. The major concern of this final part of the discourse on the bread from heaven is not eucharistic, but the midrashic commentary on the verb "to eat" (cf. v. 31) summons up a rich tradition of eucharistic language: "bread," "food," "flesh," "blood," "to eat," "to drink," "will give," "for your sakes." The discourse, from v. 25 down to v. 59, presents Jesus as the true bread from heaven, replacing the former bread from heaven, the manna of the Law. The believer must accept the revelation of God that will take place in broken flesh and spilled blood (vv. 53-54), a never-failing nourishment (v. 35) that the Son of Man will give (v. 27). But at the end of the first century Johannine readers, and the Christian readers of subsequent centuries, have every right to ask: where do we encounter this revelation of God in the flesh and blood of the Son of Man? The author's insinuation of eucharistic language into the final section of the discourse provides the answer: one encounters the flesh and blood of Jesus Christ in the eucharistic celebration. The use of the word *klasmata* to refer to the bread consigned by Jesus to his disciples (vv. 12-13) has lurked behind the discourse, reminding the reader of such celebrations.

The author is working at two levels. The main thrust of the discourse is to point to Jesus as the revelation of God, the true bread from heaven, perfecting God's former gift, the bread of the manna. However, the word *klasmata* in vv. 12-13, the promise in v. 27 of a future gift of food that the Son of Man would give, the reference to the satisfying food and drink in v. 35, and the further promise in v. 51c of the gift of the flesh of Jesus for the life of the world keep the eucharistic question alive. The midrashic unfolding of the verb "to eat" (cf. v. 31) in vv. 49-58 naturally led to the use of eucharistic language to insinuate a secondary but important theme. The Eucharist renders concrete, in the eucharistic practice of the Christian reader, what the author has spelled out throughout the discourse. The Eucharist is a place where one comes to eternal life. Encountering the broken flesh and the spilled blood of Jesus, "lifted up" on a cross (vv. 53-54), the believer is called to make a decision for or against the revelation of God in that encounter (vv. 56-58), gaining or losing life because of it (vv. 53-54).

NOTES

52. *The Jews then disputed among themselves:* The disputing *(emachonto oun . . . hoi Ioudaioi)* continues the theme of the "grumbling" from Exodus 16. It appears in LXX Exod 17:2 with the same meaning as the verb *gongyzein* in LXX Exod 16:7-8 and John 6:41, 43. See also LXX Num 11:4. On the misunderstanding involved in the question of "the Jews" see Leroy, *Rätsel und Mißverständnis* 121–124.

53. *Amen, amen, I say to you:* The presence of the double "amen" in v. 53 makes this the third use of the expression to introduce Jesus' response to the misunderstanding interruptions that mark the beginning of each section (cf. vv. 26, 32). It is an indication of the staged unfolding of the argument.

    eat the flesh of the Son of Man and drink his blood: For a detailed study of v. 53, arguing that its primary reference is the crucifixion, see Moloney, *Son of Man* 115–120. See also Schürmann, "Die Eucharistie als Representation" 30–45, 108–118.

54. *those who eat my flesh:* The use of *trōgein* for the action of "eating" is found throughout vv. 53-58 (cf. vv. 54, 56, 57, 58). The claim that the verb is used to express the physical experience, "to munch," "to crunch" (cf. BAGD 829; LSJ 1832) is sometimes questioned. See, for example, Barrett, *Gospel* 299; Schuchard, *Scripture Within Scripture* 112; Menken, "John 6:51c-58" 16–18; Obermann, *Die christologische Erfüllung* 255–258, 263–265. In defense of the position taken in the interpretation see Spicq, *"Trōgein"* 414–419. Those who reject this physical meaning point to the presence of *phagein* in the immediate context (cf. v. 53), and thus claim that the verbs are interchangeable. This does not respect the fact that the verbs *phagein* and *esthiein* are found in a number of places and contexts in the Fourth Gospel, but *trōgein* is found *only* in 6:54-58 and 13:18. Both of these passages have eucharistic background (see below on 13:18). It is often suggested that the vigor of this language combats emerging docetic ideas about Jesus. See Schnelle, *Antidocetic Christology* 201–208. The idea that the Law was consumed and absorbed like food is not foreign to Jewish thought. For a collection of many Jewish texts that make this point see Odeberg, *The Fourth Gospel* 238–247.

and I will raise them up at the last day: The practice of introducing the traditional end-time eschatology into a passage that is dominated by a more realized view continues here. Many would remove this as the addition of an ecclesiastical redactor, but it is coherent with the overall Johannine understanding of death and resurrection.

55. *food indeed . . . drink indeed:* Following the first hand of Sinaiticus, Bezae, Koridethi, Athos, Old Latin, Vulgate, Sinaitic Syriac, Curetonian Syriac, and the Peshitta, the translation reads the adverb *alethōs* ("indeed"), rather than the adjective *alethēs* ("true").

57. *the living Father:* The concentration on the theme of "life" and its communication from Father to Son to believer produces the expression "the living Father" *(ho zōn patēr)*, a *hapax legomenon* in the NT.

    because of the Father . . . because of me: The Greek *dia* followed by the accusative case could mean "through, by means of," rather than "because of." In support of "because of," adopted in the interpretation, see Bernard, *Commentary* 1:213–214; Brown, *Gospel* 1:283. For the contrary view see Lagrange, *Evangile* 185–186.

58. *This is the bread that came down from heaven:* Interpreters generally read the whole discourse as eucharistic (sacramental) or as non-sacramental. In the latter interpretation the passage is sapiential, concerned with the motif of belief and eternal life. Many accept that vv. 51c-58 are unavoidably eucharistic, but then regard them as a secondary addition to an originally sapiential text. See the influential study of Bornkamm, "Die eucharistische Rede" 161–169, and Brown, *Gospel* 1:285–291. For documented surveys of this discussion see Moloney, *Son of Man* 87–107; Roberge, "Le discours sur le pain de vie" 265–299; Menken, *Numerical* 186–188. Others have suggested, as in the interpretation, that there are eucharistic hints in an otherwise sapiential discourse. These hints are resolved in the final section of the discourse, which continues the themes of belief and eternal life, but in language that situates belief within the context of the eucharistic celebration of the community. See, for example, Hoskyns, *Gospel* 297; van den Bussche, *Jean* 148–153; Lee, *Symbolic Narrative* 148–153.

For Reference and Further Study

Barrett, C. K. "'The Flesh of the Son of Man' John 6.53." In idem, *Essays in John.* London: S.P.C.K., 1982, 37–49.

Borgen, Peder. *Bread from Heaven: An Exegetical Study of the Conception of Manna in the Gospel of John and the Writings of Philo.* NT.S 10. Leiden: E. J. Brill, 1965.

Bornkamm, Günther. "Die eucharistische Rede im Johannesevangelium," *ZNW* 47 (1956) 161–169.

Gärtner, Bertil. *John 6 and the Jewish Passover.* CNT 17. Lund: Gleerup, 1959.

Geiger, Georg. "Aufruf an Rückkehre: Zum Sinn des Zitats von Ps 78,24b in Joh 6,31," *Bib.* 65 (1984) 449–464.

Gourgues, Michel. "Section christologique et section eucharistique en Jean VI: Une proposition," *RB* 88 (1981) 515–527.

Grob, Francis. "'Vous me cherchez, non parce que vous avez vu des signes . . . ' Essai d'explication cohérente de Jean 6/26," *RHPhR* 60 (1980) 429–439.

Hare, D. R. A. *The Son of Man Tradition*. Minneapolis: Fortress, 1990.

Jeremias, Joachim. *The Eucharistic Words of Jesus*. London: SCM Press, 1966.

Kilmartin, E. J. "Liturgical Influence on John 6," *CBQ* 22 (1960) 183–191.

Lindars, Barnabas. *Jesus Son of Man. A Fresh Examination of the Son of Man Sayings in the Gospels in the Light of Recent Research*. London: S.P.C.K., 1983.

Menken, M. J. J. "John 6,51c-58: Eucharist or Christology?" *Bib.* 74 (1993) 1–26.

_____. *Numerical Literary Techniques in John* 138–188.

_____. "Some Remarks on the Course of the Dialogue: John 6,25-34," *Bijdragen* 48 (1987) 139–149.

Moloney, Francis J. "John 6 and the Celebration of the Eucharist," *DR* 93 (1975) 243–251.

_____. *Signs and Shadows* 42–59.

_____. *Son of Man* 87–123.

Phillips, G. A. "This is a Hard Saying. Who Can Be Listener to It? Creating a Reader in John 6," *Sem* 6 (1983) 23–56.

Roberge, Michel. "Jean 6,26 et le rassasiement eschatologique," *LTP* 45 (1989) 339–349.

_____. "Le discours sur le pain de vie (Jean 6,22-59): Problèmes d'interprétation," *LTP* 38 (1982) 265–299.

Schenke, Ludger. "Die formale und gedankliche Struktur von Joh 6,26-58," *BZ* 24 (1980) 21–41.

Schürmann, Heinz. "Die Eucharistie als Representation und Applikation des Heilsgeschehens nach Joh 6," *TThZ* 68 (1959) 30–45, 108–118.

_____. "Joh 6,51c—ein Schlüssel zur grossen Brotrede," *BZ* 2 (1958) 244–262.

Spicq, Ceslas. "*Trōgein*: Est-il synonyme de *phagein* et d'*esthiein* dans le Nouveau Testament?" *NTS* 26 (1979–1980) 414–419.

f) *The Crisis Created by the Word of Jesus* (6:60-71)

60. Many of his disciples, when they heard it, said, "This is a hard saying; who can listen to it?" 61. But Jesus, knowing in himself that his disciples murmured at it, said to them, "Do you take offense at this? 62. Then what if you were to see the Son of Man ascending where he was before? 63. It is the spirit that gives life, the flesh is of no avail; the words that I have spoken to you are spirit and life. 64. But there are some of you who do not believe." For Jesus knew from the first who those were that did not believe, and who it was that would betray him. 65. And he said, "This is why I told you that no one can come to me unless it is granted

by the Father." 66. Because of this many of his disciples drew back and no longer went about with him.

67. Jesus said to the twelve, "Do you also wish to go away?" 68. Simon Peter answered him, "Lord, to whom shall we go? You have the words of eternal life; 69. and we have believed, and have come to know, that you are the Holy One of God." 70. Jesus answered them, "Did I not choose you, the twelve, and one of you is a devil?" 71. He spoke of Judas the son of Simon Iscariot, for he, one of the twelve, was to betray him.

INTERPRETATION

Introduction to 6:60-71. The form of a discourse disappears as a twofold response to Jesus' words is recorded:

  (a) *Vv. 60-66:* "Many of his disciples" find Jesus' word hard (v. 60), and Jesus addresses their difficulties (vv. 61-65), mentioning a future betrayal (v. 64). However, "many of his disciples" no longer go with Jesus (v. 66).

  (b) *Vv. 67-71:* The Twelve, represented by Peter, confess belief in the word of Jesus (vv. 68-69), but Jesus foretells that even from among these believing disciples one will betray him (vv. 70-71).

The possibility of acceptance or rejection of the word of Jesus has been canvassed regularly, from the Prologue (cf. 1:11-13) onward (cf. 3:11-21; 31-36), and various examples of how one might respond to the word formed the core of the journey from Cana to Cana (2:1–4:54). As Jesus' discourse on the bread from heaven concludes, some of the disciples who had seen him on the waters, heard his self-revelation of *egō eimi*, and had come safely to land (cf. vv. 16-21) leave him (vv. 60-66). Others are told that failure is always possible, even among those who believe (vv. 67-71).

Disciples no longer go with Jesus (vv. 60-66). Many disciples have *heard* what Jesus said (v. 60a: *polloi oun akousantes ek tōn mathētōn*). The disciples have reached a crucial moment. They have been the privileged recipients of Jesus' self-revelation on the stormy sea: "It is I; do not be afraid *(egō eimi, mē phobeisthe)*" (v. 20). They, more than the other characters in the story, the crowd and "the Jews," have been shown (vv. 5-13, 16-21) and told (vv. 25-59) *who it is* who speaks to them. But they regard Jesus' discourse as unacceptable, harsh, offensive (60b: *sklēros*). They find that it is not possible to "listen" *(akouein)* to this word.

Jesus challenges them with a further word directed specifically to them. Do they take offense at what he has said? He has claimed to make God known in a way that transcends the revelation of God in the gift of the Torah; he is the true bread from heaven. Thus he suggests to his disciples that they may be looking for further support for his claim to be the definitive revelation of God. Jesus' unfinished question, "What if you were to see the Son of Man ascending where he was before?" (v. 62), is high rhetoric. Understood is the conclusion: "would that satisfy your doubts?" The question presupposes all that has been said so far about the Son of Man, but especially Jesus' words in 3:13: "No one has ascended into heaven, but one has descended from heaven, the Son of Man." Throughout the discourse of vv. 25-59 Jesus has pointed to himself as the bread that has come down from heaven (vv. 32-33, 35, 38, 51). When "the Jews" questioned his origins (vv. 41-42) he affirmed that he is from God (vv. 46-47). The Son of Man has come from heaven (3:13), but perhaps the disciples would like to see him ascend to heaven, matching the ascent of traditional revealers, Abraham, Moses, Isaiah, and Enoch. Within the Passover context it is particularly the Jewish tradition of the ascent of Moses to receive the Torah (cf. *Exod. Rab.* 28:1; 40:2; 41:6-7; 43:4; 47:5, 8; *Deut. Rab.* 2:36; 3:11; 11:10; *Pesiqta Rabbati* 20:4) that lies behind this half-asked question. But Jesus transcends all that Moses said and did. To make God known Jesus has no need to ascend from earth to heaven (v. 62a). He comes from there; he has been there before (v. 62b), and on the basis of his previous union with God (1:1: *pros ton theon;* cf. 17:5) his words have ultimate authority.

The disciples fail because they are attempting to assess Jesus' words and actions by the superficial judgment of human expectation. Such an approach to Jesus is "fleshly," and "the flesh is of no avail" (v. 63b). Jesus warns the disciples against a "fleshly" lack of courage and understanding when they are faced with his words (cf. Isa 40:6-8). The words of Jesus are spirit and life (v. 63c), but the disciples want Jesus to conform to their expectations (v. 62). He rejects their pretensions as worthless, as only the spirit gives life (v. 63a), not the superficiality of the flesh (v. 63b). What matters is the life-giving power of the Spirit, made available to the disciples in and through the revelation of God in and through the word of Jesus (v. 63). But Jesus is aware that no matter how much has been revealed to the disciples some do not believe, and one among them would betray him (v. 64). The relationship between Jesus and the disciple is crucial, but the initiative of God is the ultimate explanation for the disciple who comes believingly to Jesus and never turns away (v. 65).

The disciples have seen the miracle of the loaves and the fish (vv. 5-15), witnessed Jesus' coming across the waters announcing *egō eimi* (vv. 16-21), and heard the discourse on the true bread from heaven (vv. 25-59). But many of them (*polloi . . . ek tōn mathētōn*) have found the word of Jesus impossible (v. 60), and because of this (*ek toutou*) rejection of the word of Jesus "many of his disciples" (*polloi ek tōn mathētōn*) drew away from him (v. 66). The true disciple is the one to whom discipleship is given by the Father and who believes in the Son (vv. 64-65). It is not information that makes a disciple, but a Spirit-filled response to the Father made known in the word of Jesus. Behind this negative response to the word of Jesus lies the experience of early Christians, and Christians of all times. The word of Jesus is the essential nourishment of the community, its spirit and life. However, many are unable to accept this, and would prefer that Jesus conform to their ideas. Some members of the Johannine community would rather have had Jesus conform to the Mosaic pattern of a heavenly revealer. When he refused to accommodate their expectations they "drew back and no longer went with him" (v. 66).

Belief and the possibility of failure (vv. 67-71). Nevertheless, another response is possible, and Jesus challenges the Twelve, a restricted group within the larger crowd of disciples. He asks if they too *(kai hymeis)* would like to leave him, to return to the world of their own securities (v. 67; cf. vv. 62-63). Simon Peter answers for them all, indicating that the Father does not fail to draw believing disciples toward Jesus (cf. v. 65): "Lord, to whom shall we go? You have the words *(rhēmata)* of eternal life" (v. 68). Reflecting the unconditional openness to the word of Jesus that marked certain characters in the Cana to Cana journey (cf. 2:5: the Mother of Jesus; 3:29: John the Baptist; 4:42: the Samaritan villagers; 4:50: the royal official), Simon Peter tells Jesus that Jesus is the only possible focus for the Twelve (v. 68a). The Father has drawn them to him and they recognize that his earlier statement to the larger group of disciples is true: "The words that I have spoken to you are spirit and life" (v. 63; cf. v. 68b).

Peter's confession goes further. Looking back across the story thus far, his next words tell of the experience of the Twelve: "we have believed and we have come to know" *(hēmeis pepisteukamen kai egnōkamen)* (v. 69a). They have arrived at belief in Jesus and are living from that faith and knowledge. Thus in the name of the Twelve Peter can confess, "You are the Holy One of God" (v. 69b). For the first time in the narrative a character has expressed faith in Jesus for the right reason: *his origins.* The holiness of Jesus comes from the fact that he is *of God.* But even among this group failure is possible. Jesus responds to this confession of authentic belief by announcing that there will be a betrayer, Judas Iscariot (vv. 70-71). Jesus has chosen the Twelve but there is a larger design in God's leading some to Jesus (cf. v. 64), and each believer is free to accept or refuse this gift. The fragility of the human response remains, even among believers. More than a confession of faith is called for. If there is a betrayer, then there will be a betrayal. The shadow of a violent death, which has fallen across much of the celebration of the Passover (cf. vv. 12-13, 15, 27, 51, 53-54), again emerges as the account of Jesus' activity on the occasion of the feast comes to a close (vv. 70-71). The confession of Simon Peter is excellent . . . so far! How will this expression of faith survive in the difficult moments that will bring this story to an end? How will the believers respond to the "lifting up" of the Son of Man (cf. 3:14) that will provide a food that will endure to eternal life (6:12-13, 27, 35, 51, 53-54)?

Conclusion to 6:1-71. The Passover provides the essential chronological, literary, and theological background to John 6. Jesus does not deny the Jewish Passover memory of the gift of the manna, present in the nourishment provided by the Law that makes God known in Israel. But the revelation of God in the Law is not the end of God's action in history. "The Jews" and many of the disciples are unable to go any further than the Mosaic traditions in their response to God. For them Moses, the manna, and the Law exhaust all possibilities. At the end of the first century, deprived of their traditional priesthood, cult, and Temple, "the Jews" focus on the gift of the Law, but the Johannine community is asked to accept Jesus' claim: "I am the bread of life" (6:35; cf. vv. 41, 48, 51). There is no longer need to celebrate the former gift of the bread from heaven given through Moses. Such a tradition was a sign and a shadow of what has taken place in and through Jesus Christ. Christians are asked to accept that Jesus is the true bread from heaven, the one who gives life to all who believe in him. Jesus is the perfection of the Mosaic gift of the bread from heaven: he is the *true bread* from heaven.

As the final verses of this section of the Gospel reveal (cf. vv. 60-71), this Christian reinterpretation of the Mosaic traditions brought pain and division to the Johannine community. Not only were "the Jews" outraged by the words of Jesus; so were "many of the disciples" (vv. 60, 66). It is one thing for a Christian community to establish a theology and a christology that respond to the crises created by faith in Jesus Christ (cf. 9:22; 12:42; 16:2). It is another for everyone in the community to accept these notions and to live by them. Many could not accept that Jesus' words were spirit and life (v. 63), and thus "drew back and no longer went about with him" (v. 66).

NOTES

60. *This is a hard saying:* The Greek adjective *sklēros* does not mean "difficult" in an intellectual sense. The expressions "unacceptable, hard, offensive" best capture its meaning (cf. Barrett, *Gospel* 302).

Decisions concerning the originality of vv. 51c-58 influence the interpretation of v. 60. Is the "hard word" an objection to Jesus' words on the necessity to eat his flesh and drink his blood (vv. 53-55), or only to the earlier part of the discourse (vv. 25-51b)? Those who regard vv. 51c-58 as an addition to the original discourse (e.g., Bornkamm, "Die eucharistische Rede" 161–169; Brown, *Gospel* 1:299–303) see vv. 25-51c as the "hard word," while those who understand vv. 25-59 as a literary unit apply it to the whole discourse (e.g., Barrett, *Gospel* 284; Schenke, "Das johanneische Schisma" 108–111; Menken, "John 6,51c-58" 23–26; Moloney, *Signs and Shadows* 60–64).

62. *What if you were to see the Son of Man ascending where he was before?:* This clumsy
    sentence requires completion. It contains a question beginning with "if" (a
    protasis) and therefore requires completion (an apodosis). Interpreters must
    supply the apodosis, and there are three main solutions. Some suggest that if
    the disciples were to see Jesus ascend to where he was before, their difficul-
    ties would be greater. Others say that the use of *anabainein* refers to the cross,
    and similarly suggest that the offense would be greater. A third group claims
    that if they were to see him ascend where he was before their problems would
    be diminished, as they would know that he had authority to make such state-
    ments (e.g., Bauer, *Johannesevangelium* 101; Hoskyns, *Gospel* 300; Lightfoot,
    Gospel 169; Lagrange, *Evangile* 187. See the survey in Moloney, *Son of Man*
    120–121). The above interpretation is a development of this third option, link-
    ing it to Jewish speculation that surrounded the ascensions of the great re-
    vealers of Israel (cf. notes on 1:18 and 3:13). If the disciples were to see Jesus
    ascend—just as they believed the greater revealers from Israel's sacred his-
    tory, and especially Moses, had ascended—then would they be prepared to
    accept his "hard word"?

63. *the flesh is of no avail:* These words provide the key to the influential essay by
    Bornkamm ("Die eucharistische Rede") which suggests that there is an un-
    resolvable tension between the positive use of "flesh" *(sarx)* in vv. 51c-58 and
    the negative evaluation of "flesh" in v. 63. This contradictory use of the same
    word *(sarx)* within such close literary proximity indicates that vv. 51c-58 are a
    eucharistic addition to an originally sapiential discourse. But this is not nec-
    essarily the case. In the Fourth Gospel one must distinguish between the *sarx*
    of Jesus and the *sarx* of human beings. *Sarx* is used thirteen times in the
    Fourth Gospel, and its use is consistent. The *sarx* of Jesus tells the story of God
    (1:14, 18), and is essential for life (cf. 6:51, 52, 53, 54, 55, 56). But the *sarx* of
    human beings is confined to the human sphere, that which is "below" (1:13;
    3:6; cf. 8:23), and is the source of judgment limited by the superficial criteria
    provided by the physically observable (8:15; cf. 7:24). In 17:2 "all flesh" *(pasēs
    sarkos)* is used to render a Hebraism that means "every created thing." There
    is no contradiction between the use of *sarx* in vv. 51-58, where Jesus speaks of
    his own flesh, and v. 63 where he speaks of the superficiality of the limited
    human expectations the disciples have of Jesus (v. 62): "the flesh is of no
    avail." See Stenger, "Der Geist" 116–122; Schnelle, *Antidocetic Christology*
    194–195.

66. *Because of this:* The Greek expression *ek toutou* could mean "for this reason" or
    "from this time." I am opting for the former, although both meanings may
    have been in the mind of the author (cf. Barrett, *Gospel* 306).

67. *the twelve:* There are only two places in the Fourth Gospel where this group of
    disciples is mentioned, here and in the description of Thomas as "one of the
    Twelve" (20:24). The group plays no significant role in the Gospel's theology
    of discipleship, but the grouping of "twelve" within the larger following of
    Jesus is by now traditional. The author uses it here to differentiate between
    "many of the disciples" (vv. 60, 66) and a smaller group who have come to au-
    thentic belief in the word and person of Jesus.

69. *"we have believed, and have come to know":* Both verbs are in the perfect tense (*hēmeis pepisteukamen kai egnōkamen*). Peter tells of belief and knowledge that began in the disciples some time in the past, and that is still part of their association with Jesus. In the Fourth Gospel the verbs "to believe" and "to know" can be almost synonymous. See Brown, *Gospel* 1:298.

You are the Holy One of God: This title appears in only one other place in the NT (Mark 1:24; cf. 1 John 2:20). Within the Johannine context it is the "of God" part of the confession that is crucial. The idea of Jesus' being the agent of God is also associated with the title (cf. Domeris, "The Confession of Peter" 155–167; Joubert, "The Holy One of God" 57–69). Borgen, "John 6" 286–287, agrees that the idea of "agency" is present but suggests that one should draw together vv. 27, 29, and 68-69 to understand this final confession as "consecrated by God and sent into the world."

71. *one of the twelve, was to betray him:* The fact that disciples leave Jesus on account of his word, that the Twelve make a fine confession of faith through the words of Simon Peter, and then that one of the Twelve is singled out as the future betrayer reflects the tensions that the Johannine perspective created for people in the community. Even "insiders" were not able to stay with the community as it developed its exalted theological and christological story of Jesus. See Schenke, "Das johanneische Schisma" 105–121.

For Reference and Further Study

Domeris, W. R. "The Confession of Peter according to John 6:69," *TynB* 44 (1993) 155–167.

Joubert, H. L. N. "'The Holy One of God' (John 6:69)," *Neotest.* 2 (1968) 57–69.

Moloney, Francis J. *Signs and Shadows* 59–64

_____. *Son of Man* 120–123.

Schenke, Ludger. "Das johanneische Schisma und die 'Zwölf' (Johannes 6,60-71)," *NTS* 38 (1992) 105–121.

Stenger, Werner. "'Der Geist ist es, der lebendig macht, das Fleisch nützt nichts'," *TThZ* 85 (1976) 116–122.

iii. Jesus and Tabernacles: I (7:1–8:59)

The Feast of Tabernacles: 7:1–10:21. The appearance of "after this" (*meta tauta*) in 7:1 indicates the beginning of a new series of events (cf. 5:1; 6:1). This is reinforced by the announcement in v. 2 of another feast of "the Jews," the feast of Tabernacles. No other feast will be mentioned until 10:22: "It was the feast of the Dedication in Jerusalem." Thus 7:1–10:21 is entirely dedicated to the presence of Jesus in Jerusalem for the celebration of Tabernacles. A number of indications across 7:1–10:21 point to a succession of events that takes place during the feast:

1. The expression *meta tauta* appears in 7:1, but never again in 7:1–10:21.
2. The Jews' feast of Tabernacles was at hand (v. 2).
3. The brothers and Jesus go up to Jerusalem for the feast (v. 10).
4. Encounters take place "about the middle of the feast" (v. 14).
5. Further encounters take place "on the last day of the feast" (v. 37).
6. In 8:12 Jesus speaks "again" *(palin)*, indicating that the feast is still being celebrated.
7. The same expression reappears in v. 21, maintaining the time line.
8. Although there is a continuation of time, a change of place occurs in v. 59. As "the Jews" took up stones, Jesus hid himself and then went out *(exēlthen)* of the Temple.
9. Jesus' exit from the Temple leads directly into 9:1. "Passing by" *(paragōn)*, he sees the man born blind (9:1). The events of chs. 8 and 9 follow one another, but the location has changed.
10. The temporal unity across 7:1–10:21 is not broken until the narrator announces the feast of the Dedication in 10:22.

The celebration of Tabernacles forms the background for 7:1–10:21. However, Jesus' departure from the Temple in 8:59 divides the account of the events that took place during the feast into two parts, 7:1–8:59 and 9:1–10:21 (cf. Schenke, "Joh 7–10" 172–192).

Tabernacles in the Jewish Tradition. Tabernacles was the most popular of the three pilgrimage feasts and was known as "the feast of YHWH" (Lev 23:39; Judg 21:19) or simply "the feast" (1 Kgs 8:2, 65; 2 Chron 7:8; Neh 8:14; Isa 30:29; Ezek 45:23). Josephus describes Tabernacles as "especially sacred and important to the Hebrews" *(Ant.* 8:101). Earlier a feast of ingathering (cf. Exod 23:16; 34:22) and booths (Hebrew *sukkōt*), it was later historicized, associated with the covenant and God's care and guidance as the people dwelt in tents during the wilderness experience of the Exodus (cf. Deut 16:13, 16; Lev 23:34; Neh 8:13-19). This feast, however, was not only historicized, it was also eschatologized, celebrated in terms of the end time (cf. Bienaimé, *Moïse et le don de l'eau* 200–229). The essential elements of the celebration are provided by the Mishnah *(Sukkah)* and other rabbinic material (cf. Str-B 2:774–812; Goodman, *The Sukkot*). It is notoriously difficult to use the later rabbinic material to establish first-century practices, and the following description of the celebration must be regarded as somewhat speculative.

The celebration began on the fifteenth day of the seventh month, Tishri (September–October). It was highlighted by the building of "tabernacles," representing the tent experience of the Israelites in the desert, cared for by YHWH, with whom Israel now had a covenant. The men celebrating Tabernacles slept and ate meals in the booth for seven days, the duration of the feast *(m. Sukk.* 1–2; cf. Lev 23:42-43; Hos 12:10). After the seven days of the celebration in the booths there was an additional day, an eighth day, almost a feast in its own right, recalling the protection of YHWH during the Exodus period. This day was also dedicated to Israel's request for a superabundance of rain as a sign of YHWH's special and continuing care for the people. Within this time frame three major elements formed the ritual.

1. The Water Libation Ceremony (m. Sukk. 4:9-10)

On the morning of each of the seven days a procession led by priests and singing Levites, accompanied by a milling crowd of people, went down to the Pool of Siloam to gather water in a golden container. Accompanied by the milling people and blasts of the *shofar,* the procession returned to the Temple area through the Water Gate. According to rabbinic literature the Water Gate had an eschatological significance. Rabbi Eliezer ben Jacob identified it as the south gate of Ezek 47:1-5, through which the waters of life issuing from the threshold of the Temple would flow (cf. *t. Sukk.* 3:2-10; *Gen. Rab.* 28:18; *m. Šeqal.* 6:3; *m. Mid.* 2:6). On arrival at the Temple area they processed around the altar and sang Psalms 113–118 (the Hallel). The *lulab,* a collection of twigs of myrtle, palm, and willow, bound together along with a citron, were waved at the words of Ps 118:1: "O give thanks to the LORD for he is good," and again at v. 25: "Save us, we beseech you O LORD! O LORD, we beseech you, give us success!" On arrival at the altar the priest whose turn of duty it was poured the water from Siloam and wine into two vessels positioned on the altar, allowing the water and wine to flow out on to the altar (cf. *m. Sukk.* 4:9). On the seventh day of the feast the procession round the altar was repeated seven times (cf. *m. Sukk.* 4:5).

The association of water with the celebration linked the feast with the gift of rain. Zechariah 14 makes this link, but also associates Tabernacles with the end of time. After the destroying plague of the Lord, which will wipe out those who wage war on Jerusalem (14:12), all the surviving nations will go up to Jerusalem for the feast of Tabernacles. If they do not go up "there will be no rain upon them" (14:17). There is also evidence that the water ceremony was linked with messianic expectation in which a Moses-like teacher (cf. *m. Sukk.* 3:3-9) repeats the gift of the well of the Torah (cf. Num 21:18; CD 6:2-11; Ps.-Philo, *LAB* 10:7; 11:15; 28:7-8; *Targum Onkelos* on Num 21:18) that follows the Israelites (cf. targums on Num 21:18; *t. Sukk.* 3:10-12). The targums on Gen 49:10 play on the digging of the scribes described in the biblical text to promise a future Messiah who digs from the well of the Torah, a final "giving of water" from the Torah, the well of God (cf. Bienaimé, *Moïse et le don de l'eau* 58–194).

Jewish messianic expectation seems to have linked the Messiah with the definitive gift of water from the well, the interpretation of the Law, as expressed in *Eccl. Rab.* 1:8:

> As the former redeemer made a well to rise, so will the latter redeemer
> bring up water, as it is stated, "And a fountain shall come forth of the
> house of the LORD, and shall water the valley of Shittim" (Joel 4:18).

A parallel remark about a Mosaic gift of bread is found earlier in *Eccl. Rab.*
1:8: "As was the first redeemer, so is the latter redeemer . . . as the first
redeemer brought down the manna, so will also the latter redeemer bring
down the manna." This link between a messianic gift of bread and water
throws light on the successive presentation of Jesus as "bread" (6:35, 41,
48, 51) and "water" (7:37-38; 9:7). The antiquity of this tradition is suggested by the similar association found in other documents (cf. Ps.-Philo,
LAB 10:7; *Mekilta* on Exod 15:27), some of which date from "around the
time of Jesus" (D. J. Harrington, "Pseudo-Philo," *Old Testament Pseudepigrapha* 2:299). The association of the end time and the appearance of the
Messiah with Tabernacles plays a large part in the discussions between
Jesus and his various interlocutors during the Johannine description of
the feast of Tabernacles (7:1–10:21).

2. The Ceremony of Light (m. Sukk. 5:1-4)

Four menorahs were set up in the center of the court of the women.
The men of piety and good works who were celebrating the feast (cf. *m.
Sukk.* 5:4) danced under the lights, while the Levites sang Psalms 120–134.
This celebration lasted most of the night for each of the seven days of the
feast. The Mishnah describes the light from the Temple: "There was not a
courtyard in Jerusalem that did not reflect the light of the House of Water
Drawing" (*m. Sukk.* 5:3). Again Zechariah 14 is present:

> On that day there shall not be either cold or frost. And there shall be con-
> tinuous day (it is known to the LORD), not day and not night, for at
> evening time there shall be light. On that day living waters shall flow
> out from Jerusalem, half of them to the eastern sea and half of them to
> the western sea; it shall continue in summer as in winter (Zech 14:6-8).

There may also have been a connection between the light ceremony and
the pillar of fire that led Israel through the wilderness (cf. Exod 13:21).
The pillar of fire was expected to return at the end of time (cf. Isa 4:5; Bar
5:8-9; *Song Rab.* 1:7, 3). The light ceremony, as well as the water ritual,
probably helped in the eschatologization of Tabernacles (cf. Talbert, *Reading John* 153).

3. The Rite of Facing the Temple (m. Sukk. 5:4)

At cockcrow on each of the seven days the priests proceeded to the
east gate of the Temple area and gazed away from the Temple toward the
east. At the moment of sunrise they turned their backs on the sun and

faced the sanctuary of the Temple, reciting: "Our fathers when they were in this place turned with their backs toward the Temple of the Lord and their faces toward the east, and they worshiped the sun toward the east [see Ezek 8:16]; but as for us, our eyes are turned toward the Lord" (*m. Sukk.* 5:4). The spirit of Zech 14:9 is captured by these sentiments: "And the LORD will become king over all the earth; on that day the LORD will be one and his name one." The final words of the *Hallel,* sung in the procession, are also present: "You are my God, and I will give thanks to you; you are my God, I will extol you. O give thanks to the LORD for he is good, for his steadfast love endures forever" (Ps 118:28-29). YHWH was recognized as the one true God to whom all praise and allegiance were due.

General Introduction to 7:1–8:59. The length and complexity of this section of the Gospel, dealing largely with Jesus' presence in the Temple on the occasion of the feast of Tabernacles, calls for an arrangement of the commentary that parallels the treatment of 6:1-71. After an overall presentation of the detailed structure of the passage the sections and sub-sections will be dealt with separately, and suggestions For Reference and Further Study will be provided after the commentary on 8:48-59. This approach to a difficult text is adopted for clarity, without compromising the conviction that the various parts of 7:1–8:59 form a single literary unit.

The narrative unfolds in four major sections, of which two have subsections.

> (a) *7:1-9: Before the feast.* A *schism (schisma)* arises between Jesus and his brothers about going to the feast.
> (b) *7:10-13: At the feast.* In Jerusalem there is a *schism* about Jesus: is he a good man, or does he lead the people astray?
> (c) *7:14-36: About the middle of the feast.*
> > i. *Vv. 14-24:* Jesus teaches in the Temple and *conflict* emerges.
> > ii. *Vv. 25-31:* The question of Jesus' messiahship and his origins create *schism.*
> > iii. *Vv. 32-36:* A *conflict* arises over the destiny of Jesus.
> (d) *7:37–8:59: On the last day of the feast.*
> > i. *7:37-52:* Jesus' self-revelation as the living water leads to *schism.*
> > ii. *8:12-30:* Jesus reveals himself as "the light of the world."
> > iii. *8:31-59:* Jesus and "the Jews" in *conflict* over their respective origins.

Three elements determine the shape of the narrative. There is *schism* among various characters in the story, who divide over Jesus' claims (for the Greek word *schisma* to indicate this, see 7:43, 9:16; 10:19). Second, *conflict* intensifies between Jesus and "the Jews," and finally, there are rhythmic indications of the passing of time (7:2, 10, 14, 37). The issues that generate the *schism, conflict,* and the passing of time are determined by the Jewish celebration of Tabernacles.

a) *Before the Feast* (7:1-9)

1. After this Jesus went about in Galilee; he would not go about in Judea because the Jews sought to kill him. 2. Now the Jews' feast of Tabernacles was at hand. 3. So his brothers said to him, "Leave here and go to Judea, that your disciples may see the works you are doing. 4. For no one who wants to be widely known acts in secret. If you do these things, show yourself to the world." 5. For even his brothers did not believe in him. 6. Jesus said to them, "My time has not yet come, but your time is always here. 7. The world cannot hate you, but it hates me because I testify of it that its works are evil. 8. Go to the feast yourselves; I am not going up to this feast, for my time has not yet fully come." 9. So saying, he remained in Galilee.

INTERPRETATION

After the events at the Sea of Tiberias (v. 1: *meta tauta*) Jesus continues to "go about" in Galilee. He was not prepared to "go about" (the same verb is used: *peripatein*) in Judea because the decision of "the Jews" that Jesus must be killed (cf. 5:18) still holds (v. 1). But the Jewish feast of Tabernacles is at hand (v. 2), and all male Jews had a duty to go to Jerusalem for this "pilgrim feast" (cf. *m. Sukk.* 2:8-9). His brothers (*hoi adelphoi sou*; cf. Mark 6:3; Matt 13:55) ask him to leave Galilee for Judea, but not to be in Jerusalem for the feast. They want his works *(ta erga)* seen by the disciples (v. 3). Jesus has done wonderful works *(erga)* at Cana (2:1-11; 4:46-54) and by the Sea of Tiberias (6:1-13, 16-21). The brothers of Jesus have been in the background since journeying from Cana to Capernaum with Jesus, his mother, and the disciples (cf. 2:12). Rightly they state that no person seeking to be known openly works in secret (v. 4a). Wrongly they think that Jesus will come to be known through his *erga* alone. The brothers' conditioned statement about Jesus' miracle-working activity, "If you do these things" (v. 4b), indicates doubt (cf. Bernard, *Commentary* 1:267). At a deeper level they misunderstand the purpose of the *erga* of Jesus, asking that he show *himself (phanerōson seauton)* to the world by means of these works. Jesus has not come to show *himself* to the world, but to make God known (cf. 1:18, 51; 3:13; 4:10; 5:19, 23, 30; 6:28-29, 46). The narrator confirms the impression of the reader by commenting frankly "For even *(oude gar)* his brothers did not believe in him" (v. 5). The use of *oude gar* ("for even") indicates a wider scenario of disbelief. If not even his brothers believe in him, then there are also many others who do not believe.

Jesus' response draws a sharp distinction between two "times": "my time" that has not yet come, and "your time" that is always here (v. 6). The use of "but" *(de)* shows there is conflict between the two "times." The *kairos* of Jesus is not at hand as the unfolding of his life is measured. His response to his mother (2:4) and his continual reference to the one who sent him (cf. 3:17, 34; 4:34; 5:23, 24, 30, 36, 37, 38; 6:29, 38-39, 44, 57) indicate that the Father is master of Jesus' destiny. But *(de)* his brothers are not part of God's design that is to be made known in and through Jesus; they are free to do what they want, when they want. Jesus and his brothers belong to different worlds. The world of ordinary *kairoi* and ordinary events will not hate the brothers of Jesus, but *(de)* it does hate *(misei)* Jesus. "The light has come into the world" (3:19) but the world can reject the light and turn to evil deeds. Jesus bears witness to these evil deeds, and thus conflict and hatred are inevitable (v. 7). The brothers experience none of this hatred and can proceed to the festival (v. 8a), but Jesus is not going up to *this particular* celebration (v. 8b: *eis tēn heortēn tautēn*), for his time has not yet come. The emphatic use of "this" *(tautēn* at the end of the sentence) hints that he plans to attend *another* feast, but not this one. At some moment in the future the "time" of Jesus will be associated with one of the feasts of "the Jews." The narrator closes the episode by telling the reader that Jesus stayed in Galilee (v. 9). The celebration of Tabernacles and Jesus' subordination to the design of God are two themes that will continue to be important throughout 7:1–8:59.

NOTES

1. *Jesus went about in Galilee:* The use of the imperfect tense, *periepatei*, indicates that Jesus kept on moving about in Galilee. It is iterative (cf. BDF 166, § 318 [3]; 169, § 325).

   he would not go about in Judea: Some witnesses (Curetonian Syriac, Old Latin, Freer Gospels, some other Greek manuscripts, Chrysostom, and Augustine) read that he "did not have the ability" *(ou gar eichein exousian)* to go about in Judea. Some scholars accept this reading, but the weight of the external textual evidence (especially 𝔓⁶⁶.⁷⁵) indicates that it is better to retain the less theologically significant "would not" *(ou gar ēthelen)*.

   "the Jews" sought to kill him: The same words *(ezētoun auton hoi Ioudaioi apokteinai)* are used in 5:18 and 7:1. The present order of the text makes sense. Violence is threatened in Jerusalem in 5:18. Misunderstanding, but not violence, is encountered throughout 6:25-71. Thus Jesus continues to go about in Galilee, but not in Judea.

2. *the Jews' feast of Tabernacles was at hand:* The prominent place of this indication of time sets the scene for the importance of the celebration of the feast as background for 7:1–10:21. On the Jewish celebration see the above introduction to 7:1–10:21. In a very helpful study Cory, "Wisdom's Rescue" 95–116, suggests that "the Tabernacles discourse becomes an apologetic for a community trying to make sense of the death of Jesus, the Wisdom of God, while coming to terms with the meaning of its own persecution" (p. 95). Cory un-

covers important links between 7:1–8:59 and the "Wisdom tale." However, she neglects the setting of the feast (but see pp. 114–115) and devotes no attention to 9:1–10:21, which have the same temporal setting as 7:1–8:59.

3. *So his brothers said to him:* Even though the reason for the brothers' request that he go up to Jerusalem is not the feast, the use of "so" *(oun)* to link vv. 2 and 3 shows that it is part of the motivation.

   that your disciples may see the works you are doing: Who these "disciples" in Jerusalem might be is the subject of debate. In such close proximity to 6:60-66, however, the reference is most probably to the *mathētai* who have just left him (v. 66). The brothers are urging some miraculous works in Jerusalem to convince these disciples who have wavered and then failed to believe in his word (cf. 6:60, 66).

6. *my time . . . your time:* The word *kairos* appears in the Fourth Gospel only at 7:6, 8. "It is not distinguishable from the more common *hōra*" (Barrett, *Gospel* 312). The "not yet" *(oupō)* of Jesus' *kairos* in 7:6 looks back to the "not yet" *(oupō)* of Jesus' *hōra* in 2:4.

7. *The world cannot hate you:* The use of "you" *(hymas)* is emphatic. It thus further opens the gap between Jesus and his brothers. See also the *hymeis* in v. 8.

8. *Go to the feast yourselves:* Jesus' instructions are not a further criticism of the brothers, but an indication of the general situation of all "others." It is the author's way of pointing to the singular nature of the story of Jesus, intimately linked with the Father's direction of that story (cf. 4:54; 5:19, 30).

9. *I am not going up to this feast:* Instead of *egō ouk anabainō* some witnesses read "I am not *yet* going up to this feast" *(egō oupō anabainō)*. This reading is almost universally rejected as an attempt by early scribes to avoid the difficulty created by Jesus' going to Jerusalem in v. 10.

b) *At the Feast in Jerusalem (7:10-13)*

10. But after his brothers had gone up to the feast, then he also went up, not publicly but in private. 11. The Jews were looking for him at the feast and saying, "Where is he?" 12. And there was much muttering about him among the people. While some said, "He is a good man," others said, "No, he is leading the people astray." 13. Yet for fear of the Jews no one spoke openly of him.

INTERPRETATION

The brothers go up to the feast (v. 10a), and Jesus *(kai autos)* makes the pilgrimage. The main affirmation of the sentence is that Jesus went up to

Jerusalem (v. 10b). His earlier decision is reversed. As in 2:4-7 and 4:48-50 an initial unwillingness to be part of an action is reversed. Jesus responds to the will of someone greater than his mother (2:3), the royal official (4:47), and his brothers (7:3-4). What was said in vv. 5-7 prepares the way for Jesus' unconditional response to the greater design of his Father (cf. Giblin, "Suggestion, Negative Response" 206–208). His brothers demanded of Jesus, "Show yourself to the world" *(phanerōson seauton tǭ kosmǭ)* (v. 4). In deliberate contrast to the plans of the brothers Jesus goes up to the feast "not publicly but in private" (v. 10b: *ou phanerōs alla en kryptǭ*). In the discussions and the *schismata* that follow, the reader is aware that Jesus is in Jerusalem but "the Jews" are not. "The Jews" are looking for him *(ezētoun auton)*. This search is ominous, as it recalls 5:18 and 7:1 where the same verb *(zēteō)* was used for their designs on his life. Their question, "Where is he?" *(pou estin ekeinos)* raises an issue that runs across the Gospel and is one of the major points of conflict during the celebration of Tabernacles: where Jesus is from and where he is going. Earlier "the Jews" have muttered *(egongyzon)* over Jesus' claims to have come from heaven (cf. 6:41, 43, 61). Now "the people" join them in muttering *(gongysmos)* over another matter. Is Jesus a reliable authority *(agathos)*, or is his teaching false, in league with the devil, leading the people astray *(planos)?* The people remain divided over the issue. "The Jews" have made up their minds about Jesus, however much the people might be wondering. They are frightened to speak publicly about a man whom "the Jews" have already decided to eliminate (v. 13).

The scene is set for Jesus' presence in Jerusalem for the celebration of Tabernacles. The question of Jesus' revelation of himself to the world has been raised (vv. 1-9). Jesus, disciples, "the Jews," and "the people" are gathered in Jerusalem (vv. 10-13). Serious questions are being asked: where is Jesus (v. 11), and what is he doing (v. 12)? A conflict unto death (vv. 10, 13) is under way.

NOTES

10. *after his brothers had gone up to the feast:* The technical verb "to go up" *(anabainein)* is used twice in v. 10, once for the ascent of the brothers and then for Jesus, for the "going up" to Jerusalem for a pilgrim feast.

    not publicly, but in private: A number of textual witnesses say that Jesus went up "as it were in secret" *(hōs en kryptǭ)*. It is rightly omitted by others. It was probably added to lessen the impression of contradiction and deceit (cf. Barrett, *Gospel* 313).

11. *The Jews were looking for him at the feast:* A distinction must be maintained between "the Jews" and "the people." Brodie, *Gospel* 313, 317–318, interprets

"the Jews" and "the people" as "allusions to the diversity of the world—Jews and Gentiles" (p. 313). Such an interpretation cannot be pursued into the narrative, where all characters ("the Jews," the Pharisees, the people, the Jerusalemites) are Jews, but some are "the Jews" (cf. Introduction; Ashton, *Understanding the Fourth Gospel* 131–159).

12. *He is leading the people astray:* On the charge of Jesus' being a false teacher (*planos*), leading the people astray, see Pancaro, *The Law in the Fourth Gospel* 77–116.

13. *for fear of the Jews:* This remark from the narrator is a further indication that "the Jews" are a group of people who have already made up their minds about Jesus and the Johannine community. It is not a reference to the Jewish people, as "the Jews" and "the people" in v. 13 are all Jews.

   The use of different interlocuters within chs. 7–8 has sometimes been employed as a key for rearrangements or seen as an indication of various strata in the tradition. See, for example, Ashton, *Understanding the Fourth Gospel* 332–334. Whatever may have been the prehistory of the text, these interlocutors play an important role in tracing the unfolding logic of this dense passage in its present shape. See Schenke, "Joh 7–10" 175–178; Robert, "Étude littéraire" 71–84.

c) *About the Middle of the Feast* (7:14-36)

The structure of 7:14-36. This section of the text can be read in three sub-sections:

   i. *Vv. 14-24:* The origins of Jesus' teaching and authority are questioned by "the Jews."
   ii. *Vv. 25-31:* The Jerusalemites wonder whether Jesus can be the Christ, as they know his origins. But many of the people recognize him as the miracle-working Messiah.
   iii. *Vv. 32-36:* "The Jews" show their inability to understand Jesus' destiny.

This narrative is dense, as the characters involved and the issues debated chop and change. Its plot is heavily subordinated to the theological point of view of the Gospel as a whole. A similar intensity continues until 8:59. Attention to the progressive articulation of the author's presentation of Jesus in the midst of heated conflict and rejection reveals a coherent, if complicated, marriage between a narrative dealing with an episode in the life of Jesus and the author's theological point of view.

1. Jesus, "the Jews," and "the People" (7:14-24)

> 14. About the middle of the feast Jesus went up into the temple and taught. 15. The Jews marveled at it, saying, "How is it that this man has learning, when he has never studied?" 16. So Jesus answered them, "My teaching is not mine, but his who sent me. 17. Anyone who resolves to do the will of God will know whether the teaching is from God or whether I am speaking on my own authority. 18. Those who speak on their own authority seek their own glory; but the one who seeks the glory of the one who sent him is true, and in him there is no falsehood. 19. Did not Moses give you the law? Yet none of you keeps the law. Why do you seek to kill me?" 20. The people answered, "You have a demon! Who is seeking to kill you?" 21. Jesus answered them, "I did one deed, and you all marvel at it. 22. Moses gave you circumcision (not that it is from Moses, but from the fathers), and you circumcise a man upon the Sabbath. 23. If on the Sabbath a man receives circumcision, so that the law of Moses may not be broken, are you angry with me because on the Sabbath I made a man's whole body well? 24. Stop judging by appearances; adopt a right judgment."

INTERPRETATION

The celebration of the feast—the water and light rituals and the early-morning profession of faith in the one true God—is in full swing: "about the middle of the feast" (v. 14a) Jesus went up *(anebē)* into the Temple and taught (v. 14b). It is his teaching that creates a negative reaction from "the Jews," who have already decided that he must be slain (5:18; 7:1, 11). They marvel at his teaching (v. 15a). This "marveling" *(ethaumazon)* is an emotional rejection of Jesus' teaching (cf. BAGD 352). Authoritative teaching, or knowledge of letters *(grammata oiden)*, presupposes that one is working from a traditional basis, explaining the Torah. Traditions were passed on authoritatively by the teachers, and a newcomer teaching in the Temple would necessarily be known as a disciple of a certain teacher. This "traditional" understanding of a teacher became central to the establishment of authority in post-70 rabbinic Judaism. Jesus can lay claim to no authoritative teacher and therefore there can be no authority in what he has to teach (v. 15b). At stake are the origins of Jesus' authority. Jesus' response (vv. 16-24), repeats what has already been said to "the Jews" in chs. 5–6, especially in 5:19-47.

Everything Jesus says and does has its origins in his Father (cf. 5:19-20); thus his teaching is the teaching of the Father who sent him (v. 16). The issue at stake is not whether "the Jews" accept Jesus, but whether they accept their traditional God, now revealed as the Father of Jesus. Is God revealed in the traditions of the rabbis or in the teaching of Jesus? In

vv. 17-18 "the Jews" are challenged to make their decision. Jesus asks his opponents whether they willfully accept or refuse the intervention of God in and through his Son: "If anyone's will is to do his will" (v. 17a: *ean tis thelē to thelēma autou poiein*). Those genuinely seeking to do the will of God will be able to make their decision about the origins of Jesus' teaching. Is it "from God" (v. 17b: *ek tou theou*) or "from Jesus" *(egō ap'emautou lalō)*? As in 5:44, Jesus plays on the double meaning of the Greek word *doxa:* human esteem or the revelation of God. He condemns the authoritative utterances of the synagogue, which has rejected Jesus as the Christ and excommunicated his followers (cf. 9:22; 12:42; 16:2), as a search for their own *doxa:* "Those who speak on their own authority seek their own glory *(doxa)*" (v. 18a). But Jesus points to himself as the one who seeks the glory *(doxa)* of the one who sent him (v. 18b). He is not on a mission of self-glorification, and thus is true *(alethēs estin)*. He reveals the truth, and in him there is no falsehood *(adikia)*. "It is because the Jews do not value the teaching of Jesus for what it is (revelation) that they consider him a false prophet, in league with the devil, who leads the people astray, away from the Law and orthodoxy" (Pancaro, *The Law in the Fourth Gospel* 100).

The discussion of Moses that follows (vv. 19-23) indicates that "the Jews" have not been moved by Jesus' words. The authority of the rabbis claims to reach back to Moses, who had his teaching directly from God. Thus "the Jews" can claim that their teaching is "from God" through the mediation of Moses. But "the Jews" have decided to kill Jesus (cf. 5:18; 7:1, 11), and Jesus claims that this is a refusal to accept the Law (v. 19). For the Johannine Jesus there is a direct line from God through Moses to Jesus. In their violent attempt to eliminate Jesus, "the Jews" are placing themselves outside God's designs, partially revealed in the former gift of the Law, now perfected in the fullness of the gift through Jesus Christ (cf. 1:16-17). Jesus can therefore charge "the Jews": "None of you is keeping *(poiei)* the Law. Why do you seek to kill me?" (v. 19). Any attempt to eliminate the Sent One of God (cf. v. 16) is a refusal to do the will of God (cf. v. 17) and thus a breach of the Law of Moses (v. 19). An absoluteness about this situation is indicated by Jesus' words, "none of you *(oudeis ex hymōn)* keeps the Law." "Whereas the Jews consider belief in Jesus a betrayal of the Law, Jn is tracing the Law back to its source and doing away with the opposition between the Law and belief in Jesus" (Pancaro, *The Law in the Fourth Gospel* 379).

In v. 20 the interlocutors change, as "the people" *(ho ochlos)* raise a question. "The Jews" and "the people" are separate groups, as the former have already decided that Jesus must be killed (cf. 5:18; 7:1, 11), while "the people" are puzzled by Jesus' words of v. 19. They have no plan to kill him, nor do they know of any. Their words, "You have a demon," are not rejection, but an indication that they think he is insane. Two groups are in dialogue with Jesus. One group, "the Jews," have already made their decision, while the other, "the people," have not. Jesus' words in v. 21 are directed to "them" *(eipen autois)*. The "them" *(autois)* involves all who have discussed Jesus' authority. Jesus recalls the events of the Sabbath healing (cf. 5:1-18), telling them that he did one deed and they *all* marveled at it *(kai pantes thaumazete)*. Both "the Jews" of 5:1-18 and 7:20 and "the people" of 7:14-24 are addressed. The discussion initiated in v. 19 concerning his opponents' claim to have Moses as their authority continues (vv. 22-23). A tradition coming from God through Moses teaches that if the eighth day after the birth of a male child falls on a Sabbath, that child is to be circumcised on the Sabbath (cf. *m. Šabb.* 18:3; 19:2; *m. Ned.* 3:11). The gift of circumcision, which Israel claims was from Moses even though it was practiced before the time of Moses (cf. Gen 17:10), was a sign of entry into the covenanted people, the fulfillment of the Law, and the completion of an individual man's perfection (cf. *m. Ned.* 3:11). A matter of such life-giving importance overrides the Law. If this is the case, why object to Jesus' activity on a Sabbath when he restores the fullness of a human being's potential: "I made a man's whole body well" (v. 23: *holon anthrōpon hygiē epoiēsa;* cf. 5:6, 9, 11)! Not to see this is to refuse to see the gradual unfolding of the revelation of God, first through Moses and then through Jesus Christ (cf. 1:16-17).

This episode closes with Jesus' accusation that his opponents' judgments are totally conditioned by appearances *(kat'opsin)*. They judge by what they can measure, see, and touch, and thus the Law is sufficient. They refuse to look beyond what they can control, to accept the word of Jesus, the Son of God. To do that would be to "judge with right judgment" *(tēn dikaian krisin)*. During the celebration of the feast of Tabernacles the priests are each morning turning their backs to the rising sun, looking toward the sanctuary, and proclaiming their rejection of all false gods. Ironically, in their rejection of God as Jesus' authority they are making a lie of their daily ritual. In their rejection of Jesus they reject the one who sent him, the one true God to whom they proclaim their unswerving loyalty.

NOTES

14. *About the middle of the feast:* This indication of time locates the following events and encounters in the heart of the celebration. All the daily rituals are being performed. It need not be the Sabbath day of the feast or any special day (cf. Barrett, *Gospel* 317).

    Jesus . . . taught: This is the first time Jesus has "taught" in Jerusalem. Michaels, "Temple Discourse" 204–206, suggests that the teaching of Jesus in John 7–8 is the teaching referred to in 18:19: "The high priest then questioned Jesus about his disciples and his teaching."

15. *How is it that this man has learning?:* The use of "this man" *(houtos)* is pejorative. "The Jews" have made up their minds about Jesus, even though "the
people" are still guessing (cf. vv. 10-13, 20). On the Jewish understanding of a
true teacher as one who can link his teaching, via an authoritative rabbi, with
the tradition of Moses, and thus ultimately back to God, see Pancaro, *The Law
in the Fourth Gospel* 82–83, 88, 106–108.

17. *Anyone who resolves to do the will of God:* The interpretation adopted reads
Jesus' words as focusing on the issue of doing God's will ("his will" = God's
will). Debates between a postwar Jewish synagogue and Johannine Christianity may lie behind this discussion. Are "the Jews" correct in their insistence on the tradition in which teaching authority is passed on from teacher to
pupil, or is it true that Jesus of Nazareth as the Son of God teaches with divine authority? Jesus' teaching transcends the debate over the question of
"doing the will of God." Ethical performance, while not denied, is transcended. It is not at the center of this author's measure of true faith. See Lightfoot, *Gospel* 178; Haenchen, *John* 2:13-14.

18. *in him there is no falsehood:* This is the only place where the word "falsehood"
(adikia) appears. It is the opposite of "true" *(alēthēs).* The background to the
contrast between *alēthēs* and *adikia* is found in Qumran (e.g., 1QS 3:13–4:26;
5:10; 6:15; 8:9-10; 9:17; 1QH 4:25; 15:25; CD 2:13; 3:14, 15); *T. 12 Patr.* (e.g., *T. Reub.*
3:5-8; *T. Dan* 5:1; 6:8-9; *T. Asher* 5:3-4; 6:1-4; *T. Levi* 16:1-2; *T. Naph.* 3:2-3; *T. Gad*
3:1-4, *T. Jud.* 14:8; *T. Issach.* 4:6; *T. Benj.* 10:3); and Jewish wisdom literature
(e.g., Ps 118:10; Job 6:24; 12:24; 19:4; Prov 7:25; 12:26; 13:9; 21:16; 28:10; Sir 9:8;
Wis 5:6; 12:24). Its usage can be summed up as "true revelation" as opposed
to "false revelation." See Pancaro, *The Law in the Fourth Gospel* 92–101.

19. *Did not Moses give you the Law?:* On the tradition that Moses received the Law
from God, and that all subsequent rabbinic interpretation of the Law belonged to a line that reached back to the gift of God see Zaiman, "The Traditional Study" 1:27-36.
    none of you keeps the law: There is a possible link between Jesus' earlier state-
    ment (v. 17) on the need to do the will of God *(to thēlema autou poiein)* and
    Jesus' accusation that none of "the Jews" keeps the Law (v. 19: *oudeis ex hymōn
    poiei ton nomon*). Any attempt to eliminate the Sent One of God (v. 16) is a re-
    fusal to do the will of God (v. 17) and thus a breach of the Law of Moses (v.
    19).

20. *The people answered:* The sudden introduction of another group is dramatically
effective. The reader knows of the decision of "the Jews" (5:18; 7:1, 11) and follows their attempts to bring it into action. The people know nothing of this,
and thus act as a foil both to Jesus' knowledge of the decision to kill him and
to the duplicity of "the Jews," who are attempting to debate with Jesus.

22. *you circumcise a man on a Sabbath:* On the Jewish background to this Johannine
subtlety (*m. Šabb.* 18:3; *m. Ned.* 3:11) see Thomas, "The Fourth Gospel" 173–174.

23. *If on the Sabbath . . . are you angry with me because on the Sabbath:* There is no
conflict between the Sabbath legislation, subsequent Jewish understanding of

that legislation, and Jesus' actions. Rather there is a progression. To make this point the Jewish legal technique of moving from a lesser to a greater case, called *qal waḥōmer*, is employed. The latter does not contradict the former but is greater than the former and thus even more legitimate than the former. See Manns, *L'Evangile* 313–314.

24. *Stop judging by appearances; adopt a right judgment:* This translation, which stresses the accusatory nature of Jesus' words, calls for two forms of the verb "to judge" *(krinein)*. The former is a present imperative: "stop judging" *(mē krinēte)*, asking that a habitual way of judging come to an end, and the latter an aorist, insisting that a new way of judging be initiated: "judge" *(krinate)*. In some important manuscripts (e.g., 𝔓⁶⁶.⁷⁵, Vaticanus, Bezae) both verbs are present imperative, but the present imperative + aorist makes better sense, and is slightly better attested (e.g., Sinaiticus, Koridethi, Freer Gospels). See Barrett, *Gospel* 321. Cory, "Wisdom's Rescue" 100–102, suggests that this theme of superficial judgment is one of the many wisdom themes found in 7:1–8:59.

2. The Jerusalemites and "the People" (7:25-31)

> 25. Certain people from Jerusalem therefore said, "Is not this the man whom they seek to kill? 26. And here he is, speaking openly, and they say nothing to him! Can it be that the authorities really know that this is the Christ? 27. Yet we know where this man comes from; and when the Christ appears no one will know where he comes from." 28. So Jesus proclaimed, as he taught in the Temple, "You know me, and you know where I come from? But I have not come of my own accord; the one who sent me is true, and him you do not know. 29. I know him, for I come from him, and he sent me." 30. So they sought to arrest him; but no one laid hands on him, because his hour had not yet come. 31. Yet many of the people believed in him; they said, "When the Christ appears, will he do more signs than this man has done?"

INTERPRETATION

A further group enters the discussion with the introduction of "certain people from Jerusalem" *(tines ek tōn Hierosolymitōn)*. While "the people" *(ho ochlos)* knew nothing of the plot to kill Jesus (cf. v. 19), certain people from Jerusalem do. This group, privy to the fact that "the Jews" seek to kill him (v. 25: *zētousin apokteinai*; cf. 5:18; 7:1, 11), are puzzled. Despite the plot, Jesus appears at the feast and speaks openly, but nothing is said to him (vv. 25-26). How is this silence and inactivity from "the Jews" to be interpreted? Perhaps "the Jews" know that Jesus is the Messiah, that his claim to come from God as the authentic teacher of God is true, and therefore he cannot and must not be silenced? A *schisma* emerges. The people from Jerusalem have no hesitation in declaring that Jesus cannot be the Messiah. The Messiah would be hidden by God, and when he finally appeared his origins would be unknown. They "know" *(oidamen)* the Messiah's origins are to be hidden, "not known" *(oudeis ginoskei)*. As they "know" where Jesus comes from, they also "know" that he cannot be the Messiah. Such confident knowledge repeats earlier responses to Jesus, all of which were mistaken (cf. 1:41, 45; 3:2; 4:25; 6:42).

The setting of the feast of Tabernacles is recalled (v. 28a) as Jesus solemnly proclaims *(ekraxen)* a response that shatters their confidence. The Jerusalemites' claim to know where Jesus comes from is false. Whatever their knowledge of his geographical origins, they have no notions of who Jesus is or where he comes from. The discussions of vv. 14-24 led to the messianic question (vv. 26-27) and the question of the origins of the Messiah. Jesus describes his origins with the one who sent him, and adds that a refusal to accept what he teaches means that the Jerusalemites do not know the one who is true (v. 28). As they celebrate their loyalty to the one true God at the feast, they are rejecting Jesus, the Sent One of the one true God *(alēthinos ho pempsas me)*. Their morning protestations are a sham. The polemic increases as Jesus affirms his knowledge of God, the one who sent him (v. 29). The tables have been turned against the all-knowing Jerusalemites who dismiss Jesus as a possible Messiah. They have been accused of ignorance, not only of the Messiah but also of the God who sends him. The Jerusalemites attempt to arrest him, but they are unable to lay hands on him "because his hour had not yet come" (v. 30). The "not yet" *(oupō;* cf. 2:4; 7:6, 8) indicates that eventually the hour will arrive. At Cana (2:5), "the hour" looked forward to some future messianic revelation; in his discussion with his brothers Jesus linked "the hour" with a future Jewish feast (7:6, 8). Here it is associated with violence, a laying on of hands that is "not yet" possible (7:30).

The Jerusalemites are suddenly replaced by "the people" (v. 31: *ho ochlos*). While the former have decided that Jesus cannot be the Messiah, many of the people are being won over. They believe in him, prepared to accept that this man might be the Messiah because of the signs he did (v. 31). "The people" join a growing number of characters who believe because of Jesus' signs: the many in Jerusalem (2:23-25), Nicodemus (3:2), the Samaritan woman (4:25), and the crowds at the Sea of Tiberias (6:2). Although not as dramatic as the Jerusalemites' violent rejection of Jesus, the belief of "the people" falls short of substantial Johannine faith.

NOTES

25. *certain people from Jerusalem:* On the basis of what the different characters know or do not know about the plot to kill Jesus a distinction must be made

between "the people" (vv. 20, 31) and "certain people from Jerusalem" (v. 25). There is, however, an identity between "the authorities," "the Jews," and "the Pharisees," used without distinction in vv. 11, 13, 15, 32, 35, 47-48.

26. *that this is the Christ:* It is sometimes claimed that "this instant raising of the messianic question is surprising" (Schnackenburg, *Gospel* 2:146). If full attention is given to the context of the feast of Tabernacles (cf. v. 28), the emergence of the messianic question is not at all surprising (see "The Feast of Tabernacles" in the interpretation above).

27. *no one will know where he comes from:* There is ample Jewish background to the notion of the hidden Messiah, whose origins will be unknown (e.g., Isa 7:14-17; Mal 3:1; Dan 7:13; *b. Sanh.* 97a; *1 Enoch* 46; 48:2-6; *Esdr.* 7:28; 13:32; *2 Bar* 29:3; Justin, *Dial.* 8:4; 110:1). See the detailed treatment by Sigmund Mowinckel, *He That Cometh* (Oxford: Blackwell, 1959) 304–308. For Cory, "Wisdom's Rescue" 100–102, the question of origins, which is so central to 7:1–8:59, links the passage with wisdom traditions.

28. *the one who sent me is true:* This translation reads the expression "true" (*alēthinos*) as a strong adjectival (the one true God) rather than an adverbial sense (he is true, that is, does not tell lies).

31. *Yet many of the people:* There is a contrast between "the people" (v. 31) and "certain people from Jerusalem" (v. 25). They are different groups in the narrative, and they have different responses to Jesus. This is not always recognized (e.g., Barrett, *Gospel* 323). There is, however, also a continuation, as the messianic question raised by the Jerusalemites in v. 26 is still present in the words of "the people" in v. 31.

When the Christ appears, will he do more signs?: Popular messianism did not associate the Messiah with miracles. For a discussion of this question see Painter, *Quest* 294–295, and Ashton, *Understanding the Fourth Gospel* 273–278. Yet there was the expectation that signs and wonders would accompany the Mosaic eschatological prophet (cf. Meeks, *Prophet-King* 162–164). Bittner, *Jesu Zeichen* 245–258, has shown the importance of Isaiah 11 in pointing to a Davidic Messiah who would work miracles to show his goodness.

3. Jesus and "the Jews" (7:32-36)

32. The Pharisees heard the crowd thus muttering about him, and the chief priests and Pharisees sent officers to arrest him. 33. Jesus then said, "I shall be with you a little longer, and then I go to him who sent me; 34. you will seek me and you will not find me; where I am you cannot come." 35. The Jews said to one another, "Where does this man intend to go that we shall not find him? Does he intend to go to the Dispersion among the Greeks and teach the Greeks? 36. What does he mean by saying, 'You will seek me and you will not find me,' and, 'Where I am you cannot come'?"

INTERPRETATION

"The Pharisees" and "the chief priests" are not happy with this division among the people (cf. vv. 30-31), and they send officers *(hyperētas)* to arrest Jesus (v. 32). They temporarily (cf. v. 45) disappear from the scene. Within this angry context Jesus warns his opponents to make the most of the short time that remains for them. Jesus will remain with them *(meth'* · *hymōn)* for a brief time, after which he will return to the one who sent him. The reader of the Gospel recognizes in these words Jesus' active acceptance of God's designs, but "the Jews" are unable to enter into that world. Locked in their own world, which rejects anything but human origins for Jesus, they will search for Jesus *(zētēsete me)* there, but will not find him. The world of Jesus, the world of the Father, is beyond their ability either to understand or enter (v. 34). The discussion of the Messiah preceding this encounter moved within the world of Jewish messianic expectation: the hidden Messiah (vv. 27-28) and the Messiah who worked signs (v. 31). "The Jews" are attempting to eliminate Jesus from the human story in which they exercise authority (cf. v. 32). They cannot understand that their plot is being thwarted because there is another world where an ultimate authority reigns, and Jesus' story is determined by that world.

There is one place where Jesus would be outside the reach and control of "the Jews." They suggest that he may be planning to go to the Diaspora, the world outside the confines of the sacred land of Israel, so that he might teach the Greeks (v. 35). There is irony here. Jesus is speaking of his return to the Father, not about a journey into a foreign land. Yet earlier parts of the Gospel (cf. 1:9-13; 3:16; 4:42; 6:35, 40, 45, 51) promised that Jesus would bring God's saving presence to the whole world, even to those who were not Jews. Jesus may not be going into the Diaspora, but his going to the one who sent him (v. 31) promises the possibility of life to the whole world. As yet this promise lies unfulfilled.

"The Jews" opened their encounters with Jesus on the occasion of the celebration of Tabernacles by questioning the authority of his teaching (cf. vv. 14-15). Now they are in some consternation over the possibility that he might go into the Diaspora to teach the Greeks (v. 35), worried that a teaching they once rejected might be taken to the Greeks. The events that took place "about the middle of the feast" (v. 14) come to a conclusion with "the Jews" in considerable disarray. This disarray, however, comes from their lack of preparedness to hear the words of Jesus and respond to them positively. Thus they continue to ask questions to which Jesus has already provided answers: "What does he mean?" What is meant by "You will seek me and you will not find me," or "Where I am you cannot come" (v. 36)?

The attempts to understand who Jesus might be have been determined by traditional messianic expectation: the hidden Messiah (vv. 27-28) and the Messiah who does signs (v. 31). The mystery of Jesus can only be understood in terms of his origins and his destiny in God (vv. 33-34). His ministry is provoking *schismata* (vv. 25-26, 31, 35-36), conflict (vv. 28-29, 33-34), and violent rejection (vv. 30, 32). It is leading toward "the hour" (vv. 6, 30). The presence of Jesus at the Jewish feast of Tabernacles does not nullify traditional Jewish messianic thought, but transcends and transforms the hopes normally expressed within the context of this great feast. Conflict is generated by an unwillingness to accept that Jesus' origins and destiny transcend the limitations of the feasts of "the Jews," perfecting—not replacing—God's former gift in and through Moses (cf. vv. 19-24; 1:16-17).

NOTES

32. *the chief priests and the Pharisees:* Barrett (*Gospel* 324) rightly remarks of the author's naming of Jesus' opponents, "He simply takes *hoi Ioudaioi* as a general term for the enemies of Jesus, analyzing it on occasion into *hoi archiereis* (or *hoi archontes*) together with *hoi Pharisaioi*." The reason for the singling out of the names here may be to support the impression through the following passage that these are authoritative figures among "the people."

    sent officers to arrest him: The "officers" (*hyperētai*) mentioned here were Temple officers, available only to the chief priests (see previous note). This is a further indication that Jesus is still in the Temple area, where all the celebrations are taking place.

33. *a little longer:* The expressions "a little longer" and "a short time" have OT backgrounds (cf. Isa 10:25; 54:7; 55:6; Jer 51:33; Hos 1:4; Hag 2:6), as does the idea of seeking and not finding (cf. Deut 4:29; Hos 5:6). They also carry a note of apocalyptic urgency. See Korteweg, "You will seek me" 349–354.

    I go to him who sent me: A favorite Johannine word to express Jesus' active return to the Father emerges: *hypagō* (cf. 8:14, 22; 13:3, 33, 36; 14:4, 5, 28; 16:5, 10, 17).

34. *you will seek me:* The use of the verb "to seek" (*zēteō*) to describe the action of Jesus' opponents always has a hint of violence (cf. 5:18; 7:1, 11, 18, 20, 25, 34, 36).

    where I am: The interpretation accentuates the place of Jesus, and does not call for reading *hopou eimi egō* as an allusion to the christological use of *egō eimi*, as some would claim.

35. *The Jews said to one another:* The expression "the Jews" must still be read as an all-embracing term referring to the groups mentioned in v. 32.

    the Dispersion among the Greeks: On the background to the complex situation and Jewish understanding of "the Dispersion among the Greeks" (the Diaspora) see W. C. van Unnik, *Das Selbstverständnis der Jüdischen Diaspora in der hellenistisch-römischen Zeit* (ed. P. W. van der Horst. AGJU 17. Leiden: E. J. Brill, 1993).

teach the Greeks: On the irony created by the suggestion of "the Jews" that his departure will lead to his teachings being made available to the Greeks see Kysar, *John's Story* 46.

d) *On the Last Day of the Feast (7:37–8:59)*

The Structure of 7:37–8:59. There are three major sections to the narrative reporting events that take place in the Temple on "the last day of the feast" (v. 37).

  i. *7:37-52:* Jesus' revelation of himself as the living water leads to *schismata* among "the people" and the Pharisees.
  ii. *8:12-30:* Jesus' revelation of himself as "the light of the world" and the consequences, both positive and negative, of his revealing presence.
  iii. *8:31-59:* Jesus and "the Jews" enter into unresolvable conflict and acrimonious accusations about their respective origins.

The density of the argument increases as Jesus and "the Jews" become locked in bitter accusation and counter-accusation.

1. Jesus, "the People," and the Leaders (7:37-52)

37. On the last day of the feast, the great day, Jesus stood up and proclaimed, "Let anyone who is thirsty come to me, 38. and let the one who believes in me drink. As the scripture has said, 'Out of his heart shall flow rivers of living water.'" 39. Now this he said about the Spirit, which those who believed in him were to receive; for as yet the Spirit had not been given, because Jesus was not yet glorified. 40. When they heard these words some of the people said, "This is really the prophet." 41. Others said, "This is the Christ." But some said, "Is the Christ to come from Galilee? 42. Has not the scripture said that the Christ is descended from David, and comes from Bethlehem, the village where David was?" 43. So there was a division among the people over him. 44. Some of them wanted to arrest him, but no one laid hands on him.

45. The officers then went back to the chief priests and Pharisees, who said to them, "Why did you not bring him?" 46. The officers answered, "Never has anyone spoken like this!" 47. The Pharisees answered them, "Are you led astray, you also? 48. Have any of the authorities or of the

Pharisees believed in him? 49. But this crowd, who do not know the law, are accursed."

50. Nicodemus, who had gone to him before, and who was one of them, said to them, 51. "Does our law judge people without first giving them a hearing to know what they do?" 52. They replied, "Are you from Galilee too? Search and you will see that no prophet is to rise from Galilee."

INTERPRETATION

The eighth day of the feast, the last day, was similar to a Sabbath (cf. Lev 22:33-43). It was a day of great rejoicing, and the singing of the *Hallel* continued (cf. *m. Sukk.* 4:8; Josephus, *Ant.* 3:245, 247). The celebratory use of water and light, however, ceased on the seventh day. On the day when these *symbols* had been eliminated from the ceremony Jesus stood up *(eistēkei)* and proclaimed *(ekraxen)* in the Temple that he is the provider of water (vv. 37-38) and the light of the world (8:12; cf. 9:5). For this reason the narrator calls this day "the great day." Jesus, the giver of water that will raise up to eternal life (4:14), the perfection of the creating God of the Sabbath (5:19-30), and the gift of God's bread from heaven (5:25-58), proclaims: "Let anyone who is thirsty come to me, and let the one who believes in me drink. As the scripture has said, 'Out of his heart shall flow rivers of living water'" (vv. 37b-38) (on this punctuation and translation, see note). Within the context of a Jewish feast marked by libations and the promise of the coming Messiah who will repeat the Mosaic gift of water Jesus presents himself as the source of living water. He proposes another source of living water. No longer is there need to hold daily ritual lustrations, carrying water from the pool of Siloam. Jesus is the source of living water for *all* who believe in him *(ean tis dipsa . . . ho pisteuōn);* he transcends the ritual of the Jewish feast. The only criteria for admission to the lifegiving refreshment of Jesus are movement toward Jesus (v. 37: *erchesthō pros me*) and faith in him (v. 38a: *ho pisteuōn eis me*).

Jesus also claims he fulfills the Scriptures, promising rivers of living water flowing from within him (v. 38b), quenching the thirst of all who believe and come to him (vv. 37-38a). In Ezek 47:1-11 ever-deepening waters flow out from the Temple (vv. 3-6), enlivening the desert regions of the Arabah, via En-gedi and En-eglaim (vv. 8-11). Ezekiel 47:9 promises: "Everything will live where the river goes." Given the link between Zechariah 14 and the celebration of Tabernacles (cf. Zech 14:16-19), there may also be a reference to Zech 14:8: "On that day living waters shall flow out from Jerusalem, half of them to the eastern sea and half of them to the western sea; it shall continue in summer as in winter" (cf. also 14:17). Jesus transcends all attempts to understand him within the categories of Jewish messianic expectation (cf. vv. 14-36). In Ezek 47:1-11 the lifegiving waters flowed from the Temple, the very center, the navel of Jerusalem and the earth (cf. Ezek 38:12; *Jub.* 8:19; *b. Sanh.* 37a). Jesus proclaims that the lifegiving waters flow from within him (*ek tēs koilias autou.* See note.). "John uses this word as a means to transfer the prophecy from the city to a person" (Barrett, *Gospel* 328). Jesus' person is now the origin of lifegiving water. He perfects the symbol of the definitive mediation of God's gift of water from the well of the Torah promised by the water celebrations of the feast of Tabernacles.

Jesus' proclamation, however, points to a future time: "Out of his heart *shall flow (rhesousin)* rivers of living water" (v. 38b). Later rabbinic reflection on the feast of Tabernacles asked of the water ceremony: "Why do they call it the house of drawing?" and responded: "Because thence they draw the Holy Spirit" (*Gen. Rab.* 70:1). This link between the drawing of the water and the gift of the Spirit may lie behind Jesus' words, but the perfection of this gift of God lies in a future moment marked by the glorification of Jesus. The Spirit has not yet been given because Jesus has not yet been glorified (v. 39). When will this be? Is this gift of the Spirit related to the traditional expectation of the effusion of the Spirit that will take place at the end of time (cf. Ezek 11:19; 36:26-27; 39:29; Isa 44:3; Joel 2:26; 3:1)? What is the link between the perfection of the messianic symbol of the water, the gift of the Spirit, and Jesus' glorification? When will this glorification take place? The growing threats of violence surrounding Jesus' presence in Jerusalem for the feast of Tabernacles (cf. 7:19-20, 23, 25, 30, 32), and his earlier hint to his brothers that his "time" would come at another feast of "the Jews" (7:5-8), point toward his death. A further prolepsis that seeks resolution has been created by Jesus' words and the narrator's comment (vv. 37-39). The perfection of the messianic promise, the gift of the Spirit, and the glorification of Jesus are linked to Jesus' death by crucifixion.

Jesus' words have been heard (v. 40a). His self-revelation as the perfection of the Mosaic gift of water, however, leads to a confession from some that he is "the prophet" (v. 40b) and from others that "this is the Christ" (v. 41). They are following a path already traveled by the Samaritan woman (cf. 4:13-26). The celebration of the feast of Tabernacles that recalled Jewish messianic ideas of the second gift of water, perfecting the Torah, explains the people's response (vv. 40-41) to Jesus' words (vv. 37-38). Jesus' self-revelation creates a situation in which the people and "the Jews" must come to a decision: is he the Messiah or not? The people, not privy to the narrator's comment in v. 39, continue their discussion on the basis of Jewish hope of the Davidic Messiah (cf. 2 Sam 7:12-16; Pss 18:50; 80:3-4, 35-37; Isa 11:1, 10; Jer 23:5). Some accept that Jesus is the Messiah on the basis of his words (cf. vv. 37-38), but others point out that Jesus comes from Galilee, and the Christ is not to come from there (v. 41b). The Messiah would come from the Davidic line, and the Scriptures even indicate the city of his origins: Bethlehem, the village where David was (v. 42; cf. Mic 5:2). A Christian reader is aware of the tradition that Jesus was from Bethlehem, and Galilee is a place he visits to go away from his own country (cf. 4:42). But the irony runs deeper, as Jesus is "from God," not "from Galilee." There is a uniqueness about who Jesus is and what he is doing that cannot be resolved by Jewish messianic categories. Faced with this uniqueness, the people can only fall into disarray. There is a *schisma* over who Jesus is (v. 43), but some of the people *(tines . . . ex autōn)* join the Jerusalemites (cf. v. 30) and "the Jews" (cf. v. 32): they want to arrest Jesus (v. 44a), but are unable to do so. The reason for their ineffectual attempts has been given in v. 30: his hour has not yet come.

The messianic background to the celebration of Tabernacles has been strongly present in the attempts of the Jerusalemites and the people to locate Jesus within their messianic categories:

> – the hidden Messiah (the Jerusalemites: vv. 26-27)
> – the miracle-working Messiah (many of the people: v. 31)
> – the Messiah who provides living water (some of the people: vv. 37-41a)
> – the Davidic Messiah (some of the people: vv. 41b-42).

These attempts have led to confusion and violent threats among the people (vv. 43-44), but the Pharisees have made up their minds about Jesus (vv. 48-52). It has been some time since the temple officials *(hyperētai)* were sent to arrest Jesus (v. 32). They were sent out "about the middle of the feast" (v. 14), and they return "on the last day of the feast" (v. 42. Cf. v. 37). Thus they have heard Jesus' self-proclamation as the living water (vv. 37-38) and have attended the discussions between the people, wondering about his messianic status (vv. 40-44). They return to their masters empty handed, and they are asked to explain why (v. 45).

The officials recognize the uniqueness and the authority of the word of Jesus in their answer: "No man ever spoke like this man" *(oudepote elalēsen houtōs anthrōpos)*. Unable to see beyond "this man," they are nevertheless rendered powerless by his word, and are accused of being led astray. The narrative began with some people suggesting that Jesus was leading the people astray (v. 12: *planai ton ochlon)*, but they were afraid to speak openly about him for fear of "the Jews" (vv. 12-13). On the last day of the feast, after debates about Jesus' messianic status, "the Jews" openly challenge: "Are you led astray, you also?" (v. 47: *mē kai hymeis peplanēsthai?)*. Jesus is publicly accused of being a deceiver *(planos)* whose teaching is deceptive *(planē)*. In their accusations the Pharisees are using language found in rabbinic Judaism to speak of a pseudo-Messiah (cf. Pancaro, *The Law in the Fourth Gospel* 101–105). They claim that none of the leaders or the Pharisees have fallen to the subtleties of this man's words (v. 48). The authorities exclude themselves from all discussion over Jesus as Messiah, and regard those who engage in it as accursed, ignorant of the Law (v. 49).

Nicodemus, "one of them" (v. 50), raises questions concerning the interpretation of "our Law" (v. 51) and challenges the arrogant affirmation of v. 48. The Pharisees claim that *not one* of them had fallen to Jesus' trickery, but "one of them" emerges to defend Jesus. Nicodemus does not raise the messianic question, but queries the correctness of the procedure used against Jesus (v. 51). The officers claimed that no one has ever spoken as Jesus speaks (v. 46), but Nicodemus takes this further, asking the Pharisees why they condemn Jesus without first hearing from him *(ean mē akousē proton par'autou)* and coming to know what he does *(gnǭ ti poiei)*. No legal precept in the OT or in rabbinic Judaism demands that the accused be heard and that the accuser come to know what he does. Nicodemus enunciates a new understanding of the Law: no judgment can be announced against Jesus unless his word first be heard in faith and his signs and works be recognized for what they are: the action of God in the Son. Nicodemus challenges the Pharisees by informing them that the only ones able to make a right judgment of Jesus are those who believe in him. The Pharisees and "the Jews" have never entered into dialogue with Jesus, but one of them, Nicodemus, has allowed himself to be challenged, and baffled, by the word of Jesus (3:1-11). He now advocates a new way of understanding God's design for the people; it is found in the words and deeds of Jesus (v. 51).

The Pharisees are not prepared to move away from their traditions and their sense of self-righteous control (cf. vv. 47-49). They attempt to escape from Nicodemus' accusations by heaping abuse on him (v. 52), just as they did with the Temple officers (v. 47) and the "crowd who do not know the Law" (v. 49). Ironically, the Pharisees are refusing to do the will of God (cf. v. 17) and they are no longer practicing the Law (cf. v. 19). They join that group of the people who rejected any messianic status for Jesus because they knew his origins (cf. v. 27, 41) and they call upon the evidence of the Scriptures that no prophet ever came from Galilee (v. 52). But Jesus did not come from Galilee, and there were prophets from Galilee (e.g., Jonah, Hosea, Nahum). Jesus is not just a prophet, and he is not "from Galilee." He is "from God."

NOTES

37. *On the last day of the feast:* It is not clear exactly which day is meant. There is no Jewish background for calling the seventh or the eighth day "the great

day." Many have suggested that the seventh day is intended (e.g., Brown, *Gospel* 1:320; Schnackenburg, *Gospel* 2:152; Str-B 2:490–491). The fact that neither the water nor the light ceremony took place on the eighth day, and that this is the day when Jesus reveals himself as the source of living water (7:37-38) and the light of the world (8:12; 9:5), indicates that "the last day" is the eighth day (cf. Bauer, *Johannesevangelium* 112; Hoskyns, *Gospel* 320; Barrett, *Gospel* 326; Lindars, *Gospel* 297–298).

come to me and drink: Three major problems are associated with the interpretation of vv. 37-39.

(1) *The question of punctuation.* Do the words of Jesus come to a full stop after "come to me and drink"? This would give the RSV translation, based on the text of Nestlé-Aland: "If anyone thirst, let him come to me and drink. He who believes in me, as the scripture has said, 'Out of his heart shall flow rivers of living water.'" This option (cf. Barrett, Bernard, Haenchen, Lightfoot, Léon-Dufour, Lindars, Segalla) is largely based on the punctuation suggested by the second-century $\mathfrak{P}^{66}$.

Is there a lesser break after "come to me," reading on until "the one who believes in me" for the full stop? This produces the translation adopted in the commentary: "Let anyone who is thirsty come to me, and let the one who believes in me drink. As the scripture has said, 'Out of his heart shall flow living water.'" There is increasing modern support for this punctuation (e.g., Bauer, Becker, Bultmann, Beasley-Murray, Boismard, Brown, Dodd, Hoskyns, Schnackenburg, Westcott, NRSV). There is also second-century evidence for this reading. See R. E. Brown, "The Gospel of Thomas and St John's Gospel." *NTS* 9 (1962–1963) 162.

(2) *The question of meaning.* Out of whose heart does the living water flow? The RSV translation leads to an interpretation that has the living water flowing from the heart of the believer. The NRSV continues this interpretation. But living water might flow from Jesus, to whom the believer has gone for refreshment. The heart (*koilia:* see below) mentioned in the quotation would refer back to Jesus as the provider of the drink. This would be the more likely meaning, but it is still possible that water might flow from inside the one who has gone to Jesus for refreshment, as a result of the association with Jesus. For the possibility that both Jesus and the believer are intended see F. Manns, *Le symbole eau-esprit dans le Judaïsme ancien.* SBFA 19. Jerusalem: Franciscan Printing Press, 1983, 287–291.

(3) *The origins of the biblical text referred to in v. 38.* No text in either the MT or the LXX matches John 7:38b. Some (e.g., Obermann, *Die christologische Erfüllung* 38–39) claim that an OT source cannot be found. Yet the use of the singular *graphē* would appear to refer to some specific text. See the detailed summary of the discussion in Bienaimé, "L'annonce" 418–431. The choice of the texts from Ezekiel and Zechariah (see interpretation) is determined both by the context and by the evidence that a link between them had already been made in pre-Christian times. See Grelot, "Jean VII,38: eau du rocher" 43–51. For the later rabbinic combination of these ideas see *t. Sukk.* 3:18.

38. *out of his heart:* There is some discussion whether the expression *ek tēs koilias autou* means out of the heart or out of the belly. This is further complicated by the possibility that the Aramaic word *gūph* may lie behind the Greek, with possible reference to the rock of the wilderness or the rock of the Temple. For a documented survey of the discussion see Brown, *Gospel* 1:323–324. The basic meaning demanded by the context is that living waters flow from within Jesus. For Cory, "Wisdom's Rescue" 100–102, the theme of water comes from a wisdom background.

39. *this he said about the Spirit:* As well as the Jewish material provided in the interpretation, the same link between the gift of the water and the gift of the Spirit is found in *j. Sukk.* 55a; *Ruth Rab.* 4:8. See the excellent collection of texts, and commentary on them, in Manns, *Le symbole* 220–232.

42. *comes from Bethlehem, the village where David was:* It is not certain whether the use of Mic 5:2 as a prophecy about the birthplace of the Messiah is of Jewish or Christian origin. It is here presumed for the story of Jesus. See Lindars, *Gospel* 303. For greater detail on the question of Jesus' birthplace see R. E. Brown, *The Birth of the Messiah: A Commentary on the Infancy Narratives in Matthew and Luke.* 2nd ed. Garden City, N.Y.: Doubleday, 1993, 513–516.

45. *The officers then went back:* The distance in time between the sending of the officers "about the middle of the feast" (v. 32) and their return "on the last day of the feast" (v. 45) has led some (e.g., Brown, *Gospel* 1:325) to regard their reappearance as artificial. This arrangement is called for so that the officers can come back to the authorities impressed by the word of Jesus. They have been listening to what both Jesus and his interlocutors have said from v. 32 to v. 44 (see Schnackenburg, *Gospel* 2:159).

47. *The Pharisees answered them:* This is one of the several places in the Gospel where the roles of "the Pharisees" and "the Jews" are identical. The Pharisees are united (cf. v. 48) in their rejection of Jesus and their commitment to the Law (cf. v. 49). In v. 32 the chief priests and the Pharisees sent the officers to arrest Jesus. In v. 45 the officers return to the chief priests and the Pharisees, but only the Pharisees speak in vv. 47-52. What was said of "the Jews" in the introduction applies to "the Pharisees."

48. *Have any of the authorities or of the Pharisees:* The irony in vv. 48-49 depends on the Greek. Verse 48 is an affirmation of the rock-solid agreement of Jewish leadership in their rejection of the word of Jesus: *mē tis ek tōn archontōn . . . ē ek tōn Pharisaiōn.*

49. *this crowd, who do not know the Law:* "The Jews" or other members of the Jewish leadership (chief priests and Pharisees) have never shown signs of being receptive to the word of Jesus. This has happened only with the people and certain Jerusalemites, but now some of the Temple officers are falling victim to Jesus' deception. They are told they are joining the ignorant and accursed ones, that part of the people that does not know the Law. This section of the Jewish population was known as "the people of the Land" (*ʿam haʾāreṣ*), and was looked down upon by the political and religious authorities of Judaism.

See Pancaro, *The Law in the Fourth Gospel* 103–105; Schnackenburg, *Gospel* 2:160.

are accursed: Those accused by the authorities as ignorant and accursed accept the word of Jesus. The authorities exclude themselves from all discussion of Jesus as Messiah. The members of the Johannine community, expelled from the synagogue because of their acceptance of Jesus as the Christ (cf. 9:22; 12:42), recognize the irony. See Martyn, *History and Theology* 90–100; Pancaro, *The Law in the Fourth Gospel* 101–105.

50. *Nicodemus . . . who was one of them:* The claim of the Pharisees in v. 48, *mē tis . . . ek tōn Pharisaiōn,* is ironically rendered untrue as Nicodemus is described in 3:1 as an *archōn* of the Jews, and further described as *heis ōn ex autōn.* The security of the claim that "none of them" has listened to Jesus is disturbed by "one of them." For Cory, "Wisdom's Rescue" 107, Nicodemus plays a role from the wisdom tale: a helper who attempts to intervene on behalf of the protagonist.

51. *Does our law judge people:* Most commentators regard Nicodemus' question as a mere wondering about which detail of the Law is being used to judge Jesus. Deuteronomy 1:16-17; 17:4; Exod 23:1; Josephus, *Ant.* 6:6.3; 14:167; *War* 1:209, and *Exod. Rab.* 21:3 are cited to respond to Nicodemus' question (e.g., Bauer, *Johannesevangelium* 115). But none of these examples responds adequately to Nicodemus' question concerning *both* hearing what he has to say for himself *and* coming to know what he does. Thus there is no legislation that corresponds to his objection.

without first giving them a hearing to know what they are doing?: In the Fourth Gospel "to hear" and "to know what he does" are intimately associated with the revelation of God in and through the word and actions of Jesus. See Pancaro, *Law in the Fourth Gospel* 138–157. Pancaro concludes: "Jesus no longer appears as a violator of the Law, but as the one who fulfils it (cf. Jn 7:21-23). *Jn brings this home in 7,51 by having the Law of the Jews establish conditions for the judgement of Jesus which can be met only by those who believe on him*" (p. 156; emphasis in original). See also Pancaro, "The Metamorphosis of a Legal Principle" 340–361; Léon-Dufour, *Lecture* 2:243–246.

52. *no prophet is to rise from Galilee:* On the strange ignorance of the Pharisees concerning prophets who come from Galilee see Westcott, *Gospel* 125. Perhaps in light of this lapse on the part of the Pharisees, but most likely as a result of an assimilation of v. 40, some early readings ($\mathfrak{P}^{66.75}$) have "the prophet" *(ho prophētēs).* This is accepted by Mehlmann, "Propheta a Moyse promissus" 79–88, and Schnackenburg, *Gospel* 2:161.

Excursus on John 7:53–8:11: The Woman Taken in Adultery

7:53. They went separately to their own houses, 8:1. but Jesus went to the Mount of Olives. 2. Early in the morning he came again to the Temple; all the people came to him, and he sat down and taught them.

3. The scribes and the Pharisees brought a woman who had been caught in adultery, and placing her in the midst 4. they said to him, "Teacher, this woman has been caught in the act of adultery. 5. Now in the law Moses commanded us to stone such. What do you say about her?" 6a. This they said to test him, that they might have some charge to bring against him.

6b. Jesus bent down and wrote with his finger on the ground. 7. And as they continued to ask him, he stood up and said to them, "Let him who is without sin among you be the first to throw a stone at her." 8. And once more he bent down and wrote with his finger on the ground. 9. But when they heard it, they went away, one by one, beginning with the eldest, and Jesus was left alone with the woman standing before him.

10. Jesus looked up and said to her, "Woman, where are they? Has no one condemned you?" 11. She said, "No one, Lord." And Jesus said, "Neither do I condemn you; go, and from this moment on do not sin again."

INTERPRETATION

For sound textual reasons it is universally admitted that the account of Jesus and the woman taken in adultery (7:53–8:11) does not belong to the Fourth Gospel (cf. Brown, *Gospel* 1:332–338; Barrett, *Gospel* 589; Pickering, "John 7:53–8:11" 6–7). As this commentary is dedicated to an analysis of the dynamic of the Johannine narrative, John 7:53–8:11 is regarded as an intrusion. This popular ancient tradition about Jesus, which "floated" in written Jesus material, was incorporated into various manuscripts at different places in early textual traditions, mainly in the Fourth Gospel (after 7:36; 7:44; 7:52; or 21:25), but also in Luke (after Luke 21:38). Scribes were rightly anxious to preserve this remarkable story in its written form, and a place had to be found for it. It finally settled after John 7:52 as most copyists apparently thought it created least disturbance at that point of the Johannine narrative (cf. Metzger, *Textual Commentary* 187–190; Becker, *Jesus und die Ehebrecherin* 25; Blank, "Frauen" 83; Schnackenburg, *Gospel* 3:171). But this synoptic-like story, which does not relate to the broader context of the Gospel and interrupts the already complex thought of 7:1–8:59, disturbs the storyteller's systematic account of Jesus' presence at the feasts of "the Jews" (despite Heil, "The Story of Jesus" 182–191, and "A Rejoinder" 361–366. cf. note to v. 1). "It is certain that this narrative is not an original part of the gospel" (Barrett, *Gospel* 589). However, given the value of John 7:53–8:11 as a witness to Jesus of Nazareth, its role within the accepted biblical tradition and in the life, liturgy, and imagination of Christians, a brief treatment of the passage is called for.

The interaction among the different characters in the narrative produces the following literary shape:

> (a) *Introduction (7:53–8:2).* An unspecified crowd and Jesus are separated, but the following day Jesus and "all the people" are in the Temple. Jesus teaches them.
>
> (b) *The Scribes and Pharisees and Jesus (8:3-6a).* The Scribes and Pharisees challenge Jesus by asking what he has to say about a woman who has been taken in adultery.
>
> (c) *Jesus and the Scribes and Pharisees (8:6b-9).* The challenge is reversed as Jesus asks the one without guilt to cast the first stone, and the Scribes and Pharisees and probably "all the people" depart.
>
> (d) *Jesus and the Woman (8:10-11).* For the first time the woman becomes an active character, drawn into the action by a question from Jesus who does not condemn but gives life.

The movement from the setting into the reversal of roles between Jesus and his interlocutors culminating in the dialogue between Jesus and the woman is a finely constructed and unified narrative (cf. McDonald, "The So-Called" 422–423). It provides a striking account of an event that probably has its roots in a memory of an event from the ministry of Jesus (cf. Becker, *Jesus und die Ehebrecherin* 174; Schnackenburg, *Gospel* 3:170–171).

Introduction (7:53–8:2). Jesus is isolated from the crowd as they go to their homes and he to the Mount of Olives (7:53–8:1). This is a Lukan touch, as often in Luke's Gospel Jesus withdraws on his own for prayer before major events (e.g., Luke 4:42; 6:12; 9:18; 11:1; 21:37-38; 22:39-46). A new day begins with the assembly of "all the people" in the Temple being taught by Jesus (v. 2). There are again echoes of Jesus' teaching role in the Gospel of Luke, after a night on the Mount of Olives (Luke 21:38). A large gathering in the Temple attentive to Jesus' teaching is the setting for the action that follows.

The Scribes and Pharisees and Jesus (vv. 3-6a). The Scribes and Pharisees lead a woman who had been caught in adultery into the gathering of Jesus and the attentive crowd. The woman has been "caught" *(kateilēmenēn)* in adultery. She has been taken *in flagranti,* seized while actively involved sexually with a partner who was not her husband. This detail adds drama to the narrative as they set her in the middle of Jesus and the crowd (v. 3). In a situation of considerable distress, half-clad, and aware that she is facing death, the woman is of no concern to the Scribes and Pharisees. They accuse her and challenge Jesus (vv. 4-5). In a way reminiscent of "the Jews" in the Fourth Gospel they know what Moses would do in such a situation (v. 5a; cf. 6:30-31; 9:29), but they are anxious to place Jesus in a situation where he may appear to be in conflict with Moses and the Law. This is the point of their question: "What do you say about her?" (v. 5b), indicating a contrived use of the woman to pit the judgment of Jesus against the teaching of Moses. To clarify this the narrator adds: "They said this to test him, that they might have some charge to bring against him" (v. 6a). They are not interested in either the fate of the woman or the injured husband who is never mentioned, but in the possibility of finding fault with Jesus. The polemic is strong and very public (cf. v. 2: "all the people"), and the woman is but a trapping in the conflict. There is a process in place: Jesus is being challenged by the Law of Moses and the woman's public, and possibly tragic, exposure is an excuse to debate the Law. She is being instrumentalized for the purposes of the Scribes and Pharisees "that they might have some charge to bring against him" (v. 6a).

Jesus and the Scribes and Pharisees (vv. 6b-9). It is impossible to identify the precise purpose of Jesus' bending down and writing with his finger on the ground (v. 6b). It is even more impossible to guess what he might have written. In the face of this challenge from the Scribes and Pharisees, where the accused woman has become a chattel in a legal debate, it is best understood as a sign of indifference, and even disappointment with the proceedings. Jesus turns away from this dramatic scene and ignores the question asked of him. These are the touches, however well elaborated in the tradition, that tell of an event from the life of Jesus. There is no need to resort to symbolic interpretations (cf. note). But as the Scribes and Pharisees continue to ask their question (v. 7a) Jesus resumes a standing position, entering the debate as he reestablishes communication, insisting that the one without sin cast the first stone (v. 7b; cf. Lev 24:1-16; Deut 13:10; 17:2-7). Although Jesus' challenge is not explicitly stated, it is most likely that it refers to sin in the sexual area. Having challenged those who have challenged him, he resumes his position, doodling in the dust (v. 8). Unwatched, as Jesus bends to the ground, the Scribes and Pharisees drift away, one by one. Nothing is said of the people. They may also have departed, leaving Jesus alone with the woman (v. 9). None of them can lay claim to be without such sin, and their departure in order of seniority is a chain reaction in which the exit of the most significant Jewish leader leads to departure of the next in line until all have disappeared. One can only speculate about the historical possibilities of such an order of events (cf. Schnackenburg, *Gospel* 2:167), but the gradual disappearance of the accusers, who have now become the accused, and probably also "all the people," is a striking way of leaving Jesus alone with the sinful woman. As Augustine states it: "Only two remain, the wretched woman and the incarnation of mercy" (*In Iohannis Evangelium* 33:5; CCSL XXXVI, 309: *Relicti sunt duo, misera et misericordia*).

Jesus and the Woman (vv. 10-11). Jesus' words to the woman, "Woman, where are they? Has no one condemned you?" (v. 10: *oudeis se katekrinen?*) are the first words addressed to the woman in the story. She is addressed

as "you" (se) and is now no longer an object, a necessary evil, but someone who can enter into a relationship with Jesus. Addressing him as
"Lord" (kyrie), displaying her reverence for him, she tells Jesus that no
one condemns her (v. 11a). On the basis of the relationship that is established by this dialogue Jesus can challenge her to sin no more. From this
moment on (apo tou nun), the moment of her encounter with Jesus, he offers her the double possibility of a new life: "Go, and from this moment
on do not sin again" (cf. note). The men (Scribes and Pharisees) in the earlier part of the story would not even allow her physical life. That has been
restored to her through the intervention of Jesus. But the command to sin
no more offers her the possibility of a newness of life in a right relationship with God.

Conclusion. Although it plays no role in the Johannine account of
Jesus' presence in Jerusalem for the feast of Tabernacles (cf. 7:1–10:21),
this passage is an ancient and precious witness to Jesus of Nazareth. It
has no doubt been shaped into its present form in the storytelling tradition of the early Church (cf. Ehrmann, "Jesus and the Adulteress" 24–44;
McDonald, "The So-Called" 416–420), but at least three issues point to its
association with the life of Jesus: the punishment for adultery was discussed in the time of Jesus (cf. Mark 10:2; 12:15; Matt 22:35; Luke 10:25.
For the discussion, cf. Blank, "Frauen" 86); second, Jesus opposes the traditional defenders of the Mosaic tradition; and third, on his own authority he unconditionally forgives a sinner. Jesus stands traditional values
upside down if adherence to such values means that a woman is made a
chattel, in this case a necessary evil in a debate over a point of the Law
(cf. Moloney, *Woman* 8–25; Blank, "Frauen" 89–91). Maria Boulding's
commentary on this episode is worth recording:

> The Pharisees are tense, but he is calm and relaxed throughout; he ac-
> cepts the woman openly and lovingly, as an adult and as a person. He
> has a sureness of touch; he can handle the situation and the relationship
> with her because he has nothing to be afraid of in himself. . . . He must
> have completely accepted and integrated his own sexuality. Only a man
> who has done so, or at least begun to do so, can relate properly to
> women. (D. Rees and Others, *Consider Your Call. A Theology of Monastic
> Life Today.* London: SPCK, 1978, 169. Cf. also McDonald, "The So-Called"
> 426–427).

NOTES

7:53. *They went separately to their own houses:* It is difficult to be certain whether this
   indication is a scribal attempt to associate the following passage with the immediately preceding passage, or whether it is a remnant of an original larger
   narrative setting. On the basis of the textual evidence the latter is more likely

(cf. Blank, "Frauen" 85). In a recent debate (cf. Heil, "The Story of Jesus" 182–191, and idem, "A Rejoinder" 361–366; Wallace, "Reconsidering" 290–296), J. P. Heil has claimed that the passage has linguistic, literary, and thematic links with its present setting and was probably part of the original Gospel, dropped early in the manuscript tradition. D. B. Wallace has replied that Heil's arguments only further indicate the non-Johannine nature of the passage. The debate has not disturbed scholarly unanimity that 7:53–8:11 is an addition to an already completed narrative.

8:1. *But Jesus went to the Mount of Olives:* The parallel with the Lukan practice of Jesus' drawing aside for prayer in solitude is striking, particularly as this is found in Luke 21:37b: "and at night he would go out and spend the night on the Mount of Olives, as it was called."

2. *all the people:* This is an exaggerated statement, again also found in Luke (cf. 21:38), used to indicate a very large group of people.

   he came again to the temple . . . and he sat down and taught them: The parallel noted above between John 8:1 and Luke 21:37b continues here. Luke 21:38 reads: "And all the people would get up early in the morning to listen to him in the temple."

3. *The scribes and Pharisees:* This grouping of opponents of Jesus is never found in the Fourth Gospel, but is regular in the synoptic tradition (e.g., Mark 2:16; 7:1, 5; Matt 5:20; 12:38; 15:1; 23:2, 13-15; Luke 5:21, 30; 6:7; 11:53; 15:2).

   placing her in the midst: The disheveled and distressed woman is placed in full public view. There is irony in the fact that the woman is placed in the center of the gathering of Jesus, "all the people," and the Scribes and Pharisees, but she plays no part in the discussion, and is thus peripheral to it. This heightens the impact of vv. 10-11.

4. *Teacher:* This recognition of Jesus' status introduces the question concerning the punishment of the woman. It gives him the status necessary to enter into the debate. The evocation of themes from the story of Daniel and Susanna (cf. Dan 13:1-64) is often noticed (cf. McDonald, "The So-Called" 420–422; Schnackenburg, *Gospel* 3:167).

5. *What do you say about her?:* The answer to this question would depend on the woman's marital condition, details of which are not provided. Was she a married woman or a betrothed girl (cf. Str-B 2:519–521)? The punishment for these two situations, equally judged as adultery, was death and, at one level, Jesus might be asked which one should be applied (cf. Schnackenburg, *Gospel* 3:164). At another level (cf. interpretation) he is placed on trial. On the issue of lynch-justice that may be present here see Derrett, "Law in the New Testament" 10–11.

6. *Jesus bent down and wrote with his finger on the ground:* The interpretation of this gesture is not simple. In addition to the interpretation given above, it is sometimes understood symbolically (cf. the survey in Schnackenburg, *Gospel* 2:165–166). Some (e.g., Schnackenburg, *Gospel* 3:166–167; Blank, "Frauen" 86–87; McDonald, "The So-Called" 421) see it as a reference to LXX Jer 17:13:

"Those who turn away from you shall be recorded in the earth, for they have forsaken the fountain of living water, the LORD." There is also a rabbinic text (*m. Šabb.* 13:5) which refers to the guiltlessness of writing in the sand, or anything impermanent, on the Sabbath. These texts, however, do not match the situation of the Scribes and Pharisees. They are not being judged by Jesus' writing, but they are forced to judge themselves as a result of his words in v. 7.

7. *Let him who is without sin among you be the first to throw a stone at her:* These words reflect the legislation of Lev 24:1-16; Deut 13:10; 17:2-7, according to which the witnesses should throw the first stone. In this case the Scribes and Pharisees who claim to have caught her in the act of adultery (cf. vv. 3-4) should throw the first stone. Only after those who are genuine witnesses have cast the first stones could "all the people" (cf. v. 2) join the execution process. For some (e.g., Blank, "Frauen" 87–88) these words have the ring of Jesus' authority behind them.

9. *they went away:* Some (e.g., Becker, *Jesus und die Ehebrecherin* 83) claim that the story has the literary form of a conflict story. If that were the case the account would end here, as Jesus' opponents leave the scene defeated. But the story runs on, as its real point is not the defeat of Jesus' opponents but his encounter with the woman in vv. 10-11. Nothing is said of "all the people" (v. 2) in v. 9a, and the indication of v. 9b: "Jesus was left alone with the woman standing before him," suggests that they have also departed.

10. *Jesus looked up and said to her:* Since casting his eyes to the ground in v. 8 Jesus has played no further part in the activity. He now "looks up" and again reestablishes communication, this time with the woman. As Schnackenburg remarks: "The scene between Jesus and the woman is . . . described with a perfection of skill: not a word too few or too many" (*Gospel* 3:167).

11. *and from this moment on do not sin again:* A number of manuscripts, and most translations, read "and sin no more" (cf. RSV). The reading *apo tou nun* should be retained. It is not a superfluous addition to *mēketi*, which has the meaning of "again" (rather than the more usual "no longer") in this exhortation (cf. BAGD 518, s.v.). Jesus pinpoints the lifegiving nature of the woman's encounter. It is a turning point for her and she must not fall back into the way that leads to death: "do not sin again *(mēketi hamartane)*".

FOR REFERENCE AND FURTHER STUDY

Becker, Ulrich. *Jesus und die Ehebrecherin. Untersuchungen zur Text- und Überlieferungsgeschichte von Joh 7,53–8,11.* BZNW 28. Berlin: Töpelmann, 1963.

Blank, Josef. "Frauen in der Jesusüberlieferung." In Gerhard Dautzenberg, Helmut Merklein, and Karlheinz Müller, eds., *Die Frau im Urchristentum.* QD 95. Freiburg: Herder, 1983, 9–91.

Derrett, J. D. M. "Law in the New Testament: The Story of the Woman Taken in Adultery," *NTS* 10 (1963–1964) 10–11.

Ehrman, Bart D. "Jesus and the Adulteress," *NTS* 34 (1988) 24–44.

Heil, John Paul. "The Story of Jesus and the Adulteress (John 7,53–8,11) Reconsidered," *Bib.* 72 (1991) 182–191.

_____. "A Rejoinder to 'Reconsidering "The Story of the Adulteress Reconsidered"'," *EeT* 25 (1994) 361–366.

McDonald, J. I. H. "The So-Called *Pericopa de Adultera*," *NTS* 41 (1995) 415–427.

Moloney, Francis J. *Woman: First Among the Faithful. A New Testament Study.* London: Darton, Longman & Todd, 1985, 15–16.

Pickering, S. R. "John 7:53–8:11. The Woman Taken in Adultery," *New Testament Textual Research Update* 1 (1993) 6–7.

Wallace, D. B. "Reconsidering 'The Story of Jesus and the Adulteress Reconsidered'," *NTS* 39 (1993) 290–296.

2. Jesus Reveals Himself as the Light of the World (8:12-30)

Among the various interlocutors, on two earlier occasions during the celebration of Tabernacles Jesus has debated with "the Jews" and the Pharisees (7:14-24, 45-52). The only two groups mentioned in 8:12-30 are the Pharisees (v. 13) and "the Jews" (v. 22). The account now focuses on an audience that rejects the claim that Jesus is the Messiah (7:32) and has decided to kill him (5:18; 7:1, 11, 19, 25). Scholars discuss the division of 8:1-59 (for a survey see Moloney, *Son of Man* 125–127), but there are two moments in this further revelation of Jesus, each of which begins with the expression "again" *(palin):* v. 12 ("again Jesus spoke to them") and v. 21 ("again he said to them"). For the sake of clarity these two passages will be examined separately, although together they form Jesus' self-proclamation as the light of the world and the response of "the Jews" to this revelation.

John 8:12-20

12. Again Jesus spoke to them, saying, "I am the light of the world; whoever follows me will not walk in darkness but will have the light of life." 13. The Pharisees then said to him, "You are bearing witness to yourself; your testimony is not true." 14. Jesus answered, "Even if I do bear witness to myself, my testimony is true, for I know whence I have come and whither I am going, but you do not know whence I come or whither I am going. 15. You judge according to the flesh. I judge no one, 16. yet even if I do judge, my judgment is reliable, for it is not I alone that judge, but I and the one who sent me. 17. In your law it is written that the testimony of two persons is true; 18. I bear witness to myself, and the Father who sent me bears witness to me." 19. They said to him therefore, "Where is your Father?" Jesus answered, "You know neither me nor my Father; if you knew me, you would know my Father also." 20. These words he spoke in the treasury, as he taught in the Temple; but no one arrested him because his hour had not yet come.

INTERPRETATION

Jesus announces, "I am the light of the world" (v. 12a) within the context of a feast in which the Temple became the light of Jerusalem (cf. *m. Sukk.* 5:3). Further background for Jesus' words comes from the identification of the Torah as the light that was to be given to the world in Jewish wisdom traditions (cf. Wis 18:4; see also Ps 119:105; Prov 6:23; Sir 24:27; Bar 4:2). The rabbis also spoke of the Law as a lamp or light (cf. *T. Levi* 14:4; *Exod. Rab.* 36:3). Jesus claims to be the light of the world within the context of discussion, doubt, and *schisma*. The presence of the light calls for decision, as the light of Jesus brings a double possibility. One can remain in the darkness or walk in the light of life by following Jesus (v. 12b; cf. 1:11-12; 3:19). The christological affirmation of v. 12a and its consequences, spelled out in v. 12b, form the program for the remainder of ch. 8. On the one hand Jesus perfects the liturgy of Tabernacles (v. 12a); on the other his revelation of light brings judgment (v. 12b). The acceptance or refusal of Jesus' revelation of the Father is at the heart of every discussion that follows.

A legal question arises immediately (v. 13). According to the legal demands of Num 35:30 and Deut 17:6, Jesus' witness to himself (cf. v. 12a) is invalid *(ouk estin alēthēs)*. But this is only the case if one accepts that Jesus' words are witness *(martyria)* in a forensic sense, and Jesus is not a defendant searching out witnesses to state his case as in 5:31. In ch. 5 Jesus accepted the situation of a trial. Here there is no trace of a trial as the Pharisees attempt to understand and control Jesus by means of their legal system. To quibble over Jesus' claims to personify, perfect, and universalize the light of the Temple and the light of the Law on the basis of a legal tradition is to miss the point. The Pharisees attack the value of Jesus' *martyria*, but he is claiming to be the unique revelation of God in the world (v. 12). What the Law once was to Israel, Jesus is now to the world. To question Jesus' claim by judging it as a forensic *martyria* is not to recognize the nature of the claim: Jesus is the revealing and judging presence of God. Because of his origin and destiny (v. 14), Jesus' witness cannot be measured by traditional norms. He may be witnessing to himself, but such witness is true *(alēthēs estin hē martyria mou)*. He has already argued this case with the Pharisees (cf. 7:32-36) but they have not accepted his claims. Again there is a conflict between Jesus' claim to origins with the Father and the mundane, earthly attempts of the Pharisees to control and condemn Jesus on the basis of the Mosaic Law. They are unable to transcend what they can measure, see, touch, and control; they are judging "according to the flesh" (v. 15a). This repeats Jesus' earlier accusation against "the Jews," whom he charged with judging according to what they could see, "by appearances" (7:24: *kat' opsin*). "The Jews" and the Pharisees are unable to go beyond external experiences because they stop at the fleshly Jesus, what their eyes can see. They are not open to his words on his origin and his destiny with the Father, a reality beyond their sight and control.

In contrast to the Pharisees, Jesus judges no one on the basis of his own authority (vv. 15b-16). He judges no one, but a judging activity flows from the union he has with the one who sent him (v. 16; cf. 5:22-23a). There is a Johannine logic behind this apparent contradiction. Jesus, the one sent by the Father, makes God known (v. 16b; cf. v. 12a), and a reliable judgment *(krisis alēthinē)* flows from his presence among women and men as they accept or refuse this revelation (vv. 15b-16; cf. v. 12b). The judgment flowing from the acceptance or refusal of the revelation that takes place in Jesus, the light of the world (v. 12a), has no trace of falsity. It is judgment as it should be—reliable, dependable, and genuine *(alēthinē)*. The accusation of the Pharisees (v. 13) has been countered.

Jesus accepts that the Law of "the Jews" demands the witness of two persons for true testimony (v. 17; cf. Deut 17:6; 19:15; *m. Ketub.* 2:9), but such legislation does not apply in his case. Jesus is able to bear witness to himself because he was sent by the Father who also bears witness to him (v. 18). To stop short at the historical Jesus *(kata tēn sarka)* and apply the niceties of the Law to him is to miss the point. The Law has been perfected by the revelation of God in the person and message of the one sent. A knowledge of God has come through the Law, but Jesus cannot be understood, much less judged, by such knowledge. "All supposed 'knowledge' about God and salvation becomes shattering ignorance where there is no faith in him who possesses the true knowledge of God and reveals the way to salvation" (Schnackenburg, *Gospel* 2:195). Jesus' aggressive affirmation of his origins puts the validity of his witness outside the reach of the questioning of the Law. As Nicodemus has told his fellow Pharisees, the only way to right judgment of Jesus is to hear what he has to say and to see what he does (7:51).

The all-pervading question of Jesus' origins brings the Pharisees back into the dialogue asking a puzzled question: "Where is your father?" (v. 19a). Unable to move outside their legal system, they take it for granted he is speaking of two witnesses: himself and his father. They are happy to ask questions that might help them to identify the geographical location of Jesus' father but they avoid the crucial question: "Who is your Father?" Jesus condemns their ignorance. In v. 19bc the verb "to know" is used four times, twice negatively and twice positively, to stress the importance of true recognition of Jesus. The closed-mindedness of the Pharisees leads them into an ignorance of who Jesus is and who his Father is. To know one is to know the other (v. 19bc). Such claims have already been countered with violence. In 5:17 Jesus claimed, "My Father is still working and

I am also working," and "the Jews" responded to that claim with a decision that Jesus must die (5:18). Violence also hovers behind the response to his reprimand of v. 19, which depends on the same intimacy between Jesus and the Father. No one arrested him, as "his hour had not yet come" (v. 20b). The "not yet" *(oupō)* maintains the tension in the narrative. The hour has "not yet" come, but it will eventually be part of the story of Jesus. For the moment Jesus remains in the Temple during the feast of Tabernacles, teaching in the treasury. The focus on the celebration of a feast of "the Jews" is maintained.

NOTES

12. *Again Jesus spoke:* The expression "again" *(palin)* is used regularly in the Fourth Gospel to link one section of the narrative to another (e.g., 1:35; 4:3, 54; 6:15). See Tsuchido, "Tradition and Redaction" 59–60.

    the light of the world: For Jewish literature on the Law as a light or a lamp see Str-B 2:521–522, 552–553. See Brown, *Gospel* 1:340 for the Qumran parallels, and Scott, *Sophia* 119–121 for possible wisdom background. As well as the link between the light ritual at the celebration of Tabernacles and the use of the light to speak of the Torah it is also possible that there is a reminiscence of the pillar of fire leading the wandering Israelites through the desert (cf. Exod 13:21; 14:24; 40:38). As with other Mosaic elements (the manna, a prophet), this pillar of fire was expected by some to return at the end time (cf. Talbert, *Reading John* 153). For Cory, "Wisdom's Rescue" 100–102, light is another theme that comes from a wisdom background.

13. *your testimony is not true:* The discussion between Jesus and the Pharisees goes nowhere because the Pharisees are attempting to understand Jesus' witness in purely forensic terms, but Jesus is pointing to himself as the revelation of God to the world (cf. de la Potterie, *La vérité* 1:83–87). Some commentators attempt to show that Jesus' response points to another way in which the Law is fulfilled.

14. *you do not know whence I come or whither I am going:* A number of scholars have argued that vv. 14c-16, which deal largely with Jesus' origins and destiny, interrupt the flow of a narrative concerned with a forensic question. Once the passage is understood as Jesus' attempt to indicate that he transcends the forensic discussion these verses fit well. Indeed, they are the basis for Jesus' claims. See Pancaro, *The Law in the Fourth Gospel* 264–265.

15. *I judge no one, yet even if I do judge:* It is necessary to link v. 15b to v. 16. Jesus' claim to judge nobody looks back to the superficial judgment of the Pharisees. He judges no one in this way (v. 15b). However, he does bring about judgment as a result of his unity with the Father. There is, therefore, no contradiction between v. 15b and v. 16 (see also 3:17; 5:27). See Brown, *Gospel* 1:345.

16. *my judgment is reliable:* Some witnesses (e.g., 𝔓⁶⁶, Sinaiticus) read *alēthēs* ("true"). This is probably the result of assimilation to vv. 13, 14, and 17. The reading *alēthinē* ("reliable, dependable") is well supported (e.g., 𝔓⁷⁵, Vaticanus, Bezae, Regius, Freer Gospels), and should be retained.

17. *In your law it is written:* Critics who read this passage as Jesus' attempt to show his conformity to the Jewish legal tradition read v. 17 as a statement of an acceptable legal principle. Jesus then shows he fulfills the principle in the two witnesses of himself and his Father (v. 18). The interpretation reads vv. 17-18 as an indication that the prescription of the Law (v. 17) does not apply to the uniqueness of Jesus' revelation (v. 18). See also Schnackenburg, *Gospel* 2:194. Jesus creates a distance between himself and "the Jews" (here the Pharisees) by his description of the Law as "*your* Law."

18. *I bear witness to myself:* The Greek *egō eimi ho martyrōn* should be linked with Isa 43:10. It is a further claim (see v. 12) to be the authentic revelation of God. See Moloney, *Son of Man* 129–130.

    I bear witness . . . and the Father . . . bears witness: For the forensic interpretation of vv. 17-18 (Jesus and the Father are two witnesses) see Pancaro, *The Law in the Fourth Gospel* 275–278; Neyrey, "Jesus the Judge" 512–515; Cory, "Wisdom's Rescue" 104–105.

19. *Where is your father?:* It is unlikely that the issue of Jesus' illegitimacy lurks behind this question, as is suggested by Hoskyns, *Gospel* 332–333, following Cyril of Alexandria. It is another misunderstanding on the part of the Pharisees, who ask the wrong question. See Westcott, *Gospel* 129.

20. *These words he spoke in the treasury:* The "treasury" was situated between the court of the women and the inner court. A location is maintained close to the lights blazing every night in the court of the women.

John 8:21-30

21. Again he said to them, "I go away, and you will seek me and die in your sin; where I am going you cannot come." 22. Then said the Jews, "Will he kill himself, since he says, 'Where I am going you cannot come'?" 23. He said to them, "You are from below; I am from above. You are of this world; I am not of this world. 24. I told you that you would die in your sins, for you will die in your sins unless you believe that I am he." 25. They said to him, "Who are you?" Jesus said to them, "What is the point of talking to you? 26. I have much to say about you and much to judge; but the one who sent me is true, and I declare to the world what I have heard from him." 27. They did not understand that he spoke to them of the Father. 28. So Jesus said, "When you have lifted up the Son of man, then you will know that I am he, and that I do nothing on my own authority but speak thus as the Father taught me. 29. And the one who sent me is with me; he has not left me alone, for I always do what is pleasing to him." 30. As he spoke thus, many believed in him.

INTERPRETATION

The dialogue is resumed by the use of the expression "again" *(palin)*. In v. 21 Jesus brings to the fore his origin and destiny, an issue providing background to vv. 12-20. He tells his opponents he is going to a destiny beyond their reach. He has spoken to them of this on two earlier occasions (cf. 7:33-34; 8:14), but here a threat is added: they will seek him but die in their sins. The verb "to seek" *(zēteō)* has been used several times to indicate that they would seek but not find him (cf. 7:34, 36). It has also been used on those occasions when the narrator pointed to the plans of "the Jews" to kill Jesus (cf. 5:18; 7:1, 19, 20, 25, 30). Jesus now reverses the process. His going away will produce the death of those who seek him! The "going away" of Jesus may be through the violent intervention of "the Jews," but this going away is to be part of the hour of Jesus, the design of God that Jesus return to where he came from. It will lead to "the death" of his opponents. It may not be the same as the physical death of Jesus, but it will be a spiritual death resulting from a rejection of the revelation of God in and through Jesus (cf. 5:24).

The death theme remains as "the Jews" wonder if Jesus will kill himself (v. 22). At one level this is nonsense, as Jesus is not on a suicide mission (cf. Gen 9:5; 2 Sam 17:23; Josephus, *War* 3:375), but on another level Jesus will do whatever the Father wishes him to do (cf. 4:34; 5:36). In some sense, therefore, there is a death willed by the Father and accepted by Jesus that will take him back to the Father, to a place where "the Jews" can never come. The misunderstanding of "the Jews" is based on Jesus' origins (v. 23). In words that recall the discussion with Nicodemus (3:12-15) Jesus tells "the Jews" that they fail because they *(hymeis)* are "from below" *(ek tōn katō)*, while he *(egō)* is "from above" *(ek tōn anō)*. This gulf must be overcome if "the Jews" wish to be saved from their sins. The words and actions of Jesus are to be understood and judged in terms of the link between himself and his origins and destiny "above." "The Jews" are only able to respond to these words and actions in terms of the horizontal, humanly conditioned traditions of "below."

But the gulf can still be overcome. "The procession of the Jews along the road of sin which leads to death is imposed upon them by no categorical necessity" (Hoskyns, *Gospel* 334). Jesus sounds a note of hope. He has told them they will die in their sins (v. 24a), but this need not necessarily be the case: "You will die in your sins *unless you believe that I am he*" (v. 24b). "The division between what is above and what is below need not be absolute. For the Revealer who comes down from above enables man to ascend the heights. The division is only made final by unbelief" (Bultmann, *Gospel* 348). Jesus instructs "the Jews" that they can avoid spiritual death by believing in him as I AM *(egō eimi)*. The LXX, and especially LXX

Deutero-Isaiah, uses the expression *egō eimi* to insist that YHWH is revealed as the unique God of Israel over against all other claimants (cf. LXX Isa 41:4; 43:10, 13; 45:18; 46:4; 48:12). Using the same formula Jesus reveals his *unique* claim to be the presence of the divine in the human story. If "the Jews" believe that Jesus is the revelation of the Father they will bridge the gulf between "below" and "above" that is leading them to death in their sins.

The "who are you" of v. 25a is not a rejection of Jesus but an honest question indicating that many of the pretensions of "the Jews" are, at least temporarily, laid aside. However, they may be asking this question too late, as many decisions against Jesus have already been taken, and it is the question that he has been answering throughout the story thus far. He responds to them with a question, however rhetorical, of his own (v. 25b) that reflects "a mood of yearning impatience" (Strachan, *Fourth Gospel* 209). Throughout the encounters between Jesus and "the Jews" in chs. 7–8 "the Jews" have not been able to reach beyond what they can see, touch, and control. Their measure is always a fixed understanding of the Mosaic tradition. In vv. 23-24 Jesus has described the gap that must be bridged if "the Jews" are to be saved from their sins, but their question of v. 25a still displays puzzlement. In the face of such obtuseness Jesus asks: "What is the point of talking to you?" (v. 25b). Jesus may express exasperation, but hope continues. There is much that he could say and bring against "the Jews" because of their hardheadedness (v. 26a), but *(alla)* this is not the way of Jesus. He has not come to do what *he* might regard as opportune. The truth lies in the one who sent him, and Jesus comes to declare to the world what he had heard from him (v. 26b). The all-determining significance of the Father who sent Jesus is indicated by the narrator's comment in v. 27: "They did not understand that he spoke to them of the Father." Jesus is concerned with "the Jews'" response to the one who sent him, but they are unable to grasp this. Their question, "who are you" (v. 25a) can only be understood in terms of the Father, but they did not understand that he spoke to them of the Father (v. 27).

Jesus makes a final attempt to convince his audience (vv. 28-29), and his attempts are rewarded (v. 30). Throughout the story Jesus has claimed that he makes God known, and that anyone who believes in him will come to eternal life. Both dark and bright sides of the story coalesce in v. 28 where "the Jews" are told that they will lift up the Son of Man. This can mean nothing else than that they will crucify him (cf. 3:13-14). However, in the elevated Son of Man, a "lifting up" performed by "the Jews," the revelation of God will take place. Then they will know of the oneness between Jesus and the Father. "The Jews" have been told they will be freed from their sins if they believe Jesus' claim: *egō eimi* (v. 24). The promise of v. 28a is about neither salvation nor condemnation, but about the possibility of both offered to people of all times. The linking of the term *egō eimi* with the lifting up of Jesus is further explained in v. 28b: Jesus' claim to be the revelation of God in his lifting up flows from his total dependence on the Father. Everything Jesus says and does is ultimately the word and action of the Father (cf. 5:19-30), authentic revelation, further clarification of Jesus' claim in v. 12. He is the light of the world who will bring the light of life to all who follow him (cf. 3:16-21, 31-36). The ongoing reliability of Jesus' revelation of the Father comes from the continual presence of the Father with the Son. The oneness of Father and Son (v. 28b-29) is the basis for Jesus' claim to be the unique revelation of God (v. 28a: *egō eimi*). The Father is always with Jesus (v. 29a) and because of this all the Son does is pleasing to the Father, in perfect concurrence with his will (v. 29bc). Without any further detail the narrator announces that many *(polloi)* of "the Jews" are led to belief in Jesus *(episteusan eis auton)* by these words of Jesus *(tauta autou lalountos)*. The threats (v. 24) and promises (v. 28) have not gone unrewarded (v. 30). There are "Jews" in Jesus' audience who become followers of Jesus. Indeed, the Johannine community existed because this was true.

Conclusion to 8:12-30. During the celebration of Tabernacles Jesus has revealed himself as the light of the world, perfecting and rendering universal the celebration of the Temple as the light of all Jerusalem and the Law as the lamp and light that lead to God. The discussion that follows this revelation turns upon God as the Father of Jesus. The obtuseness and resistance from the Pharisees (vv. 12-20) and "the Jews" (vv. 21-30) are created by their determination to judge everything by their Law (cf. v. 17). They are controlled by "below" and Jesus and the Father can only be understood by an openness to "above" (cf. v. 23). Thus they know neither Jesus nor the Father (v. 19). Only acceptance of God as the Father of Jesus will solve the mystery of Jesus, living water (7:37-38) and light of the world (8:12). But "they did not know that he spoke to them of the Father" (v. 27). As each day the priests proclaim their allegiance to the one true God (cf. *m. Sukk.* 5:4), turning their backs on the rising sun, they are now running the danger of turning their backs on the source of living water (7:37-38) and the light of the world (8:12), the one sent by God (8:16, 18, 26, 29).

Jesus fulfills, universalizes, and transcends the symbols and expectations of Tabernacles because of his union with God (8:28-29). He tells "the Jews" of a future event when they will lift up the Son of Man. Then they will recognize his oneness with God (v. 28-29). Surprisingly, many of "the Jews" accept him (v. 30). But "many" does not mean "all." The threat of death (cf. 7:1, 11, 19, 25) and the violence surrounding Jesus' presence in Jerusalem for the celebration of Tabernacles (cf. 7:30, 32, 44; 8:20) have not disappeared.

NOTES

21. *Again he said to them:* Despite suggestions to the contrary, vv. 12-20 and 21-30 are closely linked. One of the causes for separating them is the change in Jesus' opponents. They are the Pharisees in vv. 12-20 (cf. 7:33-34; 8:13) and "the Jews" in vv. 21-30. Strictly, he is still speaking to the Pharisees in 8:21, as the *autois* ("to them") must look back to the Pharisees of v. 13. However, it is "the Jews" who are puzzled by these words. Throughout chs. 7–8 "the Jews" and the Pharisees are the same group. See Tsuchido, "Tradition and Redaction" 60.

22. *Will he kill himself?:* On the misunderstanding and the irony involved in this play on the notion of killing and dying see Leroy, *Rätsel und Mißverstandnis* 59–63; Duke, *Irony* 85–86.

23. *You are from below; I am from above. You are of this world; I am not of this world:* The repeated use of the pronouns: "you *(hymeis)* . . . I *(egō)*; you *(hymeis)* . . . I *(egō)*" accentuates the distance between "the Jews" ("you") and Jesus ("I").

24. *that I am he:* There has been much discussion over the origin and meaning of the absolute use of *egō eimi*. It may have its roots in the revelation of God to Moses in Exod 3:14, but the linguistic parallels between LXX Exod 3:14 and the NT use of the formula are fragile. It is best understood in light of the prophetic formula used in both the MT and the LXX to affirm the uniqueness of YHWH over against all other gods. For further discussion and bibliography see Moloney in *NJBC* 1423–1424. In support of this position, and with special reference to 8:24, 28, see Zimmermann, "Das absolute *egō eimi*" 54–69; 266–276; Riedl, "Wenn ihr den Menschensohn" 364–366. Freed, "*Egō eimi* in John VIII.28" 163–166, claims that *egō eimi* was a pre-Johannine title for the Messiah that "the Jews" refuse to recognize in Jesus. Bultmann, *Gospel* 348–349, draws vv. 24 and 28 together by eliminating vv. 25-27 as a clumsily inserted fragment (cf. pp. 350–351) and argues that v. 24 means "unless you believe that I am the Son of Man."

25. *What is the point of talking to you?:* The text at this point is notoriously obscure. Is it a question (as in the translation given and NRSV) or a statement (e.g., RSV)? Are the Greek words *tēn archēn* to be read as an accusative noun ("the beginning"), or an adverb ("primarily")? Should one read *hoti* ("that" or "because") or *ho ti* ("that which")? The above translation reads *tēn archēn hoti kai lalō hymin* literally as "why am I speaking to you at all?" For the textual, grammatical, and rhetorical reasons for this translation see Moloney, *Son of Man* 133–134. One of the crucial considerations for making sense of this impossible sentence is context. Miller, "Christology" 257–265, and Brodie, *Gospel* 327–328, adopt the translation "I am the One at the Beginning, which is what I keep telling you" (Miller, "Christology" 263). Neither Miller nor Brodie, however, relates this satisfactorily to v. 26.

26. *I have much to say . . . but the one who sent me:* There is a deliberate contrast between what Jesus could say about the unwillingness of "the Jews" to hear his words (v. 26a) and the greater design of God, accepting what God is doing

in and through Jesus (v. 26b). This is created by the use of "but" *(alla)*. See Barrett, *Gospel* 284.

28. *When you have lifted up the Son of Man:* For a detailed study of vv. 28-29 see Moloney, *Son of Man* 135–141. In support of John 8:28 as a combination of the violent action of "the Jews" and the revelation of God in and through the crucified Jesus see Riedl, "Wenn ihr den Menschensohn" 360–361; Morgan-Wynne, "The Cross and the Revelation" 219–220. For Cory, "Wisdom's Rescue" 105–111, the "lifting up" is the moment when Jesus, the Wisdom of God (cf. 1:1-18), is rescued at the moment of death (cf. 8:24, 28) and those who conspire against Wisdom are warned that they will be punished: they will die in their sins (cf. 8:24).

    then you will know: Bultmann, *Gospel* 349–350, claims that these words indicate it is already too late for "the Jews." The response in v. 30 surely suggests that they are a message of hope. See also Léon-Dufour, *Lecture* 2:274–275; Riedl, "Wenn ihr den Menschensohn" 362–370.

    and that I do nothing on my own authority: The affirmations of v. 28b are governed by the "you will know that *(hoti)*" of v. 28a. "The Jews" will know *that* Jesus makes God known *(hoti egō eimi)*, and that *(hoti)* he does nothing on his own authority (cf. Bernard, *Commentary* 2:303). They will come to know both truths.

29. *he has not left me alone:* After the present tense "he who sent me is with me" *(met' emou estin)*, one would expect a perfect tense. Instead one finds an aorist *(aphēken)*. This could be a reference to the incarnation. God is present with the Word before (cf. 1:1-2) and after the incarnation (cf. 1:14). See Morgan-Wynne, "The Cross and the Revelation" 221–223.

30. *many believed in him:* The expression *pisteuein eis* (to believe in) is sometimes claimed as a sure indication of correct Johannine faith, while *pisteuein en* or *pisteuein* followed by the dative is regarded as a limited expression of faith. In v. 30 *pisteuein eis* appears, and it does indicate true faith. However, this distinction should not be applied too rigidly. The context must play an important part in each interpretation.

3. Jesus and "the Jews" in Conflict Over Their Respective Origins (8:31-59)

The passion of the encounters that follow and the bitterness of the accusation and counter-accusation make 8:31-59 the most difficult section of the Gospel. A unifying narrative effect is created by the relentless increase in hostility between the only protagonists in the story, Jesus and "the Jews," and by regular reference to Abraham (cf. vv. 33, 37, 39, 40, 52, 53, 56, 57, 58). As with 8:12-30 the passage should be regarded as a literary unit, but for the sake of clarity it will be read in three parts: vv. 31-38, vv. 39-47, and vv. 48-59.

John 8:31-38

31. Jesus then said to the Jews who had believed in him, "If you abide in my word you are truly my disciples, 32. and you will know the truth, and the truth will make you free." 33. They answered him, "We are descendants of Abraham and have never been in bondage to any one. How is it that you say, 'You will be made free'?" 34. Jesus answered them, "Amen, amen I say to you, every one who commits sin is a slave to sin. 35. The slave does not abide in the house for ever; the son abides for ever. 36. So if the Son makes you free, you will be free indeed. 37. I know that you are descendants of Abraham; yet you seek to kill me, because my word finds no place in you. 38. I speak of what I have seen with my Father, and you do what you have heard from your father."

INTERPRETATION

Jesus continues to speak to "the Jews" (v. 31) but the narrative demands that the many who believed in him (v. 30: *polloi episteusan eis auton*) and the group now described as "the Jews who had believed in him" (v. 31: *tous pepisteukotas autǭ Ioudaious*) cannot be the same. The change in the tense of the verb from aorist (v. 30) to perfect (v. 31), and the change in syntax from *pisteuein eis* (v. 30) to *pisteuein* followed by the dative (v. 31) indicate that an ongoing section of "the Jews" have the beginnings of belief in Jesus but still have some way to go (cf. 2:23-25). The many who believed in Jesus in v. 30 because of his promise in vv. 28-29 have departed from the scene, but some of "the Jews" remain. They have come to partial faith in Jesus and remain there (perfect tense). Jesus attempts to draw them into authentic belief. He exhorts them to persist, to go on "abiding" *(ean hymeis meinēte)* in his word. There is a dynamic in the journey of faith from partial to full faith (cf. 2:1–4:54), and by committing themselves to that journey by "abiding" in the word of Jesus that they are struggling to grasp they can be regarded as disciples *(mathētai)* of Jesus. A disciple is always at the school of Jesus. "It is not immediate assent but steadiness of faith that gives character to genuine discipleship" (Bultmann, *Gospel* 434). Their journey into true faith will lead "the Jews" into a knowledge of the truth *(tēn alētheian)*, the knowledge of God made possible through the revelation that takes place uniquely in Jesus (cf. 1:18; 3:13; 6:46). This revelation will produce freedom. To believe in the revelation of God that comes through Jesus Christ gives one power to become a child of God (cf. 1:12-13). But Judaism taught that the study of the Law made people free (cf. *Exod. Rab.* 12:2; *Sifre Lev.* 11; *Sifre Num.* 115:5, 1-3; *Pirqe ʾAbot* 3:5; 6:2) and *Targum Neofiti* on Gen 15:11 even promises delivery of the wicked "in the merits of their father Abram" (cf. Sabugal, "'Y la Verdad'" 177–181). This promise is transcended by the words of Jesus as he tells "the Jews" that through acceptance of his revelation of God *(he alētheia)* they will be set free.

"The Jews" have no need for any such freedom (v. 33). They have it because they are descendants of Abraham *(sperma Abraam)*. The ensuing conflict (vv. 34-47) presupposes that the revelation of Jesus promised in vv. 31-32 would give "the Jews" the freedom that is power to become *tekna theou* (1:12), but they are unable to look beyond what they can control and understand. They insist they have never been slaves to anyone because they are *sperma Abraam* (v. 33a), and they question Jesus' right and ability to tell them he has a way that will lead them into freedom (v. 33b). Again the clash emerges between two differing understandings of the way in which God is made known. Jesus' words, beginning with the double "amen," link what follows with what has gone before. "The Jews" claim freedom because they are *sperma Abraam* (v. 33), but Jesus replies that physical descent is not the measure of freedom or slavery (v. 34). Sinfulness arises in what a person *does:* "everyone who commits sin is a slave to sin." This does not depend on bloodline. Of the two possible categories of people in a home, slaves and "sons," "the Jews" claim to be "sons" on the basis of their physical descent, but are they? At the beginning of this encounter Jesus exhorted them to "abide" in his word (v. 31). Such an "abiding" in the word of Jesus produces true freedom (v. 32). Slaves do not abide in the household, while "sons" remain forever (v. 35). Are Jesus' listeners able to accept his recommendation that they "abide" in his word (v. 31), or are they to be judged as slaves because they do evil things (v. 34)? Is their presence in the household temporary, or is it "forever" (v. 35)?

The answer to these questions is provided by means of a shift in the meaning of "son." It is Jesus, the Son, who sets people free in a genuine freedom that will last (v. 36). Jesus knows that at the level of their bloodline "the Jews" can claim physical descent from Abraham. They are *sperma Abraam*, but "the Jews" are living proof that physical descent does not determine sonship and freedom (v. 37). Jesus makes known, by means of his word, what he knows from his oneness with the Father (v. 38), but "the Jews" are unable to "make space" *(ou chōrei)* for the word of Jesus (v. 37c). The verb *chōreō* means to "make space," and it involves an active opening up of the recipient so that something or someone might enter (cf. Mark 2:2; Matt 19:11-12). There is no active openness among "the Jews" to the word of Jesus. Indeed, they are involved in a plot to kill him (v. 37b). They may claim to be *sperma Abraam*, but they are not his children. If they were they would never seek to rid themselves of the Son of God. Their paternity must be judged according to their actions, and they must be the children of another father (v. 38b). The criterion for sinfulness provided in v. 34 is being used in this judgment of "the Jews":

"everyone who commits sin is a slave to sin." Jesus has offered a way out of this slavery into freedom, but it is being rejected. A rapid and dramatic change of atmosphere has occurred. In v. 31 Jesus addressed "the Jews" who had the beginnings of belief. In v. 38 he accuses the same group of belonging to another father because of their deeds and their refusal to make space for his revealing word. Who might this father be? Obviously, it cannot be the Father of Jesus.

NOTES

31. *Jesus then said to the Jews:* The unity of this passage, created by the continual presence of the same protagonists (Jesus and "the Jews") and the theme of Abraham, makes it difficult to divide into neat literary sections. See the important suggestions of Dodd, "Behind a Johannine Dialogue" 41–42; Robert, "Étude littéraire" 71–84; Schenke, "Joh 7–10" 185–187; Tuñí Vancells, *La verdad* 104–124; Neyrey, "Jesus the Judge" 509–542. The divisions found here are offered as approximations. See UBSGNT; Lindars, *Gospel* 323, 327, 331; Brodie, *Gospel* 340–341.

    who had believed in him: The verb *pisteuein* is followed by the dative case to indicate a situation of limited belief. See, however, the note to 8:30, and Moloney, *Belief* 104–106. The problem of "the Jews" who believe in vv. 30-31 and then attempt to murder Jesus in v. 59 is the source of much debate. In a celebrated study Dodd, "Behind a Johannine Dialogue" 42–47, claims that the "believing Jews" are the same, and that they are Judaizing Christians. Most, however, would separate the groups. See, for example, Westcott, *Gospel* 133; Lightfoot, *Gospel* 192; Brodie, *Gospel* 328–329. Brown, *Gospel* 1:354–355, explains the difficulty as a gloss, using "the Jews" as the inhabitants of Jerusalem. For a survey see Swetnam, "The Meaning" 106–107. Swetnam (pp. 107–109) suggests that the verb is pluperfect in meaning: "the Jews" once believed, but no longer do so. For a response to Swetnam and a position very close to the one adopted in the interpretation see Segalla, "Un appello alla perseveranza" 387–389.

32. *If you abide in my word:* The use of *ean* ("if") followed by the aorist subjunctive *meinēte* ("you abide") indicates a desire on the part of Jesus that an action already initiated be brought to its impending fruition. See BDF 188–190, §§ 371-372.

    the truth will make you free: This is one of the more celebrated Johannine phrases. Scholars are divided over the meaning of "the truth" (*hē alētheia*). For a general study of the use of the expression, indicating that it means the revelation of God that takes place in Jesus, see de la Potterie, *La vérité* 1:23–26. Other scholars see the expression as coming from the Gospel's gnostic background and as pointing not to the revelation of God, but to the very reality of God. See, for example, Bultmann, *Gospel* 434: "God's *alētheia* thus is God's reality, which alone is reality because it is life and gives life." See also the studies of 8:32 by Atal, "Die Wahrheit" 283–289; Tuñí Vancells, *La verdad* 125–164;

Lategan, "The truth that sets man free" 71–74. The interpretation given above is largely inspired by the exhaustive study of de la Potterie, *La vérité* 2:789–866. For the link between Law and freedom see 2:811–814, and for an evaluation of the Stoic and gnostic parallels see 2:792–805.

33. *We are descendants of Abraham:* On the importance of the Jewish claim to be the physical descendants of Abraham see Joachim Jeremias, *Jerusalem in the Time of Jesus: An Investigation into Economic and Social Conditions during the New Testament Period.* London: SCM Press, 1969, 271–302.

    never been in bondage to anyone: It is sometimes pointed out by the commentators that this claim is not true, and had not been true for several hundred years (e.g., Bauer, *Johannesevangelium* 125). The freedom involved, however, may refer to their spiritual freedom, no matter what their political situation (e.g., Carson, *Gospel* 349).

34. *is a slave to sin:* Some witnesses (Sinaitic Syriac, Bezae, Clement of Alexandria) omit "to sin" *(tēs hamartias).* The weight of superior textual support (e.g., $\mathfrak{P}^{66.75}$, Sinaiticus, Vaticanus, Ephraemi Rescriptus) supports the claims of several scholars (Bauer, Dodd, Tuñí Vancells) that the reading "a slave to sin" makes better sense in the context.

35. *the slave does not abide in the house forever:* The argument from v. 31 to v. 35 is unified by the use of "abide" *(menein)* in v. 31 and v. 35, "to be in bondage" *(douleuein)* in v. 33 and "slave" *(doulos)* in vv. 34-35, and "seed/descendant" *(sperma)* in v. 33 and the allied "son" *(huios)* in vv. 34-35.

36. *if the Son makes you free:* Several scholars (e.g., Dodd, *Tradition* 381–383; Lindars, "Slave and Son" 270–286) argue that 8:35-36 was originally an independent parable about slaves and sons incorporated into the Johannine text.

38. *my Father . . . your father:* The possessive pronouns "my" and "your" are not found in the best manuscript tradition, although they have been added by many scribes in an attempt to clarify. They are in the translation because this meaning is made clear by the presence of the personal pronouns *egō* ("what I have seen") and *hymeis* ("what you have heard").

    my word finds no place in you: The use of the verb *chōrein* with the idea of "to make space for" is effective, but somewhat clumsy. See the discussion in Bernard, *Commentary* 2:309. Not all would interpret the expression as "to make space" (cf. Hoskyns, *Gospel* 341), and some suggest that it means "to make progress" (cf. Bauer, *Johannesevangelium* 125).

    from your father: Jesus is not telling "the Jews" at this stage that they are children of the devil. A question has been raised: if they slay the Son of God, then whose children are they? It will be answered later in the discussion (v. 44).

John 8:39-47

39. They answered him, "Abraham is our father." Jesus said to them, "If you were Abraham's children you would do what Abraham did, 40. but now you seek to kill me, a man who has told you the truth that I heard

from God; this is not what Abraham did. 41. You do what your father did." They said to him, "We were not born of fornication; we have one Father, even God." 42. Jesus said to them, "If God were your Father you would love me, for I proceeded and came forth from God; I came not of my own accord, but God sent me. 43. Why do you not understand what I say? It is because you cannot bear to hear my word. 44. You are of your father the devil, and your will is to do your father's desires. He was a murderer from the beginning, and has nothing to do with the truth because there is no truth in him. When he lies he speaks according to his own nature, for he is a liar and the father of lies. 45. But because I tell the truth you do not believe me. 46. Which of you convicts me of sin? If I tell the truth, why do you not believe me? 47. Whoever is of God hears the words of God; the reason why you do not hear them is that you are not of God."

INTERPRETATION

The question of a father has been raised. Who is the Father of Jesus and who is the father of "the Jews"? "The Jews" lay claim to Abrahamic paternity on the basis of their physical roots, but Abraham's status as the father of the nation has its roots in his openness to the word of God. He was a man of faith who from his setting out from Ur of the Chaldees (cf. Gen 12:1-9) to risking the life of his only son (cf. Gen 22:1-17) "made space" for the word of God as it came to him. If "the Jews" were the genuine children of Abraham (*tekna tou Abraam*) they would behave as he did (v. 39). But they have rejected the revelation of God in the word of Jesus. Indeed, they seek to kill the one who makes known the truth that comes from God, and in doing so they have lost their claim to be children of Abraham. Abraham welcomes the heavenly messengers (cf. Gen 18:1-18), but "the Jews" reject a man who brings a message from God. They do not behave as Abraham did (v. 40). As this is the case, their paternity must lie elsewhere (v. 41a), as Jesus has already suggested (v. 38b). To be a child of God one must accept the word of God. To refuse his word is to choose another father. The argument of vv. 37-38 has been repeated in vv. 39-41a.

"The Jews" respond by accusing Jesus of birth in fornication, while they are children of the one God (v. 41b). This accusation is based on the OT use of the imagery of fornication to speak of spiritual infidelity to or apostasy from God (cf. Hos 1:2; 4:46; 4:15; Ezek 16:15, 33-34. See also *Num. Rab.* 2:17-26). They then move logically from their claim to have Abraham as their father (v. 39) to say they "have one Father, even God" (v. 41c). Because of the covenant forged between YHWH and a people, "the Jews" regard themselves as God's children (cf. Exod 4:22; Deut 14:1; 32:6; Jer 3:4, 19; 31:9; Isa 63:16; 64:7). They associate themselves with the early morning

confession of the priests, celebrated each day during the feast of Tabernacles (cf. *m. Sukk. 5:4*), but Jesus responds that if they were truly the children of God they would love Jesus who proceeded and came forth from
God as God's Sent One (v. 42). The narrator's comment in 3:35, that the
Father loved the Son, is the basis for 8:42: children of the same father love
one another. The anger and mounting violence surrounding Jesus at this
celebration of the one true God show that Jesus and "the Jews" cannot be
children of the same Father.

Jesus asks why "the Jews" do not understand what he says (v. 43a),
and then answers his question. They do not hear the spoken word of
Jesus (v. 43a: *lalian tēn emēn*) because they are not open to his revealing
message (v. 43b: *logon ton emon*). Not only are they not willing to make
space for the word of Jesus (v. 37), they are now accused of not being capable *(ou dynasthe)* of hearing the word of Jesus because of their origins
(v. 43b), because their father is the devil (v. 44a). They speak and act according to their origins: "your will is to do your father's desires" (v. 44b).
Jesus' words and actions are driven by the will of his Father (cf. 4:34;
5:36), just as the words and actions of "the Jews" are driven by the will of
their father, the devil (v. 44b). The description of the devil that follows (v.
44cd) is based on the actions of the devil "from the beginning" (v. 44c: *ap'
archēs*). By means of lies and deceit he robbed Adam of YHWH's original
promise of immortality. He is thus a liar and a murderer (cf. Gen 3:1-24;
Wis 2:24). His deceits also led to the first murder, Cain's slaying of Abel
(Gen 4:1-15). In the beginning the devil was against God, deceiving and
murdering humankind (contrast John 1:1-5). Everything about the devil
is opposed to Jesus: he "has nothing to do with the truth because there is
no truth in him" (v. 44c). Jesus reveals the truth as he tells the story of God
(cf. 1:14, 17-18; 8:32, 40), while the devil is the denial of all truth. It was
the devil's role at the beginning of human history, instituting a situation
of lies, deceit, and death, that made him "the father of lies" (v. 44d). There
are, therefore, two powers at the beginning of the human story: God who
is true, and the devil who is the father of lies. Jesus speaks the truth (v. 45:
tēn alētheian legō). The word of Jesus is the revelation of truth in the
human story, reflecting his origins with God, his Father. But "the Jews,"
reflecting their origins in one who of his nature speaks a lie (v. 44d: "when
he lies he speaks according to his own nature"), do not believe in Jesus'
word (v. 45). The revelation of the truth among the children of one who is
the father of lies leads inevitably to rejection and denial.

Jesus closes this section of the discussion with an accusation formed
by two rhetorical questions (v. 46). The second of these questions is answered in v. 47, while the first question remains unanswered because it is
unanswerable. Jesus challenges "the Jews," children of the father of lies,
to convict him of sin (v. 46a). This is impossible, as a liar is in no position

to convict the one who speaks the truth. That "the Jews" are liars is at the heart of Jesus' second question (v. 46b). It is against their very nature as the children of the devil to accept the word of truth. They belong to untruth. The only answer "the Jews" could give to Jesus' question, "Why do you not believe me?" is "Because we cannot." Earlier he asked them, "Why do you not understand what I say?" (v. 43a). He then answered for them: "Because you cannot *(hoti ou dynasthe)*" (v. 43b).

In the Johannine view of God and the world two classes of people are involved in this discussion: those who are "of God" *(ek tou theou)* and those who are "not of God" *(tou theou ouk este)*. "The Jews" belong to the latter group (v. 47). The word of Jesus is the revelation of God, and a person who is "of God" will hear it. Such "hearing" is impossible for those who are children of the devil (v. 44). The discussion of the two fathers has come full circle since "the Jews" claimed Abraham as their father in v. 39.

NOTES

39. *If you were Abraham's children:* Jesus changes the language used to speak of the relationship between "the Jews" and Abraham. They had claimed they were descendants (literally "seed") of Abraham *(sperma Abraam)* in vv. 33 and 37. Jesus is now testing whether or not they are children of Abraham *(tekna Abraam)* with words possibly reminiscent of the Prologue's promise that the believers would become children of God (1:12: *tekna theou*).

    you would do what Abraham did: Some ancient manuscripts (Vaticanus; 𝔓66) have the imperative *poieite:* "If you are Abraham's children, do Abraham's works." This does not change the meaning of the passage a great deal, and is followed by a number of commentators (e.g., Westcott, *Gospel* 135; Lagrange, *Evangile* 245–246; Bernard, *Commentary* 2:310). See the discussion in Barrett, *Gospel* 347.

40. *you seek to kill me, a man:* The expression "a man" *(anthrōpon* without an article) should not be made to bear any theological significance. It simply means "the one" *(tis)*. See BDF 158, § 301 (2).

    this is not what Abraham did: A distinction is made by the later rabbis between people who act like Abraham and others who act like Balaam *(Pirke Abot* 5:19, 29). See Talbert, *Reading John* 156.

41. *We were not born of fornication:* It is possible that the background to these words is the widespread later Jewish tradition that Jesus was the illegitimate son of Mary. The interpretation does not adopt this position, as it is hard to be sure whether such a reference is possible as early as the late first century, given the late dates of the rabbinic material that reports these traditions. See John P. Meier, *A Marginal Jew: Rethinking the Historical Jesus*. ABRL. Garden City, N.Y.: Doubleday, 1991, 222–229, 245–252.

42. *I proceeded and came forth from God; I came not of my own accord but he sent me:* A
    series of terms stresses Jesus' dependence on God: "I proceeded . . . I came
    . . . he sent" (*exēlthon, hēchō, apesteilen*). These verbs refer to the event of
    Jesus' coming into the world (cf. Schnackenburg, *Gospel* 2:212). The verb *hēchō*
    was familiar in the religious language of the time, used for the saving ap-
    pearance of a deity (cf. Barrett, *Gospel* 348).

43. *you do not understand what I say . . . you cannot bear to hear my word:* The noun
    lalia is used to speak of Jesus' audible word. It may be related to current lan-
    guage associated with revealer figures (cf. Bultmann, *Gospel* 316 n. 7). Unable
    to understand his spoken word *(lalia)*, "the Jews" cannot grasp and obey
    ("hear") his revelation of God (his *logos*). See Barrett, *Gospel* 348.

44. *You are of your father the devil:* This may mean "you are of the father of the
    devil" (cf. Westcott, *Gospel* 137), which has traces of gnostic doctrine. For this
    background and early Christian reflection upon the idea, see Bauer, *Johannes-*
    evangelium 127–129. The dualism in the Fourth Gospel is moral, not meta-
    physical. Among many, see Schnackenburg, *Gospel* 2:214–215.

    your father the devil: Jesus' words in vv. 44-47 are the most negative said
    against "the Jews" in the NT (cf. Becker, *Evangelium* 1:304). But, as was pointed
    out in the Introduction, "the Jews" in the Fourth Gospel are never the Jewish
    people as such. The term reflects the christological polemic that led to the
    breakdown between the Johannine community and the local synagogue. For
    interpretations along these lines see Grässer, "Die Juden als Teufelsöhne"
    154–167; Porsch, "Ihr hat den Teufel zum Vater" 50–57. This is missed by the
    attempt of Reim, "Joh 8.44—Gotteskinder/Teufelskinder" 619–624, to link the
    passage with Cain and Abel speculation via a remanaging of the text.

47. *whoever is of God . . . you are not of God:* This final comment from Jesus points
    to the crucial nature of the question of origins. In this passage the origins of
    both Jesus and "the Jews" have been developed in terms of two contrasting
    "father-son" relationships. The concept is "central to the whole argument"
    (Lindars, *Gospel* 330).

John 8:48-59

48. The Jews answered him, "Are we not right in saying that you are a
Samaritan and have a demon?" 49. Jesus answered, "I have not a demon;
but I honor my Father, and you dishonor me. 50. Yet I do not seek my
own glory; there is One who seeks it and he will be the judge. 51. Amen,
amen, I say to you, anyone who keeps my word will never see death."
52. The Jews said to him, "Now we know that you have a demon. Abraham died, as did the prophets; and you say, 'Anyone who keeps my
word will never taste death.' 53. Are you greater than our father Abraham, who died? And the prophets died! Who do you claim to be?" 54.
Jesus answered, "If I glorify myself, my glory is nothing; it is my Father
who glorifies me, of whom you say, "He is our God." 55. But you have
not known him; I know him. If I said I do not know him, I should be a

liar like you; but I do know him and I keep his word. 56. Your father Abraham rejoiced that he was to see my day; he saw it and was glad." 57. The Jews then said to him, "You are not yet fifty years old, and have you seen Abraham?" 58. Jesus said to them, "Amen, amen I say to you, before Abraham was, I am." 59. So they took up stones to throw at him; but Jesus hid himself, and went out of the Temple.

INTERPRETATION

This final moment in the encounter between Jesus and "the Jews" in the Temple is a genuine dialogue during which two points of view clash. "The Jews" interrogate (vv. 48, 53, 57), affirm their point of view (v. 52), and react (v. 59a). Jesus answers their questions (vv. 49, 54-55), affirms his point of view (vv. 50-51, 56, 58), and reacts (v. 59b).

"The Jews" defend themselves against Jesus' claim that they are children of the devil by confidently ("are we not right in saying") accusing him of being a Samaritan, a member of a mixed and apostate race, and charging that he has a demon and therefore is insane (v. 48; cf. 7:20). They are setting their word *(legomen)* against the accusing word of Jesus. He responds by returning to the issue at stake: the Father. His words to "the Jews" flow from his union with the Father whom he seeks to honor *(timō)*, just as they seek to dishonor *(atimazate)* Jesus (v. 49). Judgment flows from the acceptance or refusal of Jesus (cf. 3:16-21, 36; 5:27; 8:16), and to honor the Father one must honor the Son (cf. 5:23). Jesus does not seek to establish his own fame *(doxa)*, but because he is the Sent One of the Father such fame will come in the Father's time and in the Father's way. The Father is the One who seeks *(zētōn)* it and who judges *(krinōn)* (v. 50). Behind the judgment that flows from the acceptance or refusal of the *doxa* of Jesus is God, the Father who sent Jesus. Everlasting life, therefore, flows from keeping the word of Jesus, holding on to it, carrying out its demands, and thus living by it (v. 51). Jesus' response to "the Jews'" rejection of his person (v. 48) is to reaffirm the central function of the revelation of God that takes place in him, leading to either life or death (vv. 49-51).

But "the Jews" will not be moved. They again lay claim to their ancestry in Abraham and the prophets (vv. 52-53). The familiar "we know" *(nun egnōkamen)* returns. They *know* their charge against Jesus (cf. v. 48) is true because the very words of Jesus condemn him. There is no openness to the word of Jesus that comes *from above*, as they remain in their world *of below* (cf. v. 23). Their words recall the Samaritan woman's inability to accept that Jesus could be greater than Jacob (cf. 4:11-12) as "the Jews" ask: "Are you greater than our father Abraham . . . the prophets?" (v. 53). They died; how can Jesus offer eternal life? They *know* that Jesus is not greater than Abraham or the prophets. The reader knows that he is! The question of death leads Jesus to repeat that he does not seek his own *doxa*. This depends entirely on the Father (v. 54. Cf. v. 50). An intervention of the Father will establish the *doxa* of Jesus. The enigma is that "the Jews" lay claim to the one true God (cf. also v. 41), but this is untrue; their father is the father of lies (v. 44). They cannot dishonor (v. 49) and seek to kill (cf. 5:18; 7:1) the Son of God and claim that his Father is also their one true God. "The Jews" do not know this God because they refuse to acknowledge the Son and accept his word (v. 55a), while Jesus knows God. If he were not to admit this knowledge he would join "the Jews" in their lies (v. 55b). Abraham may be at the source of the physical origins of "the Jews," but he is separated from them by the fact that he accepted God's design; he rejoiced that he was to see the day of Jesus, while they do not (v. 56). The faith of Abraham as it is recorded in the stories from Genesis was an example of one who looked forward to the accomplishment of God's plan. Early Jewish tradition held that Abraham had been privileged with a disclosure of the secrets of the ages to come, especially the messianic age (cf. *Targum Onkelos* on Gen 17:16-17; *Gen. Rab.* 44:22, 28; *4 Ezra* 3:14; *T. Levi* 18:14; *2 Bar* 4:4; *Apoc. Abr.* 31:1-3; *Tanh. Ber.* 6:20; *b.Sanh.* 108b), and this further claim to fame probably lies behind the words of Jesus. But this is tantamount to claiming that "the work of salvation . . . was actually complete in Jesus" (Barrett, *Gospel* 352). "The Jews," despite their claims to physical generation from their father Abraham, are separated from him by a huge gulf: he rejoiced to see the coming of Jesus while "the Jews" seek to kill him.

"The Jews" query how a man less than fifty years old could claim to have seen Abraham (v. 57). As throughout this debate (cf. vv. 52-53) they have not listened to the words of Jesus. He did not say he had seen Abraham, but that Abraham had rejoiced to see the day of Jesus. Introducing his final words with the double "amen," Jesus solemnly closes the discussion by speaking in a way incomprehensible to "the Jews," but true for anyone who has read and accepted the Prologue (1:1-18): "Amen, amen, I say to you, before Abraham was, I am." (v. 58) Jesus calls upon his having existed as the *logos*, turned in loving union toward God from before the beginning (1:1). Abraham, for all his greatness, belongs to the sequence of events that mark the passing of time. His story has finished; he has come and gone. This is not the case with Jesus. He speaks to "the Jews" from within the story time of the events of the feast of Tabernacles, but he transcends this time in an analepsis, a reference back to a point before and beyond the time of the story. Before the time of Abraham he was already in existence (1:1: *en archē ēn ho logos*). The expression "I am" (*egō eimi*) does not have the christological significance of other absolute uses of this expression (cf. 8:24, 28). It is an example of the present tense of the verb "to be" reaching outside all time, recalling the use of the imperfect tense of the same verb that highlighted the early part of the Prologue (1:1-4).

It has been said of 1:1: "If this be not true, the book is blasphemous" (Barrett, *Gospel* 156). Because "the Jews" stand outside the world of the Prologue they necessarily judge Jesus as a blasphemer and take up stones to slay him (v. 59a), but Jesus will not be slain by stoning. He must be "lifted up" (cf. 3:14; 8:28). Jesus hides himself (v. 59b: *ekrybē*), an action that recalls his manner of arrival in the Temple in 7:10 *(en kryptǭ)*. A major section of the narrative is closed by this return to the theme of secrecy, as Jesus leaves the Temple for the first time since 7:10 (8:59c).

Conclusion to 7:1–8:59. The story of Jesus' presence at the feast of Tabernacles makes christological claims that correspond with the major celebrations of the feast:

- Jesus is the revealer of the one and only God. He makes God known with a unique authority, over against all forms of idolatry (cf. *m. Sukk.* 5:4; John 7:14-24; 8:39-59).
- Jesus is the Messiah. Israel's messianic hopes are not nullified, but transcended and transformed (cf. Zech 14:16-19; John 7:25-31, 32-36).
- Jesus is the personification and universalization of the celebration of the gift of living water. The messianic hopes attached to such a gift are transformed and transcended (*m. Sukk.* 4:9-10; John 7:37, 48-52).
- Jesus is the personification and universalization of the celebration of the light of the Temple and of the city of Jerusalem (cf. *m. Sukk.* 5:2-4; John 8:12).
- The morning celebration of Israel's traditional God is at stake (cf. *m. Sukk.* 5:4). "They did not understand that he spoke to them of the Father" (John 8:27). "The Jews," who attempt to kill Jesus, are not children of Abraham or of the one true God, but children of the devil (8:37, 59; cf. 5:23).

What had been done in the Jewish Temple on the feast of Tabernacles was but a sign and a shadow of the perfection of the gift of God in the person of Jesus Christ (cf. 1:16-17), the Son of the one true God (7:14-24), the Messiah who could not be contained within Jewish messianic expectations (7:25-31, 32-36), the perfection of the gift of the Law as living water (7:37-39) and the light of the world (8:12). The Christians of the Johannine community had not lost contact with the celebration of the feast of Tabernacles, the *zikkarōn* of God's liberating, nourishing, and caring presence to God's people. In their unconditional commitment to the word of Jesus (cf. 2:1–4:54) they could claim: "We are the Lord's, and our eyes are turned to the Lord" (*m. Sukk.* 5:4). In Jesus Christ Tabernacle traditions are enfleshed, not destroyed. The Johannine community belonged to the Mosaic tradition, a tradition now perfected in the fullness of the gift of Jesus Christ (1:17). Those who would use the legislation of the former gift of the Law had no claim to be children of Abraham or children of God. They were children of the devil, a murderer from the beginning of time and the father of all lies. "The Jews" have lost their way in their rejection of God's design to perfect the former gift of the Law through Moses in the fullness of the gift that took place through Jesus Christ.

NOTES

48. *you are a Samaritan and have a demon:* The association between being a Samaritan and being possessed could come from the Jewish belief that Samaritan prophets were possessed by demons (cf. Bauer, *Johannesevangelium* 130–131).

49. *I have not a demon . . . you dishonor me:* The contrast between Jesus and "the Jews" is heightened by the use of the pronouns "I" . . . "you" *(egō . . . hymeis).*

51. *amen, amen, I say to you:* As throughout the Gospel, this unique Johannine use of the double "amen" links what has been said with what is about to follow by means of a major statement.

54. *it is my Father who glorifies me:* One should not limit the meaning of *doxa* to "honor" here (as does, for example, Bernard, *Commentary* 2:319). Jesus' words probably hint already at the link between his hour, his death, his being lifted up, and his glorification (cf. Brown, *Gospel* 1:366; Carson, *Gospel* 356). This link will become a major theme later in the Gospel.

   you say "he is our God": The Greek reads *hoti theos hēmon estin,* and should be rendered in direct speech. Scribes have attempted to render the passage as indirect speech, but not only is direct speech grammatically better (cf. Lagrange, *Evangile* 253), it points to the falsity of "the Jews'" claims. They must not associate the God of Jesus with their God who is, after v. 44, the devil.

56. *Abraham rejoiced that he was to see my day:* As is obvious in the interpretation, copious evidence from Jewish sources indicates that the background to Jesus' words is the idea that Abraham was privileged to see the secrets of the messianic age (cf. Schnackenburg, *Gospel* 2:221–223). It forces the issue to claim that Jesus speaks of a heavenly Abraham who is seeing him during his ministry (cf. Cavaletti, "La visione messianica" 179–181; Lindars, *Gospel* 334–335). There may be a link between Abraham's rejoicing in v. 56 and his joy in Gen 17:17 (cf. Hoskyns, *Gospel* 347–348).

57. *you are not yet fifty years old:* The number fifty indicates the common view of the end of a man's working life (cf. Num 4:2-3, 39; 8:24-25), but Edwards, "'Not Yet Fifty Years Old'" 449–454, has pointed out that the book of *Jubilees* uses "fifty years" to measure the eras since the creation. As Jesus' opponents apply this measure, his reply in 8:58 mocks them. He is outside any measure of the span of time.

58. *I am:* Lindars, *Gospel* 336, points to the unifying use of *egō eimi* in John 8: "'I am the light of the world' (v. 12) becomes 'I am (he),' i.e. the light and all other predicates which denote salvation (vv. 24 and 28); and this in turn becomes

the simple 'I am' of the present verse, denoting timeless pre-existence." There are no metaphysical claims here, for example "the timeless being of Deity" (Bernard, *Commentary* 2:322; Brodie, *Gospel* 336). Freed, "Who or What Was?" 52–59, claims that Jesus' words point to the Jewish belief in the preexistence of the Messiah. Jesus is that Messiah, "hidden to Jewish understanding" (p. 57).

For Reference and Further Study

Atal, Dosithée. "'Die Wahrheit wird euch freimachen' (Joh 8,32)." In Helmut Merklein and Joachim Lange, eds., *Biblische Randbemerkungen: Schüler-festschrift für Rudolf Schnackenburg zum 60. Geburtstag.* Würzburg: Echter Verlag, 1974, 283–299.

Bienaimé, Germain. "L'annonce des fleuves d'eau vive," *RTL* 21 (1990) 282–302.

_____. *Moïse et le don de l'eau dans la tradition juive ancienne: Targum et midrash.* AnBib 98. Rome: Biblical Institute Press, 1984.

Boismard, M.-É. "De son ventre couleront des fleuves d'eau," *RB* 65 (1958) 523–546.

Cavalletti, Sofia. "La visione messianica di Abramo (Giov. 8,58)," *BeO* 3 (1961) 179–181.

Cory, Catherine. "Wisdom's Rescue: A New Reading of the Tabernacles Discourse (John 7:1–8:59)," *JBL* 116 (1997) 95–116.

Dodd, C. H. "Behind a Johannine Dialogue." In idem, *More New Testament Studies.* Manchester: Manchester University Press, 1968, 41–57.

Edwards, M. J. "'Not Yet Fifty Years Old': John 8:57," *NTS* 40 (1994) 449–454.

Freed, Edwin D. "*Egō eimi* in John VIII.28 in the Light of its Context and Jewish Messianic Belief," *JThS* 33 (1982) 163–166.

_____. "Who or What Was Before Abraham in John 8:58?" *JSNT* 17 (1983) 52–59.

Giblin, C. H. "Suggestion, Negative Response and Positive Action in St John's Portrayal of Jesus (John 2.1-11.; 4.46-54.; 7.2-14.; 11:1-44)," *NTS* 26 (1979–1980) 206–208.

Goodman, Philip. *The Sukkot and Simhat Torah Anthology.* Philadelphia: Jewish Publication Society of America, 1973.

Grässer, Erich. "Die Juden als Teufelsöhne in Joh 8,37-47." In idem, *Der Alte Bund im Neuen.* WUNT 35. Tübingen: J. C. B. Mohr (Paul Siebeck), 1985, 154–167.

Grelot, Pierre. "Jean VII,38: eau du rocher ou source du Temple?" *RB* 70 (1963) 43–51.

Korteweg, T. "'You will seek me and you will not find me' (Jn 7,34). An Apocalyptic Pattern in Johannine Theology." In Jan Lambrecht, ed., *L'Apocalypse johannique et l'Apocalyptique dans le Nouveau Testament.* BETL 53. Gembloux: Duculot, 1980, 349–354.

Lategan, B. C. "The truth that sets man free. John 8:31-36," *Neotest.* 2 (1968) 70–80.

Lindars, Barnabas. "Slave and Son in John 8:31-36." In W. C. Weinrich, ed., *The New Testament Age: Essays in Honor of Bo Reicke.* Macon, Ga.: Mercer University Press, 1984, 270–286.

MacRae, George W. "The Meaning and Evolution of the Feast of Tabernacles," *CBQ* 22 (1960) 251–276.

Mehlmann, John. "Propheta a Moyse promissus in Io 7,52 citatus," *VD* 44 (1966) 79–88.

Menard, J. E. "L'interpretation patristique de Jo 7:38," *Revue de l'Université d'Ottawa* 25 (1955) 5–25.

Michaels, J. R. "The Temple Discourse in John." In R. N. Longenecker and M. C. Tenney, eds., *New Dimensions in New Testament Study.* Grand Rapids: Zondervan, 1974, 200–212.

Miller, E. L. "The Christology of John 8:25," *ThZ* 36 (1980) 257–265.

Moloney, Francis J. *Signs and Shadows* 65–116.

Morgan-Wynne, J. E. "The Cross and the Revelation of Jesus as *egō eimi* in the Fourth Gospel (John 8.28)." In E. A. Livingstone, ed., *Studia Biblica 1978 II: Papers on the Gospels: Sixth International Congress on Biblical Studies. Oxford 3–7 April 1978.* JSNT.S 2. Sheffield: JSOT Press, 1980, 219–226.

Neyrey, Jerome H. "Jesus the Judge: Forensic Process in John 8,21-59," *Bib.* 68 (1987) 409–442.

Pancaro, Severino A. "The Metamorphosis of a Legal Principle in the Fourth Gospel. A Closer Look at 7,51," *Bib.* 53 (1972) 340–361.

Pickering, S. R. "John 7:53–8:11: The Woman Taken in Adultery," *New Testament Textual Research Update* 1 (1993) 6–7.

Pinto da Silva, Alcides. "Giovanni 7,37-39," *Salesianum* 45 (1983) 575–592.

Porsch, Felix. "'Ihr hat den Teufel zum Vater' (Joh 8,44)," *BiKi* 44 (1989) 50–57.

Rahner, Hugo. "'Flumina de ventre Christi.' Die Patristische Auslegung von Joh 7:37-38," *Bib.* 22 (1941) 269–302.

Reim, Günter. "Joh 8.44—Gotteskinder/Teufelskinder: Wie antijudaistisch ist 'Die wohl antijudaistischste Äusserung des NT?'" *NTS* 30 (1984) 619–624.

Riedl, Johannes. "Wenn ihr den Menschensohn erhöht habt, werdet ihr erkennen (Joh 8,28)." In Rudolf Pesch and Rudolf Schnackenburg, eds., *Jesus und der Menschensohn: Für Anton Vögtle.* Freiburg: Herder, 1975, 355–370.

Robert, René. "Étude littéraire de Jean VIII.21-59," *RThom* 89 (1989) 71–84.

Sabugal, Santos. " . . . 'Y la Verdad os hará libres (Jn 8,32 a la luz de TPI Gen 15,11)," *Aug.* 14 (1974) 177–181.

Schaefer, Konrad R. "The Ending of the Book of Zechariah," *RB* 100 (1993) 165–238.

Schenke, Ludger. "Joh 7-10: Eine dramatische Szene," *ZNW* 80 (1989) 172–192.

Segalla, Giuseppe. "Un appello alla perseveranza nella fede in Gv 8,31-32?" *Bib.* 62 (1981) 387–389.

Swetnam, James. "The meaning of *pepisteukotas* in John 8,31," *Bib.* 61 (1980) 106–109.

Tsuchido, K. "Tradition and Redaction in John 8:12-30," *Annual of the Japanese Biblical Institute* 6 (1980) 56–75.

Tuñi Vancells, J. O. *La verdad os hará libres Jn 8:32: Liberación y liberdad del creyente en el cuarto evangelio.* Barcelona: Herder, 1973.

Zaiman, J. H. "The Traditional Study of the Mishnah," in Jacob Neusner, ed., *The Study of Ancient Judaism.* 2 vols. New York: KTAV, 1981, 2:27–36.

Zimmermann, Heinrich. "Das absolute *egō eimi* als neutestamentliche Offenbarungsformel," *BZ* 4 (1960) 54–69, 266–276.

iv. Jesus and Tabernacles: II (9:1–10:21)

John 9:1-38

1. As he passed by he saw a man blind from his birth. 2. And his disciples asked him, "Rabbi, who sinned, this man or his parents, that he was born blind?" 3. Jesus answered, "It was not that this man sinned, or his parents, but that the works of God might be made manifest in him. 4. We must work the works of the one who sent me while it is day; night comes when no one can work. 5. As long as I am in the world I am the light of the world."

6. As he said this he spat on the ground and made clay of the spittle and anointed the man's eyes with the clay, 7. saying to him, "Go, wash in the pool of Siloam" (which means the Sent One). So he went and washed and came back seeing.

8. The neighbors and those who had seen him before as a beggar said, "Is not this the man who used to sit and beg?" 9. Some said, "It is he"; others said, "No, but he is like him." He said, "I am the man." 10. They said to him, "Then how were your eyes opened?" 11. He answered, "The man called Jesus made clay and anointed my eyes and said to me, 'Go to Siloam and wash'; so I went and washed and received my sight." 12. They said to him, "Where is he?" He said, "I do not know."

13. They brought to the Pharisees the man who had formerly been blind. 14. Now it was a Sabbath day when Jesus made the clay and opened his eyes. 15. The Pharisees again asked him how he had received his sight. And he said to them, "He put clay on my eyes, and I washed, and I see." 16. Some of the Pharisees said, "This man is not from God, for he does not keep the Sabbath." But others said, "How can a man who is a sinner do such signs?" There was a division among them. 17. So they again said to the blind man, "What do you say about him, since he has opened your eyes?" He said, "He is a prophet."

18. The Jews did not believe that he had been blind and had received his sight until they called the parents of the man who had received his sight 19. and asked them, "Is this your son, who you say was born blind? How then does he now see?" 20. His parents answered, "We know that this is our son, and that he was born blind; 21. but how he now sees we do not know, nor do we know who opened his eyes. Ask him; he is of age, he will speak for himself." 22. His parents said this because they feared the Jews, for the Jews had already agreed that anyone who should confess him to be Christ was to be put out of the synagogue. 23. Therefore his parents said, "He is of age, ask him."

24. So for the second time they called the man who had been blind and said to him, "Give God the praise; we know that this man is a sinner." 25. He answered, "Whether he is a sinner I do not know; one thing I know, that though I was blind, now I see." 26. They said to him, "What did he do to you? How did he open your eyes?" 27. He answered them,

"I have told you already, and you would not listen. Why do you want to hear it again? Do you too want to become his disciples?" 28. And they reviled him, saying, "You are his disciple, but we are disciples of Moses. 29. We know that God has spoken to Moses, but as for this man, we do not know where he comes from." 30. The man answered, "Why, this is a marvel! You do not know where he comes from, and yet he opened my eyes. 31. We know that God does not listen to sinners, but if any one is a worshiper of God and does his will, God listens to him. 32. Never since the world began has it been heard that anyone opened the eyes of a man born blind. 33. If this man were not from God he could do nothing." 34. They answered him, "You were born in utter sin, and would you teach us?" And they cast him out.

35. Jesus heard that they had cast him out, and having found him he said, "Do you believe in the Son of Man?" 36. He answered, "And who is he, sir, that I may believe in him?" 37. Jesus said to him, "You have seen him, and it is he who speaks to you." 38. He said, "Lord, I believe"; and he worshiped him.

INTERPRETATION

Introduction to 9:1–10:21. This passage is widely recognized as one of the masterpieces of Johannine storytelling. Its literary beauty has been captured in the early oratorio (1896) of Sir Edward Elgar, *The Light of Life* (Opus 29). The passage is marked by a unity of time, space, and theme. It is taken for granted that the celebration of Tabernacles continues. There is no indication of a change of time, but Jesus left *(exēlthen)* the Temple (8:59), and passing by *(paragōn)* he saw a man blind from birth (9:1). The closing of one episode with an aorist tense *(exēlthen)*, and the opening of the next with a present participle *(paragōn)* link Jesus' exit from the Temple and his encounter with the man born blind. Somewhere outside the Temple a blind man comes to sight and faith in the Son of Man, while Jewish leaders move toward blindness (9:1-38). They are condemned as blind, thieves, robbers, strangers, and hirelings who do not care for their sheep (9:39–10:13). The celebration of Tabernacles closes with Jesus' revelation of himself as the messianic Good Shepherd (10:14-18) and further division among "the Jews" (vv. 19-21).

There is an "ancient maxim that no more than two active characters shall normally appear on stage at one time, and that scenes are often divided by adherence to this rule" (Martyn, *History and Theology* 26). On this basis the narrative of John 9:1–10:21 can be divided into eight scenes.

    I.   *9:1-5:* Jesus and the disciples.
    II.   *9:6-7:* Jesus and the man born blind.
    III. *9:8-12:* The blind man and his neighbors.

IV. *9:13-17:* The blind man and the Pharisees.
V. *9:18-23:* The Pharisees and the blind man's parents.
VI. *9:24-34:* The Pharisees and the blind man.
VII. *9:35-38:* Jesus and the blind man.
VIII. *9:39–10:21:* Jesus and the Pharisees.

The first scene (9:1-5) opens and the final scene (9:39–10:21) closes with reference to the man born blind.

The story of the man born blind and Jesus' discourse on shepherds continue his words and actions during the feast of Tabernacles.

1. Jesus proclaims *that* he is the light of the world (9:5; cf. 8:12), and the journey of the man born blind toward being the believer who confesses faith in the Son of Man whom he sees and hears (9:34-35) shows *how* this is true.
2. Jesus announced *that* he was the lifegiving water (7:37-38). The water of Siloam, which effects the cure of the once blind man, is interpreted as "the Sent One" (9:7) and shows *how* Jesus' claims are true.
3. The celebration of Tabernacles has been marked by debate and conflict over Jesus' messianic status (7:27-29, 31, 37-38, 41a, 41b-42). His claim to be the Good Shepherd who lays down his life for his sheep (10:14-18) tells *how* he exercises his messianic role.

Although 9:1–10:21 must be regarded as a literary unit, it is considered here in two sections. The man born blind moves toward full sight in 9:1-34, but this journey is also marked by the growing "blindness" of the Pharisees. As the once blind man has a final encounter with Jesus (vv. 35-38), so do the Pharisees (9:39–10:21). The length of the section dedicated to Jesus' words to the Pharisees and the importance of his self-revelation as the messianic Good Shepherd (10:14-18) call for a separate treatment.

Jesus and the disciples (vv. 1-5). Jesus sees a man who has never experienced sight or light (v. 1). Working from a biblical principle that God cannot be credited with the evil that happens to people (cf. Exod 20:5; Num 14:18; Deut 5:9; Tob 3:3-4), the disciples pose a logical question. Who is responsible for the evil suffered by the man: sinful parents, or the child who committed a sin while still in the womb (v. 2)? The disciples wonder about human responsibility, and address Jesus as "Rabbi" (cf. 1:38, 49; 3:2; 4:31; 6:25), but he transcends this discussion. He tells them this situation exists "that the works of God might be made manifest in him" (v. 3). God is to reveal his works in the events of the life of the man that are about to be told. Jesus' point of view has been established. Until now Jesus has indicated that he does not perform his works on his own authority (cf. 3:11-21; 31-36; 5:19-30). He now includes his disciples in his work: "We must work the works of the one who sent me" (v. 4a). They are associated with the task of Jesus, to work the works of the one who sent him. Limitations have been imposed upon this work of making God known. Jesus' revelation of God brings light into the world (1:4-9). Indeed, Jesus is the light of the world (8:12). But the darkness of "night" brings the day to an end when Jesus is absent from the human story. In this situation no one is able to make God known (v. 4b). Jesus associates the disciples with his work so that this will not happen. The presence of light in the world, as the Father continues to be revealed, will not be limited to the historical life of Jesus; it will continue in the presence of Jesus in his associates, the disciples. Tabernacle themes continue to be the focus of the narrative as Jesus reaffirms what he claimed in 8:12: he is the light of the world (v. 5). The disciples of Jesus continue the works of Jesus (v. 4a), but it is the presence of Jesus in the world that brings light into the world (v. 5).

Jesus and the man born blind (vv. 6-7). Jesus adapts a traditional practice as he forms mud from the dust of the earth and places it on the man's eyes (v. 6). This creates a situation in which Jesus can command, and the narrator can comment: "Go, wash in the Pool of Siloam (which means the Sent One)" (v. 7a). The man responds unquestioningly. Radical response to the word of Jesus is indicated by the use of four verbs: he went, he washed, he came back seeing (v. 7b: *apēlthen oun kai enipsato kai ēlthen blepōn*). As earlier in the story (cf. 2:1-12; 4:46-54; 5:2-9a), acceptance of the word of Jesus leads to a miracle. But there is little focus on the physical event of the restoration of sight. Within the context of the celebration of Tabernacles the waters of Siloam are crucial, and the narrator adds an explanation to make this clear. It is not the contact with the waters of Siloam that effects the cure, but contact with the Sent One. This identification, made on the basis of linguistic proximity and perhaps some messianic associations with Siloam, serves the story well. Jesus' claim to be the living water (7:37) and the light of the world (8:12) during his time in the Temple has been put to the test. Jesus, the light of the world (9:5), the Sent One (9:7; cf. 3:17, 34; 5:36), has restored sight to a man who has never seen the light. The first two scenes of the drama serve as promise (vv. 1-5) and fulfillment (vv. 6-7) (cf. Staley, "Stumbling in the Dark" 64–65).

The blind man and his neighbors (vv. 8-12). The action of Jesus does not lead to the praise of God, but to *schisma*: Is this the man (v. 8)? Some say that it is the same person but others say that it is only a look-alike (v. 9a). In a way similar to Jesus' own self-identification (cf. 4:26; 6:20; 8:58), the cured man speaks for himself: "I am the man" (v. 9b: *egō eimi*). He does not know how or why these things have happened to him. When interrogated he can only retell the physical facts: the miracle, the clay, the anointing, the command, the obedience, and the sight (vv. 10-11). This is the first time the question is raised of *how* the man received his sight. The answer to that oft-repeated question will remain the same (cf. vv. 10, 15, 16, 19, 21, 26). As to *who* healed him, he can only reply "that man called

Jesus" (v. 11: *ho anthrōpos ho legomenos Iēsous*). When asked of Jesus' whereabouts he responds, for the first time, "I do not know" (v. 12: *ouk oida*). The man is unable to recognize that he has been given the light through the intervention of the Sent One of God, but he admits his ignorance: "I do not know."

The blind man and the Pharisees (vv. 13-17). The neighbors and acquaintances bridge the scenes as they take the man to the Pharisees (v. 13). Another factor is introduced into the story by the remark from the narrator that the day on which Jesus made the clay was a Sabbath (v. 14). The Pharisees ask *how* the miracle occurred, and the cured man reports (v. 15). In this way the Pharisees learn of the Sabbath offense: Jesus made clay. They now show interest in the miracle as they fasten their attention on Jesus' breach of the Law (cf. *m. Šabb.* 7:2; 8:1). They are not interested in the person of Jesus as they focus on the preservation of a legal tradition (cf. 5:16-18). But a further *schisma* emerges. Some of the Pharisees claim that Jesus cannot be from God, as he does not keep the Sabbath (v. 16a), while others point to Jesus' signs as an indication that he cannot be a sinner (v. 16b). They turn to debate his origins. In their earlier conflict with Jesus he has explained his activity on the basis of his origins (5:19-30), but this has been forgotten. Some Pharisees deny Jesus' origins with God (v. 16a), while others are still open to such a possibility (v. 16b). One thing is not questioned: the fact of the miracle, and so they return to the cured man and ask his assessment of the man who cured him. He had earlier described Jesus as "the man" (v. 11), but he now confesses, "He is a prophet" (v. 17).

The Pharisees and the blind man's parents (vv. 18-23). As the man progresses (vv. 7, 11, 17), the Pharisees move in the opposite direction. "The Jews did not believe *(ouk episteusan)* that he had been blind and had received his sight" (v. 18a). Belief is beyond them; they must have the facts. They now attempt to prove that a man born blind did not come to sight and light, by summoning the people best qualified to testify: the people who bore him (v. 18b). They are attempting to disprove that the light of the world (v. 5) gave sight (v. 7), but their attempts fail. They subject the parents to a subtle abuse, suggesting that they have been lying about their son. The interrogation by "the Jews" presupposes that the man was not born blind and the parents should not claim that he was (v. 19a). Still unwilling to go beyond the question of *how* such things happened, they continue to ask, "How then does he now see?" (v. 19b). The parents can only affirm the fact of his being born blind (v. 20), and withdraw from the discussion (v. 21). The fact of the miracle has by now been told and retold three times (vv. 11, 15, 20-21). Faith in Jesus does not hinge on such facts, but on the identity of Jesus, the light of the world (v. 5), the Sent One of God (v. 7), who is being tried *in absentia*.

The parents were afraid of "the Jews" because they had decided that anyone who confessed that Jesus was the Christ was to be put out of the synagogue (v. 22: *aposynagōgos genētai*). For this reason they avoid christological debate with "the Jews" and send them back to their son (v. 23). As far as the story is concerned there is a threat to both the parents and the son, and the parents are not prepared to face such a threat. It remains to be seen how the son will behave. The first readers of the story, the Johannine Christians, also discovered their experience in the story. They had forged their christology within a context of hostility and conflict. "The Jews" rejected Jesus' claims and thus rejected all those who accepted them (cf. 12:42; 16:2). It was probably not only the parents of the man born blind who decided that they did not wish to be involved in a debate about the christological status of Jesus of Nazareth. Subsequent generations have experienced a similar faintness of heart.

The Pharisees and the blind man (vv. 24-34). The cured man is summoned again. Earlier he said he did not "know" the whereabouts of Jesus (v. 12), but "the Jews" have no such hesitations about their "knowledge." Using an oath formula employed before taking testimony or a confession of guilt (cf. Josh 7:19; 1 Chron 30:6-9; Jer 13:16; 1 Esdr 9:8; *m. Sanh.* 6:2), they command the man to give praise *(doxa)* to God. But it is to a God of their own making, not the God of Jesus Christ, because they "know" *(hēmeis oidamen)* that Jesus is a sinner. The cured man is not prepared to accept such "knowledge," as he does not "know" *(ouk oida)* whether Jesus is a sinner, but he is aware of the miracle. He poses the question asked by some of the Pharisees in v. 16, before they closed their minds against Jesus: can a man who does such signs be a sinner? As the man continues his defense on the basis of the fact of the miracle the Pharisees again ask for information about *how* it happened (v. 26). The issue of *how* rather than *who* is still at the center of their discussion. The man wonders why they want to hear the story again. They have resisted "listening" *(ouk ēkousate)* up to this point; why do they want to hear it now? Perhaps they are interested in becoming disciples of Jesus? The question is not without its irony, but he is not mocking "the Jews." They want to hear the story of the deeds of Jesus. This is part of the process of becoming a disciple of Jesus (cf. 2:11), even though true discipleship demands more than faith in miracles (cf. 2:23-25).

But "the Jews" will not be moved. They are followers of Moses while the cured man is a disciple of "that fellow" (v. 28). Their discipleship is based on the certain "knowledge" *(hēmeis oidamen)* that God has spoken through Moses (v. 29a). One thing they do not know *(ouk oidamen)*, and that is the origins of Jesus: "We do not know where he comes from" (v. 29b). Herein lie the roots of the failure of "the Jews" to accept Jesus. They are locked into adhesion to the former gift of God that came through

Moses, and they reject the perfection of God's gift that comes through Jesus Christ (cf. 1:17-18) because they will not accept that he is "from God." Having touched upon this central question, the cured man tries to press it further. There must be a link between the fact that someone opened the eyes of a man born blind and his origins (v. 30). There is a principle at stake, "known" *(oidamen)* by both "the Jews" and the man born blind. They should be working out of this common ground: God listens to people who do his will, and not to sinners (v. 31). But in their fascination with the *how* of the miracle and in their aggressive affirmation of their superior "knowledge" they have not been able to look to the *who* of Jesus. The cured man points this out to them. The miracle has no precedent. Never before in the recorded history of God's people, from the creation to the events that are happening around them, has a person who was born blind been given sight (v. 32). Thus there must be a special relationship between the person who does such things and God who makes this new creation possible (cf. v. 1: *typhlon ek genetēs*).

Earlier "the Jews" debated whether or not Jesus could be "from God" (v. 16a). They decided against such a possibility (vv. 24, 29). Earlier the cured man described Jesus as "the man called Jesus" (v. 11), but now he declares, "If this man were not from God *(para theou)* he could do nothing" (v. 33). There is still some hesitation in the man *(ei mē ēn houtos para theou)*, as he continues to base his understanding of Jesus on the fact of the miracle (v. 33b), but the response of "the Jews" to any such suggestion is rapid and violent. They accuse the man of being born in utter sin (v. 34a; see Ps 51:5) resolving a question asked by the disciples in v. 3 but dismissed by Jesus as irrelevant in v. 4. This "sinful" man is behaving ignorantly and outrageously, questioning the knowledge of "the Jews." He is attempting to teach them that their understanding of God and the one through whom God has spoken may be wrong (v. 34b). Because of this they cast him out from their midst (v. 34c: *exebalon auton exō*).

Jesus and the blind man (vv. 35-38). Jesus, hearing that the man had been cast out, finds him and asks: "Do you believe in the Son of Man?" (v. 35). Earlier references to the Son of Man (cf. 1:51; 3:13-14; 5:27; 6:27, 53, 62) have indicated that Jesus uses this term to refer to his role of making God known in the human story. His presence among us as the Son of Man is critical, revealing God and bringing judgment, but the consummation of his revealing role is yet to come. The man is puzzled by the question and he responds with a question of his own. He does not know enough (cf. vv. 12, 25, 36) to be able to make a decision. He turns to Jesus, addressing him as "Sir" *(kyrie)*, seeking further information on the Son of Man (v. 36). Jesus' response is solemn and satisfying: "You have seen him, and it is he who speaks to you" (v. 37). Terms central to the Gospel's christology are combined. It is impossible for anyone to *see* God or come to the knowledge of God (cf. 1:18; 5:37), but Jesus reveals what he has *seen* (cf. 1:34; 3:11, 22; 8:38). He *speaks* what he has seen with the Father (cf. 6:46; 8:38). Those who believe in Jesus will *see* (1:50-51), while those who *refuse to see* are condemned (cf. 3:36; 5:37-38; 6:36). The supreme revelation of God will take place when the believer *looks upon* the Son of Man (3:13-15). Jesus is challenging the man to recognize that God is made known to him in the Son of Man. Similarly, when Jesus *speaks* he makes God known. He is the incarnation of the *logos* of God (1:1-2, 14). Jesus *speaks* of what he knows from the Father (cf. 3:11, 34; 8:25-26, 38), and he *speaks* with an unquestionable authority (cf. 7:17, 18, 26, 46). His word gives life, peace, and joy (cf. 6:63), but also condemns those who refuse to listen (cf. 8:40). Jesus can say to the Samaritan woman that the one who reveals God in a unique way, the *ego eimi, speaks* to her (4:26).

The cured man is being asked to make a further step in his journey into true light and sight. Is he is prepared to accept that in Jesus, the man standing before him, whom he can see and hear, he will find the revelation of God? He responds: "Lord, I believe" (v. 38a). His earlier question of Jesus addressed him as "Sir" (v. 36: *kyrie*), but the same word has its full christological meaning of "Lord" as he bows down in an act of worship and acceptance of Jesus (v. 38b: *kai proskynēsen autǭ*). Doubted by friends and neighbors (vv. 8-12), abandoned by his parents (vv. 18-23), questioned, insulted, and cast out by "the Jews" (vv. 13-17, 24-34), he has stumbled from belief in Jesus as "a man" (v. 11) to "a prophet" (v. 17) to a suggestion that he must be "from God" (v. 33). He finally prostrates himself in belief before Jesus, the one who makes God known, the Son of Man, the Sent One of God, the light of the world. Jesus' earlier words to the disciples have come true. This man's journey from blindness to sight was "that the works of God might be made manifest in him" (v. 3).

NOTES

1. *As he passed by:* The unity of John 9:1–10:21 is a matter of some controversy. Some would see 10:1-21 as an intrusion; others would trace its insertion to a later stage in the development of the Johannine tradition. This interpretation regards it as essential to the argument of 9:1-41. For surveys see Schnackenburg, "Die Hirtenrede" 131–143; Tragan, *La parabole du "pasteur"* 55–175.

   he saw a man blind from his birth: It is theologically significant, and important to the story as a whole, that this man has *never* seen, as he has been blind "from birth" *(ek genetēs)*. What happens in the gift of sight, light, and faith to the man is a new creation.

2. *Rabbi, who sinned:* For some examples of later rabbinic reflection on prenatal sin see Str-B 2:527–529.

3. *that the works of God might be made manifest in him:* It is just possible that *hina phanerōthę* is imperative: "Let the works of God be displayed in him" (cf. Beasley-Murray, *John* 151). This interpretation eases this hard word of Jesus but loses a contact, which will appear later, between 9:3 and 11:4.

4. *We must work the works:* Reading "we must" *(hēmas dei)*, following 𝔓⁶⁶.⁷⁵, the first hand of Sinaiticus, Vaticanus Regius, Freer Gospels, Sinaitic Syriac, etc., rather then the more natural "I must" *(eme dei)* found in some witnesses. A change from the plural to the singular by the copyists is more likely. The plural reading is "unquestionably right" (Lindars, *Gospel* 342).

5. *I am the light of the world:* Although the English translation of 8:12 and 9:5 is identical, the Greek is not. In 9:5 the *egō eimi* does not appear *(phōs eimi tou kosmou)*. As Schnackenburg, *Gospel* 2:242, points out, the sign itself performs the function of the *egō eimi.*

6. *He spat on the ground and made clay of the spittle and anointed the man's eyes with the clay:* On the use of spittle on the eyes of a person afflicted with sight problems see Mark 8:23; Pliny, *Nat. Hist.* 28.7; Tacitus, *Hist.* 4.81; Suetonius, *Life of Caesar* 8.7.2-3; Dio Cassius 66.8. For rabbinic parallels see Str-B 2:15–17.

7. *Siloam (which means the Sent One):* The word "Siloam" literally means a discharge (of waters), and thus does not mean "the Sent One" *(ho hermēneuetai apestalmenos)*, although consonants of the verb "to send" (Hebrew: *šālaḥ*) are in the name. "Siloam" is close enough for popular etymology to make the link. Such an individualizing and messianic interpretation may have been current. See Müller, "Joh 9,7" 251–256; Reim, "Joh 9" 245–253, and especially Manns, *L'Evangile* 196–203.

9. *I am the man:* Some commentators regard the man's answer as the first sign of his representing Jesus. He uses the *egō eimi* and he creates schism around himself.

11. *The man called Jesus:* For Manns, *L'Evangile* 203–207, this confession is already messianic, evoking Jewish messianic use of *geber* and *īš*.

13. *They brought to the Pharisees:* The alternation between "the Pharisees" (cf. 9:13, 15, 16, 40) and "the Jews" (cf. 9:18, 22, 10:19) as major protagonists in 9:1–10:21 again (as in chs. 7–8) indicates that they represent the same group opposed to Jesus. See Thyen, "Johannes 10" 123. For Martyn, *History and Theology* 31 n. 29, "the Pharisees" represent a reading back into the story of Jesus the experience of the Johannine Christians before the *Bet Din* (religious court) in Jamnia.

14. *Now it was a sabbath day:* On the literary effect of this delay in announcing that the day was a Sabbath see Staley, "Stumbling in the Dark" 65–66. Staley also points out (pp. 66–67) that the ex-blind man's careful reporting of the incident did not provide material for the Sabbath accusation. The cured man shows adroitness, and the Pharisees show malice.

16. *This man is not from God:* An unusual word order is used here to indicate that the Jews reject Jesus' claims to be on the one hand a human being and on the other "from God": *ouk estin houtos para theou ho anthrōpos.*

do such signs: The plural "signs" indicates that they look back to the miracle of ch. 5. This recalling of the earlier miracle and their ongoing inability to accept that Jesus is "from God" show that "the Jews" have rejected his teaching in the two-part discourse of 5:19-47.

22. *was to be put out of the synagogue:* "John speaks of the cost of discipleship in terms of the conditions with which his readers were familiar" (Lindars, *Gospel* 347). While scholarship is correct in seeing the Johannine narrative as a "two-level drama" (cf. Martyn, *History and Theology* 30) reflecting the story of Jesus and the story of the Johannine community, Reinhartz, *Word in the World* 1–6, 16–47, has pointed out that there is a third level to the drama: a cosmic tale. She describes it as "the meta-tale which provides the overarching temporal, geographical, theological and narrative framework of the other two tales" (p. 5).

23. *He is of age, ask him:* The parents thus avoid the christological challenge. Among others, Brown (*Community* 71–73) has suggested that there were crypto-Christians who recognized the truth about Jesus but did not have the courage to confess their belief. They remained within the security of the Mosaic traditions.

24. *Give God the praise:* There may be a subtle irony here as the man born blind will eventually give glory to God in his witness to Jesus. See Pancaro, *The Law in the Fourth Gospel* 20–21.

27. *Do you too want to become his disciples:* It is sometimes argued that the cured man is mocking his judges at this stage (e.g., Staley, "Stumbling in the Dark" 68). This hardly fits the overall characterization of the man and his progress toward the light. See Holleran, "Seeing the Light" 373–374.

31. *We know:* This is the only time in the narrative when the knowledge of the man born blind and the knowledge of the Pharisees are at one. Haenchen, *John* 2:40, paraphrases this use of *oidamen:* "It is generally acknowledged."

32. *Never since the world began:* This is true of the biblical record (cf. Brown, *Gospel* 1:375). Reim, "Johannesevangelium und Synagogengottesdienst" 101, sets these words within a synagogue reading, beginning with Gen 1:1, passing through the great prophetic texts (reflected in John 9). Something new and unheard of is happening with the gift of sight to a man born blind.

34. *And they cast him out:* Again the experience of the Johannine community, however local such experience might have been, lies behind this expulsion. See, among many, Rensberger, *Johannine Faith* 26–27; Beck, "Narrative Function" 152–153.

35. *Do you believe in the Son of Man?:* For a detailed study of the use of "the Son of Man" in 9:35 see Moloney, *Son of Man* 149–159. The claim of Müller, "Have you Faith?" 291–294, that "Son of Man" in 9:35 is a circumlocution for "me" makes little sense of the climactic nature of this final encounter between Jesus and the cured man, and renders Jesus' dense explanation of v. 37 pointless.

37. *it is he who speaks to you:* There is a close parallel between 9:37, *ho lalōn meta sou ekeinos estin* ("it is he who speaks to you"), and Jesus' self-revelation to the

Samaritan woman in 4:26: *egō eimi ho lalōn soi* ("'I am' is the one who speaks to you").

38. *He said, "Lord, I believe"; and he worshiped him:* Some scholars regard vv. 38-39a as an addition. This is based on some manuscript evidence that only here in the Fourth Gospel does *proskynein* (v. 38: "to worship") appear, and that *ephē* (v. 39a: "said") is rare (elsewhere only at 1:23). See C. L. Porter, "John 9,38, 39a: A Liturgical Addition to the Text," *NTS* 13 (1966–1967) 387–394. Almost all commentators would agree that on both external and internal grounds such skepticism is unwarranted.

For Reference and Further Study

Gourgues, Michel. "L'aveugle-né (Jn 9). Du miracle au signe: typologie des réactions à l'égard du Fils de l'homme," *NRTh* 104 (1982) 381–395.

Holleran, J. W. "Seeing the Light: A Narrative Reading of John 9," *EThL* 49 (1993) 5–26, 354–382.

Moloney, Francis J. *Signs and Shadows* 117–129.

_____. *Son of Man* 149–159.

Müller, Karlheinz. "Joh 9,7 und das jüdische Verständnis des Siloh-Spruches," *BZ* 13 (1969) 251–256.

Müller, Mogens. "Have You Faith in the Son of Man?" *NTS* 37 (1991) 291–294.

Reim, Günter. "Joh 9—Tradition und zeitgenössische messianische Diskussion," *BZ* 22 (1978) 245–253.

_____. "Johannesevangelium und Synagogengottesdienst—eine Beobachtung," *BZ* 27 (1983) 101.

Sabugal, Santos. *La curación del ciego de nacimiento (Jn 9,1-41): Análisis exegético y teológico.* BEsB 2. Madrid: Biblia y Fe, 1977.

Staley, Jeffrey L. "Stumbling in the Dark, Reaching for the Light: Reading Characters in John 5 and 9," *Sem* 53 (1991) 55–80.

John 9:39–10:21

39. Jesus said, "For judgment I came into this world, that those who do not see may see, and that those who see may become blind." 40. Some of the Pharisees near him heard this, and they said to him, "Are we also blind?" 41. Jesus said to them, "If you were blind, you would have no guilt; but now that you say, 'We see,' your guilt remains."

10:1. "Amen, amen, I say to you, anyone who does not enter the sheepfold by the door but climbs in by another way is a thief and a robber. 2. The one who enters by the door is the shepherd of the sheep. 3. To him the doorkeeper opens; the sheep hear his voice, and he calls his own sheep by name and leads them out. 4. When he has brought out all his own, he goes before them, and the sheep follow him, for they know his voice. 5. A stranger they will not follow, but they will flee from him, for they do not know the voice of strangers." 6. This figure Jesus used with them, but they did not understand what he was saying to them.

7. So Jesus again said to them, "Amen, amen, I say to you, I am the door of the sheep. 8. All who came before me are thieves and robbers; but the sheep did not heed them. 9. I am the door; whoever enters by me will be saved, and will go in and out and find pasture. 10. The thief comes only to steal and kill and destroy; I came that they may have life, and have it abundantly. 11. I am the good shepherd. The good shepherd lays down his life for the sheep. 12. The hireling who is not a shepherd, and does not own the sheep, sees the wolf coming and leaves the sheep and flees; and the wolf snatches them and scatters them, 13. because he is a hireling and does not care for the sheep.

14. I am the good shepherd; I know my own and my own know me, 15. as the Father knows me and I know the Father; and I lay down my life for the sheep. 16. And I have other sheep that are not of this fold; I must bring them also, and they will heed my voice. So there shall be one flock, one shepherd. 17. For this reason the Father loves me, because I lay down my life that I may take it again. 18. No one takes it from me, but I lay it down of my own accord. I have power to lay it down, and I have power to take it again; this charge I have received from my Father."

19. There was again a division among the Jews because of these words. 20. Many of them said, "He has a demon, and he is mad; why listen to him?" 21. Others said, "These are not the sayings of one who has a demon. Can a demon open the eyes of the blind?"

INTERPRETATION

Introduction to 9:39–10:21. No break occurs between 9:41 and 10:1. The final encounter between Jesus and the man born blind in 9:35-38 is matched by the encounter between Jesus and the Pharisees in 9:39-10:21. Jesus addresses an unnamed audience in v. 39, and "some of the Pharisees" respond in v. 40. Their words, in turn, generate Jesus' reflection that begins in v. 41 but develops into the discourse of 10:1-18. It is on the basis of 9:39-41 that 10:1-21 unfolds. In 10:6 the narrator interrupts words of Jesus to comment on the inability of the Pharisees to understand what Jesus is saying to them, and vv. 19-21 report the *schisma* that results from the teaching of Jesus. Jesus uses *egō eimi* with a predicate in vv. 7, 11, and 14, and these passages are sometimes used to divide the discourse. But other features must be taken into account. Only one of these sayings marks a change of direction in the discourse. In vv. 7-13 Jesus speaks polemically, comparing his care for the sheep with that of others who are called thieves, robbers (vv. 8, 10), and hirelings (vv. 12-13). His identification of himself as "the door of the sheep" (v. 7) and "the Good Shepherd" (v. 11) are part of this polemic. He is good while others are wicked. In vv. 14-18 all such contrasts disappear. Without polemic Jesus describes the identity and mission of the Good Shepherd (vv. 14-16), based upon the relationship he has with the Father (vv. 17-18). The passage is therefore divided into five sections:

(a) *9:39-41:* Introduction. Jesus is questioned by the Pharisees and he condemns them for their blind arrogance.

(b) *10:1-6:* Jesus tells a parable about entering the sheepfold and the Pharisees cannot understand.

(c) *10:7-13:* Jesus contrasts himself, the door and the Good Shepherd, with others who are thieves, robbers, and hirelings.

(d) *10:14-18:* Jesus the Good Shepherd, out of union with the Father, lays down his life for his sheep.

(e) *10:19-21:* Conclusion: A *schisma* among "the Jews."

Background to "the Good Shepherd." It is widely acknowledged that there is no direct citation from the OT in 10:1-18 even though there is a strong biblical tradition presenting unfaithful leaders of Israel as bad shepherds who consign their flock to the wolves (cf. Jer 23:1-8; Ezekiel 34; 22:27; Zeph 3:3; Zech 10:2-3; 11:4-17). This theme is continued in other Jewish literature that is pre-Christian or contemporaneous with the Fourth Gospel (cf. *1 Enoch* 89:12-27, 42-44, 59-70, 74-76; 90:22-25; *T. Gad* 1:2-4). Throughout the OT God is repeatedly spoken of as the shepherd of God's people (cf. Willmes, *Die sogenannte Hirtenallegorie* 279–311). When the exile caused many to doubt, God was presented as the future shepherd of the people (cf. Jer 31:10; 13:17; 23:3; Isa 40:11; 49:9-10). Ezekiel 34:11-16 speaks of God as the future good shepherd gathering the flock. This image is continued into later writings (cf. Zeph 3:19; Mic 2:12; 4:6-7; Qoh 12:11; Sir 18:13). As the monarchy disappeared prophets spoke of a future Davidic figure who would be shepherd to the people (cf. Mic 5:3; Jer 3:15; 23:4-6; Ezek 34:23-24; 37:24; Zech 13:7-9). The notion emerges of "one shepherd" who will form "one flock."

> I will set up over them one shepherd, my servant David, and he shall feed them; he shall feed them and be their shepherd. And I, the LORD, will be their God, and my servant David shall be prince among them (Ezek 34:23-24; cf. 37:24).

The image continues and strengthens in other Jewish literature (cf. LXX Ps 2:9; *PsSol* 17:24, 40; CD 13:7-9; *2 Bar* 77:13-17), and no doubt provides the background for Jesus' words in John 10:1-18.

Introduction (9:39-41). Jesus did not come into the world to judge (cf. 3:17; 5:24; 8:15), but judgment takes place as a result of his presence in the world (cf. 5:27). The light of the world (8:12; 9:5) has come *eis krima* (v. 39: "for judgment"). His judgment is "the judicial decision which consists in the separation of those who are willing to believe from those who are unwilling to do so" (BAGD 451). As commentary upon what has happened so far Jesus describes the judgment he brings to the blind who come to

sight and those whose seeing moves toward blindness. The insistence of
the man born blind that he did not know (*ouk oida;* cf. vv. 12, 25, 26) and
his search for the Son of Man that he might believe (v. 36) contrast with
"the Jews'" arrogant affirmation of their knowledge (*oidamen;* cf. vv. 24,
29, 31). It leads to their decision that Jesus is a sinner, a person whose origins are unknown (vv. 24, 29). They are content with the knowledge that
God has spoken to Moses, and in their self-sufficiency they have become
blind and Jesus tells them they have brought judgment upon themselves
(v. 39). Arrogance continues as they question why Jesus dares to suggest
that they are blind (v. 40). Jesus' response closes this discussion and opens
the shepherd discourse and its aftermath (10:1-21). Had they been prepared to admit their need for light they would have no guilt, but because
they claim all knowledge (v. 41: *blepomen*) there is no room for the revelation of the light that comes through Jesus. Thus they fall under judgment.

The parable on entering the sheepfold (10:1-6). A double "amen" (10:1)
links 9:41 and the parable that follows (vv. 1-6). The parable plays on the
use of a "door" in pastoral practice. The background for this play on
words is the widespread use of the image of the shepherd to speak both
positively and negatively of Israel's leaders. There are two ways to enter
a sheepfold, depending on whether one wishes to shepherd or to harm
the sheep. One might enter the fold by subterfuge (v. 1), or through the
doorway of the fold (v. 2). The one who does the former is a thief and a
robber (*kleptēs estin kai lēstēs*), while the latter is the shepherd (*poimēn estin
tōn probatōn*). Another figure is introduced, the gatekeeper (v. 3: *ho
thyrōros*), but he is a minor figure called for by the pastoral background to
the parable. He has no hesitation in allowing the shepherd to enter (v. 3a),
just as the sheep have no hesitation in responding to the voice of the one
who leads and nourishes them. Each sheep knows its familiar name and
responds immediately to the voice of the one calling it by that name (v.
3b). Once the sheep have been called by name, assembled, and taken out
of the fold to frequent their pasture the shepherd walks ahead of them,
and they gladly follow the one whose voice is familiar to them (v. 4). The
opposite happens in the case of a stranger (*allotrios*), whose voice the
sheep do not know. They will not follow, and they flee in panic (v. 5).

Jesus continues his words to the Pharisees (cf. 9:39-41), applying a
significant biblical image to them. Jesus has healed (9:6-7) and sought out
(v. 36) the blind man while the Pharisees have treated him with disdain
and arrogance, throwing him out from their midst (v. 34). The narrator
explicitly identifies the Pharisees with the thieves and robbers in v. 6.
They did not understand that Jesus' parable was saying something to
them (*tina ēn ha elalei autois*). The parable's (*paroimia*) themes of shepherd,
door, thieves, and robbers will be further used and developed in vv. 7-18.
The *paroimia* of vv. 1-6 provides the material out of which the rest of the

discourse is formed. The *paroimia,* therefore, is best described as an "image field" that will provide Jesus with the raw material for the formation of the later parts of the discourse (cf. note). The sheep hear the voice of the shepherd (vv. 3-4), but the Pharisees do not hear his voice. They are unable to recognize what he is saying to them because, as throughout the Gospel, they will not listen to what he is saying (v. 6).

The contrast between the Good Shepherd and others (vv. 7-13). The discourse is resumed *(palin)* with a further use of the double "amen" (v. 7a) as Jesus reveals himself as "the door of the sheep" (v. 7b: *egō eimi hē thyra tōn probatōn*). The parable used the door as the place of right access to the sheep (cf. vv. 1-2), and Jesus presents himself as that door throughout vv. 7-10. Only Jesus is the door of the sheep, and only through him can one have right access to the sheep, and the sheep have exit to good pasture (v. 7; cf. v. 9). Again looking back to expressions from the parable Jesus claims that those who came before him were thieves *(kleptai)* and robbers *(lēstai).* "The Jews" who came before Jesus have rejected Jesus and rejected all who move toward his revelation. This has been dramatically portrayed in 9:1-34. The claims of "the Jews" to be the leaders of God's people are false. They are thieves and robbers, purveyors of a messianic hope of their own making. As the response of the man born blind to their interpretation of the Mosaic tradition has shown (cf. 9:24-33), the sheep have not listened to them. This forced him out of their company (v. 34) into belief in the Son of Man and the company of Jesus (vv. 35-38).

The image of v. 7 returns in v. 9 as Jesus explains what it means to be the door of the sheep: Jesus is the mediator who will provide what the sheep need for life. Again the experience of ancient pastoral life is background to Jesus' contrasting two ways in which people might "come" to the sheep. The thief comes only to steal, kill, and destroy. There is nothing lifegiving about those who have come before Jesus claiming to be shepherds but who are, in fact, thieves and robbers. Jesus has come that the sheep may have pasture (cf. Ezek 34:14), thus have life and have it more abundantly (cf. Ezek 34:25-31). Jesus is the "door" *through whom* access to good pasture is made available and by means of which a sheepfold is protected. Those who enter (v. 9: *eiselthē*) are saved; those who go out (v. 9: *exeleusetai*) find pasture. Jesus, the door (v. 7), offers both salvation and pasture and provides the sheep with abundant life (v. 10). It is through him (v. 9: *di' emou*) that others have life (cf. 1:3-4, 17). In this polemic with the Pharisees "the door" of v. 2 has been rendered christological in vv. 7-10.

The contrast between Jesus and others continues as he claims, "I am the Good Shepherd" (v. 11a: *egō eimi ho poimēn ho kalos*). The positioning of the adjective after the noun stresses that Jesus is the good shepherd in contrast to bad shepherds, but more is being said. The shepherd of v. 2 is rendered christological in vv. 11-13. The introduction of the image of the Good Shepherd links Jesus with the tradition of a messianic shepherd of the people of God. However, from the very first use of the image in his self-revelation Jesus also introduces his uniqueness: "the Good Shepherd lays down his life for the sheep" (v. 11b). This self-gift of the shepherd unto death for his sheep has no parallel in the Jewish texts that speak of the messianic shepherd. It is possible to read these words as "to risk one's life," but too much of the story already points toward the violent end of Jesus' life (cf. 2:20-22; 3:13-14; 5:16-18; 6:27, 51, 53-54; 7:30; 8:20). Jesus does not fit the model of the expected Davidic shepherd-messiah. In contrast to the self-gift of the Good Shepherd, the hireling flees in the face of danger, leaving the sheep exposed to the murdering and scattering presence of the wolf (v. 12). Already Jewish tradition had spoken of its false leaders as those who did not perform their God-given responsibilities, but left the people prey to the wolves (cf. Jer 23:1-8; Ezekiel 34; 22:27; Zeph 3:3; Zech 10:2-3; 11:4-17; 1 *Enoch* 89:12-27, 42-44, 59-70, 74-76; 90:22-25; *T. Gad* 1:2-4).

In a final word of condemnation Jesus stresses the negative nature of the relationship between the hireling and the sheep (v. 13). The Good Shepherd gives his life for his sheep, and the hireling is only interested in personal gain. The hireling's flight flows from the nature of his relationship with the sheep. The reader links the hireling with "the Jews" who have repeatedly refused to accept Jesus' claims that he is from God, that he will return to God, and that he makes God known. Nothing Jesus says or does shakes "the Jews" from their unflinching adherence to the former gift that came through Moses. Their self-interest blocks them from accepting the fullness of the gift that comes through Jesus Christ (cf. 1:16-17).

Jesus, the messianic Good Shepherd (vv. 14-18). All conflict disappears as Jesus again announces, "I am the good shepherd" (v. 14a). Jesus no longer concerns himself with others who claim to be shepherds but with the relationship he has with his flock (vv. 14-16) and with his Father (vv. 17-18). This is made clear by a spiraling play on the use of the verb "to know" *(ginōskein)*. Jesus is the Good Shepherd who *knows* his sheep, and his sheep *know* him (v. 14b), but behind the mutuality of the Good Shepherd and his sheep lies the fundamental mutuality between the Father and Jesus: as the Father *knows* Jesus so also does Jesus *know* the Father (v. 15a). The use of *kathōs* (as) . . . *kagō* (and I) expresses an intimacy between the mutual knowledge of Father and Son. This mutuality can be seen in the self-gift of the Good Shepherd. The sharing of knowledge and oneness between Jesus and the sheep and between Jesus and the Father leads logically to the Good Shepherd's laying down his life for the sheep (v. 15b). The expected Davidic shepherd-messiah has been eclipsed by Jesus, the

Good Shepherd Messiah who lays down his life for his sheep. The image of the Good Shepherd may come from Jewish messianic traditions, but Jesus' being the Good Shepherd flows from his oneness with God (vv. 14-15). It is precisely this issue that "the Jews" will not accept. Indeed, they seek to kill Jesus because he makes such a claim (cf. 5:16-18).

Jesus further astounds his audience by announcing that there are other sheep who are not "of this fold" (v. 16: *ek tēs aulēs tautēs*). "The *aulē* is Israel and it contains some who are Christ's own sheep and some (the unbelieving Jews) who are not" (Barrett, *Gospel* 376). Others will be brought into the fold so that there will be one shepherd, one fold. The idea of one shepherd leading one people of God came from biblical tradition (cf. Mic 5:3-5; Jer 3:15; 23:4-6; Ezek 34:23-24) and continued in later Jewish literature (cf. *PsSol* 17:24, 40; CD 13:7-9; *2 Bar* 77:13-17), but something more is claimed by Jesus. He does not abandon the traditional image of the Good Shepherd, but he expands it in a way unknown to Jewish tradition. The Good Shepherd lays down his life for his sheep because of the union between himself and the Father (v. 15). The world outside Israel will be drawn into the fold of Jesus through his willing gift of himself unto death (v. 16).

The crucial function of the relationship between Jesus and the Father dominates Jesus' final words on the Good Shepherd (vv. 17-18). The Father's love for Jesus is shown in Jesus' laying down his life so that he might take it up again (v. 17). "What is being said here is that in his sacrifice the Father's love for him is truly present, and that this sacrifice is therefore a revelation of the Father's love" (Bultmann, *Gospel* 384). The death of Jesus has been prominent in his revelation of himself as the Good Shepherd (cf. vv. 11, 15), but his laying down his life leads to his taking it up again (v. 17b). Jesus will willingly die a violent death but will take his life again because the Father loves him. Many questions are raised by these words. How can death be the action of the Good Shepherd (v. 14)? How is it that he shows the Father's love for him as he lays down his life for the sheep (v. 15)? How can this death lead to a gathering of others who are not yet of this fold (v. 16)? What does it mean to say that God's love is shown in a free giving of one's life, only to take it again (v. 17)? Questions are emerging that lead the reader further into the story and cause wonder at how all this will take place in subsequent events.

Jesus closes his discourse by speaking of his authority (v. 18b: *exousia*). The story that lies ahead will report the suffering, death, and resurrection of Jesus. But these events will not fall upon Jesus like some terrible accident or merely as a result of the ill will of those who hate and persecute him. It is Jesus' decision, the exercising of his authority, that he will lay down his life and take it again (v. 18b). No one *(oudeis)* takes it from him (v. 18a). But the final words of the Good Shepherd (cf. vv. 11, 14) look back to the Father. Jesus' transformation of the traditional messianic expectation of a Davidic shepherd-messiah gathering one flock under one shepherd by means of the unconditional gift of himself unto death, only to take his life again, is a charge received from the Father (v. 18c). Jesus' self-revelation as the messianic Good Shepherd has come full circle. It began with his teaching on the union of knowledge that exists between the Father and the Son (v. 15), and closes with an admission that whatever he does is the fulfillment of the command *(entolē)* of the Father (v. 18).

Conclusion: Schisma among "the Jews" (vv. 19-21). Regularly throughout the celebration of Tabernacles Jesus' words have produced a *schisma* among "the Jews" (cf. 7:12, 25-27, 31, 40-41; 9:16). The report of Jesus' presence at the feast closes with a further *schisma* (v. 19). On the one hand the majority of them *(polloi ex autōn)* totally reject his word, judging him to be possessed by a demon and insane. His words, therefore, are not worth listening to (v. 20). But a minority group *(alloi)* are still open to the possibilities of his word. The curing of the man born blind, the event that led to Jesus' words on sheep and shepherding, is recalled (v. 21). Two details indicate that Jesus may not be possessed: he does not speak as if he were possessed, and he has cured the blind man. The question of who Jesus might be still remains open with a section of his audience, however decisive his rejection by the larger group might be. The story of Jesus' encounter with "the Jews" has not come to an end. Some are still prepared to listen to him (v. 21) even though "many" have decided that both Jesus and the words he speaks are worthless (v. 20).

Conclusion to 7:1–10:21. During the celebration of the feast of Tabernacles Jesus has been presented as the living water (7:37-38), the light of the world (8:12; 9:5), the Son, the Sent One, and thus the revealer of the one true God (7:14-24; 8:39-59; 9:7). The messianic question has been repeatedly posed (7:25-31, 40-44). Jesus leaves the Temple to escape the violence of "the Jews" (8:59), and his words and actions in 9:1–10:21 bring these tabernacle themes to a close. Jesus, the Sent One, transforms the waters of Siloam (9:7) and gives light to a man who has never seen. The physical miracle triggers a journey of faith that leads the man to prostrate himself before Jesus, the Son of Man, confessing "Lord, I believe" (9:38). "The Jews" who turned toward the Holy of Holies each day to celebrate their unswerving loyalty to the one true God have rejected Jesus' claim to be the revelation of the Father. They have now moved from an initial sight into blindness and darkness. Condemned as blind (9:39-41), they are shown to be thieves and robbers, strangers and hirelings, in contrast to Jesus the Good Shepherd (10:1-13).

But what of the messianic question? Jesus transcends all suggested messianic expectations—the hidden Messiah (7:26-27), the miracle-working Messiah (7:31), the Messiah who gives living water (7:37-41a), and the

Davidic Messiah (7:41b-42). He repeatedly affirms his relationship with God, his Father, and the mystery of his origins and destiny. The report of the celebration closes with Jesus finally accepting a traditional Jewish messianic expectation: he is the Good Shepherd (10:11, 14). The roots of this messianic figure lie solidly within Jewish tradition, but Jesus transcends and explodes the possibilities of the image. His shepherding flows from his knowledge and love of the Father, reciprocated by the knowledge and love the Father has for him. Accepting the charge the Father has given him, Jesus will lay down his life for his sheep, but he will take it again. "The Jews" know that God spoke to Moses, but they do not even know where this man came from (9:29). Many of them consider Jesus' words worthless, the words of one possessed (10:20).

In a document that appeared about the same time as the Fourth Gospel, written to address the problems of the loss of Jerusalem and its Temple, the author of *2 Baruch* reports:

> The whole people answered and they said to me:
> ". . . For the shepherds of Israel have perished, and the lamps which gave light are extinguished, and the fountains from which we used to drink have withheld their streams. Now we have been left in the darkness and in the thick forest and in the aridness of the desert."
> And I answered and said to them:
> "Shepherds and lanterns and fountains came from the Law and when we go away, the Law will abide. If you, therefore, look upon the Law and are intent upon wisdom, then the lamp will not be wanting and the shepherd will not give way and the fountain will not dry up" (*2 Bar* 77:11, 13-16).

As postwar Judaism and the Johannine form of postwar Christianity struggled to establish their different identities, both looked to their Jewish heritage. The author of *2 Baruch* looked to the Law for the never failing presence of shepherd, light, and water. These symbols, intimately associated with the celebration of the feast of Tabernacles, have not been abandoned by Johannine Christianity. The Johannine story of Jesus' presence at the celebration of Tabernacles announces access to living water, to light, and to the shepherd. However, Jesus is the living water for *any one who thirsts* (7:37), the light *of the world* (8:12; 9:5), and the Good Shepherd who lays down his life for his sheep, *to gather into one fold sheep who as yet do not belong to this fold* (10:15-16). "The Jews" insist they know that God has spoken to Moses (9:29), and are thus in agreement with the author of *2 Baruch* on the need to hold fast to the Law. It is essential to the evolving postwar identity of Judaism. But the Johannine Christians respond that God has perfected the former gift given through Moses. God is made known to them through Jesus Christ. Gone are national boundaries, and gone is the centrality of the former gift of the Law. The signs and shadows of the celebration of Tabernacles in the Temple, and only for the Jews, have become flesh in the person of Jesus, the Sent One of the Father. Water, light, and shepherd are available to all who believe in Jesus, of whatever race or nation.

Notes

39. *For judgment I came into this world:* There is increasing scholarly consensus that 9:1-39 and 10:1-21 form a literary unity. Introducing a recent study of John 10, Johannes Beutler and Robert T. Fortna regard the unity of 9–10 as "one of the most important results of the two-year study" (*The Shepherd Discourse* 3). See also de Villiers, "The Shepherd and his Flock" 90–91; Busse, "Open Questions" 8–9. Menken, *Numerical* 193–197, claims that vv. 39-41 both close 9:1-39 and serve as a starting point for what follows.

40. *Some of the Pharisees:* "The Jews" and the Pharisees continue to be used interchangeably as Jesus' opponents throughout this narrative. On the irony of this question, see Stibbe, *John* 110–111.

1. *is a thief and a robber:* The expression *lēstēs* ("robber"), applied to "the Jews," perhaps hints that those who are supposed to lead Israel are in fact intent on their own messianic choices. On the use of *lēstēs* to speak of the Zealot movement see Martin Hengel, *The Zealots: Investigations into the Jewish Freedom Movement from Herod until 70 A. D.* Edinburgh: T. & T. Clark, 1989, 24–46; T. Rajak, *Josephus: The Historian and His Society.* Philadelphia: Fortress, 1984, 78–103, and especially Simonis, *Die Hirtenrede* 127–142. The possibility of this interpretation becomes more probable at v. 12.

3. *To him the doorkeeper opens:* Allegorical readings of this passage attempt to identify the doorkeeper with some figure in the conflict between Jesus and "the Jews." This is not necessary, as the doorkeeper belongs to the overall pastoral background to the passage and is a sub-shepherd of some sort. See Léon-Dufour, *Lecture* 2:360 n. 69. Several scholars (e.g. Robinson, "The Parable" 233–240; Dodd, Brown, Lindars, Talbert) claim that vv. 1-5 are the result of the fusion of two parables. Vv. 1-3a are a challenge to the doorkeepers of Israel while vv. 3b-5 present the shepherd. Against this see, among many, Painter, *Quest* 346–349.

4. *He goes before them, and the sheep follow him:* Numbers 27:17 ("who shall go out before them and come in before them, who shall lead them out and bring them in, so that the congregation of the LORD may not be like sheep without a shepherd") is close to vv. 3-4, and several scholars (e.g., Barrett, *Gospel* 369) suggest that even at this stage of the discourse a messianic interpretation is given to the OT passage. This is not necessary, as the Numbers and Johannine passages both reflect pastoral practice.

6. *This figure Jesus used with them:* Jesus' words in vv. 1-5 have the form of a parable but function more as a similitude, and there has been scholarly discus-

sion over the Johannine use of the term *paroimia*. For a survey see Reinhartz, *Word in the World* 50–70. Both the more Synoptic *parabolē* and the Johannine *paroimia* translate the Hebrew *māšāl* in the LXX. What must be seen is that the major words and themes of vv. 1-5, shepherd, door, thieves, and robbers, reappear in vv. 7-18. The *paroimia* provides the material out of which the rest of the discourse is formed. The *paroimia*, therefore, is best described as an "image field" (cf. Klaus Berger, *Formgeschichte des Neuen Testaments*. Heidelberg: Quelle, 1984, 38–40), approached later in the discourse from a number of different angles (cf. Schneider, "Zur Komposition" 220–225). Allegorical readings of vv. 1-5 are myriad. Most interpret the passage in an ecclesiological sense. Christ the shepherd creates a new community (Temple, etc.) over against bankrupt Judaism. For different perspectives see de la Potterie, "Le Bon Pasteur" 2:936–943, and Becker, *Evangelium* 1:326–328.

they did not understand what he was saying to them: The immediately previous narrative (9:1-38) provides background for this situation of "the Jews." They do not belong to the flock of the shepherd because they do not recognize his voice and they do not follow him. They are now blind (9:41), thieves, robbers (10:1), and strangers (v. 5). This reversal of the experience of the man born blind (cf. 9:34) by means of the narrator's comment in v. 6 is a further indication of the unity of 9:1–10:21.

7. *I am the door of the sheep:* There is ancient textual evidence ($\mathfrak{P}^{75}$, Sahidic, Coptic) for the reading "I am the shepherd of the sheep." This reading would make excellent sense and for that reason must be rejected. See Brown, *Gospel* 1:386, but it is supported by Tragan, *La Parabole* 182–90, and Busse, "Open Questions" 9–10. Matthew Black, *An Aramaic Approach to the Gospels and Acts*. 3rd ed. Oxford: Clarendon Press, 1967, 259 n. 1, suggests that the confusion between "shepherd" and "door" is the result of a mistranslation of an original Aramaic expression. For a survey of the rich background that may lie behind Jesus' claim to be "the door" see Barrett, *Gospel* 371. For links between "the door" and "the shepherd" in wisdom traditions, see Scott, *Sophia* 121–123. Some have attempted to trace messianic hints on the basis of Ps 118:20 (e.g., Jeremias, *TDNT* 3:179–180). The use of the door indicates that "the single means of access to all that is good is Jesus" (Barrett, *Gospel* 373).

The expression "the door of the sheep" (*hē thyra tōn probatōn*) can mean either the door to the sheep or the door that is used by the sheep. The interpretation associates both meanings.

A pastoral practice exists in the Near East, which has no literary support, wherein the shepherd is the door. He lies down across the door-space and is thus both shepherd and door. On this see Bishop, "The Door of the Sheep" 307–309. See also Morris, *Gospel* 451 n. 32.

8. *all who came before me:* It has long been suggested that "all who came before me" refers to the long history of God's people and its leadership. This is difficult as it implies criticism of the patriarchs, prophets, and righteous of the OT era. There are a number of textual variations here as different manuscript traditions attempted to soften the criticism of the great figures from Israel's past. If "the Jews" of the immediate narrative are those who are criticized as

"all those who came before" Jesus (cf. Brown, *Gospel* 1:393–394; Simonis, *Die Hirtenrede* 108–114; Kiefer, *Die Hirtenrede* 52–56), then the text *pantes hosoi ēlthon pro emou* can be accepted as the *lectio difficilior.*

11. *I am the good shepherd:* There is an obvious intention to stress the "goodness" of the shepherd in the expression *ho poimēn ho kalos.* Various suggestions have been made concerning its significance. It is obviously polemical, but does it mean "handsome shepherd," "effective shepherd," etc.? Given the context there is most likely a close parallel between *kalos* and *alēthinos* (cf. Barrett, *Gospel* 373). Jesus is the shepherd of the people of God in exactly the way a shepherd should be: the authentic shepherd over against all others who might claim to be shepherds.

    lays down his life for the sheep: Although there are no direct links between the use of the shepherd imagery and the laying down of one's life in the OT, there are several OT passages where the self-gift of the Messiah is possibly present (e.g., Isa 53:12; Zech 13:7). For a detailed study of the possible Isaian background to vv. 11 and 14 see Feuillet, "Deux références évangéliques" 556–561.

12. *who is not a shepherd . . . sees the wolf coming and leaves the sheep and flees:* The flight of Jewish leadership to Jamnia prior to the destruction of Jerusalem in 70 C.E. and subsequent events might form the background for this accusation. This would further substantiate the possible association of the expression *lēstēs* in v. 1 with the false messianic hope of the Zealots. Under the leadership of Johanan ben Zakkai some managed to escape besieged Jerusalem to establish postwar Jamnia. In this interpretation the Pharisees of John 9:1–10:21 would represent postwar Judaism, "the Jews" who preserved their own lives while the people of Jerusalem, the sheep of the flock, were snatched and scattered. The pain of the separation between the synagogue and the Johannine community is still keenly felt (cf. also 9:22; 12:42; 16:2). These passages reflect more than a "retrospective glance" (Schnelle, *Antidocetic Christology* 31).

13. *because he is a hireling:* Some manuscripts add "the hireling flees" *(ho de misthōtos pheugei)* to be the beginning of v. 13 to improve the meaning. But it should be omitted, as it is in such witnesses as $\mathfrak{P}^{45.66.75}$, Sinaiticus, Vaticanus, and others.

14. *I am the good shepherd:* Many scholars already divide the discourse into its second part at v. 11 because of Jesus' self-revelation as the Good Shepherd at that point (e.g., Brown, *Gospel* 1:395; Schnackenburg, *Gospel* 2:294; Léon-Dufour, *Lecture* 2:392; Kysar, "Johannine Metaphor" 86–88). The fact that all polemic ceases and that Jesus speaks directly of his relationship to the sheep and to the Father without reference to other "shepherds" from v. 14 onward is seldom noticed. See, however, Bultmann, *Gospel* 380; Tragan, *La Parabole* 207–208, 216–217; Kiefer, *Die Hirtenrede* 60–61.

15. *as the Father knows me and I know the Father:* The importance of "knowledge" in vv. 14-15 has led Bultmann, *Gospel* 367–370, to argue that the shepherd imagery has its background in Gnostic, not biblical sources. In defense of the biblical background to this use of the theme see Schnackenburg, *Gospel* 2:298.

The theme of "knowledge" has been present throughout John 9:1-38. It does not begin here even though it is being used in a different sense. On the intimacy communicated by the expressions *kathōs . . . kagō*, see O. de Dinechin, "*Kathôs:* La similitude dans l'évangile de Saint Jean," *RSR* 58 (1970) 198–207.

16. *there shall be one flock, one shepherd:* For Jewish material that indicates that the Messiah would gather the people see Hofius, "Die Sammlung" 289–291; Manns, *L'Evangile* 231–233.

17. *that I may take it again:* The "that" *(hina)* should not be read as stressing the purpose of Jesus' laying down his life *so that he might* take it again. It indicates consequence. One event will follow the other. Unlike most NT authors, who refer to the resurrection of Jesus as the action of God, the author of the Fourth Gospel here presents Jesus as the agent. See Brown, *Gospel* 1:399. He takes up his life. In v. 18 Jesus will say that he has *exousia* ("authority") to take it. However, this Gospel retains the traditional idea of God's initiative in its resurrection account (ch. 20). Schnackenburg, *Gospel* 2:301–302, insists on the Johannine idea of the union of the life-sacrifice and subsequent resurrection as lying "within the Father's mandate" (p. 301).

FOR REFERENCE AND FURTHER STUDY

Beutler, Johannes, and Robert T. Fortna, eds. *The Shepherd Discourse of John 10 and its Context.* MSSNTS 67. Cambridge: Cambridge University Press, 1991.

Bishop, E. F. "The Door of the Sheep—John x.7-9," *ET* 71 (1959–1960) 307–309.

Busse, Ulrich. "Open Questions on John 10," *The Shepherd Discourse* 6–17.

Feuillet, André. "Deux références évangéliques cachées au Serviteur martyrisé," *NRTh* 106 (1984) 556–561.

Hofius, Otfried. "Die Sammlung der Heiden zur Herde Israels (Joh 10:16; 11:51f.)," *ZNW* 58 (1967) 289–291.

Jeremias, Joachim. "*thyra,*" *TDNT* 3 (1965) 179–180.

Kiefer, Odo. *Die Hirtenrede.* SBS 23. Stuttgart: Katholisches Bibelwerk, 1967.

Kysar, Robert. "Johannine Metaphor—Meaning and Function: A Literary Case Study of John 10:1-8 [*sic*]," *Sem* 53 (1991) 81–111.

La Potterie, Ignace de. "Le Bon Pasteur." In *Populus Dei: Studi in onore del Cardinale Alfredo Ottaviani per il cinquantesimo del sacerdozio, 19 marzo, 1966.* 2 vols. Rome: LAS, 1968, 2:927–968.

Moloney, Francis J. *Signs and Shadows* 129–142.

Reinhartz, Adele. *The Word in the World: The Cosmological Tale in the Fourth Gospel.* SBL.MS 45. Atlanta: Scholars, 1992.

Robinson, J. A. T. "The Parable of the Shepherd," *ZNW* 46 (1955) 233–240.

Schneider, Johannes. "Zur Komposition von Joh. 10," *CNT* 11 (1947) 220–225.

Simonis, A. J. *Die Hirtenrede im Johannesevangelium: Versuch einer Analyse von Johannes 10,1-18 nach Entstehung, Hintergrund und Inhalt.* AnBib 29. Rome: Biblical Institute Press, 1967.

Thyen, Hartwig. "Johannes 10 im Kontext des vierten Evangeliums," *The Shepherd Discourse* 116–134.

Tragan, Pius-Ramon. *La Parabole du "Pasteur" et ses explications: Jean 10,1-18. La genèse, les milieux littéraires.* Studia Anselmiana 66. Sacramentum 3. Rome: Editrice Anselmiana, 1977.

Villiers, J. L. de. "The Shepherd and His Flock," *Neotest.* 2 (1968) 89–103.

Willmes, Bernd. *Die sogennante Hirtenallegorie Ez 34: Studien zum Bild des Hirten im Alten Testament.* BET 19. Frankfurt: Peter Lang, 1984.

v. Jesus and Dedication (10:22-42)

22. It was the feast of the Dedication at Jerusalem; 23. it was winter, and Jesus was walking in the Temple, in the portico of Solomon.
24. So the Jews gathered round him and said to him, "How long will you keep us in suspense? If you are the Christ, tell us plainly."
25. Jesus answered them, "I told you, and you do not believe. The works that I do in my Father's name, they bear witness to me; 26. but you do not believe because you do not belong to my sheep. 27. My sheep hear my voice, and I know them, and they follow me; 28. and I give them eternal life, and they shall never perish, and no one shall snatch them out of my hand. 29. My Father, who has given them to me, is greater than all, and no one is able to snatch them out of the Father's hand. 30. I and the Father are one."
31. The Jews took up stones again to stone him. 32. Jesus answered them, "I have shown you many good works from the Father; for which of these do you stone me?" 33. The Jews answered him, "It is not for a good work that we stone you but for blasphemy; because you, being a man, make yourself God." 34. Jesus answered them, "Is it not written in your law, 'I said, you are gods'? 35. If he called them gods to whom the word of God came (and the scripture always remains in force), 36. do you say of him whom the Father consecrated and sent into the world, 'You are blaspheming,' because I said, 'I am the Son of God'? 37. If I am not doing the works of my Father, then do not believe me; 38. but if I do them, even though you do not believe me, believe the works, that you may know and understand that the Father is in me and I am in the Father." 39. Again they tried to arrest him, but he escaped from their hands.
40. He went away again across the Jordan to the place where John at first baptized, and there he remained. 41. And many came to him; and they said, "John did no sign, but everything that John said about this man was true." 42. And many believed in him there.

Interpretation

Introduction to 10:22-42. In 10:22 the narrator announces: "It was the feast of the Dedication at Jerusalem." This relatively recent celebration was instituted to commemorate the rededication of the Temple after Judas Maccabeus' successful campaign to take possession of Jerusalem in 164 B.C.E. In 175 B.C.E. Antiochus IV ascended the throne in Syria. He planned to extend his rule into Egypt but he first had to consolidate his authority over the outlying areas of his present rule (cf. 1 Macc 1:41). The Jewish people resisted him, but he found support among segments of the Jewish aristocracy and priesthood. He deposed the rightful high priest, Onias III, and sold the priesthood to Onias' brother Joshua, who changed his name to the Greek "Jason." A gymnasium was built in Jerusalem (1 Macc 1:11-13), and Jews hid their circumcision as they participated naked in the events of the gymnasium. They disowned the sign of the covenant. Antiochus, now calling himself "Epiphanes" ("the manifest God") decreed that all should worship Zeus Olympios, so that the people "would forget the law and change all the ordinances" (1 Macc 1:49; cf. vv. 41-50). Opposition led to persecution and death (1 Macc 1:60-64; cf. 1:56-58). On the fifteenth of Chislev in 167 B.C.E. a sacrifice to Zeus was offered in the Temple on a pagan altar built over the altar of holocausts. This new altar was called "the desolating sacrilege" (1 Macc 1:59; cf. Dan 11:31).

These events led to the revolt initiated by a Jewish priest, Mattathias. Through a remarkable series of events and fortunate coincidences his son Judas eventually had the better of the Syrian forces, finally defeating them in 164 B.C.E. (1 Macc 2:1–4:35). His first task was the purification of the Temple. The "desolating sacrilege" was torn down and a new altar of holocausts erected. The Temple area was rebuilt and refurbished. Lamps were set up to illuminate the sacred ground once again, marking the restoration of Temple order (1 Macc 4:46-51; cf. 2 Macc 10:1-4). The Temple was rededicated on the twenty-fifth of Chislev, 164 B.C.E., three years after its defilement, and this event was commemorated each year in the celebration of the feast of the Dedication.

The accounts of Dedication in 1 Macc 4:52-59 and 2 Macc 10:5-8 reveal similarities between the feast of the Dedication, called "the feast of booths in the month of Chislev" (2 Macc 1:9; cf. also 2 Macc 10:6), and the feast of Tabernacles. As with Tabernacles (cf. Lev 23:42-43), the feast was celebrated so that Israel might remember God's protection during its wandering in the wilderness (cf. Nodet, "La Dédicace" 523–537). As well as recalling God's care during the Exodus, Dedication also focused on the evidence of God's ongoing care in the restoration of the Temple, where God dwelt among the chosen people. The Temple was the visible sign of God's presence. Another element in the celebration of Dedication, not present at Tabernacles, was the memory of the apostasy among the Jews that had led to the desecration and destruction of the Temple. Jews had blasphemed the Holy One of Israel and led others into idolatry. "The feast of the Dedication . . . summoned the people to remain steadfast to the law of their God and, by so doing, proclaim, 'Never again!'" (Yee, *Jewish Feasts* 88; cf. also Nodet, "La Dédicace" 337–340).

Against this background to the celebration of Dedication, the Johannine account of Jesus' presence in Jerusalem for the feast unfolds as follows:

> (a) *Vv. 22-23:* Setting: Jesus is in the Temple at the time of Dedication, wintertime.
> (b) *V. 24:* "The Jews" raise the question of the Messiah.
> (c) *Vv. 25-30:* Jesus tells them of the basis and purpose of his messianic status.
> (d) *Vv. 31-39:* In heated altercation Jesus points to his works as proof of his oneness with the Father (vv. 32, 34-35, 37-38), while "the Jews" attempt to stone him (vv. 31, 33), charge him with blasphemy (vv. 33, 36), and seek to arrest him (v. 39).
> (e) *Vv. 40-42:* Jesus leaves the Temple (v. 40). Many search for Jesus, recalling that what the Baptist said about him was true (vv. 41-42).

There are two moments of "closure" in vv. 40-42. Jesus' departure from the Temple in v. 40a brings to an end his presence there for the feast of Dedication (v. 22), but he returns to the other side of the Jordan, where John had at first baptized (v. 40bc), as many recall that what John had said was true (v. 41) and believe in him (v. 42). Words and events from the first day in the ministry of Jesus "in Bethany beyond the Jordan, where John was baptizing" (1:28) are recalled, indicating to the reader that a major stage in the telling of Jesus' story has come to an end.

The setting (vv. 22-23). Some three months after the celebration of Tabernacles, in the middle of winter, Jesus walks in the protection of the portico of Solomon on the occasion of the feast of the Dedication.

The question of the Messiah (v. 24). Although time and place have changed, the audience is still "the Jews" who gather around Jesus. Their question to Jesus continues the debates of Tabernacles. Whereas on the earlier occasion they disputed among themselves whether or not Jesus had messianic credentials, now they ask him directly. The question, however, is ironic: "How long will you keep us in suspense? . . . tell us plainly" (v. 24). The debate over the Messiah has been resolved by Jesus in his self-revelation as the Good Shepherd (10:14-18). Three months later "the Jews" are asking how much longer they must wait. They have already been told plainly *(parrēsią)* that Jesus is the Christ. As throughout the Gospel, they will not listen to the word of Jesus. Their judgments remain fleshly as they continue to assess Jesus by their own criteria (cf. 7:24; 8:15).

Jesus explains his messianic status (vv. 25-30). Jesus insists that he has already told them (v. 25b), but clearly they will not listen to his words. He thus asks them to look to his works done in the name of the Father. They give transparent witness to Jesus' claims (v. 25b). Jesus used the image of the Good Shepherd to address "the Jews" and to respond to their queries about his messianic status (10:1-18). They have not listened to these words, but he returns to the same imagery to explain why "the Jews" are unable to accept him as the revelation of God and the perfection of God's gift. They do not belong to his sheep and thus are unable to accept his word or see the revelation of God in his deeds. Neither are they able to believe that he is the Messiah. The sheep of the Good Shepherd hear his voice and respond to it (vv. 3, 4, 14, 16), but "the Jews" do not. They cannot belong to his flock. "Allegory and application merge" (Lindars, *Gospel* 368).

The image of the sheep of the Good Shepherd, who hear *(akousousin)* his voice and follow *(akolouthousin)* him so that he might give them eternal life *(zōē aiōnios)*, that they may never be lost *(ou mē apolōntai eis ton aiōna)*, conjures up major descriptions of the authentic believer. A believer "hears" (1:41; 3:8, 29; 4:42; 5:24, 28; 6:45; 8:38, 43; 10:3, 16), has "eternal life" (3:15, 16, 36; 4:14, 36; 5:24, 39; 6:27, 40, 47, 54, 68), "follows" Jesus (1:37, 44; 8:12; 10:4, 5), and "is not lost" (3:16; 6:12, 27, 39; 10:10). This evocation of the consistent teaching of Jesus insists that belief in Jesus as the Messiah *on his terms* will bring life, and no one can snatch them from Jesus (vv. 27-28). Although it is only said obliquely in a description of what will *not* happen to the believer—"they shall never perish"—the opposite is also true. An unwillingness to respond *beyond the limitations of their own terms* will lead "the Jews" to death. The sheep cannot be snatched away from Jesus because the life the believer receives from attachment to Jesus is a gift of the Father. No power is greater than God, and thus the believer's union with God is assured. The Father of Jesus is greater than all other powers (v. 29). As Israel celebrated God's presence at the feast of Dedication, Jesus tells "the Jews" that there is another way God is present to them. They can be sure they are in the Father's hand if they believe in Jesus. In celebrating Dedication "the Jews" pride themselves on their reconsecrated Temple, the physical evidence of their belonging to God and, in some way, of God's belonging to them. But Jesus insists that faith in his word ties the believer not only to him but to God, the Father of Jesus.

The affirmation of 10:30 continues this theme: "I and the Father are one." There is no longer need to look to the physical building on the Temple Mount to know of God's presence to God's people. Jesus, who stands before "the Jews," points to himself and claims that he is the visible presence of God among them. No Messiah in the Jewish expectation would claim to replace the Temple, but that is what Jesus does in v. 30. The promise of the Prologue is acted out in the story of Jesus: "And the Word became flesh and dwelt among us, the fullness of a gift that is truth. We have gazed upon his glory, glory as of the only Son from the Father" (1:14). This is not a study in metaphysics but a statement on the oneness of purpose that unites the Father and the Son, created by a union of love and obedience. The setting of these words of Jesus within the feast of Dedication indicates further that the union between God and the Temple that was seen as God's presence to the people is perfected in Jesus because of his oneness with the Father.

"The Jews" continue to reject Jesus (vv. 31-39). Jesus' claim in 10:30 forms the bedrock for the argument developed throughout chs. 5–10. Because of the oneness that exists between the Father and the Son, Jesus can claim the Sabbath privilege of judging and giving life (5:19-30) and can assert that he is the bread from heaven, perfecting the nourishment provided by the Law (6:44-50), as well as the water of life and the light of the world (7:37-38; 8:12; 9:5), the Messiah who perfects Israel's messianic hopes, celebrated at Tabernacles (10:1-18). But another memory is associated with Dedication: will "the Jews" stand by their resolve never again to betray their unique God? They take up stones against Jesus (v. 31), repeating the profanations of Antiochus IV and his representatives. They are attempting to rid Israel of the visible presence of God in their midst.

Jesus speaks again to his works (cf. v. 25b), asking which of these has led to this attempt to stone him (v. 32). Which particular revelation of the *doxa* of God (cf. 2:1-11; 4:46-54; 5:1-9a; 6:1-15; 9:1-7) has moved "the Jews" to attempt to kill him? Again the response shows they do not recognize the truth of Jesus' accusing question. They fall back on a superficial interpretation of the Law, claiming they are not stoning him for any "good work" *(kalon ergon)*, but for blasphemy. Jesus' blasphemy lies in his claim, as a man, to being divine (v. 33). As they remember the reconsecration of a Temple built in stone by human beings they ignore the claims of Jesus to be the living presence of God among them. Their understanding of Jesus as a blasphemer is deeply ironic.

Jesus' response develops what he said in v. 30. If it is correct that he and the Father are one, and there can be no avoiding that truth, then a charge of blasphemy against Jesus is a serious betrayal of the God of Israel. Jesus follows the Jewish technique of arguing from the minor to the major *(qal waḥōmer*; cf. Manns, *L'Evangile* 313–314). Referring to "your Law" *(en tǭ nomǭ hymōn)*, indicating the whole of the Scriptures, Jesus cites Ps 82:6: "I said, you are Gods." If the Scriptures, which always remain in force, call the people of God "gods" (v. 35: minor), how much more can the one whom God has created and sent call himself "the Son of God" (v. 36: major). "The Jews" stand condemned by their own Scriptures. Jesus claims that he offends nothing from the authentic tradition of Israel, but perfects what God had promised in consecrating *(hēgiasen)* and sending the Son into the world. This is the first time Jesus has been described as consecrated by God, and this consecration recalls the event behind the celebration of the feast of Dedication: the consecration of the altar of holocausts that replaced "the desolating sacrilege" of Antiochus IV. Jesus' presence at the feast as the one sent by the Father, the visible presence of God in the world, brings to perfection what was only a sign and a shadow in Judas' act of consecration in 164 B.C.E. There is no longer the need to seek God in the consecrated stone altar; God is made known in the person of the consecrated and sent Son of God (v. 36).

Jesus is the living presence of the Son of God among "the Jews" (v. 36b), and his works reflect his Father. If they wish to show their loyalty to their God, the Father of Jesus, then they are to accept all that Jesus says or does. There is an internal logic to Jesus' argument: once one accepts Jesus' origins and destiny, all else follows. If Jesus were not doing the works of God, "the Jews" would be right in not believing him; but such a situation is impossible after what "the Jews" have seen and heard (v. 37). They celebrate their allegiance to the God of Israel present in the Temple, but they are not prepared to accept that same God, visible in the works of Jesus. In a final moment Jesus summons them to accept the truth that the God of Israel, once present in the building of the consecrated Temple, is now present to them in the visible works of God's Son (v. 38). His final words at the celebration of Dedication are a restatement of v. 30. There is only one way to God, and that is through God's Son; there is only one place where the Father may be found and understood, and that is in the story of his Son. Jesus appeals to his unbelieving listeners, exhorting them to accept the revelation of God in his works. If they do they may come to understand ("that you may know and understand") the truth of v. 30, that Jesus and the Father are one: "The Father is in me and I am in the Father" (v. 38).

The feast of Tabernacles produced a *schisma* and a glimmer of hope for "the Jews." Some saw the possibility that Jesus might be a messianic miracle worker (10:21). At the celebration of Dedication, some three months later, all such hope disappears. "The Jews" have attempted to stone Jesus (vv. 31, 33), and they tried to arrest him, but he slipped through their hands (v. 39). Even though violence looms large, the reader is aware that the hour has not yet come (cf. 2:4; 7:30; 8:20): *for the moment,* "he escaped from their hands" (v. 39).

Conclusion (vv. 40-42). Despite the rejection of Jesus in vv. 31-39, vv. 40-42 keep alive the story of a response to Jesus as many come to believe in him in a different place (v. 42). Jesus leaves the violent scene of the Temple and leaves Jerusalem to cross the Jordan, to the place where John had baptized, and he remains there (v. 40). Apart from his presence in Galilee for the celebration of Passover (6:1-71) Jesus has been in Jerusalem, celebrating Jewish feasts, since the narrator announced the theme of the feasts of "the Jews" in 5:1. His return to the place where John had baptized recalls the first day of the ministry of Jesus (1:19-28), which concludes, "This took place in Bethany beyond the Jordan, where John was baptizing" (1:28). The ministry has come full circle as Jesus returns to the spot from which it began, and this mention of the "first day" may be a hint that the "last day" is at hand (cf. Thyen, "Johannes 10" 123–124). For the moment the action and the words of Jesus come to a halt in this new location (v. 40).

But many *(polloi)* seek him out. The possibility that Jesus might be the Messiah again emerges. John the Baptist did no sign, but many believe that his prophecies about Jesus are true (10:41): the Lamb of God who takes away the sin of the world (1:29, 36), a person filled with the Spirit (1:32) who baptizes with the Spirit (1:33). Jesus is the bridegroom who has the bride (3:29), and if the Baptist is not the Christ (1:20, 25; 3:28), the inference is that Jesus is the Christ. Thus many believed in him there (10:42). Hope returns as some in Israel come to believe that Jesus is the fulfillment of the prophecies of John the Baptist, the witness sent by God (cf. 1:6-8). "For the moment in a place still echoing with the cry of John the Baptist's witness and still bright with the light of his lamp (v. 35), Jesus pauses and is greeted by faith. The darkness has not yet come" (Brown, *Gospel* 1:415).

Conclusion to 5:1–10:42. On a Sabbath Jesus insisted he was working as his Father was working, exercising the authority of giving life and judging given to him by the Father (ch. 5). At Passover Jesus claimed to be the true bread from heaven (ch. 6). At Tabernacles Jesus declared he was the living water and the light of the world, and the story of the man born blind showed that his claims were true. Jesus is the authentic revelation of the one true God, the messianic Good Shepherd who freely lays down his life for his sheep, that they may have a life that no one can take from them (7:1–10:21). The stories of Jesus' presence at the celebration of the feasts of "the Jews" claim that he personifies, fulfills, and perfects the signs and shadows of the Jewish feasts, the celebration of the *zikkārōn* of God's action among God's people. The claims made for Jesus from 5:1 to 10:21 are true because Jesus and the Father are one (10:30, 38). It is because Jesus is the living presence of God among the people, the perfection of everything Israel thought of their Temple, that he can claim to be Lord of the Sabbath, the true bread from heaven, the light of the world, the living water, the revelation of the one true God and the Messianic Good Shepherd.

This Gospel does not attempt to denigrate the established and cherished ways of remembering and rendering present God's saving action among the people of Israel. The account of Jesus' presence at their feasts

—Sabbath, Passover, Tabernacles, and Dedication—affirms that the former order has been perfected, not destroyed. The crucial difference between the two orders is the person of Jesus Christ. The conflict between Jesus and "the Jews," as it is reported in these stories, is not a conflict between Jesus and Israel but rather a conflict between some from Israel who had definitively decided that Jesus was or was not the Christ; anyone who confessed he was must be put out of the synagogue (cf. 9:22). As Jesus and "the Jews" are on a collision course, so are "the Jews" and the Johannine Christians, but the latter are proud to look back upon their Jewish heritage, to see in their former festive celebrations of God in Israel the signs and shadows of the presence of Jesus among them. He is judge and lifegiver (Sabbath), the true bread from heaven (Passover), the living water, the light of the world, the messianic Good Shepherd sent by God to lay down his life freely for his own (Tabernacles), the true presence of Israel's one and only God, the living Temple of God in their midst (Dedication).

"The one Word is revealed in the witness of the Old Testament and the Word made flesh. There is a continuity of salvation history. But the coming of the Word made flesh has fulfilled the witness of the Old Testament and abolished its significance as a closed system" (Painter, *John* 32). The tragedy of "the Jews" in the Johannine Gospel lies in their decision that Jesus, the Son of God, is a blasphemer, and that he must die. In their inability to move beyond their "closed system" they reject the incarnate Word of God and thus frustrate God's saving purpose. The remaining part of the narrative will devote its attention to the enigma of a God who reveals his own glory and glorifies his Son through his death.

NOTES

22. *It was the feast of the Dedication at Jerusalem:* For the background and information on the celebration of Dedication see Rankin, *The Origins;* Nodet, "La Dédicace" 321–375; Yee, *Jewish Feasts* 83–86.

23. *it was winter:* The indications that it was the feast of the Dedication and it was winter match. They must be taken seriously (cf. Busse, "Open Questions" 6–9). Some (e.g., Westcott, *Gospel* 143 [9:1–10:39]; Talbert, *Reading John* 164–165 [10:1–11:54]; Kysar, *John's Story* 51–55 [10:1-42]) collapse the events of this section of the Gospel into a larger section, ignoring the indications of v. 22.

    and Jesus was walking in the temple, in the portico of Solomon: According to Josephus, *War* 5.184–185; *Ant.* 15.396–401; 20.220–221, the portico was on the eastern side of the Temple. On the wisdom of walking in this location in midwinter see Brown, *Gospel* 1:405. VanderKam, "John 10" 205–206, regards the mention of Solomon's portico as a reference to the only part of the original Temple still standing at the time of Jesus, soon to be replaced by the temple of Jesus' body (cf. 2:19-22).

24. *So the Jews gathered round him:* Commentators sometimes remark that the "gathering" of "the Jews" *(ekylōsan)* around Jesus is threatening.

    How long will you keep us in suspense?: The Greek for "keep us in suspense" *(tēn psychēn hēmōn aireis)* is obscure. It may also contain a hint of anger, and could be rendered as "How much longer will you annoy/vex us?" (Barrett, *Gospel* 380).

26. *you do not belong to my sheep:* This return to the imagery of sheep and shepherding has led scholars either to disregard the indications of the change of time and place in vv. 22-23a or to suggest that the narrative is confused, as vv. 26b-20 (30) are out of place. Both suggestions, while understandable, do not demand assent. The unfolding argument of the message as it stands makes sense, and the many parallels between the Jewish celebration of Tabernacles and Dedication enable the author to recall images used on the occasion of Tabernacles (10:1-18).

27. *hear my voice . . . follow me:* As can be seen from the texts provided in the interpretation, there are many links between 10:25-29 and 6:31-59. Von Wahlde, "Literary Structure" 575–584, and Stibbe, *John* 117, also see links between 10:25-29 and 8:13-59. Stibbe regards 10:22-39 as a summary of John 5–10. Many themes from earlier parts of the Gospel are gathered in these few verses.

29. *My Father, who has given them to me, is greater than all:* This translation of a contested Greek original affirms the uniqueness of the God of Israel, the Father of Jesus. There are five well-attested variations of the first part of v. 29. For the discussion see Birdsall, "John x.29" 342–344; Whittaker, "A Hellenistic Context" 241–260.

    no one is able to snatch them out of the Father's hand: The theme of God's care for the chosen people, transferred here to those who believe in Jesus, is a further link between themes common to the celebration of both Tabernacles and Dedication.

30. *I and the Father are one:* Although commentators rightly point out that this is not a metaphysical claim there is, nevertheless, a glimpse of "the metaphysical depths contained in the relationship between Jesus and the Father" (Schnackenburg, *Gospel* 2:308). See especially Bühner, *Der Gesandte und sein Weg* 209–235. For a survey of the possible interpretations of *hen esmen* ("are one") see Carson, *Gospel* 394–395. For the importance of this verse in later trinitarian debate see T. E. Pollard, "The Exegesis of John X,30 in the Early Trinitarian Controversies," *NTS* 3 (1956–1957) 334–339.

33. *you, being a man, make yourself God:* The Greek *poieis seauton theon,* without an article before *theon,* is virtually adjectival. See Lindars, *Gospel* 372. This makes a comfortable passage into Jesus' citation of Ps. 82:2, "You are gods" *(theoi este)* in v. 34.

34. *Is it not written in your law:* It is widely accepted that the Greek *nomos* ("law") here means the Scriptures as such. Some witnesses ($\mathfrak{P}^{45}$, first hand of Sinaiticus, Bezae, etc.) omit "your" *(hymōn).* It does seem strange that a Jew (Jesus) would speak to Jews of "your law." However, Jesus' words show the gulf between "the Jews'" understanding of God and his own.

you are gods: There is difficulty over the meaning of what Bauer calls "the elastic nature of the ancient expression *theos*" (Bauer, *Johannesevangelium* 147). The original psalm may regard as "gods" Israel's judges, the people of Israel, angelic powers, or the gods of the nations. For the rabbis, the Law was given to angels/gods. The interpretation reads that the people addressed, human beings, can be called "gods." See the discussion in Brown, *Gospel* 1:409–411.

35. *and the scripture always remains in force:* For this translation of *ou dynatai lythēnai* see Lindars, *Gospel* 375.

36. *him whom the Father consecrated:* Very few scholars make the link between the description of Jesus as "consecrated" and the celebration of Dedication. See, however, the excellent discussion by Brown, *Gospel* 1:411. Indeed, Brown entitles this section of his commentary, "Jesus is consecrated in place of the temple altar" (1:401). See also VanderKam, "John 10" 206–207.

38. *the Father is in me and I am in the Father:* VanderKam, "John 10" 211–214, sees Antiochus's claim to be "God Manifest" behind the presentation of Jesus' parallel, but justified, claim to oneness with God (vv. 30, 38). This claim by Antiochus also lies behind "the Jews'" accusation that Jesus, like the Syrian King (cf. 2 Macc 9:28), was a blasphemer (cf. vv. 33, 36)

    that you may know and understand: The use of the aorist subjunctive here *(hina gnōte kai ginōskēte)* denotes the beginning of knowledge and understanding at a point of time. This is Jesus' hope, and thus his exhortation (cf. Barrett, *Gospel* 386). Some good witnesses ($\mathfrak{P}^{45.66.75}$, Vaticanus, etc.) read *kai pisteuēte* ("and believe"), which would be an easier reading. For this reason it should be rejected.

41. *John did no sign:* This is consistent with all the traditions concerning the Baptist. See Bammel, "John Did No Miracles" 197–202.

FOR REFERENCE AND FURTHER STUDY

Bammel, Ernst. "John Did No Miracles: John 10:41," in *Miracles: Cambridge Studies in Their Philosophy and History.* London: Mowbrays, 1965, 197–202.

Birdsall, J. N. "John x.29," *JThS* 11 (1960) 342–344.

Moloney, Francis J. *Signs and Shadows* 143–153.

Nodet, Etienne. "La Dédicace, les Maccabées et le Messie," *RB* 93 (1986) 321–375.

Rankin, O. S. *The Origins of the Festival of Hanukkah: The Jewish New-Age festival.* Edinburgh: T & T Clark, 1930.

VanderKam, J. C. "John 10 and the Feast of the Dedication." In John J. Collins and Thomas H. Tobin, eds., *Of Scribes and Scrolls: Studies on the Hebrew Bible, Intertestamental Judaism, and Christian Origins Presented to John Strugnell on the Occasion of His Sixtieth Birthday.* College Theology Society Resources in Religion 5. Lanham, Md.: University Press of America, 1990.

Wahlde, Urban C. von. "Literary Structure and Theological Argument in Three Discourses with the Jews in the Fourth Gospel," *JBL* 103 (1984) 575–584.

Whittaker, John. "A Hellenistic Context for John 10,29," *VigChr* 24 (1970) 241–260.

D. JESUS TURNS TOWARD "THE HOUR" (11:1–12:50)

Introduction to 11:1–12:50. The clash between Jesus and "the Jews" has intensified in 5:1–10:42, yet however much the majority of "the Jews" has decided that Jesus should be arrested and slain, some have believed in him (cf. 8:30; 10:19-22, 41-42). Jesus' return to the place on the other side of the Jordan where the Baptist first witnessed to him (1:28) and where his ministry began (1:35-51) marks a turning point in the story. Although violence and death have been in the air, and Jesus has spoken about his being "lifted up" (3:14; 8:28), the inevitable end to the story of Jesus, his death by crucifixion, has been an undercurrent through the narrative thus far. In 11:1–12:50 it moves to center stage. Although thinly veiled references to the death of Jesus have studded the narrative, the verb "to die" *(apothnēskein)* has never been associated with Jesus. It appears for the first time in Thomas's words in 11:16, and regularly from that point on (vv. 50, 51; 12:24, 33). The story of the resurrection of Lazarus unfolds under the rubric of 11:4: "This illness is not unto death; it is for the glory of God, so that the Son of God may be glorified by means of it." It leads to the decision that Jesus must die (vv. 49-50), and the indication that the Passover feast is at hand (v. 55). The rest of the story is set within the temporal context of that feast. In 12:1-8 Jesus' body is prepared for the day of his burial, and in vv. 9-19 he enters Jerusalem. With the arrival of the Greeks wishing to see Jesus (vv. 20-22) he announces, for the first time, that "the hour has come": "The hour has come for the Son of Man to be glorified" (v. 23). Jesus speaks to all would-be disciples (vv. 24-26) and appeals to "the Jews" for the last time (vv. 30-36a). In v. 36b "he departed and hid himself from them." The public ministry of Jesus closes with a reflection from the narrator on why "the Jews" failed to accept Jesus (vv. 37-43) and a final proclamation of Jesus that synthesizes the significance of his revealing presence. The stage is well set for the Johannine account of Jesus' final encounter with his disciples (13:1–17:26), the story of his death and resurrection (18:1–20:29) and the closing remarks of the narrator (20:30-31).

i. A Resurrection That Will Lead to Death (11:1-54)

1. Now a certain man was ill, Lazarus of Bethany, the village of Mary and her sister Martha. 2. It was Mary who anointed the Lord with ointment and wiped his feet with her hair, whose brother Lazarus was ill. 3. So the sisters sent to him, saying, "Lord, he whom you love is ill." 4. But when Jesus heard it he said, "This illness is not unto death; it is for the glory of God, so that the Son of God may be glorified by means of it." 5. Now Jesus loved Martha and her sister and Lazarus. 6. So when he heard that he was ill he stayed two days longer in the place where he was.

7. Then after this he said to the disciples, "Let us go into Judea again." 8. The disciples said to him, "Rabbi, the Jews were but now seeking to stone you, and are you going there again?" 9. Jesus answered, "Are there not twelve hours in the day? Those who walk during the day do not stumble because they see the light of this world. 10. But those who walk at night stumble because the light is not in them." 11. Thus he spoke, and then he said to them, "Our friend Lazarus has fallen asleep, but I go to awake him out of sleep." 12. The disciples said to him, "Lord, if he has fallen asleep he will recover." 13. Now Jesus had spoken of his death, but they thought that he meant taking rest in sleep. 14. Then Jesus told them plainly, "Lazarus is dead; 15. and for your sake I am glad that I was not there, so that you may believe. But let us go to him." 16. Thomas, called the Twin, said to his fellow disciples, "Let us also go, that we may die with him."

17. Now when Jesus came he found that Lazarus had already been in the tomb four days. 18. Bethany was near Jerusalem, about two miles off, 19. and many of the Jews had come to Martha and Mary to console them concerning their brother. 20. When Martha heard that Jesus was coming she went and met him, while Mary sat in the house. 21. Martha said to Jesus, "Lord, if you had been here my brother would not have died. 22. And even now I know that whatever you ask from God, God will give you." 23. Jesus said to her, "Your brother will rise again." 24. Martha said to him, "I know that he will rise again in the resurrection at the last day." 25. Jesus said to her, "I am the resurrection and the life. Those who believe in me, even though they die, will live, 26. and whoever lives and believes in me shall never die. Do you believe this?" 27. She said to him, "Yes, Lord; I have believed that you are the Christ, the Son of God, the one who is coming into the world."

28. When she had said this she went and called her sister Mary, saying quietly, "The Teacher is here and is calling for you." 29. And when she heard it she rose quickly and went to him. 30. Now Jesus had not yet come to the village, but was still in the place where Martha had met him. 31. When the Jews who were with her in the house, consoling her, saw Mary rise quickly and go out, they followed her, supposing that she was going to the tomb to weep there. 32. Then Mary, when she came where Jesus was and saw him, fell at his feet, saying to him, "Lord, if you had been here my brother would not have died." 33. When Jesus saw her weeping, and the Jews who came with her also weeping, he was deeply moved in spirit and troubled; 34. and he said, "Where have you laid him?" They said to him, "Lord, come and see." 35. Jesus wept. 36. So the Jews said, "See how he loved him!" 37. But some of them said, "Could not he who opened the eyes of the blind man have kept this man from dying?"

38. Then Jesus, deeply moved again, came to the tomb; it was a cave, and a stone lay upon it. 39. Jesus said, "Take away the stone." Martha, the sister of the dead man, said to him, "Lord, by this time there will be an

odor, for he has been dead four days." 40. Jesus said to her, "Did I not tell you that if you would believe you would see the glory of God?" 41. So they took away the stone. And Jesus lifted up his eyes and said, "Father, I thank you because you have heard me. 42. I knew that you hear me always, but I have said this on account of the people standing by, that they may believe that you did send me." 43. When he had said this he cried with a loud voice, "Lazarus, come out." 44. The dead man came out, his hands and feet bound with bandages, and his face wrapped with a cloth. Jesus said to them, "Unbind him and let him go."

45. Many of the Jews therefore, who had come to Mary and had seen what he did, believed in him; 46. but some of them went to the Pharisees and told them what Jesus had done. 47. So the chief priests and the Pharisees gathered the council and said, "What are we doing? For this man performs many signs. 48. If we let him go on thus, everyone will believe in him, and the Romans will come and destroy both our holy place and our nation." 49. But one of them, Caiaphas, who was high priest that year, said to them, "You know nothing at all; 50. you do not understand that it is expedient for you that one man should die for the people, and that the whole nation should not perish." 51. He did not say this of his own accord, but being high priest that year he prophesied that Jesus should die for the nation, 52. and not for the nation only, but to gather into one the children of God who are scattered abroad. 53. So from that day on they took counsel how to put him to death. 54 Jesus therefore no longer went about openly among the Jews but went from there to the country near the wilderness, to a town called Ephraim; and there he stayed with the disciples.

INTERPRETATION

Introduction to 11:1-54. The story of the resurrection of Lazarus and the events leading up to it have long fascinated artists, musicians, storytellers, and readers. The account as we have it no doubt developed in the pre-Johannine storytelling tradition (cf. Marchadour, *Lazare* 33–63; Kremer, *Lazarus* 82–109; Byrne, *Lazarus* 69–83), but in its present location and literary shape "the miracle has been made to serve the purposes of Johannine theology" (Brown, *Gospel* 1:430). It unfolds in the following fashion:

(a) *Vv. 1-6:* Introduction. The place, time, characters, situation, and major themes of the narrative are introduced.

(b) *Vv. 7-16:* Two decisions are made. Jesus decides he must go to Judea, and Thomas decides the disciples should accompany him.

(c) *Vv. 17-27:* Jesus' encounter with Martha. Jesus reveals himself as the resurrection and the life but is misunderstood by Martha.

(d) *Vv. 28-37:* Jesus' encounter with Mary. After initially surpassing Martha's confession of Jesus she falters as she joins "the Jews" in their weeping and false understanding of Jesus.

(e) *Vv. 38-44:* The miracle. Jesus calls forth Lazarus, that doubting and unbelieving characters might believe he is the Sent One of God.

(f) *Vv. 45-54:* The decision of "the Jews." The leaders decide that Jesus must die. The full significance of this death is provided by the narrator as Jesus and his disciples leave the scene and go to Ephraim.

The narrative begins (vv. 1-6) and ends (vv. 45-54) with Jesus away from Bethany and Jerusalem. The words of Jesus in v. 4 and the comments of Caiaphas and the narrator in vv. 49-52 frame the story of a resurrection that will lead to death. Jesus will die in Jerusalem and his death will reveal the glory of God; the Son will be glorified by means of it (v. 4), and the children of God scattered abroad will be gathered into one (v. 52; cf. 10:16).

Introduction (vv. 1-6). Three new characters appear: Lazarus, Mary, and Martha, of Bethany (v. 1). Jesus is beyond the Jordan at another Bethany (10:30; cf. 1:28). Mary is introduced as the person who anointed Jesus and wiped his feet with her hair (v. 2ab). The participles "anointed" *(aleipsasa)* and "wiped" *(ekmaxasa)* are in the aorist tense, telling of something she had already done, but there is no record of this in the story thus far. This puzzle seeks resolution, as does the final remark of v. 2: "whose brother Lazarus was ill" (v. 2c). One reads further into the narrative to discover what Jesus will do about the ailing Lazarus and Mary's anointing of Jesus' feet.

The sisters are able to communicate directly with Jesus, addressing him as "Lord" *(kyrie)* and naming their ill brother as "he whom you love" *(hon phileis).* Jesus announces that this illness does not have the *ultimate purpose* of leading Lazarus to death *(ouk estin pros thanaton).* It will have two results that transcend the immediate illness of Jesus' friend. The illness will be the means by which *(di' autēs)* the glory of God will shine forth, and the Son of God will be glorified (v. 4). As the disciples saw the *doxa* as a result of Jesus' miracle at Cana (2:11), the reader expects that another miracle will be worked and that the *doxa* of God will be seen by means of it. But what of the glorification of the Son of God? During the account of the celebration of Tabernacles the narrator told the reader that the Spirit had not yet been given because Jesus had not yet been glorified (7:39), and later Jesus told "the Jews" that the Father would glorify him (8:52-54). As Jesus' ministry comes to an end a number of themes are gradually being drawn together. Jesus' words about his "hour" (2:4; 7:7-8, 30; 8:20) and his being "lifted up" (3:14; 8:28) suggest that his glorification will be linked with his death. If this is the case the events surrounding Lazarus will set in motion the glorification of the Son of God (v. 4).

There is an apparent contradiction in the juxtaposition of v. 5 and v. 6. Because of Jesus' love for Martha, her sister, and Lazarus (v. 5) he stays where he is for two further days (v. 6). Out of love Jesus does not go to his loved ones when they need him! As in other places in the Gospel (cf.

2:1-12; 4:46-54; 7:2-14) Jesus' actions cannot be measured by human criteria. He is responding to a design greater than any reader's expectations (cf. Giblin, "Suggestion, Negative Response" 208–210). His love for the family will be shown in deeds that will reveal the glory of God (v. 4). Themes that will emerge during the narrative have been introduced: illness and death (vv. 1, 4), Mary's anointing of Jesus yet to be reported (v. 2), familiarity (v. 3) and affection (v. 5), the glory of God, and the glorification of the Son of God that will result from this illness that is not unto death (v. 4).

Two decisions are made (vv. 7-16). Eventually *(meta touto)*, Jesus summons the disciples to go with him once again to Judea (v. 7). The disciples address Jesus as "Rabbi," indicating the limitations of their understanding of him (cf. 1:38, 49; 3:2, 26; 4:31; 6:25; 9:2). They recall recent attempts to stone Jesus (v. 8; cf. 8:59; 10:31) but the memory of violence does not dissuade him. His response transcends the prudence that recent events should impose. As Jesus indicates the critical nature of this journey to Judea (11:9-10) images of light and darkness, day and night, sight and blindness, so prominent during Jesus' presence in Jerusalem for Tabernacles, return (cf. 7:1–10:21). He has already instructed them on the need to walk in the light of the day provided by him, the light of the world (9:4-5). Using the Jewish calculation of twelve hours for the light of day and twelve hours for the darkness of night, he tells the disciples of the need to be guided by the light of the world. The disciples are invited to join him, not stumbling like "the Jews" (cf. 8:12, 24) but walking in the light (v. 9). In the days that lie ahead if the disciples have no light in them they will stumble (v. 10). The disciples are being prepared for coming events by the light of the world (8:12; 9:5).

Jesus' focus returns to Lazarus as he informs the disciples that their friend has fallen asleep and that he is going to Bethany to wake him from that sleep (v. 11). The disciples take Jesus' words at their face value and are pleased that Lazarus is asleep. This should mean that he will recover (v. 12). An intervention from the narrator informs the reader that the disciples are wrong in this understanding of Jesus' words. Jesus does not mean sleep in the normal sense of the word, but death (v. 13). He brings the disciples fully into the picture by telling them what the narrator has already told the reader: "Lazarus is dead" (v. 14), but he adds that he is rejoicing in this event for the sake of the disciples. Jesus rejoices because through the event of the death of Lazarus the disciples might come to faith (v. 15: *chairō di' hymas hina pisteusēte*). For this reason they are now to set out for Bethany. The strangeness of Jesus' delay in departure (vv. 5-6) is being explained. The motivation for Jesus' decision to go to Bethany is a response to God's designs, not to human need. Jesus decides to set out on this dangerous journey in response to the will of his Father (cf. 4:34;

5:36) so that he might raise Lazarus from the sleep of death (v. 11), and in the hope that this action might bring the disciples to true faith (vv. 14-15).

Thomas recognizes the risk involved and encourages his fellow disciples to join Jesus that they might die with him (v. 16). Jesus told the disciples he was going to Judea to wake Lazarus from the sleep of death (vv. 11, 14), in the hope that they might come to faith (v. 15). He has not asked them to join him on a suicide mission. Thomas's decision is full of the latter and makes no mention of the former. However admirable Thomas's words may appear to be, he has misunderstood Jesus' decision to go to Judea. Jesus seeks belief (v. 15), not death (v. 16). The reasons for the two decisions to go to Bethany, one from Jesus and the other from Thomas, are at cross-purposes. Misunderstanding intensifies among the disciples.

Jesus and Martha (vv. 17-27). Jesus arrives in Bethany to find that Lazarus has been in the tomb for four days (v. 17). The body would be in a state of advanced decay. Bethany is close to Jerusalem (v. 18: fifteen stadia) which makes the journey of "the Jews" from Jerusalem to console the sisters a genuine possibility (v. 18). Only "the Jews" are described as mourning; nothing is said of the emotional state of the sisters. Bethany's proximity to Jerusalem brings Jesus close to the *place* of his passion and death. The mounting hostility of chs. 5–10, the presence of "the Jews," and the theme of death in vv. 2, 4, 8, and 16 hint that the *time* of Jesus' passion and death might also be near. Although in v. 3 the message announcing that Lazarus was ill came from *both* sisters, only Martha is reported as hearing that Jesus was coming, and she goes out to meet him. Mary is described as stationary, seated in the house (v. 20). The two women respond to Jesus in different ways. Martha greets Jesus with the word she and Mary used in their message concerning the illness of their brother, *kyrie* (v. 3). She then confesses her faith in him as a miracle worker, accepting that Jesus' earlier presence would have cured her brother (v. 21). The reason for such belief in Jesus comes from her conviction that whatever he asks of God—even now—will happen (v. 22). Faith in Jesus' miracle-working authority falls short of true belief (cf. 2:23-25; 1:49-51; 3:1-11; 4:25-26; 6:25-27; 7:31). Both Nicodemus (3:2) and the man born blind (9:31-32) expressed their belief that Jesus had special access to God and was able to work miracles because of it. Martha repeats their understanding of Jesus as a rabbi from God who does wonderful signs because God is with him (vv. 21-22; see 3:2; 9:31-32).

Jesus' response *corrects her misunderstanding.* He informs her that Lazarus will rise (v. 23), and the reader knows that Jesus will raise Lazarus from the sleep of death (vv. 11, 14). Martha, who was not present when Jesus spoke to the disciples (vv. 7-15), allows no space to Jesus, as she knows *(oida hoti)* about the resurrection of the dead. Breaking into Jesus' words, she tells him that she accepts a current Jewish understanding of a final resurrection of the dead. *She tells* Jesus what resurrection means: "resurrection at the last day" (v. 24). Jesus must wrest the initiative from the energetic Martha. His words transcend the limited eschatological expectation uttered by Martha and center on his person as the resurrection and the life (v. 25). In another *egō eimi* statement Jesus first reveals himself as the resurrection and the life and then points to the essential nature of belief in him as the only way to resurrection and life (vv. 25-26). This self-revelation of Jesus to Martha announces that faith in him brings life both now and hereafter (cf. 5:19-30). The believer, even if he or she dies physically, will live spiritually (v. 25), and the believer who is alive spiritually will never die spiritually (see note). Jesus *is* resurrection and life, and thus the believer on this side of death *lives* in the spirit (cf. 3:6; 5:24-25), and the one who believes in him now *will live* on the other side of physical death (cf. 5:28-29; 6:40, 54). Jesus concludes his self-revelation by bluntly asking Martha: "Do you believe this?" (v. 26c: *pisteueis touto?*).

Martha has confessed her faith in Jesus as a miracle worker (v. 21) and attempted to tell him the true meaning of the resurrection of the dead (v. 24). She now continues her arrogance by telling Jesus that she has believed for some time (v. 27a: *egō pepisteuka*). The use of the personal pronoun (*egō:* "I") and the perfect tense of the verb (*pepisteuka:* "have believed") indicate Martha's long-held beliefs. In the past she came to a certain understanding of Jesus, and she has not moved from the belief that Jesus is the Christ *(ho Christos)*, the Son of God *(ho huios tou theou)*, the one who is coming into the world *(ho eis ton kosmon erchomenos)* (v. 27bcd). All these expressions have been used by others who fell short of true faith. The first disciples (1:41) and the Samaritan woman (4:25, 29) called Jesus "the Christ," and Nathanael (1:49) called Jesus "the Son of God." The disciples were corrected by the words of Jesus that promised the sight of "greater things" (1:50-51), and the Samaritan woman was asked to reach beyond her messianic hopes to see in Jesus the *egō eimi* (4.26), the Savior of the world (4:42). The crowds confessed that Jesus was the one who was coming into the world (6:14), but Jesus fled from such acclamations (v. 15), and later warned them not to labor for a bread that perishes but for the food that will be provided by the Son of Man (vv. 25-27). Martha has limited faith matching that of the disciples, Nicodemus (3:1-11), the Samaritan woman (4:25-26), and the crowds, who used traditional Jewish messianic expressions to voice their faith in Jesus.

No character in 11:1-27 has shown true faith, neither the disciples (v. 16) nor Martha (vv. 21, 24, 27). But Jesus does not cease from his mission to make God known to them (cf. 1:18). He has announced that God's glory will be seen and the Son of God will be glorified by means of events associated with the sickness and death of Lazarus (v. 4). He has told his disciples that he will raise Lazarus from the sleep of death so that they might believe (v. 15). None of this will be thwarted by the inability of others to see beyond what they themselves can determine. Jesus' self-revelation (cf. vv. 25-26) will continue so that the promise of v. 4 will be fulfilled.

Jesus and Mary (vv. 28-37). Martha's partial confession of faith is still present as, "having said this" *(kai touto eipousa)*, she returns to her sister, announcing that "the teacher is here" (v. 28). Her use of the title "the teacher" *(ho didaskalos)* takes her from one series of limited expressions of faith (vv. 21-22, 24, 27) to another (v. 28; cf. 1:38; 3:2). She reports Jesus' presence "quietly" *(lathrą)*, and informs Mary that Jesus is "calling her" *(kai phōnei se)*. Every reference to the "voice" *(phōnē)* of Jesus is a call to fullness of life with him (cf. 3:8, 29; 5:25, 28; 10:3, 4, 16, 27). Jesus condemns "the Jews" who never hear the voice of the Sent One (5:37). Particularly important for this calling of Mary has been the concentration on the voice of the Shepherd in the immediately previous context of 10:1-18 (10:3, 4, 16, 17). Only here does Jesus use the verb *phōneō* to speak of his own activity: "The sheep hear his voice *(tēs phōnēs autou)*, and he calls *(phōnei)* his own sheep by name and leads them out" (10:3). Mary is one of his own sheep and he is summoning her. In contrast to Martha, who took the initiative at every turn (vv. 21-22, 24, 27), Mary is called forth by the word of Jesus.

Mary's position as the first character to be introduced in v. 2 points to the fact that she is the special sister. Every carefully etched detail of v. 29 continues to enhance this positive portrayal of Mary. *This* woman (v. 29a: *ekeinē*), when she hears of his call (v. 29b: *hōs ēkousen*), responds immediately: "she rose quickly and went to him" (v. 29c: *ēgerthē tachy kai ērcheto pros auton*). As well as the general use of the verb "to hear" in a positive sense across the Gospel (cf. 1:37, 40; 3:8, 29, 32; 4:42, 47; 5:24, 25, 28, 30; 6:45; 7:40; 8:47), the verb has been used four times to describe the sheep responding to the voice of the Good Shepherd (10:3, 16, 20, 27). As Jesus is not yet in the village, but in the place where Martha met him (v. 30), Mary must move (v. 29). This movement enables the narrator to introduce "the Jews" who were with her in the house, comforting her (v. 31a). Nothing has been said of Mary's emotional state. Only "the Jews" are described as offering consolation (cf. vv. 19, 31). Mary's departure is reported through the eyes of "the Jews." They believe that she is going to wail at the tomb, and thus they follow her (v. 31b), expecting her to join them in their lamentations over Lazarus. But such is not the case; she is going to Jesus. While Mary responds to the presence of Jesus (cf. v. 28: *ho didaskalos parestin*), "the Jews" expect *(doxantes hoti)* her to follow accepted grieving practices. This indication of the attitude of "the Jews," totally focused on the dead Lazarus rather than on the presence of Jesus, is crucial for the proper understanding of the difficult v. 33.

Mary comes to the place where Jesus is, and a further difference between Mary and Martha emerges. Martha simply addressed Jesus in v. 21 ("Martha said to Jesus"), but Mary approaches Jesus in a different fashion. When she sees Jesus (v. 32b: *idousa auton*), she falls at his feet (v. 32c: *epesen autou pros tous podas*); from this position she repeats *part* of Martha's confession (cf. v. 22) in v. 32b: "Lord, if you had been here my brother would not have died." The reason for Martha's confidence is omitted ("whatever you ask from God, God will give you," v. 22). Martha's understanding of Jesus as a miracle-worker is not repeated in Mary's confession. She simply states her unconditional trust in the power of the presence of Jesus. In other words it is Mary, not Martha, who accepts Jesus as the resurrection and the life (cf. vv. 25-26). Only Mary accepts Jesus' revelation of himself as she confesses "if you had been here." Mary is the character in the story reflecting true faith (vv. 29, 32) while Martha has fallen short of such faith (vv. 21-22, 24, 27).

To this point in the story Mary has focused totally on Jesus, responding to the voice of the Good Shepherd. In v. 33 this situation suddenly and inexplicably changes, and it draws a remarkable demonstration of emotion from Jesus. The death of Lazarus should never be the center of attention, but Mary succumbs as she joins the weeping of "the Jews" (v. 33). When Jesus sees Mary weeping, and "the Jews" who are with her also weeping (v. 33ab), he is strangely moved. It is not compassion—or lack of it—that creates Jesus' being moved to anger in spirit and troubled (v. 33c: *enebrimēsato tǭ pneumati kai etaraxen heauton*). As Jesus' public ministry draws to a close he is frustrated and angrily disappointed (*enebrimēsato*), and this is manifested in a deep, shuddering internal emotion (*etaraxen*) (see notes). Mary had earlier shown every sign of transcending the limited expectations of "the Jews" (v. 31) and the failure of the disciples (vv. 12, 16) and Martha (vv. 21-22, 24, 27) to understand the significance of the death of Lazarus and Jesus' self-revelation as the resurrection and the life (vv. 25-26). Now she has joined "the Jews" in their tears (v. 33a). To this point in the narrative nothing has been said of the tears or the mourning of Mary. Only "the Jews" are reported as mourning (vv. 19, 31). Now, after a demonstration of authentic belief in Jesus, she turns away from him in tears to join "the Jews." Will no one come to belief? Has even Mary joined with "the Jews" in making the death of Lazarus the center of attention, and has she thus abandoned her earlier unconditional acceptance of Jesus? Her weeping with "the Jews" is a reversal of her earlier response to Jesus (vv. 28-32), and it generates anger and severe disappointment in Jesus. He is deeply moved by a justifiable anger and emotion, but he must proceed with the mission that has been entrusted to him. He must wake Lazarus from his sleep (v. 11), glorify God, and through this event be glorified (v. 4).

He asks to be led to the tomb of Lazarus, and "they" invite him to "come and see" (v. 34). The context demands that it is Mary and "the Jews" (v. 33) who issue this invitation. They respectfully (*kyrie;* cf. vv. 3, 21) ask Jesus to see the situation of a person who has been dead for four days (cf. v. 17). Mary's by now total association with the perspective of "the Jews" again leads Jesus to tears (v. 35). "The Jews" misunderstand the tears as a demonstration of Jesus' love for Lazarus (v. 36). The careful use of another verb for the weeping of Jesus (*dakryō* is used for Jesus' weeping, while *klaiō* is used for both Mary and "the Jews" in vv. 31, 33) indicates that Jesus' tears cannot be associated with the surrounding mourning process. He weeps because of the danger that his unconditional gift of himself in love as the Good Shepherd (cf. 10:11, 14-15), the resurrection and the life who offers life here and hereafter to all who would believe in him (11:25-26), will never be understood or accepted. While Mary moved toward Jesus (vv. 28-29) there was hope that one of the characters had come to faith. Once she joined "the Jews" in their sorrow and tears Jesus' promises seem to have been forgotten, and Jesus weeps in his frustration (v. 35). However deep the disappointment, anger (v. 33), and frustration (v. 35) of Jesus, he continues to respond to his task to make visible the glory of God and achieve his own glorification (v. 4). He asks, "Where have you laid him?" (v. 34a). Jesus has said that he will wake Lazarus from his sleep (v. 11), and his promise will become fact.

Looking back to the miracle of the man born blind (9:1-7), some of "the Jews" join Martha's misunderstanding of Jesus as a miracle-worker (cf. 11:21-22). If Jesus could cure the man born blind, why could he not prevent the death of Lazarus (v. 37)? "The Jews" and Martha have shown that they are not prepared to budge beyond their own criteria in assessing the person and mission of Jesus. They have not moved beyond the messianic expectations expressed during the Feast of Tabernacles, when some of the people asked, "When the Christ appears, will he do more than this man has done?" (7:31). However, even here Jesus has proved to be something of a disappointment. He cured the man born blind, but he failed to save Lazarus! Mary is not associated with "the Jews" in the complaints of v. 37. She has disappeared from the action, swallowed up in the human emotions surrounding the death of her brother, and is no longer with "the Jews" (cf. v. 33). The reader knows, from the announcement of the anointing of Jesus' feet in v. 2, that she will return. Her joining the mourning of "the Jews" in v. 33 cannot be the end of her part in the story, and her disassociation from their concerns about Jesus the miracle-worker in v. 37 is a hint that the promised anointing of Jesus (v. 2) may tell of her return to an unconditional dependence on him.

The miracle (vv. 38-44). The ongoing inability of "the Jews" to accept Jesus, and their persistent misunderstanding of him, again manifested in

vv. 36-37, move Jesus to anger (v. 38a) as he comes to the tomb *(erchetai eis to mnēmeion)*. In earlier episodes Jesus has delayed (v. 6), asked for belief (vv. 16, 26), and shown anger and emotion (vv. 33, 35, 38a). He asked to be shown the place where Lazarus was buried. Mary and "the Jews" offered to take him to the place that he might see (v. 34). But Jesus is not shown to the tomb; he *goes* there. From this point on Jesus is the master of the situation as he moves decisively to fulfill God's design (cf. v. 4), which involves waking Lazarus from sleep (cf. v. 11). Jesus' actions and imperative verbs dominate vv. 38-44. Only in addressing the Father in prayer does he show an attitude of dependence (cf. vv. 41-42).

The tomb "was a cave, and a stone lay on it" (v. 38b). Jesus orders, "Take away the stone" (v. 39a). Martha reappears and objects to Jesus' command (v. 39b). In a way coherent with her earlier encounter with Jesus (vv. 17-27) she tells Jesus how things are in her established world: Lazarus has been dead for four days, and there will be an odor. Unable to accept that Jesus is the resurrection and the life (vv. 25-26), she at least initially expressed faith in his miracle-working status (cf. 21-22). Her final words in the Gospel are to tell Jesus that he has no authority over a person who has been dead for four days (v. 39). Jesus recalls v. 4 as he informs Martha of the benefits of belief. If only she would commit herself in belief to the world of Jesus she would see the *doxa tou theou* ("the glory of God"). The guiding, caring, saving presence of God would become visible to her through the events she is about to witness—if only she would believe (v. 40). The verb is in the singular *(ean pisteusēs)*; it is the faith of Martha that is in question. There can be no resisting the imperative of Jesus (v. 39a), and thus Martha's attempt to stop the action (v. 39b) is ignored and the stone is taken away (v. 41a). The glory of God will be seen by those who question the absolutes of "this world" and believe in all that Jesus reveals (v. 40).

Jesus' attitude changes as he prays in a way that can be heard by all the bystanders: Martha, Mary, "the Jews," and the disciples. Adopting a position of prayer by lifting up his eyes (v. 41b), Jesus expresses his gratitude and absolute trust in the communion that exists between himself and the Father (vv. 41c-42). Jesus is turned in loving union toward God (cf. 1:1), and is thus able to tell the story of the God whom no one has ever seen (cf. 1:18). Never, through his ministry, has Jesus swerved from his oneness and his unconditional response to the Father (cf. 4:34; 5:19-30, 36-37, 43; 6:27, 37-38, 40, 45, 46, 57, 65; 8:18-19, 28, 38, 49, 54; 10:10, 15-18, 25, 29-30, 32, 37-38). Jesus and the Father are one (8:38), but the people around the tomb have not yet accepted this truth, so fundamental to a correct understanding of Jesus. The disciples, Martha, "the Jews," and even Mary still have much to learn. Thus Jesus prays loudly to proclaim to this group gathered at the tomb of Lazarus that the actions that will take place shortly come from Jesus' oneness with the Father. "He is no magician, no *theios anēr*, who works by his own power and seeks his own *doxa*" (Bultmann, *Gospel* 408). His actions indicate that he is the Sent One of the Father. The moment has come for Jesus to perform a deed that will show forth the glory of God and set in motion a process by means of which he will himself be glorified (cf. vv. 4, 40). It will create an opportunity for the disciples (cf. vv. 15, 42), for "the Jews" (cf. v. 42), and for Martha (cf. vv. 21-22, 26-27, 39, 42) and Mary (cf. vv. 33, 42) to believe that God is made known through the words and actions of the Sent One, Jesus.

Jesus' crying out with a loud voice *(phōnē megalē)* into the silence of a dead man's tomb (v. 43b) is linked with the prayer: "when he had said this" (v. 43a). The action that follows takes place so that the people around the tomb might come to believe that Jesus is the Sent One of God (cf. v. 25) and that he has total authority over the dead man, Lazarus (cf. v. 26). Lazarus comes forth from the cave, still tightly bound in the clothing of death (v. 44a). The image is striking and has captured the imaginations of artists over the centuries, but this is the way a man who has been raised from the dead would have to appear. The reader might wonder why so much detail is given to the description of the clothes of death, and this wondering will not be resolved until the story tells of another tomb (19:40-41: *mnēmeion kainon*) and another set of grave clothes (20:5-7). The account of the miracle closes with two further commands from Jesus: "Unbind him and let him go" (v. 44b). Lazarus must be freed from the trappings of death to go his way.

The resurrection and the life (v. 25), the Sent One of the Father (v. 42), has intervened. He has made the action of God visible in the lives of all who have participated in this event, not only Lazarus (cf. vv. 4, 40). The physical transformation of the dead body of Lazarus to the risen Lazarus is not the main point of the story. Jesus' action has revealed the *doxa tou theou* (cf. vv. 4, 40) so that the disciples might believe (cf. vv. 15, 42), so that Martha and Mary might believe (cf. vv. 26, 40, 42), so that Mary and "the Jews" might believe (cf. vv. 33, 42). The greater transformation would be acceptance on the part of all who witnessed the miracle that Jesus was the Son of the Father, the Sent One of God (cf. v. 42). A remarkable sign has shown the glory of God (cf. v. 4c), but the reader has yet to discover how the miracle of raising Lazarus will be the means by which the Son of God will be glorified (v. 4d: *hina doxasthē ho huios tou theou di autēs*).

The decision of "the Jews" (vv. 45-54). Many of "the Jews" believe because of the miracle (v. 45), but some inform their leaders what Jesus had done (v. 46). Those who believe are the ones who had earlier gone to Mary (v. 19) and had followed her when she responded to the call of Jesus

(v. 31). In fact, they had gone to both Martha and Mary (cf. v. 19), but the believers are linked to Mary. The miracle has led some of them to belief, as many earlier conflicts between Jesus and "the Jews" produce a remnant of "the Jews" who believe in Jesus (cf. 7:31; 8:30; 10:42). Those who report to the leaders of "the Jews" only tell of the deeds of Jesus (v. 46: *ha epoiēsen*). Nothing is said of his self-revelation as the resurrection and the life (vv. 25-26) or his prayer that they might come to faith in him as the Sent One of the Father (v. 42). They simply report the miracle (v. 46; cf. vv. 36-37). Faced with the difficulty of a rabble-rouser who might destabilize their established authority, the chief priests and the Pharisees gather the council *(synedrion)*. The misunderstanding of "the Jews" continues as Jesus is judged as a miracle-worker who is attracting the people (v. 47a). Something must be done to bring his activities to an end, or else "everyone" *(pantes)* will believe in him (vv. 47b-48a).

The delicate balance of power between Rome and the local religious and political authorities at the time of Jesus lies behind the Sanhedrin's conclusion that popular, messianic, miracle-working figures, if left unchecked, will create havoc. The experience of 65–70 C.E. lies behind their words: "The Romans will come and destroy both our holy place and our nation" (v. 48). Caiaphas, remembered as the high priest in the year Jesus was crucified, speaks up (v. 49ab). Accusing his fellow leaders of inability to think and plan correctly (vv. 49c-50), he takes a position that is at one level opportunist and at another an important interpretation of the death of Jesus. There was a recent tradition that a good person might lay down his or her life for the nation and effect God's blessing upon them all. The Maccabean martyrs had been an example of this, and the ideal of a good person dying for the nation was strong in first-century Israel. Ironically, Caiaphas speaks of ridding themselves of Jesus, a troublemaker, so that the nation might profit, but his words recall courageous and self-sacrificing martyrs whose deaths gave life to God's people. But that is only one level of possible interpretation. The narrator goes further. Understanding the high priest as a spokesman for God, the narrator further clarifies Caiaphas' prophetic words. Although he did not know what he was saying, Caiaphas rightly prophesied that Jesus would die for the nation (v. 51). But the benefits of the death of Jesus could not be limited to blessings for the nation as was the case with the deaths of the Maccabean martyrs. Jesus will die for Israel, but his death will also gather into one the children of God who are scattered abroad (v. 52; cf. 10:15-16). Hints provided by earlier parts of the narrative are now being drawn together. The hour of Jesus must be at hand (2:5; 7:20; 8:30). He will be lifted up as Moses lifted up the serpent in the wilderness, so that all who believe in him might have life (3:14). Even those who lift him up might come to believe in Jesus as the revelation of God (8:28). The death of Jesus will lead to the glorification of the Son of God (11:4) and the gift of the Spirit (7:39). But there is more to the death of Jesus than *his* hour, *his* being lifted up, *his* glorification. The death of Jesus is not *for himself* but for others. He gives his life for his sheep (cf. 6:51c; 10:15), and in giving his life he gathers sheep of other folds (10:16), the children of God who are scattered abroad (11:52).

There is little evidence that such a "gathering" is taking place. "The Jews" take counsel on the best way for Jesus to be put to death (v. 53). The story of the events surrounding the illness, death, and resurrection of Lazarus of Bethany close as they began: Jesus must depart to another place because he is unable to go about openly among "the Jews." His life is in danger (v. 54a; cf. 10:40; 11:5-8). He retires to a village close to the edge of the wilderness, still in the company of his disciples (v. 54b). But while his earlier stay in the remote village was accompanied by many who come to belief in him there (10:41), at Ephraim he is alone with his disciples (11:54).

Conclusion to 11:1-54. Jesus' stay at the edge of the desert is but a brief pause as he moves resolutely toward violence. He has announced that he will be glorified by means of it (cf. v. 4), that he is the resurrection and the life, and that his deeds show forth the glory of God so that all who witness them might come to believe that he is the Sent One of the Father (v. 42). His death will be both for the nation and to gather into one the scattered children of God (vv. 51-52). Violent events lie ahead but they will bring about the hour of Jesus, his lifting up, his glorification, the gift of the Spirit, the revelation of the glory of God, and the gathering of many.

There is an episode mentioned in 11:2 that is yet to be told: "It was Mary who anointed the Lord with ointment and wiped his feet with her hair." Of the two women in the story Mary is the one who made the most promising response to the presence of Jesus (vv. 28-32). But she fell away, joining "the Jews" in her tears (v. 33). Those who believed in Jesus as a consequence of the miracle were associated with Mary (v. 45) even though they had initially gone to console both women (cf. v. 19). Does this indicate that she has also accepted the challenge of Jesus' prayer-proclamation: "that they may believe that you did send me" (v. 42)? The story of Mary's response to Jesus has not been satisfactorily concluded.

NOTES

1. *Lazarus of Bethany:* The name "Lazarus" is a shortened form of a name that means "God helps." No explanation of this name is given in the text, and symbolism based on the meaning of the word should not be read into it.

2. *It was Mary who anointed the Lord:* The introduction of this detail about Mary's relationship with Jesus has been variously explained. Most commentators (e.g., Bernard, *Commentary* 2:372–373; Brown, *Gospel* 1:423; Schnackenburg, *Gospel* 2:322; Lindars, *Gospel* 386–387) regard it as a parenthesis that has been added to the original passage. It is regarded by the interpretation here as a deliberate literary technique that introduces the actions of a significant character before they happen. This is called a "gap" or a "blank" or a "place of indeterminacy" within the text. The technique creates a tension for the reader, who must read on to "fill the gap" with information provided later in the narrative. See Wolfgang Iser, *The Act of Reading: A Theory of Aesthetic Response*. London: Routledge & Kegan Paul, 1978, 182–187.

3. *he whom you love is ill:* The expression, "he whom you love" *(hon phileis)*, and various other expressions of affection between Jesus and Lazarus (e.g., vv. 5, 36) have led a number of scholars both past and present to suggest that Lazarus is the Beloved Disciple. For a survey see Kremer, *Lazarus* 55 n. 50. Most recently see Stibbe, *Jesus as Storyteller* 77–82.

4. *this illness is not unto death:* For the meaning of *pros* as indicating the "ultimate purpose," in this case the ultimate purpose of Lazarus' illness, see BAGD 710, s.v. *pros*, III (3c).

   Son of God: Only in 5:25, here (11:4), and in 11:25 does Jesus speak of himself as "Son of God." This relationship is implicit, however, in much of Jesus' teaching about himself and the Father. Some early manuscripts ($\mathfrak{P}^{66.45}$) omit or substitute "of God."

   by means of it: Few commentators notice the programmatic significance of *di' autēs:* the events involving Lazarus will be the catalyst that will set in motion a process "by means of which" the Son of God will be glorified. See, for example, Brown, *Gospel* 1:423: "Presumably through the sickness." For the use of *dia* as "the circumstances in which one finds oneself because of something" see BDF 119, § 223 (3).

5. *Now Jesus loved Martha and her sister and Lazarus:* The clumsy juxtapositioning of vv. 5-6 has led a number of critics (e.g., Segalla, *Giovanni* 323; Lindars, *Gospel* 388; Kremer, *Lazarus* 58) to suggest that v. 5 is a redactional conclusion to vv. 1-4, unconnected with v. 6. In this way v. 6 flows more naturally from v. 4. However, vv. 5-6 are logically linked (however difficult the logic) by *oun* (v. 6). See Lagrange, *Evangile* 297.

7. *Then after this:* The use of *palin* ("again") and the expression *epeita meta touto* indicate a further stage in the narrative that, however, looks back to the immediately previous reception Jesus has had in Judea. See Barrett, *Gospel* 391.

9. *Are there not twelve hours in the day?:* The use of the images of light and darkness, day and night, walking and stumbling point to vv. 9-10 as being "parabolic" in form. On the rhetorical structure of this parable see Rochais, *Les récits* 138–139; Byrne, *Lazarus* 43–44. Some commentators link the twelve hours with the hour of Jesus that has not yet come (e.g., Becker, *Evangelium*

2:366-367; Rochais, *Les récits* 139). For the case against this identification see Kremer, *Lazarus* 60.

10. *because the light is not in them:* The Jewish notion of the eye being the seat of light, i.e., the place where the light resides, where it is "in" a person, is invoked here. See, among many, Schnackenburg, *Gospel* 2:325–326.

11. *Our friend Lazarus has fallen asleep:* On the traditional Christian background for sleeping language for death see Westcott, *Gospel* 166; Bauer, *Johannesevangelium* 149. Surprisingly, there are no known parallels between waking from sleep and resurrection. Rochais, *Les récits* 139–140, links the connection made here with the Greek versions of Job 14:12-15.

12. *he will recover:* The disciples are involved in a subtle irony here. They have not understood the full significance of Lazarus' sleep and he will have to explain it to them (cf. v. 14). However, they use the double-meaning word *sōzein* to speak of his recovery: the verb means both physical recovery and spiritual salvation.

15. *for your sake:* This is the first of many elements in the story indicating that its real focus is not Lazarus but the people who surround and witness the events. On the lack of interest in the person of Lazarus see Léon-Dufour, *Lecture* 2:404–405. Nevertheless Marchadour, *Lazare* 126–127, rightly points out that Lazarus is the empty hole that drives the narrative until it is eventually filled. See also Stibbe, "A Tomb with a View" 42–43.

16. *that we may die with him:* It is grammatically possible that Thomas is suggesting that the disciples might die with Lazarus. Lagrange, *Evangile* 299, regards this interpretation as "fantasy." A number of critics have read this passage as a model for disciples, invited to join Jesus in his journey to death (e.g., Lightfoot, *Gospel* 220–221; Beasley-Murray, *John* 189; Brodie, *Gospel* 392). Such a suggestion, which is better suited to the Markan portrait of disciples (but see 12:24-26), misses the important point of the ongoing misunderstanding of the disciples.

17. *in the tomb four days:* As well as the physical decomposition of the body after four days, and related to it, there is a widely cited Jewish opinion that the soul hovered near the body for three days, but by the fourth day all hope of resuscitation was gone. See Str-B 2:544.

19. *to console them:* The verb used for "to console" (*paramytheisthai*) is rare in the NT (cf. v. 31; 1 Thess 2:11; 5:14). It is a word with great breadth of meanings (cf. LSJ 1318), but there is no cause to suspect the genuineness of the care shown to the bereaved family or to use this verb as describing a non-Christian concern over death. See Barrett, *Gospel* 394. For the importance of offering consolation see Str-B 4:592–607. The issue in v. 19 is not so much what "the Jews" offer the bereaved sisters but the fact that *only* "the Jews" are described as performing the expected rituals of mourning and consolation. Nothing is said of the sisters.

It is sometimes claimed that "the Jews" in this section of the Gospel represent ordinary people, not the hostile Jewish authorities. Brown, *Gospel*

1:427–428, uses this as an indication that chs. 11–12 were added to an original account of the ministry that concluded at 10:40-42. While "the Jews" in vv. 8, 11, 19, 31, 33, 36, 45, 54 are not as hostile as in earlier parts of the Gospel (cf. also Kremer, *Lazarus* 64), they cannot be regarded as indifferent. They repeatedly misunderstand the events surrounding the illness and death of Lazarus, and some of them report what Jesus did (and not what he said) to their leaders. Schneiders, "Death in the Community" 45, correctly points out that "the Jews" "serve to lace the story tightly into its Gospel context."

20. *Mary sat in the house:* The two different responses are often noticed, but scholars almost unanimously give all the credit to Martha for her creativity and initiative. They regard Mary's staying in the house as behaving in a way that one would expect from a person grieving. Far-fetched parallels are drawn between Mary's sitting in the house and Job 2:8 and Ezek 8:14 to assume that Mary is adopting a state of mourning. This reads too much into the text.

22. *whatever you ask from God, God will give you:* The belief that a miracle-worker had privileged access to God was "in accord with Jewish piety" (Schnackenburg, *Gospel* 2:239). It is incorrect, therefore, to judge these words as a satisfactory expression of Johannine faith (as do, for example, Westcott, *Gospel* 168; Bultmann, *Gospel* 401–402; Marchadour, *Lazare* 119).

24. *I know that he will rise again in the resurrection at the last day:* Martha is accepting a current Jewish understanding of a final resurrection. Belief in "the last day" seems to have its roots in the OT (cf. Isa 2:2; Mic 4:1), and the idea of a final resurrection was a constituent element of Pharisaic Judaism (cf. Dan 12:1-3; 2 Macc 7:22-24; 12:44; Acts 23:8; Josephus, *War* 2:163; *m. Sanh.* 10:1; *m. Sota* 9:15; *m. Ber.* 5:2; cf. also Mark 12:18-27 and parallels). For a full-scale discussion of this issue see Cavallin, "Leben nach dem Tod" 240–345.

25. *I am the resurrection and the life:* The words "and the life" *(kai hē zōē)* are missing from some good witnesses ($\mathfrak{P}^{45}$, Old Latin [Vercellensis], Sinaitic Syriac, Cyprian, and in some of Origen's texts). Brown, *Gospel* 1:425, claims that omission is harder to explain than addition. Barrett, *Gospel* 396, suspects that the shorter text may be original but says that it "makes little difference to the sense." This is hardly the case, given the play on the word "life" *(zōē)* in vv. 25b-26. On this play see Dodd, *Interpretation* 364–365; Stimpfle, *Blinde Sehen* 109.

26. *and whoever lives:* Commentators have differed in their understanding of the expression "lives" (see, for a summary, Beasley-Murray, *John* 190–191). Does it refer to physical or spiritual life? The blending of realized and traditional eschatologies, familiar from 5:24-29 (cf. also 6:40, 54), returns. People die physically (11:25b), but faith in Jesus ensures a life that transcends death. Thus Jesus insists that faith in him produces a spiritual life both now and hereafter. Here, as in 5:24-29, the problem of physical life and death emerges in a community that believed it already had been gifted with "life." See Stimpfle, *Blinde Sehen,* 111–116; Schneiders, "Death in the Community" 46–52; Stibbe, "A Tomb with a View" 50–54; Martin, "History and Eschatology"

332–343; McNeil, "The Raising" 269–275; Moule, "The Meaning of 'Life'" 114–125. For the relationship between John 11 and 5:21-29 see Neyrey, *An Ideology of Revolt* 81–92. For Neyrey ch. 11 demonstrates the claims of 5:21-29 and makes Jesus equal to God.

27. *I have believed:* The perfect tense is given its full value (see 8:31, where the perfect tense is also used in this way). See BDF 175–176, § 340. Most commentators either do not note the tense or explain it away as a characteristic use of *pisteuein* in the Fourth Gospel (e.g., Barrett, *Gospel* 396). The interpretation given here does not accept this view, claiming that *pepisteuka* is a genuine perfect tense indicating that Martha came to the faith she expresses in this verse *before* Jesus' words on resurrection and life in vv. 25-26. This also explains why no reference is made to Jesus' self-revelation. That is new, but Martha boasts of having already arrived at faith and thus does not take it into account.

you are the Christ, the Son of God, the one who is coming into the world: The position taken in the interpretation, that Martha's confession of faith reflects contemporary messianic expectation and is therefore at best partial, does not represent majority opinion. Indeed, it would be regarded by most as "maverick." Schnackenburg, *Gospel* 2:328, and Lindars, *Gospel* 396, regard Martha's words as the theological climax of the chapter, and Bultmann, *Gospel* 404, sees them as an expression of genuine Johannine faith. For Brown, "Roles of Women" 693–694, and Schneiders, "Women in the Fourth Gospel" 41, Martha replaces Peter as the one who makes the supreme confession of faith. For Scott, *Sophia* 199–206, Martha's confession is "both fully Johannine and . . . consistent with the pattern of the revelation of Jesus as Sophia incarnate." The list could go on (cf. Barrett, Beasley-Murray, Becker, Brodie, Carson, Gnilka, Haenchen, Kremer, Lagrange, Marchadour, Marsh, Rochais, Schnelle, Segalla, Stibbe, van Tilborg). Scholars discuss the confession's origins as a primitive creed (cf. Barrett, *Gospel* 397) and even suggest that it was a baptismal confession (cf. Günther Bornkamm, "Das Bekenntnis im Hebräerbrief," *Studien zu Antike und Urchristentum: Gesammelte Aufsätze Band II.* BEvTh 28. Munich: Kaiser, 1959, 191–192 n. 8). The Johannine context must come first (as it does, for example, in Lee, *Symbolic Narratives* 205–206), not the use of Martha's words in later creeds.

28. *saying quietly:* Brown, *Gospel* 1:425, suggests that the quietness is a "cautious whispering" to keep Jesus' presence a secret from "the Jews." Kremer, *Lazarus* 71, links it with the Johannine church's exclusion from the synagogue. It is also an indication of the weakening of Martha's role in the narrative.

she went and called her sister: Martha is reported as "calling" (*ephōnēsen*), but it is the *phōnē* of Jesus that is decisive (cf. interpretation).

The Teacher is here: On the use of *didaskalos* in imperfect confessions of faith see Moloney, *Belief in the Word* 67–68, 108–109. It is, of course, Greek for "Rabbi," which has always appeared where Jesus is addressed in contexts of limited faith (cf. 1:38, 49; 3:2; 4:31; 6:25; 9:2; 11:8). After interpreting v. 27 as a fully Johannine confession of faith Barrett, *Gospel* 397, admits that "the description is surprising after the exalted terms of Martha's confession of faith (v. 27)." It is less surprising if v. 27 is placed firmly within its Johannine theological and literary context.

29. *she rose quickly and went to him:* The positive interpretation of Mary, contrasting with her sister's imperfect belief, is again at variance with the vast bulk of commentary on this passage. See, for example, Brown, *Gospel* 1:435: "This scene does not advance the action; vs. 34 could easily follow vs. 27, and no one would know the difference." Rochais, *Les récits* 143, regards Mary's words as "filling." The list could go on, but this is a misunderstanding of the author's narrative strategy. What is one to make of v. 2, and then 12:1-8? Schneiders, "Women in the Fourth Gospel" 41–42, and Culpepper, *Anatomy* 140–142, present Mary as a model disciple on the basis of 12:1-8, but 11:2, 28-37 are crucial elements for the interpretation of 12:1-8. Historical studies tend to ignore v. 2. See, for example, Schnackenburg, *Gospel* 2:333: "Mary thus gives the impression of being nothing but a complaining woman." He has already decided (2:322) that v. 2 is a gloss.

31. *supposing that she was going to the tomb to weep there:* Some manuscripts (e.g., $\mathfrak{P}^{66}$, Alexandrinus, Koridethi) read "saying" *(legontes)* rather than "supposing" *(doxazontes)*. The sense of an inner expression of common opinion and accepted behavior must be maintained, on both textual and narrative grounds. As Schnackenburg, *Gospel* 2:334, comments: "She is *expected* to give way to her grief and weep at the tomb" (emphasis mine).

32. *fell at his feet:* Although the verbs are not the same, the actions of the man born blind and Mary are the same. They both prostrate themselves before Jesus in faith. Mary's actions are not, as Byrne, *Lazarus* 56, comments, "extremity of emotion." Equally unacceptable is the judgment of Brodie, *Gospel* 386, that Martha rises above the bitterness while Mary sinks into unrestrained mourning.
Lord, if you had been here my brother would not have died: This remark from Mary points to her acceptance of Jesus' presence, and she does not go on to speak of his privileged access to God as a miracle-worker. This marks Mary's words to Jesus as superior to those of her sister and not "a poor, truncated piece compared with Martha's" (Byrne, *Lazarus* 56).

33. *When Jesus saw her weeping:* The introduction of Mary's weeping is sudden, as is her association with "the Jews" who had followed her, thinking that she was going to weep at the tomb. The failure of Mary is that she has shifted her focus from Jesus to the mourning associated with the death of Lazarus. The events of Bethany must not be regarded as an end in themselves. See Wuellner, "Putting Life Back" 114–132.
he was deeply moved in spirit and troubled: Some variations in the textual tradition and much scholarly debate have been created by the use of the verb *embrimasthai*. It is associated with anger, and in its Johannine form its force is accentuated with the addition of a prefix. The basic meaning of the verb is to express anger outwardly, for example with a snort or some such gesture. In Jesus' case it is internalized by the addition of "in the spirit." The expressions

en pneumati ("in the spirit") in v. 33 and *en heautǭ* ("in himself") in v. 38 are parallel. There is no reference to "in the Spirit," but rather to a deep, internal, and spiritual experience. On the verb see LSJ 330, 540. See also the survey of its use in classical literature in Lindars, "Rebuking the Spirit" 92–96. The debate hinges around the seemingly impossible portrait of Jesus' anger when faced with the loss of Lazarus and the accompanying tears of his sister and "the Jews." Why should he be so fiercely angry? For surveys of the discussion see Lagrange, *Evangile* 303–305; Brown, *Gospel* 1:425–426; Barrett, *Gospel* 398–400; Moloney, *Signs and Shadows* 166–168. There is no need to resort to a softening of the context, suggesting that Jesus is moved by his sympathy for the sufferers. Barrett, *Gospel* 398, rightly dismisses suggestions that Jesus is angry with the hypocrisy of "the Jews." Lindars, "Rebuking the Spirit" 97–104, suggests that a Johannine source (parallel to the synoptic exorcisms: cf. Mark 1:43; 9:25-29) originally had Jesus rebuking the spirit. In John, not demons but death is overcome. In accommodating the source to its present context John's use of *embrimasthai* is conditioned by the use of *tarassō*, and thus comes to mean "emotionally moved." The interpretation claims that it is the *association* of Mary with "the Jews" and their mourning that creates the problem. Attempts have been made in some manuscripts to lessen the idea of anger by adding "as if" before the verb (e.g., $\mathfrak{P}^{45.66}$, Bezae). Black, *Aramaic Approach* 240–243, suggests that the two Greek words *enebrimēsato* and *etaraxen* translate one Aramaic expression meaning "to be strongly moved."

34. *Come and see:* This expression recalls Jesus' provocative use of these words in 1:39. Lightfoot, *Gospel* 233, makes much of this, drawing a contrast between the invitation of Jesus (1:39) and the invitation of humans (11:34). The repetition is probably coincidental.

35. *Jesus wept:* This is the only place in the NT where the verb *dakryō* appears. The noun *dakryon* appears in Heb 5:7 (significantly in the passage on Jesus' loud cries and tears).

38. *came to the tomb; it was a cave:* The general term for a tomb *(mnēmeion)* is further qualified as a cave *(spēlaion)*. This type of burial place was widespread in first-century Palestine.

39. *Take away the stone:* In the case of the resurrection of Lazarus this order must be given. On the day of Jesus' resurrection Mary Magdalene will find the stone already removed (cf. Kremer, *Lazarus* 75; Byrne, *Lazarus* 63).

   by this time there will be an odor, for he has been dead four days: If, as almost all scholars maintain, Martha comes to correct Johannine faith in v. 27 there is a serious contradiction in her response to Jesus' command in v. 39b. Is this the way someone who believes that Jesus is the resurrection and the life (cf. vv. 25-26) should respond? Most scholars struggle to combine v. 27 with these words of Martha. See, for example, Lindars, *Gospel* 399–400; Rochais, *Les récits* 144; Kremer, *Lazarus* 75. Some simply ignore the contradiction (e.g., Barrett, *Gospel* 402; Beasley-Murray, *John* 194). Others (e.g., Bultmann, *Gospel* 407 n. 7; Wilcox, "The 'Prayer' of Jesus" 128–129) put it down to the confused combination of different sources.

40. *you would see the glory of God:* For the interpretation of *doxa tou theou* given in the interpretation see Moloney, *Belief in the Word* 55–57. All the bystanders will see the events, but only the believer will see the *doxa*. Generally scholars do not read v. 40 as a recommendation to greater faith, as in the interpretation, but as a promise (e.g., Kremer, *Lazarus* 76).

41. *Father, I thank you:* Wilcox "The 'Prayer' of Jesus" 130–132, questions whether this is a prayer at all, and suggests that it has its origins in the pre-Johannine use of LXX Ps 117:21.

42. *I knew that you hear me always:* There is a great distance between this prayer and Martha's belief that anything Jesus asks of God, even now God would do (cf. v. 22). Jesus' prayer is expressed in terms of a relationship between himself as the Son and Sent One of the Father (vv. 41b-42). This complements the *egō eimi* statement of v. 25 but transcends Martha's belief in Jesus as Messiah, Son of David, Son of God, the one who is to come, of v. 27.

43. *he cried out with a loud voice:* This is the second time that the "voice" *(phōnē)* of Jesus is met by a positive response (cf. vv. 28-29, 43-44). See 5:25, 28 for Jesus' promise that the voice of the Son would summon the dead from their tombs. The resurrection of Lazarus is a proleptic fulfillment of that promise.

44. *The dead man came out:* It is often rightly said that the miracle is a parabolic repetition of Jesus' self-revelation in vv. 25-26. See, for example, Dodd, *Interpretation* 366–367; Byrne, *Lazarus* 65.

    his hands and feet bound with bandages: There is no need to raise the problem of a how a person so bound would be able to walk, as do Hoskyns, *Gospel* 475, and Bultmann, *Gospel* 409. They suggest that we have a "miracle within a miracle" (Hoskyns). For the patristic discussion of this issue see Bauer, *Johannesevangelium* 154.

    feet bound with bandages, and his face wrapped with a cloth: Among the many who have noticed the link between the burial cloths in the resurrection of Lazarus and the burial cloths in the resurrection of Jesus see Byrne, *Lazarus* 64–65; Reiser, "The Case of the Tidy Tomb" 47–57; Osborne, "A Folded Napkin" 437–440. It is often rightly remarked that the cloths that bind Lazarus are a sign that he will die a definitive death.

    Unbind him and let him go: It is remarkable that there are no domestic sequels to this miracle. They have been omitted to keep the focus of the account entirely on the significance of the events at a deeper level, some of which have already been indicated in vv. 4 and 40. Further elements will be added in vv. 45-54.

45. *who had come to Mary:* The Greek *hoi elthontes pros Mariam* is read as a reference to "the Jews" who had gone to mourn and console Martha and Mary in v. 19, not "who had come with Mary," looking back only to the group who have accompanied Jesus to the tomb (see RSV).

46. *went to the Pharisees:* There is no need for "the Pharisees" to be regarded as an official body, which would be historically incorrect. See Barrett, *Gospel* 405.

47. *gathered the council:* The Sanhedrin, the governing council and chief court of the Jewish nation, is meant. There are historical difficulties behind the Johannine scenario that are resolved by recourse to the Johannine understanding of "the Jews" (cf. Introduction). The Sanhedrin in this context is the assembly of those ("the Jews") who have decided against Jesus as the Christ, the revelation of God. For a fuller discussion see Grundmann, "The Decision of the Supreme Court" 297–298.

What are we doing?: Although many regard the expression as future, "What are we to do?" (e.g., Schnackenburg, *Gospel* 2:347; NRSV), a present question is posed: *ti poioumen?* This gives the following *hoti* the meaning of "for" or "because." See Barrett, *Gospel* 405. Bauer, *Johannesevangelium* 155, suggests that the question ironically expects an answer: "Nothing!"

48. *the Romans will come and destroy both our holy place and our nation:* On the delicate political, religious, and social balance that had to be maintained see Grimm, "Die Preisgabe" 135. As is regularly pointed out, this scene replaces the synoptic trial before the Jewish authorities.

our holy place: The phrase *ho topos* ("the place") refers to the Temple (cf. 4:20; Matt 24:15; Acts 6:13; 21:28), so intimately associated with the existence of Israel as a nation (cf. Cilia, *La morte di Gesù* 21–31). Irony is present, and will increase in the words of Caiaphas that follow. Robinson, *Priority* 70, 227, misses this. He regards these words as an indication that the Temple was still standing when the Fourth Gospel was written. But ironically the exact opposite is the case. For some scholars (especially Bammel, "Ex illa itaque" 20–26), the leaders are concerned not about destruction but about the loss of their authority as the Romans "take away" *(arousin)* their power base.

49. *Caiaphas, who was high priest that year:* The high priest was elected for life, not for a year. For a survey of the discussion of this unusual statement see Beasley-Murray, *John* 197–198. Some (e.g., Becker, *Evangelium* 368–369; Bammel, "Ex illa itaque" 38–39) suggest that there was some special situation singling out "that year." But an interpretation that dates back to Origen (cf. Lagrange, *Evangile* 314) is the most likely solution. It reads the passage as indicating that "Caiaphas was high priest in that memorable year of our Lord's passion" (Barrett, *Gospel* 406).

50. *it is expedient for you:* Ironically, the "expedience" comes from the saving effect of the death of this one man (cf. Duke, *Irony* 87–89). Such political opportunism is well represented in Josephus' portrait of the priests (cf. Grimm, "Die Preisgabe" 134–141).

for you: There is some confusion in the textual tradition here. Does Caiaphas say "for you" (*hymin:* e.g., 𝔓⁴⁵·⁶⁶, Vaticanus, Bezae, and some Vulgate manuscripts) or "for us" (*hēmin:* e.g., Alexandrinus, Koridethi, Freer Gospels, Paris, Leningrad)? The pronoun is omitted by Sinaiticus. The slightly superior external evidence and Caiaphas' assuming a superior position (shown in his contemptuous *hymeis* in v. 49) support *hymin* as the correct reading.

that one man should die for the nation: A number of texts (2 Sam 20:22; Jonah 1:12-15; *Gen. Rab.* 90:9; *Sam. Rab.* 32:3; *Qoh. Rab.* 9:18, 2) are regularly cited as biblical and Jewish background to the notion of one person dying for the nation (cf. Bauer, *Johannesevangelium* 156; Bammel, "Ex illa itaque" 26–32). Barker, "John 11.50" 41–46, attempts to link Caiaphas' words with current messianic expectations. All the parallels introduced into this line of interpretation are either too late or deal with genuine malefactors. For the suggestion that the Maccabean martyr cult might lie behind Caiaphas' words see Grimm, "Die Preisgabe" 140–141. On this cult see the so-called Maccabean literature (some of which [4 Maccabees] may be as recent as 40 C.E.). On the antiquity and importance of the cult to these martyrs see E. Bammel, "Zum jüdischen Märtyrerkult" 79–85.

should die for the people: Two words are used for Israel as a nation: *laos*, which is applied to the chosen people, and *ethnos*, which relates to its civic situation. Painter, "The Church and Israel" 103–112, correctly argues that the two words represent traditional Israel. He disagrees with Pancaro, "'People of God'" 114–129, and "The Relationship" 396–405, who claims that *laos* points toward the New Israel, the Church. The passage as a whole does move from the single nation to a universal people but it is focused on the *ethnos* of vv. 51-52 rather than on *laos*.

51. *being high priest that year he prophesied:* For the high priest as a prophet see Dodd, "The Prophecy of Caiaphas" 63–66; Peter Schäfer, *Die Vorstellung vom Heiligen Geist in der rabbinischen Literatur.* StANT 29. Munich: Kösel, 1972, 135–139. See also Josephus, *War* 1:68-69; *Ant.* 6:115–116; 13:282–283, 299; Philo, *Spec. leg.* 4:191–192.

52. *and not for the nation only:* The expression *ethnos* has been given a broader, all-embracing meaning. Painter, "Church and Israel" 112, is too restrictive, only allowing the images of John 10 and 15 as ecclesial. As Brown, *Gospel* 1:443, strongly contends, v. 52 argues not only for the universality of salvation but also for its communitarian nature. John may not mention "the Church," but the dispersed children of God are to be gathered and formed into one *(synagagē eis hen)*.

to gather into one the children of God who are scattered abroad: There are good OT and Jewish parallels to support the view that Jesus' words could simply mean the gathering of dispersed Israelites (cf. Barrett, *Gospel* 407). See also Beutler, "Two Ways of Gathering" 403–404. Léon-Dufour, *Lecture* 2:431–432 (cf. also Brown, *Gospel* 1:439) notices a subtle irony between the gathering of the synagogue (v. 47) and Jesus' gathering of the dispersed (v. 52). See also Beutler, "Two Ways of Gathering" 399–402.

FOR REFERENCE AND FURTHER STUDY

Bammel, Ernst. "'Ex illa itaque die consilium fecerunt . . .' (John 11:53)." In idem, ed., *The Trial of Jesus: Cambridge Studies in Honour of C. F. D. Moule.* SBT 13. London: SCM Press, 1970, 11–40.

_____. "Zum jüdischen Märtyrerkult." In idem, *Judaica: Kleine Schriften I.* WUNT 37. Tübingen: J. C. B. Mohr (Paul Siebeck), 1986, 79–85.

Barker, Margaret. "John 11.50." In Ernst Bammel, ed., *The Trial of Jesus: Cambridge Studies in Honour of C.F.D. Moule.* SBT 14. London: SCM Press, 1970, 41–46.

Beutler, Johannes. "Two Ways of Gathering: The Plot to Kill Jesus in John 11:47-53," *NTS* 40 (1994) 399–406.

Brown, Raymond E. "Roles of Women in the Fourth Gospel," *TS* 36 (1975) 688–699.

Byrne, Brendan. *Lazarus: A Contemporary Reading of John 11:1-46.* Zacchaeus Studies: New Testament. Collegeville: The Liturgical Press, 1991.

Cavallin, H. C. "Leben nach dem Tod im Spätjudentum und frühen Christentum," *ANRW* 19.1 (1979) 240–345.

Cilia, Lucio. *La morte di Gesù e l'unità degli uomini (Gv 11,47-53; 12,32): Contributo allo studio della soteriologia giovannea.* Bologna: Dehoniane, 1991.

Dodd, C. H. "The Prophecy of Caiaphas: John 11:47-53." In idem, *More New Testament Studies.* Manchester: Manchester University Press, 1968, 58–68.

Grimm, W. "Die Preisgabe eines Menschen zur Rettung des Volkes: Priesterliche Tradition bei Johannes und Josephus." In Otto Betz, Klaus Haacker, and Martin Hengel, eds., *Josephus-Studien: Untersuchungen zu Josephus, dem Antiken Judentum und dem Neuen Testament. Otto Michel zum 70. Geburtstag gewidmet.* Göttingen: Vandenhoeck & Ruprecht, 1974, 133–146.

Grundmann, Walter. "The Decision of the Supreme Court to Put Jesus to Death (John 11:47-57) in Its Context: Tradition and Redaction in the Gospel of John." In Ernst Bammel and C. F. D. Moule, eds., *Jesus and the Politics of His Day.* Cambridge: Cambridge University Press, 1984, 295–318.

Kremer, Jacob. *Lazarus: Die Geschichte einer Auferstehung. Text, Wirkungsgeschichte und Botschaft von Joh 11:1-46.* Stuttgart: Katholisches Bibelwerk, 1985.

Lindars, Barnabas. "Rebuking the Spirit: A New Analysis of the Lazarus Story of John 11," *NTS* 38 (1992) 89–104.

Marchadour, Alain. *Lazare: Histoire d'un récit. Récits d'une histoire.* LeDiv 132. Paris: Cerf, 1988.

Martin, J. P. "History and Eschatology in the Lazarus Narrative," *SJTh* 17 (1964) 332–343.

McNeil, Brian. "The Raising of Lazarus," *DR* 92 (1974) 269–275.

Moloney, Francis J. "The Faith of Martha and Mary. A Narrative Approach to John 11,17-40," *Bib.* 75 (1994) 471–493.

_____. *Signs and Shadows* 154–177.

Moule, C. F. D. "The Meaning of 'Life' in the Gospel and the Epistles of John: A Study in the Story of Lazarus, John 11:1-44," *Theol.* 78 (1975) 114–125.

Osborne, Basil. "A Folded Napkin in an Empty Tomb: John 11:44 and 20:7 Again," *HeyJ* 14 (1973) 437–440.

Painter, John. "The Church and Israel in the Gospel of John: A Response," *NTS* 25 (1978–1979) 103–112.

Pancaro, Severino. "'People of God' in St John's Gospel," *NTS* 16 (1969–1970) 114–129.

_____. "The Relationship of the Church to Israel in the Gospel of John," *NTS* 21 (1974–1975) 396–405.

Reiser, W. E. "The Case of the Tidy Tomb: the place of the Napkins of John 11:44 and 20:7," *HeyJ* 14 (1973) 47–57.

Rochais, Gerard. *Les récits de résurrection des morts dans le Nouveau Testament.* MSSNTS 40. Cambridge: Cambridge University Press, 1981.

Schneiders, Sandra M. "Death in the Community of Eternal Life: History, Theology and Spirituality in John 11," *Interp.* 41 (1987) 44–56.

_____. "Women in the Fourth Gospel and the Role of Women in the Contemporary Church," *BTB* 12 (1982) 35–45.

Stibbe, M. W. G. "A Tomb with a View: John 1:11-44 in Narrative-Critical Perspective," *NTS* 40 (1994) 38–54.

Wilcox, Max. "The 'Prayer' of Jesus in John XI.41b-42," *NTS* 24 (1977–1978) 128–132.

Wuellner, Wilhelm. "Putting Life Back into the Lazarus Story and Its Reading: The Narrative Rhetoric of John 11 as the Narration of Faith," *Sem* 53 (1991) 114–132.

ii. The Hour Has Come (11:55–12:36)

11:55. Now the Passover of the Jews was at hand, and many went up from the country to Jerusalem before the Passover to purify themselves. 56. They were seeking Jesus and saying to one another as they stood in the Temple, "What do you think? That he will not come to the feast?" 57. Now the chief priests and the Pharisees had given orders that anyone who knew where he was should let them know, so that they might arrest him.

12:1. Six days before the Passover Jesus came to Bethany, where Lazarus was, whom Jesus had raised from the dead. 2. There they made him a supper; Martha served, and Lazarus was one of those at table with him. 3. Mary took a pound of costly ointment of pure nard and anointed the feet of Jesus and wiped his feet with her hair; and the house was filled with the fragrance of the ointment. 4. But Judas Iscariot, one of his disciples (he who was to betray him), said, 5. "Why was this ointment not sold for three hundred denarii and given to the poor?" 6. This he said, not that he cared for the poor, but because he was a thief, and as he had the money box he used to take what was put into it. 7. Jesus said, "Leave her alone. The purpose was that she might keep this for the day of preparation for my burial. 8. The poor you always have with you, but you do not always have me."

9. When the great crowd of the Jews learned that he was there, they came, not only on account of Jesus but also to see Lazarus, whom he had raised from the dead. 10. So the chief priests planned to put Lazarus also to death, 11. because on account of him many of the Jews were going away and believing in Jesus.

12. The next day a great crowd who had come to the feast heard that Jesus was coming to Jerusalem. 13. So they took branches of palm trees and went out to meet him, crying, "Hosanna! Blessed is he who comes

in the name of the Lord, even the King of Israel!" 14. But Jesus found a young ass and sat upon it; as it is written, 15. "Fear not, daughter of Zion; behold, your king is coming, sitting on an ass's colt!" 16. His disciples did not understand this at first; but when Jesus was glorified, then they remembered that this had been written of him and had been done to him.

17. The crowd that had been with him when he called Lazarus out of the tomb and raised him from the dead bore witness. 18. The reason why the crowd went to meet him was that they heard he had done this sign. 19. The Pharisees then said to one another, "You see that you can do nothing; look, the world has gone after him."

20. Now among those who went up to worship at the feast were some Greeks. 21. So these came to Philip, who was from Bethsaida in Galilee, and said to him, "Sir, we wish to see Jesus." 22. Philip went and told Andrew; Andrew went with Philip and they told Jesus. 23. And Jesus answered them, "The hour has come for the Son of Man to be glorified. 24. Amen, amen, I say to you, unless a grain of wheat falls into the earth and dies, it remains alone; but if it dies, it bears much fruit. 25. Those who love their life lose it, and those who hate their life in this world will keep it for eternal life. 26. Whoever serves me must follow me; and where I am, there shall my servant be also. Whoever serves me the Father will honor. 27. Now is my soul troubled. And what shall I say? 'Father, assure my salvation from this hour.' Yes! It is for this reason that I have come to this hour. 28. Father, glorify your name." Then a voice came from heaven, "I have glorified it, and I will glorify it again." 29. The crowd standing by heard it and said that it had thundered. Others said, "An angel has spoken to him." 30. Jesus answered, "This voice has come for your sake, not for mine. 31. Now is the judgment of this world; now shall the ruler of this world be cast out; 32. and I, when I am lifted up from the earth, will draw all people to myself." 33. He said this to show by what death he was to die. 34. The crowd answered him, "We have heard from the law that the Christ remains for ever. How can you say that the Son of Man must be lifted up? Who is this Son of Man?" 35. Jesus said to them, "The light is with you for a little longer. Walk while you have the light, lest the darkness overtake you. If you walk in the darkness, you do not know where you are going. 36. While you have the light, believe in the light, that you may become children of light." When Jesus had said this he departed and hid himself from them.

INTERPRETATION

Introduction to 11:55–12:36. The Johannine account of final episodes in the ministry of Jesus is more determined by the significance of their place in the story than by the logical sequence of events that may have taken place on any one day. Characters, time, space, and argument combine to shape the narrative as follows:

(a) *11:55-57:* Introduction. The time of Passover, the major characters (leaders of "the Jews" and Jesus), and the theme of Jesus' death are introduced.

(b) *12:1-8:* Mary anoints Jesus as Judas complains. The gap created by 11:2 is resolved.

(c) *12:9-19:* Jesus enters Jerusalem (vv. 12-16) amid concerns over the raised person, Lazarus (vv. 9-11; 17-19).

(d) *12:20-36:* The coming of the Greeks (vv. 20-22) leads Jesus to a final discourse that begins with the announcement of the arrival of "the hour" (v. 23). In v. 36b Jesus departs and hides himself from "the Jews."

The theme of Jesus' death, so prominent in 11:1-54, dominates all these events. Mary prepares Jesus' body for the day of his burial, and, as Jesus enters Jerusalem, "the Jews" plot that not only Jesus, but also Lazarus, must die. In response to the request of the Greeks to see him Jesus interprets his death as "the hour," his glorification, and his being lifted up to draw everyone to himself. This Gospel narrative does not meddle with the historical *events* that brought Jesus' life to an end, but with their *significance*.

Introduction (11:55-57). The Passover feast is solemnly announced *(ēn de engys to pascha tōn Ioudaiōn),* and the loneliness of Jesus in 11:54 is contrasted with the bustling crowds from the villages who have come to Jerusalem *(polloi . . . ek tēs chōras).* They are assiduously fulfilling time-honored rituals in preparation for the feast (cf. Num 9:6-13; 2 Chr 30:15-19; Josephus, *War* 1.229; 6.290; *m. Pesaḥ* 9:1). As "the Jews" plot to slay Jesus (cf. 11:53), the people prepare for the Passover. The irony is intensified by the narrator's comment that they are "seeking Jesus" (v. 56a: *ezētoun oun ton Iēsoun).* The verb *zēteō* has been used to tell of the attempts of "the Jews" to arrest and kill Jesus (cf. 5:18; 7:1, 19-20, 25, 30; 8:37, 40; 10:39). He has become a matter for the crowd's discussions: "What do you think?" (v. 56b: *ti dokei hymin?).* They suggest he will probably not come to this particular feast. Their leaders had given orders: whoever knows where Jesus is should let them know so that they might arrest him (v. 57). In Jesus' absence (v. 54), as the Passover approaches (v. 55), "the Jews" have made public their decision that Jesus must die for the nation (vv. 50, 57), but the chattering crowds go about their ritual lustrations (vv. 55-56).

Mary anoints Jesus (12:1-8). Six days before the celebration of Passover Jesus returns to Bethany, the village of Lazarus (v. 1). He shares a meal with the family of Lazarus (v. 2a), and Martha, previously the leading figure in the narrative, adopts the role of the servant (v. 2b). Martha's earlier arrogance (cf. 11:21-24, 27, 39) has been transformed, and Lazarus' presence at the table is highlighted (v. 2c). The twofold mention of

Lazarus (vv. 1-2) recalls the fundamental point of Jesus' association with the raised man: "for the glory of God, so that the Son of God may be glorified by means of it" (11:4). Having set the scene and already insinuated the theme of Jesus' death, the narrator introduces Mary and her anointing of Jesus. The gap created by the prolepsis of 11:2 is filled and she is described as anointing Jesus' feet and wiping them with her hair (v. 3a). The verbs "to anoint" and "to wipe" return. The choice of the feet is strange as such an anointing is neither a royal anointing nor the welcoming of an honored guest. The meaning of this gesture will not be made clear until Jesus explains it in v. 7.

The abundance of affection is accentuated by the further remark from the narrator that the house was filled with the fragrance of the ointment (v. 3b). In 11:39 Martha objected that an evil odor would come from the grave of the deceased Lazarus, but Mary's loving gesture fills the house with fragrance (cf. Lee, *Symbolic Narratives* 222 n. 2). Although Martha has come to a position of recognition and service (v. 2b) the contrast between the two women continues. It is the love of Mary, anticipated in her response to the voice of Jesus in 11:28-32, that fills the house with fragrance. Contrast enters, and the theme of Jesus' passion returns, as Judas Iscariot, already known to the reader as the betrayer (cf. 6:60, 71), is introduced (v. 4). Judas objects that such a wasteful spreading about of the precious ointment has no place in the ministry of Jesus or his disciples. It could have been sold for a large amount of money (three hundred denarii), and the proceeds given to the poor (v. 5). The fact that Judas is introduced as "he who was to betray him" (v. 4b) indicates that social concern is not the motivation for these words. He is not interested in the poor, but is a thief and has taken from the money box that he is supposed to administer (v. 6). This juxtaposing of Mary's superabundant generosity, reflecting her love, and Judas' hypocritical objection based in self-interest poses the question: has the woman or the disciple rightly understood the significance of Jesus?

Jesus' response to Judas answers that question. His words close the episode and show that Mary, who had earlier responded to the voice of the Good Shepherd (10:38-42), is the first person to understand the significance of the death of Jesus. Jesus commands Judas: "Leave her alone." He then explains the anointing: "The purpose was that *(hina)* she might keep this for the day of preparation for my burial." (cf. note). The day of his presence at the table with Lazarus is the day of preparation for the burial of Jesus. Mary's action prepares for the death of Jesus. "The reader is invited to see in Mary's action a symbolic embalming of His body for burial, as though he were already dead" (Lightfoot, *Gospel* 236). She recognizes the singular significance of Jesus' oncoming death. Human history produces poor people (cf. Deut 15:11) who will always be present.

However, the once-and-for-all event of the incarnation of the *logos* (1:14; 3:16) has cut across that story and entered it for a brief time. In a proleptic anticipation of the glorification of the Son (cf. 11:4), highlighted by Judas' selfish rejection of her gesture (12:4-6), Mary anoints his body for death. The final events of Jesus' ministry are surrounded with superficiality (cf. 11:16, 21-22, 24, 27, 39, 55-56) and the threat of a violent death (cf. 11:57; 12:4-6, 8), but the symbolic action of Mary, who had earlier recognized Jesus as the Good Shepherd (11:29-32), points toward a more positive understanding of the events that lie ahead.

Jesus enters Jerusalem (vv. 9-19). The actual account of Jesus' entry into Jerusalem is framed by two passages that focus on Lazarus and the movement of people toward Jesus (vv. 9-11; 17-19). The first of these reports a decision to kill *both* Jesus *and* Lazarus. A "great crowd of the Jews" go to Bethany (v. 9a), not only to see the miracle worker but also to see the risen Lazarus (v. 9b). The chief priests are faced with a further complication, and thus they decide they must also be rid of Lazarus, living evidence that Jesus is a miracle worker. The narrator reports that they planned "to put Lazarus *also* to death" (v. 10). The decision to kill Jesus is in place (cf. 11:57), and the death of Lazarus must be added to their plans. The reason for the priests' concern is that on account of Lazarus "many of the Jews were going away and believing in Jesus" (v. 11). Although this motion toward Jesus is motivated by a miracle-faith the promises of 10:15-16 and 11:52 return: the death of Jesus will lead to a "gathering." As the plot to kill Jesus intensifies "many of the Jews" are going away and believing in him (12:11).

The next day the crowd gathered for the feast hears that Jesus is coming into the city (v. 12). This is the crowd described in 11:55-56 performing ritual lustrations and wondering whether Jesus would come to the city for this Passover. From this superficial background of lustrations and chatter the crowd goes out to meet Jesus, armed with palm branches *(ta baïa)*, singing his praises in an adaptation of Ps 118:25-26. The people in the crowd are welcoming *their* expected national, political messiah. Like the crowds by the side of the lake in 6:14-15 they wish to make Jesus *their* king (cf. note). He fled from such acclaim at the lakeside, but now he enters the city on an ass (v. 14). Jesus faces their acclamations, correcting them in the light of a prophecy from Zechariah (v. 15; cf. Zech 9:9). The proximity of death leads Jesus to show that he is a king (v. 15b: "behold your king is coming") but one who comes into the city seated (cf. v. 14a: *ekathisen ep' auto*)—not "riding" or "mounted"—on an ass rather than a war chariot (v. 15c). He is a king, but not the one welcomed by the crowd with palm fronds and their royal acclamation. The interpretation is guaranteed by the narrator who tells the reader that the disciples did not "at first" *(to prōton)* understand the gesture. The narrator introduces another prolepsis, taking the reader out of the events of the story into a future time when the disciples had come to a fuller understanding of Jesus' entry into Jerusalem. As bystanders at the time when the events were happening around them the disciples were unable to understand (v. 16a). But later *(all' hote)* they came to recognize that the words of Zechariah applied to Jesus, and that these things had "been done to him" (v. 16c). They came to a right understanding of these events, and of the way the prophecy of Zechariah is fulfilled in them, after the glorification of Jesus (v. 16b). Jesus is not the king of Israel expected by the crowd but the Messiah promised by Zechariah. This prophecy will be fulfilled some time in the future, when something will be *done* to Jesus (v. 16).

The narrator introduces the second part of the narrative frame around the account of Jesus' entry into Jerusalem by recalling "the Jews" who had mourned with Martha and Mary (11:19, 31), had gone to Lazarus' tomb and witnessed his resurrection (11:42-44), and had come to faith in Jesus as a miracle worker (11:45). This group gave testimony *(emartyrei)* to the fact of the miracle. The imperfect tense of the verb indicates that it was regular part of their conversations about Jesus (cf. Brown, *Gospel* 1:458). The story of Lazarus' raising was the motive for the people's going out to meet Jesus. The crowds involved in vv. 9-19 are attracted to Jesus as a miracle-worker. In v. 9 they went out to see Lazarus as well as Jesus; in v. 17 they are described as the crowd that had been at the miracle, and in vv. 12 and 18 they welcome him into Jerusalem because "they heard that he had done this sign" (v. 18). The kingly welcome they have offered Jesus (vv. 12-13) is a public statement of their hope that he will respond to their messianic expectations. Yet the Pharisees are concerned (v. 19). All the plans and threats they have mounted for the elimination of Jesus are fruitless (v. 19b: "you can do nothing"). Expanding the problem of the many Jews who were going to Jesus (cf. v. 11), the Pharisees now complain: "The world has gone after him" (v. 19c). The words of Jesus (10:15-16), Caiaphas (11:50), and the narrator (11:52) are being fulfilled, but an essential part of this gathering is that the Good Shepherd lay down his life (10:15), that one man should die (11:50-52). If "the world" is attracted to Jesus (12:19) the hour of his violent death (7:30; 8:20) must also be at hand.

The hour has come (vv. 20-36). The words and deeds that announce the arrival of the hour of Jesus and spell out some of its consequences (vv. 23-36) are introduced by the arrival of some Greeks (vv. 20-22). Among the crowds who went up to Jerusalem for Passover were "some Greeks" (v. 20: *ēsan de Hellēnes tines*). Their presence in Jerusalem for the feast makes them Greeks by birth, "God-fearers" who admired and lived Judaism as best they could from within their limitations (cf. Kossen, "Who were the Greeks?" 97–110). Their desire to see Jesus (vv. 21-22) shows that the words of the Pharisees are true: "The world has gone after him" (v. 19).

Because they are Greek they approach a disciple with a Greek name, Philip, who came from Bethsaida, a town close to the Gentile Decapolis. Their request "to see Jesus" (v. 22b: *thelomen ton Iēsoun idein*) is more than curiosity. Although the verb *eidon* is often used in the Fourth Gospel for the everyday experience of "seeing," the verbs "to see" (*horaō* and its substitute *eidon*) are often found in contexts associated with the affirmation, the acceptance, or the refusal of Jesus' role as the revealer (cf. 1:18, 33, 34, 39, 50, 51; 3:3, 11, 32, 36; 4:45; 5:37; 6:2, 36, 46; 8:38, 57; 9:37; 11:32, 40). The Greeks seek such sight. Their Gentile origins are highlighted by Philip's approaching another disciple with a Greek name, Andrew, who comes from the same town as Philip (cf. 1:44; 6:7-8). Together they speak to Jesus (v. 22).

The scene has been set with the arrival and the request of some Greeks. This event triggers Jesus' announcement of the arrival of "the hour" and his further words explaining what it will mean for himself, his followers, and "the Jews." His discourse, broken only by words from heaven (v. 28bc) and the crowd (vv. 29, 34), unfolds in the following way (cf. de la Potterie, "L'exaltation du Fils de l'homme" 461–462):

1. (a) A first revelation (vv. 23-28a): the hour of the glorification of the Son of Man, explained by a heavenly voice (v. 28b).
    (b) The crowd misunderstands (v. 29) and Jesus explains further (v. 30).
2. (a) A second revelation (vv. 31-32): the judgment of the world and the lifting up of Jesus, explained by the narrator (v. 33).
    (b) The crowd misunderstands (v. 34) and Jesus explains further (vv. 35-36a).
3.   Jesus departs and hides himself from them (v. 36b).

The hour of the Son of Man (vv. 23-30). The theme of "gathering," emerging since 10:15-16, is dramatically developed as Jesus responds to the news that Greeks wish to see him. The hour has come! The tension created by the hour that had not yet come (cf. 2:4; 7:6, 8, 30; 8:20) is resolved. It can be put off no longer, as the world is coming to Jesus (cf. vv. 20-22). The gathering at the hour of Jesus is also the glorification of the Son of Man. The hour has come and is still present: the verb is in the perfect tense (*elēlythen*). The Son of Man has already been associated with a "lifting up" (cf. 3:14; 8:28), in the self-gift of Jesus as the revelation of God (cf. 6:27, 51c-53). Jesus is about to be slain, but the hour of his death is his lifting up, his exaltation, his glorification, his self-gift for the life of the world, the moment of gathering (cf. Moloney, *Son of Man* 176–181).

The eloquent image of the grain of wheat that will remain alone unless it falls into the ground further describes the death of Jesus, and the theme of "gathering" forms its background (v. 24), but it has other ramifications, as it does not concur entirely with earlier presentations of the hour of Jesus. The seed must "fall into the earth" *(pesōn eis tēn gēn)* to bear much fruit, but the death of Jesus has been described as a "lifting up." In an extremely dense passage the use of the image of "falling" to speak of death enables Jesus to associate the bystanders with his fruitful self-gift (vv. 25-26). Those who wish to come to eternal life must, like him, be pre-pared to lay down their lives in self-gift (v. 25). But there is more to this self-gift than generosity. The disciple of Jesus is called to reverse the atti-tude of Jesus' opponents who are unable to accept the revelation of the Father in and through Jesus. They fail because they are clinging with closed fists to what is theirs: they love their lives (v. 25a: *ho philōn tēn psychēn autou*). They make an absolute of what this world can offer (v. 25b: *en tǭ kosmǭ toutǭ*), and thus they lose life. The one who is prepared to let go, to hate this life *(ho misōn tēn psychēn autou),* has eternal life *(zēn aiōnion):* a totally satisfying life both here and hereafter (cf. Beardslee, "Saving One's Life" 57–62). The disciple must be where Jesus is—and there self-gift in love is critical. The follower is the servant and must be where the Master is (v. 26ab). Again there is more than this to the rela-tionship that exists between Jesus and a disciple. Jesus points to the Father and informs his listeners that service of Jesus, looking beyond the absolutes of this world, being where he is, falling into the ground in a lov-ing "letting go" of the absolutes imposed by "this world," will bear fruit and lead to the servant's being honored by the Father. All known para-digms of servants and masters are shattered as the follower of Jesus will be honored by the Father of Jesus.

Jesus turns back to his own situation and faces the terror he feels as the hour is now with him (v. 27a; cf. Mark 14:34). The use of "now" *(nun),* "*Now* is my soul troubled," links this anguish with the "hour" of v. 23. The hour of the exaltation is also the hour of his suffering. Jesus asks the Father to bring him safely through this hour (v. 27b). His life has been a continual acceptance of the will of the Father, bringing to perfection the task that the Father gave him to do (4:34; 5:36). Now that the hour has come (v. 23), Jesus has no doubt that his Father will see him through it. The very purpose of Jesus' revealing presence has been at all times de-termined by the hour that is now with him (v. 27c). Paralleling his appeal to the Father to bring him safely through the hour, Jesus further asks that the name of the Father be glorified (v. 28a). However central the story of Jesus might be, it is entirely dependent upon the Father: the Father leads Jesus safely through the hour (v. 27b), and the Father's name is to be glo-rified (v. 28a). Jesus' prayer is met by "the Father's answer" (Schnacken-burg, *Gospel* 2:387). A voice from heaven interprets all that has happened in the story thus far and all that is yet to take place. Throughout the min-istry Jesus' words and deeds have glorified the Father (v. 28ca: *edoxasa).*

Those who have believed have seen the revelation of the *doxa* (2:11; 9:3; 11:40), but the hour has come (v. 23), and these words and events are in the past. Much is still to happen in association with the completion of the hour, and these events will go on glorifying the name of God (v. 28cb: *palin doxasō*).

The word of Jesus (v. 23) and the voice from heaven (v. 28c) are misunderstood. The people in the crowd wonder about the nature of the noise they have heard. Was it a natural phenomenon or an angel (v. 29)? The mystery of Jesus can only be understood by those who are prepared to accept that he is *from God* (cf. 1:1-5), and that his story is determined by his origins and his ongoing union with God (cf. 1:18; 3:13; 6:62; 8:23). But the crowd's explanations of *the origins* of the sound place them with those who love, rather than hate, the allure of this world (cf. v. 25). Jesus explains to them that the voice from heaven was for their sake, because of their fragility. Recalling his prayer for the people gathered at the tomb of Lazarus (11:42), Jesus points out that he has no need of assurance from above, but they are still in need of something so that they might come to believe in Jesus. The voice is for their sake *(di' hymas)*, not for Jesus' *(ou di' eme)*. They must come to believe that the only explanation for the hour of the glorification of the Son of Man (v. 23), the falling of the grain of wheat into the earth so that it might bear much fruit (v. 24), must come from above (v. 30).

The judgment of the world and the lifting up of Jesus (vv. 31-36a). A second moment of revelation begins as Jesus announces the judgment of the world (v. 31: *nun krisis estin tou kosmou*). The "now" of v. 31 is closely related to the "hour" of the glorification of the Son of Man that opened the first moment of revelation in v. 23. The theme of Jesus as the revelation of God placing the world in a situation of judgment has appeared on several occasions throughout Jesus' ministry (cf. 3:19; 5:22, 24, 27, 30; 8:16). Jesus' presence necessarily brings a judgment, and the hour of the glorification of the Son of Man is the culminating moment of judgment for the prince of this world. In itself the world is neutral, but it can be made an end unto itself (cf. 7:7; 8:23), slave to the ruler of *this* world *(ho archōn tou kosmou toutou)*. The hour of the Son of Man marks the casting out *(ekblēthēsetai exō)* of this ruler. A single force is in question here, a prince of evil drawing "the world" into the prison of *this world*, which it attempts to control and understand. But in the Johannine story more is involved. Throughout Jesus' presence among them "the Jews" have made the absolutes of their own culture, history, and religion the determining principles of their world. They have never accepted Jesus' revelation of another world. Thus the *archōn tou kosmou* has very real representatives. The only *archontes* who have appeared in the story have been the leaders of "the Jews" (cf. 3:1; 7:26, 48). Jesus addresses this audience in announcing that the hour of the glorification of the Son of Man is the judgment of *this world,* and that the judgment of the *archontes* is being reversed. In mythic terms, the struggle between the light and the darkness is *now* (cf. vv. 23, 27, 32), and the darkness does not overcome the light (cf. 1:5). It is judged and cast out (v. 31). This struggle is going on in the life story of Jesus and also in the story of the Johannine community, but "the Jews" are unwilling to accept that true freedom comes from the acceptance of the revelation of God in and through Jesus (cf. 1:3c-4; 8:31-32). This makes them slaves of the *archōn tou kosmou toutou,* whose ascendancy is now coming to an end.

In contrast to the vanquished prince of this world, when Jesus is lifted up from the earth *(ean hypsōthō ek tēs gēs)* he will draw everyone to himself (v. 32). Jesus' death will bring many sheep into one fold (10:15-16). It will be a death for a nation, and not only for a nation, but to gather into one the children of God who are scattered abroad (11:50-52). Already many Jews were believing in him (12:11), and the Pharisees were complaining that the whole world is going after him (12:19). His hour and fruitful death have come (vv. 23-24). In his being raised from the ground, at the same time a physical "lifting up" and a moment of exaltation, he will draw all people to himself (v. 32). As in the earlier revelation a voice from heaven intervened to explain Jesus' words, here the narrator comments: "He said this to show by what death he was to die" (v. 33). The hour of Jesus, the glorification of the Son of Man, the lifting up, and the gathering are all associated with the crucifixion of Jesus: a death by a lifting up on a stake as Moses lifted up the serpent in the wilderness (3:14).

"The Jews" will not be moved. They are not prepared to listen to Jesus because they "know" (v. 34a: "we have heard") that God has spoken through Moses (cf. 9:24, 29, 31). Their Law tells them that the Messiah remains for ever (cf. LXX Ps 88:37). Thus they reject Jesus' revelation by asking, "How can *you* say *(legeis su)* the Son of Man must be lifted up? Who is *this (houtos)* Son of Man?" (12:34b). The pronoun *su* and the relative pronoun *houtos* make their determination clear: no Jewish Messiah can possibly be lifted up. Jesus makes a final attempt to draw "the Jews" into his world, but it is almost a warning. He recalls his earlier words as he revealed himself as the light of the world (cf. 8:12) to insist upon the uniqueness of the moment now theirs. They have the light with them for only a short time (v. 35a; cf. 7:33; 9:4; 11:9). They should walk in the light because those who walk in the darkness lose their way (cf. 9:4; 11:10) and do not know where they are going (v. 35b). If they are to walk in the light they must "believe in the light." This is the only way to life and light (v. 36b). Jesus' earlier self-revelation as "the light of the world" (8:12) was also associated with a warning: "I told you that you would die in your sins, for you will die in your sins unless you believe that I am he" (8:24). Little has happened since that encounter on the occasion of the celebration of Tabernacles to indicate a change of heart among "the Jews." Some have marveled at his authority as a miracle-worker (cf. 11:21, 37, 45, 47; 12:9-11, 12, 17). But, locked as they are within their prison of "this world" (cf. 12:15, 31) and "the Law" (cf. 12:34), there is little hope that "the Jews" will believe in the light that is to be found in Jesus (cf. 1:4-5; 8:12; 9:5; 11:9-10).

Jesus' final departure (v. 36b). Having said these words, Jesus departed and hid himself from them (v. 36b). This final departure is marked by Jesus' active and deliberate hiding *(ekyrbē ap' autōn).* On other occasions Jesus has left the scene to specific locations with named companions (cf. 3:22-25; 4:43-45; 7:1; 8:59; 10:40-42; 11:54). As his ministry comes to an end he disappears, alone, hiding himself from "the Jews" in some unknown place. A light that is hidden can no longer direct the steps of one walking (cf. v. 35). The story of Jesus' public ministry has come to an end. He will next appear in public to be lifted up on a cross (18:1–19:16). "The Jews" will next find Jesus at Gethsemane as they search for him with the aid of lanterns and torches (18:3).

Notes

55. *to purify themselves:* The technical term for purification *(agnizein)* is used. See also Acts 21:24, 26; 24:18. See F. Hauck, *TDNT* 1:123.

57. *the chief priests and the Pharisees:* This historically unlikely combination is used by the narrator to indicate leaders of "the Jews." See also 7:32, 45; 11:47. On the Johannine nature of this combination see Tsuchido, "Tradition and Redaction" 610.

12:1. *Six days before the Passover:* There is no need to read symbolic significance into the "six days." Given the indication that the celebration of the feast was "at hand" in 11:15, a number of days are called for so that the events of 12:1-36, the encounter between Jesus and the disciples of 13:1–17:26, and the trial, crucifixion, and burial of Jesus in 18:1–19:42 can take place. Jesus dies on "the day of Preparation" (19:31).

where Lazarus was: The references to Lazarus in vv. 1-2 are somewhat heavy-handed. This has led to textual variants and to suggestions that they are glosses. See the discussion in Barrett, *Gospel* 410–411. The clumsiness of these references, taken in conjunction with the use of Lazarus in vv. 9-11 and vv. 17-19 to frame the account of Jesus' entry into Jerusalem, point to the author's desire to link 11:1–12:36. Lazarus is important to both chapters.

2. *they made him a supper:* The verb "they made" *(epoiēsan)* has no subject. It is possible that someone else prepared the supper and that Lazarus, Martha, and Mary attended. This is hardly likely, however, given the context and the fact that Martha serves at table.

Martha served: Scott, *Sophia* 212–214, reads too much into this indication. For him it is a pointer that Martha continues to respond as a perfect disciple to the revelation of Jesus as *Sophia* incarnate.

3. *Mary . . . anointed the feet of Jesus and wiped his feet with her hair:* A parallel scene is reported in all three synoptic gospels (cf. Mark 14:3-9; Matt 26:6-13; Luke 7:36-50). The literary relationship among these anointing stories in the synoptic tradition is problematic. No doubt the Fourth Gospel depends on a tradition related to that of the synoptics, but a direct literary dependence on either the Markan or Lukan accounts is difficult to prove. The use of the story is entirely conditioned by its Johannine context. For the discussion see Moloney, *Son of Man* 164–166. The focus on Jesus' feet is unique to this tradition, and Lindars, *Gospel* 416–417, sees it as a gesture of humility, pointing forward to the footwashing of ch. 13.

a pound of costly ointment of pure nard: On the ointment *(nardos pistikēs)*, mentioned by both Mark (14:3) and John, see Moloney, *Son of Man* 164. Its description, although beyond exact identification in a modern fragrance, highlights its costliness.

and the house was filled with the fragrance of the ointment: Some scholars, following a rabbinic tradition and Clement of Alexandria (cf. *Eccles. Rab.* 7:1; *Song Rab.* 1:22; Ignatius, *Eph.*17:1; Clement of Alexandria, *Paedagogus* 2:8, MPG 8:466–490) understand this remark as the Johannine version of Mark 14:9: the spreading of the odor is a symbol of the spread of the message throughout the Gentile world (e.g., Bauer, *Johannesevangelium* 159; Hoskyns, *Gospel* 415; Strachan, *Fourth Gospel* 248). Loisy, *Evangile* 362–363, takes this further, understanding the whole incident as a symbol of the Gentile Church receiving the gospel message at the feet of Jesus. Brodie, *Gospel* 407, extends this to a message that fills the whole of creation (cf. Eph 1:23).

4. *Judas Iscariot, one of his disciples (he who was to betray him):* As well as the contrast between the actions of Mary and the actions of Judas that vv. 4-6 creates, the association of Judas with the death of Jesus also hints that Mary's action may be directed toward that event. See Tsuchido, "Tradition and Redaction" 610–611.

5. *three hundred denarii:* A denarius was a day's wage. This makes the ointment very expensive indeed.

7. *Leave her alone. The purpose was that she might keep this for the day of preparation for my burial:* The translation of the Greek *hina . . . tērēsē auto* is difficult. A literal translation would be "so that she might keep it for the preparation of my burial." Is Mary to keep some of the ointment for the anointing of Jesus after his death? If so, what grounds did Judas have for complaint if the ointment had not already been used (v. 5)? A major break should be made after *aphes autēn.* Jesus commands: "Leave her alone." This creates a new sentence beginning with *hina,* which must be given a strong meaning: "the purpose was that." See also Brown, *Gospel* 1:449; Kleist, "A Note" 46–48; Kühne, "Eine kritische Studie" 476–477. The word *entaphismos* does not mean "burial" but "laying out for burial" (LSJ 575). This interpretation of v. 7 rejects the idea that the

anointing is in some way royal (e.g., Bruns, "A Note on 12,3" 219–222; Barrett, *Gospel* 409).

8. *the poor you always have with you:* Prete, "I poveri," makes a link between the archetypal selfishness of Judas (vv. 5-6) and the continual presence of the poor (v. 8). Endemic to human society is the truth that the former creates the latter. Many regard this verse as having little to do with the context, or see it as an addition. For a survey see Holst, "The One Anointing of Jesus" 444–446. It is omitted by Bezae and the Sinaitic Syriac. $\mathfrak{P}^{75}$ has a shorter text. The verse must be regarded as original.

10. *the chief priests planned:* The author continues to use a selection of groups—at times historically improbable—from the Jewish leadership to indicate opposition to Jesus.

11. *many of the Jews were going away and believing in Jesus:* Based on the resurrection of Lazarus, the faith of these people is still limited to a signs-faith (cf. Becker, *Evangelium* 2:375). Some commentators (e.g., Lindars, *Gospel* 420; Carson, *Gospel* 431) regard the action of "the Jews" as leaving Judaism to become disciples.

12. *Jesus was coming to Jerusalem:* On the question of the relationship between this account and the synoptic tradition (cf. Mark 11:1-11; Matt 21:1-11; Luke 19:29-38) see the summary in Brown, *Gospel* 1:459–461. As always there is little consensus; opinions range from Markan dependence to a separate Johannine tradition.

13. *they took branches of palm trees:* The only use of *ta baïa* in the LXX is in 1 Macc 13:51, where the Jews take possession of Jerusalem after Simon had conquered the Jerusalem citadel in 142 B.C.E. Palm fronds also appear on coins minted from 140 B.C.E. to 70 C.E. bearing the inscription "for the liberation of Israel." The use of palm fronds is closely associated with Maccabean nationalism (cf. Farmer, "The Palm Branches" 62–66. See also Hart, "Judea and Rome" 172–198, and plates I-III, for evidence of the Roman use of the palm in coins used to commemorate *Judea Capta.*). Only in the Fourth Gospel does the crowd welcome Jesus into Jerusalem waving *ta baïa*. The gesture is supported by words. They add to Ps 118:25-26 "even the King of Israel" *(kai ho basileus tou Israel).*

    Hosanna: This expression is primarily a petition (cf. Ps 118:25): "give salvation." However, it is understood as an acclamation. See Carson, *Gospel* 423.

14. *But Jesus found a young ass:* The Greek particle *de* indicates that Jesus' actions are in deliberate contrast to the acclamation of v. 13: *heurōn de ho Iēsous*.

15. *Fear not, daughter of Zion:* The quotation is very loose, and is perhaps influenced by Isa 44:2; 40:9; Zeph 3:16, or Gen 49:11. See Barrett, *Gospel* 418–419, and especially Menken, *Old Testament Quotations* 89–97.

    sitting on an ass's colt: The Zechariah passage conveys the idea of the messiah who comes on a donkey rather than in a war chariot (cf. Lindars, *Gospel* 424; Schuchard, *Scripture Within Scripture* 71–84). Brown, *Gospel* 1:462–463, rightly plays down the humility theme to suggest that the real point of the passage is its reference to the context of Zeph 3:9-10, which tells of a *universal* king, as does the context of Zech 9:9 (cf. 9:11). The proclamation cannot be read as an affirmation of Jesus' entering Jerusalem as its messianic king.

17. *the crowd who had been with him when he called Lazarus out of the tomb:* This reading accepts the syntactically more difficult *hote,* along with the majority of witnesses (e.g., Sinaiticus, Vaticanus, Alexandrinus, Freer Gospels, Koridethi), rather than the smoother *hoti* (e.g., $\mathfrak{P}^{66}$, Bezae, Claromantanus). This reading links the crowd with those who had been with him at the resurrection of Lazarus, and distinguishes it from "the crowd" who went out to see Jesus and Lazarus because they heard of the miracle (v. 9) and "the crowd" that remained in the city but welcomed him with palm fronds and acclamation (v. 12).

21. *These came to Philip:* The disciples "Philip" (v. 21) and "Andrew" (v. 22) are the only disciples whose names have been transmitted in their Greek form.

    We wish to see Jesus: The use of the verb "to see" in contexts that deal with the revelation of God in and through Jesus is particularly true for the verb *horaō*. *Eidon* is generally used for everyday events. However, *idein* is used in 12:21 as a substitute second aorist for *horaō*. See BDF 54, § 101. For Beutler, "Greeks Come" 333–347 (especially 342–347), this request is linked to Isa 52:15 and forms part of a wide-ranging use of Isaian servant material and language across John 12:20-50.

23. *The hour has come for the Son of Man to be glorified:* Many commentators divide the following discourse into three parts: vv. 23-26, 27-30, 31-36a. The division adopted by the interpretation, vv. 23-30, 31-36a, 36b is largely inspired by de la Potterie, "L'exaltation du Fils de l'homme" 461–462. For a detailed study of "the Son of Man" in 12:23 see Moloney, *Son of Man* 176–181.

25. *Those who love their life:* On *psychē* (translated here as "life") in the sense of a person's human experience of life see Brown, *Gospel* 1:467. The noun has this meaning in 12:25 and also in 10:15, but not in 12:27, where it refers to Jesus' emotional inner self.

26. *there shall my servant be also:* The demand that the servant be where the master is does not primarily mean suffering, although that is the main point of this particular context. There is a hint here, which will be developed later in the Gospel (cf. 17:1-26), of the disciples' being swept up into the oneness that unites the Father and the Son.

    Whoever serves me the Father will honor: Behind this promise of Jesus lies a community coming to grips with the physical reality of death by martyrdom that forms part of following Jesus to the cross. These words were no doubt eloquent in a community suffering exclusion and death because of their faith in Jesus as the Christ (cf. 9:22; 12:42; 16:2).

27. *Now is my soul troubled:* As Schnackenburg, *Gospel* 2:387, rightly comments: "Even in John, the cross has not lost its human darkness." See also Thüsing, *Die Erhöhung* 78–82. There is a close link between the use of the verb *tarassō* ("to be troubled"), Psalm 42/43, and Gethsemane tradition. See Thüsing,

Erhöhung 79–88; Beutler, "Psalm 42/43" 34–38. Nicholson, *Death as Departure* 124, regards vv. 20-26 as directed to the disciples and vv. 27-36a as directed to the crowds. He later claims (pp. 127–129) that Jesus' emotion in v. 27 is not generated by his own concern over suffering but by concern over the future steadfastness of the disciples.

Father, assure my salvation from this hour: For the interpretation of v. 27b as a statement rather than a question, respecting that the hour has already come, see Westcott, *Gospel* 182, and the earlier discussion summarized by Lagrange, *Evangile* 332–333. It is further developed by Léon-Dufour, "Père, fais-moi passer" 156–165. See the translation of Léon-Dufour, *Lecture* 2:466.

28. *Then a voice came from heaven:* It is sometimes suggested that this is a *bat qōl*, a divine communication that replaced the prophetic word (e.g., Bauer, *Johannesevangelium* 163). This hardly fits the context of the communication between the Father and the Son.

    I have glorified it: The strategic placing of references to the revelation of the *doxa* in the first (2:11) and the last (11:40) of Jesus' public signs indicates that the whole of the ministry has been a revelation of the *doxa*. That is now behind Jesus as he moves toward his passion.

    I will glorify it again: The revelation of the glory of God (to be distinguished from the future glory of the exalted Christ) is to be limited to the cross. See Blank, *Krisis* 276–280; Dodd, *Interpretation* 372–379; Lindars, *Gospel* 432. Against, for example, the influential work of Thüsing, *Erhöhung* 193–198, who links the aorist tense with Jesus' life and the hour of the cross and the future tense with the glorification of the exalted Christ. Some commentators (e.g., Westcott, *Gospel* 182; Nicholson, *Death as Departure* 129–130) extend the future glory into the future preaching of the gospel. The use of *palin* ("again") indicates that the same glory continues to shine both in the past works of Jesus during the ministry that now concludes and in the future glorification that is about to be told. *Both* moments belong to the historical appearance of the Son and show the unfailing union between the Father and the Son (cf. 1:18).

29. *The crowd . . . said that it had thundered. Others said, "An angel has spoken to him":* On the background to voices that sound like thunder, or a revelation that may come from angels, see Schnackenburg, *Gospel* 2:389–390. The basis of the crowd's mistake is their belief that the noise is some sort of mediation rather than the presence of God. See Lagrange, *Evangile* 334.

31. *Now is the judgment of this world:* On the variety of ways in which the Greek *ho kosmos* ("the world") is used in the Fourth Gospel see Moloney, *Belief in the Word* 37–38.

    the ruler of this world: On the development of the Christian notion of the ruler or prince of this world see Schnackenburg, *Gospel* 2:391.

32. *when I am lifted up from the earth:* The lifting up "from the earth" means crucifixion. It does not look to some future journey of Jesus into the heavens, taking believers with him, as among others Nicholson, *Death as Departure*

132–136, would maintain. The narrator's comment in v. 33 must be taken seriously: "lifting up" (v. 32) = "the death by which Jesus was to die" (v. 33). See especially Thüsing, *Erhöhung* 3–12; Cilia, *La morte* 99–107. In 8:28 "the Jews" were told they would be responsible for the "lifting up" *(hotan hypōsēte)*. This "lifting up" must mean something they do to Jesus (cf. Riedl, "Wenn ihr den Menschensohn" 360–362). The parallel drawn between Moses' lifting up of the serpent and the lifting up of the Son of Man in 3:14 also points to a physical lifting up on a stake. There is no suggestion of the serpent ascending into heaven. Nicholson, *Death as Departure* 98–103 (on 3:14) and 136–138 (on 12:33) insists that the evangelist wants the reader to look *beyond* the cross, not *at* the cross. This is unacceptable. On this unresolved debate concerning the extension of the hour and the glorification of Jesus see Moloney, *Son of Man* 61–64, and the discussion there. On the cross as revelation see Forestell, *The Word of the Cross* 58–102. No doubt, *through* the hour of the cross the Son will return to the glory he had with the Father before the world was made (cf. 7:39; 11:4; 13:1; 17:5, 24). There are two separate issues that must not be confused: (1) the revelation of the glory of God (i.e., the glorification of the Son of Man [12:23], the lifting up [v. 32], the way Jesus was to die [v. 33] = *on the cross*, and (2) the glorification of Jesus as Son of the Father (7:39; 11:4) = *through the cross*.

will draw all people to myself: The neuter plural *panta* ("all things"), rather than *pantas* ("all people"), indicating that the exalted Jesus would draw all reality, is found in 𝔓⁶⁶, first hand of Sinaiticus, Old Latin, Bezae, and some of the versions. However, this variant may indicate only humanity in general.

34. *that the Christ remains forever:* Scholars debate what Scripture is meant. For the many possibilities see Bauer, *Johannesevangelium* 164. Barrett, *Gospel* 427, settles for the common messianic teaching of the Scriptures. For a documented discussion see Moloney, *Son of Man* 182–183. Beutler, "Greeks Come" 337–342, argues for LXX Isa 52:13–53:12 as background for John 12:23, 32, 34. For the choice of LXX Ps 88:37 see van Unnik, "The Quotation" 174–179.

    Who is this Son of Man?: Behind this question lie the synagogue seeking answers in their Mosaic traditions and the Johannine community claiming that Jesus is something more than the Jewish Messiah. This has been evident in 12:9-19. He is the Son of Man who draws all to himself by being lifted up (12:23, 32). The underlying debate is deeply christological. See Tsuchido, "Tradition and Redaction" 609–619; de Jonge, "Jewish Expectations about the Messiah" 246–270.

35. *Walk while you have the light, lest the darkness overtake you:* The symbol of light and walking in the light are found in Judaism and at Qumran. For a summary see Barrett, *Gospel* 429.

36. *he departed and hid himself from them:* On the relationship between the symbol of light and darkness in vv. 35-36a and Jesus' hiding himself from "the Jews" see Dodd, *Interpretation* 380; Stibbe, *John* 137. Mörchen, "'Weggehen'" interprets Jesus' departure as a symbolic final condemnation of the refusal of "the Jews" to accept his revelation.

FOR REFERENCE AND FURTHER STUDY

Beardslee, W. A. "Saving One's Life by Losing It," *JAAR* 47 (1979) 57–72.
Beutler, Johannes. "Greeks Come to See Jesus (John 20,20f)," *Bib.* 71 (1990) 333–347.
_____. "Psalm 42/43 im Johannesevangelium," *NTS* 25 (1978–1979) 33–57.
Bruns, J. Edgar. "A Note on John 12,3," *CBQ* 28 (1966) 219–222.
Farmer, William R. "The Palm Branches in John 12,13," *JThS* 3 (1952) 62–66.
Hart, H. St. John. "Judea and Rome: The Official Commentary," *JThS* 3 (1952) 172–198.
Holst, Robert. "The One Anointing of Jesus: Another Application of the Form-Critical Method," *JBL* 95 (1976) 435–446.
Jonge, Marinus de. "Jewish Expectations about the Messiah according to the Fourth Gospel," *NTS* 19 (1972–1973) 246–270.
Karris, Robert J. *Jesus and the Marginalized in John's Gospel.* Zacchaeus Studies: New Testament. Collegeville: The Liturgical Press, 1990.
Kleist, J. A. "A Note on the Greek Text of John 12,7," *CJ* 21 (1925) 46–48.
Kossen, H. B. "Who were the Greeks of John XII.20?" In *Studies in John: Presented to Dr. J. N. Sevenster on the Occasion of His Seventieth Birthday.* NT.S 24. Leiden: E. J. Brill, 1970, 97–110.
Kühne, W. "Eine kritische Studie zu Joh. 12,7," *ThStKr* 98–99; (1926) 476–477.
La Potterie, Ignace de. "L'exaltation du Fils de l'homme (Jn 12,31-36)," *Gr.* 49 (1968) 460–478.
Léon-Dufour, Xavier. "Père, fais-moi passer sain et sauf à travers cette heure (Jean 12,27)." In Heinrich Baltensweiler and Bo Reicke, eds., *Neues Testament und Geschichte: Historisches Geschehen und Deutung im Neuen Testament: Oscar Cullmann zum 70. Geburtstag.* Zürich: Theologischer Verlag, 1972, 156–165.
Moloney, Francis J. *Signs and Shadows* 178–195.
_____. *Son of Man* 160–185.
Mörchen, Roland. "'Weggehen.' Beobachtungen zu Joh 12,36b," *BZ* 28 (1984) 240–242.
Prete, Benedetto. "'I poveri' nel racconto giovanneo dell'unzione di Betania (Giov. 12,1-8)." In *Evangelizare Pauperibus: Atti dela XXIV Settimana Biblica Associazione Biblica Italiana.* Brescia: Paideia, 1978, 429–444.
Tsuchido, Kiyoshi. "Tradition and Redaction in John 12.1-43," *NTS* 30 (1984) 609–619.
Unnik, W. C. van. "The Quotation from the Old Testament in John 12,34," *NT* 3 (1959) 174–179.

iii. Conclusion to the Ministry of Jesus (12:37-50)

37. Though he had done so many signs before them, yet they did not believe in him; 38. it was that the word spoken by the prophet Isaiah might be fulfilled:

"Lord, who has believed our report, and to whom has the arm of the Lord been revealed?"
39. Therefore they could not believe. For Isaiah again said,
40. "God has blinded their eyes and hardened their heart, lest they should see with their eyes and perceive with their heart, and turn for me to heal them."
41. Isaiah said this because he saw his glory and spoke of him.
42. Nevertheless many even of the authorities believed in him, but for fear of the Pharisees they did not confess it lest they should be put out of the synagogue: 43. for they loved human glory rather than the glory of God.
44. And Jesus cried out and said, "Whoever believes in me believes not in me but in the one who sent me. 45. And whoever sees me sees the one who sent me. 46. I have come as light into the world, that whoever believes in me may not remain in darkness. 47. I do not judge anyone who hears my words and does not keep them, for I came not to judge the world but to save the world. 48. The one who rejects me and does not receive my word has a judge; the word that I have spoken will serve as judge on the last day. 49. For I have not spoken on my own authority; the Father who sent me has himself given me commandment what to say and what to speak. 50. And I know that his commandment is eternal life. What I say, therefore, I say as the Father has bidden me."

INTERPRETATION

Introduction to 12:37-50. "The Jews" have resisted Jesus' revelation, locked as they are in their knowledge of their Law (cf. v. 34). Despite a last attempt to draw them into the light (vv. 35-36a), his departure to hide himself from them (v. 36b) is ominous. The promise of 1:11 has proved to be true in the story of Jesus' public ministry: "He came to his own home and his own people received him not." Why did this happen? The narrator attempts a response to that question in vv. 37-43. The public ministry closes with Jesus calling out (v. 44: *ekraxen*) from an unknown time and place proclaiming the unique revelation of God that takes place in him and the judgment that flows from that revelation (vv. 44-50).

The unfaith of "the Jews" (vv. 37-43). The many "signs" that Jesus had done before "the Jews" have not led them to faith (v. 37). Although response to Jesus' signs is only the beginning of faith (cf. 2:1-11; 9:1-38; 11:15, 42) some promising starts (cf. 2:23; 7:31; 8:30; 10:42; 11:45, 48; 12:11) have come to nothing (cf. 2:24-25; 7:35; 8:31-33; 11:46; 12:12-15, 34). The first part of this reflection from the narrator (vv. 38-41) falls back on traditional use of Isaiah (for Isa 53:1 [v. 38b] see Rom 10:16, and for Isa 6:9-10 [v. 40] see Mark 4:11-12; 8:17-18; Matt 13:13-15; Luke 8:10; 19:42; Acts

28:26-27; Rom 11:8, 10) to explain that this failure forms part of God's design. There are no apologies for the action of God; these things happened so that the prophecy of Isaiah would be fulfilled (v. 38a: *hina . . . plērōthȩ*). After the citation of Isa 53:1 asking who has believed in the revelation of God (v. 38b) the divine necessity of the unbelief of "the Jews" is stated in a way that is without parallel in the rest of the NT. In order to fulfill the Scriptures *it was impossible for them to believe* (v. 39: *ouk ēdynanto pisteuein*). The Johannine use of this Isaian passage insists that God was responsible for their blindness and their hardness of heart, lest they should turn to Jesus for healing (v. 40). Still reflecting early Christian traditions, the narrator tells the reader that Isaiah was able to see the glory of Jesus and thus speak of it with authority. Isaiah's vision (Isa 6:1-5) was linked with this vision of God. From there it was only a short step for Christians to claim that he saw the *doxa tou theou*, the glory of God (cf. 1:14) as it existed before all time (cf. 1:1-2). Isaiah, like Abraham and all the prophets of old, was able to speak of having seen the Christ (cf. 8:56).

But this use of early Christian tradition to explain the failure of "the Jews" by the theory of the "divine hardening" conflicts with the story that has been told to this point. If "the Jews" failed it is because they made a decision against Jesus. Thus, having provided the reader with what had become a traditional explanation to a most disturbing fact of history, the narrator next offers an explanation for this fact that resonates with the rest of the Johannine story. Almost negating his use of the "divine hardening" theory, the narrator reports that some of the *archontes* did come to belief in Jesus (v. 42a). The revelation of God in and through Jesus did not fail, but those called to belief in him failed. No doubt reflecting the situation of the members of the Johannine community, cast out of the synagogue because of their faith in Jesus, the narrator tells of certain leaders of "the Jews" who did not have the courage of their convictions. They refused to confess their faith (*ouk hōmologoun*) because they were afraid they would be cast out of the synagogue by the Pharisees (v. 42; cf. 9:22).

In a concluding statement (v. 43) playing on the twofold meaning of the Greek word *doxa* (see also 5:41-44; 7:18; 8:50-54) the narrator provides a key to the failure of "the Jews" that corresponds *exactly* with what happened throughout 1:19–12:36. "The Jews" have never been able to let go of what they could understand and control: their messianic expectations (cf. 1:19-49; 3:2-5; 4:19, 25-26; 6:14-15; 7:25-31, 40-44; 12:34) and their "knowledge" (cf. 3:2; 4:25; 7:27; 9:24, 29; 11:22, 24). Thus they have never been able to grasp *ta epourania* ("the heavenly things") revealed by Jesus. They could only understand them as *ta epigeia* ("earthly things"; cf. 3:12). There is a chasm between the world of "the Jews" who are *ek tōn katō* and Jesus who is *ek tōn anō* (cf. 8:23). They love the esteem, the honor, the praise, and the respect of human beings and "this world" (*tēn doxan tōn anthrōpōn)* so much that they are prepared to ignore Jesus, the presence of the revelation of God *(tēn doxan tou theou)* (v. 43; cf. 1:14; 2:11; 11:4, 40). This double meaning of *doxa*—human glory and the revelation of God— provides the key for a correct understanding of the conflict between Jesus and "the Jews" that has developed during the ministry of Jesus. The clash between "the Jews" and Jesus is inevitable. The former will not sacrifice the *horizontal* dimension of all that this world can offer *(tēn doxan tōn anthrōpōn)*, and reject the *vertical* inbreak of God *(tēn doxan tou theou)*, who sends the Son from above so that the world might be saved (cf. 3:16-17).

Jesus "cries out" his final message (vv. 44-50). No time or place is given for these final words of Jesus gathered from across the story of his minis- try. Summarizing the significance of his revealing and judging presence, vv. 44-50 are also commentary on the closing remarks of v. 43: Jesus makes known the *doxa* of God (v. 43). In six sentences the word *egō* ("I") is used four times (vv. 46, 47, 49, 50), but the "I" of Jesus is subordinated to the Father as Jesus is the Sent One making the Father known. He is the unique revelation of *the Father who sent him* (v. 44; cf. 3:15-16; 5:36-38; 6:29, 35, 40; 7:38; 8:19, 24, 42, 45-46), and thus to see Jesus is to see *the one who sent him* (v. 45; cf. 1:18; 6:40; 8:19; 10:30, 38). Out of this relationship with the Father Jesus can claim to bring *light into the world* so that those who believe in him can emerge from the darkness and walk permanently in the light (v. 46; cf. 1:4-5; 8:12; 9:5, 39; 11:9-10; 12:35-36a). The world judges itself as it accepts or refuses this light, the revelation *of the Father,* and thus Jesus does not actively judge. In vv. 47-48 Jesus shifts the focus of his proclamation away from his mission from the Father to the crucial im- portance of "belief in the word" (cf. 2:1–4:54). He has come to save the world, but the world, free to reject his saving presence, has done so and is thus judged (v. 47; cf. 3:16-17, 34; 5:24; 8:15, 31). Jesus' word stands in judgment against all who would reject it. This judgment is acted out both now and hereafter (v. 48; cf. 3:18; 5:24, 29, 44-45; 7:51; 8:40). But even in this Jesus depends on the Father. The word of Jesus is not his own as he does not speak on the basis of his own authority. He speaks *what the Father has commanded him to say.* With absolute confidence Jesus can claim that this word brings eternal life. Jesus has spoken *the word of the Father* with uncompromising trust and confidence (vv. 49-50; cf. 4:34; 5:22, 30, 39; 6:38; 7:16-17; 8:26, 28, 38; 10:18).

As his ministry opened Jesus (3:11-21) and the narrator (3:31-36) an- nounced that Jesus is the unique revelation of God and that life or death, light or darkness flow from the acceptance or refusal of this revelation. The ministry now closes with a collection of sayings of Jesus that make the same point. Jesus is the revelation of the *doxa tou theou* and the world judges itself by its acceptance or refusal of this revelation (12:44-50). As the curtain falls on Jesus' public presence to "the Jews" (v. 36b) the roots of the emerging crisis have been exposed: "the Jews" loved the *doxa tōn anthrōpōn* rather than the *doxa tou theou* (v. 43), but Jesus did not falter in bringing to perfection the task given to him by the Father, making known the *doxa tou theou* (cf. 4:34; 5:36). The information has been provided by the two most authoritative voices in the story: the narrator (vv. 42-43) and Jesus (vv. 44-50).

Conclusion to 11:1–12:36. As the feast of Passover was at hand Jesus made a decisive journey to Bethany (11:1, 7, 12; 12:1) and then to Jerusalem (11:55; 12:1, 12, 20). This journey will be for the glory of God, so that the Son of God might be glorified by means of it (11:4, 40). In Jerusalem, as "the world" desires to see him, the hour of Jesus' glorification is announced (12:19-20, 23, 31-32). Across 11:1–12:36 the same characters are actively involved with Jesus: Lazarus (11:1-2, 5, 14, 17, 43-44; 12:1, 9-11, 16-19), Martha (11:1, 3, 18, 28-30, 39, 42; 12:2), Mary (11:1-3, 20, 28-33, 42, 12:1-8), the disciples (11:1-16, 42; 12:4-6, 16, 21-22), and "the Jews" (11:8, 19, 31, 33, 36-37, 42, 45-46, 47-50, 54, 55-57; 12:9-11, 12-13, 17-19, 29, 34). Characters, place, and time combine to form a unified story across 11:1–12:36 (cf. Giblin, "The Tripartite Narrative Structure" 449–468; de Merode, "L'accueil triomphal" 49–62). Jesus, Lazarus, Martha, Mary, and "the Jews" all play their part within the spatial and temporal context of Jesus' movement to Jerusalem at the time of a Passover that will be marked by his violent death (11:49-50, 57; 12:7, 10, 33). But this violent end will reveal the glory of God (11:4a) and the Son of God will be glorified by means of it (11:4b). It is the hour for the glorification of the Son of Man, his being lifted up from the earth (12:23, 32). The death of Jesus is not *for himself.* Jesus will lay down his life *for others.* In the midst of increasing misunderstanding (cf. 11:8, 12, 16, 21-22, 24, 27, 33, 39, 47, 55; 12:9, 13, 29, 34) and mounting violence (cf. 11:8, 16, 47-50, 54, 57; 12:10-11) the theme of "gathering" has emerged (10:15-16; 11:50-52; 12:9, 19, 20, 32). None of this, however, takes away from the enigma of the cross: "He said this to show by what death he was to die" (12:33). The story ahead must tell of a death that is also the gathering of all people (12:32: *pantas*) around the lifted up and glorified Son of Man (12:23). But Jesus' public ministry has come to an end (12:36b). In concluding this part of the story both the narrator (12:37-43) and Jesus (12:44-50) have insisted that Jesus makes God known, and that judgment flows from the acceptance or refusal of that revelation.

NOTES

37. *though he had done so many signs before them:* There is no cause for concern over the use of the expression "so many signs," even though very few have been

told. As Forestell remarks: "*tosauta sēmeia* do not refer simply to the signs narrated in the Gospel, but to the entire miracle activity of Jesus" (*Word of the Cross* 69). Brown, *Gospel* 1:485, suggests that Deut 29:2-4 lies behind this statement.

yet they did not believe in him: There have been many attempts to find a better location for vv. 44-50, but they make excellent sense in their present context. For the discussion see Moloney, *Son of Man* 163–164; Schnackenburg, *Gospel* 2:411–412. Smith, "The Setting and Shape" 90–93, suggests that vv. 37-40 were part of a source that linked the seemingly contradictory christologies of an impressive messianic claimant (ministry) and Jesus rejected and crucified (passion account). Evans, "Obduracy and the Lord's Servant" 232–236, suggested that vv. 38-41 formed part of a larger midrash of Isa 52:7–53:17 at work in John 12:1-43. In a later work, *To See and Not Perceive* 134, he agrees with Smith's suggestion.

38. *the word spoken by the prophet Isaiah:* The citation from Isa 53:1 is close to the LXX, while that of Isa 6:10 seems to be a loose citation of the Hebrew reworked by the author. See Schnackenburg, "Joh 12,39-41" 169–171; Schuchard, *Scripture Within Scripture* 85–106.

might be fulfilled: On the absolute nature of this statement, in which the *hina* must be given its full telic force, see Bernard, *Commentary* 2:449. Both the *fact* of the failure (v. 39) and the *reason* for the failure (v. 40) fulfill Scripture. See Lindars, *Gospel* 349.

who has believed our report, and to whom has the arm of the Lord been revealed: In the words of Isaiah "our report" looks to the teaching of Jesus, while "the arm of the Lord" refers to his deeds.

40. *God has blinded their eyes:* The majority of commentators attempt to show that vv. 38-41 follow the continual rejection of Jesus by "the Jews" throughout the narrative (e.g., Becker, *Evangelium* 2:408–412; Schnackenburg, "Joh 12, 37-41" 176–177; Schuchard, *Scripture Within Scripture* 98–106). This is not the case. *Never* in the earlier narrative is the impression created that God caused "the Jews" to reject Jesus. Lieu, "Blindness" 83–95, faces this difficulty. On the basis of John 9, 12:39-43, and 1 John 2:11 she suggests that blindness and unbelief were linked in the Johannine tradition. This suggestion partially explains why Isa 6:9-10 was taken from the tradition even though it hardly fits the context. Hollenbach, "Lest they should turn" 317–320, sees the difficulty and suggests that Isaiah 6 is being used ironically: "the last thing they want to see." Blank, *Krisis* 301–303, suggests that the devil is the subject of the verbs "to make blind" and "to harden." This only shifts the problem, as the rejection of Jesus throughout the ministry is not reported as motivated by the devil. The discussion in 8:39-47 ("your father is the devil") is about origins and does not take away from the freedom of "the Jews" (cf. 8:34). The use of Isaiah and the theory of "divine hardening" indicates the continuity between the older traditions and Johannine reflections on them. On this continuity see B. Lindars, *New Testament Apologetic: The Doctrinal Significance of the*

Old Testament Quotations. London: SCM Press, 1961, 161; Schnackenburg, "Joh 12, 39-41." In 12:37-43 it appears that the tradition is accepted and reworked (vv. 38-41) and then left to one side as the author pursues his own understanding of the failure of "the Jews" (vv. 42-43). This is one of the few places in the Fourth Gospel where the author's respect for the tradition creates an awkward tension.

and turn for me to heal them: The shift to the first person in v. 40e refers to Jesus.

41. *because he saw his glory and spoke of him:* A link was made between the biblical account of the vision of Isaiah reported in Isa 6:1-5 and the claim that Isaiah saw the glory of God in the Targum of Isa 6:1, 5. On the Christian passage from this vision of the glory of God to the prophet's vision of Jesus see Lagrange, *Evangile* 343; Schnackenburg, "Joh 12,37-41" 174–176. With most critics, the translation reads *hoti* ("because" he saw), rather than *hote* ("when" he saw). For the evidence see Lindars, *Gospel* 439.

42. *Nevertheless many even of the authorities believed in him:* On vv. 42-43 as a correction see Léon-Dufour, *Lecture* 2:491. Haenchen, *John* 2:101, calls v. 42 "a consoling message." While vv. 42-43 are something of a correction to vv. 37-41, they are hardly consoling, especially to a community of Christians whose belief in Jesus has led to their being forced out of the synagogue (cf. 9:22; 12:42; 16:2).

44. *And Jesus cried out and said:* There is a logical link between the narrator's comment in v. 43, created by the use of *de* in v. 44. However, the lack of indication of where and when Jesus said these words is deliberate. Such limitations cannot be imposed upon this final summary statement of the Johannine kerygma (cf. Dodd, *Interpretation* 382). For van den Bussche, *Jean* 364, Stibbe, *John* 139, and Brodie, *Gospel* 420–421, 12:44-50 forms an inclusion with 1:1-18. The present interpretation provides references to the earlier parts of the narrative where the point made in this final summary has already been made. In an overly complex suggestion (given the large number of Johannine parallels to vv. 44-50 [cf. Schnackenburg, *Gospel* 2:419–421]), Borgen, "The Use of Tradition" 18–35, claims that vv. 44-45 have a traditional Jesus logion as their basis. Starting from there, using fragments of legal and eschatological terminology, other words from the Gospel, terminology on agency, and under the influence of the OT, the evangelist has developed a passage to present Jesus as the divine agent whose words replace the role of Moses and the Torah. On the relationship between the "kerygmatic" passages in 3:11-21, 31-36, and 12:44-50 see Loader, "The Central Structure" 188–216, and idem, *The Christology* 20–34. See also Ashton, *Understanding the Fourth Gospel* 541–545.

46. *may not remain in darkness:* The idea of walking in the light (cf. 3:21; 8:12; 12:35) has been replaced by the notion of "remaining" or not "remaining" in the darkness to show the abiding effect of a decision for or against Jesus, the light of the world (cf. 8:12; 9:5). See Lindars, *Gospel* 440.

48. *The one who rejects me:* The verb "to reject" *(athetein)* is used only here in the Fourth Gospel. It has the meaning of a considered and deliberate rejection. See BAGD, 21, s.v., 1b. See also Blank, *Krisis* 308–310.

and does not receive my word: Brown, *Gospel* 1:491–493, points to a link between the many echoes of Deuteronomy in the idea of God's punishing those who do not listen to the words of a messenger from God (vv. 47-48; cf., for example, Deut 18:18-19; 31:19, 26) and in the transmission of the commandment of God so that the children of God might have life (vv. 49-50). See also M.-É. Boismard, "Les citations targumiques dans le quatrième évangile," *RB* 66 (1959) 376–378.

as judge on the last day: Stibbe, *John* 140, regards this reference to "the last day" as "a flash forward to the conclusion of the real world and real time." It creates a proleptic sense of ending.

For Reference and Further Study

Borgen, Peder. "The Use of Tradition in John 12:44-50," *NTS* 26 (1979–1980) 18–35.

Evans, C. A. "Obduracy and the Lord's Servant: Some Observations on the Use of the Old Testament in the Fourth Gospel." In C. A. Evans and W. F. Stinespring, eds., *Early Jewish and Christian Exegesis: Studies in Memory of William Hugh Brownlee.* Scholars Press Homage Series. Atlanta: Scholars, 1987, 221–236.

_____. *To See and Not Perceive: Isaiah 6.9-10 in Early Jewish and Christian Interpretation.* JSOT.S 64. Sheffield: JSOT Press, 1989.

Giblin, C. H. "The Tripartite Narrative Structure of John's Gospel," *Bib.* 71 (1990) 449–468.

Hollenbach, B. "Lest they should turn and be forgiven: Irony," *BT* 34 (1983) 312–321.

Lieu, Judith M. "Blindness in the Johannine Tradition," *NTS* 34 (1988) 83–95.

Loader, William. "The Central Structure of Johannine Theology," *NTS* 30 (1984) 188–216.

Merode, M. de. "L'accueil triomphal de Jésus selon *Jean* 11-12," *RTL* 13 (1982) 49–62.

Moloney, Francis J. *Signs and Shadows* 195–201.

Schnackenburg, Rudolf. "Joh 12,39-41: Zur christologischen Schriftauslegung des vierten Evangeliums." In Heinrich Baltensweiler and Bo Reicke, eds., *Neues Testament und Geschichte: Historisches Geschehen und Deutung im Neuen Testament: Oscar Cullmann zum 70. Geburtstag.* Zürich: Theologischer Verlag, 1972, 167–177.

Smith, D. Moody. "The Setting and Shape of a Johannine Narrative Source." In idem, *Johannine Christianity: Essays on Its Setting, Sources, and Theology.* Edinburgh: T&T Clark, 1984, 80–93.

III. THE BOOK OF GLORY (13:1–20:31)

A. THE LAST DISCOURSE (13:1–17:26)

i. Making God Known:
The Footwashing and the Morsel (13:1-38)

Introduction to 13:1–17:26. A new stage in the story opens with the narrator's solemn words in 13:1. As the Passover of Jesus' departure to the Father approaches he is with disciples whom he loved to the end. But 13:1-38 forms part of a larger literary unity, a so-called last discourse (13:1–17:26) marked by a number of well-known repetitions and apparent contradictions (cf. Brown, *Gospel* 2:581–604; Segovia, *Farewell* 1–58; Dettwiler, *Die Gegenwart* 14–33). On the basis of literary form alone 13:1-30 (a narrative) and 17:1-26 (a prayer) stand apart. The more properly discourse material (13:31–16:33) is also marked by contradictions and tensions, highlighted by the words of Jesus in 14:31: "Arise, let us go hence." The themes of Jesus' departure, its motivation, and its consequences are stated in 14:1-31 and repeated in 16:4-33 (cf. the chart in Brown, *Gospel* 2:589–591). The metaphor of the vine with its theme of abiding and the contrasting words of Jesus on hatred and violence are found in 15:1–16:3. Many see this section of the discourse as a collection of earlier brief discourses, and most see 15:1-17 and 15:18–16:4a as originally independent discourses.

No doubt the constituent parts of 13:1–17:26 had their own history in the storytelling of the Johannine community, but the process of telling and retelling produced a Gospel that is thoroughly Johannine in all its parts. Various elements from the recorded memories of the community are laid side by side to form 13:1–17:26 as the text now stands (on the process of *"relecture"* cf. Zumstein, "Der Prozess der Relecture" 394–411; Dettwiler, *Die Gegenwart* 44–52). Consequently the canonical form of the last discourse is "an artistic and strategic whole with a highly unified and coherent literary structure and development, unified and coherent strategic concerns and aims, and a distinctive rhetorical situation" (Segovia, *Farewell* 284).

However obvious the seams (cf. 13:31-32; 14:31; 17:1), the reader of 13:1–17:26 strives "even if unconsciously, to fit everything together in a consistent pattern" (Wolfgang Iser, *The Implied Reader: Patterns of Communication in Prose Fiction from Bunyan to Beckett*. Baltimore: Johns Hopkins University Press, 1978, 283). The author of the Fourth Gospel was not the only writer in antiquity to place a final testament on the lips of a hero approaching death. The peculiarly Johannine final discourse has a function within the rhetoric of the Fourth Gospel that parallels a well-established Jewish literary form. Such a practice was common in a number of religious writings from the first three centuries of the Christian era (cf. note), and there is nowadays widespread agreement that the last discourse in the Fourth Gospel is a Johannine version of the testamentary practice.

Introduction to 13:1-38. There are a number of literary tensions in 13:1-38 (cf. Richter, *Die Fußwaschung* 3–284). There appears to be a double interpretation of the footwashing scene (vv. 6-11, 12-20). Regarded as more moralistic in tone, vv. 12-20 are generally read as a later addition to an original reflection on Jesus' gift of himself (vv. 6-11). The majority of commentators regard v. 30 as the conclusion to the narrative of the footwashing and see vv. 31-38 as the introduction to 13:31–14:31, the original form of the discourse (e.g., Brown, *Gospel* 2:605–616). Others see vv. 31-38 as an introductory summary to the whole discourse (13:31–16:33) in its final form (e.g., Barrett, *Gospel* 449–453). But whatever the prehistory of the elements that form 13:1-38, there are a number of indications that the passage has been designed to read as a coherent, self-contained narrative. Verses 31-38 are not discourse, as they contain the encounter between Simon Peter and Jesus in vv. 36-38. This passage matches the earlier prophecies of the future betrayal of Judas (vv. 10-11, 21-22) and returns to Peter's earlier misunderstanding of the footwashing (vv. 6-9). A further Johannine feature that binds vv. 1-38 together is the fourfold use of the double "amen" (vv. 16, 20, 21, 38). The use of this expression at the beginning and end of the prophecies of betrayal and denial (vv. 21-38) suggests that vv. 31-38 are more closely associated with 13:1-30 than with the discourse of 14:1–16:33. The theme of the failure of both Peter and Judas plays no further role in the discourse proper.

Attention to the strategic positioning of the double "amen" sayings indicates that there may be three sections to the narrative of vv. 1-38. The narrative opens with the account of the footwashing and the dialogues that surround it, largely dealing with Jesus' instruction of the disciples, the ignorance of Peter, and the failure of Judas (vv. 1-17). This section closes with the double "amen" in vv. 16-17. In vv. 18-20, which conclude with the double "amen" in v. 20, Jesus addresses the disciples. No other person speaks. Narrative and the pattern of dialogue between Jesus and the disciples return in vv. 21-38, which both open (v. 21) and close (v. 38) with the double "amen." The narrative reports Jesus' gift of the morsel and the dialogue is dominated by his instruction of the disciples in the midst of intensifying predictions of Judas' betrayal and Peter's denials. A closer reading of these three sections indicates that the passage unfolds in the following fashion:

(a) The Footwashing (13:1-17)

    i. *Vv. 1-5:* The narrator indicates the perfection of Jesus' love for his own (v. 1) but this is followed immediately by reference to the betrayal of Judas (v. 2), which does not deter Jesus from going ahead with his preparations for the footwashing. Love and knowledge lead to action.

    ii. *Vv. 6-11:* A dialogue between Peter and Jesus leads to the first public hint of the betrayal of Judas.

    iii. *Vv. 12-17:* Jesus provides, in word and deed, the gift of his example. The lifestyle of Jesus (vv. 1-5) is now demanded of the disciple.

(b) To Make God Known (13:18-20)

Jesus knows that he has chosen failing disciples (v. 18) and sends them out as his representatives (v. 19). He is telling them these things before they happen so that when they do happen they will recognize Jesus as I AM (v. 18).

(c) The Gift of the Morsel (13:21-38)

    i. *Vv. 21-25:* Jesus is troubled in spirit and gives witness (v. 21a), followed immediately by reference to the betrayal (vv. 21b-25).

    ii. *Vv. 26-30:* A dialogue between Judas and Jesus (vv. 26-27) leads to Jesus' unequivocal reference to the betrayal of Judas (vv. 28-30).

    iii. *Vv. 31-38:* Jesus provides, in word and deed, the gift of the new commandment. As 13:1-38 opened with reference to the betrayal of Judas (v. 2), it closes with reference to the denials of Peter (vv. 36-38).

The more narrative sections of vv. 1-17 and 21-38 stress the love, knowledge, and actions of Jesus as he gives himself in symbolic gesture to his disciples in the midst of their failure: ignorance, betrayal, and denial. Between the narratives Jesus speaks (vv. 18-20), stressing the themes of his knowledge of the ones whom he sends out, loving them in their failure (cf. Simoens, *La gloire d'aimer* 81–104). He tells them these things before they happen so when they do happen they might come to believe that such love makes God known.

For ease of consultation and clarity, the translation and notes for vv. 1-17, vv. 18-20, and vv. 21-38 will be provided separately. The literature For Reference and Further Study of 13:1-38, along with some major studies of 13:1–17:26, will be gathered after the commentary on 13:21-38.

a) *The Footwashing* (13:1-17)

1. Now before the feast of the Passover, when Jesus knew that his hour had come to depart out of this world to the Father, having loved his own

who were in the world, he loved them to the end. 2. And during supper, when the devil had already made up his mind that Judas Iscariot, Simon's son, would betray him, 3. Jesus, knowing that the Father had given all things into his hands and that he had come from God and was going to God, 4. rose from supper, laid aside his garments, and girded himself with a towel. 5. Then he poured water into a basin and began to wash the disciples' feet and to wipe them with the towel with which he was girded.

6. He came to Simon Peter; and Peter said to him, "Lord, do you wash my feet?" 7. Jesus answered him, "What I am doing you do not know now, but afterward you will understand." 8. Peter said to him, "You shall never wash my feet." Jesus answered him, "If I do not wash you, you have no part in me." 9. Simon Peter said to him, "Lord, not my feet only but also my hands and my head!" 10. Jesus said to him, "One who has bathed does not need to wash, but is entirely clean; and you are clean, but not every one of you." 11. For he knew who was to betray him; that was why he said, "You are not all clean."

12. When he had washed their feet, and taken his garments, and resumed his place, he said to them, "Do you know what I have done to you? 13. You call me Teacher and Lord; and you are right, for so I am. 14. If I then, your Lord and Teacher, have washed your feet, you also ought to wash one another's feet. 15. For I have given you an example, that you also should do as I have done to you. 16. Amen, amen, I say to you, servants are not greater than their master; nor are the ones sent greater than the one who sent them. 17. If you know these things, blessed are you if you do them."

INTERPRETATION

Jesus' knowledge, love, and action (vv. 1-5). Throughout the ministry the hour had not yet come (cf. 2:4; 7:30; 8:20). As the final Passover feast drew near and Jesus turned toward death he announced that the hour had come (cf. 11:55-57; 12:20-24, 27-33). The two "times" running through the story, the feasts of "the Jews" (2:13, 23; 4:45; 5:1, 9; 6:4; 7:2; 10:22; 11:55-57; 12:1) and the "hour" of Jesus, are determined by the design of God (2:4; 4:21, 23; 7:30; 8:20; 12:23, 27). They now join, as there is a feast of "the Jews" that is also the hour of Jesus (13:1a). The hour is to be a moment when Jesus will depart from the sphere of everyday events. The one who has been sent by the Father will return to the Father, but during his ministry he has gathered disciples, a group he has called "his own" (v. 1b: *hoi idioi.* cf. 1:11-12; 10:3, 4, 12), and his passage through the hour will be a supreme demonstration of his love for them. To indicate both the time when this love will be shown and the quality of his loving an expression with two meanings is used: "to the end" (v. 1c: *eis telos*). Jesus loved them until the end of his life, and he loved them in a way that surpasses all imaginable loving. The marriage of these two meanings of *eis telos* produces one of the major themes for the rest of the story: the death of Jesus makes known his love for his own, and thus makes God known (cf. 3:16-17). The verbs are in the past tense: Jesus knew *(eidos)* . . . loved *(agapēsas)* his own . . . and loved *(ēgapēsan)* them to the end. A program has been stated: Jesus' death was the hour of his passing over to the Father and a consummate act of loving self-gift. This is "the most significant transition in the Gospel, introducing not only the scene of the foot-washing but the entire second half of the Gospel" (Culpepper, "The Johannine *hypodeigma*" 135). But it is immediately followed by further information: the devil has decided that Judas is to betray Jesus (v. 2). The design of God, manifested in and through Jesus' love for his own (v. 1), clashes with the design of Satan that one of these would betray Jesus.

Against this backdrop Jesus, acting out of his union with the Father, knowing both his origin and destiny, moves into action (v. 3). Jesus' origins and destiny, spelled out in 1:1-18, have been stated and restated many times since, especially during his debates with "the Jews" during their feasts (5:1–10:42). But these crucial elements for a proper understanding of Jesus have never been accepted. This relentless conflict, which led to the decision that Jesus must die for the nation and gather into one the children of God who are scattered abroad (11:49-53), enhances the dramatic setting of the Passover, the hour of Jesus' passing over to the Father, a consummate and final act of love (cf. v. 1). Jesus rises from the table, prepares himself to act as a servant, and begins to wash the feet of his disciples (vv. 4-5). Jesus' knowledge (v. 1), even of his betrayer (vv. 2-3), and his love for his own (v. 1) are expressed through actions (vv. 4-5).

Jesus and Peter (vv. 6-11). Simon Peter objects to Jesus' washing his feet (v. 6). The footwashing is part of God's design (cf. vv. 1-5), and Peter's objections indicate that his understanding of the actions does not agree with Jesus' motivation for performing them. There is a lack of openness to the revelation of God's ways in the words and deeds of Jesus. Jesus' response (v. 7) accepts that in the "now" of the encounter in the upper room Peter is ignorant, but there will be an "afterward" when such ignorance will have been transformed into understanding. Something will happen between the "now" and the "afterward," and the reader suspects that "the hour" of Jesus' loving his own *eis telos* will be part of the intervening events. This suspicion is guided by the account of Jesus' purification of the Temple (2:13-22) and his entry into Jerusalem (12:12-16). On those occasions the disciples did not understand Jesus' words and actions, but after he was raised from the dead (2:22), after he was glorified (12:16), they remembered, believed, and understood, and the hour has come for the Son of Man to be glorified (12:23).

The tension between Jesus and Peter intensifies as the latter refuses to allow Jesus to wash his feet (v. 8a). Jesus warns Peter that what is at stake is "having part" with Jesus (v. 8b: *ouk echeis meros met' emou*). This is a veiled reference to the Christian practice of baptism. The author is not concerned with the rite but with the relationship baptism has with the death of Jesus (cf. Rom 6:3). To "have part with Jesus" through washing means to be part of the self-giving love that will bring Jesus' life to an end (cf. v. 1), symbolically anticipated by the footwashing (v. 8). Peter continues to impose his criteria on Jesus as he limits himself to the submission of his body to the ritual, as if the number of parts of the body mattered (v. 9). But Jesus does not abandon Peter. He explains the privileges of those who have bathed and thus have no further need of washing. Jesus' knowledge, which flows from his union with the Father and his acceptance of the Father's design (cf. v. 3), extends to a knowledge of who will betray him (vv. 10-11). In the midst of ignorance (v. 6), misunderstanding (vv. 8-9), and the threat of betrayal (vv. 10-11) Jesus indicates the depths of his love for his own by washing their feet. In v. 11 the narrator draws the reader into a privileged situation: "For he knew who was to betray him." Such information only serves to heighten the impact of Jesus' gesture. The recipients of this footwashing, a symbolic action that reveals Jesus' limitless love for his own, are ignorant disciples, one of whom he knows will betray him.

A new example: disciples must know, love, and act (vv. 12-17). Despite the apparent contradiction between Jesus' words on Peter's lack of understanding in v. 7 and his question concerning the disciples' understanding in v. 12, no break occurs in the narrative at v. 12. A theory of a later moralizing interpretation of the footwashing added to the original vv. 1-11 is not needed. There is a unity of place, characters, and theme across vv. 1-17. Peter cannot, as yet, understand the link between Jesus' action of washing the disciples' feet and his unconditional love for them (v. 7). Jesus' question to the disciples in v. 12 is of a different order. It is closely linked to the footwashing, which has just been reported, but looks away from the symbol of his self-gift toward the new example it establishes, reversing accepted patterns of behavior. Peter's question in v. 6 showed his awareness that accepted practice was being subverted, and he objected to this subversion. As Jesus dresses and resumes his place at table he questions their understanding of what he had done for them (v. 12). He answers his own question in vv. 13-14.

The disciples have witnessed the footwashing and taken part in it, but more instruction is needed so that they might correctly understand Jesus as Teacher and Lord (v. 13) and thus grasp how his action as Teacher and Lord should impinge upon their lives. The footwashing is recalled as he tells them that they are to repeat among themselves what he has done for

them (vv. 14-15). Whatever may have been the possible historical and ritual background to this instruction (cf. note), within its present literary
context Jesus' instruction is a call to his disciples to repeat in their lives
what he has done for them. They are to repeat his example of the loving
gift of self symbolized in the footwashing (v. 15). The theme of death is
behind the use of the word *hypodeigma*. This expression, found only here
in the NT, in well-known Jewish texts (cf. LXX 2 Macc 6:28; 4 Macc 17:22-
23; Sir 44:16) is associated with exemplary death. Jesus' exhortation is not
to moral performance but to imitation of his self-gift. "Jesus' death . . . as
it is here interpreted through the footwashing, is the norm of life and
conduct for the believing community" (Culpepper, "The Johannine
hypodeigma" 144). The command to lose oneself in loving self-gift unto
death in imitation of the *hypodeigma* of Jesus has been ritualized in baptism (cf. v. 8: *echein meros met' emou*). Though not "about baptism" the
passage presupposes the ritual within the life and practice of the Johannine community (cf. 3:3, 5; 19:34). The Johannine Christians are called to
do as Jesus has done for them (v. 15). Entrance into the Johannine community of disciples meant taking the risk of accepting the *hypodeigma* of
Jesus, a commitment to love even if it led to death (cf. 16:2).

This section of 13:1-38 closes with the first use of the Johannine double
"amen" in vv. 16-17. It began with the narrator's insistence that Jesus'
knowledge flowed into *action*. The disciples are told that the footwashing
is not an end in itself but an instruction of servants by the master (cf. v.
14), the sent ones by the one who sent them (v. 16). They must maintain
their places as servants, followers of the master and the one who sent
them (v. 16). In a beautifully balanced Greek sentence Jesus associates
such servants and sent ones with his own knowing and doing (vv. 1-5).
They will be blessed if they *know* what Jesus has said and done, and in
their own time and situation, *do* these same things:

If you **know** THESE THINGS	*ei* TAUTA **oidate**
blessed are you	*makarioi este*
if you **do** THESE THINGS	*hean* **poiēte** AUTA

The use of the double "amen" and the return to the theme of knowing
and doing of vv. 1-5 creates a sense of closure in vv. 16-17. As the knowledge and love of Jesus (vv. 1-3) flowed into action (vv. 4-11), so must the
knowledge and love of the disciple flow into action. Therein lies blessedness (vv. 12-17).

NOTES

A final discourse and the testament tradition. The recognition of the relevance of
Jewish testamentary literature, roughly contemporary with the emergence of

a Christian literature, has contributed to an increased interest in John 13:1–17:26 as a Christian example of that literature (cf. Käsemann, *Testament*, 3–6; Becker, *Evangelium* 2:44–46; Kurz, *Farewell Addresses* 9–32, 71–120; Cortès, *Los Discursos de Adiós*; Bammel, "The Farewell Discourse" 103–116; Segovia, *Farewell* 2–20; Dettwiler, *Die Gegenwart* 14–33). It is not surprising, given the widespread use of testaments, that Jesus gathers his disciples to bequeath to them his final testament. John 13:1–17:26 is not a perfect example of this form, as Jesus' testament must continue and develop themes that emerged during the story of his unique ministry. None of the saints or patriarchs of Israel whose testaments we have ever claimed to be the sent one of the Father (cf. 3:17, 34; 5:36, 38; 6:29, 57; 7:29; 8:42; 10:36; 11:42) or one with God (cf. 10:30, 38).

The Jewish testaments were produced at different times and places, from the second century B.C.E. (e.g., *T. 12 Patr.*) till the third century C.E. (e.g., *T. Sol.*), or even later (parts of the *T. Adam*). They have often come down to us in interpolated translations. As such the Jewish testaments are not unified by a discrete literary model, yet "one can discern among them a loose format" (Charlesworth, *Pseudepigrapha* 1:773). The following features of the Johannine last discourse are also found regularly in the testament tradition:

1. *Prediction of death and departure.* The speech is understood by the departing figure as his "farewell" to disciples. The setting for these testaments can be a meal (*T. Naph.* 1:2-5; 9:2). There is some indication of oncoming death in all testaments, and the prediction of death and departure is the reason for the gathering (cf. *T. Reub.* 1:3-4; *T. Levi* 1:2; *T. Dan* 2:1; *T. Mos.* 1:15).

2. *Predictions of future attacks upon the dying leader's disciples.* This feature is also fundamental to the testaments, as the disciples are warned of future threats and dangers (cf. *T. Sim.* 3:1-2; *T. Gad* 4:1-7). There are also regular references to the present (cf. *T. Jud.* 23:1) and future (cf. *T. Levi* 4:1; 10:1-5; 14:1-8; *T. Issach.* 6:1-4; *T. Dan* 5:7-8; *T. Naph.* 4:1-5) failures of the disciples.

3. *An exhortation to ideal behavior.* The life and experience of the dying hero serve as a basis for the instruction of the surrounding behavior. All testaments found in the *T. 12 Patr.* are marked by this feature (e.g., *T. Reub.* 4:1; *T. Jud.* 14:1; *T. Zeb.* 5:1-15; *T. Jos.* 18:1-4; *T. Benj.* 3:1-3). See Bammel, "The Farewell Discourse" 111–112.

4. *A final commission.* The hero instructs disciples concerning their continuation as a group after his departure. Central is the command to love one another (cf. *T. Reub.* 6:9; *T. Sim.* 4:7; *T. Zeb.* 5:5; *T. Gad* 6:1-7; *T. Jos.* 17:1-8). See Randall, "The Theme of Unity" 377–378. Other indications are also given (cf. *T. Levi* 18:1-4; *T. Jud.* 24:1–25:5; *T. Dan* 5:7-13; *T. Naph.* 8:1-8; *T. Benj.* 10:2-11).

5. *An affirmation and a renewal of the never-failing covenant promises of God.* This theme undergirds much of the narrative, exhortation, and praise of all the testaments. It is understandably expressed strongly and explicitly in the *T. Moses* (cf. 1:8-9; 3:9; 4:2-6; 12:7-13). See the detailed treatment of this feature of the farewell genre in Kurz, "Luke 22:14-68" 251–268. Especially useful is the chart of elements common to Greco-Roman, OT, and NT testaments on pp. 262–263.

6. *A closing doxology.* Although not present in the *T. 12 Patr.*, all of which close with notice of the patriarch's death and burial, other testaments close with a brief prayer of praise rendering glory to God (cf. *T. Job* 43:1-17; *T. Isaac* 8:6-7; *T. Jacob* 8:6-9).

As the testaments were determined by the popular and biblical traditions that had gathered around the dying patriarch, so will John 13:1–17:26 be determined by the Johannine traditions surrounding the life, and especially the death, of Jesus of Nazareth.

1. *before the feast of the Passover:* On the use of the Passover across these closing chapters of the Fourth Gospel see Knöppler, *Die theologia crucis* 119–121.

   to depart out of this world: The Johannine use of the word *kosmos* ("the world") is open to several interpretations. See the survey in Moloney, *Belief in the Word* 37. Here it has a neutral meaning: the time and place of human activity.

   Jesus knew . . . having loved . . . he loved them: These aorist tenses are all "gnomic." They have universal application, valid for all time, and are not limited to one point of time. See BDF 171, § 333. For the suggestion that vv. 1-3 serve as a "minor prologue" to the book of the passion see Grossouw, "A Note" 125–131.

2. *The devil had already made up his mind that Judas would betray him:* The Greek expression *beblēkotos eis tēn kardian* can be read as "to put in mind" or "to make up one's mind" (cf. Job 22:22; 1 Sam 29:10). It should be read as "to make up one's mind" and applied to Satan, not Judas. See Delebecque, *Évangile de Jean* 183.

4. *laid aside his garments:* There are contacts between Jesus' laying aside his garments *(tithēsin)* and the use of the same verb to describe the actions and attitude of the Good Shepherd (cf. 10:11, 15, 17, 18). In the same way the verb describing Jesus' taking up his clothes in v. 12 *(elaben)* is used for the Good Shepherd's taking up his life again (cf. 10:17, 18). See Dunn, "The Washing" 248; Culpepper, "The Johannine *hypodeigma*" 137; Koester, *Symbolism* 10–11.

8. *you have no part in me:* For a strong development of the baptismal significance of this expression see de Boer, *Johannine Perspectives* 283–292. For de Boer the introduction of this theme reflects a third stage in the community's growth. Baptism "removes a disciple from jeopardy, from the danger of sin and the devil."

10. *One who has bathed does not need to wash:* In v. 10a the participle *ho leloumenos* is used for "the one who has bathed." It means a total immersion. This is to be contrasted with the use of the verb *nipsasthai* in v. 10b for "to wash," which only involves a partial washing with water. The total immersion involved in "the one who has bathed" is a further hint of both baptism and the association of the disciple with the death of Jesus. See Schnackenburg, *Gospel* 3:21–22; Hultgren, "The Johannine Footwashing" 544.

    does not need to wash, but is entirely clean: Later copyists added "except for the feet" after "need to wash" to solve the problem of further forgiveness of sin after baptism. There were many who had been washed who were not "entirely clean." For the discussion see Moloney, *Son of Man* 192–193. Recent scholarship has questioned this, and argues that *ei mē tous podas nipsasthai* is original. See, for example, Thomas, *Footwashing in John 13* 19–25, and Niemand, *Die Fußwashungerzählung* 252–256. The arguments advanced by Grelot, "L'interprétation pénitentielle" 1:75–91, to explain its insertion in the light of the later penitential practices of the early Church remain convincing.

15. *I have given you an example:* There have been many attempts to work from this "example" to identify the practices of the early Church that were based on the footwashing. See the possibilities canvassed by Thomas, *Footwashing,* 126–185. Thomas associates footwashing with the forgiveness of sins in the Johannine community (and thus insists on the originality of v. 10b). Niemand, *Die Fußwaschungerzählung* 320–402, also provides an excellent survey of possible practices that may have come from the footwashing. He argues that the footwashing (again needing v. 10b to be understood) reflects a discussion in the early Church over the need for a partial or full initiation rite for ex-disciples of John the Baptist who became Christians. Culpepper, "The Johannine *hypodeigma*" 144, rightly links the "example" in v. 12 with the death of Jesus. For more general association of the footwashing with the death of Jesus see Beutler, "Die Heilsbedeutung" 188–204; Robinson, "The Significance" 77–80; Dunn, "The Washing" 247–252; Koester, *Symbolism,* 111–118. Others have associated the footwashing with the death of Jesus in vv. 6-11, but claim that this association disappears in vv. 12-17 (e.g., Schnackenburg, *Gospel* 3:23).

17. *If you know these things, blessed are you if you do them:* The blessedness of the Johannine believer flows from the living out, the "doing" of all that is implied by entering into discipleship through baptism. For an understanding of baptism and Eucharist in the early Church see David E. Aune, *The Cultic Setting of Realized Eschatology in Early Christianity.* NT.S 28. Leiden: E. J. Brill, 1972, 16–18. On the implications of the Johannine understanding of "knowing" and "doing" here see Rensberger, *Johannine Faith* 64–86; Weiss, "Footwashing" 298–325.

b) *To Make God Known* (13:18-20)

18. "I am not speaking of you all; I know whom I have chosen; it is that the scripture may be fulfilled, 'The one who ate my bread has lifted the heel against me.'

19. I tell you this now, before it takes place, that when it does take place you may believe that I AM.

20. Amen, amen, I say to you, whoever receives one whom I send receives me; and whoever receives me receives the one who sent me."

INTERPRETATION

Jesus knows the identity of one of them who will betray him (vv. 10-11), and knows also that a change of heart will transform Peter's present ignorance into understanding (v. 7). Not all of his disciples will act on what they know (v. 18a), but Jesus knows whom he has chosen (v. 18b). He has no illusions about their fragility, and has already indicated that one of them will betray him and another is ignorant. He chose them to fulfill Scripture. One of the disciples who will not act on what he knows will share the table of Jesus, yet strike at him (v. 18c; cf. Ps. 41:9[10]). Behind this choice of fragile disciples lies a logic that defies all human logic, and Jesus informs his disciples of the events that will fulfill the Scriptures *before* they take place, so that when they do take place, they might come to know and believe he is the unique revelation of God (v. 19:b: *hina pisteusēte hotan genētai hoti egō eimi*). The absolute use of *egō eimi*, taken from the prophetic tradition, points to Jesus as the unique revelation of God over against all others who might make such a claim. Part of this revelation is his choice of a group of ignorant, failing disciples, one of whom will betray him. When this betrayal—foretold in the Scriptures—takes place, then the wonder of a God who does such things will be seen. Then the disciples might come to know and believe that Jesus' choice of them makes God known.

Not only has Jesus knowingly *chosen* fragile, failing disciples (v. 18), but he *sends them out* as his representatives (v. 20). This centerpiece of 13:1-38, poised between the accounts of the footwashing (vv. 1-17) and the gift of the morsel (vv. 21-38), closes with another use of the double "amen." To receive the disciple means to receive Jesus, and to receive Jesus means to receive God (v. 20). Jesus has chosen (v. 18) and will send out (v. 20) disciples who are ignorant, who misunderstand him, and who will betray him. One of them will strike out against him. Jesus tells the disciples of these events before they happen, but the reader knows that Jesus means his own betrayal, suffering, and death. Scripture will be fulfilled and God will be revealed in the events of an unconditional gift of self unto death (v. 1: "he loved them *eis telos*") for those whom he chose and those whom he will send, despite the fact that these very disciples fail and betray him. God is revealed in a love that surpasses all imaginable ways of loving. The narrative promises that Jesus' death will be a moment of self-gift in love that will both reveal God (v. 19) and transform fragile disciples into sent ones of the Father (vv. 18, 20; cf. v. 7).

NOTES

18. *I know whom I have chosen:* Schneiders, "The Footwashing" 84–86, presents three models of service that might be presupposed by this narrative. She

claims that Jesus' washing his disciples' feet is a model of service between friends. The interpretation given here suggests that there is a further quality of love revealed in this action that surpasses the model of service between friends. Jesus loves disciples whom he has chosen and will send out *knowing* they will fail and betray him. His love is unconditional (v. 1: *eis telos*), and he will give his life out of love for them (cf. 10:11, 17).

The one who ate my bread: The verb used for "to eat" in LXX Ps 41:9[10] is *esthiein*, but the Johannine citation of the passage uses *trōgein*. There has been some discussion on the difference between the two verbs. Classically, the former verb is used for normal human eating while the latter is a more physical word, describing the process of munching or crunching, and often used for animals. The acceptance of this difference has an important bearing on Jesus' gift of the morsel to Judas in v. 26. In support of the distinction see Spicq, "*Trōgein:* Est-il synonyme?" 414–419. Menken, *Old Testament Quotations* 128–129, notes the five Johannine uses of *trōgein* but concludes that it is a Johannine stylistic trait to link *trōgein* and *phagein* (cf. 6:53-54). See also Obermann, *Die christologische Erfüllung* 255–258, 263–265. In neither of these discussions is the eucharistic context of the uses of *trōgein* taken into account. *Phagein* is well used in other Johannine contexts where *trōgein* never appears (cf. 4:31, 32, 33; 6:5, 23, 26, 31, 49; 18:28). Why alternate its usage with *trōgein* in 6:51-58, and why does *phagein* not appear in 13:18? The eucharistic contexts influence the choice of the more physical verb for eating. Schuchard, *Scripture within Scripture* 108–110, 112–117, agrees with Menken that there is no distinction between *phagein* and *esthiein* (112), but accepts that the Johannine author may have used *trōgein* to associate 13:18 with 6:51-58.

19. *you may believe that I AM:* For further background to the understanding of Jesus' absolute use of *egō eimi* as an affirmation of the unique revelation of God see Moloney, *Signs and Shadows* 100–101. Ball, *'I Am' in John's Gospel* 110–119, 198–200, sees the importance of the "I am" in 13:19 and suggests that it forces the reader further into the narrative to discover *who Jesus is.*

20. *whoever receives one whom I send:* It is often suggested that in the Fourth Gospel, and especially in John 13–17, there is a collapsing of the present and the future (e.g., O'Day, "'I Have Overcome the World'" 153–166). While this may be true for some passages one must carefully note that several elements in the last discourse call for a sense of "now" and "afterward." This is particularly true of Jesus' teaching on the gift of the Paraclete, but it also applies to 13:7 and 13:18-20. An element of expectation is *never* eliminated completely. The reader waits for a *future time* when Peter will understand and when "these things" will take place.

c) *The Gift of the Morsel* (13:21-38)

21. When Jesus had thus spoken he was troubled in spirit and testified, "Amen, amen, I say to you, one of you will betray me." 22. The disciples

looked at one another, uncertain of whom he spoke. 23. One of his disciples, whom Jesus loved, was lying close to the breast of Jesus; 24. so Simon Peter beckoned to him and said, "Tell us who it is of whom he speaks." 25. So lying thus, close to the breast of Jesus, he said to him, "Lord, who is it?"

26. Jesus answered, "It is he to whom I shall give this morsel when I have dipped it." So when he had dipped the morsel he took it and gave it to Judas, the son of Simon Iscariot. 27. Then after the morsel Satan entered into him. Jesus said to him, "What you are going to do, do quickly." 28. Now no one at the table knew why he said this to him. 29. Some thought that because Judas had the money box Jesus was telling him, "Buy what we need for the feast," or that he should give something to the poor. 30. So after receiving the morsel he immediately went out; and it was night.

31. Thus, when he had gone out, Jesus said, "Now is the Son of Man glorified, and in him God is glorified; 32. if God is glorified in him God will also glorify him in himself, and glorify him at once. 33. Little children, yet a little while I am with you. You will seek me; and as I said to the Jews so now I say to you, 'Where I am going you cannot come.'

34. A new commandment I give to you, that you love one another; even as I have loved you, that you also love one another. 35. By this everyone will know that you are my disciples, if you have love for one another."

36. Simon Peter said to him, "Lord, where are you going?" Jesus answered, "Where I am going you cannot follow me now; but you shall follow afterward." 37. Peter said to him, "Lord, why can I not follow you now? I will lay down my life for you." 38. Jesus answered, "Will you lay down your life for me? Amen, amen, I say to you, the cock will not crow till you have denied me three times."

Interpretation

Jesus' witness (vv. 21-25). The double "amen" that closed vv. 1-17 and 18-20 opens v. 21. Jesus raises the question of the betrayer and begins a dialogue with his own that will lead to the revelation of the identity of the betrayer at the table (v. 26; cf. v. 18). The use of the double "amen" will close this section of the narrative as Jesus tells of Peter's future denials (v. 38). There is a parallel between v. 1, where the narrator reported Jesus' knowledge and love, and v. 21 where another emotional experience is mentioned: Jesus is troubled in spirit. Jesus' love for his own *eis telos* establishes a link with the cross in v. 1, and the cross again lurks in the background in the description of Jesus' being "troubled in spirit" (v. 21a: *etarachthē tō pneumati*). The verb *tarassein* echoes Psalm 42/43, which has already been used twice to make oblique reference to the passion (cf. 11:33; 12:27). Despite these important links with the earlier parts of the narrative, the solemn introduction to Jesus' words as "he testified" (v.

21b: *emartyrēsen*) indicates a break between vv. 18-20 and what follows. Jesus' brief discourse (vv. 18-20) has come to an end as Jesus testifies to the betrayal. This testimony will lead to a dialogue (vv. 23-30) that matches his earlier conversation with Simon Peter (vv. 6-11). But the dialogue with Simon Peter took place within the context of a footwashing while the present dialogue takes place within the context of the gift of a morsel.

Jesus' testimony focuses on one of the disciples at the table (cf. vv. 12, 18) who will betray him (v. 21b: *hoti heis ex hymōn paradōsei me*). These words understandably set off a reaction among the disciples around the table, but a reaction that shows they are not moving in the world of Jesus. They are "uncertain *(aporumenoi)* of whom he spoke" (v. 22). The verb *aporein* appears only here in the Fourth Gospel, but its other (rare) uses in the NT refer to perplexity (cf. Mark 6:20; Luke 24:4; Acts 25:20; 2 Cor 4:8; Gal 4:20). Ignorance, confusion, and misunderstanding continue (cf. vv. 6, 7, 9, 12-13). The Beloved Disciple appears for the first time, lying "close to the breast of Jesus" (v. 23: *en tǭ kolpǭ tou Iēsou;* cf. 1:18). Despite his position of honor, he is included in the perplexity. As will happen regularly from this point on in the story, Peter is subordinated to the Beloved Disciple as he asks: "Tell us who it is of whom he speaks" (v. 24). This request supposes that the Beloved Disciple has some privileged access to this knowledge, but such is not the case. He must ask Jesus, and his question triggers the words and actions that follow: "Lord, who is it?" (v. 25).

Jesus and Judas (vv. 26-30). Jesus responds to the disciple's question by telling him he will share an intimate gesture with the betrayer: dipping the morsel at table and sharing it with him (v. 26a). With stark brevity the narrator reports: "So when he had dipped the morsel he took it and gave it to Judas, the Son of Simon Iscariot" (v. 26b). *After* the reception of the morsel Satan enters into Judas (v. 27a). The narrator had earlier reported that Satan had decided that Judas was to betray Jesus (v. 2), and in v. 27a Satan takes possession of him. Judas is now part of a satanic program diametrically opposed to the program of God revealed in Jesus. Yet in a final gesture of love Jesus shares the dipped morsel with his future betrayer (v. 26), only to be definitively rejected as Satan enters into Judas (v. 27a).

Several indications in the text suggest that this sharing of the morsel has its roots in the eucharistic traditions of the Johannine community. Jesus' use of Ps 41:9[10]b in v. 18 is the first of these indications. The LXX of the passage "The one who ate my bread" reads: *ho esthiōn artous mou,* but the Johannine text has *ho trōgōn mou ton arton.* There appears to be the deliberate replacement of a more "proper" word for human eating (LXX: *esthieien*) with a less delicate term, "to munch," or "to crunch with the teeth" *(trōgein).* In itself this could be insignificant, but the only other place where this verb appears is in 6:54-58, the most explicit eucharistic passage in the Gospel. It is used there four times (6:54, 56, 57, 58). The use of Ps 41:9[10] may have been part of the early Church's traditional explanation of what happened at the Last Supper (cf. Mark 14:18; Luke 22:21), but the Johannine author has refashioned the psalm, linking the gift of the morsel to Judas with Christian traditions that surrounded that event. One of the many textual difficulties in v. 26b can now be resolved. Some early manuscripts do not contain "he took it" *(lambanei kai)*, words that recall Jesus' deliberate action of taking bread in all the Gospel bread miracles (Mark 6:42; 8:6; Matt 14:19; 15:36; Luke 9:16; John 6:11), and in the synoptic and Pauline reports of the Last Supper (Mark 14:22; Matt 26:26; Luke 22:19; 1 Cor 11:23). Scribes could not tolerate the idea that the sharing of the morsel between Jesus and Judas might have eucharistic overtones and thus they eliminated words that made this association explicit. Just as baptism is a sub-theme to the footwashing, eucharist is a sub-theme to the meal and the gift of the morsel. Within the context of a meal indicated as eucharistic Jesus gives the morsel to the most despised character in the Johannine narrative: Judas. Disciples always have and always will display ignorance, fail Jesus, and deny him. Some may even betray him in an outrageous and public way. But Jesus' never-failing love for *such* disciples, a love that reached out even to the archetype of the evil disciple, reveals a unique God (cf. vv. 18-20). This is what it means to love *eis telos* (v. 1).

Jesus *knows* Judas' intentions. He has reached out in a gift of love, but Satan's designs for Judas (cf. v. 2) begin to happen: Satan enters Judas (v. 27a). Jesus knows this and, always presented as in command of the situation, sends Judas on his way, recommending that he do his task as quickly as possible (v. 27b). These dramatic words and events lead into the narrator's report of the overwhelming and universal ignorance of the disciples (vv. 28-29). Not one of the people at the table understood *(oudeis egnō)*. The "not one" *(oudeis)* includes the Beloved Disciple. It is difficult to believe that *no one* understands after the clarity of the words and gestures of vv. 25-26. The Beloved Disciple, lying so close to Jesus (vv. 23, 25), who questioned Jesus on the identity of the betrayer, should have known. But universal ignorance and confusion reign. The best *some of the disciples* *(tines)* can do is guess that Jesus is telling Judas, the guardian of the money box, to make some purchases for the feast or give something to the poor (v. 29).

After receiving the morsel Judas immediately *(euthus)* went out, and it was night (v. 30). Now controlled by Satan (vv. 2, 27a), Judas walks away from the light of the world (cf. 8:12; 9:5), into the night and the darkness of those who reject Jesus and plan to kill him (cf. 1:5; 3:2; 8:12; 9:4; 11:10; 12:35, 46). As Jesus' ministry began a leader of "the Jews" moved from the night toward the light of Jesus (3:2). The journey of that particular character is still in progress (cf. 7:50-51), but as Jesus' life draws to a conclusion one of "his own" whom he has loved *eis telos* (13:1; cf. v. 26) moves away from the light into the darkness (v. 30).

A new commandment: disciples must love one another (vv. 31-38). Judas' departure into the night (v. 30) leads to a "shout of triumph" (G. H. C. Macgregor, *The Gospel of John*. London: Hodder & Stoughton, 1928, 283) from Jesus. Judas' exit and Jesus' proclamation in vv. 31-32 are closely linked to v. 30 by the words "thus when he had gone out" (v. 31a: *hote oun exēlthen*). Crucial to Jesus' self-gift in love is his being "lifted up" to make God known (cf. 3:14; 8:28) and to draw everyone to himself (12:32-33). Thus Judas' departure (v. 30) leads *logically* to the proclamation of vv. 31-32. These words do not introduce a discourse (13:31-14:31), but proclaim that the hour has come (cf. 12:33, 27, 31; 13:1). Now is the time for the Son of Man to be lifted up for his glorification, and through it for God to be glorified (v. 31). Jesus' earlier use of "the Son of Man" pointed toward the crucifixion (cf. 1:51; 3:14; 6:27, 53; 8:28; 12:23). On the cross Jesus is glorified, but his death will also reveal the *doxa tou theou*. Consistent with the author's use of the word *doxa* to refer to revelation (cf. 1:14; 2:11; 5:44; 7:18; 11:4, 40; 12:41, 43), as the *doxa* of God was made visible at Sinai (cf. Moloney, *Belief in the Word* 55–57), the cross is the time and place where God will be revealed. The arrival of the Greeks triggered Jesus' first announcement that the hour had come for the Son of Man to be glorified (12:23). Now the departure of the betrayer triggers Jesus' proclamation that *now* the Son of Man will be glorified, that the glory of God will be seen in the glorification of Jesus on the cross (vv. 31b-32b), and these intimately associated events will take place *immediately* (v. 32c: *euthus*). Judas' exit sets in motion the events promised by Jesus in vv. 18-20 as the time and the place where the disciples, chosen and sent by Jesus, might come to believe that Jesus is the revelation of God (v. 19: *hoti egō eimi*).

Jesus' unconditional love for his failing disciples is captured by his caring address in v. 33: "little children" *(teknia)*. He looks back to words spoken to "the Jews." Within the context of possible violent arrest by officers of the Pharisees, Jesus told "the Jews" that he would be with them a little longer (cf. 7:33). That moment, marked by conflict and danger, is recalled as Jesus tells his "little children" that they will seek him but not find him because, as he told "the Jews": "Where I am going you cannot come" (13:33; cf. 7:34). "The Jews" would not understand who Jesus was and where he was going in his return to the Father. Unfortunately, so it is also with Jesus' ignorant and failing disciples. Yet they remain his disciples, his "little children," lost yet loved in their misunderstanding, failure, and ignorance. He gives them a new commandment (vv. 34-35) that matches the gift of his example (v. 15). The footwashing is marked by the gift of an example (v. 15: *hypodeigma gar edōka hymin*) and the sharing of the morsel is marked by the gift of a new commandment (v. 34a: *entolēn kainēn didōmi hymin*). Both the example and the commandment are closely associated with Jesus' demand that his disciples follow him into a loving self-gift in death. This was implied in the command that the disciples do to one another *as Jesus had done for them* (15b: *kathōs egō epoiēsa hymin*), and it becomes explicit in the new commandment that they love one another *as Jesus has loved them* (v. 34b: *kathōs ēgapēsa hymas*). A unique quality of love, inspired by the love Jesus had for "his own," will single out followers of Jesus (v. 35). There will shortly be a time when Jesus will no longer be with them and they will not be able to go where Jesus is (cf. v. 33). In that time of absence they are to repeat the love of Jesus and thus render present the lifestyle of Jesus. (vv. 34-35).

In v. 7a Jesus spoke of Peter's *present* ignorance, and Peter reinforces those words by asking what is meant by the absence of Jesus, his going to a place where the disciples cannot come (v. 36a). Jesus first recalls his words of v. 33 but then harks back to the promise of a later time in v. 7b: "but afterward you will understand." Even though Peter cannot follow him *now* (v. 36b), he will follow him *afterward* (v. 36c). There is a tension between the "now" of the present moment in the story, marked by betraying, ignorant, and failing disciples (vv. 7a, 36b), and an "afterward" when this situation will be transformed (7b; 36c. See 2:22; 12:16). The story moves in the "in between time" as the reader looks confidently forward to the resolution of the tension created by this "now" and "afterward," only partially resolved by Jesus' words of v. 19: "I tell you this now, before it takes place, that when it does take place you may believe that I am."

Peter arrogantly insists that there is no tension. Repeating his earlier difficulties with Jesus over the footwashing, he asks a question that indicates there is no journey he is not prepared to make with Jesus (v. 37). Peter is thinking of human journeys into some dangerous place and time; Jesus is speaking of his return to the Father. Peter claims he is prepared to lay down his life for Jesus as the Good Shepherd has earlier said he would lay down his life for his sheep (cf. 10:11, 15, 17). This is exactly what Jesus asks of all disciples in the gift of his example (v. 15) and the gift of the new commandment (vv. 34-35). But such love flows from a radical following of Jesus and never from an imposition of one's own worldview on God's designs. Jesus prophesies that Peter will be thwarted by his own ignorance. He will fail, denying Jesus three times before the cock crows (v. 38). The "now" of Peter's ignorance and arrogant failure is to be further demonstrated, and Jesus' knowledge will be highlighted. The reader is aware that the narrative ahead will tell of the fulfillment of Jesus' prophecies: Judas will betray Jesus (cf. vv. 2, 10-11, 18, 21-30, 31a) and Peter will deny all knowledge of him (cf. vv. 36-38).

Conclusion to 13:1-38. As the first events in the Johannine account of Jesus' final night with his disciples began (vv. 1-5), three themes emerged: the arrival of "the hour" (v. 1), Jesus' love for his own no matter how sinful they might be (vv. 1-3), and Jesus' bringing his task to a perfect end by means of a consummate act of love (v. 1). At the conclusion of this account one of those themes returned: Jesus' love for his own (vv. 34-35) no matter how frail they might be (vv. 36-38). Another theme is added: the glorification of Jesus and the revelation of the glory of God (vv. 31-32). This theme was also found at the center of the passage, in Jesus' claim that his disciples would come to recognize him as the unique revelation of God in and through events that lie in the near future (v. 19). John 13:1-38 is a description of the glory shown by unconditional love, and Jesus asks that his disciples live and love in imitation of him. This is the example (v. 15), the new commandment (vv. 34-35) he gives to them. The example and the new commandment coalesce.

Many themes adumbrated during the ministry have now come to the fore: the frailty of the disciples (cf. 1:35-49; 4:27-38; 6:1-15, 60-71; 9:1-5; 11:5-16), the betrayal of Judas (cf. 6:70-71; 12:4-6), the denials of Peter (cf. 1:40-42; 6:67-69), the departure of Jesus (cf. 7:33-34; 8:21), the impossibility of following him to the Father "now" (cf. 7:33-34), an oncoming event that will transform the lack of knowledge and faith "now" into an "afterward" when disciples will know and will follow (cf. 2:22; 12:16), the knowledge of Jesus (cf. 2:24-25; 4:1; 5:42; 6:15; 10:14-15), his love for his own (cf. 3:16-17, 34-35), the cross as the moment of Jesus' glorification (cf. 1:51; 11:4; 12:23, 33), and the revelation of God in and through the event of the cross (3:13-14; 8:28; 12:23, 32-33). Puzzles produced by the story of Jesus' public ministry converge, and in this sense 13:1-38 introduces the reader to 14:1–20:31.

NOTES

21. *he was troubled in spirit:* Ferraro, "'Pneuma' in Giov 13.21" 185–211, sees the structural importance of v. 21, opening a new section and linked to the narrator's description of Jesus' love in v. 1. He attempts to make a case for a reference to the spirit in v. 21 as the Spirit of God, driving Jesus on in the face of rejection. On the link between the use of the verb *tarassein* in v. 21 and the passion of Jesus via Psalm 42/43 see Beutler, "Psalm 42/43 im Johannesevangelium" 34–37; Dodd, *Tradition* 37–38, 69–71.

23. *lying close to the breast of Jesus:* The physical position of the Beloved Disciple is described twice: v. 23: *en tǭ kolpǭ tou Iēsou* and v. 25: *epi to stēthos tou Iēsou.* This close physical proximity is a symbol of both affection and commitment. This description matches the relationship that exists between the historical Jesus and the Father, described as *eis ton kolpon tou patros* in 1:18. This does not describe "indwelling" as is often suggested. See note to 1:18.

25. *Lord, who is it?:* There is no reason to see the Beloved Disciple's use of *kyrie* as reflecting an elevated christology. It is a respectful question.

26. *when he had dipped the morsel he took it and gave it to Judas:* Because of the difficulties created by the possibility that the morsel given to Judas might be regarded as eucharistic this text is notoriously disturbed. Most importantly, the words *lambanei kai* are missing from some important early manuscripts (e.g., 𝔓⁶⁶, first hand of Sinaiticus, Bezae, and Koridethi). The expression should not be regarded as a scribal accommodation to other eucharistic texts (as, for example, Barrett, *Gospel* 447, Brown, *Gospel* 2:575, Haenchen, *John* 2:113, and Lindars, *Gospel* 459, would claim), but seen as original because it is the *lectio difficilior* and supports the other eucharistic hints that surround the passage. For its inclusion, but not necessarily its eucharistic interpretation, see UBSGNT; Bauer, *Johannesevangelium* 174; Schnackenburg, *Gospel* 3:30. The concerns of the scribes with v. 26 can be found in a number of other textual difficulties. For a summary see Metzger, *A Textual Commentary* 205.

    The Greek word *psōmion* ("morsel") could refer to a morsel of either bread or meat. The interpretation takes it for granted that bread is referred to here, although Lagrange, *Evangile* 362, argues that it was meat, and Kysar, *John* 214, suggests that it was bitter herbs. Others have argued for a eucharistic background to John 13, but in more general terms. See, for example, Suggit, "John 13:1-30," who argues that the whole passage suggests Jesus' death and the celebration of Eucharist so closely associated with it. Cancian, *Nuovo Commandamento* 311–323, has a similar approach, adding that John 6 and the Johannine understanding of a new covenant would have led to this more general appreciation of the passage as eucharistic.

    Most modern scholars either regard the use of the morsel as a method of eliminating Judas from the upper room (e.g., Schnackenburg, *Gospel* 3:30; Cancian, *Nuovo Commandamento* 140–149) or as an indication that Judas chooses Satan rather than Jesus (e.g., Brown, *Gospel* 2:578). Those who have seen the passage as eucharistic (e.g., Bauer, *Johannesevangelium* 175) use 1 Cor 11:29 to claim that Satan enters the sinful Judas because he takes the eucharistic morsel without discerning. All shy clear of a eucharistic interpretation of the type offered above because they have not given full weight to the implications of Jesus' love for his failing disciples *eis telos* (13:1). For a more detailed study of John 13 along these lines see Moloney, "A Sacramental Reading" 237–256; idem, *Body Broken* 113–150.

30. *and it was night:* On the related Nicodemus passage and the function of the story of Nicodemus in the Fourth Gospel see Moloney, *Signs and Shadows* 90–93.

31. *Thus when he had gone out:* It is surprising that so few commentators devote attention to the link between Judas' exit and Jesus' words in vv. 31b-32, *hote oun exēlthen.* There are some exceptions (e.g., de Boer, *Johannine Perspectives* 208). It is caused, no doubt, by the widespread agreement that the original discourse ran from 13:31–14:31, with v. 31a regarded as a weak Johannine link. See, for example, the detailed commentary on vv. 31-32 in Schnackenburg,

Gospel 3:49–52, which focuses entirely on the questions raised by vv. 31b-32. If the words of v. 31a are a Johannine attempt to link vv. 31-38 (originally the beginning of 13:31–14:31) to the (originally independent) narrative of vv. 1-30 they deserve special consideration for a proper appreciation of the narrative.

31. *Now is the Son of Man glorified:* For a detailed study of vv. 31-32 see Moloney, *Son of Man* 194–202. See also de Boer, *Johannine Perspectives* 186–189, for a close association of Jesus' death and the theme of glorification in vv. 31-32. De Boer understands the association of Jesus' death with glorification as a reflection of the final stages in the Johannine community's theological development. For a sketch of that development see pp. 53–82.

34. *A new commandment I give to you:* Although there are notable exceptions (e.g., Dettwiler, *Die Gegenwart* 74–79), the parallel between the two "gifts"—the example of v. 15 and the new commandment of vv. 34-35—is seldom noticed. This is particularly true of those scholars (the majority) who separate vv. 31-38 from vv. 1-30. Schnackenburg, *Gospel* 3:12, 52–54, uses the parallel as one element to prove his claim that vv. 34-35 are an addition.

35. *everyone will know that you are my disciples if you have love for one another:* The testaments are also marked by a command to mutual love (see note above). There is something specifically Christian in Jesus' presenting himself and his self-gift as the model for mutual love, and there is an intensification of the command. Nevertheless, the new commandment is an exhortation to a quality of life that flows from the life story of the departing hero, as in the testaments. See Collins, "A New Commandment" 235–262; Cancian, *Nuovo Commandamento* 275–276.

For Reference and Further Study

The following bibliography also lists some major works on 13:1–17:26

Bammel, Ernst. "The Farewell Discourse of the Evangelist John and Its Jewish Heritage," *TynB* 44 (1993) 103–116.

Becker, Jürgen. "Die Abschiedsreden Jesu im Johannesevangelium," *ZNW* 61 (1970) 215–246.

Behler, G.-M. *The Last Discourse of Jesus.* Helicon: Baltimore, 1965.

Beutler, Johannes. "Die Heilsbedeutung des Todes Jesu im Johannesevangelium nach Johannes 13,1-20." In Karl Kertelge, ed., *Der Tod Jesu. Deutungen im Neuen Testament.* QD 74. Freiburg: Herder, 1976, 188–204.

Cancian, Domenico. *Nuovo Commandamento Nuova Alleanza. Eucharistia nell'interpretazione del capitolo 13 del Vangelo di Giovanni.* Collevalenza: Edizione "L'Amore Misericordioso", 1978.

Collins, Raymond F. "'A New Commandment I Give to You . . .' (Jn 13:34)," *LTP* 35 (1979) 235–261.

Cortès, Enric. *Los Discursos de Adiós de Gen 49 a Jn 13-17.* Colectanea San Paciano 23. Barcelona: Herder, 1976.

Culpepper, R. Alan. "The Johannine *hypodeigma:* A Reading of John 13:1-38," *Sem* 53 (1991) 133–152.

Dettwiler, Andreas. *Die Gegenwart des Erhöhten. Eine exegetische Studie zu den johanneischen Abschiedsreden (Joh 13,31–16,33) unter besonderer Berücksichtigung ihres Relecture-Charakters.* FRLANT 169. Göttingen: Vandenhoeck & Ruprecht, 1995.

Dunn, J. D. G. "The Washing of Disciples' Feet in John 13:1-20," *ZNW* 61 (1970) 247–252.

Ferraro, Giuseppe. "'Pneuma' in Giov 13,21," *RivBib* 28 (1980) 185–211.

Grelot, Pierre. "L'interpretation pénitentielle du lavement des pieds." In *L'homme devant Dieu: Mélanges H. de Lubac.* 2 vols. Paris: Aubier, 1963, 1:75–91.

Grossouw, W. K. "A Note on John XIII 1-3," *NT* 8 (1966) 124–131.

Hultgren, A. J. "The Johannine Footwashing (13:1-11) as Symbol of Eschatological Hospitality," *NTS* 28 (1982) 539–546.

Kaefer, J. P. "Les discours d'adieu en Jean 13:31-17:26," *NT* 26 (1984) 251–282.

Kleinknecht, Karl-Theodor. "Johannes 13, die Synoptiker und die 'Methode' der johanneischen Evangelienüberlieferung," *ZThK* 82 (1985) 361–388.

Kurz, W. S. "Luke 22:14-38 and Greco-Roman and Biblical Farewell Addresses," *JBL* 104 (1985) 251–268.

_____. *Farewell Addresses in the New Testament.* Zacchaeus Studies: New Testament. Collegeville: The Liturgical Press, 1990.

Lombard, H. A., and W. H. Oliver. "A Working Supper in Jerusalem: John 13:1-38 Introduces Jesus' Farewell Discourses," *Neotest.* 25 (1991) 357–378.

Moloney, Francis J. *A Body Broken for a Broken People. Eucharist in the New Testament.* Peabody: Hendrickson, 1997.

_____. *Glory not Dishonor,* Chapter 1.

_____. "A Sacramental Reading of John 13:1-38," *CBQ* 53 (1991) 237–256.

_____. *Son of Man* 186–202.

Neugebauer, Johannes. *Die eschatologischen Aussagen in den johanneischen Abschiedsreden. Eine Untersuchung zu Johannes 13-17.* BWANT 140. Stuttgart: Kohlhammer, 1995.

Niccaci, A. "L'unità letteraria di Gv 13,1-38," *ED* 29 (1976) 291–323.

Niemand, Christoph. *Die Fußwashungerzählung des Johannesevangeliums. Untersuchungen zur ihrer Entstehung und Überlieferung im Urchristentum.* Studia Anselmiana 114. Rome: Pontificio Ateneo S. Anselmo, 1993.

O'Day, Gail R. "'I Have Overcome the World' (John 16:33): Narrative Time in John 13–17," *Sem* 53 (1991) 153–166.

Painter, John. "The Farewell Discourses and the History of Johannine Christianity," *NTS* 27 (1980–1981) 525–543.

Randall, J. F. "The Theme of Unity in John 17," *EThL* 41 (1965) 373–394.

Richter, Georg. *Die Fußwaschung im Johannesevangelium. Geschichte und Deutung.* BU 1. Regensburg: Pustet, 1967.

Robinson, J. A. T. "The Significance of the Footwashing." In idem, *Twelve More New Testament Studies.* London: SCM Press, 1984, 77–80.

Schneider, Johannes. "Die Abschiedsreden Jesu: Ein Beitrag zur Frage der Komposition von Johannes 13:31–17:26," in *Gott und die Götter: Festschrift für E. Fascher.* Berlin: Evangelische Verlagsanstalt, 1958, 103–112.

Schneiders, Sandra M. "The Footwashing (John 13:1-20): An Experiment in Hermeneutics," *CBQ* 43 (1981) 76–92.

Schnelle, Udo. "Die Abschiedsreden im Johannesevangelium," *ZNW* 80 (1989) 64–79.

Segovia, Fernando F. "John 13:1-20. The Footwashing in the Johannine Tradition," *ZNW* 73 (1982) 31–51.

_____. *Love Relationships in the Johannine Tradition. Agapē/Agapan in I John and the Fourth Gospel.* SBL.DS 58. Chico: Scholars, 1982.

_____. *The Farewell of the Word. The Johannine Call to Abide.* Minneapolis: Fortress, 1991.

Simoens, Yves. *La gloire d'aimer. Structures stylistiques et interprétatives dans le Discours de la Cène.* AnBib 90. Rome: Biblical Institute Press, 1981, 81–104.

Spicq, Ceslas. "*Trōgein:* Est-il synonyme de *phagein* et d'*esthien* dans le Nouveau Testament?" *NTS* 26 (1979–1980) 414–419.

Thomas, John Christopher. *Footwashing in John 13 and the Johannine Community.* JSNT.S 61. Sheffield: JSOT Press, 1991.

Tolmie, D. F. *Jesus' Farewell to the Disciples. John 13:1–17:26 in Nàrratological Perspective.* BibIntS 12. Leiden: E. J. Brill, 1995.

Weiss, Herold. "Footwashing in the Johannine Community," *NT* 41 (1979) 298–325.

ii. Departure (14:1-31)

Introduction to 14:1-31. The dialogue between Jesus and Peter (13:36-38) brings to a close the parallel stories of the footwashing (13:1-17) and the gift of the morsel (13:21-38). The question of Jesus' departure has been raised in that dialogue (cf. 13:33, 36), but in 14:1 Jesus addresses a broader audience. The literary form of the passage changes as Jesus adopts a teaching role, peppering his words to the disciples with imperatives (cf. vv. 1 [3x], 9, 11 [2x], 27 [2x], and 31 [2x]), as they struggle to follow his words and promises (cf. vv. 5 [Thomas], 8 [Philip], 22 [Judas]). There is an obvious literary link between v. 1a: "Let not your hearts be troubled" and v. 27b: "Let not your hearts be troubled." This first section of the discourse concludes with the enigmatic words of v. 31c: "Rise, let us go hence." Despite widespread opinion that "13:31-38 functions as an introduction to chapter 14" (Segovia, *Farewell* 64), there is a new development in the narrative strategy of the author in 14:1. Only with 14:1-31 does the farewell discourse proper begin (cf. Beutler, *Habt keine Angst* 9–19).

Scholars disagree on the internal structure of 14:1-31 (cf. Segovia, *Farewell* 64–65 nn. 6-13; Migliasso, *La presenza* 64–73), but a variety of syntactic elements and details of content suggest a threefold division (cf. Simoens, *La gloire d'aimer* 105–129). The imperative "believe" appears in 14:1 and dominates vv. 1-14 (cf. vv. 1, 10, 11, 12). The recommendation to "love" appears in v. 15 for the first time in 14:1-31. It reappears in vv. 21,

23, and 24, and clearly marks the beginning and ending of the section vv. 15-24. Verses 25-31 are highlighted throughout by the repetition of a similar theme: "speaking" (v. 25), "teaching" (v. 26a), "saying" (v. 26c), "saying" (v. 28), "telling" (v. 29), and "speaking" (v. 30). The themes of departure (vv. 2, 3a, 4), faith (v. 1), and encouragement (vv. 1-4, 6) open the discourse in vv. 1-6. They return in vv. 27b-31: departure (vv. 28, 31), faith (v. 29), and encouragement (vv. 27b-29, 31). The opening (vv. 1-6) and closing (vv. 27b-31) sections of the discourse both begin "Let not your hearts be troubled" (v. 1a, 27b). Between these two sections (vv. 15-24) there is the steady repetition of Jesus' command to love him through the keeping of his commandments and his word (vv. 15, 21, 23, 24). On the basis of these indications a threefold division suggests itself:

> *Vv. 1-14:* Jesus speaks encouragingly of his departure.
> *Vv. 15-24:* Jesus instructs the disciples on the fruits of belief and love.
> *Vv. 25-31:* Jesus speaks encouragingly of his departure.

For ease of consultation and clarity the translation and notes for vv. 1-14, vv. 15-24, and vv. 25-31 will be provided separately. Further subdivisions of the material within each of these sections will be presented in a brief introduction to each section. The literature For Reference and Further Study of 14:1-31 will be gathered after the commentary on 14:25-31.

Jesus speaks encouragingly of his departure (vv. 1-14)

1. "Let not your hearts be troubled; believe in God, believe also in me. 2. In my Father's house are many abiding places, and if it had not been so I would have told you, for I am going to prepare a place for you. 3. And when I go and prepare a place for you I will come again and will take you to myself, that where I am you may be also. 4. And you know the way where I am going." 5. Thomas said to him, "Lord, we do not know where you are going; how can we know the way?" 6. Jesus said to him, "I am the way, the truth and the life; no one comes to the Father but by me.

7. If you have come to know me you shall know my Father also. Henceforth you know him and have seen him." 8. Philip said to him, "Lord, show us the Father and we shall be satisfied." 9. Jesus said to him, "Have I been with you so long and yet you do not know me, Philip? Whoever has seen me has seen the Father; how can you say, 'Show us the Father'? 10. Do you not believe that I am in the Father and the Father in me? The words that I say to you I do not speak on my own authority; but the Father who dwells in me does his works. 11. Believe me that I am in the Father and the Father in me; or else believe me for the sake of the works themselves."

12. "Amen, amen, I say to you, the one who believes in me will also do the works that I do; and will do greater works than these, because I go

to the Father. 13. Whatever you ask in my name, I will do it, that the Father may be glorified in the Son; 14. if you ask anything in my name I will do it."

INTERPRETATION

Introduction to vv. 1-14. This first section of 14:1-31 is dedicated to Jesus' encouraging presentation of his necessary departure. It unfolds in three subsections.

1. *Departure to the Father (vv. 1-6).* The theme of encouragement opens the passage (v. 1: *mē tarassesthō hymōn hē kardia*), as Jesus assures the disciples that he is going to prepare a place for them. He tells the disciples that they know the way, and the question of Thomas is a rhetorical device that allows Jesus to reveal himself by means of an *egō eimi* statement with a predicate: Jesus is the way leading to the Father.
2. *To see the Father and his works (vv. 7-11).* In v. 6b Jesus spoke of knowing the way to the Father. These words indicate that Jesus points beyond himself: he is the revelation of the Father. Again a disciple, this time Philip, raises a question that serves as a rhetorical device enabling Jesus to state his oneness with the Father and his unique role as the revelation of the Father. Disciples are asked to believe in the oneness that exists between Jesus and the Father, or at least to believe in Jesus on the basis of the Father's works that he performs.
3. *To believe and to do the works of the Father (vv. 12-14).* In v. 11b Jesus asked disciples to believe in him at least on the basis of the works of the Father revealed in the Son. The double "amen" introduces this final subsection, which picks up the theme of "works." Jesus points to a time when the disciples, who will ask in his name, will do even greater works. Anyone who asks in the name of Jesus will continue the task of manifesting the Father's oneness with the Son.

However caring the symbolic gestures of footwashing and sharing the morsel have been (13:1-38), they also carry the foreboding sense of Jesus' willingness to give himself unto death for his disciples, and each event has been marked by a command from Jesus that his disciples follow his example (v. 15) and love as he has loved (vv. 34-35). A death that is also a departure (cf. vv. 33, 36) is in the air, and the first part of the discourse proper begins to explain some of the encouraging consequences of this death and departure.

Departure to the Father (vv. 1-6). The understandable consternation of the disciples after the events, commands, and prophecies of 13:1-38 must be overcome through a renewal of their faith and trust in God and in Jesus (14:1). Faith and trust in God is still a reasonable request to make of the disciples, but the imperative "believe in me" may involve a risky association with a doomed man that is more than they are prepared to give. Jesus thus turns to explain more fully the significance of his oncoming departure. He is going to the home *(oikia)* of his Father, where there will be many dwelling places *(monai)*. The house of the Father of Jesus is the realm of God, and within this realm there are many places for the disciples to abide (v. 2a). Jesus has *said* that it will be so, and the disciples are called to believe in the word of Jesus (v. 2b; cf. 2:1–4:54). Behind the noun *monai* ("abiding places") lies the Johannine use of the verb *menein*, which refers to a permanent dwelling or abiding. The verb has already been used, positively and negatively, in the earlier parts of the narrative (cf. 1:32; 7:27, 56; 8:31, 35; 12:34, 46 [positively]; 9:41; 12:46 [negatively]) with the sense of the presence or rejection of an intimate reciprocity. It will reappear shortly as the *leitmotif* of 15:1-11. The link made between the *oikia tou patros mou* and Jesus' going to prepare a "place" *(topon)* informs the disciples of a permanent, lifegiving dwelling among the many *monai*. Jesus' departure should not be a cause for sorrow, but for comfort and trust (v. 1). He is going away to prepare for them the universal and permanent possibility of an abiding communion with his Father (v. 2).

This Gospel's practice of balancing traditional and realized eschatology (cf. 5:25-29; 6:35-40, 44-48) reappears in v. 3. The use of the present tense *palin erchomai* (literally "I am coming again") side by side with the future *kai paralēmpsomai hymas pros emauton* ("and I will take you to myself") is grammatically clumsy, but the conclusion to the verse, *hina hopou egō eimi kai hymeis ēte* ("so that where I am you may also be") demands a future meaning for the sentence. Jesus is departing to prepare a place for his own in his Father's house, but he will return in the future to take his disciples to himself, to the place where he is. Uppermost is the idea of a time between Jesus' departure and his future return, but the clumsy presence of the present tenses retains a hint of the ongoing presence of Jesus. Much of the Gospel has insisted that a time is coming *and is already present* when those who believe in the Son have eternal life (cf. 3:15, 16, 36; 4:14, 36; 5:24-25; 6:27, 35, 47, 56, 63; 10:10, 28; 11:25-26; 12:50). How the one who departs will still be present is not explained. Further clarification is called for, but this is not an ordinary departure.

The departure of Jesus is central, as he reminds the disciples that they have been instructed in the way of Jesus and his destiny; they already know the way where Jesus is going (v. 4). The disciples have heard that Jesus is returning to his Father (cf. 10:38; 12:27-28) by means of an experience of death that is at the same time his glorification and renders glory to God (cf. 11:4, 40; 12:23, 32-34; 13:31-32). Thomas's question (v. 5) reflects an ongoing unwillingness to face all the implications of the end of Jesus' story (cf. 13:33, 36). They should know where he is going *(pou hypageis)* but a request for further instruction on "the way" *(tēn hodon)* is justifiable, and it opens the possibility for Jesus' self-revelation as "the way" (v. 6a: *egō eimi hē hodos*). He is the way to the Father (v. 6b), and he explains *how* this is so by means of the two words used after "and" (*kai:* cf. note). Jesus' basic affirmation is that he is the way, and the two following words describe "the way" that is the truth (*kai hē alētheia*) and the life (*kai hē zōē*). The earlier use of these Johannine expressions, from the Prologue (cf. 1:4, 14, 17) through the story itself, points to Jesus as the authoritative and saving revelation of God (*alētheia:* 1:14, 17: 5:33: 8:32, 40, 44-46; *zōē* 1:4; 6:33, 35, 48, 63, 68; 8:12; 10:10; 11:25).

Jesus' claim to be "the way" is more than self-revelation. As with all the *egō eimi* statements with a predicate, Jesus not only announces who he is but also what he does. The way leads somewhere (cf. 10:7, 9): to the Father (v. 6b). Jesus is the only way to the Father, the unique and saving revelation of God (cf. 1:18, 51; 3:13; 5:37-38; 6:46; 10:1, 7, 11, 14). God is revealed in the life and word of Jesus, and the disciples should know that Jesus' departure to go to the Father will be through a lifting up (cf. 3:14; 8:28; 12:32) and a death (cf. 10:16-18; 11:4, 49-53; 12:23-24, 32-33; 13:18-20). The way of Jesus is a loving and total gift of himself unto death (v. 6a; cf. 13:1). It must also become the way of his followers (cf. 13:15, 34-35). A passage that began with a strong exhortation to the disciples to trust and believe in both God and Jesus (v. 1) has taught the disciples of *their* departure, the consequence of Jesus' own. He departs to prepare a place for them (vv. 2-4). The passage closes with the reason why the disciples' faltering belief in Jesus must hold firm. Belief and trust in Jesus are the only "way" to their goal: oneness with the Father (vv. 5-6).

To see the Father and his works (vv. 7-11). The reference to "the Father" in v. 6b leads into the central subsection (vv. 7-11) of vv. 1-14. To know Jesus is to know the Father (v. 7a), and from the time of Jesus onward (*ap' arti*) anyone who knows the Father through seeing Jesus has also seen the Father (v. 7b). From the affirmation of the Prologue (1:18) through Jesus' defense of his Sabbath activity (5:19-30) into the rest of his ministry (cf. 8:19, 38, 58, 10:30, 38), his claim to be the presence of the Father has been boldly made despite the mounting conflict generated by such a claim (e.g., 8:20; 10:31, 39). Jesus' statement (*ei egnōkate me . . . gnōsesthe*) is a promise, as the use of the perfect tense ("If you have come to know me") indicates a knowledge already attained. In v. 4 Jesus told the disciples of things that they knew, but Thomas asked for further clarification (v. 6). The same pattern is repeated after v. 7. They have come to know Jesus and thus they also know the Father. But Philip asks Jesus to show them the Father so that they might be satisfied (v. 8). In 6:7 Philip wondered about Jesus' ability to provide satisfaction (*arkousin*) for the large crowd by the lake, and in 14:8 he asks for the sight of God so that the disciples might be satisfied (*arkei*). The disciples are ignorant of truths that are fundamental for an understanding of who Jesus is, what he is doing, and where he is going.

Jesus' response looks back across the long period of time spent with the disciples *(meth' hymōn)*. To know Jesus is to know the Father, and Philip is exasperatingly ignorant in asking Jesus to show the Father (v. 9). The problem lies in the disciples' lack of faith. They have heard and been taught the way to the Father (v. 6): Jesus is in the Father and the Father is in Jesus (cf. 10:38), but they have not come to believe in this oneness (v. 10a). Turning patiently from accusation to teaching, Jesus repeats truths from the earlier parts of the story: the words he speaks are words of the Father (cf. 3:34; 5:23-24; 8:18, 28, 38, 47; 12:49), and the deeds of Jesus are the works *(ta erga)* of the Father (v. 10b; cf. 5:20, 36; 9:3-4; 10:25, 32, 37-38). This central subsection (vv. 7-11) of vv. 1-14 concludes with an appeal to the unbelieving disciples. Belief is crucial (v. 11; cf. v. 1). One must believe that Jesus is in the Father and the Father is in him. Flowing from this oneness and making it known are the works Jesus does. If the disciples are to commit themselves to a saving belief in the oneness between Jesus and the Father, and thus see the Father (cf. vv. 8-9), they should look to the place where such oneness is to be seen: in the works *(ta erga)* of Jesus (v. 11).

To believe, and to do the works of the Father (vv. 12-14). The reference to "the works" in v. 11 leads into v. 12, where the theme of "works" and use of the double "amen" continue what has been said before and bring it to some form of conclusion. Belief in Jesus will enable the believer *(ho pisteuōn)* to do the works of Jesus and to excel the works of Jesus (v. 12ab). The fundamental theme of Jesus' departure makes possible the increased greatness of the works of the believer (v. 12c). The absence of Jesus created by his departure will not lead to the cessation of the works of the Father by which Jesus has made God known (cf. 5:41; 7:18; 8:50, 54), but the disciples will not automatically do these greater works. They are exhorted to ask in the name of Jesus so that the works will continue to be done. The increased greatness of the works lies in their being done in his name, *after his departure.* There will be a difference between the works of Jesus done during his ministry and the works of Jesus done after his departure. The departure opens a new era when the works of the disciples surpass those of Jesus, because Jesus will be *present in his absence,* as the disciples do the works he is doing (v. 12: *ha egō poiō:* present tense) and he *will do* (vv. 13-14: *egō poiēso:* future tense) what the disciples request.

Jesus has done the works of the Father during his time with the disciples (v. 9) because of his oneness with the Father (vv. 10-11). He is now departing to the house of the Father (v. 2) and he will come again (v. 3). There will be an in-between-time during which the disciples must ask in Jesus' name and he will continue do the works of the Father among them. A crucial point has been made in this exhortation: the ongoing presence of the absent Jesus will be found in the worshiping community. Its members will associate themselves with the departed Jesus, asking in his name. Jesus, the former Paraclete, doing whatever is asked in his name (vv. 13a, 14), glorifies the Father in the Son (v. 13b). The glory of God, once seen in the deeds of Jesus (cf. 2:11; 5:41; 7:18; 8:50, 54; 11:4, 40), will be seen in the deeds of worshiping disciples, greater deeds even than Jesus did (v. 12), done as a result of their asking in the name of Jesus (vv. 13-14).

NOTES

1. *Let not your hearts be troubled:* The obvious repetition of exactly these words in v. 1a and v. 27b is often seen as indicating an inclusion that closes off the material between v. 1 and v. 27. See, for example, Bultmann, *Gospel* 599; Schneider, "Die Abschiedsreden Jesu" 106. These two identical remarks from Jesus should be regarded as repetitions. They are identical, necessary statements of encouragement that open subsections (vv. 1-6 and vv. 27b-31) that deal explicitly with Jesus' departure.

    The recommendation uses the verb *tarassein*, which links their consternation with fear of the cross via Psalm 42/43. On this see Beutler, "Psalm 42/43" 46–54.

    The encouraging words of a hero who is leaving his disciples through death is part of the Jewish testamentary tradition. For more detail see Beutler, *Habt keine Angst* 15–19.

2. *are many abiding places:* The expression *monai* has numerous possible sources from contemporary religious traditions. For comprehensive surveys see Fischer, *Wohnungen* 105–290; McCaffrey, *The House* 49–75. Most translations render the expression as "dwelling places." I have translated "abiding places" to show the Johannine nature of the term. The term "abiding" best translates the repeated use of the verb *menein* in 15:1-11. Both Fischer and McCaffrey affirm the Johannine nature of the expression, despite its possible rich background.

    and if it had not been so I would have told you, for I am going to prepare a place for you: This passage has a disturbed textual tradition. The *hoti* ("that") is wrongly omitted by the first hand of 𝔓⁶⁶, Mt Athos, and Old Latin, and it is not clear whether a stop should be made after *hymin* ("told you"). Given the fact that Jesus has never before told the disciples of the Father's house or the many abiding places I am reading v. 2b, including the *hoti*, as an insistence upon the importance of the word of Jesus, building on the imperative of v. 1c ("believe also in me"): "There are many abiding places, and if it had not been so I would have told you, for I am going to prepare a place for you" (cf. Barrett, *Gospel* 457). For a fuller discussion see Fischer, *Wohnungen* 35–36; McCaffrey, *The House* 138–140.

    to prepare a place for you: Despite the future tense of the verb some use the Johannine language of abiding to conclude that believers already dwell in

Christ and await his final coming (e.g., Gundry, "In my Father's House" 68–71; Oliver and van Aarde, "The Community of Faith" 379–400). Some commentators link the use of *oikia* and *topos* with the Jerusalem Temple, claiming that Jesus' words look to the transcending of that "place" (cf. 4:20-24). This looks back to Jesus' body as a temple (cf. 2:21) and thus 14:2-3 promises "universalism in religion" created by the departure of Jesus (e.g., Marsh, *Saint John* 501).

3. *I will come again and will take you to myself:* Some (e.g., Bernard, *Commentary* 2:534–536; Delebecque, *Jean* 187) regard v. 3 as totally determined by an end-time eschatological perspective. Becker, "Die Abschiedsreden Jesu" 219–228 (among others), claims that vv. 2-3 contain a primitive Son of Man christology and eschatology that is corrected later in the discourse (i.e., vv. 6-10, 12-17, 18-24). Others (Marsh, *Saint John* 503; Lindars, *Gospel* 471; Fischer, *Wohnungen* 299–348) attempt to read vv. 2-3 in a more realized sense, supported rather than corrected by later elements in the discourse. McCaffrey, *The House* 35–45, also leaves open the "when" of Jesus' return. Initially the disciples look toward an end-time return (pp. 136–137), but later they become aware of Jesus' continual return (pp. 177–221). Stimpfle, *Blinde Sehen* 147–216, argues that the passage is open to a misunderstanding of the returning Jesus as end-time oriented and thus serves to single out true and false believers. The true believers have life *now* as the predestined children of God in the world, while others wait. For a survey see Neugebauer, *Die eschatologischen Aussagen* 14–34. The interpretation suggests that while an end-time eschatology is dominant (cf. also Gundry, "In my Father's House" 71–72; Beutler, *Habt keine Angst* 37–40), there is already a hint of the presence of the absent one. There is no need to resolve the narrative tension created by vv. 2-3. Jesus' words pose a problem that will only be resolved later in the discourse, and especially in John 20. For something of this approach see Hoskyns, *Gospels* 454; Dettwiler, *Die Gegenwart* 141–157. For de Boer, *Johannine Perspectives* 130–132, the return of Jesus refers to the coming of the Paraclete. This may be so, but the reader has not yet been told about the gift of the Paraclete.

4. *the way where:* The English "the way where" reflects the clumsy Greek *hopou egō hypagō oidate tēn hodon*, found in 𝔓[66], Sinaiticus, Vaticanus, the first hand of Ephraimi Rescriptus, Freer Gospels. See Segovia, *Farewell* 85–86 n. 49.

6. *I am the way, the truth and the life:* The fundamental study, insisting that v. 6a is a statement on Jesus as the unique revelation of the Father ("the way"), further clarified by the descriptions of the way as "the truth" and "the life," is de la Potterie, *La Vérité* 1:241–278. This exegesis interprets the use of "and" (*kai*) as epexegetical. This means that the word that follows the "and" explains the word that preceded. Both "the truth" and "the life" explain "the way." See BDF 229, § 442 (9). For Bultmann, *Gospel* 604–607 (and others) Jesus is the way (*hodos*) to the heavenly realities of truth and life (*alētheia* and *zōē*).

7. *If you have come to know me you shall know my Father also:* This translation follows the text of 𝔓[66], Sinaiticus, Bezae, as a promise (*ei egnōkate . . . gnōsesthe*). It is thus a promise rather than, with Vaticanus (*ei egnōkeite . . . an ēdeite*), a

reproach. See, among many, Barrett, *Gospel* 458–459. For the opposite view see Segovia, *Farewell* 87 n. 52. The promise is: "If you have come to know me, as you have done, you shall know my Father also."

henceforth you know him: The use of *ap' arti* meaning "from this time onward" insists that the revelation of the Father in the Son has been present throughout the time of Jesus (cf. de la Potterie, *La Vérité* 1:263–265).

and have seen him: It is sometimes conjectured that there are different levels of "seeing" in the Fourth Gospel, and different verbs (*theorein* and *horaō*) are used to make a distinction between these levels. Thus not all who "see" the physical Jesus "see" the Father (e.g., Bernard, *Commentary* 2:539–540). It appears, however, that the verbs are used indiscriminately, as the identical claim for seeing God ("the one who sent me") in seeing Jesus in 12:45 uses *theorein*, while 14:7 uses *horaō*.

8. *and we shall be satisfied:* The verb *arkein* ("to be enough") only appears twice in the Fourth Gospel (6:7; 14:8) and it is Philip who uses it on each occasion. It is often pointed out that Philip's request articulates the spiritual search of humankind, perhaps reflecting Moses' request in Exod 33:18 (cf. also Exod 24:9-11; Isa 6:1; 40:5).

10. *Do you* [singular] *not believe . . . the words that I say to you* [plural]: The shift from Jesus' opening words, addressed in the singular to Philip *(ou pisteueis?)*, to the instruction of the disciples in the plural *(legō hymin)* indicates that Jesus' response to Philip's statement in v. 8 addresses all the disciples.

11. *I am in the Father and the Father in me:* As in 10:38 this oneness is "a linguistic way of describing . . . the complete unity between Jesus and the Father" (Schnackenburg, *Gospel* 3:69). It is not metaphysics, however much this and other Johannine sayings on the relationship between the Father and the Son have been used in later trinitarian debates. The oneness between Jesus and the Father has its roots in the Jewish concept of "the sent one" who completely identifies with the "one who sent." See especially Borgen, "God's Agent in the Fourth Gospel" 121–132; Bühner, *Der Gesandte und sein Weg*. It must always be remembered that there is a uniqueness in the Johannine view that the Son's dependence on the Father is total (cf. 5:19-30). See Carson, *Gospel* 494–495.

12. *the works that I do:* The "words" and the "works" of Jesus are not to be collapsed into one theological concept called "revelation" as do Bultmann, *Gospel* 610–611, and others. Both reveal God, but there is a close association between what Jesus does *(ta erga)* and the revelation of the *doxa tou theou* (cf. 2:11; 11:4, 40) that must be respected. See Brown, *Gospel* 2:622.

will do greater works than these: Many have had recourse to the subsequent missionary successes of early Christianity to explain the "greater works" (e.g., Bauer, *Johannesevangelium* 181; Hoskyns, *Gospel* 457; Rodriguez Ruiz, *Der Missionsgedanke* 171–184). Something more theological is at stake. The departure of Jesus sets up a privileged in-between-time. A feature of that time are the greater works, done by Jesus even in his absence. Dietzfelbinger, "Die größeren Werke" 22–47, points to the uniqueness of the Johannine situation. Unable to call upon founding witnesses to the Jesus tradition, and in a situation of conflict and rejection, the community developed a confident theology of its post-Easter situation, surpassing the works of Jesus, directed and inspired by the Paraclete. See also Dietzfelbinger, "Paraklet und theologischer Anspruch" 394–408.

13. *Whatever you ask in my name, I will do it:* Becker, *Evangelium* 2:464–465, rightly points out that vv. 12-13 present Jesus as the former Paraclete responding to the prayer of the disciples. This prepares the way for the introduction of the "other Paraclete" in v. 16. On vv. 12-14 as preparation for vv. 15-27 see also Segovia, *Farewell* 90–93.

14. *If you ask anything in my name I will do it:* This verse is omitted by some manuscripts. Despite the clumsy Greek *(aitēsēte me)* and its seeming repetition of v. 13a, it should be retained (cf. Metzger, *Textual Commentary* 208; Carson 497–498). For Becker, *Evangelium* 497–498, vv. 14-15 are clumsy Johannine paraenesis, and disturb the link between v. 13 and v. 16. This ignores the important literary relationship between v. 15 ("If you love me") and v. 24 ("He who does not love me") that makes vv. 15-24 a discrete literary unit and separates vv. 15-24 from vv. 12-14. See Dettwiler, *Die Gegenwart* 125–126.

The fruits of belief and love (vv. 15-24)

15. "If you love me you will keep my commandments. 16. And I will pray the Father, and he will give you another Paraclete to be with you for ever, 17. even the Spirit of truth, whom the world cannot receive because it neither sees him nor knows him; you know him, for he abides with you and will be among you."
18. "I will not leave you desolate; I will come to you. 19. Yet a little while and the world will see me no more, but you will see me; because I live, you will live also. 20. In that day you will know that I am in my Father, and you in me, and I in you. 21. They who have my commandments and keep them are those who love me; and those who love me will be loved by my Father, and I will love them and reveal myself to them."
22. Judas (not Iscariot) said to him, "Lord, how is it that you will manifest yourself to us and not to the world?" 23. Jesus answered him, "Those who love me will keep my word, and my Father will love them, and we will come to them and make our home with them. 24. Whoever does not love me does not keep my words; and the word that you hear is not mine but the Father's who sent me."

INTERPRETATION

Introduction to vv. 15-24. This section is held together by four statements on the fruits of loving or not loving Jesus (vv. 15, 21, 23, 24). Disciples facing the departure of their master are further challenged and encouraged by promise of the Paraclete, the ongoing presence of Jesus even in his absence, and the fruits of loving Jesus and keeping his commandments. The discourse unfolds in three subsections:

1. *The Paraclete and the world (vv. 15-17).* Jesus will ask the Father to give "another Paraclete" to abide with the disciples, setting them apart from the world that cannot receive the Spirit.
2. *The revelation of the oneness of Jesus and the Father (vv. 18-21).* Jesus promises to come to and remain in an endless presence with disciples who love him and keep his commandments. Such disciples will know and share oneness with the Father and the Son and experience the life-giving consequences of being loved by both the Father and Jesus.
3. *Loving Jesus and keeping his word (vv. 22-24).* A question from Judas allows Jesus to explain further the fruits of loving and not loving him. The one who loves receives the word and will experience the abiding presence of Jesus and the Father. The one who does not love Jesus does not hear the word and thus has no access to the revelation of God.

The theme of the departure of Jesus remains central to this section of 14:1-31. His going away will not produce a situation of "lostness" but a new era gifted with the Paraclete, marked by love, the keeping of the commandments of Jesus, and the promise of a future time when the Father and the Son will abide forever with the disciple.

The Paraclete and the world (vv. 15-17). The theme of love holds vv. 15-24 together. The disciple who loves Jesus shows this union of love by holding fast to his commandments (v. 15). As he goes to death Jesus exhorts his disciples to love as he has loved (13:15, 34-35; 14:15a) by holding fast *(tērēsete)* to his commandments (v. 15b). Jesus will ask the Father to gift that situation of love and faithfulness with "another Paraclete" (16b: *allon paraklēton*) to be with them forever. Jesus' hearing the prayers of the disciples and doing for them whatever they ask (vv. 13-14) indicate that he performs the role of a Paraclete (cf. 1 John 2:1), but there will be "another Paraclete." For all the similarities that might exist between the roles of Jesus the Paraclete (vv. 13-14) and the "other Paraclete" (v. 16), the latter does not become flesh (1:14) and will not be lifted up in death to reveal God in a consummate act of love for his disciples (cf. 12:32-33; 13:1). The "other Paraclete" will remain with the disciples forever (v. 16c: *eis ton aiōna*). The Paraclete is further described as "the Spirit of truth" (v. 17a: *to pneuma tēs alētheias*), "the Spirit who communicates truth" (Barrett, *Gospel* 463), the ongoing presence of the revelation of God in the world. However, there is a world that is unable to recognize the Paraclete sent by the Father to the disciples as a result of the request of Jesus. The Paraclete belongs to the realm of Jesus, but there is another world that has responded to Jesus by rejecting his claims for himself and his revelation of the Father. It has never accepted his *origins* with the Father (cf. 1:35-51; 3:1-21, 31-36; 4:10-15; 5:19-30, 36-38, 43-44; 6:41-51; 7:25-31, 40-44; 8:12-20, 21-29; 9:24-34; 10:31-39), and it is committed to the untruth of all that it can control (cf. de la Potterie, *La Vérité* 1:345–356). As his life draws to a close and he prepares his disciples for his departure and *return* to the Father this world is unable to receive, see, or know the Spirit of truth (v. 17b).

But the disciples are part of the world of Jesus. They are "his own" (cf. 13:1: *hoi idioi*), and the Spirit of truth already abides with them (v. 17cα: *par' hymin menei*), and there will be another Paraclete who will be among them (v. 17cβ: *en hymin estai*). The interplay between Jesus as Paraclete (vv. 13-14) and the gift of another Paraclete (v. 16) continues. Jesus is the gift of the truth (cf. 1:17), the way who is the truth (cf. 14:6), who abides with them *(par' hymin menei)*, but his departure to the Father will not bring that revealing presence to an end. It will continue to be among them *(en hymin estai)*. The Paraclete is the ongoing presence of the truth as "the Spirit who communicates truth." The Paraclete is introduced into the story as the ongoing presence of the revelation of God *(hē alētheia)* to those who love Jesus and keep his commandments (cf. v. 15). Despite the physical absence of Jesus created by his departure, his revealing mission is not coming to an end. It is moving toward a new era when the revealing role of Jesus will be taken over by another Paraclete, the Spirit of truth. During the celebration of Tabernacles the narrator told the reader that the Spirit would be given when Jesus was glorified (7:39). The glorification and the gift of the Spirit are at hand, closely associated with Jesus' death (cf. 11:4, 51-53; 12:23, 32-33; 13:1, 31-32). Therefore the departure of Jesus will be no ordinary departure.

The revelation of the oneness of Jesus and the Father (vv. 18-21). Jesus is about to depart, but his children (cf. 1:12; 11:52; 13:33) will not be left as orphans (v. 18a: *orphanous*). This situation should follow the death of a parent, and Jesus' departure is associated with his death; yet it leads to his coming (v. 18b). The departure and the return coalesce! Jesus' physical departure will not be the end of his revealing presence. This theme dominates vv. 18-21. The departure ends all physical "sight" of Jesus' revelation of the truth to the world. As Jesus warned "the Jews": "The light is with you for a little while *(eti mikron)*. Walk while you have the light, lest the darkness overtake you" (12:35). That "little while" (14:19a) is now coming to an end for the world that has rejected Jesus, as Jesus will definitively depart, but the disciples, the ones who believe in him, love him, and keep his commandments (cf. vv. 1, 11, 12, 15), are promised the sight of the departed Jesus and a life that will flow from the fact that he lives beyond the departure of his physical experience of death (v. 19b). Jesus will die and depart, but the Paraclete is a gift that follows this event (7:39;

14:16). Although Jesus is going away (v. 18a) he is coming to his disciples (v. 18b: *erchomai*) and they will see him (v. 19b: *theōreite*). The death and departure of Jesus will lead to his life with the Father (v. 19cβ), and life for the disciples (v. 19cγ). Because he still lives, a consequence of his departure from the world is his lifegiving presence to the disciples (v. 19b: "because I live, you will live also"). The departure of Jesus and the gift of another Paraclete, the Spirit of truth, call for a distinction between Jesus and the Spirit-Paraclete, but what the Spirit *does* for the disciples is the prolongation and perfection of what Jesus *does* for them. None of this is possible without Jesus' return to the Father to live so that the disciples may also live.

The physical absence of Jesus is overcome by the neverending presence of the Spirit-Paraclete. There can be no notion of the return of the departed Jesus after the resurrection to be seen by the disciples. It is in the community's "experience of the exalted Jesus in the midst of the worshipping community" (Aune, *The Cultic Setting,* 133) that the absent one is present to those who believe, love him, and keep his commandments. Jesus' departure does not leave them orphans (v. 18) as he comes to them in the gift of a living presence (v. 19). The affirmation that Jesus is leaving his disciples must be taken seriously. It reflects the experience of the original Johannine readers (and all subsequent readers), for whom the fleshly Jesus is no longer present. But the experience of the *living* Jesus continues in and through the permanent presence of the Spirit-Paraclete. In the worshiping community, and especially in baptism and eucharist (cf. 3:3-5; 6:51-58), those who believe, love, and keep the commandments of Jesus experience the presence of the absent one. The "coming" of the exalted—and therefore absent—Jesus in the worship of the community is a proleptic experience of a final "coming," made possible in the in-between-time by the presence of the Paraclete.

Jesus promises a knowledge that will be granted to the believer on the day of his departure ("in that day"), the time of his coming and his gift of new life (v. 20). This knowledge, a fruit of the presence of the Paraclete, is the revelation of the oneness that exists between the Father and the Son, and the oneness that exists between Jesus and the believer. The oneness between the Father and the Son has been at the heart of much of Jesus' teaching, and the basis of his authority (cf. 5:19-30; 10:30, 38), but the introduction of the believer into a oneness with Jesus is new. The disciples of Jesus will not be left orphans through the departure of Jesus (v. 18), but granted life (v. 19), a knowledge of the relationship that exists between the Father and the Son and between themselves and Jesus (v. 20). The departure of Jesus unleashes among the disciples something hitherto unknown and unspoken. In v. 21 Jesus addresses the wider audience of the Gospel's readership: "They who have my commandments." All potential recipients of v. 20 are told that oneness with God is to be understood in terms of love. A response to the revelation of God in Jesus through the observance of his commandments is simultaneously a loving commitment to Jesus (v. 21a). Such love will be matched by the Father's love for them, Jesus' love for them, and the ongoing revelation of Jesus to them (v. 21b: *emphanizein autǭ hemauton.* Cf. Exod 33:13, 18; Wis 1:2; 17:4), even after his departure (v. 21c).

The world not open to the revelation of God in and through Jesus cannot understand the significance of his departure through death. However, as a consequence of the gift of the Spirit-Paraclete (vv. 15-16) this departure leads to a unique experience of life. This life flows from participation in the unity that exists between the Father and the Son (vv. 18-20), the intimacy of being loved by the Father and Jesus, and the ongoing revelation of God in and through Jesus (v. 21) as disciples experience the presence of the absent one in their worship.

Loving Jesus and keeping his word (vv. 22-24). The theme of loving Jesus and holding fast to his commandments appeared in v. 15. Judas' question, asking further clarification on the privilege of a revelation to the disciples that will not be given to "the world" (v. 22), leads this section of the discourse to close with the same themes (vv. 23-24). From the first pages of the Gospel it has been made clear that Jesus' revelation of himself, the sight of God's glory (cf. 1:14; 2:11; 11:4, 40), is available to those who are open to his word (cf. 1:9-13, 19-51; 2:1–4:54). This need for belief has remained central to Jesus' final discourse (cf. 14:1, 11, 12), but disciples are also to love Jesus (14:15, 21, 23-24). The departed Jesus will manifest himself to disciples who believe in his words and love him. Such revelation is unavailable to a world that refuses both belief and love.

Priority is given to loving Jesus in v. 23a. The disciple who loves Jesus will keep the word of Jesus. The latter unfailingly flows from the former as the disciple lives the in-between-time, assured by the words of Jesus that the Father will love the loving and believing disciples. But Jesus promises more: "and we will come to them and make our home with them" (v. 23b). When will this "coming" be? *Unlike* vv. 18-21, which promised the experience of the presence of the absent Jesus after his departure (cf. v. 18: *erchomai pros hymas*), in v. 23 every verb is in the future. The Father and the Son *will come (eleusometha)* and they *will establish (poiēsometha)* an abiding presence *(monē)* with the believer. At table with his disciples Jesus opened a discourse by speaking of a time between his departure and his future coming (vv. 2-3). This period will be filled by the presence of the Paraclete (vv. 16-17) and the lifegiving presence of the departed and exalted Lord in the worshiping community (vv. 18-21). The love of the Father assures the presence of the Father and the absent Jesus during the in-between-time (v. 23a). But the resumption of the image of the abiding place *(monē)* from vv. 2-3 and the two future tenses promise a future definitive and permanent presence of the Father and the Son. They will establish their *monē* with the one who loves Jesus and holds fast to his word (v. 23). The departed Jesus comes to disciples who are not abandoned as "orphans." Those who love and believe experience the presence of the absent one (vv. 18-21) and they can look forward to a final coming, when Jesus and the Father will abide definitively with them (v. 23).

These promises also have a negative side. The person who does not love Jesus and does not keep his words is rejecting the words of the Father who sent Jesus. It is not the Sent One who is rejected but the one who sent him (v. 24). The promise of the abiding presence of the Father and the Son is in the future (v. 23), but the rejection of the one who does not love Jesus or keep his commandments *(mē agapōn . . . ou terei)* is an action that takes place in the present. This is the rejection of the revelation of God in the words and works of Jesus (cf. 3:34; 5:23-24; 8:18, 28, 38, 47; 12:49), continued in the rejection of the Spirit-filled community. In a short time Jesus will depart and thus no longer be physically present. However, the revelation of God continues in and through the Spirit-filled community of disciples, enlivened by the presence of the absent one (cf. Aune, *Cultic Setting* 103–105). It can be rejected by those who refuse to love Jesus and keep his commandments, but such rejection is nothing less than the rejection of God (v. 24).

The theme of Jesus' departure (cf. vv. 1-14) is a fundamental presupposition for all that is said in vv. 15-24. The association of love (vv. 15, 21, 23-24: "love me") and loyalty (vv. 15, 21, 23-24: "keep my commandments") leads to a new promise for the in-between-time. Disciples who in the presence of the Paraclete love Jesus and keep his commandments will come to know God and be loved by God and by Jesus. Because the exalted Jesus lives, gifted by the Spirit-Paraclete (vv. 16-17), they will experience the life of love that unites the Father and the Son (vv. 20-21) until the Father and the Son finally come to abide with them (v. 23).

NOTES

15. *you will keep:* The future tense "you will keep" *(tērēsete)*, following Vaticanus, rather than the imperative (Bezae, Koridethi) or the subjunctive ($\mathfrak{P}^{66}$, Sinaiticus) makes best sense. See Barrett, *Gospel* 461.

   my commandments: This section (vv. 15-24) is marked by Jesus' demand that the disciple keep the "word," "words," and "commandments" (cf. vv. 15, 21, 23, 24). There is widespread agreement that these different terms all ask for faith in the revelation of God in and through the word of Jesus. See Segovia, *Farewell* 94–95. Léon-Dufour, *Lecture* 3:112–116, points to the close link between the demands of Jesus and the demands of the covenant, especially as they are found in Deuteronomy (cf. Deut 5:10; 6:5-6; 7:9; 10:12-13; 11:13, 22). See also Beutler, *Habt keine Angst* 55–83.

16. *another Paraclete:* For surveys of the wide-ranging discussions of possible background to the Johannine use of the term *paraklētos* see Brown, "The Paraclete" 115–126; Burge, *Anointed* 3–45; de la Potterie, *La Vérité* 1:330–341; Dettwiler, *Die Gegenwart* 181–189. The primary meaning of the word is forensic: "Legal assistant, advocate" (LSJ 1313, s.v.). This meaning is also found transliterated in Hebrew and Aramaic documents. In support of this background and meaning see Johansson, *Parakletoi,* who looks to the widespread Jewish idea of an intercessor, and Betz, *Der Paraklet* 36–116, who uses Qumran to point to an angelic being (Michael) behind the interceding Paraclete. See also Manns, *L'Evangile* 360–373. Such views are generally regarded as not responding to the *overall* Johannine use of the term, although this forensic function of the Paraclete is strongly present in 16:8-11. De la Potterie, *La Vérité* 1:336–339, argues for the forensic nature of the Paraclete sayings but sets them within the wider theological and literary framework of the Fourth Gospel understood as a trial between Jesus and "the world." Bauer, *Johannesevangelium* 182–183, and others suggest that the Johannine expression is best linked with the use of *parakalein* and *paraklēsis* in early Christianity, and with uses of *parakalōn* in LXX Greek (cf. Job 16:2, but not elsewhere) for the concept of consolation (cf. Isa 40:1). This position has been thoroughly developed by Müller, "Die Parakletenvorstellung" 31–77. For Müller (pp. 43–52) the earliest Johannine concept was "the Spirit of truth," and this notion was later associated with the Paraclete as guide, comforter, and teacher. No doubt originally separate traditions of "the Holy Spirit" and "the Paraclete" have been joined in the Fourth Gospel (cf. 14:16-17, 26), and probably within the Johannine community before the composition of the Fourth Gospel as we now have it (cf. Barrett, *Gospel* 463). On the fundamentally Johannine nature of the expression see Johnston, *The Spirit-Paraclete* 3–58; Martyn, *History and Theology* 143–151. The classic presentation of the case for the Paraclete passages as interpolations from an independent source is found in Windisch, *The Spirit-Paraclete* 1–26.

17. *he abides with you and will be among you:* The use of the present tense "abides" *(menei)* and the future "will be" *(estai)* in this one sentence is a notorious difficulty for interpreters. Some scribes attempted to smooth it out by making the *menei* into a future. It only requires a change of accent. Some contemporary scholars accept that the verb is present, but acts as a future tense (e.g., Beasley-Murray, *John* 243). Manns, *L'Evangile* 352, claims that it reflects a rabbinic practice in which both verbs simultaneously mean both present and future. See the discussion in Morgan-Wynne, "A Note" 93–96. Morgan-Wynne rightly insists that "The future *estai* points to the post-cross era" (96). Many scholars (e.g., Schnackenburg, *Gospel* 3:76; Manns, *L'Evangile* 352) explain the tenses as a reflection of the later experience of the members of the Johannine community. They have an experience of the Spirit and are confident of the future presence of the Spirit. Schnackenburg distinguishes between the prepo-

sitions to make this point: *par' hymin* refers to the present experience of the community and *en hymin* stresses the disciples' future knowledge of the Spirit's "inner presence." These suggestions are oversubtle. The position taken in the interpretation focuses on the former (vv. 13-14) and the latter (v. 16) Paracletes. The former Paraclete (Jesus) is with the disciples, and the "other Paraclete," the Spirit of truth, will be among them. This interpretation is not without its difficulties but it attempts to take into account the distinction between Jesus and the Paraclete and to take seriously the departure of Jesus through his death and glorification. The gift of the Paraclete takes place *after* and *because of* the departure of Jesus. It is imprecise to claim that the Paraclete is not time-bound (e.g., O'Day, "'I Have Overcome'" 160–161). Jesus departs before the gift of the Spirit (cf. 7:39).

18. *I will come to you:* When will this coming of the departed Jesus take place? Most scholars opt for the resurrection while others refer to different forms of a lifegiving presence of the risen Jesus among the believers (cf. the survey of Aune, *Cultic Setting* 128–129). Migliasso, *La presenza* 207–226, unites the going, the coming, and the lifegiving presence of the absent Jesus to the redemptive event of the cross. The distinction between the physical Jesus who is departing and the "other Paraclete" who will be given must be maintained. The Greek Fathers, especially Cyril of Alexandria, identified Jesus with the Paraclete. See Anthony Casurella, *The Johannine Paraclete in the Church Fathers. A Study in the History of Exegesis.* BGBE 25. Tübingen: J. C. B. Mohr (Paul Siebeck), 1983, 43–45, 143–144. This position is nowadays universally rejected. The interpretation given disagrees with most contemporary scholarship, which argues that Jesus returns in the post-resurrection period. The "coming" of Jesus in v. 18 must not replace the gift of the Paraclete of vv. 16-17, but must be interpreted as the presence of Jesus, alive after death in his oneness with the Father, drawing the disciples into that life (vv. 19-20). This will take place *because of* the gift of the Spirit-Paraclete. Even though the Paraclete is only mentioned in vv. 16-17 the figure remains part of the message of vv. 18-24.

19. *yet a little while:* The use of the expression *eti mikron* in 12:35, warning "the Jews" of the need to walk in the light while it was still present, as well as the more positive use of the term with the disciples in 13:33, are both involved in 14:19. The usage still contains something of the "oppressive element" denied by Schnackenburg, *Gospel* 3:77–78.

you will live also: Although not mentioned in the immediate context, this "life" is linked to the gift of the Paraclete (cf. Müller, "Die Parakletenvorstellung" 51). On the disciples as "successor-agents" of the working of Jesus and bearers of the presence of the Father and the Son see Woll, "The Departure" 231–239. On Jesus' coming to the disciples in the worshiping community thanks to (and not despite) the presence of the Spirit-Paraclete see Aune, *Cultic Setting* 16–18, 112–114, 126–133. On baptism and eucharist in the Johannine community as the presence of the absent one see Moloney, *Belief in the Word* 109–114 (on 3:3-5) and *Signs and Shadows* 55–59 (on 6:51-58). For further thoughts on the way this teaching of Jesus might speak to a Christian community suffering the physical absence of Jesus see Müller, "Die Para-kletenvorstellung" 40–43.

20. *In that day:* The interpretation takes the traditional eschatological expression *en ekeinę̄ tę̄ hēmerą* as proleptically introducing eschatological language into the events of the end of Jesus' life, and thus as a reference to his hour and departure (cf. Haenchen, *John* 2:126–127). This produces what Brown, *Gospel* 2:640, rightly describes as "the period of Christian existence made possible by 'the hour.'" Most read it as indicating the resurrection.

21. *reveal myself to them:* The use of *emphanizein* ("to manifest," "to reveal") appears only here in the NT, and it "is an appropriate word since it is used of theophanies" (Barrett, *Gospel* 465).

22. *Judas (not Iscariot):* For possible connections between this otherwise unknown character in the Johannine story and other "Judases," or even Thaddeus, in the NT see Schnackenburg, *Gospel* 380–381.

23. *we will come:* The future tense of the verb must be given its full weight. It looks back to the *palin erchomai* of v. 3, which is properly read as a future (despite the present form of the verb) because of the general context of vv. 2-3 and because it follows *palin*. Both vv. 2-3 and v. 23 depend upon an end-time eschatology. This is not the case with the use of *erchomai* in v. 18. There the verb must be read as a present tense ("I am coming to you"), even though this generates considerable exegetical difficulty. Here the interpretation differs from the very helpful study of Aune, *Cultic Setting* 130–131. He associates the *monē* of v. 23 (where *oikia* does not appear) with the use of *oikia* and *monē* in v. 2, claiming that both are realized. They refer to "an individual believer who is the locus for the pneumatic dwelling of the Father and the Son." The interpretation given here questions the widespread interpretation of v. 23 "in terms of the mystical abiding of God with the believer" (Barrett, *Gospel* 466), or as a collapsing of history into a totally realized eschatology (cf. Bultmann, *Gospel* 613). The almost universal agreement that vv. 18-24 refer to the *present* coming of Jesus (and the Father) to the believer does away with the need for the Paraclete. Dettwiler, *Die Gegenwart* 191–202, interprets vv. 18-24 as addressing the Easter-coming of Jesus, but he dehistoricizes Easter, claiming that it does not refer to an event in the past but is "the experience of the love of God in Jesus" (195). This leads to an unsatisfactory explanation of the distinction between Jesus and the Paraclete as "not a difference between two separate entities, but two modes of Jesus' presence" (204). The elimination of all Johannine eschatological expectation and a real distinction between Jesus and the Paraclete, of which Dettwiler's exegesis is only one example, does not do justice to this passage and its interpretation within the message of the Gospel as a whole.

Jesus speaks encouragingly of his departure (vv. 25-31)

25. "These things I have spoken to you while I am still with you. 26. But the Paraclete, the Holy Spirit, whom the Father will send in my name,

will teach you all things and bring to your remembrance all that I have said to you.

27a. Peace I leave with you; my peace I give to you; not as the world gives do I give to you.

27b. Let not your hearts be troubled, neither let them be afraid. 28. You heard me say to you, 'I go away, and I am coming to you.' If you loved me you would have rejoiced, because I go to the Father; for the Father is greater than I. 29. And now I have told you before it takes place so that when it does take place you may believe. 30. I will no longer talk much with you, for the ruler of this world is coming. He has no power over me; 31. but I do as the Father has commanded me so that the world may know that I love the Father. Rise, let us go hence."

INTERPRETATION

Introduction to vv. 25-31. The final section of 14:1-31 returns to the theme of Jesus' departure. It can be divided into three parts:

1. *The Paraclete and the disciples (vv. 25-26).* Jesus' "speaking" to the disciples is coming to an end. In the future the Paraclete will recall everything Jesus has said, instructing them in all things.
2. *The gift of peace (v. 27a).* This ongoing revelation, recalling the words of Jesus and instructing in all things, is the reason for a further gift from Jesus: a unique peace that cannot be matched by anything the world can provide.
3. *Departure to the Father (vv. 27b-31).* Jesus' return to the Father should not trouble the disciples. He is telling them of the events that are about to happen, the clash between the ruler of this world and Jesus' revelation of love, so that when it takes place they will come to greater faith. The conflict will only make clear that Jesus loves the Father. It is time to depart.

The discourse began with words exhorting Jesus' disciples to avoid all consternation in the face of his imminent departure to the Father (vv. 1-3), and it closes with the same theme (vv. 27b-31). After a narrative that spoke openly of a gift of self in love within the context of betrayal, denial, and death (13:1-38), the discourse proper of 14:1–16:33 opened with Jesus' affirmation of his imminent departure through death (14:1-14, 25-31) and the remarkable consequences for disciples who love and believe (vv. 15-24). He promises them another Paraclete (vv. 16-17) and a peace that "the world" can never give (v. 27b).

The Paraclete and the disciples (vv. 25-26). The theme of departure (cf. vv. 1-6; vv. 18-24) returns. There are two "times" in the experience of the disciples: the *now* as Jesus speaks to them (v. 25) and the future time when the Paraclete, the Holy Spirit, sent by the Father in the name of Jesus, will be with them (v. 26). The Paraclete will replace Jesus' physical presence, teaching them all things and recalling for them everything he has said (v. 26). As Jesus is the Sent One of the Father (cf. 4:34; 5:23, 24, 30, 37; 6:38-40; 7:16; 8:16, 18, 26; 12:44-49), so is the Paraclete sent by the Father. The mission and purpose of the former Paraclete, Jesus (cf. 14:13-14), who speaks and teaches "his own" will continue into the mission and purpose of the "other Paraclete" (cf. v. 16) who teaches and brings back the memory of all that Jesus has said. The time of Jesus is intimately linked with the time after Jesus, and the accepted meaning of a departure has been undermined. The inability of the disciples to understand the words and deeds of Jesus will be overcome as they "remember" what he had said (cf. 2:22) and what had been written of him and done to him (cf. 12:16). The "remembering" will be the fruit of the presence of the Paraclete with the disciples in the in-between-time. In v. 16 Jesus focused on the inability of the world to know the Paraclete, but in v. 26 the gift of the Paraclete to "his own" is developed. As Jesus was *with* the disciples (v. 25), so will the Paraclete be *with* the disciples in the midst of hostility and rejection (v. 16). As the story has insisted that Jesus' teaching has revealed God to his disciples, so will the Paraclete recall and continue Jesus' revelation of God to the disciples (v. 26).

The gift of peace (v. 27a). Jesus is leaving a precious gift with his disciples: a peace that the world cannot give. The peace Jesus offers is *his* peace *(eirēnēn tēn emēn),* and it is this qualification that makes it something the world can never match. Earlier parts of the discourse return in this promise. The peace of Jesus flows from his oneness with his Father, his return to the Father from whence he came, and the authority he has with the Father, so that whatever is asked in his name will be given (cf. vv. 13-14, 16). The gift of peace, therefore, is intimately associated with the gift of the Spirit-Paraclete, the ongoing presence of Jesus in his absence (cf. vv. 16-17, 26), the source of the disciples' being loved by the Father and the Son, the agent for the ongoing revelation of both Jesus and the Father to the one who loves Jesus and keeps his commandments in the in-between-time (vv. 20-21). But the two gifts are not identical, as Jesus' departure leads to a oneness among the believer, Jesus, and the Father that transcends the Spirit, however much it may be the result of the abiding presence of the Spirit. Jesus' gift of peace is "from God," a gift that the quantifiable and fragile peace produced by the politics of this world can never match. In this peace (v. 27a) inspired and enlightened by the Spirit of Truth, the other Paraclete (vv. 16-17, 26), a community of disciples will perform "greater works" (v. 12) than Jesus himself, continuing the revelation of the Father and the Son (vv. 18-21).

Departure to the Father (vv. 27b-31). This section of the discourse closes recalling the words of Jesus that opened it: "Let not your hearts be troubled" (v. 27b; cf. v. 1a). Jesus has insisted that the disciples love him and hold fast to his word (cf. vv. 15, 21, 23-24) even though he is about to depart by means of a violent death (13:1-38). He reminds them of the departure in words that, like v. 27b, also recall the opening passage of the discourse (cf. vv. 2-3): "I go away, and I am coming *(erchomai)* to you" (v. 28a). Untroubled hearts, without fear in the face of his departure, are the guarantee that the disciples have heard his words and are holding fast to them. A new era is dawning and there is reason for joy. Their love for Jesus should lead them to rejoice in what will happen *for Jesus* in his departure to the Father who is greater than he. Jesus is the obedient Sent One of the Father (cf. 4:34; 5:23, 24, 30, 37; 6:38-40; 7:16; 8:16, 18, 26; 12:44-49), and it as the lesser figure, the Sent One, that he delights in the greater figure: the Sender (v. 28b). But the coming of the Sent One into the world and his return to the one who sent him are not irrelevant *for the disciples.* Even these words of Jesus are "less concerned with the relation between the Father and the Son, than with the relation between the Father and the Son and the Disciples" (Hoskyns, *Gospel* 464).

Jesus is telling them all these things while he is still with them *(nun:* "now") so that afterwards *(hotan genētai:* "when it does take place") they might believe (v. 29). There is an inevitability about the events of the departure that lie in the near future that must not be cause for fear or distress. Love for Jesus and belief in his word should make them occasions for further belief. The departure of Jesus will not be a moment of tragic desolation for the disciples (cf. vv. 1a, 18, 27b), but the beginning of the time of the Paraclete (vv. 16-17), a time of love (vv. 15, 21, 23-24, 28), belief (vv. 15, 21, 23-24, 29), joy (v. 28), and peace (v. 27a). Jesus' words to the disciples are coming to an end, as the departure is nigh (v. 30a). He will not speak much more to them, as the ruler of this world is coming. The violence that marked the closing moments of Jesus' ministry is still in the air. No doubt "the ruler of this world" *(ho tou kosmou archōn)* refers to the power of evil that opposes Jesus at a meta-historical level, the darkness, in the midst of which the light still shines (cf. 1:5). But a series of *archontes* have appeared throughout Jesus' story and they all come from the world of "the Jews" (cf. 3:1; 7:26, 48; 12:31, 42). Jesus' encounters with "the Jews" have been leading inevitably toward violence (cf. 5:18; 7:1, 19-20, 25; 8:37, 40; 11:53, 57), but in his moment of violent death and departure he will be "lifted up" (cf. 3:13-14; 8:28; 12:32-33), overcoming the powers of darkness (cf. 1:5; 11:50-53; 12:7, 10, 23-24, 31-33) to return to the Father (cf. 13:1; 14:28). The departure of Jesus is unlike any other departure. Despite all appearances to the contrary the prince of this world has no power over Jesus, whose departure is the result of his loving response to his Father (v. 30c; cf. 4:34; 5:30; 6:38; 10:15, 17-18). Despite the impotence of the prince of this world Jesus accepts his departure at the violent hands of his opponents to reveal to the world his love for his Father. He has spoken of his Father's love for him (cf. 3:35; 5:20; 10:17) and now he announces the reciprocation of that love. The time for words appears to have come to an end. Jesus' violent departure will make known to the world—by deeds rather than words—how much Jesus loves the Father (v. 31a), and it will be the definitive demonstration of his unconditional acceptance of the will of his Father (v. 30b).

As Jesus announces "Rise, let us go hence" (v. 31c) the reader expects the violent encounter announced in v. 30 to begin, but no such events follow Jesus' summons to rise from the table. The promise of v. 30a, "I will no longer speak much with you," is temporarily frustrated as Jesus and the disciples do not move and Jesus continues his discourse. Tension and delay enter the experience of the reader, who must work through further elements of a farewell discourse before encountering Jesus' departure to meet the powers of darkness (18:1-11). There is more that must be told, and thus it is important that the action be "put on hold" lest these words remain unsaid. More must be said concerning the future *of the disciples,* the difficulties and blessings of living the in-between-time. Similarly, more must be said concerning the significance of the events of the departure *for Jesus.* Jesus' summons *to depart* is a fitting conclusion to that section of the farewell discourse that has dealt with the fact of his departure and its consequences for himself and his disciples. The fact of the departure is now in place, and the action that will set the departure in motion is unavoidably imminent. However, the reader and the disciples experience a frustrating delay. They must wait and hear more from Jesus concerning his departure and their living the in-between-time. Despite v. 30a there are further words that must be spoken before the advent of the prince of this world (v. 30b).

Conclusion to 14:1-31. Jesus will depart through a loving gift of himself in death (13:1-38). This departure (14:1-6, 27b-31) must not be the cause of consternation or fear (vv. 1a, 27b) as Jesus is returning to the Father to initiate an in-between-time marked by his absence, but the presence of the Spirit-Paraclete will be with the disciples, continuing the revealing task of the absent Jesus (vv. 16-17, 26). Thus the departing Jesus is going away from his disciples and coming to them (cf. vv. 3, 18, 21, 23, 28). He has opened the way to the Father (vv. 6, 20-21). Jesus has restated a central message of the Gospel: his oneness with the Father makes his words and works the unique revelation of God (vv. 7-11). His departure will not bring this revelation to an end. The gift of the Paraclete will continue this revelation "forever" (v. 16); the oneness that exists between the Father and the Son will be revealed in the disciple who loves Jesus and keeps his commandments (vv. 18-21). The experience of the presence of the absent one during the in-between-time, therefore, undermines all the reactions one might expect from disciples of a leader who is about to depart by death. In place of consternation and fear (vv. 1a; 27b) the Spirit-filled disciples will experience love (vv. 15, 21, 23-24, 28), deepening belief (vv. 15, 21, 23-24, 29), and joy (v. 28). The gift of the departing Jesus to his disciples is his peace, a peace that cannot be matched by anything the world can provide (v. 27a).

But the departure of Jesus has not created a utopia. Living in the in-between-time, the period of the abiding presence of the Spirit-Paraclete, the reader is aware that discipleship is not only marked by love, belief, joy, and peace, swept into the oneness that unites Jesus and the Father. The Johannine community (and all subsequent Christian disciples) recognize that the hostility of the world to Jesus (cf. 14:17, 19, 22, 24, 30) has not disappeared despite Jesus' claim that the prince of this world has no power over him (v. 30c). It is this experience of the in-between-time that creates the tension in the closing sentences (vv. 30-31). Jesus announces that he will no longer talk much (v. 30a), but that the prince of this world is coming (v. 30b). The reader is caught in a tension between the revelation of God in the word of Jesus, now no longer spoken but available through the gift of the Paraclete (v. 26), and the ongoing presence of the prince of this world. This is the tension that lies behind Jesus' summons to rise (v. 31c) and face the prince of this world (v. 30c) and the need for further words from him that will guide his disciples through the conflicts and hatred of the in-between-time (cf. 15:1-16:3).

NOTES

26. *the Holy Spirit:* This is the only place in the NT where the expression "the Holy Spirit" is found. It probably passed into the Johannine text from early Christian tradition and had already been associated with the Paraclete before the Gospel took its final form. See Schnackenburg, *Gospel* 3:83.

    whom the Father will send in my name: In 14:16 the Father is described as sending the Paraclete *at Jesus' request.* In v. 26 the Father sends the Paraclete, the Holy Spirit, *in Jesus' name.* There is no contradiction in these affirmations, but development. The latter expression carries with it the idea of union and ongoing revelation. See de la Potterie, *La Vérité* 1:363–367.

    he will teach you all things and bring to your remembrance: The verbs "he will teach" *(didaxei)* and "bring to your remembrance" *(hypomnēsei)* are joined by an explicative "and" *(kai).* The teaching of the Holy Spirit recalls what Jesus has said, taking it deeper and farther into the memory and consciousness of the disciples of Jesus during the in-between-time. See de la Potterie, *La Vérité* 1:367–378. The earlier passages (2:22; 12:16) that looked forward to this "remembering" that will be the work of the Holy Spirit use the verb *mimnēskō*, while 14:26, in actually describing the action of the Paraclete, has a stronger form of the verb, *hypomimnēskō*. On "remembering" as part of the Jewish testament tradition see Bammel, "The Farewell Discourse" 108. Müller, "Die Parakletenvorstellung" 52–65, draws a number of parallels between the consoling, teaching presence of the Paraclete and the period after the death of the hero in the testaments. See *As. Mos.* (post-Moses); *LAB* 19 (post-Moses); *2 Bar.* 77 (post-Baruch); *4 Ezra* 14 (post-Ezra).

27. *my peace I give to you:* On the Messiah as the bringer of *šalôm* see Isa 9:6-7; 52:7; 57:19; Hag 2:9; Acts 10:36; Rom 14:17.

    Let not your hearts be troubled: The exact repetition of these words from Jesus (*mē tarassesthō hymōn hē kardia*) in vv. 1a and 27a is noticed by all commentators, and most see the repetition as forming a literary inclusion. In this structure v. 1 and v. 27 form the external limits of a literary unit. The present interpretation sees the expression as introducing both the first subsection (vv. 1-6), and the final subsection (vv. 27b-31) of 14:1-31. It is a repetition that marks the retuːɪ to the opening sentiments of the discourse as it closes (see also vv. 2-3 and v. 28).

28. *if you loved me:* Accepting with Brown, *Gospel* 2:654, that the conditional *ei ēgapate me* is unreal. This means that the love of the disciples at the moment is not the way it should be. It is possessive, and the disciples are loath to have Jesus depart. This could lead to an inappropriate sadness at Jesus' departure.

    for the Father is greater than I: The oneness that exists from before all time between God and the Word (1:1) and the neverending union between the Son and the Father (1:18) detract nothing from the Johannine Jesus' complete subordination of his mission to the will and design of the Father. See Brown, *Gospel* 2:655, and especially Barrett, "The Father" 19–36. As Barrett remarks, "The New Testament, and not least the Fourth Gospel, is in the end about God" (p. 34). On the difficulties 14:28 created in the early Church, and especially during the Arian crisis, see Schnackenburg, *Gospel* 3:85–86. There is a useful collection of patristic discussions of this verse in Westcott, *Gospel* 213–216.

30. *the ruler of this world:* For a recent discussion of the meta-historical possibilities behind this affirmation see Kovacs, "'Now Shall the Ruler of This World'" 228–240. On the possible link between the *archōn* of v. 30 and the various *archontes* mentioned earlier in the narrative see Moloney, *Signs and Shadows* 191–192.

31. *so that the world may know that I love the Father:* The use of "the world" (*ho kosmos*) in v. 31a does not have the negative connotations of vv. 17, 19, and 22. It refers to God's creation, offered life and salvation through the revelation of God in and through Jesus (cf. 3:16; 4:42).

    Rise, let us go hence: Most commentators make reference to the close parallel between v. 31c and Mark 14:42, but this does not explain its clumsiness (cf. Dettwiler, *Die Gegenwart* 39 n. 36). Despite Jesus' command there is no movement, and the discourse and prayer continue from 15:1 till 17:26. Only in 18:1 is there a rising and going hence. This is a notorious problem and doubtless reflects an earlier stage in the development of the discourse. Before the addition of chs. 15–17, 14:31 probably led directly into 18:1. But why did the final version of this generally sophisticated story leave these words from Jesus in 14:31c? What is a reader to make of it in the canonical Gospel? Most scholars settle for the literary-critical explanation, that the words originally led directly into 18:1. Some (e.g., Bultmann, *Gospel* 631; Bernard, *Commentary* 2:557) eliminate the problem by rearranging the sequence of the chapters. More ingenious has been the suggestion of Westcott, *Gospel* 211, that 14:31 has Jesus and the disciples leaving the room and chs. 15–17 are uttered before they cross the Kidron (cf. also Haenchen, *John* 1:128; Delebecque, *Jean* 189; Carson, *Gospel* 478–479). Behler, *Last Discourse* 131–132 (following Cyril of Alexandria) suggests that the words are addressed to all Christians, as well as the disciples, summoning them to conversion (cf. also Hoskyns, *Gospel* 465; Brodie, *Gospel* 470–471). Dodd, *Interpretation* 407 (cf. also his *Tradition* 72; Léon-Dufour, *Lecture* 3:144) argues that the words mean "up, let us march to meet him." This is a spiritual acceptance of the conflict that lies ahead, not physical movement, and it leads directly into ch. 15 (see the critique of Dettwiler, *Die Gegenwart* 37–39). For the position taken in the interpretation see the similar (but not identical) suggestions from Schnelle, "Die Abschiedsreden" 70–73; Kurz, *Farewell Addresses* 72 n. 59; Simoens, *La gloire* 128–129.

For Reference and Further Study

Barrett, C. K. "'The Father is Greater than I' (John 14:28). Subordinationist Christology in the New Testament." In idem, *Essays on John*. London: SPCK, 1982, 19–36.

Betz, Otto. *Der Paraklet. Fürsprecher im häretischen Spätjudentum im Johannesevangelium und in neu gefundenen gnostischen Schriften*. AGSU 2. Leiden: E. J. Brill, 1963.

Beutler, Johannes. *Habt keine Angst. Die erste Johanneische Abschiedsrede (Joh 14)*. SBS 116. Stuttgart: Katholisches Bibelwerk, 1984.

Brown, Raymond E. "The Paraclete in the Fourth Gospel," *NTS* 13 (1966–1967) 113–132.

Bruns, J. Edgar. "A Note on John 16:33 and I John 2:13-14," *JBL* 86 (1967) 451–453.

Dettwiler, Andreas. *Die Gegenwart* 111–212.

Dietzfelbinger, Christian. "Die grösseren Werke (Joh 14:12f.)," *NTS* 35 (1989) 27–47.

Fischer, Günter. *Die himmlischen Wohnungen: Untersuchungen zu Joh 14,2f.* Europäische Hochschulschriften XXIII/38. Bern: Herbert Lang; Frankfurt: Peter Lang, 1975.

Gundry, Robert. "In my Father's House are many *Monai* (John 14:2)," *ZNW* 58 (1967) 68–71.

Heitmüller, Wilhelm, *"Im Namen Jesu." Eine Sprach- u. religionsgeschichtliche Untersuchung zum Neuen Testament, Speziell zur altchristlichen Taufe*. FRLANT 2. Göttingen: Vandenhoeck & Ruprecht, 1903.

Johansson, Nils. *Parakletoi. Vorstellungen von Fürsprechern für die Menschen vor Gott in der alttestamentlichen Religion, im Spätjudentum und Urchristentum.* Lund: Gleerup, 1940.

Johnston, George. *The Spirit-Paraclete in the Gospel of John.* MSSNTS 12. Cambridge: Cambridge University Press, 1970.

Kovacs, J. L. "'Now Shall the Ruler of This World Be Driven Out': Jesus' Death as Cosmic Battle in John 12:20-36," *JBL* 114 (1995) 228–240.

McCaffrey, James. *The House with Many Rooms. The Temple Theme of Jn. 14,2-3.* AnBib 114. Rome: Biblical Institute Press, 1988.

Migliasso, S. *La presenza dell'Assente. Saggio di analisi lettarario-strutturale e di sintisi teologico di Gv. 13,31–14,31.* Rome: Pontificia Universitas Gregoriana, 1979.

Moloney, Francis J. *Glory not Dishonor,* Chapter 2.

Morgan-Wynne, J. E. "A Note on John 14.17b," *BZ* 23 (1979) 93–96.

Müller, U. B. "Die Parakletenvorstellungen im Johannesevangelium," *ZThK* 71 (1974) 31–77.

Niccaci, A. "Esame Letterario di Gv 14," *ED* 31 (1978) 209–214.

Oliver, W. H., and A. G. van Aarde, "The Community of Faith as Dwelling Place of the Father: *Basileia tou theou* as 'Household of God' in the Johannine Farewell Discourses," *Neotest.* 25 (1991) 379–400.

Porsch, Felix. "Der 'andere Paraklet'," *BiKi* 37 (1982) 133–138.

Segovia, Fernando F. *Farewell* 59–121.

Simoens, Yves. *La gloire* 105–129.

Windisch, Hans. *The Spirit-Paraclete in the Fourth Gospel.* Facet Books. Biblical Series 20. Philadelphia: Fortress, 1968.

Woll, D. B. "The Departure of the 'the Way': the First Farewell Discourse in the Gospel of John," *JBL* 99 (1980) 225–239.

iii. To Abide, to Love, and to Be Hated (15:1–16:3)

Introduction to John 15:1–16:3. Most major commentators and editions of the NT divide 16:4 into two parts. Verse 4a serves as a conclusion to 15:1–16:4a, and 16:4b opens the final section of the discourse proper: 16:4b-31. Yet, despite the massive support for 16:4a as the conclusion to the literary unit of 15:1–16:4a there are indications that a major break takes place at 16:3, and that 16:4 introduces the section 16:4-33 (cf. Simoens, *La gloire,* 132–139; Moloney, "The Structure and Message" 35–37, 41–44).

1. A theme basic to the latter section of 15:1–16:3 is stated in 15:21 and restated in 16:3. Read within the broader argument of the discourse this formula suggests closure in both 15:21 and 16:3:

> But all this they will do *(tauta panta poiēsousin)* to you on my account, because they do not know *(hoti ouk oidasin)* the one who sent me (15:21). And they will do this *(tauta poiēsousin)* because they have not known *(hoti ouk egnōsan)* the Father nor me (16:3).

In both cases the *tauta* ("these things") looks back across the previous words of Jesus and brings a subsection to a close.

2. The expression *tauta lelalēka hymin hina* ("these things I have said to you that") is found at the end of 15:1-11 and toward the end of the section on hatred in 16:1. The second of these expressions, in 16:1, is the literary link that scholars use to close the discourse in 16:4a, where the expression is again found. Most see 16:1 and 4a as forming an inclusion, making 16:1-4a the final subsection of 15:1–16:4a. But the use of the expression in v. 4a is prefaced by an adversative *alla* ("but"), and perhaps begins a new train of thought. The expression, without the adversative, reappears in 16:33. It is possible that 16:4a and 33 form an inclusion, with the adversative *alla* in v. 4a separating 16:4-33 from 15:1–16:3. This would allow the *tauta lelalēka hymin* of v. 4 to form an inclusion with the *tauta lelalēka hymin* of v. 6, and thus vv. 4-6 would be the first subunit of 16:4-33. On these formal grounds the analysis that follows will accept that 15:1–16:3 forms a discrete literary unit followed by 16:4-33.

The outstanding feature of the opening section of 15:1–16:3 is the use of the verb *menein*, "abide." It is fundamental to the metaphor of the vine and the branches (vv. 1-8), and is present in various forms across vv. 1-11 (cf. v. 4 [3x], v. 5, v. 6, v. 7 [2x], v. 9, v. 10 [2x]). Most scholars are fascinated by the metaphor of the vine, but it serves as a vehicle to articulate the importance of abiding. The first section of this part of the discourse is not determined by the metaphor of the vine but by the theme of "abiding" across vv. 1-11. Many scholars see vv. 1-17 as a unit, but due weight must be given to the obvious inclusion between v. 12 and v. 17:

> This is my commandment, that you love one another (v. 12).
> This I command you, to love one another (v. 17).

The content of vv. 1-11 is determined by the verb "abide," and vv. 12-17 are framed by the command to "love." In 15:18–16:3 a theme of hatred and rejection emerges, matching by contrast the theme of abiding in vv. 1-11. The shape of this central section of 13:1–17:26 can thus be summarized as follows:

    i. *To abide in Jesus (15:1-11).* The need to abide in Jesus so as to bear much fruit. The Father prunes the branches. A union of love flows from the Father and Jesus to the disciples.

    ii. *The commandment to love (15:12-17).* The new situation of the disciples, which results from what Jesus has done for them, demands that they love one another as he has loved them.

    iii. *To be hated by the world (15:18–16:3).* The reality of the world's hatred for Jesus and the Father that leads to the hatred of the world for the disciples of Jesus.

John 15:1–16:3 is the centerpiece of the whole of the farewell discourse (13:1–17:26). It is marked by a tripartite literary structure, at the center of which is a passage dominated by the command to love as Jesus has loved (15:12-17). The three sections of this structure also reflect experiences crucial to the Johannine understanding of what it means to be disciples of Jesus: to abide in Jesus (15:1-11), to love one another as Jesus has loved them (15:12-17), and to be hated (15:18–16:3), a point missed by the many studies that have traced a variety of hands and redactions in 15:1–16:4a (e.g., Segovia's two early articles, predating *Farewell*, "The Theology and Provenance" 115–128, and "John 15:18–16:4a" 210–230).

For ease of consultation and clarity the translation and notes for vv. 1-11, vv. 12-17, and 15:18–16:3 will be provided separately. John 13:1-38 and 14:1-31 are dedicated to the themes of making God known (13:1-38) and departure (14:1-31). John 16:4-33 is in its own turn dedicated to the theme of departure and 17:1-26 to making God known. But 15:1–16:3 develops three independent themes at the center of the discourse: to abide (15:1-11), to love (15:12-17), and to be hated (15:18–16:3). Further subdivisions of the material within each of these sections will be presented in a brief introduction to each section (cf. Simoens, *La gloire* 132–150). The literature For Reference and Further Study of 15:1–16:3 will be gathered after the commentary on 15:18–16:3.

a) *To Abide* (15:1-11)

1. I am the true vine and my Father is the vinedresser. 2. Every branch of mine that bears no fruit he takes away, and every branch that does bear fruit he prunes that it may bear more fruit. 3. You are already made clean by the word that I have spoken to you. 4. Abide in me, and I in you. As the branch cannot bear fruit by itself unless it abides in the vine, neither can you unless you abide in me. 5a. I am the vine, you are the branches.

5b. Those who abide in me and I in them bear much fruit because apart from me you can do nothing. 6. Whoever does not abide in me is cast forth as a branch and withers; and the branches are gathered, thrown into the fire, and burned. 7. If you abide in me and my words abide in you, ask whatever you will and it shall be done for you. 8. By this my Father is glorified, because you bear much fruit and so prove to be my disciples.

9. Inasmuch as the Father has loved me, so I have loved you; abide in my love. 10. If you keep my commandments you will abide in my love, just as I have kept my Father's commandments and abide in his love. 11.

These things I have spoken to you that my joy may be in you, and that your joy may be complete.

INTERPRETATION

Introduction to 15:1-11. Many scholars trace the metaphor of the vine as far as v. 8, as the theme of the relationship between the Father and the Son becomes dominant in v. 9 (e.g., Segalla, "La struttura chiastica" 129–131). A major monograph has suggested that vv. 1-10 form a unit, partly on the basis of chiastic structures in vv. 9-10 and 4b-5 (Borig, *Weinstock* 68–76). But the frequent use of the verb *menein* determines the literary unity of vv. 1-11, rather than the metaphor of the vine. There are three subsections in vv. 1-11:

1. *Abiding in Jesus (vv. 1-5a).* The close parallel between v. 1 ("I am the true vine") and v. 5a ("I am the vine") mark off this section that stresses the importance of abiding in Jesus.
2. *The results of abiding and not abiding in Jesus (vv. 5b-8).* A parallel similar to the one that formed vv. 1-5a is found at the beginning (v. 5b: "Those who abide in me") and near the end (v. 7: "If you abide in me") of a section that deals with the fruits of both abiding and not abiding.
3. *Abiding in the love of Jesus (vv. 9-11).* Although there are no formal indications that this section is a literary unit, the theme of "abiding" is developed further: to abide in Jesus means to abide in his love.

Each of these three sections develops Jesus' teaching on "abiding," but approaches it from a slightly different perspective: the need to abide (vv. 1-5a), the fruits of abiding (vv. 5b-8), and abiding in the love of Jesus (vv. 9-11). The introduction of the theme of love in vv. 9-11 enables the easy passage from the section devoted to abiding (vv. 1-11) into Jesus' command that the disciples are to love one another as he has loved them (vv. 12-17).

Abiding in Jesus (vv. 1-5a). Jesus claims: "I am the true vine" (v. 1a: *egō eimi hē ampelos hē alēthinē*). Jesus' "I am" statement followed by a complement points to what he does by means of his saving revelation (cf. 4:26; 6:35, 51; 8:12; 9:5; 10:7, 9, 11, 14; 14:6). He provides the unique source of life and fruitfulness. The use of the adjective "true," placed emphatically at the end of the affirmation, contains a hint of polemic. Israel has been described as a vine (cf. Jer 2:21; Ezek 19:10-14; Ps 80:18-19; Isa 27:2-6), but if Jesus is the *true* vine, what can be said of the vine that is Israel? Jesus introduces the Father, the vinedresser *(ho geōrgos)* who cares for the well-being and fruitfulness of the vine. It is the Father who is ultimately responsible for all that Jesus does and makes known. The metaphor of the vine and the vinedresser is best understood in light of the everyday reality of vines and vine-keeping. Such practices bear upon what Jesus is saying about the Father and himself, and ultimately about discipleship. The Father cares for the fruitful branch on the vine, pruning it so that it will become more fruitful, and he destroys the branch that bears no fruit by separating it from the vine (v. 2). Jesus is the lifegiving vine but it is the Father who promotes growth and decides on the destruction of the unfruitful branches.

From this description of the situation of Jesus, the Father, and the branches Jesus addresses the disciples directly: "You are already made clean" (v. 3a: *katharoi este*). The disciples at the table, listening to the discourse, are fruitful branches, united to the vine and pruned by having heard the word of the Sent One of the Father. Because they have heard and accepted the word of Jesus the pruning process is already in place. The indication of 13:10 that the disciples were all "clean" (*katharoi*) is repeated, but now they are told that this cleanliness comes from the word of Jesus. Jesus has established the essential frame of reference for vv. 1-11 in vv. 1-3: Jesus is the vine, the Father is the vinedresser, and disciples, made clean by the word of Jesus, can be fruitful branches of the vine.

However, this lifegiving bond with the vine must not be taken for granted. The prophecies of the betrayal of Judas and the denials of Peter (cf. 13:2, 11, 18-20, 21-30, 36-38) have shown that "the life of union is begun but not perfected" (Westcott, *Gospel* 216). It is not enough to be with him and to have received his word; they must abide in him and he will abide in them (v. 4a: *meinate en emoi kagō en hymin*). There must be an ongoing lifegiving mutuality generated by the disciples' union with Jesus and Jesus' union with them. The metaphor of the vine continues as Jesus clarifies the need for abiding. No branch can ever bear fruit if it is separated from the vine, and no disciple will ever bear fruit alone *(aph' heautou)*. Abiding in Jesus is the *sine qua non* of fruitfulness (v. 4c: *ean mē en emoi menēte*). This first subsection closes as Jesus returns to his opening words: "I am the vine, you are the branches" (v. 5a). The disciples are the branches but the description of Jesus as the *true* vine (v. 1a) remains unexplained.

The results of abiding and not abiding in Jesus (vv. 5b-8). In v. 5bc Jesus repeats the message of v. 4. The metaphor of the vine is applied explicitly to Jesus and the disciple. It is only by mutual abiding, the disciple in Jesus and Jesus in the disciple, that fruitfulness comes. But the disciples are now told that separated from Jesus they can do nothing *(ou dynasthe poiein ouden)*. Union with Jesus with its consequent fruitfulness is not a matter of enjoying the oneness that exists between the disciple and the master; it also consists of *doing something,* and without Jesus this is impossible. To bear fruit (v. 4b) means to do something (v. 5c). That "something" has already been summarized in the command to love, which

Jesus taught would be the hallmark of his disciples (cf. 13:34-35). Two possibilities have been stated in v. 5bc and they are further spelled out in vv. 6-7. Verse 6 describes the result of a disciple's not abiding in Jesus. Such a disciple is "cast out" *(eblēthē)* and withered *(exēranthē)*. The verbs are in the gnomic aorist tense, expressing a truth valid for all time. Jesus is warning not only the people at table with him. Like the branch that the Father takes away in v. 2, any disciple not abiding in Jesus is "cast forth as a branch and withers" (v. 6a). The use of the passive voice continues as the lifeless branch is described as gathered and burned (v. 6b). This is the only possible end for dead wood no longer attached to its source of life. The positive results of abiding in Jesus are described in v. 7. The disciples' abiding in him and his words' abiding in them (cf. v. 3) will produce a situation in which whatever they ask will be done for them. The word of Jesus, the revelation of God, abides and gives life to the disciple who abides in Jesus.

After the introduction of the Father as the vinedresser in v. 1 and the description of his fundamental role in v. 2 the passive verbs in vv. 6-7 suggest that it is the Father who destroys (v. 6) and does whatever the disciple asks (v. 7). This is confirmed in v. 8. To abide in Jesus is to make the *doxa* of the Father visible. Disciples who live in mutuality with Jesus can be *identified* as such, bearing much fruit. But it is not Jesus who is glorified by this fruitfulness; it is the Father. "There is only one mission shared by the Son and his disciples. In this one mission the Father is glorified" (Brown, *Gospel* 2:662). The revelation of God, made possible because of the mutual abiding of the disciple in Jesus and Jesus in the disciple, will produce true disciples involved in the mission of Jesus: "and so prove to be my disciples." Earlier words on the criterion for discipleship return: mutual love that leads to public recognition that they are disciples of Jesus (13:34-35).

Abiding in the love of Jesus (vv. 9-11). The explicit reference to the Father, glorified in the fruitful oneness between Jesus and the disciples in v. 8, leads into vv. 9-11. The Johannine story of Jesus has always looked to God, the Father of Jesus, as the source and goal of all Jesus is and does (cf. 1:18). Jesus announces to the disciples that the source of his love for them is the love the Father has for him (v. 9a). A unity of love bonds the Sender and the Sent One (cf. 3:35; 5:20; 10:17; 14:31). Inasmuch as *(kathōs)* the Father loves Jesus, Jesus commands his disciples to become part of that oneness by abiding in his love (v. 9b); but this abiding must be shown in a way of life determined by the commandments of Jesus. To be a disciple abiding in the love of Jesus means to "do" something, and that "doing" is determined by the commandments of Jesus (v. 10a). Jesus is not the source of this abiding love, as it flows from the relationship of love that exists between the Father and the Son, the result of Jesus' having kept the

Father's commandments and abiding in his love (v. 10b). Jesus' life is based on his having kept the commandments of God, having done the will of the Father (perfect tense: *teterēka*), evident in his ongoing abiding in the love of the Father (present tense: *menō*). The disciples are to repeat, in their relationship with Jesus, what Jesus has always had with the Father: a loving mutuality shown by the unconditional observance of his commandments.

This section of the discourse closes as Jesus announces, "these things I have spoken to you that" (v. 11a: *tauta lelalēka hymin hina*). The reason for Jesus' words on abiding, loving, and keeping the commandments is that the joy that Jesus has from his relationship of oneness and obedience with the Father might also be with the disciples. Then the joy of the disciples will be complete (v. 11b: *hē chara hymōn plērōthē*). There has been a gradual movement through the metaphor of the vine, which introduced the theme of abiding (cf. vv. 4, 5a, 5b, 6, 7), into an insistence that to abide in Jesus means to abide in his love (vv. 9-11). The disciples' abiding in the love of Jesus and keeping his commandments unites them with Jesus' response to the Father in whose love he abides, and whose commandments he keeps. Keeping the commandments of Jesus inserts the disciples into "the chain of love" (cf. Segovia, *Farewell* 148–163). But what are the commandments, and how does one keep them? Jesus turns to these questions in the section that follows (vv. 12-17).

NOTES

1. *I am the true vine:* The image of the vine is used to speak both negatively (cf. Jer 2:21; Ezek 19:12-14) and positively (cf. Isa 27:2-6; Ezek 19:10-11; Ps 80:18-19; Qoh 24:27; 2 Bar 39:7) of Israel. See Jaubert, "L'image" 93–96. For the widespread rabbinic use of the vine to describe Israel see Str-B 2:563–564.

   There is little agreement on the literary form of the passage that uses the vine. Bultmann, *Gospel* 524 n. 4, objects to the use of the expression "allegory." Brown, *Gospel* 2:558–569, claims that vv. 1-6 are best described as a *mashal*. Borig, *Weinstock* 21–23, describes vv. 1-10 as a *Bildrede*. Barrett, *Gospel* 470–471, suggests that it is a Johannine use of traditional material that defies classification. The expression "metaphor" (cf. Carson, *Gospel* 511–513) will be used, as this allows for "oscillation between literal and pictorial language" (Bultmann). See the survey in Segovia, *Farewell*, 132–135; van der Watt, "'Metaphorik'" 68–71.

   and my Father is the vinedresser: A number of commentators remark that the subordinate role of the Father is somewhat un-Johannine. However, the role of the Father as vinedresser is not subordinate. There would be no life in the vine and no care for the branches (cf. v. 2) if the vinedresser did not tend it. See Westcott, *Gospel* 217; Heise, *Bleiben* 82–83.

3. *You are already made clean by the word:* To be made clean by the word of Jesus involved a receptivity to the revelation of God in Jesus. See Brown, *Gospel* 2:676–677; Lightfoot, *Gospel* 283.

   Although vv. 1-2 have spoken of Jesus, the Father, the vine, and the branches they have prepared for the introduction of the disciples in v. 3 and all that follows in vv. 3-11. On the theme of relationship among God, the departing hero, and the disciples in the Jewish testament tradition see Cortès, *Los Discursos* 436–438.

4. *Abide in me and I in you:* The fundamental meaning of the use of the verb *menein* across vv. 1-11 is already evident in its first appearance in v. 4: mutuality and reciprocity. On the reciprocal nature of the abiding see Borig, *Weinstock* 215–236. After this first use of the verb *menein* it appears ten times in vv. 1-11 and is the unifying feature of that section of the discourse. Some (e.g., Becker, *Evangelium* 2:482; Morris, *Gospel* 592–600) use the presence of the verb to unite vv. 1-17, as it reappears in v. 16. This ignores the inclusive nature of vv. 12 and 17. On the difference between v. 16 and vv. 1-11 see Heise, *Bleiben* 81–82.

6. *cast forth as a branch and withers:* The warnings of v. 6 reflect the reality of failure among members of the community addressed by the Gospel. See, among many, Schnackenburg, *Gospel* 3:101. The gnomic aorist expresses a truth valid for all time and all potential disciples. See BDF 171, § 333,1. For this interpretation of v. 6 see Brown, *Gospel* 2:661; Léon-Dufour, *Lecture* 3:170. Some suggest that the aorist expresses the immediacy of the consequences of not abiding (e.g., Bauer, *Johannesevangelium* 191), while others argue that its use is proleptic after an implied condition: that is, that the result is so certain it is described as having already happened (e.g., Lagrange, *Evangile* 404; cf. ZGB, § 257).

   thrown into the fire and burned: As throughout the use of the metaphor it is best explained by making the link with everyday practice. Destruction by fire is the usual practice with the dry wood cut off from the vine. It does not refer to an eschatological fire as some (e.g., Bernard *Commentary* 2:482) would maintain.

8. *and so prove to be my disciples:* The future tense is called for, reading with Sinaiticus and Alexandrinus (Barrett, *Gospel* 475; Segovia, *Farewell* 147 n. 36), against the well-attested subjunctive of Vaticanus, Claromontanus, Koridethi, and perhaps $\mathfrak{P}^{66}$.

9. *As the Father has loved me:* On *kathōs* as "inasmuch as" see BDF 236, § 453, 2. The introduction of the Father in v. 8 makes for an excellent passage into v. 9. See Schnackenburg, *Gospel* 3:103.

11. *your joy may be complete:* The expression *hē chara hymōn plērōthē* is best rendered "your joy may be complete" rather than ". . . be full." There is a sense of the disciples' joy being all that it should be. See Segovia, *Farewell* 153.

b) *The Command to Love* (15:12-17)

12. "This is my commandment, that you love one another as I have loved you. 13. No one has greater love than this: to lay down one's life for one's friends. 14. You are my friends if you do what I command you. 15. No longer do I call you servants, for the servant does not know what the master is doing; but I have called you friends, for all that I have heard from my Father I have made known to you. 16. You did not choose me, but I chose you and appointed you that you should go and bear fruit and that your fruit should abide, so that whatever you ask the Father in my name, he may give it to you.
17. This I command you, to love one another."

INTERPRETATION

Introduction to vv. 12-17. This section is determined by the statement and restatement of the command to love in v. 12 and v. 17. However, the first statement of the commandment continues the theme that had been first broached in vv. 9-10: the disciples are to love one another because of Jesus' prior love for them (vv. 12-14). Before restating the commandment Jesus indicates to the disciples that their situation has changed because they have been loved and chosen (vv. 15-16). There are, therefore, three subsections to vv. 12-17:

1. *The commandment to love as Jesus loved (vv. 12-14).* The disciples are to respond to the command of Jesus (vv. 12, 14) by loving one another unto death (v. 15), as Jesus has loved them.
2. *Jesus' love has established a new relationship (vv. 15-16).* Jesus has given his life for his friends, and thus they are no longer servants but loved and chosen ones of Jesus.
3. *The commandment to love (v. 17).* It is as friends and no longer servants that the disciples are to love one another.

At the very center (15:12-17) of the Johannine account of Jesus' final encounter with his disciples (13:1–17:26) he tells them of the new situation that flows from their having been loved and chosen (vv. 15-16). They are to love one another as a result of the initiative of Jesus (vv. 12-14, 17).

The commandment to love as Jesus has loved (vv. 12-14). Jesus' command that the disciples love one another is not new (cf. 13:34-35). They are to love with a love that is continuous and lifelong (v. 12a: *agapate:* present subjunctive), and the measure of their love for one another is the supreme act of Jesus' love for them (v. 12b: *ēgapēsa:* aorist). The symbol of the self-gift of Jesus in the footwashing (13:4-17) and the gift of the morsel (13:21-38), acting out Jesus' love for his own *eis telos* (13:1), comes into play.

Jesus' love is the *hypodeigma* (cf. 13:15) of all subsequent Christian love. In vv. 12-14 Jesus recalls the *quality* of his love. The greatest of all loves (v. 13: *meizona tautēs agapēn oudeis echei*) is shown by one who lays down his or her life for friends *(tōn philōn autou).* Jesus loves without limit, laying down his life for the disciples (cf. 10:11, 14, 18) despite the fact that they are still locked in their ignorance, one of them is a betrayer, and another will deny him (13:1-38). Past and present failures will not be held against them. In loving his recalcitrant *philoi* Jesus is responding to the commands of his Father (cf. v. 10). They will respond to his love by doing what he commands them (v. 14): by loving one another as he has loved them (v. 12; 13:34).

Jesus' love has established a new relationship (vv. 15-16). If vv. 12-14 told of the *quality* of Jesus' love, vv. 15-16 insist on the *priority* of his love for his disciples. The disciples, through no act of the will or physical effort on their part, have been drawn into a new relationship (v. 15). They are not servants *(douloi)* in a relationship of dependence on a master. Never throughout the Gospel have they been called "servants." They have always been followers, people who have been going through a learning process as disciples *(mathētai)* of Jesus. They are not *douloi* depending on the whim of a master, but *philoi,* intimate and equal associates of Jesus who loves them without limit (cf. 13:1: *eis telos*).

These disciples are told, "You did not choose me, but I chose you" (v. 16a). At the heart of the account of the footwashing and the gift of the morsel Jesus announced: "I know whom I have chosen. . . . The one who receives anyone whom I send receives me; and the one who receives me receives the one who sent me" (13:19b, 20). Jesus has chosen disciples and established them *(kai ethēka hymas)* as the ones who will be sent out to bear fruit that will endure (v. 16b). The initiative lies with Jesus, but in the end the disciples must turn to the Father in their need, asking in the name of Jesus (v. 16c). As the ongoing mission of Jesus, now entrusted to the disciples, is described, language taken from the metaphor of the vine returns. The disciples are the *philoi* of Jesus for whom he lays down his life in love (v. 13), and they are the branches abiding in the vine (v. 5a), bearing much fruit (v. 5b, 8), a fruit that will endure. They, in the name of Jesus who has chosen them and commissioned them to "go and bear fruit" (v. 16b), will turn to the Father (v. 16c; cf. v. 10). As they bear fruit, continuing the mission of the one who chose them, all they ask will be granted to them (v. 16c). The oneness that exists between Jesus and the Father will also be enjoyed by the disciples chosen (v. 16a) and sent out (v. 16b) by Jesus (cf. 13:18-20).

The commandment to love (v. 17). The repetition of v. 12 in v. 17 is not only an obvious literary closure. Jesus' words on his choice of the disciples and their being established as the bearers of a lasting fruitfulness

(v. 16) in their new situation as friends (v. 15) concludes with a restatement of the commandment that is the essential condition for their status.
They must accept the commandment of Jesus. They must love one another (v. 17).

Across the latter part of Jesus' ministry a close connection was made
between Jesus' death and the revelation of the glory of God (cf. 11:4;
12:23). This connection has been made even more explicit at the final meal
(cf. 13:18-20, 31-32). At that meal Jesus focused on his gift of himself unto
death for the disciples (cf. 13:1, 1-17, 21-38). The suggestion is that Jesus'
death will be the manifestation of love, the revelation of God, and the
glorification of the Son (cf. 11:4; 12:23; 13:18-20, 31-32). The disciples have
been told that by abiding in Jesus and bearing much fruit they will join
with Jesus in the glorification of the Father (cf. 15:8). They have been chosen by Jesus to bear much fruit (v. 16ab). But the disciples, the friends of
Jesus whom he loves in a way that cannot be surpassed (v. 13; cf. 13:1),
must continue the same quality of love in their love for one another (vv.
12, 17; cf. 13:34). The quality of their love will mark them out as disciples
of Jesus (13:35; cf. 15:8).

NOTES

12. Many (e.g., Bultmann, *Gospel* 546–547; Segovia, *Farewell* 125–127; Talbert,
    Reading John 211–215; Schnackenburg, *Gospel* 3:113; Niccaci, "Gv 15–16"
    43–53; Onuki, *Gemeinde und Welt* 119–130) regard vv. 1-17 as a literary unit
    while others (e.g., Tolmie, *Jesus' Farewell* 212–213) have divisions that ignore
    the inclusion created by v. 12 and v. 17 (Tolmie suggests vv. 1-8, 9-15, 16-17).
    Dettwiler, *Die Gegenwart* 80, 86–100, notes the importance of the inclusion but
    prefers to read vv. 1-17 as a unit, with vv. 9-11 introducing the love theme of
    vv. 12-17.

    This is my commandment: A feature of the farewell genre is the renewal of cove-
    nant. This is particularly strong in this central section of Johannine discourse,
    however conditioned it is by the Johannine concept of a new covenant of love.
    See Kurz, "Luke 22:14-38" 262–263; Cortès, *Los Discursos* 434–443. On the love
    command see Collins, "'A New Commandment'" 249–252.

13. *No one has greater love than this:* The interpretation links vv. 12-13. This read-
    ing makes v. 13 primarily christological, a description of Jesus' love for his
    disciples, spelling out v. 12d (cf. 13:1). It is further indication of how much the
    disciples must love one another (v. 12a). Some would link v. 13 with vv. 14-15,
    and others regard it as a later insertion. For the discussion, and the position
    adopted here, see Knöppler, *Die theologia Crucis* 209–210, and especially
    Thyen, "'Niemand hat grössere Liebe'" 467–481.

15. *No longer do I call you servants:* The Greek word *doulos* can refer to either a
    slave or a servant. Whichever translation one adopts, the question of a radi-

cal change of status from a dependent *doulos* to an equal *philos* is clear. Lee, "John XV 14" 260, makes a link with the "friend of the bridegroom" in 3:29.

16. *appointed you:* Some critics read v. 16 as the Johannine version of the appointment of the foundational disciples. It applies to all disciples of Jesus. For a survey of this discussion and support for the application of Jesus' words to all disciples see, among others, Léon-Dufour, *Lecture* 3:182–185.

17. *love one another:* The insistence on the love command (vv. 12, 17), repeating 13:34-35 (and 13:15), is a most obvious link with 13:1-38. There are many other links, some of which will be indicated in both the interpretation and the notes. On this see Dettwiler, *Die Gegenwart* 60–110, and his summary on pp. 107–110. For Dettwiler 15:1-17 is a *"relecture"* of 13:1-17, 34-35. Some scholars link John 13 and 15 in an unwarranted attempt to trace eucharistic language and practice in 15:1-11 (e.g., Hoskyns, *Gospel* 474–479; Dodd, *Interpretation* 138–139, 411–412, and especially Sandvik, "Joh 15 als Abendmahlstext" 223–228).

c) *To Be Hated by the World (15:18–16:3)*

18. If the world hates you, know that it has hated me before it hated you. 19. If you were of the world, the world would love its own; but because you are not of the world, but I chose you out of the world, therefore the world hates you. 20. Remember the word that I said to you, 'Servants are not greater than their master.' If they persecuted me they will persecute you; if they kept my word they will keep yours also. 21. But all this they will do to you on my account, because they do not know the one who sent me.
22. If I had not come and spoken to them they would not have sin; but now they have no excuse for their sin. 23. Anyone who hates me hates my Father also. 24. If I had not done among them the works that no one else did, they would not have sin; but now they have seen and hated both me and my Father. 25. It is to fulfill the word that is written in their law, 'They hated me without a cause.'
26. But when the Paraclete comes, whom I shall send to you from the Father, even the Spirit of truth who proceeds from the Father, he will bear witness to me; 27. and you also are witnesses because you have been with me from the beginning. 16:1. I have said all this to you to keep you from falling away. 2. They will put you out of the synagogues; indeed, the hour is coming when those who kill you will think that by doing so they are offering worship to God. 3. And they will do this because they have not known the Father, nor me.

INTERPRETATION

Introduction to 15:18–16:3. This section of the discourse, which deals throughout with the issues of hatred and rejection, is marked by three subsections.

1. Two conditional clauses (opening with *ei*) followed by a principal statement appear on either side of an imperative in vv. 18-21. The conditionals are obvious: "If *(ei)* the world . . . If *(ei)* you were of the world" (vv. 18-19); "If *(ei)* they persecuted me . . . If *(ei)* they kept my word" (vv. 20b-21). Between these conditionals followed by principal statements lies the imperative: "Remember the word that I said to you, 'Servants are not greater than their master'" (v. 20a).
2. A parallel structure appears in vv. 22-25. Conditionals (opening with *ei*) and a principal clause leading into a description of the present situation ("now" [*nun*] is used in each description) surround a central statement. Again the conditionals are obvious: "If *(ei)* I had not come . . . but now *(nun)* they have no excuse" (v. 22); "If *(ei)* I had not done . . . but now *(nun)* they have seen and hated" (v. 24). Between the conditionals lies the statement: "Anyone who hates me hates my Father also" (v. 23). The perfect symmetry of this subsection is disturbed only by Jesus' telling his disciples that this hatred fulfills the word of the Law (v. 25).
3. The formal elements that highlight vv. 18-21 and vv. 22-25 are not present in 15:26–16:3. The introduction of words on the Paraclete (vv. 26-27) adds a positive note to an otherwise negative section. However, themes from 15:18-21 return. Jesus describes the situation of the disciples: "because you have been with me from the beginning" (v. 27b) in a way that recalls 19b: "because you are not of the world." He insists in both the first and the final subsection that the disciples live by his word. "I have said all this to keep you from falling away" (16:1) recalls 15:20a: "Remember the word that I said to you." The closing statement of vv. 18-21, "because they do not know the one who sent me" (v. 21; cf. vv 23, 24b) returns as the closing statement of 15:26–16:3: "because they have not known the Father, nor me" (16:3).

On the basis of these syntactic and thematic indications the following internal literary structure can be suggested for 15:18–16:3:

1. *A first explanation for the hatred of the world (vv. 18-21).* There is a fundamental reason for the disciples' experience of hatred and rejection: the world has hated Jesus, the Sent One of the Father, and thus it will hate his disciples.

2. *The results of the world's hatred (vv. 22-25).* The hatred of Jesus and the Father leaves those who hate in their sin. They are accused of hating without cause and thus fulfilling the Scriptures.
3. *A further explanation for the hatred of the world (15:26–16:3).* The rejection of the disciples of Jesus takes place because certain people know neither the Father nor Jesus. A situation of sin continues in the rejection of the revelation of God that continues in the witness of the Paraclete and the Spirit-directed disciples.

The disciples have been instructed on the fundamental importance of "abiding" in Jesus and of Jesus' "abiding" in them (15:1-11). This teaching on mutuality and reciprocity is matched by Jesus' indications of the hatred, rejection, persecution, and death the disciples must experience because the world has hated both Jesus and his Father (15:18–16:3).

A first explanation for the hatred of the world (vv. 18-21). If the world hates the disciples this is but the logical consequence of its prior hatred of Jesus (v. 18). This hatred has led to a decision that Jesus must be slain (cf. 11:49-50, 53). The world has never accepted that Jesus comes from God to make God known to a world that has its own ideas about who the Christ should be (cf., for example, 12:34) and how one should relate to God (cf., for example, 9:28-29). If the disciples had been happy to reject Jesus' word and accept the world-view of his opponents they would be of the world. They would be loved, not hated, by the world (v. 19). This condition has not been realized in the story of the disciples. Jesus has associated the disciples with his own being "not of this world" (cf. 8:21-23), and thus the world hates them. He has chosen them (cf. 13:20; 15:16a), and they have been made clean by the word of Jesus (cf. 13:10; 15:3). The world's rejection of Jesus and the disciple's choice of Jesus over against the claims of the world provide a first explanation of why the world hates the disciples (vv. 18-19). The disciples should not be surprised at this, as they have already been instructed at the footwashing: "servants are not greater than their master" (v. 20a; cf. 13:16a; cf. also Matt 10:25; Luke 6:40).

Another series of conditionals begins as Jesus tells the disciples that if "they" persecuted him "they" will persecute the disciples (v. 20b). The description of the opponents of Jesus and the disciples shifts from "the world" *(ho kosmos)* to "they." Who might "they" be? Jesus' final conditional is rhetorical: if "they" had kept the word of Jesus they would also keep the word of the disciples (v. 20c). The first explanation for the hatred of the world is its rejection of Jesus' chosen ones (v. 19b). The second explanation reaches beyond the disciples themselves and begins to single out identifiable representatives of "the world." "They" reject the one who chose them and sent them out: "all this they will do to you on my account" (v. 21a). Even more critical is their rejection of the Father: "because they do not know the one who sent me" (v. 21b). Throughout

Jesus' ministry it was "the Jews" who rejected Jesus because they would not recognize that he was the Sent One of God (cf. 8:19, 27, 39-47, 54-55). "The world" that has become "they" must be "the Jews" of the earlier narrative.

The results of the world's hatred (vv. 22-25). The promises of the Prologue have been fulfilled in the life and ministry of Jesus. He has "come and spoken to them" (v. 22a: *ei mē elthon kai elalēsa autois*). The Word has dwelt among them (cf. 1:14); he has come unto his own, but they have rejected his word (cf. 1:11). If they had not been the privileged recipients of the revelation of God in and through Jesus they would have no sin. But they have hated and rejected the word of Jesus and thus have no excuse for their sin (15:22). It is now obvious that "they" are "the Jews" of the story of Jesus' ministry (cf. 9:39-41). The oneness between the Father and the Son (1:1-2, 18) leads logically to Jesus' earlier words to "the Jews": "the one who does not honor the Son does not honor the Father who sent him" (5:23b; cf. 8:49). Jesus is thus able to speak of a further and even more damning result of the world's hatred. The hatred of Jesus indicates a hatred of the Father (15:23). But the Father of Jesus is the God of Israel, and thus "the Jews" are accused of hating their traditional God. Paradoxically "the Jews'" defense of their understanding of God, over against the revelation of that God in and through Jesus (cf. 5:19-47; 8:12-20, 21-30, 39-47, 54-59; 9:24-34, 39-41), is a reflection of their hatred of God. On several occasions "the Jews" have been urged to see the revelation of God in Jesus' works if they cannot accept his word (cf. 5:36; 7:21-24, 50-52; 9:24-34; 10:31-39). What Jesus had said about his words in v. 22 is now said about his works in v. 24: "If I had not done among them the works *(ei erga mē epoiēsa en autois)* that no one else did." The rejection of the words (v. 22a) and the works (v. 24a) of Jesus manifests their hatred for both Jesus and the Father (v. 24b).

Jesus points beyond his words and works to the word of God spoken to God's people in their Scriptures. The negative response of "the Jews" to the revelation of God in Jesus, and their resulting hatred of the Father of Jesus, the God of Israel, fulfills the Law. In their determined defense of the Law "the Jews" can be accused by a word from their own Scriptures (Ps 35:19; cf. Ps 69:4-5). God speaks through the Scriptures, accusing "the Jews": "They have hated me without a cause" (v. 25). Those who hate the disciples hate Jesus and his Father. They remain in their sin (cf. 8:24), having hated and rejected God. They are accused by the word of God. Jesus does not refer to the Scriptures as "their Law" *(en tō nomō autōn)* in mockery, but ironically indicates that they are making a lie of the Law by which they claim to live (cf. Obermann, *Die christologische Erfüllung* 271–282).

A further explanation for the hatred of the world (15:26–16:3). The challenge that Jesus' words and works brings into the world will not disappear, and thus the hatred of the world will continue. The disciples will be the bearers of the challenging presence of Jesus' revelation of God. They need not fear, as the other Paraclete will always be with them (cf. 14:16-17), teaching them all things, reminding them of all that Jesus has said to them (14:25-27). The disciples have been given a new peace over against the false securities of the world (14:27), but none of this takes away from the hatred and violence of their experience (15:18-21). In the midst of this hatred the Paraclete sent from the Father will continue to bear witness to Jesus. The other Paraclete, the Spirit of truth whom Jesus will send, and who proceeds from the Father, continues this revelation (v. 26) along with disciples who have been with Jesus from the beginning, hearing his words and seeing his works (v. 27). The disciples, directed, reminded, and strengthened by the Spirit, give witness to Jesus in the midst of a hostile world. Jesus speaks of the future experience of the disciples. They suffer the same rejection as Jesus has suffered during his *earthly* ministry (cf. vv. 18, 20), but the future suffering of the disciples will take place *after the departure of Jesus* described in 14:1-31. It will form part of their lives in the in-between-time. Thus the Paraclete must play a role, continuing the revelation of God that has taken place in and through Jesus (v. 26: *ekeinos martyrēsei peri emou*) now that he is no longer present with the disciples.

Earlier in the discourse Jesus told his disciples of events that lay ahead, his suffering (13:19), the gift of the Paraclete (14:25-26), and his going to the Father (14:28-29), so that when these things took place they would understand and believe. He now foretells the ongoing hatred of the world. Jesus instructs his followers that they must face the future hatred of the world, and because of their trust in his assuring word they must not fall away (16:1). The description of Jesus' and the disciples' opponents, earlier named as "the world" (vv. 18, 19) and "they" (vv. 20, 21, 22, 24, 25), a people accused by its own Scriptures (v. 25), must be "the Jews." Jesus tells his disciples they will suffer the experience of the man born blind (cf. 9:22, 34), as the time is coming when they will be put out of the synagogue (16:2a: *aposynagōgous poiēsousin hymas*). This corresponds with the comment from the narrator, earlier in the story, that "the Jews" had already decided to put out of the synagogue (9:22: *aposynagōgos genētai*; cf. 12:42) anyone who confessed that Jesus was the Christ. "The Jews" are the only characters in the story who could be involved in such action, and Jesus' words reflect the lived experience of disciples living the in-between-time, where some are failing in the face of hatred, persecution, expulsion, and death.

More drastically Jesus tells his future witnesses (cf. v. 27) that they will be slain by people who regard the killing of disciples of Jesus as offering service to God (16:2b: *latreian prospherein tǭ theǭ*). It is difficult to document an early Christian experience of persecution at the hands of Jews that was regarded as an act of worship to God (cf. note). Whatever may have been the exact identification of the experience of Christian disciples who originally read this Gospel, such acts repeat in the life of disciples the hatred and rejection of Jesus (cf. v. 20). He is hated because "they do not know him who sent me" (v. 21). The rejection of Jesus was based upon the non-recognition of God, and the persecution and slaying of the disciples take place for the same reason: they do not know the Father. The disciples described in vv. 2-3 come from the next generation of Christians but their rejection continues the world's knowing neither the Father nor Jesus: "They have not known the Father, nor me" (v. 3). The situation of sin described in vv. 22-25 continues in the rejection of the revelation of God present in the witness of the Paraclete and the Spirit-directed disciples of Jesus in the in-between-time (cf. vv. 26-27).

Conclusion to 15:1–16:3. This section of the last discourse is unique. Only Jesus speaks, announcing at the heart of his departing discourse a message about abiding, loving, and being hated. The passage is formed by Jesus' words on two contrasting experiences, bridged by his commandment of mutual love. The first section deals with the mutuality of "abiding" that should exist between Jesus and the disciples (15:1-11). The closing section spells out the hatred and violent separation that exists between "the world" and both Jesus and the disciples (15:18–16:3). Both the abiding and the hatred are grounded in the recognition or non-recognition of the one who sent Jesus, the Father (see vv. 15:1, 8-11, and 21, 23, 16:3). They are positive and negative faces of the same truth: the all-determining function of God in the Johannine story.

The use of the expression *aposynagōgos* (16:2) indicates that this story reflects the experiences of an early Christian community. But there is more to it. The shift from "the world" to "they" in vv. 18-21 points to "the Jews" of the earlier parts of the narrative. The reference to exclusion from the synagogue confirms this. In v. 1 Jesus claimed to be the *true* vine. The actions of those who hate, exclude, and kill Jesus and the disciples are associated with the synagogue, the gathering place of a people of God who also claim to be "the vine." A paradox emerges as the vine-synagogue hates, persecutes, and excludes (16:1-3) the vine-Jesus (15:1-5a). Who is persecuting whom? Who is excluding whom? By hating, the persecutor and the executor fall into sin (see vv. 22-25), and do not bear the fruit demanded from those who are branches of the *true* vine. They are thus pruned, cut off from the vine and the branches that are tended by the Father, the vine-dresser (see 15:1-5a, 5b-8). Those who hate and reject Jesus and his disciples are not judged; they judge themselves by refusing to accept the words and works of Jesus (see vv. 22, 24). Such a perspective was no doubt formed within the context of anger, rejection, and exclusion on the part of "the Jews." Jesus is silent on the response that disciples should make to "the Jews." But "the Jews" are not Israel, however strongly they may claim to possess the definitive understanding of God's way with the world.

Those who will not abide in Jesus, and those who hate, rejecting the revelation of the love of God in and through Jesus, are in sin. They bring judgment upon themselves. Despite this self-inflicted judgment 15:12-17 insists that the message of the love of God, shown by Jesus' words and actions in the midst of ignorance, failure, betrayal, and denial, so central to the narrative of 13:1-38, continues. Jesus has chosen disciples; they did not choose him (15:16). He has loved them and made them into friends rather than servants (15:14-15), giving himself unto death out of love for them (15:13). Thus in the midst of hatred and violence one reality endures: the sovereign freedom for both Jesus and the Father to love the world *unconditionally* (cf. 3:16-17; 13:1: *eis telos*). The love of Jesus, the *true* vine, has both shown (13:1-38) and taught (15:1–16:3) that God's love knows no boundaries. There is only one *true* vine (15:1: *hē ampelos hē alēthinē*), however much some from the synagogue (16:2: *aposynagōgous poiēsousin hymas*) may have become a "degenerate plant, a bastard vine" (see Jer 2:21). Contrary to the actions of this degenerate vine (cf. 9:22, 34; 12:42; 16:2), the words of Jesus on abiding, loving, and being hated have contained no message of exclusion from the true vine, but they have stated the possibility that some will choose to exclude themselves by rejecting Jesus and the Father who sent him. For this reason Jesus instructs his fragile disciples on the need to abide (15:1-11), to love one another (15:12-17) in the midst of present and future hatred, persecution, exclusion, and martyrdom (15:18–16:3).

NOTES

18. *If the world hates you:* The six conditional clauses in vv. 18-24 carry a warning about the future (present) experiences of the Christian community. These warnings, placed on the lips of the dying hero, are a widespread feature of the farewell discourse genre.

    the world: The use of the expression "the world" in vv. 18-19 does not identify creation or humanity as such. It is theologically determined, and refers to that part of created reality that has definitively rejected both Jesus and the Father.

20. *they will persecute you:* On the relationship between the experience of Jesus and the experience of the disciples expressed in these clauses and main statements see Lindars, "Persecution of Christians" 59–62.

21. *on my account:* For this interpretation of the Greek *dia to onoma mou*, which literally means "because of my name," see Barrett, *Gospel* 481. Brown, *Gospel* 2:696–697, attempts too much in suggesting that the disciples are persecuted and hated because Jesus bears the divine name.

22. *but now they have no excuse:* The use of *nun* ("now") in vv. 22, 24 is more an indication of a current state of affairs than an indication of time (cf. Brown, *Gospel* 2:688). As Bernard, *Commentary* 2:494, puts it: "but now, as things are."

25. *that is written in their law:* Most commentators see Ps 35:19 as Jesus' reference to "the Law" taken in its broad sense of the Jewish Scriptures as a whole. Some (e.g., Obermann, *Die christologische Erfüllung* 271–276; Menken, *Old Testament Quotations* 139–145) suggest Ps 69:4-5. Marsh, *Saint John* 531, and Haenchen, *John* 2:138, suggest that both passages may be behind Jesus' words. See the discussion in Segovia, *Farewell* 194 n. 40; Schuchard, *Scripture Within Scripture* 119–123.

26. *when the Paraclete comes:* The appearance of the Paraclete saying in this context has often mistakenly been regarded as a later, clumsy insertion into the text (e.g., Bauer, *Johannesevangelium* 195; Becker, "Die Abschiedsreden Jesu" 237–238).

   who proceeds from the Father: This insistence that the Paraclete comes from the Father (cf. 14:16, 26), even though Jesus now involves himself in the sending of the Spirit of truth (cf. 14:17), points to the identity of the origin of the former Paraclete (Jesus) and that of the other Paraclete (cf. 14:16). Despite Lagrange, *Evangile* 413, this passage is not to be read in the light of fourth-century trinitarian debates. On the one who sends the Paraclete, the Father or Jesus, Brown, *Gospel* 2:689, comments: "The variation is not really significant at the theological level, for in Johannine thought the Father and Jesus are one (10:30)."

27. *you have been with me from the beginning:* Given the setting of the final meal (cf. 13:1) and the testamentary form, "from the beginning" *(ap' archēs)* means that the disciples have been with him from the beginning of his ministry (cf. Brown, *Gospel* 2:690).

16:1. *I have said all this to keep you from falling away:* Authoritative words from the departing hero to encourage and strengthen his followers are very common in the Jewish testamentary tradition. The *tauta* ("all this," literally "these things") looks back across 15:18-27 (at least), and not just to Jesus' words on the Paraclete and the disciples in vv. 26-27.

2. *They will put you out of the synagogues:* On these words of Jesus as a reflection of the experience of later Johannine Christians see, among many, Lindars, "Persecution of Christians" 48–51; Onuki, *Gemeinde und Welt* 131–143. See also Lightfoot, *Gospel* 284–286, for a series of links between John 9 and 15:18–16:3. The Johannine community has experienced expulsion from the synagogue, however local that conflict and expulsion may have been (cf. introduction). There is no need to link this expulsion with the *birkat ha-minim.* See Lieu, *Image and Reality* 130–135. For a recent restatement of the position (strongly advanced by Martyn, *History and Theology,* but since then much modified) see Davies, "Reflections on Aspects" 43–64.

   the hour is coming: The use of *erchetai hōra* does not have links with "the hour of Jesus." It is a reference to the coming of a critical time in the near future. See Léon-Dufour, *Lecture* 3:205.

those who kill you will think that by doing so they are offering worship to God: Several different attempts have been made to resolve the difficulty of setting these words of Jesus in an identifiable historical experience of the early Church. Some scholars suggest that Jesus foretells two forms of future suffering, currently part of the readers' experience: expulsion from the synagogue perpetrated by "the Jews" and martyrdom at the hands of the Romans who regarded the Christians as atheists and thus deserving death (e.g., Harvey, *Jesus on Trial* 107). The possibility of reference to Roman persecution is canvassed by Brown, *Gospel* 2:691; Cassidy, *John's Gospel* 110–113, but it is often suggested that the use of *latreia* ("cultic service") restricts the killing to "the Jews." This need not be the case. On the pagan use of *latreia* as acts of piety done in the service of religion see Augustine, *De Civitate Dei* V:15 (MPL 41:160). Most scholars look to Jewish practices (see *Num. Rab.* 21; *m. Sanh.* 9:6; Josephus, *Ant.* 20:200; *Mart. Poly.* 13:1; Justin, *Dial.* 95:4; 133:6). See, for example, Hoskyns, *Gospel* 482–483; Carson, *Gospel* 531; de Boer, *Johannine Perspectives* 61–62. Martyn, "Persecution and Martyrdom" 55–89, has suggested that it may be a memory of some form of persecution that took place while the community was still a Jewish-Christian sect. Lindars, "Persecution of Christians" 66, stresses the future tense of the verbs, and (with reference to attacks on Christians during the Bar Kochba rebellion referred to in Justin's *Dialogue*) writes of an "alarming possibility." On the second-century Christian texts see the important study of Lieu, *Image and Reality* 57–102 (on the *Martyrdom of Polycarp*) and 103–153 (on Justin's *Dialogue*).

FOR REFERENCE AND FURTHER STUDY

Borig, Rainer. *Der wahre Weinstock. Untersuchungen zu Joh 15,1-10.* StANT 16. Munich: Kösel, 1967.

Davies, W. D. "Reflections on Aspects of the Jewish Background of the Gospel of John." In Culpepper and Black, eds., *Exploring the Gospel of John* 43–64.

Dettwiler, Andreas. *Die Gegenwart* 60–110.

Heise, Jürgen. *Bleiben. Menein in den Johanneischen Schriften.* HUTh 8. Tübingen: J. C. B. Mohr (Paul Siebeck), 1967.

Jaubert, Annie. "L'image de la vigne (Jean 15)." In *Oikonomia: Heilsgeschichte als Thema der Theologie. Oscar Cullmann zum 65. Geburtstag gewidmet.* Hamburg: H. Reich, 1967, 93–99.

Lee, G. M. "John XV 14 'Ye are my friends,'" *NT* 15 (1973) 260.

Lindars, Barnabas. "The Persecution of Christians in John 15:18–16:4a." In William Horbury and Brian McNeil, eds., *Suffering and Martyrdom in the New Testament: Studies Presented to G. M. Styler.* Cambridge: Cambridge University Press, 1981, 48–69.

Martyn, J. L. "A Dark and Difficult Chapter in the History of Johannine Christianity." In idem, *The Gospel of John in Christian History. Essays for Interpreters.* New York: Paulist, 1978, 55–89.

Moloney, Francis J. "The Structure and Message of John 15.1–16.3," *ABR* 35 (1987) 35–49.

_____. *Glory not Dishonor,* Chapter Three.

Niccaci, A. "Esame letterario di Gv 15–16," *Anton.* 56 (1981) 43–71.

Sandvik, Björn. "Joh 15 als Abendmahlstext," *ThZ* 23 (1967) 323–328.

Segalla, Giuseppe. "La struttura chiastica di Giov. 15,1-8," *BeO* 12 (1970) 129–131.

Segovia, Fernando F. "John 15:18–16:4a: A First Addition to the Original Farewell Discourse," *CBQ* 45 (1983) 210–230.

_____. "The Theology and Provenance of John 15:1-17," *JBL* 101 (1982) 115–128.

_____. *Farewell* 123–212.

Simoens, Yves. *La gloire* 130–150.

Thyen, Hartwig. "Niemand hat grössere Liebe als die, daß er sein Leben für seine Freunde hingibt." In C. Andresen and G. Klein, eds., *Theologia Crucis—Signum Crucis. Festschrift für Erich Dinkler zum 70. Geburtstag.* Tübingen: J.C.B. Mohr (Paul Siebeck), 1979, 467–481.

Watt, J. G. van der. "'Metaphorik' in Joh 15,1-8," *BZ* 38 (1994) 67–80.

iv. Departure (16:4-33)

Introduction to 16:4-33. Only Jesus spoke in 15:1–16:3. In the next section of the discourse (16:4-33) disciples question and interrupt Jesus' words as they did in 14:1-31. In a way also reminiscent of 14:1-31 Jesus speaks of his departure (16:4-6, 25-31), the gift of the Paraclete (vv. 7-15), and the challenges of living in the in-between-time (vv. 20-24). There are a number of links between v. 4 and v. 33. The expression *tauta lelalēka hymin hina* in v. 4a is repeated in v. 33, but there is almost universal agreement that this part of the discourse begins with v. 4b (cf. UBSGNT, NTG, RSV, NRSV, JB, NJB, TOB, NAB, NEB). This division separates the things Jesus has said (v. 4a) and his not having said these things from the beginning (v. 4b). But both "these things" *(tauta)* look back to what has been said in the discourse thus far, especially his departure (14:1-31) and the difficulties of the in-between-time (15:18–16:3). Over against these difficulties (v. 4a: *alla*) Jesus' words of prophecy and assurance have been delivered in this final period of his being with them (cf. v. 4b: *de;* cf. note). Much has been said about Jesus' love for his own (13:1, 18-20), the future gift of the Paraclete (14:16-17, 26; 15:26), the oneness that exists among the Father and the Son and the disciple who believes and loves Jesus (14:20-24), and those who abide in Jesus (15:1-11). The hatred and rejection promised in 15:18–16:3 cannot be the end of the story. The adversative *alla* (v. 4a: "but") reintroduces the events and consequences of Jesus' departure (16:4-33) in a way that both matches and develops Jesus' earlier words on his departure (14:1-31).

As with 14:1-31, the first part of 16:4-33 is dedicated to the themes of Jesus' departure and the role of the Paraclete in the in-between-time (vv.

4-20). This section closes with the use of the Johannine double "amen" (v. 20). The image of a woman in childbirth and the play on the theme of "before" and "after" are used in the following section, addressing the situation of the disciples "before" and "after" (vv. 21-24). In another parallel with 14:1-31 a final section returns to the theme of Jesus' imminent departure and the peace he leaves with the disciples as they face the difficulties of the in-between-time (vv. 25-33). The overall structure of 16:4-33 can be described in the following fashion (cf. Simoens, *La gloire* 151–167):

i. *The departure of Jesus (vv. 4-20).* Jesus describes a departure that creates sorrow and confusion but is marked by the critical, judging presence of the Paraclete.

ii. *Now and afterwards (vv. 21-24).* The symbol of a woman in childbirth provides an image of the now and afterward experience of the disciples, who are now facing life in the in-between-time.

iii. *The departure of Jesus (vv. 25-33).* Jesus' departure is described as the return of the Son to the Father. The disciples still languish in the limitations of their belief in Jesus as the Sent One, not as the one who must depart, but Jesus promises them the gift of peace.

The literary form and many of the themes of 14:1-31 return, but there is an increased focus on the disciples. Their sorrow at Jesus' departure is misplaced because it is for their benefit that Jesus is going away so that the Paraclete might bring judgment against the world and further unfold the revelation of God. The disciples must pass through "the hour" that they may overcome the sorrow of the "now" to attain the perfect joy of "afterward." As the discourse draws to a close Jesus speaks openly of his departure to the Father, and the disciples express belief and knowledge. They accept that Jesus came from God. They have accepted his origins, but how will they deal with his departure and destiny?

For ease of consultation and clarity the translation and notes for vv. 4-20, vv. 21-24, and vv. 25-33 will be provided separately. Further subdivisions of the material within each of these sections will be presented in a brief introduction to each section. The literature For Reference and Further Study of 16:4-33 will be gathered after the commentary on 16:25-33.

The Departure of Jesus (vv. 4-20)

4. "But I have said these things to you that when their hour comes you may remember that I told you of them. I did not say these things to you from the beginning, because I was with you. 5. But now I am going to the one who sent me, yet none of you asks me, 'Where are you going?' 6. But because I have said these things to you sorrow has filled your hearts.

7. Nevertheless I tell you the truth: it is to your advantage that I go away, for if I do not go away the Paraclete will not come to you; but if I go I will send him to you. 8. And when he comes he will expose the world concerning sin and righteousness and judgment: 9. concerning sin, because they do not believe in me; 10. concerning righteousness, because I go to the Father and you will see me no more; 11. concerning judgment, because the ruler of this world is judged. 12. I have yet many things to say to you but you cannot bear them now. 13. When the Spirit of truth comes he will guide you into all the truth, for he will not speak on his own authority, but whatever he hears he will speak, and he will declare to you the things that are to come. 14. He will glorify me, for he will take what is mine and declare it to you. 15. All that the Father has is mine; therefore I said that he takes what is mine and will declare it to you.

16. "A little while and you will see me no more; again a little while and you will see me." 17. Some of his disciples said to one another, "What is this that he says to us, 'A little while and you will not see me, and again a little while and you will see me,' and 'because I go to the Father'?" 18. They said, "What does he mean by 'a little while'? We do not know what he means." 19. Jesus knew that they wanted to ask him, so he said to them, "Is this what you are asking yourselves, what I meant by saying 'A little while and you will not see me, and again a little while and you will see me'? 20. Amen, amen, I say to you, you will weep and lament, but the world will rejoice; you will be sorrowful, but your sorrow will turn into joy."

INTERPRETATION

Introduction to vv. 4-20. The argument and literary shape of this passage are dominated by the words of Jesus on the Paraclete in vv. 7-15. There is a brief introduction to these words in which Jesus insists upon his departure (vv. 4-6), and he returns to this theme after his words on the Paraclete to bring the subsection to a close (vv. 16-20). Thus vv. 4-20 unfold in the following fashion:

1. *The departure of Jesus (vv. 4-6).* This section begins and closes with the expression *tauta lelalēka hymin* (v. 4 and v. 6: "these things I have said to you"). Jesus speaks of his departure, informing the disciples that their ignorance is creating sorrow.
2. *The role of the Paraclete (vv. 7-15).* Teaching on the Paraclete determines this section. Jesus' departure is to the advantage of the disciples as it leads to the sending of the Paraclete who will judge the world and continue the revelation of Jesus.
3. *The departure of Jesus (16-20).* This section is marked by the continual use of "a little while" (vv. 16 [2x], 17 [2x], 18, 19 [2x]: *mikron*) and closes with the use of the double "amen." Jesus returns to the theme of departure, addressing disciples who remain ignorant.

The themes of the departure of Jesus and the gift of the Paraclete, already part of Jesus' teaching in 14:1-31, return as 16:4-33 opens. However, 16:4-20 does not simply repeat what was said earlier in the discourse. There is an increasing focus on frail disciples and a presentation of the Paraclete as the one who will expose the sinfulness of the world.

A departure that creates sorrow (vv. 4-6). Jesus has told the disciples of many experiences that lie ahead of them so that *afterward,* when they happen, the memory of Jesus' words will be with them (v. 4a; cf. 13:19; 14:25, 29; 15:11; 16:1). Difficulties will come: the departure of Jesus (14:1, 18, 27), hatred, rejection, and even death (15:18–16:3). But they will also receive the gift of the Spirit-Paraclete (14:16-17, 26; 15:26-27). Jesus has not spoken of these things from the beginning of his ministry (*ap' archês:* see 15:27) as it was neither necessary nor appropriate during those formative days (v. 4b). But the days of Jesus' being with his disciples are drawing to a close as "their hour" (v. 4a: *hē hōra autōn*) is coming. The hour of Jesus (cf. 2:5; 7:8, 30; 8:20; 12:23; 13:1) associated with his death might appear to indicate defeat, but it will be the moment of his exaltation to glory (cf. 12:23, 32-33; 13:1). The hour of his enemies (16:4a) will appear to be their victory but it will in fact be their defeat (cf. Barrett, *Gospel* 485).

The time of his departure is at hand as Jesus goes to the one who sent him (v. 5a). Jesus has said this often to his disciples and he rebukes them because not one of them is asking where he is going (v. 5b). But Simon Peter asked exactly that question *(pou hypageis?)* in 13:36a. Within the context of the footwashing (13:1-17), the promise that the revelation of God would take place in events that were near at hand (13:18-20), and the gift of the morsel (13:21-28), Peter's question was related to Jesus' human experience of death. Jesus attempted to transcend Peter's time-conditioned understanding of his destiny (cf. 13:33, 36b), but the disciple continued to ask why he could not follow *now,* swearing that he would lay down his life for him (13:37). Much has been said to the disciples since then, and all suggestions that Jesus' departure can be limited to the human and historical experience of death have been eclipsed (cf. 13:33, 36b; 14:2-4, 6, 12, 18, 19-20, 28, 31; 15:26). Despite this further explicit instruction of the disciples they are still not asking the correct question. The passing of time across the discourse generates this statement from Jesus. At a moment that comes some time *after* Peter's question (13:36a) Jesus points out that still not one of them *is questioning* (present tense: *erōta*) Jesus' destiny. They are not asking where he is going (16:5) because they are not able to reach beyond the identification of departure with physical death. Thus "grief has pervaded, taken possession" (Barrett, *Gospel* 486) of their hearts because Jesus continues to talk of his departure ("these things": *tauta*) in a way that they are unable to comprehend (v. 6). The misunderstanding of Peter's earlier question has not been overcome.

The role of the Paraclete (vv. 7-15). Despite their desire to keep their master with them (v. 7a: *alla;* cf. v. 4a), it is to the disciples' advantage that Jesus depart. Rather than adding to their suffering (cf. 15:18–16:3), his departure will overcome their sorrow. Jesus must depart to send the Paraclete (v. 7). The sending of the Spirit has been linked to the departure of Jesus since the narrator's remark in 7:39: "As yet the Spirit had not been given, because Jesus was not yet glorified." The link between the end of Jesus' life through death and departure, his glorification, and the gift of the Spirit-Paraclete is increasingly strengthened (cf. 11:4; 12:23, 32-33; 13:1, 31-32). Jesus first describes the role of the Paraclete who comes to expose the world concerning sin, righteousness, and judgment (v. 8). This passage is made notoriously obscure by the use of the Greek verb *elenchein,* a rich expression with a number of possible meanings across the semantic fields of blame, conviction, convincing, exposure, shame, and investigation (cf. de la Potterie, *La Vérité* 1:399–406, and note on v. 8 below). Earlier in the narrative the verb was used to describe the person who would not walk in the light lest evil deeds be brought out into the open (3:20: *hina mē elenchthē ta erga autou*), and to challenge the opponents of Jesus to make evident that he is a sinner (8:46: *elenxei me peri hamartias*). A further element useful for the interpretation of the expression in v. 8 is the parallel between Jesus and the Paraclete. Jesus did not come to judge, but his presence as the revelation of God brings about *krisis* (cf. 3:19-21; 5:22; 7:7; 8:24; 9:39; 12:31). Jesus' presence reveals truth and light that *expose* the surrounding darkness (cf. 12:45-47). The Paraclete also exposes the darkness of the world and thus brings it to judgment. The Johannine story has resembled a trial during which Jesus is the accused, but his accusers are ironically judged throughout (cf. 3:19; 5:22, 27, 30, 44-45; 8:16; 9:39). This process will continue after the departure of Jesus. The Paraclete continues the critical, judging function that flows from the revelation of God, so clearly attributed to Jesus (cf. 5:27). The ongoing presence of this authority in the Paraclete is described in vv. 9-11 as three moments of exposure:

- The Paraclete will expose the sin of the world because *(hoti)* it has not believed in Jesus (v. 9). Sin exists where the decision is made not to believe in Jesus: "The one who rejects me and does not receive my word has a judge" (12:48a; cf. 8:44-47).
- The Paraclete will expose the false righteousness of the world because it is radically mistaken in its attempt to understand Jesus in terms of "this world" (v. 10). Jesus' opponents have consistently failed to accept that Jesus is from the Father and that he is returning to the Father and will no longer be seen among his disciples (v. 10bc). Yet they have made claim to righteousness as children of Abraham (cf. 8:39-59), disciples of Moses (cf. 6:30-31; 9:28-29), subject to Torah (cf. 5:16-18, 39-40, 45-47; 7:12, 18, 20-24, 48-49; 9:16, 24; 8:58-59; 10:24-38; 11:48-50; 16:2).

The problem of 12:43 has never been overcome: the opponents of Jesus preferred the *doxa tōn anthrōpōn* to the *doxa tou theou*. In their *horizontally* determined understanding of a righteousness worked out within the human story (Abraham, Moses, and Torah), they have rejected the *vertical* inbreaking of the Word become flesh in Jesus Christ (v. 10).

* The Paraclete will expose the false judgment of the world (v. 11) because, despite all appearances to the contrary, Jesus' departure through death is at the same time his being "lifted up" in exaltation (3:14; 8:28; 12:32-33), his revelation of the glory of God and his own glorification (11:4; 12:23; 13:31-32), his "gathering" of the scattered (11:50, 52; 12:11, 19, 32), the moment of his return to the Father (13:1). The apparent victory of the ruler of this world in the death of Jesus will be exposed as Jesus' death and glorification reverse the judgment of history (v. 11; see 14:30).

The rhythmic repetition of Johannine expressions appears in vv. 13-15 to indicate *how* and *when* this exposing activity will take place. The Paraclete will continue the revealing activity of Jesus, in the in-between-time. The Paraclete will speak (v. 13: *lalēsei* [2x]) and declare all truth (vv. 13, 14, 15: *anangelei*). Jesus' presence with his disciples is coming to an end. There is tension between Jesus' desire to communicate much to them (v. 12a) and the disciples' *present* (you cannot bear them all now [*arti*]) inability to cope with all the implications of the revelation of God that takes place in Jesus (v. 12b). It is not as if more revelation is still to follow, to be delivered by the Paraclete. The problem lies with the fragile disciples "now." God has been made known to all who have seen Jesus Christ (cf. 1:14-18), but in the Spirit-directed time after the departure of Jesus the full implications of this revelation will unfold. This is another reason why it is advantageous for the disciples that Jesus depart (cf. v. 7). Jesus must leave the many things *(polla)* he would like to tell them to the revealing activity of the other Paraclete (cf. 14:16), the Spirit of truth (16:12b-13a). This figure *(ekeinos)* will guide the disciples *(hodēgēsei hymas)* into the fullness of truth. The journey into "all the truth" *(en tē alētheia pasē)* has not yet been completed, even though Jesus has been with the disciples as "the way" (14:6a: *hē hodos*). He is about to depart, but "the way" goes on. The in-between-time will be marked by the ongoing presence of the light and the truth (cf. 14:6b) of Jesus, through the presence of the Spirit of truth who will lead *(hodēgēsei)* disciples unerringly toward the fullness of truth. A dynamic sense of a steady unfolding of a revelation has not yet been fully grasped or experienced. Given the guide, the disciple journeys with unconditioned confidence (v. 13).

Neither Jesus nor the Paraclete is the ultimate source of the revelation they communicate. Like Jesus (cf. 3:32-35; 7:16-18; 8:26-29, 42-43; 12:47-50; 14:10) the Spirit will speak whatever he hears (v. 13a: *hosa akousei lalēsei*).

The period of the Spirit-Paraclete is an in-between-time, as there are things that are "yet to come" *(ta erchomena)*. The revealing task of the Paraclete points forward toward those things that are yet to come (v. 13b). The gift of the Spirit does not mark the end of the story but signals a new stage, after the death and glorification of Jesus (cf. 7:39), the period of the Spirit-filled community of worshiping disciples looking forward to the *eschata*, things that are yet to come. As Brown rightly insists:

> We find no evidence that Johannine theology ever abandoned the hope of the final return of Jesus in visible glory, although the Gospel clearly puts more emphasis on all the eschatological features that have already been realized in Jesus' first coming. The question is not one of the presence of Jesus in and through the Paraclete *as opposed* to the coming of Jesus in glory, but one of the relative importance of each (Brown, "The Paraclete" 131 [emphasis in the original]).

Perhaps more than most early Christian communities the Johannine Church lived the tension between the givenness of the "now" and the promise of the "not yet." The Paraclete is Jesus' gift to bring peace into that tension (cf. 14:27).

Jesus' revealing mission, described biblically as the vision of the *doxa* (12:43; cf. Exod 19:16-20; John 2:11; 11:40; 12:23; 13:31), will continue in the revealing mission of the Paraclete who will take all that is of Jesus and declare it *(ek tou emou lēmpsetai kai anangelei)*, thus bringing to remembrance what Jesus has said to the disciples (v. 14; cf. 14:26). But this affirmation calls for further clarification lest the disciples think that what the Paraclete declares has its *source* in Jesus. Both Jesus and the Paraclete are sent by the Father (cf. 14:16, 26; 15:26). Jesus states that everything belonging to the Father also belongs to him. Not only does Jesus receive everything he has from the Father (cf. 5:19, 30), but *everything the Father has* is his. The oneness between Jesus and the Father (cf. 1:1-2, 18; 10:30, 38) is so complete that what is of the Father is also of Jesus. Jesus is thus the perfect and ideal revelation of the Father, and nothing of the Father can be hidden, as Jesus possesses everything of the Father (16:15; see 1:1c). This unique Johannine understanding of Jesus flows into the author's presentation of the Paraclete, who takes all that is from Jesus and will declare it to the disciples in the in-between-time (v. 15).

Jesus' teaching on the critical presence of the Paraclete over against the sin, false righteousness, and false judgment of the world (vv. 8-11) is new, but it is the logical development of what he has already said about the inability of the world to receive the Paraclete (14:17). The Paraclete brings *krisis* into the world, exposing its darkness (vv. 8-11) as the ongoing presence of the revelation of God in the in-between-time (vv. 12-15).

The departure of Jesus (vv. 16-20). In v. 16 Jesus speaks of "a little while" *(mikron)*, an expression he has used on several occasions (v. 5; cf. 7:33; 12:35; 13:33; 14:19), to return to the theme of his departure. In a short while no longer will he be seen, but there will be a time in the future when his disciples will see him once more *(palin . . . opsesthe me)*. As so often, the disciples fail to understand Jesus' consistent teaching on the two brief times that lie ahead: the *mikron* after which they will no longer see Jesus, and the *mikron* after which they will again see him (v. 17b). Yet they recall Jesus' words on the deeper implications of his departure. Without any prompting they link Jesus' departure with his return to the Father and question the meaning of both. Not only do they question the meaning of the two "times," but also the "place" to which Jesus is going: to the Father (v. 18d; cf. 14:28). The disciples have heard of the relationship between the departure of Jesus and the return to the Father but reject it as they plead ignorance on the meaning of *mikron:* "we do not know what he means" (v. 18). In their questioning they have provided the answer to their own question: it is *because* Jesus is going away from them that they will see him again. It is for their benefit that he departs (cf. v. 7). Despite the eightfold use of *mikron* in vv. 16-19 the issue in question is the *fact* of Jesus' departure, not merely its *timing*. The disciples, like Nicodemus (3:1-11) and the Samaritan woman (4:16-30), are unable to reach beyond their own categories to accept the word of Jesus.

The puzzled disciples have been the focus of vv. 17-18, but Jesus returns to center stage in vv. 19-20. He knows the subject matter of their discussion, and their unspoken desire to ask him for an explanation (v. 19; cf. v. 16). The use of the double "amen" (v. 20) links Jesus' closing words in this subsection with what has just been said and points forward to the next theme (cf. 13:16, 20, 21; 14:12). He does not answer the precise question the disciples are asking, as he does not explain the meaning of *mikron* (cf. v. 18) nor does he elaborate on what he means when he tells them of his return to the Father (cf. v. 17d). He resumes the theme of the in-between-time, addressing the problem of the immediate future of the disciples and the experience through which they must pass as they broach this time. Jesus' words on the future of the disciples recall earlier sayings that create a tension between the experiences of the present that must be undergone to produce belief, joy, memory, and peace in the future (cf. 13:18-20; 14:25-27, 29; 15:11; 16:1, 4). The shadow of the cross looms as Jesus tells his disciples they are approaching a moment when they will weep and lament *(klausete kai thrēnēsete)*, and the world will rejoice (v. 20). Jesus' being lifted up in a death upon a cross lies in the immediate future (cf. 12:32-33), and this death will bear all the appearances of a victory for those who are lining up against Jesus (cf. 11:49-50, 53, 57; 12:10-11), but their rejoicing will be hollow because, for this author, the brute facts of history do not reflect the true significance of the death of Jesus.

The departure of Jesus through the cross will create the *mikron* when Jesus will not be seen (cf. v. 16a), but the sorrow of the disciples will be turned into joy. How this will take place is still to be told, but enough has already been said to indicate that the Paraclete will play a crucial role in that transformation and that it will be a result of Jesus' departure to the Father (cf. v. 7). Jesus' departure will be a genuine departure and he will not return to be seen again as he was seen during the ministry (cf. v. 16a). However, the absent one will be present in the worshiping community (cf. v. 16b). The cross may appear to be defeat but, enigmatically, the opposite is the case. The lifting up of Jesus is also his exaltation (cf. 3:14; 8:28; 12:32), and it marks "the hour" of the judgment of this world (cf. 12:23, 27-33). But neither Jesus nor the disciples can avoid the experience of the cross, the unavoidable loss and pain of a departure by death. The author is not about to rewrite the *events* of history but is telling a story that attempts to give these events *new meaning*.

NOTES

4. *I have said these things . . . I did not say these things:* Most scholars and commentators claim that the "these things" *(tauta)* of v. 4a looks back to 15:1–16:3 and thus closes 15:1–16:4a, while the "these things" *(tauta)* of v. 4b looks forward to the theme of departure and thus opens 16:4b-33. Both uses of *tauta* look back to all that has been said in the discourse thus far. The *alla* in v. 4a is adversative, and the *de* of v. 4b continues the thought of v. 4a (cf. Simoens, *La gloire* 134). In this way v. 4 is to be read as a unit introducing 16:4-33.

    when their hour comes: The expression *hē hōra autōn* refers to the immediately preceding *tauta* and thus is linked to the various indications Jesus has already given to the disciples of the "things" that are about to happen (especially 15:18–16:3). United as the first verse in the division of 16:4-33, the *tauta, autōn, autōn, tauta* of v. 4 all look back to Jesus' predictions earlier in the discourse of things that are to happen in the near future.

5. *I am going to the one who sent me:* The return of the theme of Jesus' departure to the Father resumes one of the major themes of 14:1-31. On 16:4b-33 as a "*relecture*" of 13:31–14:31 see Dettwiler, *Die Gegenwart* 266–292.

    none of you asks me, 'Where are you going?': Commentators regularly point out that Philip's question in 14:5 is also a request to know where Jesus is going. However, 13:36a and 16:5 are the major cause for concern as exactly the same words are used. The contradiction has created difficulty for interpreters. Some rearrange the order of the text (e.g., Bernard, *Commentary* 1:xx; Bultmann, *Gospel* 459–461) while others have claimed there is no contradiction (e.g., Lagrange, *Evangile* 417–418; Dodd, *Interpretation* 412–413 n. 1; Hoskyns,

Gospel 483), and a slightly different text has been proposed by da Cagliari, "'. . . E nessuno di voi'" 233–244. The most common contemporary explanation is that it is the result of the final editor's placing two versions of a discourse side by side (e.g., Brown, *Gospel* 2:710; Schnackenburg, *Gospel* 3:126; Beasley-Murray, *John* 279). Carson, *Gospel* 533, resorts to desperate measures when he asks whether Peter and Thomas were "really asking the question formally represented by their words."

6. *sorrow has filled your hearts:* On the inability of the disciples to accept the word of Jesus and let go of their own pretensions as the source of their sorrow at the news of Jesus' departure see van den Bussche, *Jean* 435: "What remains of their messianic dream? A poignant sorrow wrenches their hearts. Each one of them looks at the debris of his illusions."

7. *I will send him to you:* The first Paraclete saying indicated that the one who sent the Son also sent the Paraclete, as the result of Jesus' request (14:16). Almost immediately Jesus announces that the Father and Son are united in the sending of the Spirit (14:26). From that point on it must be taken for granted that the Father is ultimately responsible for the sending of the Spirit. This remains the case even in those sayings in which Jesus claims to be sending the Spirit (15:26; 16:7). The cumulative reading experience of the Paraclete sayings informs the reader of the active role of Jesus in sending the Spirit, intimately linked with his departure, but the Father who sends Jesus also sends the Paraclete (14:16, 26).

8. *he will expose the world:* As well as the reference to de la Potterie in the interpretation, see Friedrich Büchsel, *TDNT* 2 (1964) 473–476, Porsch, *Pneuma und Wort* 281–282, and Stenger, "DIKAIOSUNE" 3–6 on the problem of interpreting the wide-ranging word *elenchein*. For the meaning "to expose" in 14:8 see Porsch, *Pneuma und Wort* 282–283; Beasley-Murray, *John* 280–281; Lindars, "DIKAIOSUNE" 5–6. The forensic nature of the verb must not be lost from sight, as the Paraclete exercises a judging role in vv. 8–11 (cf. Bultmann, *Gospel* 561–562; Blank, *Krisis* 335; de la Potterie, *La Vérité* 1:410–416). On the continuation of the legal process behind much of John 5–12 and the function of the Paraclete who judges those who have judged Jesus see Léon-Dufour, *Lecture* 3:225–226. Carson, "The Function of the Paraclete" 551–558, rejects the interpretation of a judgment that comes from the exposure of sin, insisting that many other NT passages show the meaning here must be "to convict of" or "to convince of." On the continuation of Jesus' judging function in the Paraclete see Dettwiler, *Die Gegenwart* 221–222, and for the link between revelation and judgment in 5:27 see Moloney, *Son of Man* 77–86. Müller, "Parakletenvorstellung" 66–75, has shown that the judging, forensic role of the Paraclete, taken by many scholars as the original meaning of *paraklētos*, is a development within the Johannine tradition.

9. *concerning sin, because:* On the many possible meanings of *hoti* ("because") in this context see Barrett, *Gospel* 487. Carson, "The Function of the Paraclete" 561–563, rightly insists that *hoti* be understood in exactly the same way across vv. 9-11.

10. *concerning righteousness:* Discussion of the meaning of *dikaiosunē* in this context must limit itself to the possible Johannine meaning of this famous Pauline concept. It should be given one of its basic meanings in vv. 8 and 10: "fulfilling the divine statutes" (BAGD 196). In the Fourth Gospel "the Jews" lay claim to such righteousness but they are in breach of God's design, revealed in Jesus. On this see Pancaro, *The Law in the Fourth Gospel* 9–125. It is not necessary to explain how this positive word can be the subject of judgment, as many attempt to do (e.g., Lindars, "DIKAIOSUNE" 279–285). Although this is not explicit in the text, "the Jews'" understanding of their "righteousness" is exposed and judged by the Paraclete. The nature of their "righteousness" is displayed in the immediately preceding 16:2: "Whoever kills you will think he is offering service to God" (cf. Westcott, *Gospel* 229).

because I go to the Father: A reprehensible *dikaiosunē* is exposed by "the Jews'" unwillingness to accept the *hypagein* of Jesus and all that is associated with it (his origins with the Father, his being the revelation of God, etc.). See Blank, *Krisis* 336–338; Stenger, "DIKAIOSUNE" 6–8. This situation has been programmatically stated in 12:43: "For they loved the *doxa tōn anthrōpōn* more than the *doxa tou theou*." See Moloney, *Signs and Shadows* 196–198.

you will see me no more: There is a clumsy blend of third and second person in v. 10 that must be explained by the fact that Jesus is addressing his disciples. In v. 10a Jesus addresses the failure of the world to accept that Jesus departs to the Father. However, as Jesus is speaking directly to the disciples he is able to describe the consequence of his departure to the Father (which the world will not accept), in the second person future: *ouketi theōreite me.* See Lagrange, *Evangile* 419.

13. *he will guide you into all the truth:* The use of the expression "truth" *(alētheia)* further indicates the link between the mission of the Paraclete and the ongoing task of the revelation of God. Here, however, the stress is on *pasę̄*. See the rich study of Kremer, "Jesu Verheißung des Geistes" 247–273, claiming that John 16:13 (along with Mark 13:11) is legitimation for the Christian community's ongoing interpretation of the message of Jesus in the post-Easter period. The translation "into all the truth" is based on the *lectio difficilior* found in Sinaiticus, Cantabrigiensis, Freer Gospels, and other witnesses *(en tę̄ alētheią pasę̄)*. Some scholars (e.g., Porsch, *Pneuma und Wort* 294–295; de la Potterie, *La Vérité* 1:431–438) read (with Vaticanus) *eis tên alētheian*, and interpret the passage as saying that the Spirit will lead the disciple "to the very heart of all truth."

he will declare to you: The steady use of *legein* and *lalein* across vv. 12-15 can be associated with the widespread use of these verbs for Jesus' revealing word. The Paraclete continues this revelation (cf. Porsch, *Pneuma und Wort* 295–297). This cannot be said for *anangellein* (vv. 13, 15: "to declare") that, up to this point in the Gospel, has only been found twice (cf. 4:25; 5:15). Brown, *Gospel* 2:708, claims that its widespread use in the LXX, and especially in Isaiah, has provided background for its Johannine use. For Brown it contains the idea of "seeking a deeper meaning in what has already happened." See also Young, "A Study of the Relation of Isaiah" 224–226.

the things that are yet to come: Scholars divide over the interpretation of the role of the Paraclete declaring "the things that are yet to come" *(ta erchomena)*. Some claim that it is fully eschatological, that is, the Paraclete instructs the disciples concerning the end of time (e.g., Bernard, *Commentary* 2:511; Windisch, *Spirit-Paraclete* 12; Johnson, *Spirit-Paraclete* 38–39; Betz, *Der Paraklet* 191–192). For others it is an indication of the apocalyptic nature of primitive Christian prophecy (e.g., Bauer, *Johannesevangelium* 198–199; Bernard, *Commentary* 2:511; Lindars, *Gospel* 505). For others again it is a reference to the events of "the hour" that are about to come in the story of Jesus (e.g., Thüsing, *Die Erhöhung* 149–153; Marsh, *Saint John* 538–539). The position taken in the interpretation combines these views. The Paraclete points the disciples forward to the many things that will flow from the event of Jesus, from "the hour" (and including "the hour") until the traditional end of time.

15. *he takes what is mine and will declare it to you:* The verbs that speak of the revealing mission of the Paraclete in vv. 12-15 are in the future tense with the exception of "he takes" *(lambanei)* in v. 15b. Most translations (e.g., RSV, NRSV) render the present as a future. The author's point of view is best respected by maintaining the present tense (cf. translation). One of the consequences of the Prologue (cf. 1:1-2) is stated in v. 15a: "All that the Father has is mine *(ema estin)*." Thus all that is of Jesus has always been his because of the oneness that exists between God and the Word (1:1-2). The Paraclete therefore *takes* (v. 15b: *lambanei*) what *is* (v. 15a: *estin*).

It is the Spirit-Paraclete who fills the post-Easter period, and not the risen Jesus as so many insist. See, most recently, Stimpfle, *Blinde Sehen* and Dettwiler, *Die Gegenwart*. Both Dettwiler and Stimpfle overstate the centrality of Johannine realized eschatology and underestimate the in-between-time role of the Paraclete during the period of the absence of Jesus. Stimpfle is correct in claiming that the Johannine eschatology cannot be described as a tension between the "now" and the "not yet" (cf. p. 278), but the notion of a final return of Jesus is still in place, however much the Johannine believer already experiences "eternal life."

16. *A little while . . . again a little while:* Scholarship is widely in agreement that these two "times" are the short time between the discourse and Jesus' death ("you will not see me"), and the time after the resurrection ("you will see me"). See, for example, Bauer, *Johannesevangelium* 199; Hoskyns, *Gospel* 487; Dietzfelbinger, "Die eschatologische Freude" 422–423. The interpretation given here suggests that the period of not seeing the physical Jesus is (as the disciples correctly suggest) associated with the departure of Jesus and his return to the Father (cf. v. 17d). The time of "not seeing" is the in-between-time when the physical Jesus is no longer present to them, but the "seeing" is associated with the worshiping community and the time of the Paraclete. The times of not seeing and then seeing in v. 16 are the time of suffering produced by the departure of the former Paraclete, Jesus (cf. 14:13-14), through the cross, and the time of joy when the other Paraclete is sent as a result of the departure of Jesus (cf. v. 7; cf. also 14:18-21). See Aune, *Cultic Setting* 132–133. Onuki, *Gemeinde und Welt* 152–156, also makes the link with the Paraclete but

introduces the temporal dimension of the Lukan Pentecost, foreign to the Fourth Gospel, to explain two different points of time.

Most commentators make a major break at v. 16, read vv. 16-33 as a unit, and then trace further subdivisions within those verses. See Brown, *Gospel* 2:727–729; Dietzfelbinger, "Die eschatologische Freude" 420–421. Segovia, *Farewell* 220–224, and Stibbe, *John* 170–171, have three divisions with a major break at v. 16 (vv. 4b-15, vv. 16-24, vv. 25-33), depending on the progressive role of the disciples (cf. vv. 5, 17, 29).

20. *you will weep and lament:* The verb *thrēnein* is regularly linked with the singing of funeral dirges (cf. Matt 11:17; Luke 7:32; 23:27). See BAGD 363. *Klaiein* is used in this Gospel only in connection with death (cf. 11:31, 33).

Now and Afterward (vv. 21-24)

21. "When a woman is in travail she has sorrow because her hour has come; but when she is delivered of the child she no longer remembers the anguish for joy that a child is born into the world.
22. So you have sorrow now, but I will see you again and your hearts will rejoice and no one will take your joy from you. 23a. In that day you will ask nothing of me.
23b. Amen, amen, I say to you, if you ask anything of the Father he will give it to you in my name. 24. Hitherto you have asked nothing in my name; ask, and you will receive, that your joy may be full."

INTERPRETATION

Introduction to vv. 21-24. This brief section, based on the image of a woman in childbirth, develops the theme of "now" and "afterward" in three stages.

1. *The now and afterward of the woman (v. 21).* Jesus presents the image of a woman who passes from tribulation to joy by means of her "hour."
2. *The now and afterward of the disciples (vv. 22-23a).* On the basis of the image of the woman's experience Jesus corrects and instructs the disciples on their need to pass through their experience of sorrow "now" to experience joy "afterward" when they will no longer need to ask for anything.
3. *Living between now and afterward (vv. 23b-24).* Jesus further instructs the disciples on the way they are to correct their "now," never asking in the name of Jesus, into an "afterward" when whatever they ask of the Father will be given to them in Jesus' name.

This brief section dominated by the theme of "now" and "afterward" states the principle of transformation in the image of the woman (v. 21) and applies it to the definitive transformation of the end time (vv. 22-23a) and the need for the disciples to ask in the name of Jesus in the in-between-time (vv. 23b-24).

The now and afterward of the woman (v. 21). There is an easy progression from Jesus' closing words to the disciples about the transformation of sorrow into joy (v. 20) and his further instruction on how they are to live the oncoming anxiety of broaching the in-between-time (vv. 21-24). Jesus uses the experience of a woman in childbirth to explain how the disciples' sorrow will turn into joy. There are contrasting moments in the woman's experience that cannot be avoided. *Before* the birth the woman experiences the sorrow of physical pain and anxiety because she has come to her "hour" (v. 21a). *After* the child has been born the memory of the anguish *(tēs thlipseōs)* disappears (v. 21b) because a child *(anthrōpos)* has been born to the world (v. 21c). The experience of a woman at the birth of a child serves as a symbol of the way joy can be attained through sorrow and anxiety.

Certain elements in this symbol hint that a deeper meaning might lie behind the image of the woman in childbirth. There is a close link between Jesus' words and the use of the same image in Isa 26:16-19 and 66:7-14. The Isaian texts announce a messianic salvation that will relieve the afflictions that must intervene before the final consummation (cf. Bauer, *Johannesevangelium* 199, for further biblical and Jewish background). Earlier in the narrative (cf. 2:4) "the hour" *(hē hōra)* was announced by Jesus as "not yet" when approached by his mother, whom he called "woman" *(gynē)*. The subsequent miracle at Cana was a foretaste of the messianic fullness that would mark "the hour," and the *doxa* was seen by the disciples (2:11). The language is also reminiscent of a widespread early Christian expression for the pains of the end time *(hē thlipsis;* cf. Mark 13:19, 24; Matt 24:9, 21, 29; Acts 14:22; 1 Cor 7:26; 10:11; 2 Cor 4:17; Rev 2:10; 7:14). This language and its links with biblical and other Johannine traditions suggest that something of messianic and final significance is being mooted.

The now and afterward of the disciples (vv. 22-23a). Before Jesus' departure *(nun)* the disciples wait in sorrow and anxiety just as the woman awaits the birth of her child (v. 22a; cf. v. 21a). But *afterward* sorrow will be turned into joy and they will no longer need to ask Jesus for anything (vv. 22c-23a). *When* will this time be? Although this is almost universally understood as a reference to Jesus' seeing the disciples again after the resurrection, such a reading hardly fits what Jesus says. The readers of this Gospel are living the in-between-time, which is marked by hatred, rejection, and murder (cf. 15:18–16:3). This cannot be the time described by Jesus as full of a joy that no one can take from them (22c) so that there is no longer any need to ask anything of Jesus (v. 23a).

The traditional eschatological expression "in that day" (v. 23a: *en ekeinę tę hemerą*) retains its usual meaning (cf. Mark 13:11, 17, 19; 14:25; Acts 2:18; 2 Tim 1:12, 18; Heb 8:10; Rev 9:15). Jesus' future coming back to "see" (v. 22b: *opsomai hymas*) his disciples will produce a joy that no one will ever take away, and it will remove all need for them to turn to him in prayer. The disciple will shortly *see* the revelation of God in Jesus in and through the Paraclete (cf. vv. 16 and 19c: *palin mikron kai opsesthe me*), but in v. 22b Jesus announces that *he will see the disciple.* Verses 22-23a contrast the difficulties of the in-between-time (v. 22a: "now": [*nun*]) and the definitive return of Jesus at the end of time to see his own (vv. 22b-23a: "I will see" . . . "your hearts will rejoice" . . . "you will ask nothing"). "On that day" they will no longer have need to ask for anything (v. 23a). The weight of the Johannine realized eschatology has not eliminated a traditional view of an end time. Jesus tells his disciples of a time when the ambiguities and the suffering of the in-between-time will be finally resolved.

Living between now and afterward (vv. 23b-24). Still the problems and difficulties of the in-between-time remain (cf. 15:18–16:3). A double "amen" opens the final statement of this subsection. In the in-between-time disciples are to turn to the Father, and whatever they ask of him will be given to them in the name of Jesus (v. 23b). The physical Jesus experienced during the earthly ministry will be absent, but the Father will respond to the prayers of the disciples in union with the absent Jesus. The exalted—and therefore absent—Jesus can be experienced in community worship as disciples pray in the name of Jesus. The in-between-time will be marked by requests granted by the Father in the name of Jesus (v. 23b) and the presence of the Paraclete, sent in the name of Jesus (cf. 14:26; 16:7).

Jesus returns to his earlier use of the scheme of *before* and *afterward* (v. 24). Until this time, as Jesus speaks to them at the meal-table (*heōs arti*), the disciples have asked nothing in the name of Jesus. This situation *before* the events of "the hour" will change. *Afterward,* if they ask the Father in the name of Jesus they will receive what they ask for, and their joy will be full. There is a difference in the character of Jesus' words in v. 24 and his earlier words on "before and after" in vv. 21 and vv. 22-23a. In his earlier use of this time-scheme Jesus was able to speak with authority: the pain of the woman *will be overcome* by the birth of a child (v. 21); the sorrow of the disciples and the need to ask things of Jesus *will disappear* when he comes again and sees them (vv. 23b-24). These are truths that do not depend on the disciples' response because they are a part of God's design. This is not the case in the in-between-time. Here an imperative appears (*aiteite*) instructing the disciples on what they must do, followed by a subjunctive: so that their joy might be complete (*hina hē chara hymōn ę peplerōmenē*). The imperative and the subjunctive of v. 24 are an indication of how disciples living in the in-between-time *might* be part of God's design. Whether or not disciples respond to the initiative of God in the sending of the Son and the Paraclete is entirely their concern as they face the ambiguities of that time. It is in the worshiping community that the exalted Jesus gives life to those who ask in his name (cf. 14:18-21), and he promises that asking in his name will lead to a joy-filled experience of the in-between-time (16:24).

NOTES

21. *she no longer remembers the anguish:* The theme of "anguish" *(thlipsis)* is important to biblical language and imagery surrounding the end time (cf. Heinrich Schlier, *TDNT* 3 [1965] 143–148) and has a correspondingly important place in the Jewish testamentary tradition (cf. Bammel, "The Farewell Discourses" 109).

22. *you have sorrow now:* For the play on a time-scheme of "before and afterward," critical to the interpretation, see Simoens, *La gloire* 163–167. It is given insufficient attention by most critics, who generally exclude any reference to the parousia (e.g., Dettwiler, *Die Gegenwart* 239–252. For his rejection of any reference to the parousia see pp. 240–241).

    I will see you again: The indication that Jesus will see the disciples rather than vice-versa is unique and calls for an explanation. Scholars generally remark on the importance of the initiative of God or make true but vague generalizations about the use of *opsomai hymas:* "It is better to be seen of God than to see him (cf. Gal 4:9)" (Bernard, *Commentary* 2:515). Some commentators take it for granted that this is the same as the disciples' seeing Jesus (e.g., Brodie, *Gospel* 500), or that it is what is demanded of v. 22 in the light of vv. 16, 17, 19 (e.g., Carson, *Gospel* 545).

    and no one will take your joy from you: The situation of undisturbed joy when the disciple asks nothing of Jesus must look beyond the ambiguity of the human story into the time after the parousia (cf. Neugebauer, *Die eschatologischen Aussagen* 136–137). Schnackenburg, *Gospel* 3:159, represents majority opinion in rejecting this suggestion (cf. most recently, Dettwiler, *Die Gegenwart* 248–249). Like most, Schnackenburg claims that the time referred to is post-Easter. He argues that interpreters who read it as the end time "have misunderstood the joy of the Johannine community." But what internal wrangling might lie behind the insistence on the need to abide in 15:1-11, and to love one another in 15:12-17? See Segovia, "The Theology and Provenance" 125–128. What is to be made of the suffering imposed on the community by outside people and authorities, described in 15:18–16:3? See Segovia, "John 15:18–16:4a" 225–230. What internal divisions lie behind the account of the disciples who left Jesus in 6:61? See Moloney, *Signs and Shadows* 62–63. What of the division in the communities described by 1 John 2:19: "They went out from us, but they were not of us; for if they had been of us, they would have continued with us; but they went out, that it might be plain that they are all not of us"? See the possible reconstruction by Brown, *The Epistles of John* 47–115. The joy of the Johannine community may represent the dream of the interpreter more than the world behind the text.

23. *you will ask nothing of me:* Among others, Hoskyns, *Gospel* 488–489, and Barrett, *Gospel* 494, distinguish between the use of the Greek verbs *erōtan* (v. 23) and *aitein* (v. 24), claiming that the former means "to ask a question" and the latter "to ask for something." See also Segovia, *Farewell* 257–258. Given the Johannine stylistic tendency to couple words having similar meanings, the translation renders both verbs as "to ask for something" (in this case, to ask for nothing!). As well as suiting the context it eliminates the conflict with Jesus' saying that the disciples do not ask questions when the discourse is studded with them.

The Departure of Jesus (vv. 25-33)

25. "I have said this to you in figures; the hour is coming when I shall no longer speak to you in figures but tell you plainly of the Father. 26. In that day you will ask in my name; and I do not say to you that I shall pray to the Father for you, 27. for the Father himself loves you because you have loved me and have believed that I came from God. 28. I came from the Father and have come into the world; again I am leaving the world and going to the Father."
29. His disciples said, "Ah, now you are speaking plainly, not in any figure! 30. Now we know that you know all things and need none to question you; by this we believe that you came from God."
31. Jesus answered them, "Do you now believe? 32. The hour is coming, indeed it has come, when you will be scattered each to your own home, and will leave me alone; yet I am not alone, for the Father is with me. 33. I have said this to you that in me you may have peace. In the world you have tribulation; but be of good cheer, I have overcome the world."

INTERPRETATION

Introduction to vv. 25-33. The words *tauta . . . lelalēka hymin* open (v. 25a) and close (v. 33a) this section. The three stages in the unfolding of the discourse are marked by the characters who speak. In vv. 25-28 Jesus speaks of his departure and in vv. 29-30 the disciples respond. In vv. 31-33 Jesus corrects the overconfident disciples and returns to the theme of departure. The section can be divided as follows:

1. *The return of the Son to the Father (vv. 25-28).* Jesus resumes his presentation of his necessary departure, explaining openly that this departure is the return of the Son to the Father.

2. *The disciples' knowledge and belief (vv. 29-30).* The disciples' response shows they have come part of the way to a proper understanding of Jesus, but they still have not grasped the significance of his departure.

3. *The peace Jesus gives (vv. 31-33).* Responding to the disciples' partial belief, Jesus points out that the hour of his departure may produce a physical scattering but it cannot take away the peace he gives. He has overcome the world.

The significance of Jesus' departure is spelled out as the return of the Son to the Father (vv. 25-28), but the disciples can only accept half of this story's christological equation: Jesus has come from God (vv. 29-30). How will they deal with his departure? They will suffer scattering and tribulation when he departs, but in Jesus they can find peace and joy (vv. 31-33).

The return of the Son to the Father (vv. 25-28). The image of the woman in childbirth leads into Jesus' telling his disciples that he will no longer speak to them *en paroimias* (v. 25a: "in figures"), but *parrēsią* (v. 25b: "openly"). There is a change in the way Jesus announces the Father and this change is associated with the coming hour *(erchetai hōra).* The hour is coming when words, which are always approximations of the truths that lie behind them, will be surpassed by a public proclamation of the Father: "I will tell you plainly of the Father" (v. 25c). This promise looks forward to Jesus' public revelation of the Father on the cross: the glory of God will shine forth in and through the death of Jesus (cf. 11:4; 12:23, 32-33; 13:1, 31-32). But the hour of this public revelation will not only be marked by a change in the way *Jesus is present to the disciples.* The way *they are present to him* will also be transformed by the coming hour of Jesus. No longer will the disciples approach the Jesus they have known; they will make their requests in the name of Jesus (v. 26a). They will not need his intercession with the Father (v. 26b) because the events of "the hour of Jesus" and the revelation of God so closely associated with it will change the nature of the relationship between the Father of Jesus and the disciples of Jesus. In a way that recalls 14:23 Jesus tells his disciples that because they have loved him and believed he came from God they will be swept into the love of the Father (vv. 26-27).

This new situation is demanded by the message that lies at the heart of 16:4-33: the departure of Jesus to the Father. Jesus tells of his origins with God (v. 28a: *para tou theou*), from whom he once came in the event of the incarnation (aorist: *exēlthon*). He has come into the world, and the significance of his coming endures (v. 28b: *elēlutha*). Balancing the statement of his coming, he tells of his imminent departure from the world (v. 28c: *palin aphiēmi ton kosmon*) and return to the Father *(poreuomai pros ton patera).* Jesus' departure to return to the person and place of his origins leaves the disciples in an in-between-time. This departure (v. 28), linked with the public proclamation of the Father (v. 25), demands the oneness that will exist between the Father and the disciples in this in-between-time (vv. 26-27).

·*The disciples' knowledge and belief (vv. 29-30).* With one voice *(legousin hoi mathētai autou)* the disciples acclaim Jesus' having spoken in clear words *(parrēsią),* and not in a way that can be misunderstood (v. 29). The time of clarity ("now" [*nun*]) has done away with the obscurities of the past ("not in any figure"). As a result of this clarity the disciples think they can already *(nun)* lay claim to perfect knowledge and authentic belief (v. 30): Jesus knows all things and no one can question him. The encounters of the past, especially as they have been reported in the conflicts that marked 5:1–10:42, have been studded with sharp and unbelieving questions (cf. 5:12, 18; 6:5, 7, 9, 30-31, 34, 41-42, 52, 7:3-4, 20, 25-27, 31, 35-36, 40-42, 45-51; 8:13, 19, 22, 25, 33, 39, 41, 48, 52-53; 9:40; 10:6, 19-21, 33). As recently as 16:19 the disciples have posed questions. They now claim that such a relationship with Jesus is a thing of the past. An awareness of Jesus' knowledge of everything is an admission that Jesus is "the only true revealer of God" (Brown, *Gospel* 2:726). Their knowledge (v. 30a) leads them to state their belief: Jesus came from God (v. 30b).

The disciples have already shown their inability to cope with Jesus' words on his departure to the Father (vv. 17-19), and he has only just spoken to them about his departure and return to the Father (v. 28). The departure of Jesus is not part of their knowledge (cf. v. 30a) or their belief (v. 30b). They must believe he is returning to the Father, and thus the disciples have arrived at a confession of a partial faith parallel to that of Nicodemus and the Samaritan woman. What they know and believe is correct (v. 30), but there is more to Jesus than his knowledge and his origins. His words in v. 28 instruct that both the incarnation *and* his return to the Father must be accepted. The disciples are still unable to commit themselves to an unconditional acceptance of the word of Jesus (cf. vv. 28, 30).

The peace Jesus gives (vv.31-33): The limitations of the disciples' belief are laid bare by Jesus' question: "Do you now believe?" (v. 31: *arti pisteuete;* cf. 11:26-27). The "now" *(nun)* of the disciples' claim in v. 29 is undermined by the "now" *(arti)* of Jesus' response in v. 31. Jesus returns to his promise of v. 25: a critical time is rushing upon them: "the hour is coming, indeed it has come" (v. 32a). This hour may be associated with the revelation of God (v. 25), but there are other events that will be coupled with it: the disciples will abandon Jesus, be scattered to their own homes *(eis ta idia),* thus fulfilling the prophecy of Zech 13:7: "strike the shepherd that the sheep may be scattered" (v. 32b; cf. Mark 14:27). The flight *eis ta idia* is a rejection of the challenge of Jesus as each "disciple is concerned with his own safety, and not at all with Jesus" (Schnackenburg, *Gospel* 3:165). In 1:11 the narrator announced that Jesus came to his own home *(eis ta idia)* and his own people *(hoi idioi)* did not accept him. A fulfillment of this promise is found in 16:32b. "The hour" is at one and the same time the revelation of the Father (v. 25) and a moment of flight and abandonment (v. 32b). A partial explanation for this enigma is immediately provided: Jesus may be abandoned at "the hour" but he is not alone (cf. 8:16, 29). The oneness that has always existed between Jesus and the Father is not taken away by the violence that will surround Jesus' death (v. 32c). Indeed there are many hints that this oneness will become most visible at "the hour."

Jesus returns to a theme that has been present across the discourse. He is telling them of the coming "hour" and its significance so that they might be aware of the riches that will flow from it (cf. 13:18-20 [belief]; 14:25-27 [peace]; 14:29 [the prevention of failure]; 16:4a [that they might remember]). He has also reprimanded his disciples because his telling them these things is leading to sorrow caused by their unbelief (16:4b-6). He returns to this motif in v. 33. He is telling them of the dramatic events that lie ahead and of their significance, so that when these things take place the disciples will not remain in their flight and confusion but will have peace (v. 33a). Jesus' promise of tribulations no doubt reflects the experience of the first readers of this Gospel (cf. 15:18–16:3), but they should not become the all-determining element in their lives as disciples of Jesus. In the midst of their suffering they are to be of good cheer (cf. 14:1, 27), as they are disciples of Jesus who is victorious even in his darkest moments of abandonment and death.

The oneness between Jesus and the Father (cf. v. 32c) is Jesus' assurance of victory, no matter how convincingly the forces of this world may appear to have won the day in the violence that will terminate Jesus' life (v. 33c). In the God-directed view of reality that is all-determining in this story Jesus has overcome the world. This victory enables him to promise the gift of peace to his failing (cf. vv. 29-30) and troubled (cf. v. 33b) disciples. The disciples have been promised that the events of "the hour" will lead to an unequivocal revelation of the Father (v. 25) and unmediated oneness between the Father and the disciples (vv. 26-27). The peace and victory of Jesus, which flow from his oneness with the Father (v. 33), will also be granted to disciples who love and believe in him even though, for the moment, they are unable to accept his departure (vv. 29-30). They are summoned to be one with Jesus *(en emoi)*, rather than in the world *(en tō kosmō)* if they are to be part of his victory. In the midst of their confusion (vv. 16-17) and limited faith (vv. 29-30) the disciples of Jesus have every reason for good cheer (v. 33; cf. vv. 25-27).

Conclusion to 16:4-33. In anticipation of the prayer of Jesus, which will follow immediately, the need for the disciples to turn to the Father in the name of Jesus is central to this passage. Jesus addresses the experience of disciples *before* and *after* "the hour" (vv. 21-24). The in-between-time will be highlighted by asking and receiving in the name of Jesus (v. 23b). *Before* this time the disciples have not prayed in the name of Jesus, but *after* the hour of Jesus their prayer will bring them to the fullness of joy (v. 24). This time will come to an end when Jesus will see his disciples once more and they will no longer ask anything in his name (vv. 22-23a). During the time of the Christian reader there is a fundamental need for disciples of Jesus to ask for things from the Father so that their joy may be full (cf. vv. 23b-24). The ambiguities of the in-between-time will be overcome because of the lifegiving presence of the absent one to a worshiping community (cf. 14:18-21; 16:16-19, 23b-24).

As the disciples have believed that Jesus comes from the Father, the Father loves them (cf. vv. 25-27), but they are challenged to go farther in their love and belief. Jesus came from the Father and is returning to the Father (v. 28), but the disciples are only able to accept half of that equation. They are not prepared to understand or accept that Jesus must depart (vv. 29-30). Between the "now" of the upper room and the "then" of perfect faith, when they will ask nothing of Jesus (cf. v. 23a), they must live through the anguish of the in-between-time. During that time they will be scattered, abandoning Jesus in his "hour" (v. 31). But Jesus' suffering and loneliness are overcome by his oneness with the Father (v. 32). Jesus has overcome the world, and the disciples' eventual awareness of his victory should bring them courage and joy in the midst of their many tribulations (v. 33). Jesus has now concluded his discourse with his disciples. His remaining words in the upper room will be a prayer to the Father (17:1-26). He closes with a cry of triumph and a promise that disciples can be associated with that triumph. He has instructed them on his departure (vv. 4-6, 25-28) and their frailty (vv. 16-20, 31-33) in the in-between-time. As they live through the challenges that will face them he has promised the critical yet revealing presence of the Spirit-Paraclete during his absence (vv. 7-15). He has promised them that despite his absence—indeed *because of* his absence through departure (cf. v. 7)—love, faith, joy, and peace can be theirs (cf. vv. 27, 30, 33).

NOTES

25. *tell you plainly of the Father:* The verb "to tell" (*apangellō*) is to be preferred to the more forceful "to declare" (*anangellō*) found in some witnesses. The latter reading is the result of assimilation with the use of this strong verb in vv. 13, 14, 15.

27. *the Father himself loves you:* The Greek *autos gar ho patēr* is a classic way of emphasizing the Father himself, acting of his own accord. See Bernard, *Commentary* 2:520.

from God: There is a finely balanced textual problem behind the choice of the reading "from the Father" *(para tou patros)* rather than "from God" *(para tou theou).* The reading chosen has the support of, among other witnesses, $\mathfrak{P}^5$, the first hand of Sinaiticus, and Alexandrinus. See the discussion, coming to this conclusion, in Segovia, *Farewell,* 265 n. 73.

28. *I came from the Father:* Bezae, Freer Gospels, Old Latin, and Siniatic Syriac have a shorter reading, omitting *exēlthon para tou patros* at the beginning of v. 28, thus linking the belief of the disciples in v. 27 with Jesus' coming from God and into the world in vv. 27-28. See the discussion in Barrett, *Gospel* 496, and the support of the longer reading for both textual and Johannine reasons in Brown, *Gospel* 2:724–725; Lindars, *Gospel* 512.

30. *need none to question you:* Bream, "No Need to be Asked Questions" 49–74, surveys the discussion of this affirmation and concludes interpreters should notice the contrast that is made between Jesus and revealers from the Greek and Jewish worlds. Unlike them Jesus does not need to be questioned, as he is the authentic revelation of God.

    we believe that you came from God: The interpretation claims that this is ironic, as the disciples make a claim to full knowledge and faith but then express this knowledge and faith in terms that are only partially correct. See also Duke, *Irony* 57–58. Some see this as a climactic post-Easter confession of faith (e.g., Dettwiler, *Die Gegenwart* 258–259, 262–263), but this fails to take account of the immediate and total context of the disciples' words.

31. *Do you now believe?:* There is a significant parallel between this question from Jesus in which he exposes the partial belief of the disciples *(arti pisteuete?)* and the question Jesus poses to Martha's faith in 11:26 *(pisteueis?).* See Moloney, *Signs and Shadows* 161–162.

32. *the hour is coming, indeed it has come:* The interpretation links the use of *erchetai hōra hote* in v. 25 and *erchetai hōra hote* in v. 32. They both refer to the cross, the "lifting up," the glorification, the gathering, and the gift of the Spirit. The addition of "and indeed has come" adds intensity to the passage, building on the information already supplied in 12:23, 27; 13:1.

    when you will be scattered: There is no explicit citation of Zech 13:7, but both the text and the context are so close to Mark 14:27 *par.* Matt 26:31 that an implicit reference to the passage should be supposed. On the use of Zech 13:7, and the relationship between John 16:32 and Mark 14:27, see Brown, *Gospel* 2:736–737; Dodd, *Tradition* 56–58.

    yet I am not alone, for the Father is with me: On the possible relationship to 16:32c, correcting or affirming Jesus' cry of abandon in Mark 15:34, see the summary in Brown, *Gospel* 2:737.

33. *I have overcome the world:* O'Day, "'I Have Overcome'" 162–164, pays too little attention to the subtle play on the time-scheme behind this passage. Jesus' victory is in place because "the hour" is already under way (cf. 12:23, 27; 13:1; 16:32), but Jesus' words in v. 33 *will have* an inspirational and guiding function in the future experience of the disciples. Time has not been collapsed into a Spirit-filled present.

Dettwiler, *Die Gegenwart* 294–304, rightly interprets 13:31–16:33 as the fruit of a *"relecture"* within the Johannine community by means of which the absent Jesus is rendered present. However, he collapses the presence of the Paraclete in the post-Easter period into the presence of the glorified Christ and thus underestimates the impact of the *physical* absence of Jesus on the Johannine experience.

For Reference and Further Study

Bream, Howard N. "'No Need to be Asked Questions: A Study of John 16:30." In Jacob M. Myers, Otto Reimherr, and Howard N. Bream, eds., *Search the Scriptures. New Testament Studies in Honor of Raymond T. Stamm.* Gettysburg Theological Studies 3. Leiden: E. J. Brill, 1969, 49–74.

Cagliari, F. da. "'. . . E nessuno di voi mi domanda:—dove vai?'—(Giov. 16,5)," *Laur.* 10 (1969) 233–244.

Carson, D. A. "The Function of the Paraclete in John 16:7-11," *JBL* 98 (1979) 547–566.

Dettwiler, Andreas. *Die Gegenwart* 217–292.

Dietzfelbinger, Christian. "Die eschatologische Freude der Gemeinde in der Angst der Welt," *EvTh* 40 (1980) 420–436.

Kremer, Jacob. "Jesu Verheißung des Geistes. Zur Verankerung der Aussage von Joh 16:13 im Leben Jesu." In Rudolf Schnackenburg, Josef Ernst, and Joachim Wanke, eds., *Die Kirche des Anfangs. Für Heinz Schürmann zum 65. Geburtstag.* Erfurter Theologische Studien 38. Leipzig: St. Benno, 1977, 247–273.

Lindars, Barnabas. "DIKAIOSUNE in 16.8 and 10." In Albert Descamps and André de Halleux, eds., *Mélanges Bibliques en hommage au R. P. Béda Rigaux.* Gembloux: Duculot, 1970, 275–285.

Moloney, Francis J. *Glory not Dishonor,* Chapter Four.

O'Day, Gail R. "'I Have Overcome the World' (John 16:33): Narrative Time in John 13–17," *Sem* 53 (1991) 153–166.

Segovia, Fernando F. *Farewell* 213–282.

Simoens, Yves. *La gloire* 151–173.

Stenger, Werner. "DIKAIOSUNE in Jo XVI 8.10," *NT* 21 (1979) 2–12.

v. Making God Known: Jesus' Final Prayer (17:1-26)

Introduction to 17:1-26. The narrator breaks into the discourse to describe Jesus' adopting a formal pose for prayer (17:1; cf. 11:41). Jesus prays to the Father, without interruption, till 17:26. The disciples are present, listening to the prayer (cf. vv. 6-8, 9-19, 20, 24-26), much of which concerns the listeners and those who believe in Jesus through their word (v. 20). The prayer concludes Jesus' final encounter with the disciples. In

18:1 he sets out with them, crossing the Kidron valley to a garden. There is widespread agreement among scholars that the prayer has three parts: vv. 1-5, vv. 6-19, and vv. 20-26. Critical studies have remarked on the unequal length of the sections of the prayer and wonder about the place of vv. 24-26. Developing the suggestions of earlier scholars (Bernard, *Commentary* 2:559; Loisy, *Evangile* 441; Hoskyns, *Gospel* 496–497; Lightfoot, *Gospel* 296–297; van den Bussche, *Jean* 448), Brown (*Gospel* 2:748–751) has proposed a threefold division based on formal indications of prayer (cf. v. 1: "he lifted his eyes up to heaven"; v. 9: "I am praying for them"; v. 20: "I do not pray for these only").

As one division closes it opens the way to the subject of the following section. Thus in v. 4 Jesus tells the Father, "I glorified you on earth, having accomplished the work that you gave me to do." This theme is spelled out in vv. 6-8. Jesus does not pray for the disciples, but tells the Father he has accomplished the work among the disciples. Having *described* the disciples (vv. 6-8), he then *prays* for them (vv. 9-19). Toward the end of his prayer for them he parallels his mission with their mission (vv. 17-19). There are people who believe in Jesus through the word of the disciples. Having *described* the mission of the disciples he *prays* for "those who believe in me through their word" (v. 20). As the prayer closes Jesus prays for all those whom God has given him (v. 24). This final petition looks back across the prayer, that all who believe might be swept into the love that unites the Father and the Son (vv. 25-26). The resolution of this petition will be provided by the rest of the story (18:1–20:31). A tripartite shape emerges:

  i. *Jesus prays to the Father (vv. 1-8).* He prays for his own glorification and points to his having glorified the Father in the completion of his task of *making God known.*
  ii. *Jesus prays to the "holy Father" (9-19).* After describing the *disciples' fragile situation* he asks a "holy Father" to be father to the disciples and to make them holy.
  iii. *Jesus prays to the Father (vv. 20-26).* Reaching outside the limitations of the upper room, Jesus prays that those who believe in him through the word of the disciples may be one, *making known the one who sent him.* He concludes the prayer by asking that all be swept into the love that unites the Father and the Son.

The themes of glory, love, fragile disciples, Jesus' self-gift, and the revelation of God, which were at the heart of 13:1-38, return in 17:1-26 despite the fact that 13:1-38 is narrative and 17:1-26 is a prayer.

For ease of consultation and clarity the translation and notes for vv. 1-8, vv. 9-19, and vv. 20-26 will be provided separately. Further subdivisions of the material within each of these sections will be presented in a brief introduction to each section. The literature For Reference and Further Study of 17:1-26 will be gathered after the commentary on 17:20-26.

To make God known (vv. 1-8)

1. When Jesus had spoken these words he lifted up his eyes to heaven and said, "Father, the hour has come; glorify your Son that the Son may glorify you, 2. since you have given him power over all flesh, to give eternal life to all whom you have given him. 3. And this is eternal life, that they know you the only true God, and Jesus Christ whom you have sent. 4. I glorified you on earth, having accomplished the work that you gave me to do; 5. and now, Father, glorify me in your own presence with the glory I had with you before the world was made."

6. "I have manifested your name to those whom you gave me out of the world; they were yours, and you gave them to me, and they have kept your word. 7. Now they know that everything that you have given me is from you; 8. for the words that you gave to me I have given to them, and they have received them and know in truth that I came from you, and they have believed that you sent me."

INTERPRETATION

Introduction to vv. 1-8. The prayer opens with a series of petitions from Jesus to the Father concerning the glorification of God and the Son. The petitions are made on the basis of Jesus' having brought to perfection the task given him by the Father. The first part of the prayer has two subsections:

1. *Glorify! (vv. 1-5).* Jesus asks for the consummation of both God's glory and his own glorification, to bring eternal life into the human story by making God known. The petition "glorify" *(doxason)* both opens (v. 1) and closes (v. 5) this part of the prayer.
2. *God has been made known (vv. 6-8).* Jesus has perfected the task the Father gave him to do: he has made God known to the disciples. This section is marked by the repeated use of the verb *didōmi,* "give" *(edōkas* [2x in v. 6], *dedōkas* [v. 7], *edōkas, dedōka* [v. 8]).

The Son will glorify the Father and will himself be glorified through Jesus' having brought to completion the task given to him by the Father: he has made God known.

Glorify! (vv. 1-5). Despite 14:31 the setting of 13:1-4 continues. It is at the supper table that Jesus closes his discourse (17:1a: "When Jesus had spoken these words" [*tauta elalēsan*]) and raises his eyes to heaven in a formal position of prayer. As Jesus' final encounter began the narrator commented, "Jesus knew that his hour had come" (13:1); as it closes Jesus announces, "Father, the hour has come" (17:1b). As the ministry closed Jesus announced that the arrival of the hour also marks the time of the glorification of the Son: "The hour has come for the Son of Man to be glorified" (12:23; cf. vv. 32-33). The prayer that follows this introductory statement leads more deeply into the enigma of a departure by crucifixion that is also the revelation of the glory of God and part of the process of Jesus' glorification (17:1c). The prayer unfolds under the shadow of the hour (cf. Thüsing, *Herrlichkeit* 10–13).

Jesus' role as the one who will glorify God and thus be glorified is associated with his having been given prerogatives traditionally belonging to God (cf. v. 2a: "since" [*kathōs*]). Jesus' power *(exousia)* over all flesh, that he might give eternal life to all *(pan)* that God has entrusted to him (v. 2; cf. 6:37; Sir 17:1-4), conjures up the Prologue (cf. 1:12-13) and Jesus' words on his authority as lifegiver and judge in 5:19-30. The glorification of the Father and the Son (v. 1; cf. 5:23) flows from the Son's giving eternal life to those entrusted to him (v. 2; cf. 5:21, 24). Further clarification of what is meant by "eternal life" is provided in v. 3. Widely regarded as an addition to the original prayer, v. 3 can also be seen as its *leitmotif*. Knowledge of God comes through the revealing words and actions of the Sent One (cf. 1:14, 16-18; 3:14-15, 16-17, 31-36a; 4:13-14; 5:24-25; 6:35, 51; 7:37-38; 8:12; 9:5; 10:27-29; 11:42; 13:18-20; 14:6-7). This is not a gnostic promise of a saving "knowledge," but the promise of life that can be had by those who believe that Jesus Christ has told the saving story of God (cf. 1:18). The believer has eternal life by knowing the God revealed by Jesus, the *logos* of God. The revelation that makes eternal life possible for "all flesh" (vv. 2-3) has taken place in Jesus' revealing words and works.

The fundamental orientation of the life of Jesus was to complete the task given him by the Father (cf. 4:34; 5:36). Jesus tells the Father that this has now been accomplished (v. 4), and because of that a decisive turning point in Jesus' story has been reached (v. 5a: *kai nun*). The revelation of God in and through the words and action of Jesus is complete (v. 5b), and thus Jesus can ask the Father to glorify him *(nun doxason me)* by restoring him to the Father's presence with the glory that was his before the world was made (v. 5c; cf. 1:1-2; 6:62; 8:58). But this can only happen through the "hour" of the "lifting up," that the glory of God may be revealed and the Son may be glorified (cf. 11:4; 12:23, 32-33; 13:31-33). This "hour" has come (v. 1: *elēluthen hē hōra*). Crossing the threshold into his "hour," Jesus looks back across his life and ministry. He is able to point to the people at table with him as proof of his claim that he has brought to perfection the task the Father gave him (vv. 6-8; cf. v. 4), but the climactic moment for the revelation of the glory of the Father, through which the Son will be glorified, lies in the near future (cf. 3:13-14; 7:39; 8:28; 11:4; 12:23, 32-33; 13:18-20, 31-32). At that time and place the love of God revealed in Jesus' love for the Father and for his own will be seen (cf. 13:1, 18-20; 14:30-31; 17:1-2). Through the "hour" Jesus will return to the glory that was his before the world was made (17:5: *nun doxason me;* cf. v. 1: *doxason sou ton huion*).

God has been made known (vv. 6-8). If the hour has come, and its completion will not be achieved until Jesus passes through it, how can he claim to have perfected the task given him by the Father (cf. v. 4)? Jesus provides the answer by pointing to the fragile group of disciples sharing his table (vv. 6-8). There is a close link between vv. 3-5 and vv. 6-8. Jesus has said that eternal life flows from the knowledge of God, the result of the acceptance of the revelation that takes place in Jesus Christ (v. 3). He has made God known, his revealing ministry is at an end (cf. 12:36b), and he is about to return to the glory he had with the Father before the world was made (vv. 4-5). But Jesus is able to point to the group at table with him, disciples given to him by the Father "out of the world." A theme from 15:12-17 (cf. vv. 14-16), the center of the discourse, returns as Jesus points out that the disciples are such only because of the initiative of God. The Father "gave" them to Jesus (v. 6: *edōkas . . . edōkas*); they are a part of God's larger gift of all things to Jesus (v. 7: *panta hosa dedōkas moi*), and Jesus, the Son of the Father, has "given them" (v. 8aβ: *dedōka autois*) the words that the Father "gave" to him (v. 8aα: *edōkas moi*). Jesus' positive assessment of his disciples cannot be regarded as the result of their achievements. Jesus has made known the name of God (v. 6: *ephanerōsa sou to onoma*) to them. The use of the complexive aorist tense looks back across the earlier part of the story and sums up Jesus' ministry (cf. v. 4). To reveal "the name" of God means to make known all that can be known of the reality of God. "The name stands for God's being and nature, his holiness, 'justice' and love" (Schnackenburg, *Gospel* 3:175).

Jesus has completed the task given him by the Father because these people have kept the revelation given to Jesus by the Father. Made clean by the word of Jesus (cf. 13:10; 15:3), abiding in Jesus and in God as Jesus abides in God (cf. 15:9-10), the disciples know that everything Jesus has passed on to them is from God (v. 7; cf. 15:15). "Gifted" in a remarkable way, they have now (v. 7: *nun*) reached a greater maturity of faith and knowledge. The disciples are described in terms that make them models of the Johannine believer: they have received from Jesus the revelation of God that comes to Jesus from God (v. 8: *ta rhemeta ha edōkas moi dedōka autois*). They have thus accepted that Jesus is the Sent One of the Father (v. 8).

NOTES

1. *When Jesus had spoken:* Some Jewish testaments end with a brief prayer of praise, rendering glory to God (cf. *T. Job* 43:1-17; *T. Isaac* 8:6-7; *T. Jacob* 8:6-9).

A doxology is also found in John 17 (cf. vv. 1-5, 24). Other biblical and Jewish literature indicates that the practice of the final "prayer" was reasonably common (cf. Deut 32; *Jub.* 1:19-21 [Moses]; 10:3-6 [Noah]; 20–22 [Abraham]). In some cases prayers are used to link diverse sections of an apocalypse (e.g., 4 Ezra 8:20-36; 2 *Bar* 21; 34; 48:1-24; 84-85). However remote these prayers may be from John 17, the form of a prayer is present (cf. also Marzotto, "Giovanni 17" 375–388; Manns, *L'Evangile* 394–396, for possible contacts between John 17 and the Targums of Exodus 19–20 [Marzotto] and of Deuteronomy 32 [Manns]). Closer contacts have been traced in the Hermetic writings (cf. *Poimandres* I:31-32; *Corpus Hermeticum* XIII:21-22) where God is praised and there are certain verbal similarities, and in the Mandean writings (cf. *Book of John* 236–239; Mandean Liturgy [*Qolastā* 58:9-20]) where "the Great Life" is asked to raise up and give the splendor of light to disciples and children who are locked in the darkness of the lower world. There is no convincing evidence that John 17 depended on these traditions, but "the language and ideas would . . . be familiar and acceptable" (Dodd, *Interpretation* 422). Other Johannine prayers (cf. 11:41-42; 12:27-28) and the so-called "bolt from the Johannine sky" in Matt 11:25-27 (Luke 10:21-22) have literary and theological contacts with this final prayer, but as with the use of the Jewish testamentary tradition in the discourse section of this report of Jesus' final encounter with his disciples, so also in the composition of the final prayer "the author of the prayer had received ideas from different directions, but . . . in the last resort he produced something quite distinctive and unique, firmly marked by the Johannine Christology" (Schnackenburg, *Gospel* 3:200). For a thorough survey of possible background see Appold, *The Oneness Motif* 194–211. For a survey of the debates over the tradition history of the prayer see Ritt, *Das Gebet zum Vater* 59–91, and for its possible liturgical origins see Marzotto, "Giovanni 17" 375–388; Walker, "The Lord's Prayer" 237–256.

these words: The words referred to *(tauta)* are the discourses of 14:1–16:33. Westcott, *Gospel* 237, hypothesizes that Jesus uttered the prayer in the Temple courts. Léon-Dufour, *Lecture* 3:273, points out that Jesus' departures from "the Jews" and from the disciples open with the same words: *tauta elalēsen Iēsous* (cf. 12:36; 17:1).

"Father, the hour has come": Jesus' recourse to intimate prayer to the Father, immediately after 16:4-33, is proof of his claim in 16:32b: "I am not alone, for the Father is with me." The connection between 13:1 and 17:1 is one of many links with 13:1-38, as was pointed out in the interpretation. Bultmann's recognition of these links led to his reordering of the text. Part of 13:1 is linked to Judas' departure in 13:31, and 17:1-26 follows (Bultmann, *Gospel* 486–489). On these links see also Segalla, *Giovanni* 416–417; Stibbe, *John* 175–176.

2. *since you have given him power . . . to give eternal life to all:* The use of the aorist *edōkas* ("you have given him") looks back to the incarnation (1:14), and the use of the neuter singular *pan* ("all") rather than the masculine plural suggests the oneness of the group of disciples. Some limit the *hina*-clause to v. 2: "You have given him power . . . that" (e.g., Lagrange, *Evangile* 440; Barrett, *Gospel* 502). It is more likely that there is a link between the two *hina*-clauses

in v. 1 ("glorify your Son . . . *that* the Son might glorify you") and in v. 2 ("since you have given him power . . . *to* give eternal life"). The Father's glorification (v. 1) is reflected in Jesus' gift of life to all (v. 2). The use of *kathōs* ("since") linking the two statements supports this view (cf. Bernard, *Commentary* 2:560; Brown, *Gospel* 2:740–741).

3. *And this is eternal life:* No doubt v. 3 is a traditional "summary" inserted here to provide an explanation of what is meant by "eternal life" (cf. Marzotto, *L'Unità* 172–173; Thüsing, *Herrlichkeit* 40–41), and may well have been added to an earlier form of the prayer. The use of "Jesus Christ" on the lips of Jesus is strange (for its only other use—by the narrator—see 1:17), and the expression *ton monon alēthinon theon* ("the only true God") is found only here. The question that must be resolved in the interpretation of the prayer is: *why* was it added? For gnostic background to the notion of eternal life resulting from the knowledge of God see Bultmann, *Gospel* 494–495; Käsemann, *Testament* 6. However, on the widespread biblical background to the crucial importance of "knowledge of God" see Barrett, *Gospel* 503, and Brown, *Gospel* 2:752–753.

4. *I glorified you on earth:* However much the later experience and thought of the Johannine community may be determining the shape and message of the prayer, its place in the narrative *after* the ministry of Jesus and *before* his death and resurrection must be kept in mind. Jesus looks both backward and forward. The often-repeated claim that the prayer is written *sub specie aeternitatis* (e.g., Lagrange, *Evangile* 437) is inaccurate, as it detaches the interpretation of the prayer from its present literary setting (cf. Rigaux, "Les destinataires" 299 n. 32).

   having accomplished the work that you gave me to do: Many point to Phil 2:9-11 as parallel to John 17:1-5, but two different christologies are involved. It is *as a consequence* of the humiliation of crucifixion that the Pauline Jesus is lifted up into glory (cf. Phil 2:9: *dio kai ho theos auton hyperypsōsen*), while the Johannine *hypsōsis* takes place *on the cross* (cf. John 3:14; 8:28; 12:32-33).

6. *I have manifested your name:* To make known "the name" is both biblical and gnostic (cf. Barrett, *Gospel* 505). The traditional story of Jesus is being told, but in a way that resonates with a newer readership. There is no need to see the revelation of a particular name as do Dodd, *Interpretation* 417 n. 2, and Brown, *Gospel* 2:754-756.

8. *know in truth that I came from you; and they have believed that you sent me:* On the links between v. 4 ("I glorified you on earth") and vv. 6-8 ("I have manifested your name") see Segalla, *Giovanni* 419; Rigaux, "Les destinataires" 300–302. The positive assessment of the current situation of the disciples does not eliminate the possibility of future failure. The doxologies that conclude some of the Jewish testaments (e.g., *T. Job* 43:1-17; *T. Isaac* 8:6-7; *T. Jacob* 8:6-9) render glory to the wonder of God in the midst of the ambiguity of Israel's situation. The disciples' *knowledge* and *belief* reflect Jesus' accomplishment of the task his Father gave him: he has made God known to them (vv. 3-4). How they will respond to the challenges that lie ahead of them, the necessary consequence of their knowledge and faith (cf. 15:1–16:3), is yet to be seen. There

is more to *the story of Jesus* (cf. 18:1–20:29), but an even longer story lies ahead *of the disciples* (cf. 13:1–17:26). On the ambiguity of the community that received this Gospel see Culpepper, *Anatomy* 118–119; Carson, *Gospel* 559–560.

Keep them and make them holy (vv. 9-19)

9. "I am praying for them; I am not praying for the world but for those whom you have given me, for they are yours; 10. all mine are yours, and yours are mine, and I am glorified in them. 11a. And now I am no more in the world, but they are in the world and I am coming to you.

11b. Holy Father, keep them in your name, which you have given me, that they may be one, even as we are one. 12. While I was with them I kept them in your name, which you gave me; I have guarded them, and none of them is lost but the son of perdition, that the scripture might be fulfilled. 13. But now I am coming to you; and these things I speak in the world that they may have my joy fulfilled in themselves. 14. I have given them your word; and the world has hated them because they are not of the world, even as I am not of the world. 15. I do not pray that you should take them out of the world, but that you should keep them from the evil one. 16. They are not of the world, even as I am not of the world. 17. Make them holy in the truth; your word is truth. 18. As you sent me into the world, so I have sent them into the world. 19. And for their sake I make myself holy that they also may be made holy in truth."

INTERPRETATION

Introduction to vv. 9-19. There are indications that the central section of the prayer has three parts. It opens with Jesus' statement that he is praying for the disciples (v. 9), and he describes their situation in the world. In v. 11b Jesus addresses God as "Holy Father" and asks God to care for his fragile disciples, to be "father" to them. Finally, in v. 17, picking up the theme of the holiness of God, Jesus asks that he sanctify the disciples, making them holy as Jesus is holy. The section unfolds in the following fashion:

1. *Jesus prays for the disciples in the world (vv. 9-11a).* Jesus is about to depart from this world, but the disciples will remain. This subsection is highlighted by Jesus' addressing the situation in which the disciples will find themselves: "the world." Such words both open (v. 9: "I am not praying for the world") and close (v. 11a: "I am no more in the world, but they are in the world") the subsection.
2. *That the holy Father be "father" to the fragile disciples (vv. 11b-16).* Addressing God as "holy Father," Jesus first asks the Father to be "father" to them, to keep them safe and protect them. A petition that the Father "keep" the disciples opens (v. 11b: *tērēson autous*) and closes (v. 15: *hina tērēseis autous*) the subsection.

3. *That the holy Father make the disciples holy (vv. 17-19).* Jesus asks that the Father extend his holiness to the disciples that they may repeat the holiness of Jesus, sent into the world, as Jesus was sent into the world. A petition for the holiness of the disciples both opens (v. 17: *hagiason autous*) and closes (v. 19: *hina ōsin kai autoi hēgiasmenoi*) the subsection.

The section focuses almost entirely on the disciples of Jesus, and the Father is asked to care for these fragile followers of Jesus to make them holy. This theme of the fragility of the disciples was strongly present in the accounts of the footwashing (13:1-17) and the gift of the morsel (13:21-38), *flanking* the central statement of John 13:18-20. In John 17 it is found at the *center* of the prayer. They are sent into the world as Jesus was sent into the world (v. 18), but this points to another group for whom Jesus will pray, those who believe in Jesus through their word (vv. 21-26).

Jesus prays for the disciples in the world (vv. 9-11a). Having pointed to the disciples as proof that he has brought to perfection the task given to him by the Father (vv. 4, 6-8), he now announces that he is praying for them (v. 9: *egō peri autōn erōtō*). Jesus does not pray for the world (cf. 14:30; 15:18-19, 21; 16:3), but for those whom the Father has given him (cf. vv. 6-8). Everything belonging to the Father has been given to the Son (cf. 16:15), and the disciples are part of this gift (v. 10a), but they have their own responsibility: Jesus is glorified in them (v. 10b). The repetition in the life of the disciples of the loving self-gift of Jesus will reveal that they are disciples of Jesus (cf. 13:34-35; 15:12, 17). Jesus' words to the Father indicate that as his perfection of the task given him by the Father glorifies the Father (v. 4), so the ongoing presence of the same quality of love among his disciples glorifies Jesus (v. 10b).

At the threshold of "the hour" Jesus tells the Father that he is no longer in the world (v. 11aα). In strictly physical terms Jesus is at table with his disciples (cf. 13:1-5) and thus still part of the human story. His public revelation of God to the world has come to an end (cf. 12:36b), but a number of events lie ahead: "the hour" (cf. 12:23, 31-32; 13:1; 17:1), the lifting up on the cross (3:14; 8:28; 12:32), the gathering of the whole world (cf. 10:16; 11:52; 12:11, 19, 32), the revelation of the glory of God and the glorification of the Son (cf. 11:4; 12:23; 13:31-32; 17:1, 5). Jesus does not speak from outside the constraints of time. The disciples will remain in the world (v. 11aβ), but Jesus is returning to the Father (v. 11aγ). Jesus has not yet returned to the Father, but a process has begun by means of which Jesus will be glorified (cf. 11:4; 13:23; 17:1, 5). He is passing from this world to the Father (cf. 13:1; 17:5) but he has one further task: he must · love his own *eis telos* (13:1). Through the performance of that task he will return to the Father and the disciples will be the ongoing bearers of the mission of Jesus (cf. 13:15, 34-35; 15:12, 17; 17:10). Jesus' mission in and to "the world" has come to an end (v. 11aα; cf. 12:36), but that of the disciples is about to begin (v. 11aβ; cf. 10b).

That the holy Father (cf. v. 11b) be "father" to the disciples (vv. 11b-16). Throughout the prayer Jesus addresses God as "Father," but here he adds a qualification: "Holy Father" (v. 11b: *pater hagie*). These two elements, *hagios* and *pater*, determine the remaining subsections of this central section of the prayer (vv. 11-16: *pater*; vv. 17-19: *hagios*). Jesus asks the Father to be "father" to the disciples, to care for them *(tēreson autous).* Despite Jesus' words on the disciples in vv. 6-8 they remain fragile in a hostile world (cf. 13:2, 10-11, 12, 18, 21-30, 36-38; 16:29-31) and they will not survive unless the Father keeps them in his name. All Jesus is and does flows from his oneness with the Father (cf. 10:30, 38), a consequence of his being the Sent One of the Father. All that is of the Father is also of the Son (cf. 16:15), and thus "the name" of the Father has been given to Jesus (17:11b). Jesus has made known to the disciples all that one can know of the reality of God: "the name" of the Father (17:6; cf. 15:15). The Son's possession of "the name" enables his revelation of "the name" of the Father, which does not belong to him by right but because it has been given to him *(hō dedōkas moi).* Jesus asks the Father to keep them in his name, to care for the fragile disciples by gathering them into all that can be known of the reality of God *(tēreson autous en tō onomati sou),* creating a unity among them, repeating the oneness that has always existed between Jesus and the Father. Jesus used the expression "the name" of God in v. 6 to show that he had made known all that could be known of God. Jesus was "gifted" with this knowledge, the basis of his oneness with the Father (v. 11c). He prays that his disciples, to whom he has manifested "the name" (cf. v. 6), might be kept in that name by the Father and thus experience the same oneness (v. 11d).

Jesus looks back upon his own care for them. He has done what he now asks of the Father: he has kept them in God's name (v. 12a). As he asks the Father to be "father" to the disciples he points out that he has guarded them, surrounding them with care (v. 12b: *ephulaxa*) so effectively that not one of them has been lost, with the exception of "the son of perdition" (v. 12c: *ho huios tēs apōleias*). Often regarded as a reference to Judas, this expression must be given the meaning it has in the only other place it appears in the NT: Satan (2 Thess 2:3, 8-9). The only figure in the story Jesus could not "care for" is Satan who planned the betrayal (cf. 13:2). Jesus washed the feet and shared the morsel with Judas despite Satan's designs (cf. 13:2). Nevertheless, Satan entered Judas (cf. 13:27) "that the Scripture might be fulfilled" (17:12d; cf. 13:18). There is a divine order in the events of the life and death of Jesus beyond his control. The son of perdition is beyond the control of Jesus, but he has cared for his disciples. During their time with him they have been made clean by his

word (cf. 13:10; 15:3) that they have kept (17:6), and they have believed
that he is the Sent One of the Father (cf. 16:30; 17:8). He has manifested
the name of God to them (cf. 17:6). Jesus has kept and cared for all the disciples entrusted to him by the Father, including Judas. As his gestures in
13:1-17, 21-38 indicate, not even Judas can be judged as lost. The intervention of the son of perdition is part of the larger plan of God manifested in the Scriptures, but so is the limitless love of God revealed in the
unfailing love of Jesus for fragile disciples (cf. 13:18-20). He is asking the
Father to be "father" to all the disciples, including Judas.

The time of Jesus' presence with the disciples is at an end, as Jesus has
begun the process of coming (v. 13a: *erchomai*) to the Father. It is important that while he is still speaking in the world the disciples hear his petition to the Father, asking that the Father keep them after his departure.
In this way all anxiety about their future will be overcome and their joy
will be full, matching the joy of Jesus (v. 13). The promises of earlier parts
of the discourse, that the disciples' openness to the Father in the in-between-
time will bring them a fullness of joy (cf. 15:7-11; 16:24), are now solidly
based on a request that Jesus makes of the Father in the hearing of the disciples. This section of the prayer, asking that the Father "keep" and care
for the fragile disciples, closes (vv. 14-16) with the repetition of themes
from across the discourse and the earlier parts of the prayer. The disciples
are not "of the world" *(ek tou kosmou)* as Jesus is not "of the world" *(ek tou
kosmou)* (v. 16; cf. 15:19). This does not mean that the disciples form an
otherworldly enclave. The expression *ek tou kosmou* indicates that they do
not belong to the prince of this world, to the son of perdition (cf. v. 12), to
the power of darkness, to the forces of evil that are lining up against Jesus
in order to kill him (e.g., 11:49-50, 57; 12:9-11). Jesus has come to make
God known, but "the world" has rejected him, the one who sent him, and
his disciples (v. 14; cf. 15:18–16:3). In the face of this opposition, and even
violence (cf. 16:2), the revelation of God will continue. Jesus is departing
from the world (v. 13) but he is leaving behind disciples who do not belong to this world, so that they may continue to glorify him (v. 10). The
disciples will continue to make God known as they continue to glorify
Jesus. Jesus does not pray that they be removed from their situation in the
world, but that the Father keep them *(hina tērēsēs autous)* from the evil
one.

That the holy Father (cf. v. 11b) make the disciples holy (vv. 17-19). Disciples of Jesus cannot simply bask in the protection of God (vv. 11b-16).
Jesus asks that they be made holy by a holy God (vv. 17, 19; cf. v. 11b: *pater
hagie*), that they be made holy in the knowledge of God, in truth *(en tē
alētheią)* (v. 17). Identification with the design of God will make the disciples holy. To be *hagios* means to be one with a *patēr hagios* (cf. v. 11b). The
disciples are the recipients of the manifestation of God in Jesus, and they

have come to believe that he is the Sent One of God (cf. v. 8). Jesus prays that they might live holy lives corresponding to the holiness of God, revealed to them in and through Jesus *(en tē alētheia)*. As Jesus' association with the Father determined his life, the disciples' association with Jesus, who has revealed the truth to them, determines theirs. The disciples are to become the sent ones of the Sent One. They are to make God known in the world. As Jesus made God known in and through his mission as the Sent One of a holy God (v. 18a), so also the disciples continue to make the same God known as sent ones of Jesus (v. 18b). The revelation of a holy God calls for a holy Sent One. It is the mission to make God known that determines the demand for holiness (vv. 17 and 19).

Jesus has come to the moment of his final self-gift in love so that the glory of God might be revealed. For the sake of the disciples—those at table with him, and all disciples—his consummate act of love will be accomplished. Jesus' total identification with the design of God (cf. 4:34; 5:36; 17:4) and his being associated with the judging and lifegiving action of God (cf. 5:19-30) are the basis of his holiness. Thus Jesus can lay claim to a final and consummate act of holiness *(egō hagiazō emauton)* in "the hour," the lifting up, the gathering, the revelation of the glory of God and the glorification of the Son, the final revelation of his love for his own (cf. 13:1). But Jesus' holiness is not an end in itself (cf. 3:16-17; 10:14-18; 13:1; 15:13). Addressing God in the presence of the disciples, he commits himself to a final act of holiness for their sake *(hyper autōn)*, so that in his total self-gift, making known the love of God, he makes known to them the holiness that must be theirs (v. 19). The present tense of the verb *hagiazō* associates this moment of final revelation of holiness with the departure of Jesus, which is already under way (cf. 13:1; 17:1, 11, 13). As his oneness with the Father is the basis of his holiness, the disciples' oneness with the God who has been revealed to them (v. 19b: *en alētheia*; cf. v. 17) is the basis of their holiness. Jesus prays that they be made holy in the truth. The holiness of God, made visible in the human story in the holiness of Jesus' gift of himself for his own (v. 19a), is to be matched by the holiness of the disciples (v. 19b) as Jesus is sending them into the world to make God known, just as God sent him (v. 18). To succeed in this mission they must be holy, as God is holy (cf. Lev 11:44; John 17:11b, 17, 19).

NOTES

9. *I am not praying for the world:* The Johannine use of the expression "the world" *(ho kosmos)* continues to have a number of possible meanings. See Moloney, *Belief in the Word* 37–38; Koester, *Symbolism* 249–253. Here the meaning is negative.

11. *I am no more in the world . . . and I am coming to you:* The temporal aspect of the narrative must be maintained although many see v. 11a as an indication that Jesus is speaking "as if" the Passover events are behind him. Jesus has begun a prayer for his disciples (v. 9). They are in the world and will remain in the world (v. 11aβ), but Jesus is returning to the Father (v. 11aγ; cf. 13:1; 17:1). The present tense *(kagō pros se erchomai)* indicates that Jesus has not yet returned to the Father, but that a process has begun by means of which Jesus will be glorified (cf. 11:4; 12:23; 17:1, 5). There has been a presence of Jesus "in the world," teaching and doing "signs," which Jesus has brought to an end (v. 4; cf. 12:36b). This presence "in the world" is past, however much the narrative points forward to further "completion" in the lifting up of the Son of Man to reveal the glory of God and to initiate the glorification of Jesus (cf. 3:14; 8:28; 11:4; 12:23, 31-33; 13:1; 17:1).

Holy Father: This expression, based upon a fundamental Hebrew concept of the holiness of God (cf. 2 Macc 14:36; 3 Macc 2:2 for use of *hagie* in addressing God in prayer), is found only here in the NT. See de la Potterie, *La Vérité* 2:737–740, for background to *hagiazein* as the presence of the holiness of God in the human sphere.

keep them in your name: For the use of *tērein* ("keep") in the sense of "caring for" someone see Delebecque, *Jean* 197. For the interpretation of "the name of God" as all that one can know of God see M. Rose, *ABD* 4:1001–1011, especially 1002. Some scholars regard "in the name of" here as "by the power of your name" (e.g., Heitmüller, *Im Namen Jesu* 132–134; Hoskyns, *Gospel* 500; Bultmann, *Gospel* 503). Marzotto, *L'Unità* 177–180, argues that it also has the notion of being in a sacred place. For the interpretation it is read as "in adherence to what Jesus has revealed to the disciples of the character of God" (Beasley-Murray, *John* 299); see Lagrange, *Evangile* 445; Lindars, *Gospel* 523; Schnackenburg, *Gospel* 3:180.

which you have given me: The perfect tense is read rather than the aorist found in some manuscripts. Also, with 𝔓⁶⁶ the dative neuter singular relative pronoun is read, referring back to "in your name." See Metzger, *Textual Commentary* 213.

12. *I kept them:* The verb *ephulaxa* is stronger than *tērein* (v. 11), but here "it is probably no more than a synonymous variation" (Barrett, *Gospel* 508).

the son of perdition: There is an almost universal identification between Judas and the son of perdition. Danielou, "Le fils de perdition" 187–189, suggests that Judas anticipates the Antichrist, but the Antichrist is responsible for the betrayal of Judas (cf. 13:2), whom Jesus has loved, and whom he continues to love and care for (cf. 13:18-20). Satan is more likely "the son of perdition."

13. *these things I speak in the world:* This claim, that Jesus is still speaking "in the world" does not contradict v. 11a, "I am no longer in the world." Jesus is firmly located in a room on the face of the earth (v. 13) but he is no longer involved in a revealing mission to the world (v. 11a; cf. 12:26b).

14. *even as I am not of the world:* This phrase is missing in 𝔓⁶⁶. This does not represent a textual tradition, but an accidental omission through *homoioteleuton;*

that is, the scribe's eye moved from the first *ek tou kosmou* in v. 14, referring to the disciples, jumping the second appearance of *ek tou kosmou*, referring to Jesus, and thus moved immediately into the present v. 14. See Metzger, *Textual Commentary* 213.

15. *keep them from the evil one:* As the word "evil one" *(ponērou)* is in the genitive case it is impossible to be certain if the neuter "evil" *(ponēron;* cf. 3:19; 7:7) or the masculine "evil one" *(ponēros)* is meant. In light of 12:31; 14:30; 16:11, and 1 John 2:13-14; 3:12; 5:18-19, and especially the reference to Satan as "the son of perdition" in v. 12, the "evil one" is preferable.

17. *Make them holy:* The translation renders the verb *hagiazein* as "to make holy" throughout vv. 17-19 rather than "to consecrate." The latter translation is closely associated with a tradition that has its beginnings at least as early as Cyril of Alexandria (*In Joannis Evangelium* XI, 8; MPG 74:545). It was made popular in the sixteenth century by David Chytraeus (1530–1600), who contended that this prayer was priestly, associating the disciples with Jesus' self-oblation. Some (e.g., Hoskyns, *Gospel* 501–504; Lindars, *Gospel* 528–529; Kysar, *John* 261) argue that *hagiazein* means "make holy" in v. 17 and "consecrate" in v. 19. For a more detailed discussion, rejecting this shift of meaning, see de la Potterie, *La Vérité* 2:740–746, and especially his rich study, "Consécration ou sanctification" 339–349. Against the sacrificial-priestly interpretation in general see Appold, *The Oneness Motif* 194–198. The use of *hagios* in v. 11b determines the meaning of *hagiazein* in this context. In v. 11b it does not mean that the "Holy Father" is consecrated and separated from the profane, nor does the use of the verb *hagiazein* in vv. 17-19. Feuillet, *The Priesthood of Christ* 37–48, traces the passage from the Suffering Servant in Isaiah 53 into the Jewish liturgy of *yôm kippûr* to show that John 17:19 is both priestly and sacrificial. For a detailed discussion and rejection of this suggestion see Delorme, "Sacerdoce du Christ" 199–219.

    in the truth: For a full discussion of *en tē alētheiᵩ,* concluding that it serves as a *place* of holiness, a *means* for sanctification closely related to the "in your name" of v. 11b, see de la Potterie, *La Vérité* 2:747–758.

18. *I have sent them into the world:* The mission of the disciples *eis ton kosmon* ("into the world") must be taken seriously and not explained away as an addition aimed at Church order (e.g., Käsemann, *Testament* 29–30) or, aided by a source theory, as a reflection of the fact that the Johannine community was a sectarian conventicle (e.g., Becker, *Evangelium* 2:524–525). On this see Segalla, *La preghiera* 73–84.

19. *for their sake I make myself holy:* It is this "consecration for their sake" that is often read as priestly. But Jesus' final act of holiness is an act of self-gift in love, the perfect fulfillment of his God-given task (cf. 4:34; 5:36; 17:4), so that he might make God known and thus enable eternal life (cf. 17:3). See Schnackenburg, *Gospel* 3:187–188; Forestell, *Word of the Cross* 78–82; Thüsing, *Herrlichkeit* 79–85; de la Potterie, *La Vérité* 2:761–767; Knöppler, *Die theologia Crucis* 210–215. Jesus' holiness flows from his oneness with the holy God, whose love leads him to lay down his life and to take it up again (cf. 10:17-18). This

is revealed to the disciples. He prays that they may be caught up in the same oneness as a result of his manifestation of God to them (cf. v. 6) and thus be holy as he is holy. See especially de la Potterie, *La Vérité* 2:767–775. For some this is a "priestly" concept.

that they also may be made holy in truth: In itself the expression "in truth" *(en alētheiǫ)* could simply mean "indeed." However, the use of the expression *en tę alētheiǫ* in the parallel v. 17 makes a more theological reading of v. 19 probable. The disciples are to be made holy through their acceptance of the revelation of God. See de la Potterie, *La Vérité* 2:773–775.

To make God known (vv. 20-26)

20. "I do not pray for these only, but also for those who believe in me through their word, 21. that they may all be one, even as you, Father, are in me, and I in you, that they also may be in us, so that the world may believe that you have sent me. 22. The glory that you have given me I have given to them, that they may be one even as we are one, 23. I in them and you in me, that they may become perfectly one, so that the world may know that you have sent me and have loved them even as you have loved me.

24. Father, I desire that they also, whom you have given me, may be with me where I am, to behold my glory, which you have given me because you loved me before the foundation of the world. 25. O righteous Father, the world has not known you, but I have known you; and these know that you have sent me. 26. I made known to them your name, and I will make it known, that the love with which you have loved me may be in them, and I in them."

INTERPRETATION

Introduction to vv. 20-26. The prayer opened with two subsections: Jesus, who has made God known, prays for his own glorification (vv. 1-5) and points to the faith and knowledge of the disciples (vv. 6-8). A parallel shape returns in the final section. Jesus prays that God will be made known in the oneness of all who believe in him (vv. 20-23), resulting in a oneness of love among the Father, the Son, and all believers, a sharing in his glorification, which will continue to make God known (vv. 24-26). The section unfolds as follows:

1. *A oneness that makes God known (vv. 20-23).* Jesus prays that a oneness among those who believe in him as a result of the word of the disciples might make God known. This subsection of the prayer is highlighted by the request "that they may be one" (vv. 21, 22, 23).
2. *Glorify! (vv. 24-26).* Jesus asks that all believers see the glory of Jesus, swept up into the oneness that unites the Father and the Son, thus

making God known. This subsection opens with a change of literary form. Jesus expresses his will (v. 24: *thelō hina*) rather than a petition (cf. vv. 1, 9, 20).

The theme that highlighted the *center* of 13:1-38, making God known in a hostile world (13:18-20), *flanks* the centerpiece of 17:1-26 (vv. 1-8, vv. 20-26). Jesus has made God known (vv. 1-8), and he passes on this task to his disciples and subsequent generations who come to believe in him because of their word (vv. 20-26). However, the themes of love (cf. 13:1, 34-35) and glory (cf. 13:31-32) that highlighted 13:1-17 and 13:21-38 return in 17:1-8 (vv. 1, 4-5: glory) and 17:20-26 (vv. 21-23, v. 26: love; v. 24: glory). Despite the difference in literary form, ideas crucial to 13:1-38 return in 17:1-26. John 13:1–17:26 began with a proclamation of the love of Jesus for his own (13:1), and it closes with his prayer that all disciples be swept into the love that unites the Father and the Son (17:26). At the center of the report of Jesus' final encounter with his disciples lies the command that the disciples love one another as he has loved them (15:12-17). These are major indications that—whatever the prehistory of its component parts might have been—13:1–17:26 is a carefully designed literary unit (cf. Simoens, *La gloire* 52–80).

A oneness that makes God known (vv. 20-23). Jesus prays not only for the disciples at table (v. 20a), but also for those who will be the fruit of their missionary activity: "for those who believe in me through their word" (v. 20b). The situation at table must not be lost from view. In contrast to the synoptic tradition (cf. Mark 6:1-13; Matt 10:1-11:1; Luke 9:1-6; 10:1-12), no report has been provided of any missionary activity of the disciples during the story, although there has been a hint of it in 4:35-38 (cf. Moloney, *Belief in the Word* 163–168). But Jesus now prays for those already believing *(peri tōn pisteuontōn)* because of the word of the disciples. Remaining strictly within the story-time of the passage, Jesus prays for his disciples present with him at the table, and for other believers not present. However, readers across the generations rightly read themselves into Jesus' words "for those who believe in me through their word." They are the continuing presence of those believers who were part of the story, fruit of the preaching of the original disciples (cf. 4:35-58).

Jesus' having made God known to the disciples has opened a new possibility: that they share in the oneness that exists between the Father and the Son (cf. v. 11b). This petition is repeated in v. 21ab, and a further element is added in v. 21c. Jesus now prays that this group of believers be taken into the oneness that exists between the Father and the Son. Jesus first asks the Father that believers be united as one (v. 21a: *hina pantes hen ōsin*). The juxtaposition of the "many" *(pantes)* and the "one" *(hen)* expresses the point of Jesus' prayer, but a unique model of oneness is given (cf. also v. 11b). As the Father is in the Son and the Son is in the Father, so also might it be among believers (v. 21b). But the unity among believers is not an end in itself; it is "so that the world may believe that you have sent me" (v. 21c). Jesus may not be praying for "the world" (v. 9), but he has been sent into the world (cf. 3:16; 17:18) and he sends his disciples into the world (17:18). Because of the mission of the original disciples others have come to believe that Jesus is the Sent One of the Father (v. 20). The missionary chain, however, runs on unendingly. A further group of believers is to mirror in the human story the oneness between the Father and the Son that "the world" might be led to belief that Jesus is the Sent One of God.

A slight deviation from the form of a prayer occurs in v. 22 as Jesus tells the Father, in an aside heard by the listening disciples, that the mutuality between himself and the Father that he passes on to believers is the *doxa* ("glory"). Consistent with the use of this expression across the Gospel, the biblical idea of the revelation of God returns. God was made known through Israel's history in the *kābôd* YHWH, especially in and through the Law. But the love and oneness existing between the Father and the Son from all time (cf. 1:1-2; 17:5) have been made visible in and through the gift of the Son (cf. 1:14; 3:16). Jesus' life, teaching, and signs have been the revelation of the *doxa* of God (cf. 2:11; 5:44; 7:18; 8:50-54; 11:4, 40), a *doxa tou theou* rejected by "the Jews" because they preferred the *doxa tōn anthrōpōn* (see 12:43). But there are some to whom the love of God, made visible in the *doxa* of Jesus, has been given (cf. vv. 6-8). Jesus has already prayed for their oneness (cf. v. 11b). He now prays for oneness among those who have come to believe, through their word, that Jesus is the Sent One of God (v. 20). Jesus has given the love and oneness shared by the Father and the Son to believers. The *doxa*, which is the love bestowed upon the Son by the Father (v. 22a: *tēn doxan hēn dedōkas moi*), is present in the human story in the *doxa* that Jesus has given to the believers (v. 22a: *dedōka autois*). Jesus prays that the oneness of love among believers might reflect the oneness of love that exists between the Father and the Son (v. 22b: *hina ōsin hen kathōs hēmeis hen*).

After this brief pause the form of prayer returns, but the chain of relationships continues into v. 23. Jesus now *prays for* the mutual indwelling *stated* in v. 22. Recalling 15:1-11, he asks the Father that the mutual abiding be realized in a mutual indwelling between Jesus and the believers, and the Father and Jesus (v. 23a). The realization of this indwelling is to have two consequences, one internal and the other external. In the first place it will produce a situation in which the Father enables the perfection of oneness among a newer group of believers (v. 23b: "that they may become perfectly one"). But—as throughout the prayer—Jesus does not make intense communion among the believers an end in itself. The oneness is to be there *that God might be made known*. The gift of the *doxa* given to Jesus by the Father and passed on to the believer by Jesus (cf. v. 22) reaches beyond the boundaries of a unified believing community into the world. The end result of Jesus' request for a oneness between the Father, Jesus, and the believers is that the glory of the love that unites them makes God known to the world (v. 23c). The love of Jesus and the mutual love of believers make known the love that lies behind the sending of the Son: God (cf. 3:16). Jesus' loving his own is not for their comfort and encouragement. It inevitably leads into a mission, matching his mission (cf. vv. 17-19): to make God known (v. 23b; cf. v. 3).

Glorify (vv. 24-26). A change of tone enters the prayer as Jesus expresses a desire (v. 24: *thelō hina*) that all those the Father has given him may be with him "there" *(hopou egō eimi)*. The expression "whom you gave me" could be limited to the disciples, described in this way in vv. 6-7, but the cumulative effect of the prayer makes such an interpretation improbable. Those who believe in Jesus because of the word of the disciples (v. 20) are also involved. Jesus prays for all who have been touched by his love, which makes known the union existing between the Father and the Son (cf. vv. 21-23). He expresses his desire that the gulf be bridged between the Father-Son oneness and the ambiguous situation of fragile disciples and believers *in the world* but not *of the world* (cf. vv. 11, 14-15, 16). In a transformed situation all fragility will be overcome, and they will join Jesus in a new "place" (cf. 14:2-3), to behold the *doxa* that Jesus has as a result of the Father's love from before all time (v. 24). Such a transformation is, for the moment, impossible for the disciples *in the story of Jesus*. They have seen the *doxa* in Jesus' revealing life and actions (cf. 2:11; 11:4, 40). They wait for its consummation in the lifting up, the gathering, the revelation of the glory of God, the glorification of the Son, and the gift of the Spirit-Paraclete. They also wait for the return of Jesus to take them to the place he has prepared for them (14:1-3). But believing disciples who are *readers of the story of Jesus* are also involved, and they experience a similar "waiting." The prayer draws to an end, and brings the story closer to Jesus' death, with a message of transcendent hope. Jesus' words to the Father open the mind and heart of readers to the possibility of "a world" that lies beyond "this world": the vision of the glory of Jesus that existed, as a result of the Father's love for the Son "before the foundation of the world" (v. 24b).

In a way that parallels Jesus' addressing the Father as "holy Father" (v. 11b) he now prays to a "righteous Father" (v. 25: *pater dikaie*). A just God will act justly with a world that does not know him, as also with those who turn to him as Father. Part of this action will be the exposing task of the Paraclete, bringing righteousness and judgment into a hostile world (cf. 16:7-11). Despite the world's rejection of the Father of Jesus as

God, Jesus has never failed in his knowledge of the Father. Disciples in the world but not of the world have come to know the one true God in and through their belief in Jesus. The sound of a single theme tolls across the opening and closing sections of the prayer: making God known (cf. Jaubert, "Jean 17,25" 347–353). In v. 3 Jesus stated the principle that eternal life comes from knowing God and Jesus Christ whom God has sent. In v. 8 he affirmed that his disciples had come to know God and the one whom God had sent. In the final section of the prayer, in vv. 21 and 23, he asks the Father that such knowledge be the fruit of a oneness among believers. Jesus has made God known, and his disciples and other believers have come to know the God and Father of Jesus as their God and Father (v. 25). Jesus has made known all that can be known of God (v. 26a: *to onoma sou*; see vv. 6, 11), and this revealing task will continue in the brief time that remains for Jesus (v. 26b). Indeed, the reader is aware that the high point of Jesus' revelation of the love of God still lies ahead (see 13:1, 19, 34-35; 15:12-13). The enigma of the revelation of love upon a cross looms large (see 13:1; 15:13).

Jesus has made God known to the disciples so that the love that bonds the Father and the Son might bond the disciples, that they might be loved by God in the same way that the Father has loved the Son, and that this love will be their experience of the never-failing presence of Jesus to his own (17:26c). It is crucial to the ongoing story of disciples who will be known as followers of Jesus: only through God's being father to them by bonding them in the love that unites the Father and the Son will disciples make God known. They are to live in the world in a way that responds to the commandment of Jesus: "By this they shall know that you are my disciples, if you love one another as I have loved you" (13:34-35; 15:12, 17).

Jesus' first request in this closing passage (v. 24) offers hope to all believers. It transcends their life in the world and their mission to the world: that they might behold the glory the Son possessed before the foundation of the world. His closing prayer (v. 26bc) missions the disciples for the world, united by the same love that unites the Father and the Son, making God known in loving self-gift as Jesus has made known the name of his Father. Between these requests lie words of Jesus telling of his having made God known (vv. 25-26a). The first two sections of 17:1-26 (vv. 1-8; vv. 9-19) closed with a subsection that served as a bridge from one section of the prayer into the next (vv. 6-8; vv. 17-19). The final section of the prayer (vv. 20-26) closes with words that end Jesus' prayer to his Father (vv. 24-26). They point the reader into the remaining moments of *the story of Jesus* (see vv. 25-26a), into *the future story of Jesus' disciples* (v. 26b), and into *a place that transcends the story-time of both Jesus and his followers,* beyond the in-between-time, contemplating the glory given to the Son by the Father before the world was made (v. 24; see 14:2-3).

Conclusion to 17:1-26. Jesus has completed the task the Father gave him (17:4). *He has made God known* (v. 3), and there is a group of people given to Jesus by the Father who are the fruit of Jesus' *having made God known* (vv. 6-8). They believe that Jesus is the Sent One of God (v. 8). He has also completed his prayer for these first believers, the disciples at the table (vv. 9-19). He has asked that they may be one as the Father and the Son are one (v. 11b), that they be both protected and made holy in a hostile world so that they may perform their mission (vv. 11-19). As Jesus was sent into the world, Jesus sends them into the world (v. 18). The revealing task of Jesus is passed on to the disciples whose performance of that task, *making God known,* glorifies Jesus (v. 10). They too have been successful in this mission, and thus Jesus has prayed for a newer group of believers who have come to believe that Jesus is the Sent One of God through their word. They too must be one, as the Father and the Son are one, so that they might *make God known* (vv. 20-23). The love that unites them will reveal to the world the love that unites the Father and the Son, and will continue to make known that Jesus is the Sent One of God. Jesus, the disciples, and the believers have an identical mission: *to make God known* (see vv. 3; 10, 18; 21, 23). The prayer comes to a close as all those for whom Jesus has prayed are recalled. The final words of Jesus' prayer reach beyond the limits of the time and place of the prayer, into the proximate glorification of Jesus (v. 24) and the desired future glorification of the disciples and the first believers, through their association with his love and the love that unites him and the Father. Jesus *has made God known* to the disciples, and the believers' loving oneness with the Father and the Son will further *make God known* to a world that *has not known God* (vv. 25-26). A rich interweaving of themes has been present throughout 17:1-26. However, one theme predominates: the mission *to make God known* (cf. Segalla, *La preghiera* 193–207). Jesus prays for himself now that he has made God known (vv. 1-8). He prays to his holy Father for his fragile disciples so that, in the midst of a hostile world, cared for and made holy, they might make God known (vv. 9-19), thus continuing their initial success (see v. 20). He also prays that all who believe in Jesus as the Sent One of God might make God known (vv. 20-26) until such time as they are with Jesus in the place he has prepared for them (see 14:2-3), beholding the glory that was his before the foundation of the world (17:24). This is eternal life, that they know God, a knowledge now possible through the revelation that has taken place in and through Jesus Christ, whom God has sent (see v. 3).

Conclusion to 13:1–17:26. This interpretation of John 13:1–17:26 claims that the Johannine account of Jesus' last encounter with the disciples is marked by a discernible unified literary structure and theological argument. The literary form and a number of important themes of the account

come from the Jewish testament tradition, but the final product is profoundly Johannine in its structure and message. The following outline
provides a summary of that literary structure and theological argument,
drawing together elements that have been argued at various points
throughout the interpretation and the notes.

> **13:1-38: *Jesus makes God known in the perfect love he shows for his
> fragile disciples. In and through his loving Jesus is glorified, and God is
> glorified in him. The disciples are to be recognized as the sent ones of
> Jesus in the unity created by the love they have for one another.***

>> *14:1-31: Jesus instructs his failing disciples on his departure and on the
>> conditions and challenges that will face them. They will be guided by the
>> Paraclete in his physical absence; love, faith, joy, and peace should be
>> theirs as they are swept into the love that unites the Father and Jesus, the
>> Sent One.*

>>> 15:1-11: Oneness, joy, and fruitfulness come from abiding in
>>> Jesus, the true vine, and being drawn into his abiding one-
>>> ness with the Father.

>>>> **15:12-17: *The disciples of Jesus are to love as he has
>>>> loved, as a consequence of what he has done for them.***

>>> 15:18–16:3: Hatred, rejection, expulsion, and slaying will
>>> come from "the Jews," the false vine that has rejected Jesus
>>> and the Father.

>> *16:4-33: Jesus instructs his failing disciples on his departure and on the
>> conditions and challenges that will face them. They will be guided by the
>> Paraclete in his physical absence; joy and confidence should be theirs, as
>> they are loved by the Father who sent Jesus.*

> **17:1-26: *Jesus makes God known in the perfect love he shows for his
> fragile disciples. In and through his loving Jesus is glorified, and God is
> glorified in him. The disciples are to be recognized as the sent ones of
> Jesus in the unity created by the love they have for one another.***

Using the language and some of the ideas forged by Dettwiler *(Die Gegenwart)*, this presentation of 13:1–17:26 suggests that 17:1-26 is a *"relecture"*
of 13:1-38, 16:4-33 is a *"relecture"* of 14:1-31, and 15:1–16:3 is an initial
"relecture" of 13:1-38. Crucial to this presentation of the departure of Jesus
(14:1-31; 16:4-33) is the ongoing *"relecture"* of 13:1-38 into 15:1–16:3, climaxing in 17:1-26. The death of Jesus is the hour (13:1; 17:1: *hē hōra*) of an
act of consummate (13:1; 17:4: *telos*) love (13:1, 34-35; 15:12-17; 17:24-26:
agapē) that reveals the glory of God (13:31-32; 17:1-5: *doxa*).

The account of Jesus' final evening with his disciples looks further
into the story for the resolution of the many questions that flow from this
insistence *that Jesus' loving is the revelation of God.* One must read on to discover *how this happens in the life (and death) of Jesus.* But the narratives, dis-

courses, and prayer of John 13–17 also raise questions that point the readers beyond the boundaries of the Jesus-story. "Farewells . . . explicitly look ahead beyond the time of the narrative itself" (Kurz, *Farewell Addresses* 15). Questions emerge powerfully at the structural heart of the story of Jesus' last encounter with his disciples (15:1–16:3). Is God still being made known by fruitful disciples of the Johannine Jesus? Are they abiding in him (15:1-11) in the midst of a hostile world (15:18–16:3)? Does their love for one another proclaim that they are no longer servants (15:12-17)? This should be the case, as they have been chosen by Jesus and have heard all that the Father has made known to him (15:15-16).

NOTES

20. *also for those who believe in me:* The present participle *pisteuontōn* could be a hint of the fruits of the disciples' mission (cf. 4:35-38), although v. 20 is almost universally read as addressing the time of the Church. The idea that the prayer is "timeless," or to be read entirely from the point of view of the later Church is widely accepted by critics. For this perspective see O'Day, "'I Have Overcome the World'" 153–166. This view is challenged by the interpretation, which respects the time and place of the prayer within the Gospel's story of Jesus. Strongly influenced by the experiences and understanding of the later Christian community, it nevertheless reports the last encounter between Jesus and his disciples, set at the table that, despite 14:31, they have never left.

21. *that they may all be one:* For a comparison between this request for unity and "the unity" (*yaḥad*) that was the Qumran community see Brown, *Gospel* 2:277; Beasley-Murray, *John* 302. On the threefold use of "that . . . as" (*hina . . . kathōs . . . hina . . . kathōs . . . hina . . . kathōs*) in vv. 21-23 see Brown, *Gospel* 2:769. The theological focus on the relationship between Jesus and the Father is all-determining.

22. *the glory:* The position adopted in the interpretation is only one of many possible. Westcott, *Gospel* 246–247, saw it as "the revelation of the divine in man realised through Christ." For Bultmann, *Gospel* 515–516, the *doxa* is paralleled with the name of God and the words of God given to Jesus (cf. vv. 8, 11, 14). Schnackenburg, *Gospel* 3:191–192, sees it as the anticipation of eternal life, and Barrett, *Gospel* 513, suggests that it is unity with the death and resurrection of Jesus, from which life flows. The interpretation here depends on the principle that the use of *doxa* and *doxazein* across the story will retain the same basic meaning throughout, linked to the revelation of God.

23. *that they may become perfectly one:* The word "perfectly" translates a passive participle *(teteleiōmenoi)* and could be accurately (but clumsily) rendered "that they might be perfected into one." The less clumsy translation, however, loses the sense of God's being the agent who enables this perfect oneness. The use of this verb associates the "perfection" with Jesus' accomplishment of the task

given him by the Father (cf. 4:34; 5:36; 17:4). See Rigaux, "Les destinataires" 312–316.

so that the world may know: On the identity between "so that the world may believe" (v. 21) and "so that the world may know" (v. 23) see, among many, Rigaux, "Les destinataires" 304–305. The *hina* ("so that") associates the mission to the world with the very purpose of Jesus' petition. See Rodriguez Ruiz, *Der Missionsgedanke* 247–255, and especially Appold, *The Oneness Motif* 157–193, 227–235, 287–289.

24. *that they . . . may be with me where I am:* The interpretation regards this petition as a prayer for the final union between the believer and the glorified Jesus, outside time, in the place where Jesus had his glory before the world was made (cf. 17:5). In this "place" the difficulties and challenges of the in-between-time, so much a part of the message of 14:1–16:33, will finally be overcome. Few would read the passage in this way. Recently Stimpfle, *Blinde Sehen* 217–243, has argued that the Johannine "insider" is aware of being already a part of a predestined sect, while the "outsider" mistakenly waits for an end-time solution. But, as the interpretation has regularly argued, an end-time solution is part of the Johannine vision, however central realized eschatology is to its understanding of life and eternal life.

26. *I made known your name to them, and I will make it known:* Jesus is situated at the end of his ministry, during which he has revealed the *doxa*. He will shortly consummate that revelation (cf. 13:1). A parallel exists between 17:26 and 13:31-32. The past revelation of the name of God will shortly lead to the accomplishment of its future revelation (17:26), just as Jesus proclaimed his past revelation of the glory of God *(edoxasthē . . . edoxasthē)* and God's future glorification of the Son of Man *(. . . doxasei auton)* (13:31-32). This is a further link between 13:1-38 and 17:1-26.

For Reference and Further Study

Agourides, Savras. "The 'High Priestly Prayer' of Jesus," *StEv* 4 (1968) 137–145.

Appold, Mark L. *The Oneness Motif in the Fourth Gospel. Motif Analysis and Exegetical Probe into the Gospel of John.* WUNT 2nd ser. 1. Tübingen: J. C. B. Mohr (Paul Siebeck), 1976.

Becker, Jürgen. "Aufbau, Schichtung und theologiegeschichtliche Stellung des Gebets in Johannes 17," *ZNW* 60 (1969) 56–83.

Danielou, Jean. "Le fils de perdition (Joh. 17,12)." In *Mélanges d'histoire des religions offerts à Henri-Charles Puech.* Paris: Presses Universitaires de France, 1974, 187–189.

Delorme, Jean. "Sacerdoce du Christ et ministère. (A propos de Jean 17). Sémantique et théologie biblique," *RSR* 62 (1974) 199–219.

Feuillet, André. *The Priesthood of Christ and His Ministers.* Garden City, N.Y.: Doubleday, 1975.

Jaubert, Annie. "Jean 17,25 et l'interprétation gnostique," *Mélanges Puech,* 347–353.

Käsemann, Ernst. *The Testament of Jesus. A Study of John in the Light of Chapter 17.* London: SCM Press, 1965.

La Potterie, Ignace de. "Consécration ou sanctification du chrétien d'après Jean 17?" In Enrico Castelli, ed., *Le Sacré. Etudes et Recherches. Actes du colloque organisé par le Centre International d'Etudes Humanistes et par l'Institut d'Etudes Philosophiques de Rome.* Paris: Aubier-Montaigne, 1974, 339–349.

_____. *La vérité* 2:706–787.

Laurentin, André. "*Weʾattah—kai nun.* Formule charactéristique des textes juridiques et liturgiques (à propos de Jean 17,5)," *Bib.* 45 (1964) 168–197, 413–432.

Malatesta, Edward. "The Literary Structure of John 17," *Bib.* 52 (1971) 190–214.

Marzotto, Damiano. "Giovanni 17 e il Targum di Esodo 19-20," *RivBib* 25 (1977) 375–388.

_____. *L'Unità degli Uomini nel Vangelo di Giovanni.* RivBibSupp 9. Brescia: Paideia, 1977.

Moloney, Francis J. *Glory not Dishonor,* Chapter 5.

_____. "To Make God Known. A Reading of John 17:1-26," *Sal.* 59 (1997) 463–489.

Randall, J. F. "The Theme of Unity in John 17," *EThL* 41 (1965) 373–394.

Rigaux, Beda. "Les destinataires du IVe Évangile à la lumière de Jn 17," *RTL* 1 (1970) 289–319.

Ritt, Hubert. *Das Gebet zum Vater. Zur Interpretation von Joh 17.* FzB 36. Würzburg: Echter, 1979.

Schnackenburg, Rudolf. "Strukturanalyse von Joh 17," *BZ* 17 (1973) 67–78, 196–202.

Segalla, Giuseppe. *La preghiera di Gesù al Padre (Giov. 17). Un addio missionario.* SB 16. Brescia: Paideia, 1983.

Simoens, Yves. *La gloire* 174–199.

Thüsing, Wilhelm. *Herrlichkeit und Einheit. Eine Auslegung des Hohenpriesterlichen Gebetes Jesu (Joh. 17).* 2nd ed. Münster: Aschendorff, 1975.

Walker, W. O. "The Lord's Prayer in Matthew and John," *NTS* 27 (1982) 237–256.

B. THE PASSION (18:1–19:42)

Introduction. An account of the suffering and death of Jesus is fundamental to the early Christian storytelling tradition (cf. the summary of the scholarly discussion of this question in Donald Senior, *The Passion of Jesus in the Gospel of Mark.* Wilmington: Michael Glazier, 1984, 7–11). The passion account in the Fourth Gospel is no exception. Jesus' suffering has its place in this Gospel (cf. Thüsing, *Erhöhung* 78–82; Koester, *Symbolism* 188–191), but the Johannine story must do more than repeat the earlier story. The Johannine version of the life of Jesus has looked toward the event of the cross as the high point of Jesus' human experience, his being "lifted up" (cf. 3:14; 8:28; 12:32-33). Associated with this lifting up is the notion of Jesus' "hour" that during the major part of the public ministry has pointed to some future moment (cf. 2:4; 7:6, 30; 8:20). Jesus announced that the hour has come as the ministry draws to an end (cf. 12:23). Jesus' final encounter with his disciples opens (13:1) and closes (17:1) by acknowledging that the hour has come. More subtle suggestions have also been made in the narrative of a future time when the Son of Man would give a gift that will not perish (cf. 6:27), when the disciples would come to understand the words of Jesus and the Spirit would be given when Jesus was glorified (cf. 2:22; 7:39; 12:16). Toward the end of Jesus' ministry a close link emerges between the death of Jesus and the glorification of God and Jesus' being glorified (cf. 11:4; 12:23, 28). During a final meal these suggestions are further confirmed (cf. 13:31-32; 17:1-5). The lifting up of Jesus on a cross will lead to the gathering of many who were formerly "dispersed" (cf. 10:16; 11:52; 12:11, 19, 32). During his final evening with his disciples he has instructed them on the need for a oneness of love (cf. 13:34-35; 15:12-17), the fruitfulness of being drawn into the love that exists between the Father and the Son (cf. 14:23; 15:9-11; 16:26-27). He has prayed to the Father that this oneness be such that others might come to believe that Jesus was the Sent One of God (cf. 17:23-24, 26).

Regularly throughout the Fourth Gospel new places and new characters have been introduced at the beginning of a fresh sequence of events (cf. 2:1-2, 13-14; 3:1-2a; 4:1-7a; 5:1-5; 6:1-4; 7:1-14; 9:1-5; 10:22-23; 11:1-4; 12:1-2). On the basis of this formal criterion (cf. Giblin, "Confrontations" 211–212) John 18:1–19:32 can be divided into five distinct scenes:

   i.   *18:1-11:* Jesus and his enemies in a garden (cf. vv. 1-3 for the introduction).
   ii. *18:12-27:* Jesus' appearance before "the Jews" (cf. vv. 12-16 for the introduction).
  iii. *18:28–19:6a:* Jesus before Pilate (cf. v. 28 for the introduction).
  iv. *19:16b-37:* The crucifixion of Jesus (cf. vv. 16b-18 for the introduction).
   v. *19:38-42:* The burial of Jesus in a garden with his newly-found friends (cf. vv. 38-39 for the introduction).

The account begins (18:1: *ēn kēpos*) and ends (19:41: *ēn . . . kēpos*) with scenes in a garden and has the report of the trial before Pilate at the heart of the story.

i. Jesus and His Enemies in a Garden (18:1-11)

18:1. When Jesus had spoken these words he went forth with his disciples across the Kidron valley where there was a garden, which he and his disciples entered. 2. Now Judas, who betrayed him, also knew the place, for Jesus often met there with his disciples. 3. So Judas, procuring a band of soldiers and some officers from the chief priests and the Pharisees, went there with lanterns and torches and weapons. 4. Then Jesus, knowing all that was to befall him, came forward and said to them, "Whom do you seek?" 5. They answered him, "Jesus of Nazareth." Jesus said to them, "I am he." Judas, who betrayed him, was standing with them. 6. When he said to them, "I am he," they drew back and fell to the ground. 7. Again he asked them, "Whom do you seek?" And they said, "Jesus of Nazareth." 8. Jesus answered, "I told you that I am he; so if you seek me let these others go." 9. This was to fulfill the word that he had spoken, "Of those whom you gave me I lost not one." 10. Then Simon Peter, having a sword, drew it and struck the high priest's slave and cut off his right ear. The slave's name was Malchus. 11. Jesus said to Peter, "Put your sword into its sheath; shall I not drink the cup the Father has given me?"

INTERPRETATION

Commentators generally refer to 18:1-11 as "the arrest" of Jesus (e.g., Bauer, *Johannesevanglium* 208; Stibbe, *John* 180), but this hardly reflects Jesus' domination of the events in the garden. He is not arrested until v. 12. Jesus and his disciples move to an unknown location "where there was a garden *(hopou ēn kēpos),*" as opposing forces, Judas, a cohort of Roman soldiers *(tēn speirēn),* and some Temple officers *(hypēretas)* gather and approach Jesus, bearing lanterns, torches, and weapons (vv. 1-3). Such a combination is historically improbable, but elements from the darkness combine against Jesus, the light of the world (cf. 8:12; 9:5). Armed for violence, Jesus' enemies, Judas, Romans, and Jews, representing "the world," come in search of the light of the world, carrying their own light, lanterns and torches (cf. Culpepper, *Anatomy* 192; Giblin, "Confrontations" 216–217; Heil, *Blood and Water* 19–20).

Jesus knows what will befall him (v. 4a) and comes forward asking whom they are seeking, only to level them to the ground with his self-identification as *egō eimi* after their request for "Jesus of Nazareth" (v. 4b-6). Repeating the formula of self-revelation *(egō eimi),* he *informs* his opponents that their designs upon Jesus of Nazareth can be pursued if they allow the disciples to go free (vv. 7-8). The narrator recalls words from Jesus' prayer: "Of those whom you gave me I lost not one" (v. 9; cf. 17:12. Cf. also 6:69; 10:28). Not even Judas, the betrayer, is excluded from those who must be allowed to go free. The fact that even in this hostile context no exception is made in v. 9: "I lost not one," is an indication that this Gospel makes no *final* judgment upon the disciple Judas. However bad his performance, he has now been given into the care of the Father whose remarkable love has been revealed by Jesus (cf. 17:11-12). Judas is "with" Jesus' opponents (v. 5: *met' autōn*) but he plays no active role in the arrest (contrast Mark 14:42-45, *parr.*). Jesus prayed for his disciples (cf. 17:9-19) and for those who have heard the word through their ministry (vv. 20-26), that they might be drawn into the oneness of love that existed from all time between the Father and the Son, "so that the world might know that you have sent me and have loved them even as you have loved me" (17:23). As Jesus initiates the process that will lead to his being lifted up (cf. 3:14; 8:28; 12:32) he demands that the disciples go their way to perform their missionary task (cf. 13:20, 34-35; 15:5-8, 16, 26-27; 17:18-19, 20-23).

Peter fails to understand the significance of what lies ahead and draws a sword in a violent attempt to change the course of events (18:10), but he is rebuked as the passion must now begin. Peter is thwarting God's design as Judas is thwarting God's design. The prophecies of 13:1-17, 21-38 are being fulfilled. Jesus willingly drinks the cup the Father gives him (v. 11; cf. 12:27), and the Johannine passion story begins because Jesus allows it to begin. He is the master of the situation. From this very first scene, 18:1-11, the disciples are singled out for special attention. Unlike the parallel scene in the synoptic tradition, where Jesus' loneliness is stressed (cf. Mark 15:32-42; Matt 26:26-46; Luke 22:40-46), Jesus is in the garden with his disciples (John 18:1). They are mentioned three times in two verses (vv. 1-2), while Judas, another disciple of Jesus, is described as standing with Jesus' enemies (v. 5). In the face of hostility and violence Jesus demands that the disciples go free (v. 8). The passion of Jesus in the Fourth Gospel may not only be about what happens to Jesus, but may also determine the future of disciples. The first scene in the garden begins a series of events during which Jesus will love his disciples *eis telos* (cf. 13:1), a love that makes God known (cf. 13:18-20).

NOTES

1. *where there was a garden:* Patristic sources and some commentators make a link between the Garden of Eden where the first Adam fell and this Garden where the saving action of Jesus, the second Adam, began (cf. Hoskyns, *Gospel* 509). Links have also been made between Jesus' journey across the Kidron valley and the journey of David fleeing from his son Absalom in 2 Sam 15:30-31 (cf. Glasson, "Davidic Links" 118–119). The former is a valuable reflection but not part of Johannine thought, and the latter may be remotely present to the scene. However, there is no sense of flight or suffering and wailing in John.

3. *Judas, procuring a band of soldiers and some officers:* Judas' assembling this collection of a large group of Roman soldiers (*hē speira:* six hundred troops) and some Temple guards (*hypēretai*) described as "of the chief priests" and "of the

Pharisees" is both unlikely and historically inaccurate. As throughout the Johannine passion account, historical accuracy and political correctness are often subordinated to the Johannine theological point of view. For a detailed analysis of the historical difficulties and their theological significance see Brown, *Death* 1:248–252. Schnackenburg (*Gospel* 3:223) remarks: "He (the evangelist) would have Jesus confront the whole unbelieving cosmos."

4. *Jesus, knowing . . . came forward and said to them:* From the first moment Jesus directs the action. Jesus is not betrayed, led out, or questioned. He knows, comes forward, and initiates the encounter.

 Jesus of Nazareth: There may be a pejorative note in the name "Jesus of Nazareth." This is only the second time in the Gospel that Jesus' origins in Nazareth are mentioned. Earlier Nathanael had commented, "Can anything good come out of Nazareth?" (1:46).

5. *Jesus said to them, "I am he":* On the use of *egō eimi* in 18:4-8a see Brown, *Death* 1:259–262. Some speculate that there is allusion to OT theophanic texts such as Isa 11:4 (cf. Schnackenburg, *Gospel* 3:225) or Ps 56:9 (cf. Barrett, *Gospel* 520). Not all would accept that the expression is anything more than self-identification for the people who have come to arrest him (e.g., Bligh, *The Sign* 18–19). Ball, *'I Am' in John's Gospel* 137–145, 201, claims that in themselves the words say little, but the reader has by now (and especially after 13:19) come to recognize that Jesus is applying Isaian ideas of YHWH as God and Savior to himself.

6. *they drew back and fell to the ground:* This response from Jesus' enemies demands that his self-revelation be more than a simple identification of the man they were looking for. Brodie, *Gospel* 325–326, however, exaggerates in his claim that the scene is God's "going out into the world and overcoming the forces of darkness" (vv. 4-6), followed by "divine self-giving" that brings salvation to others (vv. 7-9).

9. *I lost not one:* The position taken in the interpretation, that the absolute nature of Jesus' claim both here and in 17:12 includes Judas, is further indication that "the son of perdition" in 17:12 is not Judas, but Satan (cf. 2 Thess 2:3, 8-9). Against, for example, Senior, *Passion*, 48: "John's Gospel has no sympathy whatsoever for Judas and sees behind his terrible apostasy the face of the demon."

10. *Peter, having a sword, drew it:* Becker, *Evangelium* 2:544, claims that Peter's actions serve no purpose except to introduce Jesus' aggressive acceptance of the Father's will in v. 11. But see Stibbe, *John* 181; Senior, *Passion* 54–55 for a better theological understanding of Peter's failure. Heil, "Jesus as the Unique High Priest" 736–737, understands Peter's gesture as a misguided attempt to stop Jesus' high priestly sacrifice, and Brodie, *Gospel* 526–527, plays on the name "Malchus" to show that Peter misunderstands the nature of Jesus' kingship.

 cut off his right ear: Critics have speculated on the significance of this mutilation of the *right* ear. Was Peter left-handed? Is the mutilation of the right ear more hideous? Does this prevent Malchus from attending the high priest in the Temple? None of these questions can be answered with confidence. See Senior, *Passion* 54 n. 17.

ii. Jesus' Appearance Before "the Jews" (18:12-27)

12. So the band of soldiers and their captain and the officers of the Jews seized Jesus and bound him. 13. First they led him to Annas, for he was the father-in-law of Caiaphas, who was high priest that year. 14. It was Caiaphas who had given counsel to the Jews that it was expedient that one man should die for the people.
15. Simon Peter followed Jesus, and so did another disciple. As this disciple was known to the high priest he entered the court of the high priest along with Jesus, 16. while Peter stood outside at the door. So the other disciple, who was known to the high priest, went out and spoke to the maid who kept the door, and brought Peter in.
17. The maid who kept the door said to Peter, "Are not you also one of this man's disciples?" He said, "I am not." 18. Now the servants and officers had made a charcoal fire because it was cold, and they were standing and warming themselves; Peter also was with them, standing and warming himself.
19. The high priest then questioned Jesus about his disciples and his teaching. 20. Jesus answered him, "I have spoken openly to the world; I always taught in synagogues and in the Temple, where all Jews come together; I said nothing secretly. 21. Why do you ask me? Ask those who have heard me what I said to them; they know what I said." 22. When he had said this one of the officers standing by struck Jesus with his hand, saying, "Is that how you answer the high priest?" 23. Jesus answered him, "If I have spoken wrongly, bear witness to the wrong; but if I have spoken rightly, why do you strike me?" 24. Annas then sent him bound to Caiaphas the high priest.
25. Now Simon Peter was standing and warming himself. They said to him, "Are not you also one of his disciples?" He denied it and said, "I am not." 26. One of the servants of the high priest, a kinsman of the man whose ear Peter had cut off, asked, "Did I not see you in the garden with him?" 27. Peter again denied it; and at once the cock crowed.

INTERPRETATION

Jesus and Peter are introduced in vv. 12-16 in a way unparalleled in the synoptic tradition. Only now is Jesus seized (v. 12) and led to the house of Annas (v. 13a). The narrator links Annas and Caiaphas and recalls the words of Caiaphas from 11:49-52: Jesus' death is not for himself, but to gather into one the children of God who are scattered abroad (vv. 13b-14). Introductions continue as two disciples are described as following Jesus (v. 15: *ēkolouthei de tǭ Iēsou*). Simon Peter is a leading disciple (cf. 1:41-43; 6:8, 68-69; 13:6-9, 24, 36-38), and an anonymous disciple has also appeared earlier in the narrative (cf. 1:37-42). There are two *mathētai* ("disciples") in the court of the high priest along with Jesus (v. 15).

The action begins as Peter gains entry to the court through the mediation of the other disciple, described as "known *(gnōstos)* to the high priest." Peter's being one of the *mathētai* of Jesus is the focus of the question of the maid who kept the door: "Are not you also one of this man's disciples?" Peter's first denial reverses the words of Jesus, who revealed his identity at Gethsemane with the words *egō eimi* (cf. vv. 5, 8). Peter tells a lie as he responds *ouk eimi* (v. 17: "I am not"). Without comment the narrator shifts the focus briefly from Peter to the *hypēretai* and some servants who have prepared a charcoal fire against the cold. The *hypēretai* had come out carrying lanterns and torches (18:2) to arrest Jesus, the light of the world (cf. 8:12; 9:5). They had seized him, bound him, and taken him to Annas (vv. 12-13a). The focus returns to Peter who, paralleling Judas' association with the *hypēretai* in the garden, is described as *met' autōn* (v. 18; cf. v. 5). He approaches the false warmth and light created by characters in the narrative who have sided with the powers of darkness. Peter is joining Judas, moving away from the light of the world toward the darkness (cf. 13:30).

The account of Peter's first denial (vv. 15-18) has been highlighted by the fourfold use of the term *mathētes*. In addition, the description of Peter as "disciple" recalls that he is an important disciple (cf. 1:41-42) who has confessed Johannine belief in the word of Jesus (cf. 6:68-69). His name has appeared six times in this context. But the same disciple is fragile and has been shown to misunderstand the significance of Jesus' actions (cf. 13:6-9, 24, 36-38). In a story of discipleship denied, coming before a centerpiece in which Jesus will be asked about his disciples (cf. v. 19) and will send his listeners to "those who have heard me" (cf. v. 21), the theme of the disciple of Jesus has appeared nine times (v. 15 [3x]; v. 16 [3x]; v. 17 [2x]; v. 18).

In a way unique to the Fourth Gospel the denials of Peter are interrupted as Jesus is questioned "about his disciples and his teaching *(peri tōn mathētōn autou kai peri tēs didachēs autou)*" (v. 19). Jesus' response reverses the order as he first speaks of his *didachē* (v. 20) and then of "those who have heard me" *(tous akēkootas)*, those who know what Jesus has said (v. 21). Jesus looks back across his public revelation of God that closed in 12:36b as he informs his interrogator of two events, both in the past but described with different tenses. In v. 20b Jesus speaks of his preaching to "the Jews": "I have always taught *(edidaxa)* in synagogues and in the

Temple, where all Jews come together" (v. 20b). The verb *edidaxa* is in the aorist tense. He has taught in Jewish centers in the past, the synagogues and the Temple, but he will do so no longer. There can be no going back on the definitive separation between Jesus and "the Jews" (cf. 12:36b). "The statement of Jesus no longer signifies an indirect appeal for decision or for faith; rather it affirms, 'You have already decided!' It is too late for discussion, the confrontation with Judaism is at an end" (Bultmann, *Gospel* 646). But Jesus continues, "I have spoken openly *(parrēsiǫ lelalēka)* to the world *(tǫ kosmǫ)* . . . I said nothing secretly" (v. 20a.c). The verb *lelalēka* is in the perfect tense. The word of Jesus has been proclaimed in the world. The Gospel's rich use of *ho kosmos* cannot be equated to "the Jews" (cf. Koester, *Symbolism* 249–253). The world that is the saving object of God's love (cf. 3:16) is in question in 18:20a. Jesus' historical presence as a teacher proclaiming his word has come to an end (12:36b), but his word spoken in the past was never hidden or limited (18:20c: *en kryptǫ elalēsa ouden*). The perfect tense "I have spoken" placed in close proximity with the aorist "I taught" indicates that, although the teaching of Jesus to "the Jews" has come to an end, the word of Jesus is still available. It was proclaimed in the past and its consequences are still abroad.

If the presence of Jesus "in synagogues and in the temple" (v. 20b) is no longer available, where is the word once spoken so openly to the world (v. 20a.c) to be found? One must ask those who have heard him *(tous akēkootas)* what he said *(elalēsa)* to them. During the ministry of Jesus the word was spoken (complexive aorist) to "those who heard." They are in possession of the word to the world, and anyone who wishes to hear that word must ask them (v. 21b). They know *(oidasin)* what Jesus said (v. 21c). Many commentators remark that Jesus is asking his accusers "to take testimony in the legal manner" (Barrett, *Gospel* 528), but "those who have heard" are the *mathētai* of Jesus, those who have learned at the school of Jesus (cf. K. H. Rengstorf, *TDNT* 4, 444–450). Jesus is no longer present, but in his absence the disciples who know what he said are to be approached. The high priest's question concerning Jesus' disciples has been answered, as the *didachē* and the *mathētai* belong together. The "teaching" of Jesus is to be found among his "disciples" (v. 19; cf. Hoskyns, *Gospel* 514).

One of the *hypēretai* (cf. vv. 2, 12, 18), out of loyalty to the high priest, slaps Jesus. He refuses to accept the promise of Jesus (v. 22), but Jesus' response to the slap returns to the true significance of the events. Jesus asks that if has spoken evilly *(ei kakōs elalēsa)*, his assailant bear witness; but if he has spoken well *(ei kalōs elalēsa)*, then the officer must explain his action (v. 23). *Kakōs lalein* is used in the LXX for blasphemy (cf. Exod 22:7; Lev 19:14; 20:9; Isa 8:21; 1 Macc 7:42). If the slap is punishment for blasphemous speech, then witnesses must be brought; but if Jesus is proclaiming what is right *(kalōs)*, a truthfulness that opposes blasphemy, then the officer stands condemned by his action (cf. Brown, *Death* 1:415–416). The tradition of the guiltlessness of Jesus, found in both the synoptic and Johannine trial before Pilate (cf. Mark 15:14; Matt 27:4, 19, 24; Luke 23:13-16, 22; John 18:38; 19:4, 6), emerges here. But Jesus is not only guiltless; he has revealed the truth, he has spoken well *(kalōs)*, and the truth has been rejected.

The narrator returns to one of the founding members of the community, Peter, one of those who have heard what Jesus said (cf. v. 21) but who has joined Judas in the darkness (v. 18: *met' autōn;* cf. v. 5). The "other disciple" has disappeared, but Simon Peter, still "with them" at the fire (v. 18), is again asked whether he is *ek tōn mathetōn autou.* He repeats his first denial: *ouk eimi* (v. 25). The almost exact repetition in v. 25 of what was done and said in Peter's first denial in v. 17 creates a tight frame around Jesus' directions that those who wish to know his teaching must go to those who have heard him (vv. 20-21). Jesus' encounter with his enemies in the garden provides background for both the denials of Peter and the witness of Jesus (cf. vv. 5, 8 and vv. 17, 18, 25; v. 3 and vv. 12, 22). A further link emerges as Peter's active intervention with a sword to cut off Malchus' right ear is recalled (v. 26; cf. v. 10). The accusation, made by a blood relative of the injured man, cannot be denied. But Peter insists that he has no association with Jesus (v. 27a). The third denial implies that there never was a garden, a place known to Judas because "Jesus often met there with his disciples" (v. 2). Peter, who has drawn closer to the darkness represented by the *hypēretai*, denies all links with Gethsemane, Jesus, and his disciples who often met there. Peter denies something that even Judas acknowledged (cf. vv. 2a, 26b-27a).

"And at once the cock crowed" (v. 27b). Jesus' words addressed to Peter in 13:38 come true. What Jesus said would happen (13:38) does happen (18:27b). This final remark from the narrator brings the episodes reported in vv. 12-27 to a fitting conclusion. Jesus has indicated that his word is abroad in the world (v. 20) and that it can be found among those who have heard him; they know what he said (v. 21). One of them is denying that he had any association with Jesus (vv. 15-18, 25-27), and another has betrayed him (vv. 1-5), but the fulfillment of Jesus' promise in the crowing of the cock indicates a more fundamental truth: Jesus' promises comes true. However badly Peter and Judas may perform, Jesus' teaching can be heard from those who—like Peter and Judas—have heard him. Within the context of his earlier prophecies of the betrayal of Judas and the denials of Peter, Jesus had made another promise: "I tell you this now, before it takes place, that when it does take place you may believe *hoti egō eimi*" (13:19). It is in his unconditional love for those who fail him, including Judas and Peter, that Jesus makes God known (cf. Moloney, "John 18:15-27" 231–248).

13. *who was high priest that year:* Staley, "Subversive Narrator" 91–98, uses this first reference to the *archiereus* as the beginning of the narrator's design to victimize the reader. Only in v. 24 does the reader discover that the *archiereus* was Annas, not Caiaphas. See also idem, *Reading with a Passion* 85–109. On the continuing use of *archiereus* for former high priests see Pancaro, *The Law in the Fourth Gospel* 66–67. For Stibbe, *John as Storyteller* 173, the trial before Annas is historical, coming from the witness of Lazarus, the Beloved Disciple.

15. *another disciple:* There is considerable difference of opinion over the possible identification of "another disciple" with the Beloved Disciple. The debate is exhaustively surveyed by J. H. Charlesworth, *The Beloved Disciple. Whose Witness Validates the Gospel of John?* Valley Forge: Trinity Press International, 1995, 336–359. For Stibbe, *John as Storyteller* 98–99, "the anonymous believer here is undoubtedly the BD" (i.e., Lazarus). The issue is further complicated by textual confusion. Some manuscripts add a definite article before *allos mathētēs* in v. 15. Others read "that disciple," while some have neither "other" nor "that." Van Tilborg, *Imaginative Love* 93–94, perhaps rightly, suggests that it is "polyinterpretable."

16. *known to the high priest:* There has been much speculation, none of which can be verified, surrounding the relationship that might have existed between this disciple and the high priest. See Brown, *Gospel* 2:822–823; idem, *Death* 1:404–411. On the possibilities behind the use of the word *gnōstos* see Barrett, *Gospel* 525–526.

18. *the servants and officers had made a charcoal fire:* There are some contacts with the Markan and Lukan traditions at this point: the female doorkeeper, the kindling of a fire, and, in Luke, Peter's presence among the people who had seized Jesus. See Dauer, *Passionsgeschichte* 62–63, 91–99; Quast, *Peter and the Beloved Disciple* 71–76; Brown, *Death* 1:78–79 (Mark); 87–88 (Luke); 418–419 (synoptic chart).

    Peter also was with them: The parallel between Judas' being "with them" and Peter's being "with them" is seldom noticed. Knöppler, *Die theologia Crucis* 220–227, studies the role of Judas and points to Judas' being "with" the Romans in v. 7 (p. 227), but fails to notice that Peter joins him in vv. 18, 25.

19. *The high priest then questioned Jesus:* Only the Fourth Gospel inserts Jesus' encounter with Jewish authority (vv. 19-24) between the first (vv. 15-18) and the remaining two denials of Peter (vv. 25-27). This has led to suggestions that the text should be rearranged, that the evangelist has changed his sources, that the source itself is uncertain, or that the Johannine text is the result of editorial additions (cf. the survey in Schnackenburg, *Gospel* 3:228–233). The Sinaitic Syriac version brought forward v. 24 to make Caiaphas the interrogating high priest and took Peter's three denials together. On this see the remarks of Bultmann, *Gospel* 643–644. This transposition has been followed by Lagrange, *Evangile* 459–462, and Schneider, "Zur Komposition" 111–119. In reading vv. 18-27 in its traditional order we must "reckon with his (the evangelist's)

strong and individualistic shaping of the material" (Schnackenburg, *Gospel* 3:233).

questioned Jesus: The aorist *erōtēsen* ("questioned") is complexive, describing an event from the past that went on for some time. See BDF 171, § 332.

about his disciples and his teaching: The link between the interrogation over the *mathētai* and the *didachē* in v. 19 and Jesus' response in vv. 20-21 is rarely noticed, not even in studies that focus on this section of the narrative. See, for example, Giblin, "Confrontations" 221–230; Heil, "Unique High Priest" 739–740. Barrett, *Gospel* 523, states that Jesus "refuses to answer." Pancaro, *The Law in the Fourth Gospel* 64–71, rightly points out that vv. 19-24 cannot be regarded as a trial. All "trials" (Jesus by "the Jews" and "the Jews" by Jesus) have taken place during the public ministry. See also Brown, *Death* 1:423–426.

20. *I have spoken openly to the world:* The clumsy juxtaposition of the aorist and the perfect tenses is noticed by Brown, *Gospel* 2:825, but he suggests that the perfect has an aorist sense. The interpretation given here claims that the full sense of the perfect tense must be retained: "The perfect combines in itself, so to speak, the present and the aorist in that it denotes the *continuance* of a *completed action*" (BDF 175).

  I always taught in synagogues: The aorist *edidaxa* is complexive. It is an action of Jesus that took place in the past but that went on for some time. This is heightened by the use of "always" *(pantote)*. The fact that Jesus' revelation to "the Jews" is regarded as closed reflects the Johannine situation and says nothing about God's revelation to Israel (cf. Introduction).

  I said nothing secretly: The aorist *elalēsa* is another complexive aorist, referring to the whole period of Jesus' once-and-for-all revelation of the Father during his ministry.

22. *struck Jesus with his hand:* One must not eliminate the physical gesture and the pain inflicted, but the striking with the hand is more a sign of rejection than the infliction of punishment. Staley, "Subversive Narrator" 96, misses this in his description of the *hypēretēs* as "the chief priest's brutalizing assistant." For the more theological interpretation adopted above see de la Potterie, *The Hour* 72–74; Bernard, *Commentary* 2:239; Brown, *Death* 1:413.

25. *Now Simon Peter was standing and warming himself:* It is often remarked that there are no indications of the passing of time across vv. 12-27 (e.g., Quast, *Peter and the Beloved Disciple* 76). This is part of the literary form adopted, well described by R. M. Fowler, *Let the Reader Understand: Reader-Response Criticism and the Gospel of Mark.* Minneapolis: Fortress, 1991, 143–144: "Intercalation is narrative sleight of hand, a crafty manipulation of the discourse level that creates the illusion that two episodes are taking place simultaneously."

26. *a kinsman of the man whose ear Peter had cut off:* The charge that Peter had drawn a weapon and injured a servant of the high priest was, in fact, more serious than his being a disciple of Jesus (cf. Bernard, *Commentary* 2:603).

27. *at once the cock crowed:* Despite some commentators who see no significance in the cock-crow (e.g., Bultmann, *Gospel* 648), the fulfillment of Jesus' prophecy

in 13:38 is fundamental to the message of part of the passion story. As that prophecy came true, so will Jesus' prophecy about the availability of the word among those who heard Jesus, even Simon Peter. See Schnackenburg, *Gospel* 3:240.

iii. Jesus Before Pilate (18:28–19:16a)

28. Then they led Jesus from the house of Caiaphas to the praetorium. It was early. They themselves did not enter the praetorium so that they might not be defiled, but might eat the Passover.

29. So Pilate went out to them and said, "What accusation do you bring against this man?" 30. They answered him, "If this man were not an evildoer we would not have handed him over." 31. Pilate said to them, "Take him yourselves and judge him by your own law." The Jews said to him, "It is not lawful for us to put any man to death." 32. This was to fulfill the word that Jesus had spoken to show by what death he was to die.

33. Pilate entered the praetorium again and called Jesus, and said to him, "Are you the King of the Jews?" 34. Jesus answered, "Do you say this of your own accord, or did others say it to you about me?" 35. Pilate answered, "Am I a Jew? Your own nation and the chief priests have handed you over to me; what have you done?" 36. Jesus answered, "My kingship is not of this world; if my kingship were of this world my servants would fight that I might not be handed over to the Jews; but my kingship is not from the world." 37. Pilate said to him, "So you are a king?" Jesus answered, "You say that I am a king. For this I was born, and for this I have come into the world, to bear witness to the truth. Everyone who is of the truth hears my voice." 38a. Pilate said to him, "What is truth?"

38b. After he had said this he went out to the Jews again and told them, "I find no crime in him. 39. But you have a custom that I should release one man for you at the Passover; will you have me release for you the King of the Jews?" 40. They cried out again, "Not this man, but Barabbas!" Now Barabbas was a robber.

19:1. Then Pilate took Jesus and scourged him. 2. And the soldiers plaited a crown of thorns and put it on his head, and arrayed him in a purple robe; 3. they came up to him, saying, "Hail, the King of the Jews!" and struck him with their hands.

4. Pilate went out again and said to them, "See, I am bringing him out to you that you may know that I find no crime in him." 5. So Jesus came out, bearing the crown of thorns and the purple robe. Pilate said to them, "Behold the man!" 6. When the chief priests and the officers saw him they cried out, "Crucify him, crucify him!" Pilate said to them, "Take him yourselves and crucify him, for I find no crime in him." 7. The Jews answered him, "We have a law, and by that law he ought to die, because he has made himself the Son of God."

8. When Pilate heard these words he was the more afraid; 9. he entered the praetorium again and said to Jesus, "Where are you from?" But Jesus gave no answer. 10. Pilate therefore said to him, "You will not speak to me? Do you not know that I have power to release you and power to crucify you?" 11. Jesus answered him, "You would have no power over me unless it had been given you from above; therefore the one who delivered me to you has the greater sin."

12. Upon this Pilate sought to release him, but the Jews cried out, "If you release this man you are not Caesar's friend; every one who makes himself a king sets himself against Caesar." 13. When Pilate heard these words he brought Jesus out and sat down on the judgment seat at a place called The Pavement, and in Hebrew, Gabbatha. 14. Now it was the day of Preparation of the Passover; it was about the sixth hour. He said to the Jews, "Behold your king!" 15. They cried out, "Away with him, away with him, crucify him!" Pilate said to them, "Shall I crucify your king?" The chief priests answered, "We have no king but Caesar."

16a. Then he handed him over to them to be crucified.

INTERPRETATION

The synoptic tradition had already used the trial of Jesus before Pilate and the sign on the cross to proclaim Jesus as "king" (cf. Mark 15:2, 9, 12, 18, 26, 32; Matt 27:11, 29, 37, 42; Luke 23: 2, 3, 27, 38), but in the Johannine story the theme of Jesus' royal status dominates the interrogation of Jesus by Pilate (cf. 18:33, 37, 39; 19:3, 12, 14, 15) and continues into the scene of the crucifixion (cf. 19:19, 21). The "trial" is marked by an introduction (18:28), seven brief scenes that take place either inside or outside the praetorium (18:29-32, 33-38a, 38b-40; 19:1-3, 4-7, 8-11, 12-15), and a conclusion (19:16a). The narrator uses verbs of motion to show that Pilate and/or Jesus comes in or goes out. There are two "trials" in progress: one follows from the encounter between the Roman authority of Pilate and "the Jews" (cf. 18:29-32, 38b-40; 19:5-7, 12-15) and the other from the encounter between Pilate and Jesus (cf. 18:33-38a; 19:8-11). The decisive issue is how Pilate and "the Jews" respond to Jesus' royal status. There is only one scene, 19:1-3, where there is no verb of motion and no dialogue. This central scene (the fourth in a series of seven) takes place in the praetorium. Jesus is crowned, dressed as a king, and ironically proclaimed: "Hail, the King of the Jews" (v. 3). Although the synoptic tradition has a parallel scene (cf. Mark 15:18; Matt 27:29) only the Johannine Gospel has the soldiers use the definite article in addressing Jesus as *the* King in their ironic salutation: *chaire ho basileus tōn Ioudaiōn* (19:3).

Introduction (v. 28). The scene is set at the praetorium and all the characters are introduced: Jesus, Pilate, and the Jewish leaders. As the first light of day breaks the leaders present Jesus, the Lamb of God (cf. 1:29,

34), for trial, while they remain outside the praetorium to avoid ritual impurity on the eve of the Passover (v. 28). The dawning of the day may be a subtle hint of an ironic victory that is being initiated (cf. Bultmann, *Gospel* 651; Brown, *Gospel* 2:866). As "the Jews" struggle to maintain their ritual purity on the occasion of the Passover (cf. 11:55-57) they seek the death of the Lamb of God.

Outside (vv. 29-32). "So Pilate went out" (v. 29a). In response to Pilate's question concerning Jesus' crime (v. 29b) "the Jews" indicate that they have already made up their minds that Jesus is an evildoer (v. 30) and must die by the Roman method of execution: "lifted up" in crucifixion (v. 31). The narrator recalls the earlier word of Jesus about the manner of his death: "When I am lifted up from the earth I will gather everyone to myself" (12:32). The death of Jesus is not for himself but for the gathering of others.

Inside (vv. 33-38a). "Pilate entered the praetorium" (v. 33a). Pilate will have none of Jewish stories of kings and messiahs (vv. 33-35), but he is told of the nature of Jesus' messianic kingship: he exercises his royalty in making God known to the world, bearing witness to the truth, and drawing all those who are of the truth into his kingdom (vv. 36-37). Although Pilate questions Jesus about his royal status Jesus does not speak of himself, but about the "kingdom" (cf. Bultmann, *Gospel* 654). There is a gratuitous offer of truth from Jesus to his Roman interrogator as he tells Pilate that he reveals the truth and draws the people of the truth into a kingdom of truth as they hear his voice. The term "kingdom" *(basileia)* has been used on only one other occasion in the story: Nicodemus was told of the need to be born again from above *(anōthen)* by water and the Spirit in order to "see" and "enter" the kingdom (3:3-5). The kingdom is a "place" where God reigns, a community, and those who are of God, of the truth, respond to the voice of Jesus and "see" *(idein)* and "enter into" *(eiselthein eis)* that kingdom (cf. Moloney, *Belief in the Word* 109–114). But Pilate rejects Jesus' revelation-invitation with his brusque refusal of the word of Jesus: "What is truth?" (v. 38).

Outside (vv. 38b-40). "He went out to the Jews again" (v. 38b). Despite Pilate's inability to step into Jesus' kingdom of truth he goes out to "the Jews," proclaims Jesus' innocence and, responding to custom *(synētheia)*, offers to free Jesus, "the King of the Jews" (v. 39). But "the Jews" ask for Barabbas, a *lęstēs*, a man of violence and a false messianic choice (cf. Giblin, "John's Narration" 228; note on v. 40 below).

Inside (19:1-3). There is no indication of change of place, but Pilate takes Jesus and scourges him (v. 1), and the soldiers crown him with thorns and array him in a purple robe (v. 2). Following hard upon Pilate's proclamation of Jesus as "the King of the Jews" (8:39) he is mockingly dressed and proclaimed by the soldiers as "the King of the Jews" (v. 3).

Many elements in the synoptic account of Jesus' scourging and mocking are not found: the blindfolding, the punches, the spitting, the mocking genuflections, and the striking on the head with a rod (cf. Mark 14:65; 15:16-17; Matt 26:67-68; 27:27-30; Luke 22:63-64). The Johannine account is simplified. It is highlighted by a coronation, a clothing, and an ironic proclamation of the truth: Jesus is the King of the Jews. Despite the rejection involved in the scene Jesus is crowned, clothed, and acclaimed as "the King of the Jews."

Outside (vv. 4-7). "Pilate went out again" (v. 4a). Emerging from the praetorium, Pilate again declares that Jesus is innocent (v. 4b). Jesus, dressed and crowned as a king, "came out" *(exēlthen . . . exō);* he is not "led out," as he is still master of his own destiny. He is "bearing" *(phorōn)* the signs of his royal status (v. 5a). Unlike the parallel report in the synoptic tradition (cf. Mark 15:20; Matt 27:31), the royal trappings of the crown and the cloak are never taken from Jesus to be replaced by his own clothing. Jesus goes to the cross dressed as a king. This is the setting for Pilate's presentation of Jesus: "Behold the man (v. 5b: *idou ho anthrōpos*)." Paralleling his earlier declaration of Jesus' innocence and his presentation of Jesus as "the King of the Jews" (18:38b-40) Pilate again declares Jesus innocent and gives him another title of honor "the Man." (19:5). But as before his coronation and investiture "the Jews" had asked for the release of Barabbas (cf. 18:40), they now demand that Jesus be crucified (v. 6a). This sequence of events summons up 8:28: "When you have lifted up the Son of Man, then you will know that I am he." The first part of this prophecy is being fulfilled: they are taking it upon themselves to "lift up" in crucifixion the royal figure presented to them by Pilate as "the Man." As Greeks came to see Jesus he announced, "The hour has come for the Son of Man to be glorified" (12:23), and further clarified his words: "When I am lifted up from the earth I will draw everyone to myself" (12:32). The narrator explains what is meant by "lifting up": "He said this to show by what death he was to die" (12:33). "The Jews" are demanding that the innocent Son of Man be lifted up (cf. Moloney, *Son of Man* 202–207). They claim that he challenges their Law in his claim to be Son of God. The real reason for their rejection of Jesus, so obviously present throughout all the clashes between Jesus and "the Jews" in 5:1–10:42, has at last surfaced: they cannot and will not accept that Jesus is "of God."

Inside (vv. 8-11). "He entered the praetorium again" (v. 9a). Pilate is frightened, "more afraid" at the suggestion that Jesus is the Son of God (v. 8). Thus in his second encounter with Jesus (cf. 18:33-38) he asks the fundamental question of Johannine christology: "Where are you from?" but he receives no answer (v. 9). In Pilate's earlier encounter with Jesus, Jesus openly and gratuitously revealed to him the possibility of being drawn into the kingdom of truth: "Everyone who is of the truth hears my voice" (18:37). But this offer was brusquely rejected (cf. 18:36-38). In this second private encounter "inside" the praetorium Jesus' response matches his refusal to speak to "the Jews" in 18:20-21. He had already spoken to them "openly" *(parresią)* throughout his ministry (v. 20). He has also given witness "to the truth" *(tę alētheią)* to Pilate (18:37), but this witness has been rejected (v. 38). Thus he refuses to be drawn into any further self-revelation to Pilate (19:9), who asks his question from a position of human authority and non-belief. Pilate blusters against Jesus about his political authority and his power over life and death (v. 10), but Jesus' response rings true. The one who handed him over *(ho paradous;* cf. note) has the greater guilt, but Pilate must recognize that all authority over life and death comes from above. In many ways Jesus has answered Pilate's question of v. 9: "Where are you from?" Jesus has everything "from above" because that is where he is from (cf. v. 11) (cf. Zeller, "Jesus und die Philosophen" 88–92).

Outside (vv. 12-15). "He brought Jesus out" (v. 13b). Whatever the Roman soldier may have made of Jesus' words, he seeks to release Jesus (v. 12a) only to find that "the Jews" ironically attempt to teach the Procurator a lesson on the universal authority of the Roman emperor (v. 12b). The challenge that his attempt to free Jesus indicates Pilate is not Caesar's friend leads him to bring Jesus out either to seat himself or (less likely) to have Jesus take the judgment seat (v. 13). On the day of preparation for the Passover Pilate proclaims Jesus as king: "Behold your King!" (v. 14), but "the Jews" demand crucifixion, and Pilate expresses his surprise that they wish to crucify their king. At the "sixth hour" *(hōra ēn hōs hektē),* precisely at the moment when the Passover lambs were being ritually slaughtered in the Temple, "the Jews" scream out for the death of Jesus, the Lamb of God (vv. 14-15; cf. 1:29, 35). Despite Pilate's initial refusal to listen to "the truth" (18:38), Jesus' subsequent refusal to answer his question concerning his origins (19:8-9), "the Jews'" baying for the blood of Jesus (v. 6), and their threat concerning his allegiance to Caesar (v. 12), he continues to insist on the kingship of Jesus (v. 14). This may not make much sense of Pilate's psychological coherence when judged by modern-day criteria, but it enables the author to use the Roman official's surprising insistence on Jesus' royal status to proclaim ironically the truth about Jesus. In the end Pilate capitulates to "the Jews" who betray the Mosaic tradition they have so stoutly used to accuse Jesus throughout the latter part of his ministry (cf. especially 5:1–10:42), and during the trial (cf. 19:7: "We have a law, and by that law he ought to die"). They now announce: "We have no king but Caesar" (v. 15). "The Jews" match their choice of Barabbas the *lęstēs* rather than Pilate's offer of the King of the Jews (cf. 18:39-40) when they choose Roman authority over against their king. They forsake all attachment to the promised kingdom of God and ask that a Roman form of execution be used to eliminate their king. "Their repudiation of Jesus in the name of a pretended loyalty to the emperor entailed their repudiation of the kingdom of God, with which the gift of the Messiah is inseparably bound in Jewish faith, and Israel's vocation to be its heir, its instrument, and its proclaimer to the nations" (Beasley-Murray, *John* 39).

Conclusion (v. 16a). The account of Jesus before Pilate began with "the Jews'" leading Jesus before Roman authority (v. 28). It concludes with the Roman authority handing Jesus over to them that they might lift up the Son of Man (v. 16a; cf. 8:28; 19:5). The story has come full circle. Jesus has been proclaimed king both before (18:38b-40) and after (19:4-7) his coronation (19:1-3), but the response of "the Jews" has been to choose false messianic hopes (18:40: Barabbas; 19:12-15: Rome) and to seek the crucifixion of their king (18:29-32; 19:4-7, 13-15). The trial of Jesus before Pilate has really been a trial of Pilate and "the Jews." Both have been found wanting, and the irony of their failure is that Pilate hands Jesus over to "the Jews" to be crucified, to be lifted up (19:16a).

A violent end to Jesus' life has been in the making from the earliest days of his ministry. Jesus has spoken of the need for the Son of Man to be lifted up (3:14; 8:28; 12:32), and he has also looked forward to this moment as his glorification. At the feast of Tabernacles the narrator commented that the Spirit had not yet been given because Jesus had not yet been glorified (7:39). In 11:4 he informed his disciples that the illness of Lazarus would lead to the revelation of the glory of God and that the Son would be glorified by means of it. Further words of Jesus have reinforced his earlier claims (cf. 12:16, 23; 13:31-32; 17:1-5). The crucifixion that must now follow will be a moment of royal glory, a lifting up (3:14; 8:28; 12:32), a glorification (12:23), the enthronement of Jesus as "King of the Jews."

NOTES

28. On the irony involved in "the Jews'" refusal to enter the praetorium as they hand over Jesus see Brown, *Death* 1:744–776; Heil, *Blood and Water* 47–48. It is not entirely clear how entry into the praetorium would have incurred impurity. For the discussion see Brown, *Death* 1:744–745. For a useful list of the ways in which John 18:28–19:16a has used earlier traditions surrounding the passion of Jesus see Ehrman, "Jesus' Trial" 124–126.

29. *So Pilate went out:* The pattern of "outside" and "inside," creating an overall episode marked by seven scenes, is widely recognized by scholars. See Westcott, *Gospel* 258; Janssens de Varebeke, "La Structure" 504–522. Baum-Bodenbender, *Hoheit in Niedrigkeit* 28–96, traces two acts (1: 18:28–19:5 and 2: 19:6-16a) in which the scenes "outside" (18:28-32, 38b-40; 19:6-8, 12b-16a) carry the supporting theme of the rejection of Jesus while the scenes "inside" (18:33-38a;

19:1-5, 9-12a) form the main axis of the narrative, instructing the reader in Johannine christology. Giblin, "John's Narration" 221–224, argues for a mounting tension across two narrative sections, both of which conclude with *tote oun* and an action of Pilate: 19:1-3 and 19:16a. Giblin, "John's Narration" 226–227, 238, and Rensberger, *Johannine Faith* 87–106, rightly reject a once popular interpretation of the encounter between Jesus and Pilate as an encounter between State and Christianity. Dauer, *Passionsgeschichte* 102, argues that revelation takes place "inside," as only there does Jesus speak, while "outside" belongs to the godless world. This is not the case, as Pilate regularly, however ironically, proclaims the truth about Jesus to "the Jews."

31. *It is not lawful for us to put anyone to death:* It is inconclusively debated whether or not the Jews could put people to death while they were under Roman rule. For a survey of the discussion see Brown, *Death* 1:747–749. Pancaro, *The Law in the Fourth Gospel* 310–326, rightly shows that the motivation for the statement of v. 31 (and also 19:6) is theological. He argues that according to the Law Jesus was innocent of the charge "the Jews" are bringing against him (v. 30: he was an evildoer) and thus they could not put him to death. Their real problem is that he is "Son of God." Jesus will be put to death by Pilate because such is the will of the Father, and Pilate executes Jesus in virtue of the *exousia* he receives from God (cf. 19:11).

32. *by what death he was to die:* Historical concerns are again subjected to Johannine theology. Whether or not the Jews had authority to execute anyone is debated, but Jesus must be "lifted up" on a cross, a Roman form of execution (cf. Bammel, "The Trial" 414–451; Senior, *Passion* 75–76).

36. *My kingship is not of this world:* "These words are saturated with Johannine theology" (Senior, *Passion* 80). The *basileia* of Jesus may not be "of the world," but this does not mean that it cannot be found "in the world" (cf. interpretation of 17:14). The physical and spatial nature of the language must be given its full weight. For a detailed interpretation of *basileia* in 3:3, 5 as the Christian community see Moloney, *Belief in the Word* 109–114. See also Lagrange, *Evangile* 477.

37. *to bear witness to the truth:* For the meaning of "truth" (*alêtheia*) in the Fourth Gospel as the revelation of God see de la Potterie, *La vérité*. On 18:37 as a statement on the fundamental purpose of Jesus' mission to make God known in his person, i.e., "to bear witness to the truth," see 1:100–116.

    everyone who is of the truth hears my voice: On the link between "hearing the voice" of Jesus and the proper response of the sheep to the Good Shepherd in 10:3-4, 8, 16 see Meeks, *The Prophet-King* 66–67.

38. *What is truth?:* Pilate's question is a dismissive rejection of the word of Jesus and not the sign of a searching, philosophical mind, however much the passage has been used in that way over the centuries. The criterion for authentic belief in Jesus is an openness to his word. Pilate fails because like many before him in the story, especially "the Jews," he dismisses the word of Jesus. On this criterion for belief see Moloney, *Belief in the Word* 192–199.

39. *you have a custom:* It is difficult to find evidence for this "custom" *(synētheia).* Some see it as possible background to *m. Pesaḥ* 8:6 and *b. Pesaḥ* 91a, but others challenge the suggestion. For a comprehensive but inconclusive assessment of the evidence see Brown, *Death* 1:814–820.

40. *Barabbas was a robber:* Josephus used the term *lēstēs* of the Zealots, whose false messianic pretensions, according to Josephus, caused God to abandon God's people and thus led to the destruction of the City and the Nation (cf. Simonis, *Die Hirtenrede* 130–139). Against this understanding of "robber" in 18:40 see Brown, *Death* 1:808. A link with 10:1-18, however, is likely where the discourse culminates in the revelation of Jesus as the messianic Good Shepherd (cf. 10:14-18). But "the Jews" have chosen a *lēstēs*, a thief and a robber who came before him to plunder the sheep (cf. 10:1, 8). See Meeks, *The Prophet-King* 67–68. On the possibility that the name "Bar-abbas" might be a false "Son of the father" (Aramaic/Hebrew) see Brown, *Death* 1:796–800. Brown surveys the discussion and rejects the suggestion.

19:3 *saying "Hail, King of the Jews!" and struck him with their hands:* On the irony in this scene see Duke, *Irony* 131–132; Blank, "Verhandlung" 73–74; de la Potterie, *The Hour* 101–103. Brown, *Death* 1:869, misses this by claiming that the slap is the equivalent of the spitting and the striking. He does not mention the omission of the mocking genuflections.

4. *I am bringing him out to you:* Pilate claims to be master of the situation, bringing Jesus out, but this is not what happens. Jesus "came out" (v. 5: *exēlthen*), enigmatically in control of his own actions.

5. *bearing the crown of thorns and the purple robe:* For *phoreō* as a regal bearing of clothes or of armor see LSJ 1950–1951, s.v. *phoreia.*

   Behold the Man!: For more detailed argument in support of the presentation of Jesus as the Son of Man adopted in the interpretation see Moloney, *Son of Man* 202–207; Blank, "Verhandlung" 75–77; Dauer, *Passionsgeschichte* 264–265; de la Potterie, *The Hour* 78–80; Giblin, "John's Narration" 230; Stibbe, *John* 191; Heil, *Blood and Water* 64–65. Schnackenburg, *Gospel* 1:532–533, is more cautious ("at most . . . an indirect allusion"). Bultmann, *Gospel* 659, claims that Jesus' miserable state is the ultimate consequence of the Word's becoming flesh. See also Brown, *Death* 1:827–828. For Becker, *Evangelium* 2:572–573, Pilate presents Jesus as a "laughable King." Baum-Bodenbender, *Hoheit* 66–67, shows that both lowliness and majesty are present. Panackel, *IDOU HO ANTHRŌPOS* 215–338, claims too much, seeing 19:5b as the culminating use of the expression *anthrōpos* to proclaim that in the humanity of Jesus the Son of God is revealed.

7. *he has made himself the Son of God:* This is the theological reason for "the Jews'" presentation of Jesus to the Romans for trial. All other claims (e.g., 18:30: "If he were not an evildoer") are false, but this accusation is—ironically—correct. See Pancaro, *The Law in the Fourth Gospel* 310–326 (cf. note to v. 31).

8. *he was the more afraid:* Scholars discuss what is meant by Pilate's being "the more afraid." See Brown, *Death* 1:830. Rightly Brown concludes: "Pilate is afraid because it becomes clearer and clearer that he will not be able to escape making a judgment about truth."

9. *Where are you from?:* On the central function of this question in the Johannine christology and its function in the narrative at this point see Dewailly, "D'où es-tu?" 481–496.

11. *he who delivered me to you:* This is not a reference to Judas, a disciple now consigned to the care of the Father (cf. 17:2; 18:9). It is sometimes suggested that "the Jews" are those responsible (e.g., Brown, *Death* 1:842; Heil, *Blood and Water* 73–74). The singular form of the noun *(ho paradous),* however, points to an individual. Strictly in terms of the narrative it is Caiaphas who made the final decision (cf. 11:49-53) and who sees to it that Jesus is led to Pilate (18:27-28). For this suggestion see also Beasley-Murray, *John* 340. It may also be a further reference to the son of perdition (= Satan) of 17:12.

12. *If you release this man you are not Caesar's friend:* It is most unlikely, historically, that any Jewish crowd would have articulated this form of threat against the Roman procurator (but see the attempt of Beasley-Murray, *John* 340–341, to reconstruct such a possibility). Dramatic irony, not history, is the major feature of the episode. See Duke, *Irony* 134–136. On the possible reference to "Caesar's friend" *(philos tou Kaisaros)* as a technical term of honor see Bammel, *"Philos tou Kaisaros"* 205–210; Brown, *Death* 1:843–844.

13. *and sat down on the judgment seat:* It is possible that the verb "sat down" *(ekathisen)* is transitive, meaning that Pilate sat Jesus down, rather than the intransitive, indicating that Pilate sat down. For the transitive meaning, among many (Haenchen, Loisy, Lightfoot, Meeks, Brodie) see de la Potterie, *The Hour* 108–111. Against this see Dauer, *Passionsgeschichte* 269–274; Brown, *Death* 1:844–845. The most likely meaning is that Pilate sat down, while the careful reader might suspect that the transitive meaning is possible. For a detailed survey of the discussion, concluding that Pilate sits on the judgment seat, see Brown, *Death* 2:1388–1393.

   The Pavement, and in Hebrew, Gabbatha: For a survey of the discussions over the place of the praetorium (the Antonia Fortress and "the Palace of the King"), closely associated with the identification of this "pavement" *(lithostrōtos)* with the Roman floor uncovered in the site of the former Antonia Fortress (today the *Ecce Homo* Convent of the Sisters of Our Lady of Sion) see Brown, *Death* 1:705–710.

15. *We have no king but Caesar:* For the remarkable nature of this statement from a Jewish crowd and its function in the Johannine presentation of "the Jews" in this passion account see also Brown, *Death* 1:848–849, and especially Genuyt, "La comparution de Jésus" 133–146.

16a. *he handed him over to them:* The reversal of the process initiated in 18:28 has led many scholars to point to the chiastic nature of 18:28–19:26. See, for example, Brown, *Gospel* 2:858–859; Stibbe, *John* 187. But however obvious chiasms are to the scholar, readers do not read in chiasms (cf. Fowler, *Let the Reader Understand* 151–152). Senior, *Passion* 68–71, warns against overplaying the chiasm in interpretation to the detriment of the linear "dynamism of the narrative" (p. 69). See also Stibbe, *John* 187, on "progression" across the trial before Pilate.

iv. The Crucifixion of Jesus (19:16b-37)

16b. So they took Jesus, 17. and he went out, bearing his own cross, to the place called the place of a skull, which is called in Hebrew Golgotha. 18. There they crucified him, and with him two others, one on either side, and Jesus between them. 19. Pilate also wrote a title and put it on the cross; it read, "Jesus of Nazareth, the King of the Jews." 20. Many of the Jews read this title, for the place where Jesus was crucified was near the city, and it was written in Hebrew, in Latin, and in Greek. 21. The chief priests of the Jews then said to Pilate, "Do not write, 'The King of the Jews,' but, 'This man said, I am King of the Jews.'" 22. Pilate answered, "What I have written I have written."

23. When the soldiers had crucified Jesus they took his garments and made four parts, one for each soldier; also his tunic. But the tunic was without seam, woven from top to bottom; 24. so they said to one another, "Let us not tear it, but cast lots for it to see whose it shall be." This was to fulfill the scripture,

"They parted my garments among them,
and for my clothing they cast lots."

So the soldiers did this.

25. But standing by the cross of Jesus were his mother, and his mother's sister, Mary the wife of Clopas, and Mary Magdalene. 26. When Jesus saw his mother, and the disciple whom he loved standing near, he said to his mother, "Woman, behold, your son!" 27. Then he said to the disciple, "Behold, your mother!" And from that hour the disciple took her to his own home.

28. After this Jesus, knowing that all was now finished, said (to fulfill the scripture), "I thirst." 29. A bowl full of vinegar stood there; so they put a sponge full of the vinegar on hyssop and held it to his mouth. 30. When Jesus had received the vinegar he said, "It is finished"; and he bowed his head and handed over the Spirit.

31. Since it was the day of Preparation, in order to prevent the bodies from remaining on the cross on the Sabbath (for that Sabbath was a solemn day), the Jews asked Pilate that their legs might be broken and that they might be taken away. 32. So the soldiers came and broke the legs of the first, and of the other who had been crucified with him; 33. but when they came to Jesus and saw that he was already dead they did not break his legs. 34. But one of the soldiers pierced his side with a spear, and at once there came out blood and water. 35. He who saw it has

borne witness—his testimony is true, and he knows that he is telling the truth—that you also may believe. 36. For these things took place that the scripture might be fulfilled, "Not a bone of him shall be broken." 37. And again another scripture says, "They shall look on him whom they have pierced."

INTERPRETATION

Introduction. The account of Jesus' crucifixion and its consequences are told in five brief scenes:

1. *Vv. 16b-22:* The crucifixion, the title on the cross, and the response of "the Jews."
2. *Vv. 23-24:* The decision not to tear apart the seamless garment.
3. *Vv. 25-27:* The Mother of Jesus and the Beloved Disciple at the cross.
4. *Vv. 28-30:* The death of Jesus and the gift of the Spirit.
5. *Vv. 31-37:* The aftermath of the death: the gift of water and blood.

It is sometimes suggested that these scenes have been arranged in a chiastic literary structure with the gift of mother to son and son to mother at its center (e.g., Brown, *Death* 2:907–909; Stibbe, *John* 193–194), but it is important to appreciate "the forward motion of the story" (Senior, *Passion* 99–100).

The crucifixion (vv. 16b-22). The scene is set at the place of the skull (v. 17b) and the characters are introduced: Jesus, handed over to "the Jews" (v. 16b), carrying the cross (v. 17a), "sole master of his own destiny" (Brown, *Gospel* 2:917). But the Romans are involved as he is crucified at Golgotha between two others. The synoptic gospels record that they were bandits (cf. Mark 15:27; Matt 27:38) or evildoers (cf. Luke 23:39-43), but this is not said in the Johannine account. In his very "lifting up" there is a gathering, and he is at its center. The focus is on Jesus, occupying a central place among the crucified. The physical crucifixion is described in the briefest terms (v. 18b: *auton estaurōsan*) as the narrator does not wish to dwell on the bloody reality of a Roman crucifixion. After making Jesus the centerpiece of a triptych of crucified people the narrative moves immediately to the issue of the title on the cross: "Jesus of Nazareth, the King of the Jews" (v. 19). Pilate, who had insisted on Jesus' royal status during the trial (cf. 18:33, 37, 39; 19:14, 15), continues this ironic proclamation of the truth in Hebrew, Latin, and Greek (v. 20b), the languages of the cultured world of the Roman empire. The kingship of Jesus is proclaimed universally and can be read by all who pass by (v. 20a). The multilingual proclamation of the crucified Jesus as King is another indication that Jesus is drawing everyone to himself (cf. 10:16; 11:49-52; 12:32). "The Jews" reject this proclamation, insisting that Jesus is only a pretender to such claims, but Pilate will not allow the inscription to be changed. What he has written, he has written—because it is true (vv. 21-22).

The seamless garment (vv. 23-24). Romans *(hoi stratiōtai)* continue to play a role as they divide Jesus' garments into four parts but cast lots for the seamless inner garment so that it not be torn asunder (vv. 23-24). Scripture is fulfilled as the soldiers do as Ps 22:19 had foretold. But there must be more to the focus on the fact that the inner garment of Jesus is not to be torn asunder. Is there something precious that belongs to Jesus whose unity must be maintained? In 17:20-26 Jesus asked the Father to preserve the unity of his own disciples and all those who have come to believe in him through his word. This unity was not an end it itself, but announced to the world that God had sent his Son and that God loved the world just as he loved his Son. The passion story has already told of Jesus' demand that his disciples be allowed to leave the garden freely (cf. 18:8-9), on which occasion the narrator referred back to Jesus' prayer (cf. 17:12). At the heart of that prayer is a plea for the unity of those who are and who will be his followers (cf. 17:11, 22-24). Jesus has instructed his Jewish interrogators that if they wished to know his teaching *(didachē)* they ask those who had heard him *(tous akēkootas)* (cf. 18:21). This instruction presupposes that his prayer for the disciples has been heard. The patristic interpretation of the Fourth Gospel has suggested that this garment, which cannot be torn apart even when it falls into the hands of Jesus' crucifiers, is a symbol of those who have heard his word: the community of the disciples. The patristic interpretation is strengthened by a communitarian reading of the passage that follows (19:25-27).

The Mother of Jesus and the Beloved Disciple (vv. 25-27). Lifted up on the cross, Jesus speaks to the woman who was the first character in the narrative to commit herself unconditionally to his word (cf. 2:3-5), and commands her to see *(ide)* the Beloved Disciple and accept him as her son. He then turns to the Beloved Disciple, by now clearly indicated as the model disciple who has lain close to the breast of Jesus at the meal table (cf. 13:23), and commands him to see *(ide)* the Mother of Jesus and accept her as his mother. His words are unquestioningly obeyed, as the narrator comments: "and *ap' ekeinas tēs hōras* he took her to his own home." The cross is "the hour of Jesus" (cf. 12:23; 13:1; 17:1), and hence there is a play on two possible meanings for the Greek *ap'ekeinas tēs hōras.* First, it has a temporal meaning: "from that particular time." Second, the theological and dramatic significance of "the hour of Jesus" can give the preposition *apo,* followed by the genitive case, a causative sense: "because of that hour" (BDF 113, § 210). As a result of the lifting up of Jesus on the cross the Beloved Disciple and the Mother become one. The disciple leads the Mother *eis ta idia.* The situation described in the Prologue, when the Word came *eis ta idia* but was not received (1:11: *ou parelabon*), has been reversed. Because of the cross and from the moment of the cross a new family of Jesus has been created. The Mother of Jesus, a model of faith, and the disciple whom Jesus loved and held close to himself are one as the disciple accepts the Mother (19:27: *elaben . . . autēn*) in an unconditioned acceptance of the word of Jesus.

Exaggerated mariological claims have been made for this passage, but there can be no avoiding the fact that at the cross and because of the cross the crucified Jesus has established a new family. The promise of the "gathering" emerging from the closing scenes of Jesus' public ministry (cf. 10:16; 11:49-52; 12:11, 19, 20-24, 32-33) has been achieved. Within the space of three verses (vv. 25-27) the expression "mother" *(mētēr)* has appeared no less than five times (vv. 25 [2x], 26 [2x], 27). The earlier use of "Mother of Jesus" in 2:1-5, where she was the first to accept the word of Jesus, comes into play as the Mother of Jesus becomes the Mother of the Disciple in 19:25-27. At such a dramatic moment in this sophisticated and symbolic narrative the passage cannot simply mean that the Beloved Disciple is to look after the widowed mother of Jesus once her only son has died (e.g., Dauer, *Passionsgeschichte* 322–326; but cf. Brown, *Gospel* 2:923). The passage affirms the maternal role of the Mother of Jesus in the new family of Jesus established at the cross (cf. Moloney, *Mary* 31–50).

The death of Jesus (vv. 28-30). The account of the death of Jesus is highlighted by a series of statements indicating fulfillment and perfection. Jesus knows that he has come to the end of his life (v. 28: *ēdē panta tetelestai*) and his words in 13:1 are recalled: "he loved them to the end *(eis telos)*." To fulfill *(hina teleōthē)* the Scriptures he cries out in his thirst and is assuaged with vinegar on "hyssop" *(hyssōpǭ)*. He has drunk the cup the Father gave him (cf. 18:11). There is a possible link between Jesus' role as the Passover Lamb and the explicit reference to "hyssop." Exodus 12:22-23 instructs the Israelites to sprinkle their lintels by using a "hyssop" at the moment of the exodus. Jesus is offered hyssop in the moment of his "passing over" through his death (cf. 13:1). There may also be an echo of LXX Psalm 68, already used in 2:17 and 15:25, as Jesus says, to fulfill the Scripture: "I thirst" (cf. LXX Ps 68:22: "for my thirst they gave me vinegar to drink"). Climaxing these indications of fulfillment, Jesus cries out *"tetelestai"* (v. 30a), an exclamation of achievement, almost of triumph. The task given to him by the Father (cf. 4:34; 5:36; 17:4) has now been consummately brought to a conclusion.

Jesus has now perfected the task given to him, and the narrator confirms this as he comments: "He bowed his head and *paredōken to pneuma*" (v. 30b). At the celebration of Tabernacles the narrator had remarked that the Spirit had not yet been given because Jesus was not yet glorified (7:39). Now the Spirit is poured out. If the seamless robe was a symbol of the community of disciples and the gift of the Mother to Son and Son to Mother foreshadowed the unity of faith, faith that is the *ekklēsia* of God (cf. Hoskyns, *Gospel* 530), then it is upon the nascent community that the Spirit is poured. The words of the narrator are not a euphemism for death. The text does not say that Jesus "gave up his spirit" (cf. RSV, NRSV, JB, NJB, CEI. See, by way of contrast, Mark 15:37: *exepneusen* [*par.* Luke 23:46]; Matt 27:50: *aphēken to pneuma*). The verb used has the primary meaning of "to hand over, to deliver, to entrust" (BAGD 614), and the definite article used indicates "the Spirit." In bringing to perfection the task the Father had given to him Jesus hands over, entrusts, *the* Spirit to his new family gathered at the foot of the cross (vv. 25-27).

The aftermath of the death of Jesus (vv. 31-37). The preparation for the Passover necessitates the removal of the crucified from their place of torture. The concern for cultic purity, evident in "the Jews'" ritual purifications in preparation for this Passover (11:55-57) and their unwillingness to enter the praetorium (18:28) is ironically pursued to the end of the passion story (19:31). The two who have been crucified with Jesus have their legs broken, but this does not happen to Jesus. He is already dead. His side is pierced with a lance, and blood and water flow from his pierced side (vv. 31-34). Scripture is fulfilled as the Passover Lamb is slain without a bone being broken (cf. Ps 34:20-21; Exod 12:10, 46; Num 9:12). Once allowance is made for the reinterpretation of these events as the fulfillment of Scripture the narrative could be nothing more than a reporting of events that could have taken place, including the flow of blood and water from the wound in the deceased body of Jesus (cf. Wilkinson, "The Incident of the Blood and Water" 149–172). But the narrator unexpectedly launches into a personal comment that has no parallel in the rest of the Gospel. The narrator insists on personal witness and on the truthfulness of his testimony. The narrator's concern in passing on the account of these events to another generation is "that you also may believe" (v. 35). The blood and water must mean something to the readers of the Gospel, and the narrator is anxious that the readers have no doubt about the fact that blood and water flowed from the crucified Jesus.

Jesus has entrusted the Spirit to the community (v. 30); now he entrusts the blood and water of Eucharist and Baptism. The promise of Jesus' words and the narrator's comment in 7:37-39 are realized: "Let any one who is thirsty come to me, and let the one who believes in me drink. As the scripture has said, 'Out of his heart shall flow rivers of living water.' Now this he said about the Spirit, which those who believed in him were to receive; for as yet the Spirit had not been given because Jesus was not yet glorified." The "not yet" is "now," and the Spirit (v. 30b) and the water (v. 34) are given to the community of Jesus' disciples by the crucified one who has brought to perfection the task given to him (v. 30a).

The author presupposes the readers' knowledge and experience of the "water" of Baptism (cf. 3:5) and the "blood" of Eucharist (cf. 6:53, 54, 55-56), and links them with the cross. The Johannine passion account deals both with what happened to Jesus and with how this affects the community of the absent Jesus. Where is the pierced one in the life of a Christian community that looks back across at least two generations to the events of Jesus' death? It is precisely the *absence* of the physical, historical Jesus in the community that lies behind the narrator's passionate intervention in v. 35. Despite his *physical* absence Jesus is still present in the blood and water of the practices of a worshiping community.

Jesus has fulfilled the Scriptures in two ways. He is the perfect Paschal Lamb, as not one of his bones was broken (v. 36; cf. Exod 12:10; 12:46; Num 9:12). The earlier indications of John the Baptist that Jesus was the Lamb of God (cf. 1:29, 35) come to their conclusion in v. 36. Second, despite his absence the community of his disciples of all generations will be able to find the presence of the absent one and gaze upon the one whom they have pierced (v. 37; cf. Zech 12:10). God has been revealed in the pierced one, and this revelation of God continues in the flowing water and the spilled blood of Baptism and Eucharist as the worshiping community experiences the presence of the absent one. The urgency of this question for a community that no longer sees Jesus has led to the intervention of the narrator in v. 35: "He who saw it has borne witness—his testimony is true, and he knows that he is telling the truth—*that you also may believe.*"

NOTES

16. *So they took Jesus:* "The Jews" were the ones who cried out that Jesus be crucified in v. 15, to whom Jesus is "handed over" in v. 16. They are the subject of "took" *(parelabon)* in v. 16b (cf. Senior, *Passion* 101–102; Heil, *Blood and Water* 84). A number of scholars insist that the "they" in v. 16b must be the Romans (e.g., Beasley-Murray, *John* 344; Brown, *Death* 1:856–857). Brown argues that the readers knew that the Romans crucified Jesus and thus had no illusions about the identity of "they." He claims that "one should not press grammatical antecedents" (p. 856). Apart from the grammar, which points clearly to "the Jews" as "they," a combination of what the reader knows and what the text says indicates that both "the Jews" and the Romans collaborate in the execution of Jesus. This is borne out by the narrative (cf. vv. 18, 23).

17. *bearing his own cross:* The synoptic tradition has Simon of Cyrene bear the cross of Jesus (cf. Mark 15:21; Matt 27:32; Luke 23:26). Awareness of this tradition heightens the impression that in the Johannine Gospel even on his way to Golgotha Jesus is master of his own situation. See also Barrett, *Gospel* 549; Schnackenburg, *Gospel* 3:270. For a survey of other possible motifs that may be operating here see Beasley-Murray, *John* 345.

18. *and with him two others, one on either side, and Jesus between them:* The detailed description of the positioning of the three crucified men has led to a number of interpretations. Senior, *Passion* 103, sees the two flanking figures as part of a royal retinue. Brodie, *Gospel* 545, rightly suggests that from his position "in the middle" *(meson de ton Iēsoun)* Jesus is already drawing people to himself.

22. *What I have written, I have written:* On the unchangeable nature of Pilate's words in the title on the cross see Dauer, *Passionsgeschichte* 275; Brown, *Death* 2:964–967. Kysar, *John* 287, comments: "John has the unwilling Pilate proclaim the fulfillment of the redemptive act of God, which can never be changed now that it is done."

23. *the tunic was without seam:* The clothes in general are called *ta himatia,* but this garment is called *ho chitōn,* a "tunic," an inner garment. See Brown, *Death* 2:955–956.

24. *Let us not tear it:* There is a long and strong patristic interpretation of the passage as a symbolic statement on the unity of the Christian community. For a survey of the patristic data see Aubineau, "La tunique sans couture" 1:100–127. See especially Cyprian, *De unitate ecclesiae* 7 (MPL 4:520–521) and Augustine, *In Iohannis Evangelium* 118:4 (MPL 35:1949). In support of this interpretation see also de la Potterie, *The Hour* 124–132; Schuchard, *Scripture Within Scripture* 127–132; Longenecker, "The Unbroken Messiah" 433–434. For a survey of the discussion, concluding that the communitarian interpretation is possible, see Brown, *Death* 2:955–958. Others make a link with priestly garments. For example, Schnackenburg, *Gospel* 3:274, points to the fact that Jesus' garments are taken from him, and makes a link with the symbol of Jesus' laying aside his garments in 13:4. He uses Josephus, *Ant.* 3:161, to claim that there is reference to a priestly garment. Heil, *Blood and Water* 89–92, and idem, "Unique High Priest" 741–744, broadens this discussion by adding further OT and Jewish background and claiming that this episode serves as a climax to a number of "high priestly" episodes. Kysar, *John* 288, rightly points out that clear signals to the correct interpretation of the passage cannot be found in the passage itself. The reader must proceed farther into the account of the crucifixion to discover its significance. The communitarian interpretation is greatly enhanced by vv. 25-27, vv. 28-30, and vv. 31-37.

This was to fulfill the scripture: On this use of the Lament Psalms, and especially Psalm 22, in the passion tradition see D. J. Moo, *The Old Testament in the Gospel Passion Narratives.* Sheffield: Almond Press, 1983, 224–232. On Ps 22:19 in John 19:24 see pp. 252–257. Moo decides against the symbol of the unity of the Christian community in vv. 23-24. Obermann, *Die christologische Erfüllung* 282–297, suggests that Jesus fulfills the Psalm (LXX Ps 21:19) in his experience of rejection by God.

25. *his mother:* On the faith of the Mother of Jesus in 2:3-5 see Moloney, *Belief in the Word* 80–85. R. G. Maccini, *Her Testimony is True. Women as Witnesses according to John.* JSNT.S 125. Sheffield: Sheffield Academic Press, 1996, 184–206, argues against an interpretation of the passage as singling out the Mother of Jesus and giving her a role in the community. He focuses on the four female

witnesses at the cross but does not give enough consideration to the communitarian nature of the immediate narrative context.

26. *Woman, behold your son:* On 19:25-27 as a revelatory moment in the Fourth Gospel see M. de Goedt, "Un Schème de Révélation dans le Quatrième Évangile," *NTS* 8 (1961–1962) 145–150. For surveys of the Marian interpretation of this passage see R. F. Collins, "Mary in the Fourth Gospel—a decade of Johannine Studies," *Louvain Studies* 3 (1970) 99–142; Senior, *Passion* 108–113; Brown, *Death* 2:1019–1026. The evocative nature of this scene continues to stimulate suggestions that claim more than the passage can provide. For example, Ignace de la Potterie, *Mary in the Mystery of the Covenant.* New York: Alba House, 1992, 229–235, claims John 19:25-27 as a biblical source for later reflection on "the 'Marian Countenance' of the Church."

27. *he took her to his own home:* On the *eis ta idia* in 19:27 as a reversal of the *eis ta idia* in 1:11 see de la Potterie, *Mary* 225–228. There is broadly-based support for the reading of vv. 25-27 as the Johannine version of the foundation of the Christian community by the crucified King. For a selection see Hoskyns, *Gospel* 530; Serra, *Contributi,* 370–429; Becker, *Evangelium* 591–592; Gourgues, "Marie, la 'femme'" 174–191; Koester, *Symbolism* 214–219; Heil, *Blood and Water* 94–98; Boguslazwski, "Jesus' Mother" 106–129; Zumstein, "L'interprétation johannique" 3:2131.

28. *I thirst:* For a comprehensive interpretation of vv. 28-30 that reaches beyond the request for a drink but tells of the perfection of Jesus' task, the revelation of glory as he returns to the Father, and the gift of the Spirit see Witkamp, "Jesus' Thirst" 489–510.

29. *on hyssop:* On the link between this reference to "hyssop" and the use of hyssop to sprinkle the lintels prior to the Exodus see Senior, *Passion* 117–118; Stibbe, *John* 196; Beetham and Beetham, "A Note" 163–169. Brawley, "An Absent Complement" 427–443, rightly argues that more than Exod 12:22-23 may be involved in the fulfillment of Scripture. He suggests that Psalm 69 serves as intertext, allowing the reader to sense the fulfillment of a Scripture that spoke of opposition to Jesus, at the cross and in the experience of the later community. But as the psalm is an absent complement it makes the reader aware that "the divine power that embraces the death of Jesus remains a mystery beyond understanding" (p. 443). On the possible presence of Psalm 69 see also Obermann, *Die christologische Erfüllung* 350–364; Witkamp, "Jesus' Thirst" 502–509.

30. *It is finished:* On the importance of this final cry of triumph, bringing to a conclusion Jesus' earlier promise of the perfection of a task that had been given to him by the Father (cf. 4:34; 5:36; 17:4), see Dauer, *Passionsgeschichte* 20; Brown, *Death* 2:1077–1078; Koester, *Symbolism* 193–196; Bergmeier, "TETELESTAI" 282–290; Obermann, *Die christologische Erfüllung* 362–363; Witkamp, "Jesus' Thirst" 489–510.

    and handed over the Spirit: As suggested in the interpretation, the Greek must be taken seriously, and *paradidomi* should be rendered as "handed over" (rather than "gave up") and *to pneuma* as "the Spirit" (rather than "his spirit"). For the case against this interpretation see Senior, *Passion* 119–120. In support see Porsch, *Pneuma und Wort* 327–332; Hoskyns, *Gospel* 532; Bampfylde, "John XIX 28" 247–260; Gourgues, "Marie 'la femme'" 187–188; Beasley-Murray, *John* 353; de la Potterie, *The Hour* 163–165; Swetnam, "Bestowal of the Spirit" 563–567.

33. *they did not break his legs:* As well as the reference to Exod 12:10, 46; Num 9:12, there may also be reference to the righteous sufferer (cf. Ps 34:20-21). Menken, *Old Testament Quotations* 147–166, shows that elements from the psalm and the Pentateuchal texts have been combined in a way common in contemporary Jewish and Christian exegesis. Psalm 34:21 is the primary text but the addition of the Pentateuchal texts indicates the evangelist's understanding of Jesus as *both* the righteous sufferer *and* the Paschal Lamb.

34. *there came out blood and water:* The sacramental reading adopted in the interpretation is regularly challenged, and it is regarded as the addition of an antidocetic element to the Gospel. See, for example, Richter, "Blut und Wasser" 1–21; Kysar, *John* 292. Dodd, *Interpretation* 428, claims that the blood and water from the side of Jesus are a "sign" of the life that flows from the crucified and risen Christ. This is true, but the context further suggests that the members of the new family of Jesus receive this life from the pierced one upon whom they gaze (cf. 19:37). This "life" includes Eucharist and Baptism, where they experience the presence of the absent one. In support of the sacramental reading see Zumstein, "L'interprétation johannique" 3:2132–2133; Heil, *Blood and Water* 105–113; Moloney, "When is John Talking about Sacraments?" 10–33. For a survey of patristic interpretations along these lines see Westcott, *Gospel* 284–286. On the passage as a late baptismal addition in the development of the final Gospel see de Boer, *Johannine Perspectives* 292–303.

35. *He who saw it has borne witness:* This remarkable intervention from the narrator is only matched by the concluding words of 20:30-31. Concluding words, however, might be expected from the narrator, while the direct address to the reader in 19:35 comes as a surprise. Many scholars link it with 21:24 and thus regard it as an editorial addition to the Gospel (e.g., Bultmann, *Gospel* 678; Brown, *Gospel* 2:945; Becker, *Evangelium* 2:600; Beasley-Murray, *John* 354). Even if this were the case there is still need to explain *why* v. 35 was inserted into its present place and *what it means* within that context. Not all are sure of the secondary nature of v. 35 (e.g., Schnackenburg, *Gospel* 3:287, 291; Lindars, *Gospel* 589). For a detailed history of the interpretation of this passage see Sr. Thomas More Bertels, *His Witness is True*.

36. *Not a bone of his shall be broken:* Cf. note to v. 33.

37. *another scripture says:* On the twofold fulfillment of Scripture see Brown, *Death* 2:1184–1188; Schuchard, *Scripture Within Scripture* 133–140. For Pancaro, *The Law in the Fourth Gospel* 331–363, not only is there a literal fulfillment of biblical prophecies but Jesus' death as the Son of God can be regarded as *kata ton nomon* ("according to the Law"). For Obermann, *Die christologische Erfüllung* 298–310 (on 19:36) and 311–325 (on 19:37), the Johannine community looks to

the Scriptures as both source for understanding Jesus and for the recognition of its members as the privileged recipients of the fulfillment of Scripture.

They shall look on him whom they have pierced: The interpretation reads the "they" who shall gaze on the pierced one as the members of the Johannine community and all who will later believe through them. See Schnackenburg, *Gospel* 2:292–294; Obermann, *Die christologische Erfüllung* 320–323, and especially Menken, *Old Testament Quotations* 167–185.

v. Jesus Is Buried in a Garden by His New-found Friends (19:38-42)

38. After this Joseph of Arimathea, who was a disciple of Jesus, but secretly for fear of the Jews, asked Pilate that he might take away the body of Jesus, and Pilate gave him leave. So he came and took away his body. 39. Nicodemus also, who had at first come to him by night, came bringing a mixture of myrrh and aloes, about a hundred pounds' weight. 40. They took the body of Jesus and bound it in linen cloths with the spices, as is the burial custom of the Jews. 41. Now in the place where he was crucified there was a garden, and in the garden a new tomb where no one had ever been laid. 42. So because of the Jewish day of Preparation, as the tomb was close at hand, they laid Jesus there.

INTERPRETATION

The account of the burial of Jesus, told in gentler tones by the narrator, closes the story of the passion and points to events that will take place beyond the tomb of Jesus. A link is made with the events just narrated: "after this" (v. 38: *meta de tauta*), and the story tells of the first actions of a community founded at the cross. Two characters emerge, one of whom is known: Nicodemus (v. 39). He had earlier come to Jesus by night for fear of "the Jews" (cf. 3:1). Joseph of Arimathea is introduced as another disciple who had also remained hidden for fear of "the Jews" (v. 38). These *secret* disciples now become *public*. Joseph of Arimathea goes to the person who had handed Jesus over to be crucified and successfully asks for the body of Jesus (v. 38). Nicodemus brings a very large quantity of myrrh and aloes (v. 39). Together they anoint and bind the body of Jesus in a way that is unknown to the synoptic tradition. Jesus, proclaimed and crowned as a king before Pilate (cf. 18:28–19:16a), further proclaimed as a king by the sign on the cross (19:19-22), and who acted as a king in founding a new people of God from the cross (vv. 25-27), is anointed with an exaggeratedly large quantity of spices, bound in burial clothes, and placed in a new tomb. He is buried as a king (vv. 40-42). The narrator points out that these things took place in a garden (v. 41: *ēn . . . hopou . . . kēpos*), recalling that the passion account began in a garden (cf. 18:1: *hopou ēn kēpos*). Now he is surrounded by his new-found friends, a community that handles his crucified body in a royal way. Much has taken place since Jesus encountered his enemies in a garden alone, betrayed by Judas and misunderstood by Peter (cf. 18:1-5, 10-11).

Conclusion to 18:1–19:37. The first and final scenes (18:1-11; 19:38-42), both set in a garden, witness a significant reversal made possible by the events that have happened during the passion story. The second scene, Jesus' interrogation by "the Jews," is framed by Peter's denials (18:12-27). It points to the future community of disciples who had heard what Jesus said as the place where the teaching of Jesus could now be found. This reference to the community is matched by the description of Jesus' crucifixion and death (19:16b-37): the royal moment of lifting up, the gathering, and the foundation of a community of faith and love. In death Jesus perfects all that he was sent to do, giving the Spirit and the blood and water that flowed from the side of the pierced one. The God who so loved the world that he gave his only Son (cf. 3:16) is now revealed to all who gaze upon the one who has laid down his life for his friends, the greatest gesture of love possible (cf. 15:13). The central scene (18:28–19:16a) stands alone. It is devoted to Jesus' proclamation and coronation as king and the ironic judgment of those who appear to be judging. They show by word and deed that they do not belong to the truth.

Many of the prolepses of the narrative have now been resolved: the lifting up (cf. 3:14; 8:28; 12:32), "the hour" (cf. 2:4; 7:6, 30; 8:20; 13:1; 17:1; 19:27), the gift of the Spirit (cf. 7:37-39), the revelation of a God who so loved the world that he gave his only Son (cf. 3:16). (On the passion as the fulfillment of the proleptic nature of much of the Gospel cf. Zumstein, "L'interprétation johannique" 3:2119–2127). The crucified Jesus has been proclaimed as king (cf. 18:28–19:16a) and has exercised his royal authority (19:16b-37). He has brought to completion the task given him by the Father (cf. 4:34; 17:4; 19:28-30). He has revealed the glory of God (cf. 11:4; 13:31-32; 17:1-5) and in doing so he is himself glorified (cf. 11:4; 12:23). (On the cross as Jesus' glorification cf. Knöppler, *Die theologia Crucis,* 154– 183). The promise of the gift of the Spirit-Paraclete, which was not to take place until Jesus was glorified through his departure, returning to the Father by death (cf. 14:16-18; 15:26; 16:7), has now been fulfilled (cf. 19:30).

In light of the farewell discourse (13:1–17:26), however, there are other prolepses that are partially resolved. They require a time beyond the life and death of Jesus for their complete resolution and can only be resolved by the *readers of the story.* The "gathering" of all people around the one lifted up from the earth (cf. 10:16; 11:51-52; 12:11, 19, 32) has its beginnings in the foundation of a new community of faith and love at the foot of the cross (19:25-27), nourished by the blood and water that flow from the side of the pierced one (cf. 6:27; 19:31-37). Despite the ongoing frailty of those who have heard the word of Jesus, always capable of denying him (Peter) and betraying him (Judas), they are now the bearers of the teaching of Jesus (cf. 18:12-27), cleansed by the word (cf. 13:10; 15:3), entrusted to the care of the Father (17:11-12), chosen and sent (13:18-20) (cf. Koester, *Symbolism* 214–219). Their fragility has not disappeared. Indeed, Jesus' choice and sending of them is a further indication of a love that reveals God (13:19). These fragile disciples—no matter how much they have failed—are challenged to love as he has loved (13:34-35; 15:12-17) so that they might be swept into the oneness of love that unites the Father and the Son (cf. 14:23; 15:9-11; 16:26-27; 17:24-26). Gazing upon the one whom they have pierced, future generations of believers will see the revelation of the glory of God and the glorified Jesus (cf. 19:37). In the absence of Jesus they will always have the Paraclete, the Spirit of truth (14:16-17; 16:7), who will teach them and call to their remembrance all that Jesus has taught them (14:26). They will witness to Jesus, along with his disciples, in his absence (15:26-27) laying bare the falseness of a world that has become an end unto itself (16:8-10), and continue the revelation of God initiated by Jesus (16:12-15). There is an in-between-time filled by the presence of the "other Paraclete" during which the followers of Jesus confidently await the fulfillment of another of his promises: "I will come again and will take you to myself, that where I am you may be also" (14:3). Jesus has told the story of God (cf. 1:18), but the reader is aware that the cross is not the end of his story. A community of his disciples, the founding group for a later community, is reading this particular version of Jesus' story (cf. 17:20). They are divided (cf. 6:60-71), hated, excluded and even slain (cf. 15:18–16:3). A story of suffering and death that is at the same time *doxa* addresses this situation (cf. Zumstein, "L'interprétation johannique" 3:2134–2138). Yet despite the sense of completion created by the Johannine passion account questions remained unresolved.

NOTES

38. *for fear of the Jews:* The choice of Joseph of Arimathea and Nicodemus, previously "secret disciples," may be an encouragement for so-called crypto-Christians (cf. 7:13; 9:22; 12:42-43; cf. also Brown, *Death* 2:1265–1268).

39. *Nicodemus . . . a mixture of myrrh and aloes, about a hundred pounds weight:* There are a number of suggestions concerning Nicodemus and the significance of the large amount of spices. In support of the reading of this as a royal burial adopted in the interpretation see Schnackenburg, *Gospel* 3:296–297; Brown, *Gospel* 2:259–260; Senior, *Passion* 130–133. Others read Nicodemus' gesture as an indication that he has not progressed from the limited faith dis-

played in 3:1-11 (e.g., Rensberger, *Johannine Faith* 40; Duke, *Irony* 110). Sylva, "Nicodemus and His Spices" 148–151, suggests that the binding and the spices indicate that Nicodemus has no understanding of a life after death. See pp. 150–151 nn. 7, 12, for a comprehensive survey of scholarly opinion on Nicodemus' actions in the burial scene. Some overstate the significance of the reception of the body of Jesus by Nicodemus, even seeing eucharistic hints (Suggit, "Nicodemus" 90–110; Hemelsoet, "L'ensevelissement" 47–65; Auwers, "La Nuit de Nicodème" 481–503).

41. *there was a garden:* There is a Jewish, patristic, and scholarly association of "the garden" (both in 18:1-11 and 19:38-42) with Paradise and of the crucified Jesus as the New Adam (cf. Manns, *L'Evangile* 401–429).

For Reference and Further Study

Aubineau, Michel. "La tunique sans couture de Christ. Exégèse patristique de Jean 19:23-24." In Patrick Granfield and Josef A. Jungmann, eds., *Kyriakon. Festschrift Johannes Quasten.* 2 vols. Münster: Aschendorff, 1970, 1:100–127.

Auwers, J.-M. "La Nuit de Nicodème (Jean 3,2; 19,39) ou l'ombre du langage," *RB* 97 (1990) 481–503.

Bammel, Ernst. *"Philos tou Kaisaros,"* TLZ 77 (1952) 205–210

_____. "The Trial before Pilate." In Ernst Bammel and C. F. D. Moule, eds., *Jesus and the Politics of His Day.* Cambridge: Cambridge University Press, 1984, 414–451.

Bampfylde, G. "John XIX 28: A Case for a New Translation," *NT* 11 (1969) 247–260.

Baum-Bodenbender, Rosel. *Hoheit in Niedrigkeit. Johanneische Christologie im Prozess vor Pilatus (Joh 18,28-19,16a).* FzB 49. Würzburg: Echter, 1984.

Beetham, F. G., and P. A. Beetham. "A Note on John 19:29," *JThS* 44 (1993) 163–169.

Bergmeier, Roland. *"TETELESTAI* Joh 19:30," *ZNW* 79 (1988) 282–290.

Bertels, Sr. Thomas More. *His Witness is True: John and His Interpreters.* American University Studies, Series 7: Theology and Religion 42. Bern: Peter Lang, 1988.

Blank, Josef. "Die Verhandlung vor Pilatus Jo 18:28–19:16 im Lichte johanneischer Theologie," *BZ* 3 (1959) 60–81.

Bligh, John. *The Sign of the Cross. The Passion and Resurrection of Jesus According to St John.* Slough: St Paul Publications, 1975.

Boguslazwski, S. "Jesus' Mother and the Bestowal of the Spirit," *IBSt* 14 (1992) 106–129.

Brawley, R. L. "An Absent Complement and Intertextuality in John 19:28-29," *JBL* 112 (1993) 427–443.

Brown, Raymond E. *The Death of the Messiah. From Gethsemane to the Grave. A Commentary on the Passion Narratives in the Four Gospels.* 2 vols. ABRL. Garden City, N.Y.: Doubleday, 1994. For a comprehensive general bibliography on the Johannine passion narrative see 1:104–106.

Collins, Raymond F. "Mary in the Fourth Gospel—a decade of Johannine Studies," *Louvain Studies* 3 (1970) 99–142.

Dauer, Anton. *Die Passionsgeschichte im Johannesevangelium. Eine traditions-geschichtliche und theologische Untersuchung zu Joh 18,1–19,30.* StANT 30. Munich: Kösel, 1972.

Dewailly, L.-M. "D'où es-tu? (Jean 19,9)," *RB* 92 (1985) 481–496.

Ehrman, Bart D. "Jesus' Trial Before Pilate," *BTB* 13 (1983) 124–131.

Genuyt, François M. "La comparution de Jésus devant Pilate. Analyse sémiotique de Jean 18,28–19,16," *RSR* 73 (1985) 133–146.

Giblin, C. H. "Confrontations in John 18,1-27," *Bib.* 65 (1984) 210–232.

_____. "John's Narration of the Hearing Before Pilate," *Bib.* 67 (1986) 221–239.

Glasson, T. F. "Davidic Links with the Betrayal of Jesus," *ET* 85 (1973–1974) 118–119.

Goedt, Michel de. "Un Schème de Révélation dans le Quatrième Évangile," *NTS* 8 (1961–1962) 142–150.

Gourgues, Michel. "Marie 'la femme' et la 'mère' en Jean," *NRTh* 108 (1986) 174–191.

Heil, John Paul. "Jesus as the Unique High Priest in the Gospel of John," *CBQ* 57 (1995) 729–745.

_____. *Blood and Water. The Death and Resurrection of Jesus in John 18–21.* CBQ.MS 27. Washington: The Catholic Biblical Association of America, 1995.

Hemelsoet, B. "L'ensevelissement selon Jean." In *Studies in John: Presented to Professor Dr. J. N. Sevenster on the Occasion of His Seventieth Birthday.* NT.S 24. Leiden: E. J. Brill, 1970, 47–65.

Janssens de Varebeke, A. "La structure des scenes du récit de la passion en Joh. xviii-xix," *EThL* 38 (1962) 504–522.

La Potterie, Ignace de. *The Hour of Jesus. The Passion and Resurrection of Jesus according to John: Text and Spirit.* Slough: St Paul Publications, 1989.

Longenecker, B. W. "The Unbroken Messiah: A Johannine Feature and Its Social Functions," *NTS* 41 (1995) 428–441.

Moloney, Francis J. *Glory not Dishonor,* Chapter Six.

_____. "John 18:15-27: A Johannine View of the Church," *DR* 112 (1994) 231–248.

_____. *Mary: Woman and Mother.* Collegeville: The Liturgical Press, 1989.

Panackel, Charles. IDOU HO ANTHRŌPOS *(Jn 19,5b). An Exegetico-Theological Study of the Text in the light of the use of the term* ANTHRŌPOS *designating Jesus in the Fourth Gospel.* Analecta Gregoriana 251. Rome: Gregorian University Press, 1988.

Quast, Kevin. *Peter and the Beloved Disciple. Figures for a Community in Crisis.* JSNT.S 32. Sheffield: JSOT Press, 1989.

Richter, Georg. "Blut und Wasser aus der durchbohrten Seite Jesu (Joh 19,34b)," *MThZ* 21 (1970) 1–21.

Senior, Donald. *The Passion of Jesus in the Gospel of John.* Collegeville: The Liturgical Press, 1991.

Staley, Jeffrey L. "Subversive Narrator/Victimized Reader: a Reader Response Assessment of a Text-Critical Problem," *JSNT* 51 (1993) 79–98.

_____. *Reading with a Passion. Rhetoric, Autobiography, and the American West in the Gospel of John*. New York: Continuum, 1995.

Suggit, J. N. "Nicodemus—The True Jew," *Neotest.* 14 (1981) 90–110.

Swetnam, James. "Bestowal of the Spirit in the Fourth Gospel," *Bib.* 74 (1993) 556–576.

Sylva, D. D. "Nicodemus and His Spices," *NTS* 34 (1988) 148–151.

Wilkinson, John. "The Incident of the Blood and Water in John 19.34," *SJTh* 28 (1975) 149–172.

Witkamp, L. T. "Jesus' Thirst in John 19:28-30: Literal or Figurative?" *JBL* 115 (1996) 489–510.

Zeller, Dieter. "Jesus und die Philosophen vor dem Richter (zu Joh 19,8-11)," *BZ* 37 (1993) 88–92.

Zumstein, Jean. "L'interprétation johannique de la mort du Christ." In Frans van Segbroeck et al, eds., *The Four Gospels 1992. Festschrift Frans Neirynck*. 3 vols. BEThL 100. Leuven: Leuven University Press, 1992, 3:2119–2138.

C. THE RESURRECTION (20:1-29)

Introduction. The Johannine story *of Jesus* has come to an almost satisfying conclusion, as on the cross Jesus perfects the task given him by the Father (cf. 4:34; 5:36; 17:4; 19:30). His exaltation and the revelation of the glory of God take place on the cross. But the story *of the disciples*, the other major characters in the story, is unresolved. Despite Jesus' challenging final discourse and prayer and his promise of the Paraclete who will be with them throughout the in-between-time, they languish in misunderstanding (cf. 16:17-18, 29-31). They will not survive in the hostile world unless the holy Father of Jesus (cf. 17:11a) looks after them (17:11b-16) and makes them holy (17:17-19). The passion narrative has reinforced this presentation of the disciples. Judas has betrayed Jesus (cf. 18:1-5) and Peter resorted to violence (cf. 18:8-11). Like Judas, Peter stands with Jesus' opponents (cf. 18:5, 18, 25), and he denies any knowledge of him (vv. 15-18, 25-27). Yet as the passion story opens Jesus' earlier words are recalled: "Of those whom you gave me I lost not one" (18:9; cf. 17:12). The first signs of the future role of the disciples appear as the Beloved Disciple is at the cross (cf. 19:25-27) and Nicodemus and Joseph of Arimathea emerge from the darkness for Jesus' burial (cf. 19:38-42), but the reader looks forward to a further resolution of the story of the larger group of the disciples who have been with Jesus from the beginnings of the narrative (cf. 1:35-51; 2:11).

The opening pages of this story of Jesus were highlighted by a hymn and a narrative that dealt with who Jesus is (1:1-18) and how one might respond to him (1:19–4:54). The story of the passion and death of Jesus has brought the story *of Jesus* to a close: the light has shone in the darkness, but the darkness has not overcome it (cf. 1:5). What of *the disciples'* response to Jesus? Following the first disciples' hesitant and partial attempts to express their belief in him (1:35-51) there were stories dealing with a variety of responses to Jesus, the Word become flesh (cf. 1:14): the Mother of Jesus (2:1-12), "the Jews" (2:13-25), Nicodemus (3:1-21), John the Baptist (3:22-36), the Samaritan Woman (4:1-38), the Samaritan Villagers (4:39-42), and the Royal Official (4:43-54) (cf. Moloney, *Belief in the Word* 192–199). It could be said that the Gospel of John *began* with a series of faith journeys through which different characters responded to Jesus in different ways. How does it close? Large sections of the Johannine narrative open and close in a parallel fashion (cf., for example, 1:1-5 and 1:18; 2:1-12 and 4:43-54; 13:1-38 and 17:1-26; 18:1-11 and 19:38-42), and it would not be surprising to find that this story *ends* by looking back to its *beginning*. It is often pointed out that the narrator's final words (20:30-31) look back to the prologue, the words of the narrator that opened the book (1:1-18) (e.g., Mlakuzhyil, *Christocentric* 137–143, 238–240), but does the contact cease there? The *first reported episodes* of the life of Jesus highlighted a journey of faith (1:19–4:54), and the reader might suspect that the *final reported episodes* will return to this theme.

Early Christian traditions associated with the resurrection form the basis of the Johannine account: a woman at an empty tomb (20:1-2), appearances to a woman and to the disciples as a group (vv. 11-18, 19-23), a command to a woman to announce the risen Jesus (v. 17), and a missionary commission (vv. 21-23). These traditions have been thoroughly johannized. Only Mary Magdalene is at the empty tomb and she alone is commanded to announce the risen Lord. Thus the missionary command of John 20:21-23 is unlike Matt 28:16-20 or Luke 24:44-49 (cf. Lüdemann, *Resurrection* 151–165). The narrative of the disciples' running to the tomb may come from the same traditions that produced Luke 24:12 and 24 (cf. Mahoney, *Two Disciples* 41–69; Lüdemann, *Resurrection* 138–139); the encounter with Mary Magdalene may be the johannization of the Matthean report of Jesus' encounter with the women returning from the empty tomb (Matt 28:8-10); and the story of the doubting Thomas may be the dramatization of the theme of doubt that marks all the synoptic resurrection accounts (cf. Mark 16:8; Matt 28:8, 17; Luke 24:10-11, 19-24, 37-43; cf. also Mark 16:14; and see Riley, *Resurrection Reconsidered* 100–107).

Scholars have made valuable suggestions concerning the tradition history of the passage (e.g., Lindars, "The Composition" 142–147; Hartmann, "Die Vorlage" 197–220; Ghiberti, *I racconti pasquali* 51–141; Dauer, "Zur Herkunft" 56–76; Lorenzen, *Resurrection and Discipleship* 168–173), but the present form of John 20 is a unified literary unit, a story plotted by the passing of time and the change of characters and places. With time, characters, and place as criteria we see that John 20:1-29 has the following literary shape.

1. **Vv. 1-18: Scenes at the Tomb**. Two sets of characters are involved in these scenes: the two disciples who run to the tomb and Mary Magdalene. The events take place "on the first day of the week" (v. 1).
   a. *Vv. 1-10: Visits to the empty tomb*
      vv. 1-2: Mary Magdalene establishes the emptiness of the tomb.
      vv. 3-10: Peter and the Beloved Disciple hasten to the tomb; the Beloved Disciple comes to faith, but this is not the end of the journey of faith (cf. v. 9).
   b. *Vv. 11-18: Jesus appears to Mary Magdalene*
      vv. 11-13: Mary Magdalene looks into the empty tomb but does not repeat the Beloved Disciple's experience of faith.
      vv. 14-18: The appearance of Jesus to Mary Magdalene leads her from no faith to a conditioned faith, until she finally accepts his command, returning to the disciples to announce: "I have seen the Lord" (v. 18).
2. **Vv. 19-29: Scenes in the House**. Two sets of characters again determine the shape of the narrative. Jesus appears to the disciples as a group and then to Thomas who has joined the disciples. The two appearances occur in the same place but are separated by changes in time: "On the evening of that day" (v. 19) and "eight days later" (v. 26).
   a. *Vv. 19-23: Jesus appears to the disciples without Thomas*
      On the evening of the same day Jesus appears to the disciples amid great joy. He gives them the Holy Spirit and the commission to forgive and retain sins.
   b. *Vv. 24-29: Jesus appears to the disciples and to Thomas*
      Eight days later Jesus appears to the disciples, but the previously absent Thomas is now present. He did not share the faith and joy of the disciples, but the risen Jesus leads him from his conditioned faith to proclaim: "My Lord and my God" (v. 28). Thomas is told that this moment of faith is not the end of possible journeys of faith (v. 29).

A pattern of growth occurs across the story. In vv. 1-10 there is a development in the objects seen. Mary Magdalene sees a stone that has been taken away (v. 1), the Beloved Disciple sees the linen cloths that had once encased the dead body of Jesus (v. 5), and Peter sees the same linen cloths, but also the napkin that had wrapped the head of Jesus lying apart from the linen cloths (vv. 6-7). Once the accounts of appearances begin Jesus appears to an increasing number of people. He appears to Mary Magdalene (v. 14) and then to the disciples, but Thomas is absent (v. 24). Finally he appears to all the disciples including Thomas (v. 26). The account concludes with a universal blessing of all who will believe without seeing (v. 29).

i. Scenes at the Tomb (20:1-18)

a) *Visits to the Empty Tomb* (20:1-10)

1. Now on the first day of the week Mary Magdalene came to the tomb early, while it was still dark, and saw that the stone had been taken away from the tomb. 2. So she ran, and went to Simon Peter and the other disciple, the one whom Jesus loved, and said to them, "They have taken the Lord out of the tomb, and we do not know where they have laid him." 3. Peter then came out with the other disciple and they went toward the tomb. 4. They both ran, but the other disciple outran Peter and reached the tomb first; 5. and stooping to look in he saw the linen cloths lying there, but he did not go in. 6. Then Simon Peter came, following him, and went into the tomb; he saw the linen cloths lying, 7. and the napkin, which had been on his head, not lying with the linen cloths but rolled up in a place by itself. 8. Then the other disciple, who reached the tomb first, also went in, and he saw and believed; 9. for as yet they did not know the scripture, that he must rise from the dead. 10. Then the disciples went back to their homes.

INTERPRETATION

Mary Magdalene comes to the tomb on the first day of the week (v. 1a: *tȩ de mią tōn sabbatōn*). This "day" links the Johannine story with the earliest Christian tradition, that the tomb was found empty on the third day after Jesus' crucifixion on the day before the Passover, which that year fell on a Sabbath (cf. 19:31). The indication of the time of the day (cf. also Mark 16:1) focuses on the fact that it was still dark (v. 1b: *prōï skotias*). Throughout the story the darkness of the night has been linked with unfaith (cf. 1:5; 3:2; 6:17; 9:4; 8:12; 11:10; 12:35, 46; 13:30; 19:39) (cf. Maccini, *Her Testimony is True* 207–208). Mary Magdalene sees that the stone has been removed *(ton lithon ērmenon)* from the tomb. The use of the passive *(ērmenon)* hints at the action of God (cf. Mollat, "La découverte du tombeau vide" 137–138). Mary sees the open tomb but no such thought crosses her mind.

In the darkness, a setting of unfaith, Mary runs *away from the tomb* to the two most important disciples in the story: Peter (cf. 1:40-42; 6:8, 66-69; 13:5-11, 24, 36-38; 18:10-11, 15-18, 25-27) and the other disciple, the one whom Jesus loved (cf. 1:35[?]; 13:23-25; 18:15-16; 19:25-27). She announces that the body has been taken away by an unnamed plural "they." She makes no suggestion of God's action or the possibility of resurrection. Further, she associates the two disciples with her lack of faith by creating another plural "we." For Mary Magdalene there are two groups involved: the "they" who have taken away *(ēran)* the corpse of the Lord, and the "we" who do not know *(ouk oidamen)* where they have laid it. The first person plural in v. 2 associates two foundational figures from the Johannine story with Mary's situation of unfaith. The situation in vv. 1-2 is one of confusion and no faith, as the group of Mary Magdalene, Simon Peter, and the other disciple stands still in the darkness. Verses 1-2 "allow the view of the unbeliever to be stated" (Evans, *Resurrection and the New Testament* 120). A woman communicates the message of an empty tomb to the disciples, but she is an unbelieving character *with whom two disciples are intimately associated.* It is as unbelievers that the two disciples turn toward the tomb in v. 3.

There is a sense of a new beginning as Peter "came out" *(exēlthen oun)* with the other disciple and they "went" *(ērchonto)* toward the tomb. Initially it is Simon Peter who leads the way and the other disciple follows. The newness of the situation is reinforced by Mary's *running away from the tomb* to the disciples in v. 2 and the disciples' *going toward the tomb* in v. 3. Much has been made of the running to the tomb, and it has sometimes been called a "race" (e.g., Bauer, *Johannesevangelium* 229; van Tilborg, *Imaginative Love* 101–102). There is no race, but two disciples turn their backs on the situation in which they found themselves through association with the unfaith of Mary Magdalene and move toward the place of the action of God: an empty tomb (vv. 3-4). They are now in a position of partial faith. Consistent with the priority accorded to the Beloved Disciple in 13:23-26 and 19:25-27 he is the one who arrives first at that place. However, the reader also knows that Simon Peter is the one appointed to the position of "the Rock" (cf. 1:42) and that—with mixed success—he has represented other disciples on several occasions (cf. 6:66-69; 13:36-38; 18:10-11). There is a tension between these two figures: one is the disciple whom Jesus loved in a special way (cf. 20:2) while the other is the bearer of authority. The disciple whom Jesus loved demonstrates a greater urgency to come to a knowledge of the truth concerning the one who loved him and thus arrives at the tomb before Simon Peter. Although he initially followed Peter (v. 3) he arrives first at the tomb (v. 4). The two most important disciples in the Johannine story of Jesus experience unfaith (vv. 1-2) yet move away from that static situation toward the place where the action of God in Jesus can be seen (vv. 4-5). Once at the tomb the other disciple stoops to look in and sees the linen cloths *(ta othonia).* He does not enter the tomb but waits for Simon Peter (v. 5).

As this scene began Simon Peter led the way (v. 3). This situation has been reversed: Simon Peter, now following the other disciple, arrives and penetrates farther into the tomb. He not only sees the *othonia* but the napkin used to wrap around Jesus' head *(to soudarion).* It is lying apart, carefully folded and placed to one side. Lazarus came forth from the tomb still wrapped in the clothing of death, his face still covered with the *soudarion* (11:44). Not only is the tomb empty but the trappings of death are also empty. Lazarus was raised from the dead but he came forth bearing the clothing of death. The risen Jesus has no such trappings. Another use of the passive voice (cf. 20:1) to indicate that the napkin that covered Jesus' head *(to soudarion)* had been folded *(entetuligmenon)* and that it was now lying to one side, separated from the cloths used to cover his body *(ta othonia)*, reinforces the impression that God has entered the story (vv. 6-7). Simon Peter enters the tomb and sees the evidence but nothing is said of his response. This delaying tactic leads the reader into the climax of v. 8. The other disciple's greater urge to arrive at the tomb that brought this disciple there ahead of Simon Peter is recalled (v. 8a). He sees the vanquished signs of death: the empty tomb, the empty cloths including the *soudarion*. The other disciple's sight of these things leads him to faith: *kai eiden kai episteusen* (v. 8c).

Paralleling the experience of *several* characters in the opening pages of the Gospel who moved from no faith through partial faith to full faith (2:1–4:54), the foundational disciple of the Johannine community (cf. Introduction) and the model of Johannine discipleship has moved from no faith (vv. 1-2) through partial faith (vv. 4-5) into the fullness of resurrection faith by seeing that God had overcome the death of Jesus (vv. 7-8). All the signs of death have been overcome.

Yet despite this moment of faith at the empty tomb the narrator comments that as yet *(oudepō)* these disciples were not aware of the Scripture that told that Jesus *must* rise from the dead (v. 9: *dei auton ek nekrōn anastēnai*). This is an important concluding statement from the narrator, directed to the reader of the story. Two foundational disciples have witnessed the action of God and one of them has seen and believed. But God also speaks through the Scripture: Jesus *must* rise from the dead. The disciples did *not yet* know this truth: "as yet they did not know the scripture." They are in a "not yet" situation of ignorance that will be overcome by a later generation of believers who will read the Scripture and recognize the revelation of the action of God in the resurrection of Jesus. The Johannine narrative is itself "scripture," but the characters, Simon Peter and the Beloved Disciple, are *in the story* and are thus are not able to be *readers of the story*. They are in a "not yet" situation as far as the *graphē* ("scripture") of the Johannine narrative is concerned. A later generation may not be able to penetrate the tomb and see the cloths but it will have the Scripture, especially the Johannine story, and in every way match the faith experience of the Beloved Disciple.

The Beloved Disciple was not given specially privileged access to a unique "sight" that made his belief superior to those who would never be able to match such an experience. The disciples did not know the "word of God" about the resurrection of Jesus from the dead, but the reader does! Having made this point, which leads the narrative away from the past and applies it to the broader worlds of the generations of readers of this story, the narrator dismisses the two disciples from the scene: they return to their homes (v. 10). These foundational disciples have played their part in the drama of the life, death, and resurrection of Jesus. The Beloved Disciple has come to faith without seeing Jesus, but he must leave the scene to allow room for other "disciples" to follow him in a journey of faith. Both the Beloved Disciple and later generations believe without seeing *Jesus*. A later generation of believers has no cause to lament the fact that they are living in the in-between-time, in the time after Jesus' departure, and thus in his *absence*. During this time they are able to read the Scriptures under the direction of the Paraclete (cf. 14:25-26; 16:12-14) who will be with them until the final return of Jesus (cf. 14:16-17; see also 14:2-3, 18-21). Faith motivated by the Scriptures, especially the Johannine version of the life, death, and resurrection of Jesus, matches the faith of the Beloved Disciple. Those living in the absence of Jesus (cf. 14:2-3, 28; 16:5, 28) but in the presence of the Paraclete (cf. 14:16-17) have evidence that Jesus must rise from the dead (cf. v. 9b).

NOTES

1. *on the first day of the week:* The Greek uses the cardinal number "on the one day of the week" (*tȩ de mią tōn sabbatōn*), for the ordinal number ("on the first day"). This is Semitic. See BDF 129, § 247:1, and the discussion in Barrett, *Gospel* 562. Although the traditional expression "on the third day" never appears in the Johannine resurrection account there is a close link with the tradition in the use of "the first day" (Brown, *Gospel* 2:980; Schnackenburg, *Gospel* 3:307–308). The expression "on the third day" is found in 2:1 and is often interpreted there as having resurrection overtones (cf. Moloney, *Belief in the Word* 57–60, 77). Carson, *Gospel* 635, suggests that the use of "the first day" in all four gospels (cf. Matt 28:1; Mark 16:2; Luke 24:1) presents the resurrection as "the beginning of something new." See also Blanquart, *Le premier jour* 20–21.

2. *the other disciple, the one whom Jesus loved:* This is the first time in the Gospel that "the other disciple" has been linked with "the one whom Jesus loved." The latter expression has been added to the former in 20:2 so that earlier descriptions of "the other disciple" or the "Beloved Disciple" can now be identified as referring to the same disciple (cf. 18:15-16 [the other disciple]; 13:23-26; 19:25-27 [the Beloved Disciple]).

They have taken the Lord: Mary's description of Jesus as "the Lord" (*ton kyrion*) is to be read as a respectful title, not a high christological confession.

we do not know where they have laid him: Most scholars argue that the plural *oidamen* is a remnant of an earlier tradition associating other women with the discovery of the empty tomb (cf. Mark 16:1; Matt 28:1; Luke 24:1, 10). See, for example, Bauer, *Johannesevangelium* 229; Maccini, *Her Testimony is True* 208–210. Others suggest that it is a Semitic turn of phrase (e.g., Bultmann, *Gospel* 684 n. 1). Would it not have been obvious to an author who was capable of writing such elegant passages as John 9, 11, 18–19 that, whatever the sources may have had, this was an unpardonable error in Greek? For Kitzberger, "Mary of Bethany" 564–586, on arrival at the account of Mary Magdalene at the empty tomb as well as the earlier reference to her at 19:25 the reader is influenced by the other "Mary" who was at a tomb (cf. 11:1-46; 12:1-8). She links Mary of Bethany and Mary Magdalene through "configuration" and "interfigurality" in which a reader understands one character in terms of the other (cf. also Bernard, *Commentary* 2:657). The "we" in v. 2 is also a text-signal that evokes interfigurality with the Easter morning presence of other women at the empty tomb (cf. pp. 581–582). The "them" and "us" of John 20:2 may reflect an early tradition found in Matt 28:11-15. See also *Gos. Peter* 5:30; Justin, *Dial.* 108:2; Tertullian, *Spect.* 30 (MPL 1:737–738); *Apol.* 23 (MPL 1:474). See Minear, "We don't Know" 125–139, who links the "we" with other "we-passages" in the Gospel (cf. 1:14; 3:11) reflecting the response of the Johannine Christians to Jewish opponents.

3. *Peter then came out:* There is sufficient evidence within the Fourth Gospel to indicate that Simon Peter was understood as an authority and a spokesperson, however fragile he may have been. See Raymond E. Brown, Karl P. Donfried, and John Reumann, eds., *Peter in the New Testament. A Collaborative Assessment by Protestant and Roman Catholic Scholars.* Minneapolis: Augsburg, and New York: Paulist, 1973, 129–147.

4. *the other disciple outran Peter:* The interpretation claims that this detail, which reverses the situation of v. 3 where Peter leads the way, indicates a greater eagerness and the beginnings of belief that God has entered the story. Some claim that "the race itself is not undertaken with any flickering of faith in the resurrection" (Byrne, "Beloved Disciple" 86). Mahoney, *Two Disciples* 245–251, argues against any *personal* significance for Simon Peter and the Beloved Disciple, claiming that they only have a *function* within the narrative. He further argues that Simon Peter must establish the facts while the Beloved Disciple, i.e., disciples in general, must "see" these facts and "believe" (pp. 251–260).

6. *Then Simon Peter came, following him:* The description of Simon Peter as *akolouthōn autǭ* ("following him") indicates a serious reversal of the situation in v. 3 where Peter led the way. The other disciple must be "followed," and this adds weight to the suggestion that the Beloved Disciple's earlier arrival at the tomb is a first sign of belief.

6-7. *the linen cloths lying, and the napkin:* The link with the resurrection of Lazarus, described as emerging from the tomb still clothed with the linen cloths, has often been noticed (cf. Reiser, "The Case of the Tidy Tomb" 47–57; Osborne, "A Folded Napkin" 437–440). The careful disposition of the cloths is probably also part of the apologetic against the claim that the tomb was robbed. See Chrysostom, *In Joannem Homeliae* 85,4 (MPG 59:465) for the early use of the Johannine text in this way.

rolled up in a place by itself: Byrne, "The Beloved Disciple" 87–89, rightly insists on the significance of the *soudarion* and its position, seen on entering the tomb, as the motive for the Beloved Disciple's faith. However, he misses the importance of the divine passives, claiming on the basis of 10:18 that while Lazarus was raised, Jesus "actively raised himself" (p. 88). Brodie, *Gospel* 562–563, argues in the light of Exod 34:33-35 that Jesus has put aside the veil (cf. also Schneiders, "The Face Veil" 94–97), and on the basis of the undivided tunic in John 19:23-24 sees the folded cloths as a symbol of the unity made possible by the death and resurrection of Jesus.

8. *he saw and believed:* Some scholars have questioned the significance of the Beloved Disciple's faith, especially in light of vv. 9 and 29. For example, Nicholson, *Death as Departure* 69–71, joins Augustine and other Fathers of the Church in seeing the disciple's belief as an acceptance of Mary Magdalene's witness. Among others de la Potterie, *The Hour* 202–207, argues that the faith of the disciple is only beginning and has yet to be fully illuminated (cf. v. 9). Lee, "Partnership in Easter Faith" 39–40, argues that "v. 8 has no narrative impact" and that v. 9 leaves both the Beloved Disciple and Peter in a situation of unfaith not resolved until John 21. Brown, "John 20" 197–198, uses v. 9 to support the claim that Beloved Disciple comes to perfect faith. He not only believed without seeing Jesus but he did not even need the help of the Scriptures.

     The use of Peter and the Beloved Disciple in this narrative is determined by their being founding figures of the Christian community. Others have claimed that Peter represents Jewish Christianity while the Beloved Disciple represents the Gentile Church (e.g., Bultmann, *Gospel* 685), or that Peter represents the pastoral ministry while the Beloved Disciple represents the prophetic ministry (Kragerud, *Der Lieblingjünger* 29–32). Brodie, *Gospel* 563–564, suggests that the Beloved Disciple represents the contemplative while Peter represents the official face of the Church.

9. *as yet they did not know the scripture:* The interpretation claims that the author regards the Johannine story as "scripture." The two disciples are characters in the narrative and thus "as yet" *(oudepō gar)* do not know this story. The readers of the Gospel belong to a "later" time not excluded by the "as yet" and thus "know the scripture" of the Johannine Gospel. On the Johannine understanding of its own story as *logos* (Word), *graphē* (Scripture), and *rhēmata zōēs aiōniou* ("words of eternal life") see Obermann, *Die christologische Erfüllung* 409–422, especially 418–422.

     On the transferral of interest from the faith of the foundational disciple to the possibility of faith for future generations see Siedensticker, *Die Auferstehung Jesu* 122–125. This is missed by most commentators who attempt to identify some OT references that might be regarded as the Scripture that the disciples had "not yet" known. Most suggest Ps 16:10 (e.g., Westcott, *Gospel* 290; Lagrange, *Evangile* 508–509).

10. *Then the disciples went back to their homes:* The interpretation regards the dis-
missal of the disciples as the moment when the Beloved Disciple finally
leaves the action so that other "disciples" can be challenged to follow his journey into faith. For de la Potterie, *The Hour* 205–207, they return into the darkness with which the passage opened in v. 1. He regards this action as a
"reditus ad sua" in the sense of a turning back on themselves.

b) *Jesus Appears to Mary Magdalene* (20:11-18)

11. But Mary stood weeping outside the tomb, and as she wept she
stooped to look into the tomb; 12. and she saw two angels in white, sitting where the body of Jesus had lain, one at the head and one at the feet.
13. They said to her, "Woman, why are you weeping?" She said to them,
"Because they have taken away my Lord and I do not know where they
have laid him."
14. Saying this, she turned round and saw Jesus standing, but she did
not know that it was Jesus. 15. Jesus said to her, "Woman, why are you
weeping? Whom do you seek?" Supposing him to be the gardener, she
said to him, "Sir, if you have carried him away, tell me where you have
laid him and I will take him away." 16. Jesus said to her, "Mariam." She
turned and said to him in Hebrew, "Rabbouni!" (which means Teacher).
17. Jesus said to her, "Do not cling to me, for I have not yet ascended to
the Father; but go to my brethren and say to them, 'I am ascending to my
Father and your Father, to my God and your God.'" 18. Mary Magdalene went and said to the disciples, "I have seen the Lord"; and she told
them that he had said these things to her.

INTERPRETATION

There is no explanation for the appearance of Mary Magdalene at the
tomb that she had earlier abandoned (cf. v. 2). The disciples have been
dismissed (cf. v. 10), thus enabling the author to reintroduce the discon-
solate Mary Magdalene into the story. Although one would expect an
indication of Mary's return to the tomb, this is bypassed. Another foundational character from the early Christian community (cf. Mark 15:40;
16:1; Matt 27:56, 61; 28:1, 9-10; Luke 8:2; 23:49, 55-56; 24:1-9, 10-11) is at
center stage. Mary Magdalene and the two dismissed disciples (cf. v. 10)
formed the "we" of v. 2. They were aware of the empty tomb but showed
no recognition of resurrection. The two disciples, and especially the
Beloved Disciple, have gone beyond the experience of Mary, moving to-

ward (vv. 3-4) and away from (v. 10) the empty tomb. As the focus returns to Mary she is portrayed as stationary, standing still in the darkness of the unbelief she shared with them in vv. 1-2. Her standing outside the tomb in tears shows her continued inability to believe or understand what might have happened (v. 11a: *estēkei pros tǭ mnēmeiǭ exō klaiousa*). The faithless wailing *(klaiein)* that accompanied the death of Lazarus (cf. 11:31, 33) is recalled. It only generated the deep frustration and weeping *(dakruein)* of Jesus (cf. 11:35). Mary matches the initiative of both the Beloved Disciple (cf. 20:5) and Simon Peter (cf. v. 6) as she stoops and peers into the tomb for the first time (v. 11b). There is no mention of the cloths and the head covering (cf. vv. 6-7). They have been replaced by two angels in white, one seated at the head and the other at the feet, in the place where Jesus had been laid (v. 11). The angels *(angeloi)* are further evidence that God has entered the story, and the point of view of God is reflected in the angels' question: "Woman, why are you weeping?" (v. 13a).

She answers with almost the same words she used to tell the disciples of the open tomb: "they" have taken away *(ēran)* the body of Jesus, whom she calls her "Lord." There is a slight change from her earlier words. In v. 2 she associated the disciples with her lack of faith and knowledge, claiming that "we" did not know *(ouk oidamen)* where the body has been laid. Now she states "I do not know" *(ouk oida)*. The shift from the plural to the singular accurately reflects the present situation of the characters in the unfolding story. Now it is only Mary who does not know (v. 13b; cf. vv. 3-10). The portrayal of the depths of her unbelief is heightened as she turns to behold Jesus standing in front of her but is incapable of recognizing the figure as Jesus (v. 14). Jesus repeats the question asked by the angels, but adds: "Whom do you seek?" (v. 15a), recalling similar questions from earlier parts of the narrative (1:41; 18:4). Ironically, the one whom she seeks asks her whom she is seeking, but her lack of faith is intensified as she mistakenly identifies Jesus as the gardener *(ho kēpouros)*. With deepening irony the earlier "they" now becomes "you." Jesus, the supposed gardener, is asked where he, taken as a representative of the violent "they" who crucified Jesus, has laid his body! The one whose body she is seeking is asked for a solution to the mystery of the empty tomb. Mary persists in her belief that the body has been "taken away" *(airein:* see vv. 2, 13; *bastazein:* 15a). She asks that she might be the one who takes away the body: "Tell me where you have laid him, and I *will take him away (kagō auton arō)*" (v. 15b). There is no suggestion of resurrection and there is no recognition of the risen one. Mary Magdalene remains in a situation of unbelief as she concerns herself with the removal of a corpse.

Mary's unbelief has been described with considerable detail across vv. 1-2 and 11-15. Her transformation, although not immediate, is reported more rapidly. Fulfilling the promise made in the Good Shepherd discourse (cf. 10:3, 14), Jesus calls Mary by her name: *"Mariam."* She turns again, recognizes him, and knows him, addressing him with the Aramaic name used throughout Jesus' ministry, attaching the first person possessive ending, *Rabbouni:* "my master" (v. 17; cf. 1:38, 49; 3:2; 4:31; 6:25; 9:2; 11:8). The first (1:38) and last (20:16) appearances of this title in the story are followed by implicit commentary from the narrator: "which means teacher." The reader recognizes that Mary has made a partial confession of faith. She recognizes Jesus as the Rabbi whom she had known throughout the ministry. "Both by her address to Jesus as a teacher, and physical contact, she is trying to recapture the past" (Barrett, *Gospel* 565). Like Nicodemus and the Samaritan Woman, used to exemplify the journey of faith at the beginning of the story (3:1-21; 4:16-26), Mary Magdalene has arrived at a partial faith, a belief in the Jesus who best responded to her present hopes and needs.

Associated with this confession is a desire to cling to Jesus (v. 17). Jesus' words, *mē mou haptou,* instruct her that she must desist from her attempt to reestablish the relationship she once had with him. The hour is still in progress, and Jesus not only forbids her to cling to him but explains why all clinging should cease. In and through the cross Jesus has revealed God and has brought to perfection the task given to him (cf. 4:34; 5:36; 17:4; 19:30). The disciples are yet to experience the fruits of Jesus' glorification, but the days of being associated with the historical Jesus are over. An entirely new situation is being established through the hour that is in progress. Jesus has "not yet" *(oupō)* fulfilled his promise to the disciples (cf. 14:12, 28; 16:10, 28) that he would return to the Father; it is about to take place. But Jesus' words to Mary go farther than the promises made before the hour of Jesus. Throughout the earlier part of the narrative there has been a studied avoidance of any relationship between Jesus' disciples and the Father of Jesus, *as their Father.* Although the reader has been told that those who believe in Jesus have the *exousia* to become *tekna theou* (cf. 1:12), this has never been said to the disciples. Only Jesus is "the Son of God." Jesus' words to Mary indicate that this situation is about to change. He is ascending to the Father (v. 17a), and Mary is to inform the disciples, now called Jesus' brethren (v. 17b: *tous adelphous mou*), that he is ascending *pros ton patera mou kai patera hymōn kai theon mou kai theon hymōn* (v. 17c). The hour of Jesus, shortly to culminate in Jesus' ascension to the Father, will create a new situation where the God and Father of Jesus will also be the God and Father of Jesus' brethren. Because of this new relationship, made possible by Jesus' passing from this world to the Father through the hour (see 13:1), they are no longer Jesus' disciples, but his brethren.

Mary does exactly as Jesus commanded: she "went and said to the disciples" (v. 18a; cf. v. 17b). This episode began with a tearful Mary stationary at the tomb, still in the darkness of unfaith. It closes as she moves again, away from the tomb. Responding to the command of Jesus who tells her to go *pros tous adelphous mou* (v. 17), she goes *(erchetai)*. This renewed movement indicates to the reader that Mary has reached another stage in her journey of faith. This is confirmed by her words. In vv. 2, 13, and 15 Mary used the respectful term *ho kyrios* to speak of the dead body of the man she had followed during his public ministry. The meaning of this term is transformed as she is the first to tell the disciples of Jesus' resurrection: "I have seen the Lord *(ton kyrion)*" (v. 18b). Her journey of faith has come full circle. From the darkness of unfaith (vv. 1-2, 11-15) she has passed through the conditioned faith that led her to recognize Jesus as her Rabbi (vv. 16-17a). She now announces that she has seen the risen Lord. Mary informs the disciples of the words that Jesus had spoken to her concerning his return to the Father and the establishment of the oneness between Jesus' Father and God and the Father and God of the disciples (v. 18c; cf. v. 17c). Mary was not capable of understanding the words of the *angeloi* as this scene at the tomb began (vv. 12-13), but as it closes she becomes the messenger, announcing *(angelousa)* the words of Jesus to the disciples (v. 18) (cf. Maccini, *Her Testimony is True* 225–233). Another foundational character from the earliest Christian community has journeyed from the darkness of unfaith through a partial faith into perfect belief.

NOTES

11. *But Mary stood weeping:* The introduction of Mary at the tomb is strange. In almost every case the narrator of the Fourth Gospel indicates movement of characters from one place to another (e.g., 2:1, 13; 3:22; 4:3-6; 5:1; 6:1; 7:10; 8:59; 10:22; 11:5, 17, 38, 54; 12:1, 12, 36b). The present state of the text is probably the result of the insertion of the passage on the two disciples into what was originally a Mary Magdalene story (cf. Brown, *Gospel* 2:996–1004). For Kitzberger, "Mary of Bethany" 582, the reader has supposed from the Lazarus story that Mary would come weeping to the tomb. But this is a misreading of 11:31. See Moloney, *Signs and Shadows* 164–165. The link with 11:31-35 supports the negative interpretation of Mary's weeping (cf. Moloney, *Signs and Shadows* 167–169) despite some suggestions (e.g., Okure, "The Significance" 180; Lee, "Partnership in Easter Faith" 41) that the weeping reveals love and determination.

    outside the tomb: The "outside" *(exō)* is omitted by several manuscripts but should be regarded as original. See Barrett, *Gospel* 564.

12. *two angels in white:* On their white garments as "the symbol of the heavenly world" see Bernard, *Commentary* 2:663. It is fanciful to link the angels with the cherubim at the two ends of the mercy seat on the ark of the covenant as does Siminel, "Les 2 anges" 71–76.

14. *she turned round and saw Jesus:* There is no need to read anything symbolic in Mary's action. Her turning round *eis ta opisō* ("backward") simply indicates that the angels are in front of her and, on turning round, she sees another figure behind her. See Bernard, *Commentary* 2:665.

15. *whom do you seek?:* On the irony of this question from the one she is seeking see Kitzberger, "Mary of Bethany" 582–583. Kitzberger, like others, rightly makes a link with 1:37-38.

    Supposing him to be the gardener: This is perhaps the earliest literary evidence of a Jewish response to the Christian story of the resurrection. While early Christians explained the tradition of an empty tomb by claiming that God had raised Jesus from the dead, early Christian documents report a Jewish response that the body had been stolen from the tomb by a gardener. For this suggestion see von Campenhausen, "The Events of Easter" 66–69. There is a trace of this legend in Tertullian, *Spect.* 30 (MPL 1:662A). Hoskyns, *Gospel* 542, sees the use of "the gardener" as a hint of "the true, life-giving ruler of the Paradise (Garden) of God." See also Blanquart, *Le premier jour* 64–66, and the study of Jewish literature in support of this position by Wyatt, "Supposing Him" 21–38.

16. *she turned:* As with Mary's turning away from the angels to see Jesus in v. 14 there is no need for a symbolic reading of this second turning. From a partial looking back to Jesus she now turns completely to face him. See Lindars, *Gospel* 606.

    Mariam . . . Rabbouni: The name Jesus calls Mary and her response are Greek transliterations of Aramaic, although the narrator explains that it is Hebrew. There is a level of intimacy implied by the recourse to an original language in both the naming and the response (cf. Maccini, *Her Testimony is True* 212–213). Some (e.g., Westcott, *Gospel* 292; Marsh, *Saint John* 637) mistakenly argue that *Rabbouni* is quasi-divine. A number of scholars (e.g., Hoskyns, *Gospel* 542; Marsh, *Saint John* 633, 636–637; Rigaux, *Dio l'ha risuscitato* 324–325; Schneiders, "John 20:11-18" 162–164) regard Mary's addressing Jesus as *Rabbouni* as an authentic confession of faith. Others (Feuillet, "La recherche du Christ" 93–112; Stibbe, *John* 205; Okure, "Jesus' Commission" 181) trace in this encounter the experience of the bride seeking the spouse in the early hours of the dawn in Song of Songs 3:1-3.

17. *Do not cling to me:* For the translation "do not cling to me" see BAGD, s.v. *haptō*, 2a; Delebecque, *Jean* 210. "To cling" is used here to indicate the ongoing holding of someone and does not have any pejorative significance (cf. Lee, "Partnership in Easter Faith" 42 n. 10). The conflict between the prohibition of touch in v. 17 and its encouragement in v. 27 is often overplayed, as the long history of critical discussion of this issue shows. The verbs are different

(v. 17: *haptomai;* v. 27ab: *pherein;* v. 27c: *ballein*), and the significance of the touching (or clinging) is entirely determined by its immediate context.

I have not yet ascended: The "not yet" of v. 17 is to be associated with the conclusion of the hour of Jesus' return to the Father. It is not to be linked with a time "later on" reflected in the Thomas episode when it will be possible to cling to Jesus (cf. v. 27). See previous note. The importance of the "process" of the hour is highlighted by the use of the perfect tense to indicate that Jesus has "not yet" ascended *(oupō gar anabebēka),* and the present tense of Jesus' instruction to Mary concerning the report she must make to the disciples: "I am ascending" *(anabainō).* Jesus has not yet ascended but is in the midst of a process that will come to its conclusion once he has returned to the Father. This is what the brethren must be told. See Lagrange, *Evangile* 511–512; Hoskyns, *Gospel* 542–543; Burge, *Anointed* 136–137; Maccini, *Her Testimony is True* 214–216. Among others Carson, *Gospel* 641–644, 652–654, argues that the resurrection and the ascension must be kept as distinct moments, as 20:22 is a "symbolic promise" from Jesus assuring the disciples of the gift of the Spirit at Pentecost. For a discussion of this proposal see Hatina, "John 20,22 in Its Eschatological Context" 196–219. D'Angelo, "A Critical Note" 529–536, describes Jesus' appearance to Mary Magdalene as an indication of the numinous state he is in prior to the completeness of his ascension. He is no longer in this state when he appears to Thomas and thus can be touched. There is no hint of this in the text. Indeed, in v. 26 the doors are shut, and thus Jesus could still be regarded as in the "numinous" state of v. 17.

to my Father and your Father, to my God and your God: On the new and unique relationship these words promise see Mollat, *Études johanniques* 173–174. Barrett, *Gospel* 566, rightly points out that there are still two forms of filiation: that of Jesus and that of the Christian. As Bernard, *Commentary* 2:668–669, points out, for the Fourth Gospel *anabainein* ("to ascend") is "practically equivalent" to the more frequently used verbs *hypagein* and *poreuesthai* to speak of Jesus' return to the Father.

18. *"I have seen the Lord"* . . . *that he had said these things to her:* The Greek of v. 18 is a strange blend of direct speech ("I have seen the Lord") and indirect speech ("that he had said these things to her"), and it has generated a number of attempts to correct the text (cf. Lagrange, *Evangile* 513). It is probably an attempt to avoid the need to repeat Jesus' words from v. 17 in direct speech.

ii. Scenes in the House (20:19-29)

a) *Jesus Appears to the Disciples but not Thomas* (20:19-23)

19. On the evening of that day, the first day of the week, the doors being shut where the disciples were for fear of the Jews, Jesus came and stood among them and said to them, "Peace to you." 20. When he had said this

he showed them his hands and his side. Then the disciples were glad when they saw the Lord. 21. Jesus said to them again, "Peace to you. As the Father has sent me, even so I send you." 22. And when he had said this he breathed on them and said to them, "Receive the Holy Spirit. 23. If you forgive the sins of any, they are forgiven; if you retain the sins of any, they are retained."

INTERPRETATION

There are indications that vv. 19-23 form a bridge between the scenes at the tomb and the final scene in the house reported in vv. 24-29. Mary obediently responds to the command of Jesus (vv. 17-18). The following events take place "on the evening of that day *(ousēs oun opsias tę hēmerą ekeinę)*" (v. 19). As Mary went *from* the tomb to announce Jesus' message *to* the disciples (v. 18a), the place is now "*where* the disciples were *(hopou ēsan hoi mathētai)*" (v. 19a). Thus Mary's presence at the tomb ends (v. 18) where the following scene begins (v. 19): with the characters to whom Mary announced Jesus' message. The day, place, and characters involved in the events of vv. 19-23 were already part of the closing moments of the immediately previous scene reported in vv. 11-18. The conclusion of the report of Mary Magdalene's experience of the risen Jesus is sufficiently "missionary" (vv. 17-18) to suggest to the reader that the faith experience of Mary Magdalene might be communicated beyond the boundaries of the characters and the time of the present story.

Jesus has been briefly present in the story to send Mary Magdalene to the disciples (v. 17). Despite their having heard Mary's message from the risen Lord, they are locked in a room "for fear of the Jews" (v. 19a). There are no names given to the *mathētai* present in the upper room, nor is there a number. From the beginning of this brief scene "disciples" *as such* are the focus of attention. The story of the original gathering of disciples reflects the experience of all disciples: the proclamation of the message of resurrection does not dispel disciples' fear. The "we" and the "they" of v. 2 are still active forces in the account. The disciples ("we") have not overcome the fear that "the Jews" ("they") have created throughout the story of Jesus. The assembled disciples of Jesus know of the resurrection (cf. vv. 17-18) but the fear of "the Jews," who might subject them to hatred, insult, and death, remains (v. 19a).

Jesus comes into this situation proclaiming his peace (v. 19b). The greeting *eirēnē hymin* may be a regular form of greeting, but within the present setting of Jesus' sudden physical presence among his fear-filled disciples (see 15:18–16:3) it brings into effect Jesus' promises of 14:27 and 16:33. The disciples are now able to be of good cheer (cf. 16:33: *tharseite*); the risen Jesus is among them. His presence despite the locked doors is an indication of his victory over the limitations that human circumstances would impose, evidenced earlier in the story by the empty cloths in an empty tomb (cf. vv. 5-7). But doubt is still possible among the disciples: is this really the crucified Jesus? The disciples may need proof that the figure they see before them is the same Jesus of Nazareth whom they followed. Thus, closely associating a gesture with the greeting of peace (v. 20a: *kai touto eipōn*), he shows them his hands and his side (v. 20b). The risen Jesus is the person they had seen lifted up on a cross and whose side had been pierced with a lance (19:18, 34). Immediately the disciples respond with joy (v. 20c). His greeting, in vv. 19 and 21, brings peace in the midst of turmoil (cf. 14:27). The certain proof that Jesus of Nazareth, the crucified one, is among them as risen Lord brings joy in the midst of confusion and suffering (cf. 16:33). The message of Mary Magdalene has been confirmed by their own experience. The Beloved Disciple and Mary journeyed from unbelief through conditioned faith to an unconditional acceptance of the risen Lord (cf. vv. 3-9, 11-18). This is not the case with the assembled disciples. They heard Mary's message, have had it confirmed, and they respond with peace and joy.

The author uses this first scene in the locked room to continue the account of Mary's journey of faith, bringing it to a conclusion that parallels the conclusion of the experience of the Beloved Disciple (cf. v. 9). The linking of time, place, and characters across vv. 1-18 and 19-23 by means of vv. 17-19 makes the latter scene the conclusion of the former. Jesus' appearance among the rejoicing disciples is not told simply to inform the reader that the promises of 14:27 and 16:33 have been fulfilled. They are not only to be at peace and rejoice, in the midst of their fear, at the physical presence of the risen Lord; they are to be the bearers of the fruits of Jesus' victory to the world beyond the characters and the time of the story of Jesus (vv. 21-23). Again bestowing his peace on them, Jesus indicates to the disciples that his prayer for them on the night before he died was not a fancy. Jesus prayed to his Father: "As you sent me into the world, so I have sent them into the world" (17:18). He has gone, through his total self-gift that makes God known (cf. 17:19), and now he sends them out. They are to be to the world what Jesus has been to the world (cf. 13:20; 17:18). But the reader also recalls Jesus' awareness of the frailty of the disciples and of their need that Jesus' holy Father be Father to them (cf. 17:11b-16) and make them holy, for they must be holy as Jesus was holy (cf. 17:17-19). Such holiness is only possible through the presence of the Paraclete, the Holy Spirit (cf. 14:16-17, 26; 15:26-27; 16:7-11, 12-15).

Much of the earlier narrative floods back as intertext to the passage. The Paraclete sayings and Jesus' prayer for the disciples return, but the words of the narrator in 7:39 are also present: "As yet the Spirit had not been given because Jesus was not yet glorified." At his death Jesus

poured down the Spirit upon the tiny community at the foot of the cross
(cf. 19:30). At the cross the promise of the narrator on the occasion of the
Feast of Tabernacles is fulfilled: Jesus has been glorified and the Spirit is
given (cf. 7:39; 19:30). What is the point of this solemn second bestowal of
the Spirit? The Paraclete sayings, and especially 15:26-27, indicate that
the Spirit was not only to dwell with the new family of Jesus founded at
the cross. As risen Lord he further gifts his disciples with the Spirit that
they may be to the world what he has been. The reader is aware that the
Spirit is *with* the community and *in* the community and will remain with
the community forever (cf. 14:16-17), but the community must reach beyond its own borders to continue the mission of Jesus, so that the world
might know and believe that he is the Sent One of the Father (cf. 17:21,
23). The Spirit will bear witness to Jesus in his absence so that the disciples, who have been with him from the beginning, might also be witnesses (cf. 15:26-27). There are not two "gifts of the Spirit." As there is
only one hour of Jesus there is only one Spirit, given to the members of
the community (cf. 19:30) so that they might be witnesses to Jesus (20:22).
At the hour of the cross and resurrection Jesus pours down the Spirit
upon the community of his followers (19:30) and breathes the Spirit into
its members that they might be in the world as he was in the world
(20:22). The oneness of the hour and all that is achieved by and through
it is nowhere clearer to the reader than in these two episodes that take
place at the hour: the founding gift of the Spirit (19:30; cf. 14:16-17) and
the commissioning of the disciples to be his witnesses empowered by the
Spirit (20:22; cf. 15:26-27).

The disciples, who have been with him from the beginning (cf. 15:27),
will continue the presence of Jesus to a later generation. The message of
the story is less concerned with those who have had the physical experience of the risen Lord than with those who have not. The disciples have
failed to believe and commit themselves unconditionally to the one
whom the Father sent. However much they have failed Jesus they have
never been failed by the love of God made manifest in Jesus. This author's presentation of Jesus' unfailing love for both Peter *and Judas* makes
this point most dramatically. The immensity of the love of God has shone
forth in Jesus' loving gift of self in the midst of their failure (cf. especially
13:19). Yet there is a positive side to the disciples who have been with him
from the beginning. Jesus describes them as having received the manifestation of the name of God, having kept God's word and knowing that
everything Jesus had came from God. They know he is the sent one of
God (cf. 17:6-8). It is for this group whose story has been marked by a
mixture of success and failure that Jesus prays to his Father, asking that
the Father keep them in his name (cf. 17:12) and make them holy as Jesus
is holy (cf. 17:19). Their experience in the locked room encapsulates their

response throughout the Gospel. They are at the same time full of fear yet joyful in the presence of the risen Jesus.

Jesus' words to the frightened yet joyful disciples on their future mission must be understood against this background. Through their ministry sins are to be forgiven and retained. Another use of the passive (cf. vv. 1, 6-7) makes it clear that the disciples are missioned to do God's work, not their own. They are to bring the peace and joy received on the evening of that first day of the week from the risen Jesus (see v. 19) to later generations of frightened disciples of Jesus (cf. 15:18–16:3). The Paraclete's ongoing—yet divisive—revelation will lay bare sin, righteousness, and judgment (cf. 16:7-11). Thus the disciples, empowered by the Spirit, in the midst of their fear and joy will be the agents for the future sanctification of generations of believers. Jesus' instruction of the disciples is recalled. The gift of the Spirit-Paraclete will render the absent Jesus present within the worshiping community (cf. 14:18-21), sharing their experience so that the world might know and believe that Jesus is the Sent One of the Father (cf. 17:21-23). The mission of the disciples renders present the holiness of the absent Jesus (cf. 17:17-19). They will bring God's forgiveness for all sin that is to be forgiven, and lay bare all sinfulness (v. 23). This latter aspect may seem harsh, but it flows naturally from the story of Jesus. This element in the new situation established through the hour of Jesus is "the power to isolate, repel and negate evil and sin, a power given to Jesus by the Father and given in turn by Jesus through the Spirit to those whom he commissions" (Brown, *Gospel* 2:1044). Sanctification may lead to blessedness before God, but it also has the hard edge of exposing all that rejects the love lavished upon the world by a God who sent his only son (cf. 3:16-17).

As the journey of faith of the Beloved Disciple led to an indication from the narrator that there would be a later generation of believers (vv. 3-10), so also does the journey of faith of Mary Magdalene (vv. 11-23). Mary was commissioned by Jesus to announce the message of a new situation initiated by Jesus' return to the Father. She goes to the disciples, now the brethren of Jesus (vv. 17-18). Despite their fear the disciples are blessed with the peace of Jesus and respond with joy when their crucified and risen Lord appears in their midst. The story of a journey of faith did not recommence with the introduction of a new set of characters, as these characters conclude Mary's journey. They are the ones who will bring the holiness of Jesus to a further generation, thus enabling the ongoing experience of the peace and joy that only faith in Jesus can bring (cf. 14:27; 16:33). Despite the struggle of foundational characters in the Christian story to move from no faith through partial faith into unconditional belief they stand at the beginning of a further generation of believers. The readers of the Gospel have come to belief in the resurrection of Jesus.

They do so through the Scripture, including the Johannine Gospel (v. 9), and through the holiness, peace, joy, and judgment made possible by the Lord's gift of the Spirit and Jesus' sending disciples to bring forgiveness of sin to a later generation (v. 23).

NOTES

19. *the doors being shut:* Jesus' victory over the constraints of human conditioning is the point at issue in the reporting of both the empty cloths and Jesus' sudden appearance in a room without coming through the door. This is Johannine proclamation, not the telling of Jesus' miraculous powers (cf. Léon-Dufour, *Resurrection* 183).

    where the disciples were: This "place" forms an obvious link with vv. 17-18, where Mary was instructed to go to the disciples (v. 17) and is reported as going and speaking to the disciples (v. 18). For a series of further links between vv. 19-23 and earlier parts of the Johannine resurrection story, and also with the rest of the Gospel (some of which are a little forced), see Heil, *Blood and Water* 133–136.

    The fact that none of the disciples is mentioned by name and no number is given indicates that disciples as such are implied here, and that the scene that follows is addressed to all disciples of Jesus (cf. Barrett, *Gospel* 568). Some (e.g., Rigaux, *Dio l'ha risuscitato* 367–368; Blanquart, *Le premier jour* 107–109) attempt too much by reading "the apostolic college" into this group of disciples.

    Jesus came and stood among them: Frequently the interpretation and the notes on John 13:1–17:26 have insisted that the return of Jesus to his disciples is at the end time. Many (e.g., Bultmann, *Gospel* 691–692; Beasley-Murray, *John* 379; Talbert, *Reading John* 253–254; Heil, *Blood and Water* 134–135) see this coming in 20:19 as the fulfillment of the promise made to the disciples during the last discourse (that he would come to them: cf. 14:18, 22-23; 16:20-22). This interpretation does not take sufficient notice of the overall message of John 20:1-29, especially Jesus' words in v. 29 that bless people who believe without seeing. This implies that Jesus' coming to the disciples in v. 19 is not his definitive return. His absence will be filled with the presence of the Paraclete.

20. *He showed them his hands and his side:* Unlike Luke 24:38-39 the showing of the pierced body in John 20:20 has no trace of apologetic. It is above all an act of revelation (cf. Mollat, *Études johanniques* 152–154; Becker, *Evangelium* 2:620–621).

21. *Peace to you:* There is no verb in the Greek *(eirēnē hymin)*, and thus the expression should be rendered "Peace to you." Jesus declares that peace is already among them. See W. C. van Unnik, "*Dominus Vobiscum:* The Background of a Liturgical Formula," in A. J. B. Higgins, ed., *New Testament Essays. Studies in Memory of Thomas Walter Manson 1893–1958.* Manchester: Manchester University Press, 1959, 270–305, especially 283–284.

As the Father has sent me, even so I send you: The identity of the mission of Jesus and the mission of the disciples is expressed by means of *kathōs . . . kagō* ("as the Father . . . even so I"). See Bernard, *Commentary* 2:675–676; Barrett, *Gospel* 569–570. Although the recipients of the mission of the disciples are not mentioned, "the world" is presupposed from 13:20 and especially from 17:18 (cf. Mollat, *Études johanniques* 156).

22. *he breathed on them:* Most commentators point to the parallel use of "he breathed on" *(enephusēsen)* in LXX Gen 2:7 (cf. also LXX Ezek 37:9-10; Wis 15:11), making the gift of the Spirit the beginning of the new creation.

    Receive the Holy Spirit: Most scholars discount 19:30 *(paredōken to pneuma)* as the gift of the Spirit (cf. interpretation and note to 19:30), regarding it as a euphemism used to describe Jesus' death. Thus 20:22 is the only Johannine gift of the Spirit, matching the Lukan Pentecost (e.g., Burge, *Anointed* 116–131, 147–149). De la Potterie, *The Hour,* who does regard 19:30 as a gift of the Spirit (cf. pp. 163–165), argues on several grounds that 20:22 is to arouse Easter faith in the disciples and thus overcome their fear and hesitation. For more detail see also de la Potterie, "Parole et Esprit" 195–201. Heil, *Blood and Water,* 137–138, who also holds that 19:30 marks the gift of the Spirit (cf. pp. 102–103), plays on the earlier use of *paredōken* (19:30) as the moment of the *gift* of the Spirit, and Jesus' subsequent command in 20:22 as his instruction that believing disciples receive *(labete)* the Spirit. Swetnam, "Bestowal of the Spirit" 571–574, claims that 19:30 is a bestowal to help all believers (symbolized by the Mother and the Disciple) to discern the meaning of Jesus' life and death, while 20:22 is a specific empowerment to a restricted group for the forgiveness of sins. Accepting that both 19:30 and 20:22 record the gift of the Spirit, the interpretation argues that there are not two "gifts of the Spirit." The one Spirit is given in the one "hour of Jesus" to the members of the Christian community (19:30) so that they might be witnesses to Jesus (20:22) (cf. Manns, *L'Evangile* 462).

    The issue of the relationship between this view of the gift of the Spirit and the Lukan tradition of Pentecost cannot be resolved here. For a full discussion see Burge, *Anointed* 114–149. Léon-Dufour, *Resurrection* 186, aptly summarizes the position adopted by this commentary: "John sets forth an essential dimension of the Easter ministry which Luke has extended in time."

23. *If you forgive . . . if you retain:* For a discussion of the possibility that John 20:23 is a variant form of Matt 16:19; 18:18 see Dodd, *Tradition* 347–349; Brown, *Gospel* 2:1039–1041. Both decide that the two traditions are probably independent. For the division that the understanding of the verse has created among Christians, some of whom would see Jesus' words as limited to a restricted ministry of the forgiveness of sins (most recently see Swetnam's position described in the note to v. 22) while others understand Jesus as commissioning all Christian disciples (cf. Barrett, *Gospel* 568), see Brown, *Gospel* 2:1041–1043. On the strange use of the verb *kratein* to refer to the retention of sins see Bauer, *Johannesevangelium* 232, who rightly points to its close association with *aphienai,* "to let go" (cf. Mark 7:8). For Emerton, "Binding and Loosing" 325–331, an original Aramaic saying based on Isa 22:22 said

"close–open" but was interpreted in the Matthean tradition as "bind–loose" and in the Johannine tradition as "retain–forgive."

if you retain the sins of any: The difficulties involved in understanding what is meant by the disciples' mission to forgive and retain sin are eased by the association of these actions with the mission of the Paraclete to "lay bare" the goodness and evil of the world (cf. 16:7-11). A further connection must be made with the Johannine understanding of the response to the revelation of God in and through Jesus. Some come to the light, but some turn away and the wrath of God rests upon them.

b) *Jesus Appears to the Disciples and to Thomas* (20:24-29)

24. Now Thomas, one of the twelve, called the Twin, was not with them when Jesus came. 25. So the other disciples told him, "We have seen the Lord." But he said to them, "Unless I see in his hands the print of the nails, and place my finger in the mark of the nails, and place my hand in his side, I will not believe." 26. Eight days later his disciples were again in the house, and Thomas was with them. The doors were shut, but Jesus came and stood among them, and said, "Peace to you." 27. Then he said to Thomas, "Put your finger here and see my hands; and put out your hand and place it in my side; do not be faithless, but believing." 28. Thomas answered him, "My Lord and my God!" 29. Jesus said to him, "You have believed because you saw me. Blessed are those who have not seen and yet believe."

INTERPRETATION

The narrative continues: "Thomas, one of the twelve, called the Twin, was not with them when Jesus came" (v. 24). There is no indication of a change in time or place. It is still that "first day of the week" (cf. vv. 1, 19) and the place is the upper room, where an atmosphere of peace and joy prevails among Spirit-filled disciples who have been commissioned to bring the holiness of God to the world. Thomas is not part of this. He was not there (v. 24: *Thōmas de heis tōn dōdeka . . . ouk ēn met' autōn*), and thus has been part neither of Mary Magdalene's message (vv. 17-18) nor of Jesus' appearance and commissioning (vv. 19-23). This is Thomas' first moment in a journey of faith. Surrounded by peace and joy, signs of Easter faith (cf. vv. 19, 20, 21), Thomas, like Peter, the Beloved Disciple, and Mary Magdalene in vv. 1-2 is in the darkness of unfaith (v. 24). His fellow disciples attempt to communicate their Easter faith to him *(elegon oun autǭ)*, repeating the confession of Mary Magdalene: "We have seen the Lord" (v. 25a; cf. v. 18). Thomas' response to the other disciples marks a second stage in his journey of faith. He is only prepared to lay aside his unfaith if the risen Jesus meets *his* criteria. "Unless" *(ean mē)* Jesus fulfills his conditions he will remain in his present situation of unbelief *(ou mē pisteusō)*. Thomas demands that Jesus be "touchable." As Mary wished to cling to the body of Jesus, Thomas asks that he experience the risen body of the person who was crucified by seeing the nail-marks and placing his finger into *(balō)* the wounds, and by placing his hand in *(balō)* his side. Of the three journeys of faith told in this narrative the conditioned response (v. 25: *ean mē*) of Thomas is the most dramatic. He does not refuse the possibility of resurrection. He insists that the risen body of Jesus fulfill his requirements (v. 25; cf. v. 17). He has progressed from his situation of absence (cf. v. 24), but the imposition of his own criteria for belief in the resurrection of Jesus indicates his conditioned commitment.

"Eight days later" *(kai meth' hēmeras oktō)* Jesus again stands among his disciples. Much of the detail that surrounded Jesus' earlier appearance returns. The doors are shut, and he greets them with his peace: *eirēnē hymin* (v. 26; cf. v. 19). The indication of time, eight days later, is also an association with the earlier appearance. Scholars have rightly suggested that the rhythmic reference to "the first day of the week" (v. 1), "the evening of that same day" (v. 19), and "eight days later" (v. 26) deliberately situates all these events on the day of the Lord. The only new element in v. 26, in comparison with v. 21, is the fact that "Thomas was with them." Surprisingly, Jesus offers to fulfill Thomas' conditions (v. 27ab), but he also commands Thomas to reach beyond his conditioned faith: *mē ginou apistos alla pistos*. The risen Jesus is the crucified Jesus. If Thomas wishes to have physical proof he can have it, but there is more at stake: "do not be faithless, but believing" (v. 27c). There is no indication in the text that Thomas performed a touching ritual. The requested ritual is forgotten as Thomas accepts the challenge of faith, responding: "My Lord and my God!" Scholars differ in their evaluation of this act of faith. For some it is the "supreme Christological pronouncement of the Fourth Gospel" (Brown, *Gospel* 2:1047). Others claim that the remarks of Jesus in v. 29: "You have believed because you have seen me. Blessed are those who have not seen and yet believe" show that there is a quality of faith without sight surpassing the faith that generated Thomas' confession (Bultmann, *Gospel* 695–696). A confession that recognizes Jesus as Lord and God at a climactic moment in the narrative corresponds to the christology developed across the earlier parts of the story. It recognizes the implications of the narrator's teaching on the *logos* in 1:1-2, Jesus' unique use of the absolute *egō eimi* (cf. 4:26; 8:24, 28, 58; 13:19), and his claim, "I and the Father are one" (10:30; cf. also 10:38). Parallel with the faith journeys of the Beloved Disciple and Mary Magdalene (cf. vv. 8, 18), this final statement of faith in Jesus concludes Thomas' journey of faith.

The faith journeys of the Beloved Disciple and Mary Magdalene looked beyond the characters *in the story* to further generations: the readers of the story. They believe on the authority of the Scripture, including the word of the Gospel itself, that Jesus rose (cf. v. 9), and they are the recipients of a holiness made possible by Jesus' commissioning fragile but peace-filled and joyful disciples (v. 23). There is a generation of believers reading the Gospel for whom the physical Jesus is *absent*. Their faith is based upon the Scriptures, including the Johannine story (v. 9), and the holiness administered by the Christian community (v. 23). Addressing the last of the foundational figures from the story who have stumbled to faith, Jesus says: "You have believed because you saw me. Blessed are those who have not seen and yet believe" (v. 29). As the Gospel closes Jesus points to two different eras. Some, not without difficulty, have made their journey of faith *in the physical presence of* the risen Jesus: Mary Magdalene and Thomas; but the experience of these disciples is past history for the readers of the Gospel who have been summoned by the narrative to believe that Jesus is the saving revelation of God. How are they, a new generation, to believe *in the absence of Jesus?* With the Scripture and this Gospel in hand (v. 9), and blessed with the holiness that only God can give (v. 23), they are to regard their situation as equally privileged to that of the foundational disciples. Indeed, they are blessed in their belief without seeing (v. 29) (cf. Judge, "A Note on Jn 20,29" 3:2183–2192).

The blessing of those who believe without seeing him recalls that one of the foundational disciples believed without seeing Jesus. The Beloved Disciple had to make his journey out of the darkness (cf. vv. 1-2) and came to faith without seeing Jesus (v. 8). He returned home and does not reappear in the narrative (v. 10). The foundational figure of the Johannine community led the way: he believed without seeing *Jesus* (cf. Byrne, "Beloved Disciple" 89–91, 93–94). This was not the case for the other two characters in the story. Their dependence on *the physical presence of Jesus* is evident in Mary Magdalene's wish to cling to Jesus (cf. v. 17) and Thomas' demand to touch Jesus' wounds and place his hand in the pierced side (v. 25) (cf. Lee, "Partnership in Easter Faith" 40–46). The risen Jesus led these fragile disciples through their hesitation into authentic belief, yet the faith of those who believe without seeing matches that of the greatest disciple (v. 29; cf. v. 8). They have come to faith *in the absence of Jesus.*

Notes

24. *Now Thomas:* The use of *de* ("now") to introduce the Thomas episode establishes a contrast between Thomas and the disciples present at the events described in vv. 19-23 (cf. Heil, *Blood and Water* 139). On Thomas' not being with them see Blanquart, *Le premier jour* 116–119.

one of the twelve: The expression "the Twelve" has become a standard formula. See Brown, *Gospel* 2:1024. In an ambitious study (cf. *JBL* 116 [1997] 147–148) Riley, *Resurrection Reconsidered* 108–110, claims that the author, who is addressing Thomas' disciples to bring them into line with his thought (just as he earlier addressed Baptist disciples for the same purposes), refers to "the Twelve" to link Thomas with Judas, the only other disciple to be associated with "the Twelve" (cf. 6:70-71). For the possibility that *didymos* carries the idea of duplicity see Bauer, *Johannesevangelium* 232. For Riley, *Resurrection Reconsidered* 110–114, the reference to "the twin" identifies Thomas for the Thomas community.

25. *So the other disciples told him:* Brown, *Gospel* 2:1025, suggests that the verb *elegon* ("told") is a conative imperfect (cf. BDF 169, § 326), indicating that the other disciples "tried to tell him."

    place my finger . . . and place my hand: The use of the verb *ballein* ("place") is much stronger than a simple "placing" of the finger or the hand. It conveys the idea of an energetic thrust (cf. Brown, *Gospel* 2:1025). Léon-Dufour, *Resurrection* 188, points out that the criteria imposed by Thomas are not his own: "He rigorously applies the categories of Jewish thought concerning the resurrection of the dead. He requires a strict continuity between the two worlds." Riley, *Resurrection Reconsidered* 126–175, argues that the Thomas community (cf. *The Gospel of Thomas, The Book of Thomas,* and *The Acts of Thomas*) represents a widespread early Christian and Jewish understanding that continued traditional Greco-Roman thought on the risen body as substantial but disembodied. The author of the Fourth Gospel reflects this false view in Thomas' words in 20:25 (cf. pp. 114–119).

    I will not believe: The Greek used for this expression (*ou mē* followed by a future tense) is particularly forceful (cf. BDF 184, § 365).

26. *Eight days later:* Although much of the description of the disciples in v. 26 repeats v. 19, there is no mention of the earlier fear of the disciples. There is no place for fear after vv. 19-23.

27. *do not be faithless, but believing:* Jesus' words summon Thomas away from unfaith into belief (cf. Brown, *Gospel* 2:1026). Some scholars (e.g., Westcott, *Gospel* 296; Loisy, *Evangile* 511; Barrett, *Gospel* 476; van den Bussche, *Jean* 553–554; Wenz, "Sehen und Glauben" 1–25) suggest that Thomas has never been an unbeliever and Jesus exhorts him to maintain his situation of belief. In this interpretation the expressions *pistos* and *apistos,* both found only here in the Fourth Gospel, are read as nouns, and this sentence is translated: "Do not become an unbeliever but a believer." For Riley, *Resurrection Reconsidered* 119–124, the author addresses the unbelievers in the Thomas community, using the figure of Thomas as a literary device to summon them away from their false understanding of resurrection.

28. *My Lord and my God:* It is sometimes suggested (e.g., Mastin, "The Imperial Cult" 352–365; Cassidy, *John's Gospel* 13–16, 69–88) that the Johannine tradition has taken this confession of faith from Domitian's (81–96 C.E.) claim to be worshiped as *Dominus et Deus noster* (cf. Suetonius, *Domitian* 13). For other

classical references see Bauer, *Johannesevangelium* 233. At best the rejection of emperor worship serves as background. The confession is not primarily *against* something, but the final affirmation of the christology of the Gospel.

29. *You have believed because you saw me:* For the translation of *hoti heōrakas me pepisteukas* as a statement rather than a question see Barrett, *Gospel* 573. Most commentators cite *Tanh.* 6:32a, where Rabbi Simeon ben Laqish is reported as eulogizing the one who takes on the yoke of the kingdom of God without having seen the events of Sinai.

For Reference and Further Study

Blanquart, Fabien. *Le premier jour. Étude sur Jean 20.* LD 146. Paris: Cerf, 1992.

Brown, Raymond E. "The Resurrection in John 20—A Series of Diverse Reactions," *Worship* 64 (1990) 194–206.

Byrne, Brendan. "The Faith of the Beloved Disciple and the Community in John 20," *JSNT* 23 (1985) 83–97.

Campenhausen, Hans Freiherr von. "The Events of Easter and the Empty Tomb." In idem, *Tradition and Life in the Church. Essays and Lectures in Church History.* London: Collins, 1968, 42–89.

D'Angelo, Mary Rose. "A Critical Note: John 20.17 and the Apocalypse of Moses," *JThS* 41 (1990) 529–536.

Dauer, Anton. "Zur Herkunft der Thomas Perikope Joh 20,24-29." In Helmut Merklein and Joachim Lange, eds., *Biblische Randbemerkungen: Schülerfestschrift für Rudolf Schnackenburg zum 60. Geburtstag.* Würzburg: Echter, 1974, 56–76.

Dupont, Liliane, Christopher Lash, and Georges Levesque. "Recherche sur la structure du Jean 20," *Bib.* 54 (1973) 482–498.

Emerton, J. A. "Binding and Loosing—Forgiving and Retaining," *JThS* 13 (1962) 325–331.

Evans, C. F. *Resurrection and New Testament.* SBT 12. London: SCM Press, 1970.

Feuillet, André. "La recherche du Christ dans la Nouvelle Alliance d'après la Christophanie de Jo 20,11-18." In *L'homme devant Dieu: Mélanges H. de Lubac.* 2 vols. Paris: Aubier, 1963, 1:93–112.

Fuller, Reginald H. *The Formation of the Resurrection Narratives.* London: S.P.C.K., 1972.

Ghiberti, Giuseppe. *I racconti pasquali del capitolo 20 di Giovanni.* SB 19. Brescia: Paideia, 1972.

Hartmann, Gerhard. "Die Vorlage der Osterbericht in Joh 20," *ZNW* 55 (1974) 197–220.

Hatina, T. R. "John 20,22 in Its Eschatological Context: Promise or Fulfillment?" *Bib.* 74 (1993) 196–219.

Heil, John Paul. *Blood and Water* 120–150.

Judge, P. J. "A Note on Jn 20,29." In *The Four Gospels 1992,* 3:2183–2192.

Kitzberger, I. R. "Mary of Bethany and Mary of Magdala—Two Female Characters in the Johannine Passion Narrative. A Feminist, Narrative-Critical Reader Response," *NTS* 41 (1995) 564–586.

Kragerud, Alv. *Der Lieblingsjünger im Johannesevangelium: ein exegetischer Versuch.* Oslo: Osloer Universitätsverlag, 1959.

La Potterie, Ignace de. "Genèse de la foi pascale d'après Jn 20," *NTS* 30 (1984) 26–49.

_____. "Parole et Esprit dans S. Jean." In *L'Évangile de Jean. Sources, rédaction, théologie.* BEThL 44. Gembloux: Duculot, 1977, 177–201.

Lee, D. A. "Partnership in Easter Faith: The Role of Mary Magdalene and Thomas in John 20," *JSNT* 58 (1995) 37–49.

Léon-Dufour, Xavier. *Resurrection and the Message of Easter.* London: Geoffrey Chapman, 1974.

Lindars, Barnabas. "The Composition of John XX," *NTS* 7 (1960–1961) 142–147.

Lorenzen, Thorwald. *Resurrection and Discipleship. Interpretive Models, Biblical Reflections, Theological Consequences.* Maryknoll: Orbis, 1995.

Lüdemann, Gerd. *The Resurrection of Jesus.* London: SCM Press, 1994.

Mahoney, Robert. *Two Disciples at the Tomb. The Background and Message of John 20,1-10.* TW 6. Bern: Herbert Lang, 1974.

Mastin, B. A. "The Imperial Cult and the Ascription of the Title to Jesus (John 20,28)," *StEv* 6 (1973) 352–365.

Minear, Paul S. "We Don't Know Where . . . Jn 20:2," *Interp.* 30 (1976) 125–139.

Mollat, Donatien. "La découverte du tombeau vide." In *Études johanniques.* Paris: Editions du Seuil, 1979, 135–147.

_____. "La foi pascale selon le chapitre 20 de l'Évangile de Jean. Essai de théologie biblique," in *Études johanniques* 165–184.

Moloney, Francis J. *Glory not Dishonor,* Chapter Seven.

Neyrey, Jerome H. *The Resurrection Stories.* Zacchaeus Studies: New Testament. Wilmington, Del.: Michael Glazier, 1988.

Okure, Teresa. "The Significance Today of Jesus' Commission of Mary Magdalene," *IRM* 81 (1992) 177–188.

Osborne, Basil. "A Folded Napkin in an Empty Tomb: John 11:44 and 20:7 Again," *HeyJ* 14 (1973) 437–440.

Perkins, Pheme. *Resurrection. New Testament Witness and Contemporary Reflection.* Garden City, N.Y.: Doubleday, 1984.

Reiser, William. "The Case of the Tidy Tomb: The Place of the Napkins of John 11:44 and 20:7," *HeyJ* 14 (1973) 47–57.

Rigaux, Beda. *Dio l'ha risuscitato. Esegesi e teologia biblica.* Parola di Dio 13. Rome: Edizioni Paoline, 1976.

Riley, G. J. *Resurrection Reconsidered. Thomas and John in Controversy.* Minneapolis: Fortress, 1995.

Schneiders, Sandra M. "John 20:11-18: The Encounter of the Easter Jesus with Mary Magdalene—A Transformative Feminist Reading." In Fernando F. Segovia, ed., *"What is John?" Readers and Readings of the Fourth Gospel.* SS 3. Atlanta: Scholars Press, 1996, 155–168.

_____. "The Face Veil: A Johannine Sign," *BTB* 13 (1983) 94–97.

Seidensticker, Philipp. *Die Auferstehung Jesu in der Botschaft der Evangelisten.* SBS 26. Stuttgart: Katholisches Bibelwerk, 1968.

Siminel, Philippe. "Les 2 anges de Jean 20/11-12," *ETR* 67 (1992) 71–76.

Swetnam, James. "Bestowal of the Spirit in the Fourth Gospel," *Bib.* 74 (1993) 556–576.

Wenz, Helmut. "Sehen und Glauben bei Johannes," *ThZ* 17 (1961) 17–25.

Wilckens, Ulrich. *Resurrection. An Historical Examination and Explanation.* Edinburgh: The Saint Andrew Press, 1977.

Wyatt, Nicolas. "'Supposing Him to Be the Gardener' (John 20,15). A Study of the Paradise Motif in John," *ZNW* 81 (1990) 21–38.

IV. THE CONCLUSION TO THE GOSPEL (20:30-31)

30. Now Jesus did many other signs in the presence of the disciples, which are not written in this book; 31. but these are written that you might go on believing that Jesus is the Christ, the Son of God, and that believing you may have life in his name.

INTERPRETATION

The Johannine story of Jesus has come full circle. It opened with the narrator's instructing the reader about *who* Jesus was and *what* he did (1:1-18). The life story of Jesus has further developed that instruction but it has, above all, been concerned with telling the reader *how* Jesus was who he was and *how* he achieved his mission. As Jesus dies on the cross the narrator again interrupts the story to speak directly to the reader. Although the Prologue was dedicated to sophisticated instruction, the clumsily passionate intervention of the narrator into the passion story makes his intentions clear. The author's chief concern is the faith of the reader (cf. 19:35). This theme returns as the narrator resumes direct address to the readers to bring the book to its end. Christians who have not seen yet believe are told that this account of the life, death, and resurrection of Jesus has been written for them (20:30-31). The Jesus proclaimed in the Prologue has lived, has been slain, and has risen through the story. But the narrative exists so that the readers of the Gospel might go farther in their faith. It is not merely a recollection of things past but a proclamation addressing the present. Foundational disciples were summoned to reach beyond their unfaith and partial faith into genuine belief (20:1-29). The Gospel has been written that Christian readers who believe without seeing might similarly go farther in their belief in Jesus (vv. 30-31).

The promise of a possible journey of faith in 1:19–4:54 comes to its completion in 20:1-29. As the public ministry of Jesus began, a series of episodes described characters who demonstrated the possibility of authentic Johannine belief (2:1–4:54). The end of the story reports the foundational Easter experience of the Beloved Disciple, Mary Magdalene, and Thomas. Faced with the evidence of God's victory (cf. 20:5-7) or the person of their risen Lord (cf. vv. 14-17, 26-27), each disciple journeyed from no faith to authentic belief (20:2-8, 11-18, 24-28). The readers of a story that began and ended in this fashion are the result of the missionary activity of the foundational members of the Christian community (cf. 17:20-23). The disciples have reaped a harvest they did not sow (cf. 4:36-38), the gathering associated with Jesus' glorification (10:16; 11:52; 12:11, 19, 32; 19:25-27). The readers are this "gathering," the fruit of Jesus' glorification and departure. Despite the absence of Jesus they are blessed in their believing (see 20:9, 23, 29). No doubt they, like the foundational members of the Christian community, will struggle through experiences of no faith and partial faith toward true belief, but they should not be discouraged. Even the Beloved Disciple, so dear to the Johannine storyteller, had to struggle toward belief. If such were the case from the beginnings of the Christian community, subsequent Christian believers have no cause for undue anxiety as they face their own struggles and hesitations (cf. 6:60-71; 15:18–16:3). As a consequence of the gift of the Spirit-Paraclete the absent Jesus is present to the members of the community in their mutual loving (cf. 13:34-35; 15:12, 17; 17:21-23), their mission (cf. 13:34-35; 15:12; 17:17-19), their sanctifying ministry (17:17-19; 20:22), and especially in their worship: cult (cf. 4:23; 14:18-21), prayer in the name of Jesus (cf. 14:12-14; 15:16; 16:23-24, 25-26), and celebration of Baptism and Eucharist (cf. 3:5; 6:51-58; 13:1-38; 19:34-37). But they do not *see Jesus.*

The members of a Christian community coming to faith in the in-between-time, the time of the absence of the physical Jesus, are being summoned to recognize that they are as blessed in their belief as were those who believed on the basis of what they saw (cf. v. 29). Like the Beloved Disciple (cf. v. 8) they believe without seeing *Jesus* (v. 29). It is the desire of the author that all those who read this book or hear its proclamation be a community of beloved disciples (cf. Byrne, "Beloved Disciple" 94). The book was written so that a narrative that reports *how* Jesus has lived his story might confirm *what* was proclaimed in the Prologue. The author believes passionately that Jesus' life story proves the claims made for him in the Prologue. Thus he has written this account, confessedly a selection from the many stories that could have been told (v. 30), so that subsequent Christians might share this passionate belief. Jesus is the Christ, but the Christ who is the Son of God. A belief that reaches beyond all human, historical, and cultural conditioning accepts that Jesus is the long-awaited Christ, but only insofar as he has come from God and returns to God and is the Son of God, the Sent One of the Father, the one who has made God known. Eternal life is possible for those who come to know God through Jesus Christ, the one whom God has sent (cf. 17:3). Jesus' being the Christ is entirely conditioned by the greater truth: he is the Son of God.

> In a mysterious way he began to be more present to them in his godhead once he had become more distant in his humanity. . . . The faith of the believers was being drawn to touch, not with the hand of the flesh but with the understanding of the Spirit, the only-begotten Son, the equal of his Father (Leo the Great, *Sermo LXXIV. De Ascensione Domini II:4* [MPL 54:398C–399D]).

The author has shared his belief in Jesus, the Christ, the Son of God, by means of the story from which the reader now rises. The journey of Jesus and the journey of the reader have been completed, but the story-telling is successful only if the one rising from the story has become part of it, led more deeply into belief in Jesus and all he has made known about God, and comes to life as a result of the reading experience (v. 31).

NOTES

30. *many other signs:* With majority opinion the interpretation takes the reference to the "signs" (*sēmeia*) that are reported (cf. v. 31) as a "look back over the *whole* book" (Schnackenburg, *Gospel* 3:337) rather than the recently reported resurrection appearances. Advocates of the existence of a pre-Johannine Signs Source (cf. notes to 2:23-25) behind the Fourth Gospel see the reference to *sēmeia* in v. 30 as the original conclusion to that source. For a recent persuasive demolition of the Signs Source theory see Schnelle, *Antidocetic Christology* 150–164.

31. *these are written:* On *tauta de gegraptai* ("these things are written") as a rubric that includes the story now coming to an end as part of the *graphē* of v. 9 see Obermann, *Die christologische Erfüllung* 418–422.

    that you might go on believing: The translation reads the present rather than the aorist subjunctive in v. 31. The textual evidence is very finely balanced (*hina pisteuēte* [present subjunctive] or *hina pisteusēte* [aorist subjunctive]). In defense of this choice see Schnackenburg, *Gospel* 3:337–338; Brown, *Gospel* 2:1056; Fee, "On the Text and Meaning" 3:2193–2206; Metzger, *Textual Commentary* 219–220. Schnackenburg suggests that even if the original was in the aorist tense it would not be ingressive ("may come to believe"), as is claimed by those who would see the Fourth Gospel as something of a missionary tract (e.g., van Unnik, "The Purpose" 382–411; Robinson, "The Destination and Purpose" 117–131; Carson, "The Purpose" 639–651). If originally aorist, Schnackenburg claims, it was a summons to "a new impulse in their faith" (cf. 11:15, 40). For the use of *hina*-clauses in the Johannine literature for community instruction see Riesenfeld, "Zu den johanneischen *hina*-Sätzen" 213–220.

FOR REFERENCE AND FURTHER STUDY

Carson, D. A. "The Purpose of the Fourth Gospel: John 20:31 Reconsidered," *JBL* 106 (1987) 639–651.

Fee, Gordon D. "On the Text and Meaning of John 20:30-31." In Frans van Segbroeck et al, eds., *The Four Gospels 1992. Festschrift Frans Neirynck.* 3 vols. Leuven: Leuven University Press, 1992, 3:2193–2206.

Riesenfeld, Harald. "Zu den johanneischen *hina*-Sätzen," *StTh* 19 (1965) 213–220.

Robinson, J. A. T. "The Destination and Purpose of St John's Gospel," *NTS* 6 (1959–1960) 117–131.

Unnik, W. C. van "The Purpose of St John's Gospel," *StEv* 1 (1959) 382–411.

V. EPILOGUE (21:1-25)

Further Resurrection Appearances (21:1-25)

Introduction. John 21:1-25 is widely regarded as an addition to a Gospel that closed with the author's words to the reader in 20:30-31. The following might indicate that an original story ended at 20:31:

1. The ending of 20:30-31 reads like a solemn conclusion to a story.
2. Many words, expressions, and literary peculiarities are found for the first and only time in the Fourth Gospel in 21:1-25 (cf. Boismard, "Le chapitre xxi" 473–502; Brown, *Gospel* 2:2:1079–1080).
3. The narrative of John 21 shows a concern for the community, its mission, and authority within the community that exceeds the interest shown in these questions throughout John 1:1–20:31 (cf. Ruckstuhl, "Zur Aussage" 339–362; Brown, "The Resurrection in John 21" 433–445).
4. The sequence of the story becomes confused. After the mission of Mary Magdalene to announce the resurrection (see 20:18) and the subsequent mission of the disciples in vv. 19-23, why do the disciples return from Jerusalem to Galilee and to their former occupations, seemingly somewhat bored by their present situation (see 21:2-3)?

5. There is an obtuseness among the disciples that makes nonsense of the joy, the mission, and the gift of the Spirit of 20:19-23. After having twice seen Jesus in the upper room (20:19-23, 26-29) why do they fail to recognize him when he appears for the third time (21:14)?
6. Is this the third time? If one includes the appearance to Mary Magdalene (see 20:10-18) it is the fourth appearance.
7. The final words in 21:25 form a literary conclusion, similar to other conclusions from ancient literature (cf. Brown 2:1130). These words repeat, in a less theological and a less reader-oriented fashion, the conclusion of 20:30.

Although it has been suggested that Tertullian knew a Gospel that ended at 20:30-31 (cf. Lattke, "Joh 20:30f als Buchschluss" 288–292), to the best of our knowledge there has never been a textual tradition that did not contain John 21. Whatever scholarship may decide about the origins of John 21 as some form of addition to an original Gospel, this collection of post-resurrection stories was important to the Christians who first wrote and passed down the Gospel to later generations. For this reason alone it must be regarded as an "epilogue," something that belongs to the Gospel as we now have it, and not just an "addendum" or "postscript" added as an afterthought (cf. Zumstein, "Der Prozess der Relecture" 401–404). Despite massive support for the theory that this chapter has been added to a story that originally concluded at 20:30-31 there have always been some who defended its place as the original conclusion to the Gospel on historical grounds (e.g., Lagrange, *Evangile* 520–521 [but he transposes 20:30-31 to follow 21:23]; Hoskyns, *Gospel* 550; Robinson, "The Relation" 120–129; Smalley, *John* 92–97; Minear, "John 21" 85–98; Carson, *Gospel* 665–668; Morris, *Gospel* 757–758). The contemporary rise of canonical and literary approaches to biblical narrative has led to increased effort among a newer generation of scholars to explain John 1:1–21:25 as a literary and theological unit. Most contemporary narrative approaches to the Fourth Gospel take this position (e.g., Hartman, Staley, Ellis, Klinger, Breck, Kieffer, Segovia, Brodie, Stibbe, Lee, Talbert, Schneiders, Okure, Thyen, Busse, Vorster, Korting, Tolmie [cf. For Reference and Further Study for details]). A reading of John 21:1-25 must be pursued in the light of the narrative of 1:1–20:31 by asking whether these additional resurrection stories form part of the original literary and theological design of the Fourth Gospel.

Introduction to 21:1-25. The narrative of John 21:1-25 unfolds in three sections determined by the characters and the action central to each section. Most commentators read vv. 24-25 as the conclusion to the passage (cf. Brown, *Gospel* 2:1065; Beasley-Murray, *John* 396), but the following structure follows the major characters, Peter and the other disciple, across vv. 15-24. Their respective roles in the community are established: Peter is shepherd and disciple (vv. 15-19) and the other disciple is the Beloved

Disciple and the author of the Johannine story (vv. 20-24) (cf. Ruckstuhl, "Zur Aussage" 352 n. 22; Delebecque, "La mission" 339–341; Brown, "John 21" 434–435). This leaves v. 25 as the solemn conclusion that has certain parallels with 20:30-31.

    i.   *Vv. 1-14:* Jesus' appearance to his disciples at the side of the Sea of Tiberias leads to a miraculous catch of fish and a meal by the lake.

    ii.   *Vv. 15-24:* A discussion between Jesus and Peter clarifies the respective roles of Peter the shepherd and the Beloved Disciple, the one who has told this story.

    iii.   *V. 25:* Conclusion.

The reader, who rises from 20:31 under the impression that both Jesus (cf. 20:29) and the narrator (cf. vv. 30-31) have had their last say, is surprised by the laconic summary statement of 21:1, that Jesus revealed himself again. After the blessing of those who believe without sight (20:29) it is surprising to find that there are to be more appearances.

i. Jesus Appears to His Disciples at the Sea of Tiberias (21:1-14)

1. After this Jesus revealed himself again to the disciples by the Sea of Tiberias, and he revealed himself in this way: 2. Simon Peter, Thomas called the Twin, Nathanael of Cana in Galilee, the sons of Zebedee, and two others of his disciples were together. 3. Simon Peter said to them, "I am going fishing." They said to him, "We will go with you." They went out and got into the boat, but that night they caught nothing.
4. Just as day was breaking Jesus stood on the beach, yet the disciples did not know that it was Jesus. 5. Jesus said to them, "Children, have you caught any fish?" They answered him, "No." 6. He said to them, "Cast the net on the right side of the boat and you will find some." So they cast it, and now they were not able to haul it in for the quantity of fish. 7. That disciple whom Jesus loved said to Peter, "It is the Lord!" When Simon Peter heard that it was the Lord he tucked in his outer garment, for he was otherwise naked, and sprang into the sea. 8. But the other disciples came in the boat, dragging the net full of fish, for they were not far from the land, but about a hundred yards off.
9. When they got out on land they saw a charcoal fire there, with fish lying on it, and bread. 10. Jesus said to them, "Bring some of the fish that you have just caught." 11. So Simon Peter went aboard and hauled the net ashore, full of large fish, one hundred fifty-three of them; and although there were so many the net was not torn. 12. Jesus said to them, "Come and have breakfast." Now none of the disciples dared ask him, "Who are you?" They knew it was the Lord. 13. Jesus came and took the bread and gave it to them, and so with the fish. 14. This was now the third time that Jesus was revealed to the disciples after he was raised from the dead.

INTERPRETATION

Introduction. The episodes on the lake and beside the lake fall easily into three sections, vv. 1-3, vv. 4-8, and vv. 9-14 (but cf. note to v. 3). In vv. 1-3 the fishing excursion is introduced. Most Johannine scenes have an introduction to the place, time, and characters of the episodes that follow. This introduction is unique, as it immediately informs the reader that what follows is about a further appearance of the risen Jesus to the disciples (v. 1). The experience of the disciples on the sea is introduced by an indication of time: "Just as day was breaking" (v. 4), and closes with the disciples heading for land, dragging their net full of fish (v. 8.). This encounter between Jesus and the group of disciples closes with a shared meal on the land (cf. v. 9) and a comment from the narrator: "This was now the third time that Jesus was revealed to the disciples after he was raised from the dead" (v. 14).

The Setting (vv. 1-3). The account opens with a laconic statement from the narrator that the Lord revealed himself *(ephanerōsen heauton)* again to the disciples by the Sea of Tiberias, and announces that the way in which he revealed himself is about to be described (v. 1). The verb *phaneroō* has never been used in John 20 (or elsewhere in the NT) to speak of resurrection appearances, and its use is extremely rare in the synoptic tradition (only at Mark 4:22 and in the longer ending to Mark [16:12,14]). However, it has been used significantly in the Fourth Gospel to speak of the revelation that takes place in Jesus (cf. 1:31; 2:11; 3:21; 7:4; 9:3; 17:6). This form of introduction is foreign to the rest of the Gospel, but a significant verb from the earlier story is used to indicate that what is about to be reported is something more than a physical appearance. "The whole verse makes the effect of the announcement of a theme" (Schnackenburg, *Gospel* 3:352).

Seven disciples "were together" (v. 2: *ēsan homou*). The statement of the "togetherness" at the beginning of the sentence, and the list of seven disciples, a symbolic representation of disciples as such, continue the theme of the creation of a new community at the cross (cf. 19:25-27). It also hints at the centrality of that theme in 21:1-25. There are some surprises in the names listed. Simon Peter is named first, as one would expect (cf. 6:67-69; 13:6-9; 20:2-7), and the identification of Thomas as "the twin" looks back to 20:24. But only here is Nathanael described as "the man from Cana of Galilee," and the sons of Zebedee appear in the Johannine story for the first time. The listing of two unnamed disciples leaves open the possibility of the presence of the Beloved Disciple, who will emerge both in the account of the appearance of Jesus to the fishermen (v. 7) and in the discussions that follow (vv. 20-24). The unnamed disciples continue a practice of the Fourth Gospel never to reveal the identity of the Beloved Disciple (cf. 1:35; 18:15, 16; 20:2, 3, 8). Two un-named disciples appear at the beginning (1:35) and at the end (21:2) of the finished Gospel.

Peter's decision to go fishing, the other disciples' decision to join him, and the information that their night in the boat produced no catch have been the source of much speculation. How is it possible that the disciples, after 20:19-23, could so easily give themselves to this prosaic return to their everyday activity? Solutions range from speculations about the mental state of the post-Easter disciples (Beasley-Murray, *John* 399–400), to Peter's symbolic leading of the mission as "fishers" of people (Barrett, *Gospel* 579), to aimless disorientation (e.g., Brown, *Gospel* 2:1096), to apos-tasy (Hoskyns, *Gospel* 552). In the end the presence of the disciples on the sea after a fruitless night's fishing does not need to be explained theo-logically or psychologically. It is an essential part of the setting for the ap-pearance that follows, but it also indicates that John 21 and its formation in the community were independent of 20:1-31.

The miracle (vv. 4-8). At a time that links this episode with Mary Mag-dalene's unbelieving visit to the empty tomb in the darkness of very early morning (cf. 20:1: *prōï*) Jesus stands on the beach "just as day was break-ing" (v. 4: *prōïas de ēdē ginomenēs;* cf. note). Another traditional resurrec-tion motif emerges: he is not recognized by those who had been with him during the ministry (cf. Luke 24:13-35, 36-38; John 20:15). As they go about their everyday affairs as if the risen Lord had never broken into their lives, like Mary Magdalene they are understandably unable to rec-ognize him. He initiates contact as he addresses them as "children" *(paidia).* This form of address, not found elsewhere in the Fourth Gospel (but cf. 1 John 2:14, 18; 3:7), indicates an intimate authority. Jesus ex-presses his interest and concern over their unsuccessful fishing trip and commands them to cast the net on the right side of the boat, promising that they will find fish (6a). There is no need to resort to popular specu-lation that the "right" side of the boat was the lucky side (cf. BAGD 174). The detail merely adds to Jesus' authority over both the elements and the disciples' behavior. The obedient response of the disciples to Jesus' com-mand bears fruit. On several occasions during his ministry Jesus exercises authority over nature (cf. 2:1-11; 6:1-15, 16-21), and the miracle that re-sults from the disciples' wordless performance of his commands does not come as a surprise (v. 6b).

In the recognition of Jesus and response to the miracle the two dis-ciples who played such an important role at the empty tomb, Peter and the Beloved Disciple (cf. 20:3-10), assume important roles. It is the Beloved Disciple who recognizes the risen Jesus, telling Peter (and not the other disciples?): "It is the Lord" (cf. 20:8). Again paralleling events re-ported in John 20, the response of these same two disciples at the empty tomb is recalled (cf. 20:4-8): the Beloved Disciple is the one who confesses his faith in Jesus as the risen Lord while Peter responds to the indications of the Beloved Disciple just as he had "followed" him in 20:6, and adjusts his scant clothing and leaps into the water (cf. note). The other disciples bring the boat to land, dragging the net with them (v. 8). The reader is not told of Peter's belief, only of his energetic response to the Beloved Disciple's confession. The other disciples serve merely to round off this part of the story, bringing the boat (presumably along with the Beloved Disciple) and the fish to join Peter and Jesus on the shore.

In reintroducing Simon Peter and the Beloved Disciple into the story the author of John 21 looks back to John 20, but overlooks the fact that in 20:10 these two disciples "went back to their homes." They were dismissed from the scene after the Beloved Disciple had seen the signs of God's victory over the death of Jesus and had believed *without seeing Jesus* (20:8). By bringing Jesus back into the lives of these disciples the author suggests that the Beloved Disciple no longer falls under the blessing of 20:29. He believes in 21:7a because he sees Jesus.

The meal (vv. 9-14). Whatever might have been the prehistory of the account of the miracle and the Easter meal, they are skillfully joined. On arrival at the shore the disciples see that a meal has been prepared: a charcoal fire with fish lying on it, and bread (v. 9). Peter's restoration is underway. He had earlier joined those who had gone out to arrest Jesus with lanterns and torches by a charcoal fire (cf. 18:3, 18: *anthrakian*) but he is now invited to join Jesus at a meal prepared on another charcoal fire (v. 9: *anthrakian*). Peter's presence links the miraculous haul of fish with the meal. He is instructed to bring some of the fish that were caught (v. 10), and he obeys, hauling the net ashore. The detail of the great catch of one hundred fifty-three large fish that, miraculously, did not tear the net, has "teased the minds" (Beasley-Murray, *John* 401) of readers of this Gospel at least from the time of Jerome (cf. *Commentarium in Ezechielem*, Liber XIV:47; MPL 25:474C). It is impossible to summarize the many suggestions that have been made over the centuries to explain the mention of one hundred fifty-three large fish (cf. Beasley-Murray, *John* 401–404), and their sheer number militates against there being a solution. No doubt the author had good reason for choosing the number one hundred fifty-three, either for symbolic meaning or as the result of a mysterious combination of possible numbers, or even because he had it on good tradition that there were exactly one hundred fifty-three fish in the net! A great miracle has been worked by the risen Jesus, and the result of that miracle is a large number of fish that *should have* torn the net. Many have been drawn into the net, but the net is not damaged. The seamless garment that could not be torn apart may be in the mind of the author (cf. interpretation of 19:23-24). At Jesus' word disciples in a boat have cast their net into the sea and gathered many fish without damaging the net. The universality of the Christian community, the result of the initiative of Jesus (cf. v. 6), the leadership of Simon Peter and the Beloved Disciple (cf. v. 7), and the participation of the disciples (cf. 4:34-38) shape the main point of the story (cf. Brown, *Gospel* 2:1075).

Jesus continues to determine the action as he commands them to eat the first meal of the day. There is a complete transformation of the disciples from v. 4, where they did not recognize Jesus. Guided by the faith of the Beloved Disciple and the actions of Simon Peter, they no longer dare to ask for the identity of Jesus. They now recognize that the risen Lord is present (v. 12: *hoti ho kyrios estin*). In v. 9 fish and bread were already prepared for a meal, and these elements recall the miracle of 6:1-15 where both bread and fish were multiplied to feed a multitude at Passover time. There were hints of early Christian eucharistic celebrations there (cf. the interpretation of 6:1-15), and they are again present in this passage, particularly in the indications that Jesus "took the bread and gave it to them, and so with the fish" (cf. 6:11). Within an overall message of a universal community gathered as the result of the initiative of the risen Christ and under the leadership of Simon Peter the eucharistic hints do nothing more than indicate the presence of one of the central acts of worship of the Johannine community (cf. 6:1-15, 51-58; 13:21-38; 19:35).

This episode closes with the announcement from the narrator that this was the third time that the risen Jesus was revealed (again *phaneroō* is used) to the disciples (v. 14). Either Mary Magdalene was not regarded as a disciple (*mathētēs*; cf. Carson, *Gospel* 675), or the author of John 21 has not counted accurately. This is the fourth appearance of the risen Jesus (cf. 20:11-18, 19-23, 26-29; 21:4-14), and this closing comment from the narrator leaves the impression "that the present story does not belong to the carefully composed narrative of ch. 20" (Barrett, *Gospel* 582–583).

A careful reading of 21:1-14 indicates several conscious links with the Gospel of John as a whole (e.g., the use of the verb *phaneroō* for the revelation of Jesus, the unnamed disciples in v. 2, the possible link between the bread and fish of 21:9 and 6:1-15) and especially with events reported in 20:1-29 (e.g., links with the experience of Mary Magdalene and the time when it took place, and the return of Simon Peter and the Beloved Disciple, who behave as they did in 20:3-10). However, a number of awkward elements emerge: the strange introduction (v. 1), the non-Johannine characters who appear in the list of seven disciples (v. 2), the "ordinariness" of the disciples' decision to go fishing (v. 3), and the fact that the number given for Jesus' post-resurrection appearances (v. 14) is incorrect. Crucially, however, the disciple who had believed without seeing (20:8) has now confessed his belief in Jesus as Lord because he recognized Jesus on the shore (v. 7). There is a curious blend of continuity and discontinuity in this first section of John 21 (cf. note).

NOTES

3. *I am going fishing:* There are a number of similarities between the fishing episode in John 21:1-14 and the synoptic tradition, especially Luke 5:4-8. Pesch, *Der reiche Fischfang,* has proposed that this account is the result of the blending of two elements: a fishing tradition (vv. 2, 3, 4a, 6, 11) that had its origins in Jesus' ministry (cf. Luke 5:1-11) and a resurrection appearance (vv. 4b, 7-9, 12-13) associated with a meal (cf. Luke 24:28-32, 41-43). Although some have objected to the dissociation of the fishing episode from the Easter narratives (e.g., Beasley-Murray, *John* 396–397), many scholars have accepted Pesch's hypothesis.

   If an explanation for this odd decision is called for, Barrett's suggestion (p. 579) is helpful. The author of John 21, aware of the commission of 20:21, uses this passage, which had its origins independent of John 20, to show the disciples responding to their commission, setting out on the missionary task of "fishing" (cf. Mark 1:16-20). The fact that they fail throws into relief their wonderful success when directed by Jesus (v. 6).

4. *Just as day was breaking:* Although, as pointed out in the interpretation, there is a contact between Mary Magdalene's arrival at the empty tomb "early" *(prōi)* and Jesus' appearance "as day was breaking" *(prōias de ēde ginomenēs),* elsewhere in the Fourth Gospel only the indeclinable form of *prōi* ("early") is found (18:28; 20:1). Even in these details there is continuity and discontinuity between the two resurrection chapters.

5. *Children:* A number of commentators render *paidia* as "lads" (e.g., Carson, *Gospel* 670), but this does not do justice to the subsequent authoritative relationship that Jesus has with the disciples or to the echo of the way in which the letter writer of 1 John addresses his subjects.

   have you caught any fish?: The question (beginning with the negative *mē*) supposes a negative answer. The word used for "fish" in this question *(prosphagion)* is not found anywhere else in either the LXX or the NT. It is rare in all Greek literature. It is the first of three different expressions used for "fish" in this brief narrative.

6. *for the quantity of fish:* The narrator uses the word *ichthus* for "fish" in the report of the miraculous catch *(apo tou plēthous tōn ichthuōn).*

7. *It is the Lord:* The words of the Beloved Disciple must be given their full post-Easter significance. He confesses his belief in the presence of Jesus as the risen Lord *(ho kyrios estin).* This confession is then reinforced by the report "when Peter heard *hoti ho kyrios estin.*" This does not necessarily indicate that Peter believes in the presence of the risen Lord, but only that he has heard what the Beloved Disciple said. Although the verb "to be" is to be expected, it may also carry the meaning "the Lord *is present*" (cf. Barrett, *Gospel* 580).

he tucked in his outer garment, for he was otherwise naked: This translation (cf. Brown, *Gospel* 2:1072) is but one way of handling the rather strange indication that Peter dressed himself to leap into the water. One would expect the opposite procedure. The verb used *(diazōnnynai)* primarily means to tuck up clothes or to tie them up with a cincture. Peter is not entirely naked, but very lightly clad in one garment *(ependytēs:* "outer garment"). To remove it would have left him entirely naked, so he tucks it up so that he might move freely in the water (cf. Lagrange, *Evangile* 525).

9. *charcoal fire:* The link made between 18:18 and 21:9 in the interpretation is disregarded by most commentators, and suspiciously regarded by some as "very subtle indeed" (Carson, *Gospel* 671 n. 2).

 with fish lying on it: The third expression for "fish" *(opsarion)* appears here. This inexplicable use of three words for "fish" within very few verses is an indication of the long and complicated prehistory of this account.

11. *one hundred fifty-three of them:* Whatever the hidden secret behind the number might be (allegory, gematria, a mathematical symbol?), it has led such diverse critics as Brown, *Gospel* 2:1075–1076, and Staley, *The Print's First Kiss* 113, to conclude that it is impossible to give it a meaning. For the recent resumption of an attempt (cf. Barrett, *Gospel* 581) to explain it on the basis of the number seventeen see Brodie, *Gospel* 587–588. In support of the missionary significance of the passage see Ruckstuhl, "Zur Aussage" 340–351; Schneiders, "John 21:1-14" 72; Marzotto, *L'Unità* 215–219; Rodriguez Ruiz, *Der Missionsgedanke* 290–304; Heil, *Blood and Water* 157.

13. *Jesus came and took the bread and gave it to them:* Associated with v. 9, the eucharistic background to the "coming" of Jesus and his distribution of the bread and fish to the disciples is clear (cf. also Brown, *Gospel* 2:1098–1100). Not all would accept that there is a eucharistic reference (e.g., Dodd, *Interpretation* 431 n. 1), and Barrett (*Gospel* 582) correctly points out that parallels with 6:51 should not be too easily drawn. Indeed, as shown in the interpretation, the major contacts come from 6:1-15 (cf. Shaw, "The Breakfast by the Shore" 12–26). Others rightly insist that it must not be exaggerated (e.g., Beasley-Murray, *John* 401–402). See, for example, Cullmann, "The Breaking of Bread" 8–16.

14. *This was now the third time:* The widespread agreement that John 21 has been added to an already completed Gospel depends heavily on the large number of words and grammatical expressions that appear only in this chapter and nowhere else in the Gospel. The most thorough treatment of this question is Boismard, "Le chapitre xxi" 473–501. See also Mahoney, *Two Disciples* 12–40. The use of this criterion alone, however, is somewhat skewed by the fact that this is the only fishing episode in the Fourth Gospel and thus necessarily has its own language (cf. Barrett, *Gospel* 576–577). It is therefore necessary to resort to a more literary analysis, recognizing both the continuation and the discontinuity of such things as themes and characterization between the Gospel and this final chapter.

ii. Jesus, Peter, and the Beloved Disciple (21:15-24)

15. When they had finished breakfast Jesus said to Simon Peter, "Simon, son of John, do you love me more than these?" He said to him, "Yes, Lord; you know that I love you." He said to him, "Feed my lambs." 16. A second time he said to him, "Simon, son of John, do you love me?" He said to him, "Yes, Lord; you know that I love you." He said to him, "Tend my sheep." 17. He said to him the third time, "Simon, son of John, do you love me?" Peter was grieved because he said to him the third time, "Do you love me?" And he said to him, "Lord, you know everything; you know that I love you." Jesus said to him, "Feed my sheep. 18. Amen, amen, I say to you, when you were young you girded yourself and walked where you would; but when you are old you will stretch out your hands, and another will gird you and carry you where you do not wish to go." 19. This he said to show by what death he was to glorify God. And after this he said to him, "Follow me."
20. Peter turned and saw following them the disciple whom Jesus loved, who had lain close to his breast at the supper and had said, "Lord, who is it that is going to betray you?" 21. When Peter saw him he said to Jesus, "Lord, what about this man?" 22. Jesus said to him, "If it is my will that he remain until I come, what is that to you? Follow me!" 23. The saying spread abroad among the brethren that this disciple was not to die; yet Jesus did not say to him that he was not to die, but "If it is my will that he remain until I come, what is that to you?" 24. This is the disciple who is bearing witness to these things, and who has written these things, and we know that his testimony is true.

INTERPRETATION

Introduction. The two disciples whose roles were singled out in v. 7 in the account of the miracle on the sea and its aftermath are next given more extended treatment. Providing a good link with the previous narrative, "When they had finished breakfast" (v. 15a), the author initially focuses on the figure of Simon Peter. Jesus demands a threefold confession of love and charges him with the care of his sheep, promising him that, as his follower, he will share in his destiny (vv. 15-19). Peter, now "following" Jesus (cf. v. 19b), turns to see another disciple "following." This disciple is identified as the Beloved Disciple, and responding to the question from Peter "What about this man?" Jesus speaks of his destiny and the narrator adds a description of the role of this significant disciple in and for the community (vv. 20-24).

Simon Peter (vv. 15-19). Jesus' thrice-repeated question asks Simon Peter to commit himself to love Jesus more than he loves the other disciples at the meal. Peter responds unconditionally, further confessing that his love for Jesus is known by the all-knowing risen Lord. On the basis of this response to his question Jesus commands Peter to pasture his sheep. A relationship between the role of Peter and the role of Jesus the Good Shepherd in 10:1-18, and especially in 10:14-18, is established. What is surprising, however, is that this same question, answer, and imperative are repeated three times (vv. 15-17). There may be precedents for a three-fold declaration in front of witnesses before contracting oneself to a binding situation (cf. Gaechter, "Das dreifache" 328–344), and there are subtle changes in the words of both Jesus and Peter that have also been exploited by interpreters (cf. notes). But the major reason for Jesus' demanding a threefold confession of love is obviously Peter's threefold denial of Jesus at the outset of the passion narrative (cf. 18:15-18, 25-27). However fragile, Peter has been close to Jesus throughout the ministry (cf. 1:40-42; 6:67-69; 13:6-10, 36-38; 18:15), a closeness dramatically destroyed by the disciple's threefold denial and the subsequent events of the crucifixion of Jesus. The royal lifting up of Jesus on the cross, the foundation of a new family of God and the gift of the Spirit (19:17-37), have been marked by the presence of the Beloved Disciple (cf. 19:25-27) and the absence of Simon Peter. The denials must be overcome, and an element in the rhythmic repetition of the same question is the hint of an accusation: "you once denied me . . . are you sure of your relationship to me now?" Peter's embarrassed but honest responses lead to the risen Lord's acceptance of Peter's protestations of love and the establishment of a new relationship: Jesus appoints Peter as the one who shepherds his sheep.

The pastoral role Peter is called to fill associates him with the Good Shepherd. He is charged to "shepherd" *(poimaine)* and "feed" *(boske)* the "lambs" *(ta arnia)* and "sheep" *(ta probata)* of Jesus. Discussions of the Petrine office in the Roman tradition of Christianity are out of place in an exegesis of this passage (cf. note). The person charged with that pastoral office, and all Christian pastors, like Peter, are challenged to repeat the relationship Jesus had with his flock. Peter's love for Jesus (vv. 15c, 16b, 17b) must be shown in his preparedness to make his own the words of Jesus, the Good Shepherd (vv. 15d, 16c, 17c): "I came that they may have life, and have it more abundantly" (10:10); "I know my own and my own know me" (10:14); "I lay down my life for my sheep" (10:15; cf. 10:11, 17, 18); "I have other sheep that are not of this fold . . . there shall be one flock, one shepherd" (10:16).

Despite the claims of some that there is no inner connection between vv. 15-17 and vv. 18-19 (e.g., Bultmann, *Gospel* 713; Brown, *Gospel* 2:1117), Jesus' further words concerning Peter's future are but the logical consequence of the christological basis for his shepherding. Introduced by the Johannine double "amen," his words remind Peter of a time in the past, the time during the ministry of Jesus when Peter showed a great deal of good will but ultimately went his own way into denial. That was the time when Peter was young, when he girded himself and went where he would (v. 18a). Those days are over. He has now overcome the scandal of his rejection of Jesus and has unconditionally committed himself to the way of the Good Shepherd (vv. 15-17). The time will come, "when you are old," when Peter will lay down his life for the sheep of Jesus that have been entrusted to his pastoral care. Another will gird him and carry him where he would prefer not to go. Despite scholarly squabbles over the exact nature of the way this might be applied to crucifixion (cf. note) there can be little doubt that by the time this episode was written Peter had already stretched out his hands, an executioner had girded him with the cross, and he had laid down his life for the flock of Jesus (cf. Haenchen, *John* 2:226–227). But Peter's commitment to the way of the Good Shepherd also associates him with the meaning of the death of Jesus. Death did not fall upon Jesus as a terrible end to a self-sacrificed life. Jesus' unconditional acceptance of his will of the Father (cf. 4:34; 5:36; 17:4) revealed the love of God for the world (3:16). In this Jesus was glorified (cf. 11:4; 12:23; 13:31-32; 17:1-5) and Jesus gave glory to God (cf. 11:4, 40; 12:28; 13:31-32; 17:1-5). Peter's unconditional acceptance of his role as shepherd of the sheep of Jesus (vv. 15-17) will also lead to the glorification of God in his self-gift in love unto death (v. 19a). Once he has explained all the implications of being the shepherd of his flock (vv. 15-19a) there is little else for Jesus to do but invite Peter to follow him down this way (v. 19b). This "following" has a physical meaning, as immediately Peter walks behind Jesus (cf. v. 20a), but it also means an "undeviating discipleship all the rest of his days" (Beasley-Murray, *John* 409).

The Beloved Disciple (vv. 20-24). There is a strong sense of "following" in v. 20. Peter is physically following Jesus in an obedient response to the command of Jesus in v. 19: "Follow me." In his following he turns and sees that the Beloved Disciple, described as the one who had lain close to Jesus' breast and asked for the identity of the betrayer (cf. 13:23-25), is also "following" (v. 20). It is Peter who poses the question that will be answered in two stages, by Jesus in v. 22 and then by the narrator in vv. 23-24: "Lord, what about this man?" (v. 21). Peter has been firmly established as a disciple and a pastor, but questions remain around the figure of the Beloved Disciple. The paths of these two characters have been entwined across the latter part of the Gospel, at the last meal (cf. 13:23-25), in the court of the high priest (18:15-16), and at the empty tomb (cf. 20:3-10). On those earlier occasions, despite Peter's obvious importance, the Beloved Disciple held pride of place (13:23), had disappeared from the scene once Peter began to deny his association with Jesus (18:17-18), and was the only one reported to have come to faith at the empty tomb (20:8). Be-

tween these moments in the narrative, in the absence of Peter who had
thrice denied that he was a disciple of Jesus (18:15-18, 25-27), the Beloved
Disciple has been consigned to the Mother of Jesus and the Mother has
been consigned to the Disciple by the crucified King (19:25-27). The Johannine community obviously regarded this figure with great respect
and looked back on him as the founding figure of the community (cf.
19:25-27, and Introduction), but if Peter has been appointed disciple and
pastor not only Peter *in the story* but also *the readers of the Gospel* might ask:
"What about this man?" (21:21).

Jesus' response addresses an issue that must have been part of the
community's wondering. They have in their recorded memory of Jesus'
words a promise that the Beloved Disciple would not die before Jesus' return, but this memory needs correction. The exact words of Jesus were:
"If it is my will that he remain until I come, what is that to you? Follow
me!" (v. 22). Jesus challenges Peter to maintain his role as a follower of
Jesus, and he is not to worry about the destiny of the Beloved Disciple.
His own destiny has been made clear to him in vv. 18-19. But the community's memory of these words seems to have focused on the wrong
issue. What is central to Jesus' words, comments the narrator, is the conditional: "If it is my will." Jesus did not say that the Beloved Disciple
would not die before the coming of Jesus but that his future would be determined by the will of Jesus. The problem behind this clarification of
what it was exactly that Jesus had said is clearly the death of the Beloved
Disciple. "The saying spread abroad . . . that this disciple was not to die"
(v. 23a), but "this saying" *(houtos ho logos)*, this expression of popular
opinion, was based on a faulty understanding of Jesus' words to Peter.
The Beloved Disciple is no longer alive, and the community should not
wonder at his death. Whatever has happened to the Beloved Disciple is
but the fulfillment of the will of Jesus for him. Both Peter (cf. vv. 18-19)
and the Beloved Disciple (vv. 22-23) have died.

The community that received this Gospel lived in a time after the
deaths of Jesus, Simon Peter, and the Beloved Disciple. The narrator,
therefore, has more to say about the Beloved Disciple. Matching Jesus' establishment of Peter as pastor and disciple (vv. 15-19), the final words
from the narrator add something further to the significance of the
Beloved Disciple. The mutual consigning of Mother and Disciple at the
cross and the gift of the Holy Spirit to this nucleus of the new family of
God (cf. 19:25-30) point unambiguously to the community's regard for
the Beloved Disciple as the founding figure of the Christian community
to which they belong. The founding figure is also the author of the community's story of the life and teaching, death and resurrection of Jesus (v.
24). The narrator's words are close to the earlier intervention of the narrator in 19:35. Living in the in-between-time, after the deaths of Jesus,

Peter, and the Beloved Disciple, the community has a link between the events of the past and the experience of the present, and the Beloved Disciple's witness provides it. He was a disciple of Jesus who both witnessed "these things" *(ho martyrōn peri toutōn)* and then became the author of a record that transmitted "these things" *(ho grapsas tauta).* The witnessing is still present *(martyrōn:* present participle) because of the record *(grapsas:* aorist participle). On the basis of this recorded witness, alive despite the death of the Beloved Disciple, the community can be confident in the knowledge *(oidamen)* that their Jesus story and the life-style they are living as a consequence of that story are true. Peter is the appointed shepherd of the flock (cf. vv. 15-17) and the Beloved Disciple is the bearer of the authentic Jesus tradition (v. 24).

The continuity and discontinuity between John 1–20 and John 21 that marked 21:1-14 are also present in vv. 15-24. The figures of Simon Peter and the Beloved Disciple (cf. 13:23-25), the use of shepherding language (vv. 15-17; cf. 10:1-18), the theme of love (vv. 15-17; cf. 3:16, 35; 13:1, 15, 34-35; 15:12, 17; 17:24-26), the knowledge of Jesus (vv. 15-17; cf. 2:23-24; 5:42; 6:15; 10:14-15, 27; 13:1; 16:19; 17:25-26; 18:4), the glorification of God that takes place in death (v. 19; cf. 11:4, 40; 12:28; 13:31-32; 17:1-5), the use of the double "amen" (v. 18), and the witnessing role of the author/narrator of the Gospel (v. 24; cf. 19:35) all look back to John 1–20. Much of this, however, could be the work of an editor with a profound knowledge and understanding of the Johannine story, and the use of the Johannine double "amen" would be easy to imitate. The elements of discontinuity are more serious. Simon Peter and the Beloved Disciple, two major characters from the story, have died, and vv. 15-24 have been partly motivated by a need to explain the *absence* of the authoritative pastor and the founding disciple. However, in order to provide this explanation the editor has added further resurrection appearance accounts to a narrative that concluded with a solemn announcement of the blessedness of belief in the *absence* of Jesus. In 21:15-24 the risen Jesus returns, and his *presence* explains the *absence* of Simon Peter and the Beloved Disciple. This return of Jesus disturbs the impact of his words blessing those who believe without seeing in 20:29.

NOTES

15-17. *When they had finished breakfast:* It is widely claimed that there is little connection between vv. 1-14 and vv. 15-19, and most cite Schnackenburg (*Gospel* 3:361) approvingly: vv. 1-14 constitute "a disciple pericope" and vv. 15-19 "a Peter fragment." The passages no doubt had their own history in the tradition, but vv. 15-19, neatly stitched together with vv. 1-14 by means of the introductory statement, develop the role of Peter, already emerging in vv. 7 and

11. The same can be said of vv. 20-24, linked to vv. 15-19 by means of v. 20a and developing the figure of the Beloved Disciple, mentioned in v. 7. An author may have been working with different elements in the traditions, but there is an overall logic to John 21:1-25 that critics often underestimate.

do you love me?: There is a change in the verb used for "to love" across vv. 15-17. In Jesus' first two questions he uses the verb *agapaō*, but Peter responds with the verb *phileō*. Jesus' final question uses *phileō*, but Peter continues to respond with the same verb. It is sometimes claimed that the stronger verb *agapaō*, used by Jesus, is too much for Peter, whose self-confidence has now failed him. He cannot reach beyond the weaker expression *phileō* (e.g., West-cott, *Gospel* 302–303; NIV). Almost all modern scholars regard this suggestion as a misunderstanding of the Johannine practice of using synonymous verbs for stylistic variety. For an extensive presentation of this case see Carson, *Gospel* 676–677.

15. *more than these:* It is sometimes suggested that the "more than these" might be the tools of the fishing trade. The more likely comparison is between Peter's love of his fellow disciples and his love of Jesus. The question does not ask Peter whether his love for Jesus is superior to the love the other disciples had for Jesus.

feed my lambs: As with the verb "to love" used across vv. 15-17, so also the word for the flock varies between *ta arnia* (v. 15: "lambs") and *ta probata* (vv. 16-17: "sheep"). Similarly there is a variation in the verb *boske* (vv. 15, 17: "feed") and *poimaine* (v. 16: "tend"). These further variations of expression to say basically the same thing (cf. Barrett, *Gospel* 584–585) to Peter three times are an additional indication that the changes in the verb "to love" (cf. above) are stylistic. The vast majority of scholars accept that the threefold repetition of the question from Jesus is linked to Peter's denials. Bultmann, *Gospel* 712–713, questions the link, finding no narrative connection and no word of absolution. He suggests that it is a variant of Matt 16:17-19, but does not offer any satisfactory explanation for the threefold repetition. He rightly comments of the pastoral role of Peter: "Any tendencies in the direction of ecclesiastical politics—for example the buttressing of the authority of the Roman community—is [*sic*] quite remote from vv. 15-17." For a discussion of the use and abuse of this text in discussions of Petrine primacy see the surveys in Beasley-Murray, *John* 406–407; Brown, *Gospel* 2:1112–1117.

18. *when you were young:* It is widely accepted that the words of Jesus that contrast "when you were young . . . but when you are old" are an adaptation of a proverb that contrasted the vigor of youth with the frailty of old age (e.g., Bultmann, *Gospel* 713). The interpretation does not deny this possibility, but links Peter's "youth" with his relationship to Jesus prior to the death and resurrection, full of vigor and self-confidence, and the "when you are old" with his subsequent experience that will be the fruit of his unconditional love for Jesus (vv. 15-17).

you will stretch out your hands: Some have developed explanations of this passage that bypass any reference to Peter's death (e.g., Bernard, *Commentary*

2:708; Bultmann, *Gospel* 713–714), and others point to the incongruity of the description of the stretching out of the hands prior to being girded (e.g., Schnackenburg, *Gospel* 3:366–370). Most would accept the judgment that "it is clear that the redactor knows that Peter has died a martyr's death" (Brown, *Gospel* 2:1118). For early Christian references to Peter's death see Schnackenburg, *Gospel* 3:482 n. 76.

20. *the disciple whom Jesus loved:* The introduction of the Beloved Disciple with the attached description of his place beside Jesus in 13:24 recalls the context of 13:23-25. It is frequently pointed out that this is clumsy, as such an introduction was not needed in v. 7. There is no need to have recourse to a different source, however. The editor is constructing a conclusion to the Gospel that associates yet distinguishes the roles of Peter and the Beloved Disciple. However clumsy, the recollection of 13:23-25 provides excellent background for this association/distinction.

21-23. *What about this man? . . . What is that to you?:* This question, placed on the lips of Peter, does not denigrate him in any way despite the apparent sharpness of Jesus' response. There are three characters in the narrative: Jesus, Peter, and the Beloved Disciple. Only Peter can ask a question that gives the author space to have Jesus ease the anxiety that may have been generated by the Beloved Disciple's death (vv. 22-23). It is the seriousness of this anxiety that creates Jesus' sharp answer (v. 23), not Peter's obtuseness. He is reminded that he must continue to follow Jesus (v. 22; cf. v. 19b).

Throughout the latter part of the Gospel these two disciples were often linked (cf. 13:23-25; 18:15-16; 20:3-10), and the Beloved Disciple is inevitably the disciple who is presented in the more favorable light. In the absence of Peter the Beloved Disciple is at the foot of the cross (cf. 19:25-27). The fragile Peter has, nevertheless, overcome his threefold denial with his threefold profession of love (21:15-17). Scholars have long discussed the significance of the contrast/comparison of the two disciples (for surveys see Brown, *Gospel* 2:1117–1122; Beasley-Murray, *John* 417–418). What is important is that Peter, with all his waxing and waning, is still a disciple (vv. 19, 22: "follow me") and a pastor (vv. 15-17) (cf. Wiarda, "John 21.1-23" 53–71). However, the hallmark of the disciple is to be found in the Beloved Disciple's relationship to Jesus: one who lies close to him in love (v. 20) and one who witnesses to him (v. 24). Peter may well represent the situation of *all disciples,* fragile followers and pastors, while the Beloved Disciple presents the *ideal disciple.* The suggestions of Westcott, Hoskyns, Schnackenburg, and de la Potterie, that the "remaining" of the Beloved Disciple is fulfilled in the proclamation of the Gospel (cf. vv. 22-23, and next note) support this suggestion. Thyen ("Entwicklungen" 259–299) argues that the presence of the narrative fiction of the Beloved Disciple in both Gospel and Epilogue is proof of the literary unity of John 1:1–21:25. But to claim that John 21 presents the Beloved Disciple as the *ideal disciple* in no way detracts from the position taken in the Introduction that he was a historical disciple of Jesus, the founder of the Johannine community, and the bearer of its Jesus story.

22-23: *that he remain until I come:* Some scholars, and especially those who identify the Beloved Disciple with the final writing author of the book, reject the suggestion that this passage indicates that the disciple is dead. For them (e.g., Robinson, *Priority* 70–71; Carson, *Gospel* 682), the advancing age of the Beloved Disciple is generating unwarranted eschatological expectation. Others (e.g., Westcott, *Gospel* 305; Hoskyns, *Gospel* 558–559; Schnackenburg, *Gospel* 3:371; de la Potterie, "La témoin qui demeure" 343–359) transcend this discussion, claiming that the point being made is that the Beloved Disciple "abides/remains" in the community in the proclamation of his Gospel. Both the fact that the Beloved Disciple is dead and the belief that his witness "remains" are involved.

24. *who has written these things:* This affirmation lies behind all claims, so consistently maintained by Christian tradition, that the Beloved Disciple (John, the son of Zebedee?) penned the whole Gospel (for an elegant defense of this position cf. W. Sanday, *The Criticism of the Fourth Gospel* [Oxford: Clarendon Press, 1905] 74–108). This need not necessarily be the case. The aorist participial form of the verb *(ho grapsas)* could have a causative sense: "he had these things written" (cf. Bernard, *Commentary* 2:713). Most modern scholars (cf. Brown, *Gospel* 2:1123) would follow Gottlob Schrenk, who looked to Paul's use of the verb in 1 Cor 4:14 and 14:37 where he is clearly dictating his message to a community to suggest that "In the light of this incontrovertible fact it might be asked whether the *ho grapsas tauta* of Jn. 21:24 might not simply mean that the Beloved Disciple and his recollections stand behind this Gospel and are the occasion of its writing. This is a very possible view so long as we do not weaken unduly the second aspect. Indeed, it would be difficult to press the formula to imply other than an assertion of spiritual responsibility for what is contained in the book" (*TDNT* 1:743). Playing on the possibilities of the English language one could say that the Beloved Disciple is "author" insofar as he is "author-ity" for the Gospel. Those who completely dismiss John 21 as a later apologetic addendum to an already finished Gospel disregard as apologetic fiction the claim of the narrator that the Beloved Disciple is the author.

we know: The "we" of this affirmation demands identification. Some have suggested the elders of the Church at Ephesus (Westcott, *Gospel* 306), or of the Church to which the Disciple belonged, without specifying Ephesus (Bultmann, *Gospel* 717–718; Barrett, *Gospel* 588). Dodd suggests that it is a way of affirming "as is well known" ("Note on John 21,24" *JThS* 4 [1954] 212–213), and it is also possible that it is the author using an editorial "we" (cf. J. Chapman, "We Know That His Testimony is True," *JThS* 31 [1930] 379–387; Carson, *Gospel* 684; Morris, *Gospel* 880–881). This commentary sits comfortably with some form of the first suggestion. One cannot be sure of the exact location although the Introduction tentatively accepts the traditional site of Ephesus, but members of the Johannine community confidently affirm the truthfulness of the tradition they have received. However, there is more to the "we" than the historical first "real readers." The work was aimed at a readership, and the very existence of this commentary indicates that it has transcended that readership. In many ways the "we" of v. 24 involves generations of Christian readers who know that this witness is true and who can give witness to their own belief that the truth sets people free (cf. 8:32). On this see Culpepper, *Anatomy* 45–49.

iii. A Second Conclusion to the Gospel (21:25)

25. But there are also many other things that Jesus did; were every one of them to be written, I suppose that the world itself could not contain the books that would be written.

INTERPRETATION

The Gospel comes to a second conclusion in a way that has parallels with the original conclusion (cf. the comparison in Beasley-Murray, *John* 416). But this second conclusion adds a reflection that forces the reader to look beyond the written pages of the Gospel text. The reader must not suspect that the story just read exhausts all that could be said about Jesus. Adopting a literary form used by other writers of the period (see Qoh 12:9-12; Minor Tractates of the Talmud, *Sopherim* 16:8; Philo, *Post.* XLIII:144; *Ebr.* IX:42; *Mos.* I:38,213), the author of John 21 repeats what the author of 20:30 said more briefly concerning the many other unrecorded signs that Jesus did in the presence of the disciples. A selection has been made. However, while 20:30-31 motivated that choice by further words to the readers telling them *why* a certain selection and a certain ordering of events has taken place, no such motivation is given in 21:25. Perhaps none was needed. It is sufficient for this readership to know that the book they have completed has the Beloved Disciple as its author (21:24).

Conclusion: Does John 21 Belong to the Story?

Interest in the integrity of John 1:1–21:25 concentrates on perceived gaps in the narrative of the Gospel (cf. note). This case has been reinforced by literary considerations (cf. note). Much erudition and imagination have been given to explanations of the role that 21:1-25 plays as the Gospel's conclusion. The number and variety of very different hypotheses (cf. notes) weaken the likelihood that any one of these explanations, or even a combination of them, is true. However subtle such explanations are, they are something of a *tour de force*. A crucial issue dominates the narrative of 20:1-31. The author desires that readers respond to a summons to greater faith (20:31) so that they might know of Jesus' resurrection from their reading of the Scriptures (v. 9), from their experience of the Spirit and the holiness granted to them through generations of disciples who retain and forgive sin (cf. vv. 22-23), and from their recognition of their blessedness in believing without seeing (v. 29). The story closes with a frank recognition of the situation of the readers: they are living in the in-between-time and they are blessed because they believe without seeing (see v. 29). The final chapter instructs a community of Christians on their blessedness and exhorts them to greater faith (vv. 30-31) even though they are living in the period of *the physical absence of Jesus*.

Earlier parts of the narrative have prepared the reader for this final instruction on the presence of the one who is now physically absent. This is particularly obvious in those few places where the reading experience depends on the community's sacramental practices. This storyteller shows no overt interest in those rituals that came to be known as sacraments. On several occasions the storyteller takes Eucharist and Baptism for granted. Living without the *physical* presence of Jesus, the Christian reading in the in-between-time asks: "How do *I see* and *enter into* this kingdom? Where do *I* find this Jesus in whom *I must believe*? How am *I to have a part* in Jesus? Upon which crucified one *must I gaze*?" The author responds by introducing material that reminds the reader of the presence of the one who is physically absent (3:3-5; 6:51-58; 13:1-38; 19:34-37) (cf. interpretation to these passages). The sacraments are never ends in themselves in this Gospel; they are taken for granted by the storyteller as part of the life of the reader. Allusion to Baptism and Eucharist at critical moments in the narrative reminds the reader of the presence of the physically absent one. The Johannine Jesus and the narrator have insisted that Jesus must depart to the Father (cf. 7:32-36; 8:14; 13:1, 33, 36; 14:2-3, 28; 16:6-7, 16, 28; 17:1-5, 11a, 13, 24), leaving the disciples in the world (13:1; 14:2-3, 18-20, 29; 15:18–16:3; 16:21-24; 17:11b, 13-16). His departure, however, is not final. He will come to them (cf. 5:28-29; 6:40, 54; 14:3, 18, 23; 16:16), but during the in-between-time he will not leave them orphans (14:18). He will send them another Paraclete to dwell with them throughout the in-between-time (cf. 14:15-17), guiding, strengthening, reminding, and teaching them during his absence (cf. 14:26; 16:12-15), enabling them to bear courageous witness in a hostile world (cf. 15:26-27), and continuing the judgment of Jesus in the world (cf. 16:7-11). Because the departed Jesus lives, the disciples will live in the unity of Father, Son, and believer (14:18-21). The reader has been well prepared for the final words of the risen Jesus in the original story: "Blessed are those who have not seen and yet believe" (20:29).

But according to 21:1-25 the risen Jesus is not absent! This subverts the impact that 1:1–20:31 should have made on readers living in the in-between-time in *the absence of Jesus*. The addition of the appearance stories of 21:1-25 contradicts the storyteller's original narrative design. The story came to a conclusion with a blessing from Jesus in 20:29 and closing words from the narrator in vv. 30-31. While the author of 1:1–20:31 creates a satisfactory sense of closure as a journey is completed in 20:1-31, the author of 21:1-25 tells the reader that the journey goes on. John 21 under-mines the message of the *absence* of Jesus by telling of the *presence* of Jesus to the infant Church. It is not possible to discover the precise identity of the historical authors who actually *wrote* John 1–20 and John 21. How-ever, as the interpretation of John 21 has shown, there is a strong element of continuity between the Gospel and the Epilogue. It is possible that the addition of chapter 21 was the work of the same author at a later stage, faced with difficulties in the ongoing life of the community that were not foreseen earlier. It may not have been enough to exhort believers to go on believing more, so that their experience of the risen one might match that of the original disciples *despite his physical absence.* It is equally possible that John 21 came from another Johannine Christian (on this discussion, cf. Culpepper, *John, the Son of Zebedee* 297–325). The one (or those) re-sponsible for the Epilogue of John 21 belonged to the same Christian community as the original author. The undeniable literary links between John 1:1–20:31 and John 21:1-25 and the fact that there is no manuscript tradition without John 21 show this conclusively.

The Johannine story *of Jesus* comes to an end in 20:30-31, but that was not the end of the story of *Johannine disciples.* Troubled by the unanswered questions concerning the nature and mission of the community and ques-tions of leadership and authority, someone had to tell the readers that although the story of Jesus had come to an end another story had begun. In order to tell this further story the author called upon other Johannine traditions concerning the risen Jesus (cf. Brown, "John 21" 246–265; Neirynck, "John 21" 321–329; Vorster, "The Growth" 2207–2214). But *the absent one has returned!* The addition of the Epilogue was pastorally effec-tive, as the ongoing presence of John 21 within accepted Christian litera-ture indicates. It must not be regarded as a mere appendix added by accident for apologetic reasons (cf. Gaventa, "The Archive of Excess" 240–252; Zumstein, "La rédaction finale" 214–230; Breck, "Appendix?" 27–28), but it has altered the design of the original narrative. There is a crucial element of discontinuity between John 1–20 and John 21 that calls for the former's being regarded as "the Gospel" and the latter as "the Epi-logue." The Christian reader who has been led from 1:1 to 20:31 to see the blessedness of the one who believes despite the *absence* of Jesus makes no sense of a further narrative in which Jesus is again *present.* After the story told in John 1:1–20:31 there is no place for the return of the ascended Jesus to guide the Church with Peter, the Beloved Disciple, and the other disciples (cf. thus Brodie, *Gospel* 582), however helpful this may have proved to be for the ongoing life of the Johannine community. Jesus has ascended to the Father to establish a new situation in which his disciples are his brethren, sons and daughters of the same Father (cf. 20:17). Another Paraclete is with the followers of Jesus, and will be with them (cf. 14:16-17) until Jesus returns to take them to his Father's dwelling place (cf. 14:2-3).

Some who lived in a community that had produced a Jesus story sensed the need to give further instructions from the risen Lord to guide them as they lived the in-between-time. Thus the Fourth Gospel appeared in its present form. John 21:25 hints that the early Christian community that listened to and read John 1:1–20:31, despite its conviction that "the world itself could not contain the books that would be written" (21:25), could not resist the temptation to add more to the book it had as a treasured part of its storytelling tradition. But there is only one book that rightly tells the Johannine story of Jesus and it ends: "Blessed are those who have not seen and yet believe. . . . These things are written that you may go on believing that Jesus is the Christ, the Son of God, and that believing you may have life in his name" (20:29, 31).

NOTES

The following notes report some contemporary attempts to link 21:1-25 with 1:1–20:31 on the basis of gaps in the narrative and other literary considerations.

Gaps in the narrative: Some of the commonly perceived gaps in the narrative of 1:1–20:31 resolved by 21:1-25 are the disappearance of the Beloved Disciple and Peter in 20:10 (e.g., Hoskyns, *Gospel* 556–561; Carson, *Gospel* 666–667; Bligh, *The Hour of the Cross* 89–90; Hartman, "An Attempt" 37–39; Minear, "John 21" 91–94; Segovia, "The Final Farewell" 173–174; Schneiders, "John 21:1-14" 73–74; Heil, *Blood and Water* 154–156), the need for clear indications of the mission of the Christian community (e.g., Hartman, "An Attempt" 41–42; Morris, *Gospel* 758; Segovia, "The Final Farewell" 176–182; Okure, *The Johannine Approach* 194–195; Brodie, *Gospel* 579–591), especially its eucharistic mission (e.g., Hoskyns, *Gospel* 552–556; Heil, *Blood and Water* 156–159), and the relationship between the evangelist and the Beloved Disciple (e.g., Minear, "John 21" 95; Thyen, "Entwicklungen" 273–299; Stimpfle, *Blinde Sehen* 248–272; Segovia, "The Final Farewell" 183; Tolmie, *Jesus' Farewell* 45–46). However, Schnelle, *Antidocetic Christology* 12–21, argues correctly that the presentation of the Beloved Disciple and Simon Peter in 21:1-25 *differs* from their presentation in 1:1–20:31.

Other literary considerations: Minear suggests that 20:30-31 does not conclude the Gospel as a whole, but only 20:1-31, and opens the narrative to the events that follow ("John 21" 87–90; cf. also Vorster, "The Growth" 2217–2221).

Segovia has developed this further by drawing a link between 20:30-31 and 21:24-25 and showing that 21:1-23 is an example of a final farewell, common in the literature of the time ("The Final Farewell" 174–175; cf. also Breck, "John 21" 29). Talbert sees 20:30-31 as an example of a technique used by the evangelist in 12:36b-37. There is an apparent "ending," but the story goes on (*Reading John* 258; cf. also Ellis, "The Authenticity" 20–21). Staley points to the literary contacts between the use of *agapaō* and *phileō* in 11:1-5 and 21:15-17 as well as the geographical parallels between 11:1–12:11 and 21:1-25. Both take place outside Jerusalem (*The Print's First Kiss* 67–69). Kieffer makes a different geographical link, pointing to the fact that the Gospel closes (21:1-25) where it began (1:19-51): in Galilee (*Le monde symbolique* 17, 90–95). Busse argues that the coming of the Greeks (12:20-22), set within the context of 11:55–12:36, looks to the miracle of the one hundred fifty-three fish and Peter as the good shepherd in John 21 for narrative resolution ("Die 'Hellenen'" 2097–2100). A chiastic structure is proposed by Ellis, who parallels 1:19-51, Jesus' first coming, the witness of the Baptist, Simon, two unnamed disciples, and Nathanael, with 20:19–21:25, which treats Jesus' second coming, Thomas' witness, Simon Peter, two unnamed disciples, and Nathanael (*The Genius* 13–15; 310–312; cf. also Breck, "Appendix?" 36–39; Smalley, *John* 92–97; Robinson, "The Relation" 120–129; Franzmann and Klinger, "The Call Stories" 7–16). Both Staley and Segovia locate 21:1-25 at the end of a series of physical and metaphorical journeys (Staley, *The Print's First Kiss* 72–73; Segovia, "The Journey(s)" 50–51). Korting structures the Gospel on the basis of a communication through "threes," and John 20:1–21:25 forms the final third of the section 13:1–21:25 (*Die esoterische* 1:425–447, 2:72–76). Brodie argues that John 21 is a culminating point in the theological argument of the Gospel as a whole. A mission of daily self-giving, especially in the Church watched over by a provident risen Lord, brings the Gospel to a fitting conclusion (*Gospel* 579–582).

For Reference and Further Study

Boismard, M.-E. "Le chapitre xxi de saint Jean: essai de critique littéraire," *RB* 54 (1947) 473–501.

Breck, John. "John 21: Appendix, Epilogue or Conclusion?" *SVTQ* 36 (1992) 27–49.

Brown, Raymond E. "John 21 and the First Appearance of the Risen Jesus to Peter." In Eduard Dhanis, ed., *Resurrexit. Actes du Symposium International sue la Résurrection du Jésus (Rome 1970)*. Rome: Editrice Libreria Vaticana, 1974, 246–265.

_____. "The Resurrection in John 21—Missionary and Pastoral Directives for the Church," *Worship* 64 (1990) 433–445.

Busse, Ulrich. "Die 'Hellenen' Joh 12,20ff. und der sogennante 'Anhang' Joh 21." In Frans van Segbroeck et al, eds., *The Four Gospels 1992. Festschrift Frans Neirynck.* 3 vols. BEThL 100. Leuven: Leuven University Press, 1992, 3:2083–2100.

Cullmann, Oscar. "The Breaking of Bread and the Resurrection Appearances." In Oscar Cullmann and F. J. Leenhardt, eds., *Essays on the Lord's Supper*. Ecumenical Studies in Worship. London: Lutterworth, 1958, 8–16.

Delebecque, Edouard. "Le mission de Pierre et celle de Jean: note philologique sur Jean 21," *Bib.* 67 (1986) 335–342.

Ellis, P. F. "The Authenticity of John 21," *SVTQ* 36 (1992) 17–25.

Franzmann, M., and Michael Klinger. "The Call Stories of John 1 and John 21," *SVTQ* 36 (1992) 7–16.

Gaechter, Paul. "Das dreifache 'Weide meine Lämmer'," *ZKTh* 69 (1947) 328–344.

Gaventa, Beverly Roberts. "The Archive of Excess: John 21 and the Problem of Narrative Closure." In R. Alan Culpepper and C. Clifton Black, eds., *Exploring the Gospel. In Honor of D. Moody Smith*. Louisville: Westminster John Knox Press, 1996, 240–251.

Hartman, Lars. "An Attempt at a Text-Centered Exegesis of John 21," *StTh* 39 (1984) 29–45.

Heil, John Paul. *Blood and Water* 151–167.

Korting, Georg. *Die esoterische Struktur des Johannesevangeliums*. 2 vols. BU 25. Regensburg: Pustet, 1994.

La Potterie, Ignace de. "Le temoin qui demeure: le disciple que Jésus aimait," *Bib.* 67 (1986) 343–359.

Lattke, Michael. "Joh 20:30f. als Buchschluss," *ZNW* 78 (1987) 288–292.

Minear, Paul S. "The Original Functions of John 21," *JBL* 102 (1983) 85–98.

Moloney, Francis J. *Glory not Dishonor*, Chapter Eight.

Neirynck, Frans. "John 21," *NTS* 36 (1990) 321–336.

Pesch, Rudolf. *Der reiche Fischfang. Lk 5,1-11/Jo 21,1-14. Wundergeschichte—Berufungserzählung—Erscheinungsbericht*. Kommentare und Beiträge zum Alten und Neuen Testament. Düsseldorf: Patmos, 1969.

Reim, Günter. "Johannes 21: Ein Anhang?" In J. K. Elliot, ed., *Studies in New Testament Language and Text: Essays in Honor of George Dunbar Kilpatrick on the Occasion of His Sixty-Fifth Birthday*. NT.S 44. Leiden: E. J. Brill, 1976, 330–337.

Robinson, J. A. T. "The Relation of the Prologue to the Gospel of St John," *NTS* 9 (1962–1963) 120–129.

Ruckstuhl, Eugen. "Zur Aussage und Botschaft von Johannes 21." In *Die Kirche des Anfangs. Festschrift für Heinz Schürmann zum 65. Geburtstag*. Erfurter Theologische Studien 38. Leipzig: St. Benno, 1977, 339–362.

Schneiders, Sandra M. "John 21:1-14," *Interp.* 43 (1989) 70–75.

Segovia, Fernando F. "The Final Farewell of Jesus: A Reading of John 20:30–21:25," *Sem* 53 (1991) 167–190.

_____. "The Journey(s) of the Word of God: A Reading of the Plot of the Fourth Gospel," *Sem* 53 (1991) 23–54.

Shaw, Alan. "The Breakfast by the Shore and the Mary Magdalene Encounter as Eucharistic Narratives," *JThS* 25 (1974) 12–26.

Thyen, Hartwig. "Entwicklungen innerhalb der johanneischen Theologie und Kirche im Spiegel von Joh. 21 und der Lieblingsjüngertexte des Evangeliums." In Marinus de Jonge, ed., *L'Évangile de Jean. Sources, rédaction, théologie*. BEThL 44. Gembloux, Duculot, 259–299.

Vorster, W. S. "The Growth and Making of John 21." In *The Four Gospels 1992.* 3:2207–2221.

Wiarda, Timothy. "John 21:1-23: Narrative Unity and Its Implications," *JSNT* 46 (1992) 53–71.

Zumstein, Jean. "Der Prozess der Relecture in der johanneischen Literatur," *NTS* 42 (1996) 394–411.

_____. "La rédaction finale de l'évangile selon Jean (à l'exemple du chapitre 21)." In Jean-Daniel Kaestli, Jean-Michel Poffet, and Jean Zumstein, eds., *La Communauté Johannique et son Histoire.* Geneva: Labor et Fides, 1990, 207–230.

INDEXES

SCRIPTURAL INDEX

Old Testament

Genesis

1	41
1:1	35
2:2-3	170
2:7	535
3:1-24	280
3:5	170
4:1-15	280
7:11	57
9:5	270
12:1-9	279
15:1	202
17:10	244
22:1-17	279
24:10-19	121
26:24	202
27:35-36	56, 61
28–29	120, 122
28:12	57
28:16-17	57
29:1-14	121
33:19	116
46:3	202
48:22	116
49:11	358

Exodus

2:15b-21	121
3:12	91
3:14	130
4:22	279
12:10	505, 506
12:22-23	504
12:46	505, 506
13:21	235
14–15	203
14:1-2	195
15:8	94
15:24	217
16:2	217
16:4	212, 213
16:7	217
16:7-8	224
16:8	198, 217
16:12	198
16:15	213
16:16	198
16:18	198
16:19-20	198
16:21	198
17:2	224
17:3	217
19	72
19:7-9	50
19:8	72
19:10-15	55
19:11	215
19:16	51, 63, 66, 73, 82
19:16-20	442
19:16-25	41
19:20	195, 215
19–20	463

20:1-26	41		*Deuteronomy*	
20:5	291		1:16-17	258
20:8	170		4:29	250
20:8-11	168, 170		5:9	291
22:7	488		5:10	406
23:1	258		5:15	170
23:16	233		5:21	39
24	72		6:5-6	406
24:3	72		7:2-7	203
24:7	72		7:9	406
24:9-11	399		8:3	192
25:8	39		9:18-29	188
29:46	39		10:12-13	406
32:11-14	188		11:13	406
32:30-33	188		11:22	406
33:13	404		13:10	264
33:18	399, 404		14:1	279
33:22	39, 233		15:11	349
34:6	39		16:13	233
34:33-35	523		16:16	233
40:35	39		17:2-7	264
			17:4	258
Leviticus			17:6	266, 267
11:44	469		18:15	52
19:14	488		18:15-18	199
20:9	488		18:15-19	132
22:33-43	252		18:18	52, 134
23:34	233		19:15	186, 267
23:39	233		29:2-4	367
23:42-43	233, 313		32	463
24:1-16	264		32:6	279
24:10-16	170		32:39	178
			34:5-8	218
Numbers				
4:2-3	286		*Joshua*	
4:39	286		7:19	294
8:24-25	286			
9:6-13	348		*Judges*	
9:12	505, 506		21:19	233
11:4	224			
14:18	291		*1 Samuel*	
15:30-31	170		2:6	178
21:8-9	95		29:10	378
21:16-18	120–121			
21:18	234		*2 Samuel*	
25:11	77		7:12-16	253
35:30	266		7:14	56

15:30-31	484
17:23	270
20:22	343

1 Kings
4:25	56
8:2	233
8:11	39
8:65	233
19:10	77
19:14	77

2 Kings
4:42-44	199
5:7	178
17:24-42	120
17:27-31	132
19:15	189

Isaiah
2:4	179
4:5	235
6:1	368, 399
6:1-5	364, 368
6:5	368
6:9-10	363
6:10	367
7:14-17	248
8:21	488
9:6-7	414
10:1	39
10:25	250
11:1	253
11:2	53, 59
11:4	485
11:10	253
14:14	170
24:18	57
25:6-8	66
25:8	178
26:9	179
27:2-6	419, 422
27:12	144
30:29	233
33:2	179
34:2-4	195
37:20	189

40:1	406
40:5	399
40:7	94
40:9	358
40:11	301
41:4	271
41:13-14	203
43:1	203
43:1-5	203
43:3	203
43:10	130, 271
43:13	271
44:2	358
44:3	94, 253
45:18	130, 271
46:4	271
48:12	271
49:9-10	301
49:10	214
49:18	144
51:9-10	203
52:7	414
52:7–53:17	367
52:13–53:12	361
53	59, 471
53:1	363, 367
53:9	56, 61
54:7	250
54:13	218
55:6	250
55:10-11	215
56:7	77
57:19	414
59:21	94
62:4-5	106
63:16	279
64:1	57
64:7	279

Jeremiah
1:8	91
2:2	66, 106
2:21	419, 422
3:4	279
3:15	301, 305
3:19	279
13:16	294

13:17	301		2:19-20	66
17:19-27	168		2:21	106
23:3	301		4:15	279
23:1-8	301, 304		4:46	279
23:4-6	301, 305		5:6	250
23:5	253		12:10	233
31:9	279			
31:10	301		*Joel*	
51:33	250		2:26	253
			3:1	253
Baruch			4:13	144
4:2	266		28:29	94
5:8-9	235			
			Jonah	
Ezekiel			1:12-15	343
1:1	57			
8:16	236		*Micah*	
11:19	253		2:12	301
11:19-20	94		4:3	179
16:8	106		4:4	56
16:15	279		4:6-7	301
16:33-34	279		5:2	254
19:10-11	422		5:3	301
19:10-14	419		5:3-5	305
19:12-14	422			
22:27	301, 304		*Habakkuk*	
23:4	106		2:14	39
28	170			
30:3	179		*Zephaniah*	
34	301, 304		3:3	301, 304
34:11-16	301		3:9-10	359
34:23-24	301, 305		3:16	358
36:26-27	94, 253		3:19	301
37:9-10	535			
37:24	301		*Haggai*	
38:12	253		2:6	250
39:29	253		2:9	414
45:23	233			
47:1-5	234		*Zechariah*	
47:1-11	252, 253		2:14	39
47:3-6	252		3:10	56
47:8-11	252		9:9	350, 359
47:9	252		9:11	359
			10:2-3	301, 304
Hosea			11:4-17	301, 304
1:2	279		12:10	506
1:4	250		13:7	454, 457

13:7-9	301
14	234, 252
14:6-8	235
14:8	252
14:9	236
14:12	234
14:14-36	253
14:16-19	252, 285
14:17	234, 252

Malachi

3:1	248
4:5	52

Psalms

2:7	56
2:9	301
16:10	523
18:15	94
18:50	253
22	200, 507
22:19	503, 507
23:1	198
23:2	198
29:3	203
32:2	56, 61
34:20-21	505
35:19	430
41:9	380, 381, 384
41:10	380, 381, 384
42/43	359, 360, 382, 387, 397
51:5	295
51:10	94
56:9	485
65:8	203
67:5	179
68	504
68:10	77, 83
68:22	504
69:4-5	430
77:18-19	204
77:20	203
78:24	212, 213
80:3-4	253
80:18-19	419, 422
80:35-37	253
82:2	320

82:6	316
85:10	189
88:37	355, 361
89:10	203
93:3-4	203
94:2	179
105:7	179
105:40	212
113–118	234
117:21	342
118:1	234
118:10	245
118:25	234, 358
118:25-26	350, 358
118:28-29	236
119	192
119:105	266
120–134	235
131:16b-17	187, 191

Job

6:24	245
9:8	203
12:24	245
16:2	406
19:4	245
22:22	378
34:14	94
38:16	203

Proverbs

6:23	266
7:25	245
12:26	245
13:9	245
21:16	245
28:10	245

Qoheleth

11:5	93
12:9-12	562
12:11	301
24:27	422

Daniel

3:25	189
7:13	183, 184, 248
11:31	313

11:31-36	170
12:1-3	338

Nehemiah
8:13-19	233
8:14	233
9:15	212, 213
13	120

1 Chronicles
30:6-9	294

2 Chronicles
7:8	233
30:15-19	348

1 Maccabees
1:11-13	313
1:41	313
1:41-50	313
1:49	313
1:56-58	313
1:59	313
1:60-64	313
2:1–4:35	313
2:24-26	77
4:46-51	313
4:52-59	313
7:42	488

2 Maccabees
1:9	313
6:28	376
7:22-24	338
9:12	170
9:28	321
10:1-4	313
10:5-8	313
10:6	313
12:44	338
14:36	470

Sirach
9:8	245
16:21	93
17:1-4	461
17:11	192, 209
18:13	301
24:8	39
24:10	39
24:21	214
24:27	266
44:16	376
45:5	192, 209
48:1	77, 187
48:10-11	52
50:25-26	117

Tobit
3:3-4	291

Wisdom
1:2	404
2:24	280
5:6	245
9:16-18	94
12:24	245
15:11	535
16:13	178
16:20	212
17:4	404
18:4	266

New Testament

Matthew
2:23	152
3:2-3	52
3:16	53, 57
5:10	93
5:20	263
6:10	93
6:33	93
8:5-13	160
10:1–11:1	473
10:25	429
11:17	448
12:38	263
13:13-15	363
13:24-30	144
13:41	184
13:55	237
13:57	151

14:19	384	27:42	493
14:20	198	27:48	81
15:1	263	27:50	505
15:36	384	27:56	524
16:17-19	559	27:61	524
16:19	535	28:1	521, 522, 524
16:21	82	28:8	516
16:28	184	28:8-10	516
17:22	101	28:9-10	524
17:23	82	28:11-15	516
18:18	535	28:16-20	516
19:11-12	276		
19:28	184	*Mark*	
20:18	101	1:2-3	52
20:19	82	1:10	53, 57
21:1-11	358	1:15	93
21:12-13	75	1:16-20	55, 61, 552
21:13	77	2:2	276
22:35	262	4:1-9	144
23:2	263	4:11-12	363
23:13-15	263	4:22	548
24:9	449	4:26-29	144
24:15	343	6:1-13	473
24:21	449	6:3	237
24:29	449	6:4	151
24:29-30	184	6:42	384
24:39	184	6:43	198
25:31	184	7:8	535
25:31-46	102	8:6	384
26:2	101	8:17-18	363
26:6-13	357	8:23	297
26:24	101	8:38	184
26:25	101	9:1	93
26:26	384	9:31	101
26:26-46	484	10:2	262
26:31	457	10:33	101
26:67-68	495	11:1-11	358
27:4	489	11:15-17	75
27:11	493	11:17	77
27:19	489	12:18-27	338
27:24	489	13:11	450
27:27-30	495	13:17	450
27:29	493	13:19	449, 450
27:31	495	13:24	449
27:32	506	13:26	184
27:37	493	14:3-9	357
27:38	502	14:9	357

14:18	384		8:2	524
14:21	101		8:10	363
14:22	384		8:11	42
14:25	450		9:1-6	473
14:27	454, 457		9:2	93
14:41	101		9:11	93
14:42-45	484		9:16	384
14:62	184		9:17	198
14:65	495		9:18	260
14:70	152		9:22	82
15:2	493		10:1-12	473
15:9	493		10:25	262
15:12	493		11:1	260
15:14	489		11:30	184
15:16-17	495		11:53	263
15:18	493		12:8	184
15:20	495		12:40	184
15:21	506		13:33-34	151
15:26	493		15:2	263
15:27	502		17:21	93
15:32	493		17:22	184
15:32-42	484		17:24	184
15:34	457		17:26	184
15:37	505		17:30	184
15:40	524		18:8	184
16:1	522, 524		18:32	101
16:2	521		18:33	82
16:8	516		19:29-38	358
16:12	548		19:42	363
16:14	516, 548		19:45-46	75
			19:46	77
Luke			21:36	184
1:47	147		21:37	263
3:4-5	52		21:38	263
3:21	57		21:37-38	260
3:22	53		21:38	260
4:24	151		22:39-46	260
4:42	260		22:21	384
5:1-11	55, 61, 552		22:22	101
5:21	263		22:40-46	484
5:30	263		22:63-64	495
6:7	263		23:2	493
6:12	260		23:3	493
6:40	429		23:13-16	489
7:1-10	160		23:22	489
7:32	448		23:26	506
7:36-50	357		23:27	448, 493

23:39-43   502
23:46   505
23:49   524
23:55-56   524
24:1   521, 522
24:1-9   524
24:7   82, 101
24:10   522
24:10-11   516, 524
24:12   516
24:13-35   549
24:19-24   516
24:24   516
24:28-32   552
24:36-38   549
24:37-43   516
24:38-39   534
24:41-43   552
24:44-49   21, 516
24:46   82

Acts
1:20   81
2:1-13   21
2:18   450
5:31   147
6:13   343
10:36   414
13:5   42
13:23   147
14:22   449
21:28   343
23:8   338
28:26-27   364

Romans
6:3   375
10:16   363
11:8   364
11:9   81
11:10   364
14:17   93, 414

1 Corinthians
4:14   561
7:26   449
10:11   449

11:23   384
14:37   561
15:4   82

2 Corinthians
4:17   449
11:2   106

Galatians
1:4   101

Ephesians
1:23   357
5:25-27   106
5:31-32   106

Philippians
2:9   464
2:9-11   464
3:20   147

1 Thessalonians
2:13   42

2 Thessalonians
2:3   467, 485
2:8-9   467, 485

2 Timothy
1:12   450
1:18   450
2:9   42

Hebrews
5:7   341
8:10   450

1 John
2:1   401
2:13-14   471
2:14   549
2:18   5, 549
2:19   451–452
2:19   4, 13
2:22   5
3:7   549
3:12   471
4:3   5

4:9	46
4:14	147
5:18-19	471

2 John
7	4, 5
10–11	6
12	6

3 John
3	6
5–6	6
9–10	5
10	6
10–11	6

Revelation
1:1	1, 8
1:4	1, 8
1:9	1, 8, 42
2:10	449
4:1	57
7:14	449
7:17	59
9:15	450
14:5	61
14:14-16	144
17:14	59
21:2	106
22:8	1, 8
22:17	106

INDEX OF ANCIENT WRITINGS

Jewish Writings

Adam and Eve
25–28   100

Apocalypse of Abraham
31:1-3   284

2 Baruch
2:1-8   100
4:4   284
21   463
29:3   248
29:8   199
34   463
39:7   422
48:1-24   463
77   414
77:11   307
77:13-16   307
77:13-17   301, 305
84–85   463

3 Baruch   100

Biblical Antiquities (Pseudo Philo)
10:7   234, 235
11:15   234
19   414
28:7-8   234

1 Enoch
46   248
48:2-6   248
71   100

89:12-27   301, 304
89:42-44   301, 304
89:59-70   301, 304
89:74-76   301, 304
90:22-25   301, 304

2 Enoch
1   100

1 Esdras
9:8   294

4 Ezra
3:14   284
8:20-36   463
14   414

3 Maccabees
2:2   470

4 Maccabees
17:22-23   376

Martyrdom of Isaiah
2:9   100
3:7-10   100

Jubilees
1:19-21   188, 463
8:19   253
10:3-6   463
10:20-22   463

Psalms of Solomon
17:24   301, 305
17:40   301, 305

Testament of Abraham
8–12   100
10–15   100

Testament of Job
43:1-17   378, 462, 464

Testament of Moses
1:15   377
1:8-9   377
3:9   377
4:2-6   377
11:17   188
12:7-13   377

Testament of Isaac
8:6-7   378, 462, 464

Testament of Jacob
8:6-9   378, 462, 464

Testaments of the Twelve Patriarchs

Testament of Reuben
1:3-4   377
3:5-8   245
4:1   377
6:9   377

Testament of Simeon
3:1-2   377
4:7   377

Testament of Levi
1:2   377
4:1   377
10:1-5   377
14:4   266
14:1-8   377
16:1-2   245
18:1-4   377

Testament of Judah
14:1   377
14:8   245
23:1   377
24:1–25:5   377

Testament of Issachar
4:6   245
6:1-4   377

Testament of Zebulun
5:1-15   377
5:5   377

Testament of Dan
2:1   377
5:1   245
5:7-8   377
5:7-13   377
6:8-9   245

Testament of Naphtali
1:2-5   377
3:2-3   245
4:1-5   377
8:1-8   377
9:2   377

Testament of Gad
1:2-4   301, 304
3:1-4   245
4:1-7   377
6:1-7   377

Testament of Asher
5:3-4   245
6:1-4   245

Testament of Joseph
17:1-8   377
18:1-4   377

Testament of Benjamin
3:1-3   377
10:3   245

Josephus

Antiquities of the Jews
3.161   507
3.245   252

3.247	252
4.219	186
4.194-95	188
6.6.3	258
8.101	233
9.288	131
9.288-90	117
10.184	117
11.297-347	120
14.167	258
15.396-401	319
20.118	116
20.200	435
20.220-221	319

Jewish War
1.209	258
1.229	348
2.163	338
2.232	116
3.375	270
5.184-85	319
6.290	348

Life
269	120

Philo of Alexandria

De Cherubim
86–90	174

De Ebrietate
IX.42	562

De Posteritate Caini
XLIII.144	562

De Vita Mosis
I.8	562
I.213	562

Legum Allegoriae
I.5-6	174

Letter of Aristeas

210	174

Qumran (Dead Sea Scrolls)

Damascus Document (CD)
2:13	245
2:14-15	209
3:14	245
3:15	245
6:2-11	234
10:10-13	109
13:7-9	301, 305

Thanksgiving Psalms (1QH)
4:25	245
15:25	245

Community Rule (1QS)
3:1-9	109
3:13–4:26	94, 245
4:20-22	52
5:10	245
5:13-14	109
6:15	245
8:9-10	245
9:11	52
9:17	245

Copper Scroll (3Q15)
11:12	117

Florigium (4QFlor)
	52

Rabbinic Literature

Targumim

Neofiti
Gen 15:11	275

Onkelos
Gen 17:16-17	284
Num 21:18	234
Deut 30:11-14	100

Pseudo Jonathan
Deut 30:11-14   100

Targum on Psalms
Ps 68:19   100

Midrashim
Tanḥuma Bereshit
6:20   284

Tanḥuma Shemot
4:19   209
4:24   200

Mekilta on Exodus
2:25   174
15:26   209
15:27   235
16:25   194, 200
19:10   51

Sifre Numbers
115:1-3   275
115:5   275

Sifre Leviticus
11   275

Genesis Rabbah
11:5   174
11:10   174
11:12   174
28:18   234
32:10   128
44:22   284
44:28   284
70:1   253
81:9   128

Exodus Rabbah
12:2   275
18:3   188
21:3   258
28:1   228
28:1-3   215

29:9   209
30:6   174
30:9   174
36:3   266
40:2   228
41:6-7   228
43:4   228
47:5   228
47:8   228

Numbers Rabbah
2:17-26   279
21   435

Deuteronomy Rabbah
2:36   228
3:11   228
8:3   209
11:10   228

Samuel Rabbah
32:3   343

Ruth Rabbah
4:8   257

Qoheleth Rabbah
9:18.2   343

Ecclesiasticus Rabbah
1:8   234, 235
1:9   200
7:1   357

Song of Songs Rabbah
1:3   235
1:7   235
1:22   235

Pesiqta Rabbati
20:4   228
53:2   215

Pirqe ʾAbot
2:8   192

3:5   275
6:2   275
6:7   192

Pirqe de-Rabbi Elizer
35–36   121

Mishnaic Literature

Tosefta Sukkah
3:18   256

Tosefta Ketubot
14   110

Tanḥuma
6:32a   540

The Mishnah

Berakot
5:2   338

Šabbat
7:2   168, 293
8:1   293
10:5   168
18:3   244
19:2   244

Šeqalim
6:3   234

Pesaḥim
8:6   499
9:1   348

Sukka
1–2   233
2:8-9   237
3:2-10   234
3:3-9   234
4:5   234
4:8   252
4:9   234
4:9-10   234, 285

5:1-4   235
5:2-4   285
5:3   235
5:4   235, 236, 272, 280, 285

Roš Haš Šana
3:1   186

Ketubot
2:9   186, 267

Nedarim
3:11   244

Sota
9:15   338

Sanhedrin
6:2   294
9:6   435
10:1   215, 338

Middot
2:6   234

Talmudic Literature

Babylonian Talmud

  Berakot
  50b   200

  Šabbat
  89b   215
  147b   200

  Pesaḥim
  91a   499

  Sanhedrin
  37a   253
  108b   284

  Ḥullin
  105b   200

  Minor Tractates
    Sopherim
    16:8   562

Jerusalem Talmud
  Sukka
    55a   257

Christian Writings

Didache
9:3   198
9:4   198

1 Clement
34:7   198

IGNATIUS

Polycarp
4:2   198

Ephesians
17:1   357

JUSTIN

Dialogue with Trypho
8:4   248
95:4   435
110:1   248
133:6   435

Martyrdom of Polycarp
13:1   435

TERTULLIAN

De Spectaculis
30   528

CYPRIAN

De Unitate Ecclesiae
7   507

CLEMENT OF ALEXANDRIA

Paedagogus
2:8   357

ORIGEN

In Johannem
13:8   131

EUSEBIUS

Historia Ecclesiastica
6.14.7   12

CYRIL OF ALEXANDRIA

In Joannis Evangelium
XI,8   471

JOHN CHRYSOSTOM

In Joannem Homeliae
85,4   523

JEROME

Commentarium in Ezekielem
XIV,47   550

AUGUSTINE

In Iohannis Evangelium
13:12   110
15:33   148, 155
33:5   261
118:4   507

De Civitate Dei
V,15   435

Gnostic Writings

HERMETIC LITERATURE

Poimandres
I:31-32   463

Corpus Hermeticum
XIII:21-22   463

MANDEAN LITERATURE

Book of John
236–239   463

Mandean Liturgy
58:9-20   463
114:4-5   37

Non-Christian Writers

PLINY

Natural History
28.7   297

SUETONIUS

Life of Caesar
8.7.2-3   297

Domitian
12   539

TACITUS

History
4.81   297

DIO CASSIUS
13   539

AUTHOR INDEX

Aarde, A. G. van, 398, 416
Abrahams, I., 76
Agourides, S., 480
Alter, R., 69
Appold, M., 463, 471, 480
Arens, E., 45
Ashton, J., 5, 11, 26, 47, 168, 182, 184, 210, 241, 248, 368
Atal, D., 277, 287
Aubineau, M., 507, 513
Auwers, J.-M., 513

Baldensperger, W., 112
Ball, D. M., 26, 381, 485
Balzac, H. de, 20
Bammel, E., 321, 343, 344, 377, 389, 414, 451, 498, 500, 513
Bampfylde, G., 509, 513
Barker, M., 344
Barrosse, T., 62
Barrera, J. T., 109
Barrett, C. K., xi, 1, 25, 26, 35, 47, 58, 61, 67, 80, 82, 83, 85, 86, 93, 97, 100, 106, 109, 111, 117, 120, 123, 132, 133, 134, 135, 142, 149, 159, 161, 171, 182, 190, 192, 203, 206, 210, 211, 212, 213, 216, 220, 224, 225, 230, 231, 239, 240, 244, 246, 248, 250, 256, 259, 274, 281, 282, 284, 285, 305, 308, 309, 310, 320, 321, 336, 337, 338, 341, 342, 343, 344, 356, 358, 361, 371, 388, 397, 399, 405, 406, 408, 414, 415, 422, 433, 445, 452, 457, 463, 464, 470, 479, 485, 490, 491, 506, 521, 526, 527, 529, 534, 535, 539, 540, 549, 551, 552, 553, 559, 561
Bassler, J. M., 102

Bauer, W., 12, 25, 71, 85, 87, 99, 111, 123, 132, 142, 144, 158, 159, 160, 171, 172, 199, 201, 206, 231, 256, 278, 282, 286, 321, 337, 342, 343, 344, 357, 360, 361, 388, 399, 406, 423, 434, 447, 449, 483, 519, 522, 535, 539, 540
Baum-Bodenbender, R., 497, 499, 513
Beardslee, W. A., 362
Beasley-Murray, G. R., 25, 76, 98, 122, 133, 159, 183, 201, 256, 297, 337, 338, 339, 341, 343, 406, 445, 470, 479, 497, 500, 506, 509, 534, 546, 549, 550, 552, 553, 556, 559
Beck, D. R., 173, 175, 298
Becker, H., 86, 87
Becker, J., xi, 1, 12, 25, 86, 87, 109, 135, 143, 159, 171, 190, 191, 196, 204, 282, 309, 336, 339, 343, 358, 367, 377, 389, 398, 400, 423, 434, 471, 480, 485, 499, 508, 509, 534
Becker, U., 259, 260, 264
Beetham, F. G., 508, 513
Beetham, P. A., 508, 513
Behler, G.-M., 389, 415
Belle, G. van, 24, 161, 163
Berger, K., 309
Bergmeier, R., 508, 513
Bernard, J., 174, 175, 183, 191, 192, 193
Bernard, J. H., 25, 45, 81, 86, 87, 97, 98, 121, 123, 132, 142, 144, 149, 159, 182, 190, 204, 216, 225, 237, 256, 274, 278, 281, 286, 287, 336, 367, 398, 399, 415, 423, 434, 444, 447, 451, 456, 459, 464, 491, 522, 528, 529, 535, 559, 561
Bertels, Sr Thomas More, 509, 513
Betz, O., 132, 133, 135, 406, 415, 447

586

Beutler, J., 26, 190, 191, 193, 308, 311, 344, 359, 360, 361, 362, 379, 387, 389, 391, 397, 398, 406, 415

Bienaimé, G., 233, 234, 256, 287

Birdsall, J. N., 320, 321

Bishop, E. F., 309, 311

Bishop, J., 91, 102

Bittner, W. J., 26, 59, 73, 161, 162, 201, 248

Black, M., 309

Blank, J., 26, 100, 102, 182, 259, 263, 264, 360, 367, 369, 445, 446, 499, 513

Blanquart, F., 521, 528, 534, 538, 540

Bligh, J., 124, 485, 513, 565

Boer, M. de, 26, 378, 388, 389, 398, 435, 509

Boers, H., 123, 124, 134, 139, 148

Boguslazwski, S., 508, 513

Boismard, M.-E., 2, 3, 8, 25, 50, 60, 62, 73, 74, 86, 87, 97, 105, 108, 110, 111, 112, 119, 132, 159, 161, 162, 171, 256, 287, 369, 545, 553, 566

Bokser, B. M., 76, 83

Borgen, P., 43, 47, 203, 204, 207, 211, 212, 213, 216, 219, 225, 232, 368, 369, 399

Borig, R., 419, 422, 435

Bornkamm, G., 225, 230, 231, 339

Bowman, J., 133, 135

Braun, F.-M., 59, 122, 124

Brawley, R. L., 508, 513

Bream, H. N., 457, 458

Breck, J., 546, 564, 566

Briend, J., 120, 124

Brodie, T. L., 3, 25, 192, 240, 273, 277, 287, 337, 339, 340, 357, 368, 415, 451, 485, 500, 507, 523, 546

Brown, R. E., xi, 1, 4, 6, 12, 25, 26, 46, 59, 62, 73, 74, 80, 81, 82, 86, 98, 100, 101, 108, 111, 132, 134, 144, 149, 152, 159, 171, 182, 190, 196, 201, 204, 210, 211, 213, 216, 217, 220, 225, 230, 232, 256, 257, 259, 268, 277, 286, 298, 308, 309, 310, 311, 319, 321, 324, 336, 337, 338, 339, 340, 341, 344, 357, 358, 359, 367, 369, 370, 371, 388, 399, 406, 408, 414, 415, 421, 422, 423, 433, 434, 435, 442, 445, 446, 448, 452, 454, 457, 459,

464, 479, 485, 489, 490, 491, 494, 497, 498, 499, 500, 502, 506, 507, 508, 509, 512, 513, 521, 522, 523, 527, 535, 539, 540, 544, 545, 546, 547, 549, 551, 553, 555, 559, 560, 561, 564, 566

Bruns, J. E., 358, 362, 415

Büchsel, F., 445

Bühner, J.-A., 26, 184, 216, 320, 399

Bultmann, R., xi, 5, 12, 25, 26, 70, 71, 73, 82, 85, 88, 98, 99, 100, 108, 109, 132, 133, 134, 143, 148, 162, 174, 184, 191, 216, 256, 273, 274, 275, 277, 282, 305, 310, 333, 338, 339, 341, 342, 397, 398, 399, 408, 415, 422, 426, 444, 445, 463, 464, 470, 479, 488, 490, 491, 494, 499, 509, 522, 523, 534, 555, 559, 560, 561

Burge, G. M., 27, 62, 406, 529, 535

Busse, U., 308, 309, 311, 319, 546, 566

Byrne, B., xii, 56, 324, 336, 340, 341, 342, 345, 522, 523, 538, 540, 543

Bussche, H. van den, 25, 83, 135, 225, 368, 445, 459, 539

Cagliari, F. da, 445, 458

Cahill, P. J., 124

Campbell, R. J., 83

Campenhausen, H. von, 528, 540

Cancian, D., 388, 389

Carmichael, C. M., 121, 123, 124

Carroll, J. T., 184

Carson, D. A., 8, 25, 278, 286, 320, 339, 358, 399, 400, 415, 422, 435, 445, 451, 458, 465, 521, 529, 544, 545, 546, 552, 553, 559, 561, 565

Carter, W., 46, 47

Cassem, N. H., 44, 47

Cassidy, R. J., 27, 435, 539

Casurella, A., 407

Cavaletti, S., 286, 287

Cavallin, H. C., 338, 345

Chance, J. K., 73

Chapman, J., 561

Charlesworth, J. H., xv, 27, 60, 377, 490

Chatman, S., 20

Chenderlin, F., 164, 175

Cilia, L., 343, 345, 361

Collins, M. S., 73, 74
Collins, R. F., 27, 74, 389, 426, 508, 513
Cortès, E., 377, 389, 423, 426
Cory, C. 238, 239, 246, 248, 257, 258, 268, 269, 274, 287
Cosgrove, C. H., 102
Cross, F. M., 120, 124
Crossan, J. D., 196, 201
Cullmann, O., 27, 72, 74, 83, 122, 132, 135, 144, 553, 567
Culpepper, R. A., 8, 13, 14, 27, 34, 47, 173, 175, 340, 374, 376, 378, 379, 389, 465, 483, 562, 564

D'Angelo, M.R., 529, 540
Dagonet, P., 121, 124, 132
Dahl, N. A. 184
Danielou, J., 470, 480
Daube, D., 121, 124, 200, 201, 210
Dauer, A., 490, 498, 499, 500, 504, 507, 508, 514, 516
Davies, W. D., 11, 171, 175, 434, 435
Delebecque, F., 25, 47, 378, 398, 415, 470, 528, 547, 567
Delling, G., 45
Delorme, J., 471, 480
Derrett, J.D.M., 71, 74, 81, 83, 263, 264
Dettwiler, A., 370, 377, 389, 390, 398, 400, 406, 408, 414, 415, 426, 427, 435, 444, 445, 447, 451, 457, 458, 478
Dewailly, L.-M., 500, 514
Dewey, K., 55
Dexinger, F., 134, 135
Diaz, J. R., 121, 124
Dietzfelbinger, C., 399, 400, 415, 447, 448, 458
Dinechin, O. de, 311
Dodd, C. H., xi, 3, 5, 27, 73, 77, 82, 83, 97, 102, 110, 119, 159, 160, 174, 182, 192, 200, 256, 277, 278, 287, 308, 338, 342, 344, 345, 360, 361, 368, 387, 415, 427, 444, 457, 463, 464, 535, 553, 561
Domeris, W. R., 232
Duke, P. D., 27, 73, 100, 121, 273, 343, 457, 499, 500, 513
Dunn, J.D.G., 378, 379, 390
Dupont, L., 540

Duprez, A., 171, 172, 175

Edwards, M. J., 286, 287
Edwards, R. B., 45, 46, 47
Ehrman, B. D., 265, 497, 514
Ellis, P. F., 25, 183, 546, 566, 567
Emerton, J. A., 535, 540
Eslinger, L., 121, 124
Evans, C. A., 367, 369
Evans, C. F., 519, 540

Farmer, W. R., 358, 362
Fee, G. D., 171, 175, 544, 545
Fennema, D. A., 47
Ferraro, G., 175, 387, 390
Feuillet, A., 159, 163, 204, 310, 311, 471, 480, 528, 540
Fischer, G., 397, 398, 415
Fish, S., 17
Forestell, J. T., 27, 59, 361, 367, 471
Fortna, R. T., 27, 62, 71, 73, 86, 88, 162, 308, 311
Fowler, R. M., 491, 501
Franzmann, M., 566, 567
Freed, E. D., 52, 62, 133, 134, 135, 136, 162, 163, 273, 287
Friedrich, G., 122, 124
Fuller, R. H., 540

Gaechter, P., 567
Gaeta, G., 97, 99, 102
Garcia Martínez, F., xv, 109, 112
Gardner-Smith, P., 3
Gärtner, G., 210, 225
Gaventa, B. R., 564, 567
Geiger, G., 213, 225
Genette, G., 85
Genuyt, F., 500, 514
Geoltrain, P., 74
Ghiberti, G., 516, 540
Giblin, C. H., 71, 74, 153, 163, 203, 204, 240, 287, 326, 366, 369, 483, 491, 494, 498, 499, 514
Glasson, T. F., 484, 514
Gnilka, J., 25, 72, 73, 86, 88, 162, 339,
Goedt, M. de, 508, 514
Goodman, P., 233, 287

Gourgues, M., 226, 299, 508, 509, 514
Grässer, E., 282, 287
Grassi, J. A., 74
Greeven, H., 133, 135
Grelot, P., 256, 287, 379, 390
Grimm, W., 343, 344, 345
Grob, F., 210, 226
Grossouw, W. K., 378, 390
Grundmann, W., 343, 345
Guilding, A., 27, 165
Gundry, R., 398, 415

Haacker, K., 132, 136
Haenchen, E., 1, 25, 27, 86, 88, 120, 121,
    133, 134, 135, 161, 162, 184, 245, 256,
    298, 339, 368, 388, 408, 415, 434, 500
Hahn, F., 27, 56, 61, 62, 87, 132, 136
Hall, B. W., 132, 133, 134, 136
Hanhart, K., 163
Hare, D.R.A., 27, 184, 210, 226
Harrington, D. J., 235
Hart, H., 358, 362
Hartman, L., 546, 563, 565
Hartmann, G., 516, 540
Harvey, A. E., 175, 190, 435
Hasel, G. F., 174, 175
Hatina, T. R., 529, 540
Hauck, F., 356
Hayward, C.T.R., 47
Heil, J. P., 204, 259, 263, 265, 483, 485,
    491, 497, 499, 500, 506, 507, 508, 509,
    514, 534, 535, 538, 540, 553, 565, 567
Heise, J., 422, 423, 435
Heitmüller, W., 415, 470,
Hemelsoet, B., 513, 514
Hengel, M., 6, 27, 308
Hiers, R. H., 83
Hodges, Z. C., 87
Hofius, O., 47, 311
Hollenbach, B., 367, 369
Holleran, J. W., 298, 299
Holst, R., 358, 362
Hooker, M. D., 47, 53, 62, 110
Horsley, R. A., 201
Horst, P. W. van der, 11
Hoskyns, E. C., xi, 25, 66, 77, 159, 182,
    192, 225, 231, 256, 269, 270, 278, 286,

342, 357, 398, 399, 411, 415, 427, 435,
    444, 447, 452, 459, 470, 471, 484, 488,
    505, 508, 509, 528, 529, 546, 549, 560,
    561, 565
Hudry-Clergeon, C., 124, 149
Hultgren, A. J., 378, 390

Ibuki, Y., 111, 112
Infante, R., 110, 112
Iser, W., 336, 370

Janssens de Varebeke, A., 497, 514
Jaubert, A., 121, 124, 422, 435, 480
Jeremias, J., 85, 120, 124, 171, 175, 192,
    193, 220, 226, 278, 309, 311
Johannsson, N., 406, 416
Johnston, E. D., 200, 201
Johnston, G., 406, 416, 447
Jonge, M. de, 28, 102, 361, 362
Joubert, H.L.N., 232
Judge, P. J., 538, 540

Kaefer, J., 390
Karris, R. J., 362
Käsemann, E., 5, 28, 47, 377, 464, 471,
    481
Kiefer, O., 310, 311
Kieffer, R., 28, 546, 566
Kilmartin, E. J., 201, 226
Kilpatrick, G. D., 162, 163
Kittel, G., 63
Kitzberger, I.-R., 522, 527, 528, 540
Klaiber, W., 111, 112
Kleinknecht, K. T., 390
Kleist, J. A., 357, 362
Klinger, M., 546, 566, 567
Knöppler, T., 28, 378, 426, 471, 490
Koester, C. R., 28, 56, 62, 80, 83, 378,
    379, 481, 488, 508, 512
Korteweg, T., 250, 287
Korting, G., 546, 566, 567
Kossen, H. B., 362
Kovacs, J. L., 414, 416
Kragerud, A., 523, 541
Kremer, J., 324, 336, 337, 338, 339, 341,
    342, 345, 446, 458
Krieger, N., 108, 112
Kuhn, H.-J., 62

Kühne, W., 357, 362
Kurz, W. S., 377, 390, 415, 426, 479
Kysar, R., 25, 28, 86, 102, 204, 251, 310,
    311, 319, 388, 471, 507, 509

La Potterie, I. de, 29, 44, 45, 46, 48, 62,
    87, 99, 102, 132, 136, 268, 277, 278,
    309, 311, 352, 359, 362, 398, 399, 402,
    406, 413, 440, 445, 446, 470, 471, 472,
    481, 491, 498, 499, 500, 507, 508, 509,
    514, 523, 524, 535, 541, 560, 561, 567
Lacan, M.-F., 48
Lagrange, M.-J., xi, 25, 71, 72, 81, 98,
    133, 134, 142, 144, 149, 159, 161, 206,
    225, 231, 281, 286, 336, 337, 339, 341,
    343, 360, 368, 388, 423, 434, 444, 446,
    463, 464, 470, 498, 523, 529, 546, 553
Lamouille, A., 2, 3, 25, 87, 97, 111, 119,
    159, 161, 162, 171
Lash, C., 540
Lategan, B. C., 278, 287
Lattke, M., 546, 567
Laurentin, A., 481
Lauterbach, J., 58
Lee, D. A., 28, 199, 225, 339, 349, 523,
    527, 528, 538, 541, 546
Lee, G. M., 427, 435
Légasse, S., 108, 109, 112
Leidig, E., 120, 124, 132, 134
Lenglet, A., 123, 125, 142
Lentzen-Deis, F.-L., 59
Léon-Dufour, X., 25, 28, 50, 51, 121,
    122, 123, 144, 149, 184, 203, 206, 220,
    256, 258, 274, 308, 310, 337, 344, 360,
    362, 368, 405, 415, 423, 427, 434, 445,
    463, 534, 535, 539, 541
Léonard, J. M., 199, 201
Leroy, H., 28, 99, 124, 143, 213, 224, 273
Levesque, G., 540
Lieu, J. M., 28, 367, 369, 434, 435
Lightfoot, R. H., 25, 99, 124, 128, 155,
    160, 173, 245, 256, 277, 337, 341, 349,
    423, 434, 459, 500
Lindars, B., 1, 25, 81, 86, 102, 121, 135,
    144, 155, 159, 161, 173, 182, 192, 210,
    226, 256, 257, 277, 278, 282, 287, 297,
    298, 308, 315, 320, 321, 336, 339, 341,

    345, 357, 358, 360, 367, 368, 388, 398,
    433, 434, 435, 445, 446, 447, 457, 458,
    470, 471, 509, 516, 528, 541
Loader, W., 28, 111, 112, 369
Loisy, A., 25, 120, 132, 160, 162, 184,
    357, 459, 500, 539
Lombard, H. A., 390
Longenecker, B. W., 507, 514
Lorenzen, T., 516, 541
Lüdemann, G., 516, 541

Maccini, R. G., 28, 507, 518, 522, 527,
    528, 529
Macgregor, G.H.C., 25, 385
Macrae, G. W., 287
Mahoney, R., 516, 522, 541, 553
Malatesta, A., 481
Manns, F., 28, 210, 212, 213, 246, 256,
    257, 297, 311, 316, 406, 463, 513, 535
Marchadour, A., 324, 337, 338, 339
Marsh, J., 26, 160, 172, 339, 398, 434,
    447, 528
Martin, J. P., 338, 345
Martyn, J. L., 2, 11, 12, 28, 72, 108, 258,
    290, 297, 298, 406, 434, 435
Marzotto, D., 463, 464, 470, 481, 553
Mastin, B. A., 539, 541
Matsunaga, K., 163
Maynard, A. H., 71, 74
McCaffrey, J., 397, 398, 416
McDonald, J., 133, 136
McDonald, J.I.H., 260, 262, 263, 265
McNeil, B., 339, 345
Mead, A. H., 160, 163
Meeks, W. A., 28, 175, 192, 248, 498,
    499, 500
Mehlmann, J., 258, 288
Meier, J. P., 281
Menard, J. E., 288
Menken, M.J.J., 28, 175, 210, 213, 220,
    224, 225, 226, 230, 308, 358, 381, 434,
    509, 510
Merode, M. de, 366, 369
Metzger, B. M., 171, 259, 388, 400, 470,
    471, 544
Michaels, J. R., 244, 288
Michaud, J.-P., 74

Michel, M., 99, 103
Migliasso, S., 391, 407, 416
Miller, E. L., 43, 48, 273, 288
Minear, P., 541, 546, 565, 567
Mlakuzhyil, G., 28, 183, 516
Mollat, D., 518, 529, 534, 535, 541
Moloney, F. J., 14, 26, 29, 48, 50, 57, 62, 63, 74, 83, 87, 101, 103, 111, 112, 125, 134, 136, 145, 150, 171, 175, 182, 183, 184, 193, 194, 196, 201, 204, 206, 210, 211, 213, 220, 224, 225, 226, 230, 231, 232, 265, 269, 273, 274, 277, 288, 298, 299, 311, 321, 339, 341, 342, 345, 352, 357, 359, 360, 361, 362, 367, 378, 379, 381, 385, 388, 389, 390, 407, 414, 416, 435, 436, 445, 446, 451, 457, 458, 469, 473, 481, 489, 494, 495, 498, 499, 504, 507, 509, 514, 516, 521, 527, 541, 567
Montgomery, J. A., 132, 136
Moo, D. J., 507
Mörchen, R., 361, 362
Morgan-Wynne, J. E., 274, 288, 406, 416
Morgenstern, J., 174, 175
Morris, L., 8, 26, 309, 423, 546, 561, 565
Moule, C.F.D., 200, 201, 339, 345
Moulton, H. K., 81
Mowinckel, S., 248
Müller, K., 299
Müller, M., 297, 298, 299
Müller, U. B., 406, 407, 408, 414, 416, 445
Murphy-O'Connor, J., 105, 108, 109, 112, 145

Neirynck, F., 2, 3, 60, 83, 160, 163, 206, 564, 567
Neugebauer, F., 398, 451
Neugebauer, J., 191, 193, 390
Neusner, J., 110
Neyrey, J. H., 29, 62, 63, 97, 103, 121, 125, 134, 269, 277, 288, 339, 541
Niccaci, A., 144, 145, 390, 416, 426, 436
Nicholson, G. C., 29, 360, 361, 523
Nicol, W., 86, 88
Niemand, C., 379, 390
Nisin, A., 204
Nodet, E., 313, 314, 319, 321

O'Day, G. R., 29, 118, 121, 122, 125, 130, 135, 136, 142, 145, 150, 381, 390, 407, 457, 458, 479
Obermann, A., 29, 213, 220, 224, 256, 381, 430, 434, 507, 508, 509, 510, 523, 544
Odeberg, H., 29, 224
Okure, T., 118, 120, 121, 122, 125, 129, 131, 134, 135, 136, 143, 144, 145, 148, 149, 150, 527, 528, 541, 546, 565
Oliver, W. H., 390, 398, 416
Olsson, B., 63, 69, 71, 72, 73, 74, 121, 122, 123, 125, 136, 142, 143, 144, 145, 150
Onuki, T., 29, 99, 426, 434, 447
Osborne, B., 342, 345, 522, 541

Pagels, E. H., 7
Painter, J., 1, 5, 6, 12, 13, 29, 125, 175, 184, 191, 193, 201, 213, 219, 248, 308, 344, 390
Panackel, C., 499, 514
Pancaro, S., 29, 61, 73, 172, 175, 191, 192, 193, 241, 243, 245, 254, 258, 268, 269, 288, 344, 345, 446, 490, 491, 498, 499, 509
Panimolle, S., 48
Patte, D., 99, 103
Pazdan, M., 125
Perkins, P., 121, 541
Perry, J. M., 196, 201, 204
Pesch, R., 552, 567
Petersen, N. R., 29
Phillips, G. A., 210, 226
Pickering, S. R., 259, 265, 288
Pinto da Silva, A., 288
Pollard, T. E., 20, 29, 320
Porsch, F. 29, 282, 288, 416, 445, 446, 509
Porter, C. L., 299
Potin, J., 58
Preisker, H., 43, 48
Prete, B., 358, 362
Pryor, J. W., 44, 48, 159, 163
Purvis, J. D., 133, 136

Quast, K., 29, 490, 491, 514

Rad, G. von, 63
Rajak, T., 308
Rahner, H., 288
Randall, J. F., 377, 390, 481
Rankin, O. S., 319, 321
Reim, G., 29, 86, 88, 160, 163, 282, 288, 297, 298, 299, 567
Reinhartz, A., 29, 298, 311
Reiser, W. E., 342, 346, 522, 541
Rengstorf, K.-H., 488
Rensberger, D., 29, 89, 99, 298, 379, 498, 513
Richter, G., 86, 88, 371, 390, 509, 514
Riedl, J., 273, 274, 288, 361
Riesenfeld, H., 545
Rigaux, B., 464, 480, 481, 528, 534, 541
Riley, G. J., 516, 539, 541
Ritt, H., 463, 481
Roberge, M., 206, 210, 225, 226
Robert, R., 47, 48, 241, 277, 288
Robinson, B. P., 162, 163
Robinson, J.A.T., 4, 8, 12, 29, 145, 168, 172, 175, 308, 311, 343, 379, 390, 544, 545, 546, 561, 566, 567
Rochais, G., 336, 337, 339, 340, 341, 346
Rodriguez Ruiz, M., 30, 399, 480, 553
Rose, M., 470
Rossetto, G., 99, 103
Roustang, F., 124, 125
Rowland, C. C., 63
Ruckstuhl, E., 545, 547, 553, 567
Rudolph, K., 45

Sabugal, S., 30, 133, 275, 288, 299
Sanday, W., 561
Sandvik, B., 427, 436
Saxby, H., 50, 63
Schäefer, P., 344
Schaefer, K., 288
Schalit, A., 160, 163
Schenke, L., 30, 63, 206, 210, 226, 230, 232, 233, 241, 277, 288
Schlier, H., 451
Schnackenburg, R., 1, 12, 26, 44, 45, 50, 60, 61, 73, 74, 78, 83, 85, 86, 99, 109, 111, 113, 123, 124, 128, 130, 132, 133, 134, 136, 143, 144, 149, 155, 159, 160, 161, 162, 163, 171, 172, 182, 184, 192, 196, 200, 204, 206, 211, 212, 216, 248, 256, 257, 258, 259, 260, 263, 269, 282, 286, 296, 297, 310, 311, 336, 337, 338, 339, 340, 343, 353, 359, 360, 367, 368, 369, 378, 379, 388, 389, 399, 406, 407, 408, 413, 414, 423, 426, 445, 451, 463, 470, 471, 479, 481, 485, 490, 491, 499, 506, 507, 509, 510, 512, 521, 544, 558, 560, 561
Schneider, G., 59
Schneider, J., 309, 311, 390, 397, 490
Schneiders, S. M., 13, 125, 338, 339, 340, 346, 380, 390, 523, 528, 541, 546, 553, 565, 567
Schnelle, U., 13, 30, 86, 88, 201, 206, 213, 224, 231, 310, 339, 391, 415, 544, 565
Schrenk, G., 561
Schuchard, B. G., 30, 213, 220, 224, 358, 367, 381, 434, 507, 509
Schulz, S., 86, 88
Schürmann, H., 220, 224, 226
Schwarz, G., 160, 163
Schweizer, E., 30, 161, 163
Scott, M., 30, 216, 268, 339, 357
Segalla, G., 26, 111, 134, 143, 145, 149, 191, 196, 256, 277, 288, 336, 339, 419, 436, 463, 464, 471
Segovia, F. F., 30, 370, 377, 391, 398, 399, 400, 405, 416, 418, 422, 423, 426, 434, 436, 448, 451, 452, 457, 458, 546, 565, 566, 567
Seidensticker, P., 523, 541
Selms, A. van, 110, 113
Senior, D., 481, 485, 486, 498, 501, 502, 506, 508, 509, 512, 514
Serra, A. M., 58, 63, 72, 74, 508
Shaw, A., 553, 567
Siminel, P., 528, 541
Simoens, Y., 372, 391, 415, 416, 418, 436, 437, 444, 451, 458, 481
Simonis, A. J., 308, 310, 311, 499
Smalley, S. S., 30, 546, 566
Smith, D. M., 5, 6, 30, 86, 88, 367, 369
Smitmans, A., 71, 73, 74
Spicq, C., 224, 226, 381, 391

Staley, J. L., 30, 173, 175, 292, 297, 298, 299, 490, 491, 514, 515, 546, 553, 566
Steiner, G., 15, 16
Stemberger, G., 30, 102
Stenger, W., 231, 232, 445, 446, 458
Stibbe, M.W.G., 26, 30, 308, 319, 336, 337, 338, 339, 346, 361, 368, 448, 463, 483, 485, 490, 499, 500, 501, 502, 508, 528, 546
Stimpfle, A., 30, 183, 191, 338, 398, 447, 480, 565
Stowasser, J., 110, 113, 191
Strachan, R. H., 30, 98, 357
Strathmann, H., 86, 88
Sturch, R. L., 163
Suggit, J. N., 74, 103, 388, 513, 515
Swetnam, J., 277, 288, 509, 515, 535, 542
Sylva, D. D., 513, 515

Talbert, C. H., 26, 46, 101, 103, 182, 204, 235, 268, 281, 308, 319, 426, 534, 546, 566
Teeple, H. M., 86, 88
Temple, S., 86, 88
Theobald, M., 43, 44, 48, 73
Thomas, J. C., 30, 172, 190, 245, 379, 391
Thompson, M. M., 30, 162, 191, 193
Thüsing, W., 30, 359, 360, 361, 447, 461, 464, 471, 481
Thyen, H., 97, 111, 113, 132, 136, 297, 311, 426, 436, 546, 560, 565, 567
Tilborg, S. van, 30, 339, 490, 519
Tobin, T. H., 48
Tolmie, D. F., 391, 426, 546, 565
Topel, L. J., 84, 87
Tracy, D., 19
Tragan, P.-R., 296, 309, 310, 312
Trocmé, E., 84
Tröger, K. W., 31
Trudinger, L. P., 63
Tsuchido, K., 268, 273, 288, 356, 357, 361, 362
Tuñi Vancells, J. O., 277, 278, 288

Unnik, W. C. van, 251, 361, 362, 534, 544, 545

VanderKam, J. C., 319, 321
Vanhoye, A., 74, 183, 184, 185, 191, 193
Vaux, R. de, 81
Vellanickal, M., 99
Villiers, J. L. de, 308, 312
Vorster, W. S., 546, 564, 565, 568

Wahlde, U. C. von, 31, 58, 86, 88, 191, 193, 320, 321
Walker, R., 148, 149, 150
Walker, W. O., 463, 481
Wallace, D. B., 263, 265
Watson, W.G.E., 144, 145
Watt, J. G. van der, 183, 184, 185, 422, 436
Wegner, U., 153, 160, 164
Weiand, D. J., 171, 175
Weiss, H., 379, 391
Wellhausen, J., 85, 88
Wengst, K., 31
Wenz, H., 539, 542
Westcott, B. F., 26, 72, 83, 87, 99, 108, 134, 135, 144, 159, 200, 206, 256, 258, 269, 277, 281, 282, 319, 337, 338, 360, 414, 415, 420, 422, 446, 463, 479, 497, 509, 523, 528, 539, 559, 560, 561
Whittaker, J., 31, 320, 321
Wiarda, T., 560, 568
Wilckens, U., 542
Wilcox, M., 341, 342, 346
Wilkens, W., 86, 88
Wilkinson, J., 505, 515
Willemse, J., 159, 164
Willmes, B., 301, 312
Wilson, J., 111, 113
Windisch, H., 406, 416, 447
Witherington, III, B., 26, 108, 113
Witkamp, L. T., 172, 176, 196, 200, 201, 203, 508, 515
Woll, D. B., 407, 416
Wuellner, W., 340, 346
Wyatt, N., 528, 542

Yarbro Collins, A., 18
Yee, G. A., 176, 314, 319
Young, F. W., 31, 446

Zaiman, J. H., 245, 288
Zappella, M., 71, 74
Zeller, D., 496, 515

Zimmermann, H., 273, 288
Zumstein, J., 31, 370, 508, 509, 512, 515, 546, 564, 568